Public Relations
STRATEGIES AND TACTICS

FOURTH EDITION

With a Foreword by Edward L. Bernays

DENNIS L. WILCOX

San Jose State University

PHILLIP H. AULT

South Bend Tribune

WARREN K. AGEE

University of Georgia

HarperCollins*CollegePublishers*

Acquisitions Editor/Executive Editor: Cynthia Biron
Developmental Editor: Betty Slack
Project Management, Text and Cover Design: York Production Services
Photo Researcher: Roberta Knauf
Electronic Production Manager: Christine Pearson
Electronic Page Makeup: Laura Leever
Printer and Binder: R.R. Donnelley & Sons Company
Cover Printer: Coral Graphics Services, Inc.

Public Relations: Strategies and Tactics, 4/e

Library of Congress Cataloging-in-Publication Data

Wilcox, Dennis L.
    Public relations : strategies and tactics / Dennis L. Wilcox,
Phillip H. Ault, Warren K. Agee. — 4th ed. / with a foreword by
Edward L. Bernays.
        p.   cm.
    Includes bibliographical references and index.
    ISBN 0-673-99309-4
    1. Public relations.   2. Public relations—United States.
I. Ault, Phillip H., 1914–   . II. Agee, Warren Kendall.
III. Title
HM263.W49   1995
659.2—dc20   94-13715
                                                  CIP

96 97   9 8 7 6 5 4

CONTENTS IN BRIEF

CONTENTS

PART TWO PROCESS   155

FOREWORD

BY EDWARD L. BERNAYS[1]

One of the basic requirements of a vocation is that it have a literature of its own. In 1923 I wrote *Crystalizing Public Opinion,* published by Boni and Liveright, the first book on public relations. It defined the principles and practices of the new vocation of public relations and the ethics by which it should be governed.

Today there are more than 16,000 items in the bibliography of public relations. Every new volume, like this one that discusses the old and new problems the vocation faces, should be welcomed.

With the increasing complexity of our society, the public relations practitioner, an applied social scientist, must gain new and old knowledge from books before he or she can practice effectively. That is the pattern pursued consistently by lawyers, medical doctors, and those in other vocations.

With people power the most dominant force in society, it is essential that the public relations practitioner have the broadest understanding possible of the vocation. This book meets that need.

The past is prelude to the future. That is why the historical treatment of public relations in this volume is so important. Historical perspective provides proof why people must be given such serious consideration. Every activity depends on people for its survival, whether profit or nonprofit. By taking up various steps to pursue, this book provides basic approaches for teacher, student, and practitioner.

In my practice of 77 years, books have been my greatest, most valuable resource.

Many people in public relations, as in other fields, think of themselves as Columbuses and Magellans in tackling their problems, as if they were the first ever to burst upon a particular issue. But the real Columbuses and Magellans read a book like this and then proceed to use books like this one as their greatest resource in the practice of their vocation.

There are serious problems concerning public relations that readers of this book must face if the vocation is to survive. The words *public relations* are in the public domain. Unlike true professions, public relations has not been defined by law. In the American language, words have the stability of soap bubbles. Anyone can misuse the term *public relations.* And many people unfitted by education, experience, or ethics use the term to mean whatever they want it to mean.

---

1. New York University commemorated the sixty-second anniversary of the teaching of public relations at a ceremony in 1985, during which NYU President John Brademas presented Dr. Bernays with a presidential citation. Dr. Bernays died in 1995 at the age of 103.

I noted in one directory of a public relations association 14 different appellations. None of them gave the least indication of an individual's education, experience, or ethics. Today any car salesperson or paperhanger can call himself or herself a "public relations practitioner." I have seen help-wanted advertisements for tourist-guide public relations practitioners who are required to "love people." It is in the interest of all the readers of this book to strengthen the status of public relations by making it a profession.

Public relations is an art applied to a science—social science—in which the public interest rather than financial motivation is the primary consideration. A professional practitioner in public relations would turn down Somoza, Franco, and Hitler as clients, as I did.

Public relations today has all the characteristics of a profession except one. Public relations lacks licensing and registration by the state with legal sanctions.

The public relations vocation has its literature, an earmark of a profession. With more than 16,000 items published as of this writing, the literature grows every year.

Public relations has its educational courses, another earmark of a profession. In this and most other countries, instruction is offered in public relations. But what is actually taught as public relations often differs from school to school. Obviously, education would be standardized if licensing and registration were adopted in public relations, as is currently the case with instruction in the professions.

Public relations has its associations. They exist both in this country and internationally. There is an International Public Relations Association, with members in more than 66 countries.

Ethics is still another earmark of a profession. The public relations societies have their codes of ethics. In the case of licensed and registered professions, these codes of ethics are enforced by law. In public relations, no legal sanctions exist.

A group of practitioners is trying to bring about needed change. A committee calling for registration and licensing with legal sanctions has been established, not only to preserve and codify the standards of the field but also to prevent unqualified individuals from calling themselves public relations practitioners. It would also standardize the teaching of public relations in the United States.

In my judgment, degrees in public relations should be given on completion of a liberal arts program. In the two years following, M.S. degree graduates in public relations would study the social science disciplines, including economics and history. Additionally, universities could set up a double-degree program for students who plan a career in a specific area of public relations—for example, degrees in medicine and public relations for a career in medical public relations.

In sum, this book promises to be a good preparation for life in a public relations career.

Edward L. Bernays received honorary doctorates from Boston University, Babson College, Ball State University, and Northeastern University for his contributions to the fields of public relations and social science.

PREFACE

The world of public relations expands and changes so rapidly that a textbook covering the entire field, as *Public Relations: Strategies and Tactics* does, requires frequent revision to stay abreast of developments. This fourth edition does precisely that. It examines public relations at the end of the twentieth century in both theory and practice, with emphasis on emerging trends.

Basic organization of the textbook remains the same as in the third edition. In a survey, users of the book told us overwhelmingly to keep it that way. Within that format, much up-to-the-minute new material drawn from real-world public relations practice has been added.

Six aspects of public relations in particular receive strong emphasis in this edition:

- Ethics and professionalism
- Diversity
- International public relations
- The environment
- Crisis management
- New technologies

Concern about ethical responsibility in public relations practice has grown as the field expands. This textbook examines numerous aspects of ethics and illustrates them with examples from professional practice. Among them is Hill and Knowlton's disputed Campaign for a Free Kuwait during the Persian Gulf War. The chapter includes the new Code of Good Practice for creators and users of video news releases (VNRs).

We discuss the significant issue of multiracial and multilingual diversity from two angles: (1) how public relations professionals can reach the diverse audiences that comprise contemporary society and (2) the need for greater minority participation in public relations practice. Accusations of racial bias against the Denny's restaurant chain and the ways in which the company responded to them provide a case study.

As more corporations expand into global marketing, trade barriers fall, and worldwide communication becomes virtually instantaneous, international public relations practice multiplies. In our chapter on international public relations, and in other references throughout the textbook, we explain how the global system operates and the opportunities it offers to individuals. Case studies include the successful campaign to "sell" the North American Free Trade Agreement (NAFTA).

Public demands for cleanup of the environment have created a challenging new role for public relations. We look at the opportunities and problems from opposite points of view. First, we discuss how corporations, governments, and other organizations identify their environmental problems, respond to criticism, and inform the public about their cleanup efforts. Second, we examine operating methods and financing of environmental activist organizations that are forcing change. A case study of the 3M Company shows how one international corporation operates a broad environmental program.

Corporations and nonprofit organizations alike constantly face the possibility of unexpected crisis. The manner in which management meets the crisis—by wisely communicating openly and quickly with the public or, alternatively, by "stonewalling" and trying to cover up the problem—can determine whether an organization can emerge from its problem virtually unscathed or critically damaged. We discuss two classic cases, the excellent performance by the makers of Tylenol in its poisoning crisis and the public relations disaster for Exxon in its Alaskan oil spill. We also examine Pepsi Cola's handling of the hoax caused by customers claiming to find syringes in Pepsi cans and the crisis that struck Sears, Roebuck & Company when two state governments revealed that its auto mechanics had been cheating customers.

The textbook also looks at developments in electronic technology that are blending the telephone, computer, and television systems into a new form of two-way communication popularly called an "information superhighway."

As every instructor knows, examples, anecdotes, and case histories are extremely valuable in helping students grasp principles and theories. *Public Relations: Strategies and Tactics* has won a reputation for its abundance of this material, mostly drawn from professional practice. This edition is filled with new material.

Chapter 1 describes the epic public relations battle waged by conflicting medical, insurance, political, and social organizations over President Clinton's health-care plan. Follow-up references to specific aspects of the fight appear throughout the textbook. Other examples drawn from the news pages include such diverse public relations episodes as Michael Jackson's career crisis resulting from child-abuse charges against him, the McDonald's organization's use of community public relations to win zoning rights for a restaurant, and a computer error that cost Pepsi millions of dollars when a half-million Filipinos held winning tickets for the grand prize in a contest drawing. Riots broke out after the company paid only a token amount to each holder of a prize ticket.

This book is divided into five parts:

- ■ Part One: Role

- ■ Part Two: Process

- ■ Part Three: Strategy

- ■ Part Four: Application

- ■ Part Five: Tactics

The organization is based on the fact that diversity exists in the teaching of introductory courses in public relations. At some colleges and universities, the course is offered as an overview of the entire field, covering theories, strategies, and on-the-job tactics. Other universities concentrate on theory and strategy, teaching the technical applications in public relations writing courses. Therefore, we concentrate on the tactical material in Part Five. Instructors may include it or not, as they desire. Thus the book may be used under both teaching approaches.

The first four parts examine the principles, theories, and strategies in a natural teaching sequence. The fifth part explains the techniques of day-by-day public relations practice—such assignments as preparing a news release, writing a speech, coaching a client for a television appearance, and staging a news conference. For the reader's convenience, we have grouped the techniques into three categories, with a chapter on each: "Written Tactics" (Ch. 22); "Spoken Tactics" (Ch. 23); and "Visual Tactics" (Ch. 24).

We also draw readers' attention to Chapter 21, "Public Relations and New Technologies." Discussion centers on the spectacular advances worldwide in message-delivery methods and electronic research sources. It explains how such tools as facsimile, video news releases, desktop publishing, and satellite transmission are used in public relations practice.

A new feature in the fourth edition will help both instructors and students. Each chapter opens with a Preview. This defines the objective of the chapter and lists in concise form the major topics covered in the text.

Also new in this edition is a four-color section titled "The Tools of Public Relations." This introduces students to some of the methods practitioners use to deliver their messages. More than 60 new black-and-white illustrations add to the textbook's up-to-the-minute "feel."

The chapter titled "The Individual in Public Relations," which appeared as Chapter 5 in previous editions, has been moved forward to become Chapter 4 in the fourth edition. This improves the natural flow of instruction.

Supplementing the body of the text are a glossary of public relations terms and a comprehensive bibliography at the back of the book, as well as lists of suggested readings and review questions at the end of each chapter.

Supplements to the textbook include the following:

- ■ an instructor's manual/test bank;

- ■ a computerized test bank, available in IBM or Mac formats.

ACKNOWLEDGMENTS

A textbook of such scope as this one could not have been written without the assistance of many academic and professional advisers and consultants. We particularly wish to thank the following academics who reviewed the manuscript for the fourth edition and provided many helpful suggestions: Philip Adler, Jr., Georgia Tech University; Jamie M. Byrne, Millersville University of Pennsylvania; Roberta L. Crisson, Kutztown University of Pennsylvania; Bill Dean, Texas Tech University; Thomas Healy, Endicott Junior College; Carl Jensen, Sonoma State University; John T. Ludlum, Otterbein College; Susan Pendleton, Mansfield University of Pennsylvania; Gene Sekeres, Youngstown State University; Tommy V. Smith, University of Southern Mississippi; and John Spengler, Franklin University.

We express our gratitude also to those who reviewed drafts of the manuscript for the first, second, and third editions: Robert L. Bishop, University of Georgia; Glenn Butler, University of Florida; Fred L. Casmir, Pepperdine University; Lois Conn, Grand Valley State College; Bill Day, University of Toledo; Michael B. Hesse, University of Alabama; Jerry Hudson, Texas Tech University; Robert L. Kendall, University of Florida; Marilyn Kern-Foxworth, Texas A&M University; Norman R. Nager, California State University at Fullerton; Bruce Renfro, Southwest Texas State University; Maria Russell, Syracuse University; Walt Seifert, Ohio State University; Judy VanSlyke Turk, University of South Carolina; and Albert Walker, Northern Illinois University.

Others in the academic world who assisted us include James E. Grunig, College of Journalism, University of Maryland, College Park; Randall Murray, California Polytechnic State University, San Luis Obispo; and Glen T. Cameron, Ruth Ann W. Lariscy, Roland Page, and R. Barry Wood, University of Georgia, Athens.

Our special gratitude is extended to Edward L. Bernays for writing the Foreword to this textbook.

Dennis L. Wilcox
Phillip H. Ault
Warren K. Agee

PART ONE
Role

What Is Public Relations?

PREVIEW   The objective of this introductory chapter is to define public relations, explain its communication and counseling roles, and clarify the relationship of public relations to journalism, advertising, and marketing.

Topics covered in the chapter include:

- The challenge of public relations

- Definitions of public relations

- Public relations as a process

- The components of public relations

- How public relations differs from journalism, advertising, and marketing

- The integrated approach

- Public relations in action: the Clinton health plan

Humanity has at its disposal tools of communication so swift, so abundant, and so pervasive that their potential is not yet fully comprehended. Messages flash around the world by satellite within seconds. Computers produce almost instantaneous calculations and pour out information at the rate of thousands of words a minute. Immense warehouses of information stored in electronic databases are available at the touch of a keyboard.

Yet in the midst of this information revolution, and in general agreement that we live in a "global information society," misunderstanding, lack of comprehension, and antagonism abound. Time after time, a crisis or conflict is caused by failure to communicate effectively.

Research and analysis also have provided knowledge of the motivation behind individual behavior, the dynamics of group conduct, and the sociological factors that create conflict among different groups. Our tools and accumulated knowledge, however, far surpass our ability to harness the concepts for effective conflict resolution, negotiation, and compromise between groups that take different sides on such varying issues as economic development and preservation of the environment, abortion, and cigarette smoking.

More than ever, today the world needs—not more information—but sensitive communicators and facilitators who can explain the goals and methods of organizations, individuals, and governments to others in a socially responsible manner. Equally, these experts in communication and public opinion must provide their employers with knowledge of what others are thinking, to guide them in setting their policies wisely for the common good.

Patrick Jackson, a former president of the Public Relations Society of America (PRSA) and publisher of *PR Reporter,* makes the case for this public relations role. He once wrote:

As soon as there was Eve with Adam, there were relationships, and in every society, no matter how small or primitive, public communication needs and problems inevitably emerge and must be resolved. Public relations is devoted to the essential function of building and improving human relationships.

Indeed, those who fill this need are in the challenging field of public relations. The U.S. Bureau of Labor Statistics estimates that 168,000 men and women are employed in public relations in the United States, up considerably from the 80,000 in 1970. Probably more public relations specialists are working than these numbers indicate. Professor Robert L. Kendall of the University of Florida, after analyzing U.S. Census Bureau figures, estimated the number of public relations people in the United States at almost 400,000.

Whatever the figure, the numbers are expected to increase during the late 1990s. A recent issue of the *U.S. Employment Opportunities Handbook* predicts a growth rate for public relations "much faster than average for all occupations through the year 2000." Areas of growth in public relations, according to the report, will be corporations, associations, and health agencies. Other growth areas and trends in employment are discussed in Chapter 5.

It is difficult to estimate worldwide figures, but *Reed's Worldwide Directory of Public Relations Organizations* (1990) lists 155 public relations organizations with an aggregate membership of 137,000 people. Such memberships usually are the tip of the iceberg, because large numbers of public relations practitioners don't belong to such organizations. The president of the China International Public Relations Association, for example, says that China has more than 100,000 public relations practitioners and that up to 500,000 are studying aspects of public relations in colleges and training institutes.

The public relations field is most extensively developed in the United States, where organizations spend an estimated $10 billion annually in such activity. However, considerable growth also is taking place in Europe and Asia.

Claudio Belli, head of international operations for the Hill and Knowlton public relations firm, estimates that European companies spend $3 billion annually on public relations, a figure that continues to increase through implementation of the European Community (EC) and the opening of Eastern Europe to private enterprise. Areas with strong growth potential in Europe are public affairs, corporate relations, health care, and marketing communications.

The second area of major growth is Asia. Shandwick, the world's second largest public relations firm, sees growth of 20 to 30 percent in Asian nations on the Pacific Rim. Increased privatization of national industries and expansion of free market economies also are fueling major growth in Latin America. A more detailed discussion on international public relations is found in Chapter 16.

In sum, public relations is a global activity with excellent prospects for growth. The challenge is to define and practice public relations in such a way that it fosters greater understanding and harmonious relationships among nations and organizations, in the public interest.

A VARIETY OF DEFINITIONS

People often define public relations by some of its most visible techniques and tactics, such as publicity in a newspaper, a television interview with an organization's spokesperson, or the appearance of a celebrity at a special event.

What people fail to understand is that public relations is a process involving many subtle and far-reaching aspects. It includes research and analysis, policy formation, programming, communication, and feedback from numerous publics. Its practitioners operate on two distinct levels—as advisers to their clients or to an organization's top management, and as technicians who produce and disseminate messages in multiple media channels.

Any number of definitions have been formulated over the years. Rex Harlow, a pioneer public relations educator, once compiled more than 500 definitions from almost as many sources. He found definitions ranging from the simple to the complex. Some of the more succinct include:

- Good performance, publicly appreciated.

- PR stands for **P**erformance and then **R**ecognition.

- Doing good and getting credit for it.

More formal definitions are provided by dictionaries and textbook authors. The *American Heritage College Dictionary* defines *public relations* as: "The art or science of establishing and promoting a favorable relationship with the public; the methods and activities used to establish and promote such a relationship."

Scott M. Cutlip, Allen H. Center, and Glen M. Broom state in *Effective Public Relations* (Sixth Edition) that "public relations is the management function that identifies, establishes, and maintains mutually beneficial relationships between an organization and the various publics on whom its success or failure depends." The management function is also emphasized in *Managing Public Relations* by James E. Grunig and Todd Hunt. They state that public relations is "the management of communication between an organization and its publics."

National and international public relations organizations, including the Public Relations Society of America (PRSA), also have formulated definitions. Here is a sampling from around the world:

■ "Public relations is the deliberate, planned, and sustained effort to establish and maintain mutual understanding between an organization and its publics." (British Institute of Public Opinion, whose definition has also been adopted in a number of Commonwealth nations)

■ "Public relations is the conscious and legitimate effort to achieve understanding and the establishment and maintenance of trust among the public on the basis of systematic research." (Deutsche Public Relations Gesellschaft of the Federal Republic of Germany—note that there is no term equivalent to *public relations* in the German language)

■ "Public relations is the sustained and systematic managerial effort through which private and public organizations seek to establish understanding, sympathy, and support in those public circles with which they have or expect to obtain contact." (Dansk Public Relations Klub of Denmark, which also uses the English term)

■ "Public relations practice is the art and social science of analyzing trends, predicting their consequences, counseling organization leaders, and implementing planned programs of action which serve both the organization's and the public's interest." (A definition approved at the World Assembly of Public Relations in Mexico City in 1978 and endorsed by 34 national public relations organizations)

Careful study of these explanations should enable anyone to formulate a definition of public relations; committing any single one to memory is unnecessary. The key words to remember in defining public relations follow:

Deliberate. Public relations activity is intentional. It is designed to influence, gain understanding, provide information, and obtain *feedback* (reaction from those affected by the activity).

Planned. Public relations activity is organized. Solutions to problems are discovered and logistics are thought out, with the activity taking place over a period of time. It is systematic, requiring research and analysis.

PUBLIC RELATIONS SOCIETY OF AMERICA OFFICIAL STATEMENT ON PUBLIC RELATIONS

Public relations helps our complex, pluralistic society to reach decisions and function more effectively by contributing to mutual understanding among groups and institutions. It serves to bring private and public policies into harmony.

Public relations serves a wide variety of institutions in society such as businesses, trade unions, government agencies, voluntary associations, foundations, hospitals, and educational and religious institutions. To achieve their goals, these institutions must develop effective relationships with many different audiences or publics such as employees, members, customers, local communities, shareholders and other institutions, and with society at large.

The managements of institutions need to understand the attitudes and values of their publics in order to achieve institutional goals. The goals themselves are shaped by the external environment. The public relations practitioner acts as a counselor to management, and as a mediator, helping to translate private aims into reasonable, publicly acceptable policy and action.

As a management function, public relations encompasses the following:

■ Anticipating, analyzing, and interpreting public opinion, attitudes, and issues which might impact, for good or ill, the operations and plans of the organization.

■ Counseling management at all levels in the organization with regard to policy decisions, courses of action and communication, taking into account their public ramifications and the organization's social or citizenship responsibilities.

■ Researching, conducting and evaluating, on a continuing basis, programs of action and communication to achieve informed public understanding necessary to the success of an organization's aims. These may include marketing, financial, fund-raising, employee, community or government relations and other programs.

■ Planning and implementing the organization's efforts to influence or change public policy.

■ Setting objectives, planning, budgeting, recruiting and training staff, developing facilities—in short, *managing* the resources needed to perform all of the above.

■ Examples of the knowledge that may be required in the professional practice of public relations include communication arts, psychology, social psychology, sociology, political science, economics and the principles of management and ethics. Technical knowledge and skills are required for opinion research, public issues analysis, media relations, direct mail, institutional advertising, publications, film/video productions, special events, speeches and presentations.

In helping to define and implement policy, the public relations practitioner utilizes a variety of professional communication skills and plays an integrative role both within the organization and between the organization and the external environment.

Performance.   Effective public relations is based on actual policies and performance. No amount of public relations will generate goodwill and support if the organization is unresponsive to community concerns. A Pacific Northwest timber company, despite an advertising campaign with the theme "For Us, Every Day Is Earth Day," became known as the villain of Washington State because of its insistence on logging old-growth forests and bulldozing a logging road into a prime elk habitat.

Public Interest.   The rationale for any public relations activity is to serve the public interest, and not simply to achieve benefits for the organization. Ideally, public relations activity is mutually beneficial to the organization and the public; it is the alignment of the organization's self-interests with the public's concerns and interests. For example, the Mobil Corporation sponsors quality programming on public television because it enhances the company's image; by the same token, the public benefits from the availability of such programming.

Two-Way Communication.   Dictionary definitions often give the impression that public relations consists only of the dissemination of informational materials. It is equally important, however, that the definition include feedback from audiences. The ability to listen is an essential part of communication expertise.

Management Function.   Public relations is most effective when it is part of the decision making of top management. Public relations involves counseling and problem solving at high levels, not just the releasing of information after a decision has been made. Public relations is defined by Denny Griswold, founder and owner of *PR News,* as "the management function which evaluates public attitudes, identifies the policies and procedures of an organization with the public interest, and executes a program of action (and communication) to earn public understanding and acceptance."

To summarize, a person can grasp the essential elements of public relations by remembering the following words: *deliberate . . . planned . . . performance . . . public interest . . . two-way communication . . . management function.*
   In his own definition, based on the interpretations of public relations that he assembled, Harlow strongly emphasized the role of management:

Public relations is a distinctive management function which helps establish and maintain mutual lines of communication, understanding, acceptance, and cooperation between an organization and its publics; involves the management of problems or issues; helps management to keep informed on and responsive to public opinion; defines and emphasizes the responsibility of management to serve the public interest; helps management keep abreast of and effectively utilize change, serving as an early warning system to help anticipate trends; and uses research and ethical communication techniques as its principal tools.

   Other definitions stress the importance of counseling management. As public relations pioneer Edward L. Bernays once explained to the World Assembly of Public Relations, professional counsel advises management on attitudes and actions to gain social objectives.

PUBLIC RELATIONS AS A PROCESS

Public relations is a *process*—that is, a series of actions, changes, or functions that bring about a result. One popular way to describe the process, and to remember its components, is to use the RACE acronym, first articulated by John Marston in his book *The*

Nature of Public Relations. Essentially, RACE means that public relations activity consists of four key elements:

1. Research—What is the problem?

2. Action and Planning—What is going to be done about it?

3. Communication—How will the public be told?

4. Evaluation—Was the audience reached and what was the effect?

Part Two of the text discusses this key four-step process.

Another approach is to think of the process as a never-ending cycle in which six components are links in a chain. Figure 1.1 shows the process.

The public relations process also may be conceptualized as follows:

Level 1

a. Public relations personnel obtain insights into the problem from numerous sources.

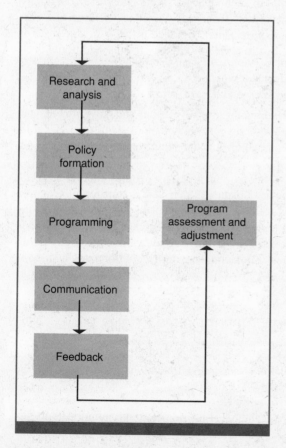

FIGURE 1.1
In the conceptualization of public relations as a cyclical process, feedback—or audience response—leads to assessment of the program, which becomes an essential element in the development of another public relations project.

b. Public relations personnel analyze these inputs and make recommendations to management.

c. Management makes policy and action decisions.

Level 2

d. Public relations personnel execute a program of action.

e. Public relations personnel evaluate the effectiveness of the action.

Step A consists of inputs that determine the nature and extent of the public relations problem. These may include feedback from the public, media reporting and editorial comment, analysis of trend data, other forms of research, personal experience, and government pressures and regulations.

In Step B, public relations personnel assess these inputs, establish objectives and an agenda of activity, and convey their recommendations to management. As previously noted, this is the adviser role of public relations.

After management makes its decisions, in Step C, public relations personnel execute the action program in Step D through such means as news releases, publications, speeches, and community relations programs. In Step E, the effect of these efforts is measured by feedback from the same components that made up Step A. The cycle is then repeated to solve related aspects of the problem that may require additional decision making and action.

Note that public relations plays two distinct roles in this process, thus serving as a "middle ground" or "linking agent." On Level 1, public relations interacts directly with external sources of information, including the public, media, and government, and relays these inputs to management along with recommendations. On Level 2, public relations becomes the vehicle through which management reaches the public with assorted messages.

Diffusion-of-knowledge theorists call public relations people "linking agents." Sociologists refer to them as "boundary spanners" that act to transfer information between two systems. As the last lines of the official statement on public relations by the Public Relations Society of America note: "The public relations practitioner utilizes a variety of professional communication skills and plays an integrative role both within the organization and between the organization and the external environment."

THE COMPONENTS OF PUBLIC RELATIONS

The basic components of public relations, according to a monograph issued by the PRSA Foundation, include the following:

Counseling. Providing advice to management concerning policies, relationships, and communications.

Research.   Determining attitudes and behaviors of publics in order to plan public relations strategies. Such research can be used to (1) generate mutual understanding or (2) influence and persuade publics.

Media Relations.   Working with mass media in seeking publicity or responding to their interests in the organization.

Publicity.   Disseminating planned messages through selected media to further the organization's interests.

Employee/Member Relations.   Responding to concerns, informing, and motivating an organization's employees or members.

Community Relations.   Planned activity with a community to maintain an environment that benefits both the organization and the community.

Public Affairs.   Developing effective involvement in public policy, and helping an organization adapt to public expectations. The term also is used by government agencies to describe their public relations activities and by many corporations as an umbrella term to describe multiple public relations activities.

Government Affairs.   Relating directly with legislatures and regulatory agencies on behalf of the organization. *Lobbying* can be part of a government affairs program.

Issues Management.   Identifying and addressing issues of public concern that affect the organization. It can include *environmental affairs*.

Financial Relations.   Creating and maintaining investor confidence and building good relationships with the financial community. Also known as *Investor Relations* or *Shareholder Relations*.

Industry Relations.   Relating with other firms in the industry of an organization and with trade associations.

Development/Fund-Raising.   Demonstrating the need for and encouraging the public to support an organization, primarily through financial contributions.

Minority Relations/Multicultural Affairs.   Relating with individuals and groups in minorities or cultural groups.

Special Events.   Stimulating an interest in a person, product, or organization by means of a focused "happening"; also, activities designed to interact with publics and listen to them.

Marketing Communications.   Combination of activities designed to sell a product, service, or idea, including advertising, collateral materials, publicity, promotion, direct mail, trade shows, and special events.

These components, and how they function, constitute the substance of this textbook. Chapter 2, for example, begins with an overview of how various kinds of organizations use public relations.

OTHER TERMS FOR PUBLIC RELATIONS

Public relations is used as an umbrella term on a worldwide basis. Sixty-four of the 69 national membership associations, from the Arab Public Relations Society to the Zimbabwe Institute of Public Relations, identify themselves with that term.

Individual companies and other groups, however, often use other terms to describe the public relations function. *O'Dwyer's Directory of Corporate Communications* (1992) identifies 135 of the *Fortune* 500 companies as having *corporate communications* departments, while another 62 use the term *public affairs.* Other titles used include *corporate affairs, corporate relations, corporate and investor relations, marketing services,* and *external affairs.*

A Conference Board survey of 150 major U.S. corporations also found a movement toward the use of other names. In 60 percent of the surveyed firms, the word *communications* is used to describe the public relations function. In some cases, as at Apple Computer, Inc., corporate communications is the umbrella term and "public relations" is considered one of several departments.

Public information is the term most widely used by social service agencies, universities, and government agencies. The implication is that only information is being disseminated, in contrast to persuasive communication, generally perceived as the purpose of public relations. Social services agencies often use the term *community relations,* and the military is fond of *public affairs.*

In many cases it is clear that companies and organizations use *public information, public affairs,* or *corporate communications* as euphemisms for *public relations.* This, in part, is a reaction to the misuse of the original term by the public and the media. On occasion, a reporter or government official will use the term *public relations gimmick* or *ploy* to imply that the activities or statements of an organization are without substance or sincerity.

The popularity of *corporate communications* is based on the idea that the term is broader than *public relations,* which is often incorrectly perceived as only *media relations.* Corporate communications, many contend, encompasses all communications of the company, including advertising, marketing communications, public affairs, community relations, and employee communications.

Other organizations use a term that better describes the primary activity of the department. It is clear, for example, that a department of investor relations deals primarily with stockholders, institutional investors, and the financial press. Likewise, a department of environmental affairs, community relations, or employee communications is self-explanatory. A department of marketing communications primarily emphasizes product publicity and promotion. The organization and functions of communications departments are discussed in Chapter 5.

*President Bill Clinton and Vice President Al Gore open
their campaign to simplify government by posing outside the
White House with stacks of federal regulations. Creating
events to dramatize a program is a frequently used public
relations technique.*

Like departments, individuals specialize in subcategories of public relations. A person who deals exclusively with placement of stories in the media is, to be precise, a *publicist.* A *press agent* also is a specialist, operating within the subcategory of public relations that concentrates on finding unusual news angles and planning events or "happenings" that attract media attention—a stunt by an aspiring Hollywood actress, for example, or an attempt to be listed in the *Guinness Book of Records* by baking the world's largest apple pie.

Unfortunately, the public and the press often use the general term *public relations expert* to describe publicists, press agents, and former government officials such as Michael Deaver who illegally traded on his Washington contacts under the guise of "public affairs." (Chapter 15 discusses the Deaver case.)

A number of newspapers, including the Washington *Post,* also continue the practice of using *flack,* a derisive slang term for a press agent or anyone else working in public relations. Some media also refer to public relations people and other communication consultants as "spin doctors," particularly in politics.

Within the public relations community, feeling also exists that "PR" is a slang term that carries a somewhat denigrating connotation. Sam Black, a public relations consultant in the United Kingdom and author of several books on public relations, says, "The use of 'PR' was probably originated as a nickname for 'press relations,'" the primary activity of public relations in its early years (see Chapter 3).

The worldwide aspect of public relations is illustrated by this publication of American Express. Many corporations have international operations that require extensive public relations programs.

Nicknames rarely have a place in formal writing, and the authors of this text have eliminated "PR" as much as possible. The authors agree with Black and others that it is difficult to take an emerging profession seriously if its complexity and broad scope are reduced to a trite abbreviation. However, the term *PR* probably never will be eliminated from daily conversation.

HOW PUBLIC RELATIONS DIFFERS FROM JOURNALISM

Writing for mass audiences is a common activity of both public relations practitioners and journalists. In addition, public relations professionals use a number of journalistic techniques to communicate with various publics.

This practice has led many people, including former journalists who enter public relations, to the incorrect conclusion that little difference exists between public relations and journalism. The two fields, however, differ fundamentally in scope, objectives, audiences, and channels.

Scope. Public relations, as stated earlier, has many components, ranging from counseling to issues management and special events. Journalistic writing and media relations, although important, are only two of these elements. In addition, effective practice of public relations requires strategic thinking, problem-solving capability, and other management skills.

Objectives. Journalists, usually employed by a news organization, are paid to gather and select information for the primary purpose of providing "objective" news and information. In such a setting, as Professors David Dozier and William Ehling explain, ". . . communication activities are an end in themselves."

Public relations personnel also gather facts and information, but their objective is different. Communications activity is only a means to end. Dozier and Ehling write, "Conceptually, the effects achieved by public relations programs include awareness, knowledge, opinions, attitudes, and behavior of those affected by the program."

Periodicals such as this magazine San Diego Gas & Electric Company publishes for its employees are an important channel of communication within a corporation. This issue gives employees goals to pursue during the coming year. Employee relations is a vital part of corporate public relations operations.

In other words, public relations personnel are not "objective" reporters, but advocates. Edward M. Stanton, former chairman of the Manning, Selvage & Lee public relations firm, describes public relations as "working with clients on strategy and messages, and then delivering these messages to target audiences in order to persuade them to do something that is beneficial to the client."

Audiences.   Journalists write primarily for one mass audience—readers, listeners, or viewers of the medium for which they work. By definition, mass audiences are usually large and ill-defined, and they have little in common with each other. In contrast, effective public relations is based on carefully defining an audience and segmenting it into demographic and psychological characteristics. Constant research allows messages to be tailored to audience needs, concerns, and interests.

Channels.   Most journalists, by nature of their employment, reach audiences through one channel—the medium that publishes or broadcasts their work. Public relations personnel use a variety of channels to reach targeted audiences. The channels employed may be a combination of mass media outlets—newspapers, magazines, radio, and television. Or they may include direct mail, pamphlets, posters, and special events. Any combination of channels may be selected to achieve message penetration and maximum understanding.

HOW PUBLIC RELATIONS DIFFERS FROM ADVERTISING

Just as many people mistakenly equate publicity with public relations, there is also some confusion about the distinction between publicity (one area of public relations) and advertising.

Publicity—or information about an event, an individual or group, or a product—is disseminated through the news media and other channels to attract favorable public notice. The practitioner who prepares and distributes the information is often called a *publicist.*

Advertising is paid space and time in print, including billboards, and in electronic media. Organizations and individuals contract to purchase space and time, and an advertisement is almost always broadcast or printed exactly as the purchaser has prepared it.

Publicity, as distinguished from advertising, appears in broadcast news programs and in newspaper and magazine stories. The prepared copy is sent to the news department (not the advertising department) and *gatekeepers* (reporters and editors) modify the material according to news requirements. In other words, there is no guarantee that an organization's news release will be used or will appear in the form in which it was prepared.

There are other differences between public relations activities and advertising. Here are some of them:

■　Advertising works almost exclusively through mass media outlets; public relations relies on a number of communication tools—brochures, slide presentations, special events, speeches, news releases, feature stories, and so forth.

- Advertising is addressed to external audiences—primarily consumers of goods and services; public relations presents its message to specialized external audiences (stockholders, vendors, community leaders, environmental groups, and so on) and internal publics (employees).

- Advertising is readily identified as a specialized communication function; public relations is broader in scope, dealing with the policies and performance of the entire organization, from the morale of employees to the way telephone operators respond to calls.

- Advertising often is used as a communication tool in public relations, and public relations activity often supports advertising campaigns. Advertising's function is to sell goods and services; the public relations function is to create an environment in which the organization can thrive. The latter calls for dealing with economic, social, and political factors that can affect the organization.

The major disadvantage of advertising, of course, is the cost. Typically, a full-page ad in *Parade* magazine, distributed weekly in almost 350 dailies, costs $421,000. Advertising campaigns on network television can run into the millions of dollars. Because of this, companies increasingly are using a tool of public relations—product publicity—that is more cost-effective and often more credible because the message appears in a news context.

HOW PUBLIC RELATIONS DIFFERS FROM MARKETING

Public relations is distinct from marketing in several ways, although their boundaries often overlap.

The functions overlap, for example, because both deal with an organization's relationships and employ similar communication tools to reach the public. Both have the ultimate purpose of assuring an organization's success and economic survival. Public relations and marketing, however, approach this task from somewhat different perspectives, or world views.

This difference is illustrated by the descriptions of each field that a distinguished panel of educators and practitioners in public relations and marketing developed during a colloquium at San Diego State University. After a day of debate, they formed this definition of public relations:

Public relations is the management process whose goal is to attain and maintain accord and positive behaviors among social groupings on which an organization depends in order to achieve its mission. Its fundamental responsibility is to build and maintain a hospitable environment for an organization.

The group defined marketing's goal in different terms:

Marketing is the management process whose goal is to attract and satisfy customers (or clients) on a long-term basis in order to achieve an organization's economic objectives. Its fundamental responsibility is to build and maintain markets for an organization's products or services.

In other words, public relations is concerned with building relationships and generating goodwill for the organization; marketing is concerned with customers and selling products and services.

James E. Grunig, editor of *Excellence in Public Relations and Communication Management,* put the differences between public relations and marketing in sharp contrast:

. . . the marketing function should communicate with the markets for an organization's goods and services. Public relations should be concerned with all the publics of the organization. The major purpose of marketing is to make money for the organization by increasing the slope of the demand curve. The major purpose of public relations is to save money for the organization by building relationships with publics that constrain or enhance the ability of the organization to meet its mission.

In this passage, Grunig points out a fundamental difference between marketing and public relations in terms of how the public is described. Marketing and advertising professionals tend to speak of "target markets," "consumers," and "customers." Public relations professionals tend to talk of "publics," "audiences," and "stakeholders." These groups may be any publics that are affected by or can affect an organization. According to Grunig, "Publics can arise within stakeholder categories—such as employees, communities, stockholders, governments, members, students, suppliers, and donors, as well as consumers."

Public relations theorists point out another fundamental difference between public relations and marketing. In their view, "excellent" public relations is devoid of persuasion; its ideal purpose is to create mutual understanding and cooperation through two-way dialogue. Marketing, by definition, is persuasive in intent and purpose—to sell products and services. The four models of public relations are discussed in Chapter 3.

HOW PUBLIC RELATIONS SUPPORTS MARKETING

Philip Kotler, professor of marketing at Northwestern University and author of a leading marketing textbook, says public relations is the fifth "P" of marketing strategy, which includes four other Ps—Product, Price, Place, and Promotion. As he wrote in the *Harvard Business Review,* "Public relations takes longer to cultivate, but when energized, it can help pull the company into the market."

When public relations is used to support directly an organization's marketing objectives, it is called *marketing communications.* This was identified as a component of public relations earlier in the chapter. Another term, coined by Thomas Harris in his book *The Marketer's Guide to Public Relations,* is *marketing public relations.* He says:

I make a clear distinction between those public relations functions which support marketing, which I call Marketing Public Relations (MPR) and the other public relations activities that define the corporation's relationships with its non-customer publics, which I label Corporate Public Relations (CPR).

Dennis L. Wilcox and Lawrence W. Nolte, in their text *Public Relations Writing and Media Techniques,* list eight ways in which product publicity contributes to fulfilling marketing objectives by

- Developing new prospects for new markets, such as people who inquire after seeing or hearing a product release in the news media

- Providing third-party endorsements—via newspapers, magazines, radio, and television—through news releases about a company's products or services, community involvement, inventions, and new plans

- Generating sales leads, usually through articles in the trade press about new products and services

- Paving the way for sales calls

- Stretching the organization's advertising and promotional dollars through timely and supportive releases about it and its products

- Providing inexpensive sales literature, because articles about the company and its products can be reprinted as informative pieces for prospective customers

- Establishing the corporation as an authoritative source of information on a given product

- Helping to sell minor products that don't have large advertising budgets

Harris summarizes:

In its market-support function, public relations is used to achieve a number of objectives. The most important of these are to raise awareness, to inform and educate, to gain understanding, to build trust, to make friends, to give people reasons to buy and finally to create a climate of consumer acceptance.

The successful promotion of the movie *Jurassic Park* shows how public relations tools can make a difference. A month before the film opened, movie studio publicists had generated more than a thousand stories in the mass media about it and had stimulated a national fascination with dinosaurs. In the week before the opening, 438 newspapers and magazines and countless television programs did advance stories about it. The result: *Jurassic Park* broke all box office records.

The key to the successful publicity was development of news releases and feature stories about all aspects of the film. Some story angles included (1) the making of the life-sized, lifelike electronically controlled dinosaurs, (2) the use of computer graphics to "create" prehistoric beasts, (3) the creation of the sounds of the dinosaurs, and (4) a description of the numerous tie-ins with merchandisers.

The human stars of the movie went on an extensive media tour and appeared on such programs as *Today* and *Good Morning, America.* Publicists arranged for a group of paleontologists to appear on *Nightline* with Ted Koppel to explore the possibility that dinosaurs could indeed be cloned in real life. For special events, models of the dinosaurs from the movie were included in museum tours around the country.

On a less spectacular level, Keebler Cookie Company used public relations techniques to introduce its Soft-Batch brand. Lacking the massive advertising resources of competitors such as Procter & Gamble and Nabisco, Keebler used a marketing public relations plan that included an unusual press kit designed in the form of Keebler's "Magic Oven." The resulting media publicity, valued at $3 million in national television exposure alone, helped Keebler take a 30 percent market share with only modest advertising expenses.

Effective use of public relations tools in an integrated marketing program should not be underestimated, and this text provides a number of case studies showing how public relations departments and firms conduct programs on behalf of marketing objectives.

At the same time, readers should remember that the specialty function of "marketing communications" or "marketing public relations" is not public relations in the full sense of the definition. To say otherwise is the same as saying "publicity and public relations are the same thing."

TOWARD AN INTEGRATED PERSPECTIVE

Although well-defined differences exist among the fields of advertising, marketing, and public relations, there is an increasing realization that an organization's goals and objectives can be best accomplished through an integrated approach.

This understanding has given rise, in the 1990s, to such terms as _integrated marketing, convergent communications,_ and _integrated marketing communications._ Don Schulz, Stanley Tannenbaum, and Robert Lauterborn, authors of _Integrated Marketing Communications,_ explain the title of their book as follows:

A concept of marketing communication planning that recognizes the added value of a comprehensive plan that evaluates the strategic roles of a variety of communications disciplines, e.g., General Advertising, Direct Response, Sales Promotion, and Public Relations—and combines these disciplines to provide clarity, consistency, and maximum communication impact.

Several factors have fueled the trend toward integration. One is the adoption of tighter budgets for organizational marketing and communications. Many organizations, to avoid the high cost of advertising, now place greater emphasis on product publicity, direct mail, and sales promotion.

Second is a realization that the marketing of products and services can be affected by public and social policy issues. Environmental legislation influences packaging and content of products, a proposed luxury tax on expensive autos affects sales of those cars, and a company's support of Planned Parenthood may spur a product boycott by pro-life forces.

The impact of such factors has led many professionals to believe that organizations should do a better job of integrating public relations and public affairs into overall marketing considerations. In fact, David Coronna, writing in the _Public Relations Journal,_ suggests marketing's sixth "P" should be public policy.

A third reason is the rise of *relationship marketing*. This term essentially means developing long-term bonds with customers by making them feel good about how the company does business and giving them some kind of personal connection to it. This approach, like a response to threats of government regulation, requires the expertise of public relations professionals and the use of two-way communication.

The concept of *integrated communications* is that marketing and public relations, as well as advertising, sales promotion, and direct response, all have a voice in determining a strategy for a campaign. Figure 1.2 shows the model for integrated marketing communications.

This model, however, is the ideal. In many organizations, marketing is the dominant voice, and public relations historically has been relegated to a market-support function, concentrating on techniques instead of strategy. This role often includes producing product publicity, planning special events, arranging media interviews at a trade show, and general media relations.

Problems arise when advertising agencies attempt to do integrated programs. One advertising agency, asked to submit a plan for an integrated campaign for a million-dollar account, proposed $941,000 for traditional advertising and $59,000 for public relations. Such examples make many public relations professionals wary of "integrated communications." They see it as a veiled attempt by marketing or advertising to reduce public relations to a product-publicity function.

It is to be hoped that the turf battles of the 1990s are only the birth pains of genuine cooperation and integrated communication strategies that recognize the value and worth of each distinct discipline in the mix.

FIGURE 1.2
This model shows hows how marketing, public relations, advertising, sales promotion, and direct response can be integrated in order to achieve a unified corporate strategy. (Source: Tom Duncan, University of Colorado)

Integrated Marketing Communication

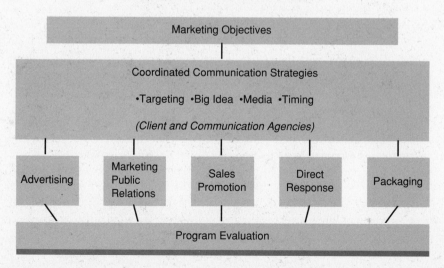

THE VALUES OF PUBLIC RELATIONS

This chapter has placed public relations within the context of definitions, activities, and process. It has also attempted to explain how public relations differs from journalism, advertising, and marketing. A good summarizing statement on the role of public relations was prepared by PRSA's Task Force on the Stature and Role of Public Relations:

Public relations is a means for the public to have its desires and interests felt by the institutions in our society. It interprets and speaks for the public to otherwise unresponsive organizations, as well as speaking for those organizations to the public.

Public relations is a means to achieve mutual adjustment between institutions and groups, establishing smoother relationships that benefit the public.

Public relations is a safety valve for freedom. By providing means of working out accommodations, it makes arbitrary action or coercion less likely.

Public relations is an essential element in the communications system that enables individuals to be informed on many aspects of subjects that affect their lives.

Public relations personnel can help activate the organization's social conscience.

Public relations (either systematic or unconscious) is a universal activity. It functions in all aspects of life. Everyone practices principles of public relations in seeking acceptance, cooperation, or affection of others. Public relations professionals practice public relations as an occupation.

CLINTON HEALTH PLAN CREATES FIERCE PUBLIC RELATIONS FIGHT

A public relations battle with extremely high stakes, involving powerful competing forces in American society, erupted when President Clinton proposed to Congress a fundamental change in the nation's health-care system.

As it evolved, the fight to win the minds of Congress and of the American people provided a vivid example of public relations in operation.

The principal competing forces were (1) Clinton, his wife Hillary Rodham Clinton, the White House publicity machine, and their political allies, selling the plan; (2) anti-Clinton members of Congress, working to prevent its passage; (3) massive commercial forces including insurance, tobacco, liquor and beer, pharmaceutical, and hospital firms, seeking to kill portions of the plan they believed would hurt them financially; and (4) major national membership organizations such as the American Medical Association, the Association of Trial Lawyers of America, the American Association of Retired People, and the National Federation of Independent Business, trying to block or reshape portions of the plan to benefit their members.

The groups used a wide range of public relations tools, including television appearances and commercials, radio talk shows, full-page newspaper advertisements, intense person-to-person lobbying, pamphlets, videotapes, banks of telephone persuaders, facsimile and electronic mail (computer) messages.

"It's the largest mobilization since the establishment of Social Security," said Frank Mankiewicz, a veteran Washington political figure now a partner in Hill and Knowlton, which lobbies for the Medical Rehabilitation Education Foundation.

Hillary Rodham Clinton testifies before the U.S. Senate Finance Committee concerning health care.

Some examples of the public relations tactics used in the struggle:

■ After his warmly applauded speech to Congress announcing the plan, President Clinton appeared in person at televised community meetings around the country to explain the program and answer questions. Hillary Rodham Clinton, principal author of the plan, spoke repeatedly before congressional committees and made innumerable TV appearances, both nationally and in interviews with local TV personalities by satellite. Clinton cabinet members spread out across the country for local speeches and TV talks. News releases and fax messages flowed from the White House in a daily torrent.

■ The American Medical Association, opposing central elements of the plan, sent a letter to 670,000 doctors and 40,000 medical students, urging them to support its position. The AMA asked doctors to lobby their patients on its behalf. Hundreds of doctors paid calls on their congressmen in the Capitol. The AMA had a $7 million budget for lobbying.

■ Restaurant owners gave a banquet for 150 members of Congress, with silver-plated Chippendale mint dishes as favors, to rally them against small business taxation in the plan.

■ The Democratic National Committee ran a TV commercial accusing the insurance industry of using scare tactics in its TV advertisements in order to protect its profits.

■ Anheuser-Busch put placards on its trucks urging beer drinkers to dial 1-800-BEER-TAX and protest a possible tax on that beverage.

■ Planned Parenthood organized a postcard campaign by members demanding retention of abortion services in the plan.

■ So many groups campaigned for their special interests in the fight that organizations with widely diverse concerns hired the same powerful lobbying firm to represent them. Patton, Boggs & Blow worked for the Federation of American Health Systems (for-profit hospitals), the U.S. Tobacco Company, the National Association of Life Underwriters, the Association of Trial Lawyers of America, Blue Cross of California, and the National Retail Federation, among others.

■ Bogged down under these conflicting pressures, the 1994 session of Congress failed to vote on a health care bill. The fight resumed in the next session.

Other aspects of the health-care battle are discussed throughout this textbook.

CASE PROBLEM

The National Company plans to introduce a new line of its battery-powered note-book and portable computers. The approach is an integrated marketing communications campaign that will incorporate public relations, direct mail, sales promotion, and advertising. The objectives are to

■ Generate awareness of the new product with business audiences.

■ Position National as the technology leader in developing and manufacturing of notebook/portable computers.

■ Increase National's sales and market share.

Do some brainstorming. Can you think of any audience research that could be done before you plan the marketing communications program? What variety of techniques and activities could help accomplish National's objectives?

QUESTIONS FOR REVIEW AND DISCUSSION

1. How many people work in public relations? Is public relations a growing field around the world?

2. There are many definitions of public relations. Of those listed in Chapter 1, select the one you find most satisfying and discuss the reasons for your preference.

3. What ten words characterize the essential elements of public relations?

4. How would you summarize the official statement on public relations issued by the Public Relations Society of America?

5. The RACE acronym is a popular way of describing the public relations process. For what step does each initial stand?

6. Public relations is described as a *loop process*. What component makes it a loop process instead of just a linear process?

7. What are the basic components of public relations practice? Which one sounds the most interesting as a career specialty for you?

8. What other terms are used by organizations to describe the public relations function? Do you have a preference for any of them? Explain your reasons.

9. What do publicists and press agents do? Should they be considered "public relations experts"? Why or why not?

10. Do you consider "PR" a slang term that should be avoided? Why or why not?

11. How does public relations differ from journalism? Advertising? Marketing?

12. How can the techniques and activities of public relations support the marketing function?

13. What is marketing communications? What is the concept of integrated marketing communications?

14. What three reasons are given for an organization to establish an integrated approach to its communications strategy?

15. What are the social values of public relations?

SUGGESTED READINGS

Blewett, Steve. "Who Do People Say That We Are." *Communication World,* August 1993, pp. 13–16. Essay on what constitutes public relations.

Broom, Glen M., and Tucker, Kerry. "An Essential Double Helix: Marketing Public Relations." *Public Relations Journal,* November 1989, pp. 39–40.

Brody, E. W. "The Domain of Public Relations." *Public Relations Review,* Winter 1992, pp. 349–365.

Coronna, David M. "Add Public Policy to Marketing Portfolio." *Public Relations Journal,* September 1993, pp. 12–13.

Culbertson, Hugh M. "Breadth of Perspective: An Important Concept for Public Relations." In *Public Relations Research Annual,* Vol. 1, ed. James and Larissa Grunig. Hillsdale, NJ: Lawrence Erlbaum Associates, 1989, pp. 3–26.

Cushman, Aaron. "Why Marketing Directors Are Listening Now." *Public Relations Journal,* May 1990, pp. 17–19.

Dozier, David M., and Ehling William P. "Evaluation of Public Relations Programs: What the Literature Tells Us About Their Effects." In *Excellence in Public Relations and Communication Management,* ed. James E. Grunig. Hillsdale, NJ: Erlbaum Associates, 1992, pp. 159–184.

Ehling, William P., White, Jon, and Grunig, James E. "Public Relations and Marketing Practices." In *Excellence in Public Relations and Communication Management,* ed. James E. Grunig. Hillsdale, NJ: Erlbaum Associates, 1992, pp. 327–356.

Harris, Thomas L. "How MPR Adds Value to Integrated Marketing Communications." *Public Relations Quarterly,* Summer 1993, pp. 13–18. Marketing public relations.

Hauss, Deborah. "Global Communications Come of Age: Five Case Histories Prove Power of Integrated Messages." *Public Relations Journal,* August 1993, pp. 22–26.

Holmes, Paul. "Brands on the Run." *Inside PR,* August 1993, pp. 15–19. The role of public relations in building credibility for products.

Holmes, Paul. "Public Relations as Conflict Resolution." *Inside PR,* June–July 1993, pp. 15–18. Practitioners as consensus builders.

Levy, Dorothy. "What Public Relations Can Do Better Than Advertising." *Public Relations Quarterly,* Fall 1989, pp. 7–9.

Paluszek, John. "Public Relations in the Coming Global Economy." *Vital Speeches of the Day,* October 15, 1989.

Sparks, Suzanne D. "Public Relations: Is It Dangerous to Use the Term?" *Public Relations Quarterly,* Fall 1993, pp. 27–28. How to increase the field's credibility.

Spicer, Christopher H. "Images of Public Relations in the Print Media." *Journal of Public Relations Research,* vol. 5, no. 1, 1993, pp. 47–61.

Tavcar, Larry. "Public Relations on the Screen: 17 Films to See." *Public Relations Quarterly,* Fall 1993, pp. 21–23. How Hollywood portrays public relations.

Webster, Philip J. "Strategic Corporate Public Relations: What's the Bottom Line?" *Public Relations Journal,* February 1990, pp. 18–21.

Types of Public Relations Work

P R E V I E W   The objective of this chapter is to identify the principal areas of public relations work, including corporations, several types of nonprofit organizations, education, government, entertainment, sports, and travel.

Topics covered in the chapter include:

- Corporations

- Membership organizations

- Social, cultural, religious, and health-care agencies

- Entertainment, sports, and travel

- Government, politics, and the military

- Education

A substantial majority of public relations professionals work to further the goals and objectives of profit-earning organizations. They do so either as members of a public relations department or as part of a counseling firm employed by the corporation. Especially in large companies, public relations programs have many facets, each of which requires development of specialized knowledge and techniques.

The primary areas of corporate public relations work are the following:

1. *Reputation—protection and enhancement.* The role of tending to company reputation involves preserving and building goodwill for a company by demonstrating to the public that the firm is an efficient producer of well-made products, an honest seller of goods and services, a fair and equitable employer, and a responsible corporate citizen. This function includes: (*a*) protecting the company against attacks; (*b*) telling its story well when controversy arises; (*c*) initiating programs to explain company goals and policies; (*d*) making early identification of developing problems so the company can act quickly to solve them; (*e*) demonstrating that the company follows good environmental practices and urging management to do so; (*f*) protecting and promoting corporate trademarks and logos; (*g*) showing that the company cares for the welfare of its employees and the communities in which its facilities are located, with special awareness of ethnic diversity; and (*h*) explaining the company's position on political, social, and economic issues.

This role, performed in many ways, uses a variety of strategies and communication tools to build a positive image of the company. "Image" in this sense means the personality or character of the company projected to the public.

Some public relations experts dislike the term *image* because it has the connotation of being illusionary, suggesting deceptive manipulation. Since effective public relations is presenting "images" that actually reflect a company's policies and actions, many companies describe this broad-based role as building *corporate identity.*

2. *Information service.* Part of building a company's reputation is the role of supplying information to a variety of publics. One important area is *media relations.* Companies send news releases to the media in order to inform the public about earnings, acquisitions, new products, and so forth. They hold news conferences, and the public relations staff sometimes arranges interviews for reporters with company executives. Companies must respond to inquiries from customers, distributors, government officials, and community residents. Prompt, comprehensive, and gracious responses build friends; perceived "brush-offs" make enemies.

3. *Marketing communications.* Public relations strategies and tactics are designed to fulfill the marketing objectives of an organization, whether these involve selling services or goods, or increasing the membership of an organization.

Much of this work is in the form of product publicity. People in the field work closely with the trade press, and with the general media as well, in placement of stories about product developments and use of products. They write articles and brochures, organize product promotions, create tie-ins with special events, and arrange press interviews. Public relations practitioners work closely with the marketing department.

When the quality and safety of a company's product are under severe criticism, public relations representatives must use a wide range of techniques either to recall the product or convince the public that the product is safe and a recall unnecessary.

4. *Investor relations.* The corporate function of investor relations is also called *stockholder communications.* Essentially, it means providing information to individuals who own stock or have a special interest in the corporation. Elaborate annual reports, quarterly reports mailed with dividend checks, and other printed materials are sent to stockholders on a regular basis. At an annual meeting stockholders may ask questions of management, voice complaints, and have their resolutions for policy changes put to a vote. If a proxy fight erupts (conflict involving rival solicitations of support from absent stockholders), or one company attempts the forced takeover of another, public relations personnel often mount a campaign to convince stockholders not to sell their stock. Conversely, staff members may be called upon to convince stockholders that an acquisition or merger is in their best interest.

For example, Lockheed Corporation successfully fought off an attempt by billionaire Harold Simmons to capture control of its board of directors in a bitter proxy battle. Solicitation of proxies by both sides was so intense that 83.4 percent of Lockheed's 63.2 million outstanding shares were voted at the annual meeting. Lockheed employees, who owned 19 percent of the stock, voted 90 percent of it in favor of their bosses—a major factor in management's victory. Total cost of the proxy fight for the two sides: $14 million. Both sides made extensive use of public relations counsel and employed such techniques as letters to stockholders, full-page advertisements in the *Wall Street Journal,* and video news releases to institutional investors.

5. *Financial relations.* A parallel function of investor relations is to provide extensive information to the financial community. Security analysts at brokerage houses, large banks, and similar institutions weigh the information and make judgments on a company's financial strength and prospects. On the basis of their recommendations, institutional investors and brokerage firms buy or sell a company's stock.

Public relations staff members prepare printed materials and arrange for high company officials to address meetings of financial analysts. Failure to communicate the company's message well can cause major losses, as in the case of the Amdahl Corporation. Its stock immediately declined three points after a key analyst covering the computer industry removed the company from a recommended list. This meant a paper loss to the company of millions of dollars.

A thorough knowledge of finance, as well as Securities and Exchange Commission (SEC) rules, is essential for a public relations person specializing in financial relations. (For a further discussion, see Chapters 13 and 14.)

6. *Community relations.* A company is a citizen in a local community, and such citizenship implies certain obligations. Corporations often take an active role in supporting community organizations. Encouraging employees to do volunteer work, giving a grant to the local symphony orchestra, lending executives to the United Way effort, having executives serve on civic advisory boards—these are a few of the steps a company can take. Good relations include an effort to assure company compliance with environmental regulations and to work with other civic groups to improve the quality of life. The swift growth of multicultural diversity challenges companies to make certain that they are reaching all elements of their communities.

7. *Employee relations.* An open flow of information from management to employees, and from employees to management, is recognized as essential by most corporations. To achieve this, the public relations department works closely with the personnel or human resources department.

Among the functions it performs are (*a*) publication of an employee magazine, newspaper, or video news magazine; (*b*) the writing of brochures for employees explaining company policies and benefits: (*c*) preparation of audiovisual materials for training and policy-transmission purposes; (*d*) the scheduling of staff meetings and seminars; (*e*) the training of speakers among managers and supervisors who serve as communicators to employees; and (*f*) coordination of employee productivity or energy conservation campaigns. The public relations staff of FMC Corporation, for example, coordinated an employee campaign to generate awareness about the company's code of ethics.

8. *Special events management.* A relatively new role for public relations personnel is special events management, as companies increasingly sponsor everything from rock concerts to marathon races. Corporate sponsorship of such events requires public relations staff members who have an eye for detail, organization, logistics, and publicity opportunities.

9. *Public affairs.* The actions of government on the local, state, and national level have major effects on corporations and how they conduct their affairs. Thus, a number of public relations people work in the area often referred to as *governmental relations.* In this role public affairs executives seek to influence legislation through contact with legislators and governmental regulatory agencies.

Public affairs work is done on several levels. On one level is the public affairs manager. He or she, according to the public affairs section of PRSA, must be "concerned with the management function covering the relationship between the organization and its external environment and involving key tasks of intelligence gathering and analysis, external action program directed at government, communities and the general public as well as strategic issue management and internal communications." A *lobbyist,* in contrast, has a narrower function: the lobbyist is "concerned with direct or indirect means of exercising influence on passage or defeat of legislative bills or regulatory actions, and [seeks] to influence their outcomes."

10. *Issues management.* The role of issues management, often carried out by public relations professionals, is the management process of determining how various public issues will affect the company. R. Howard Chase, a counselor specializing in issues management, says there are five steps in the process: (1) identifying the issue, (2) analyzing it, (3) ascertaining options open to the company, (4) initiating a plan of action, and (5) evaluating the results. (A detailed discussion of issues management appears in Chapter 8.)

The way in which an American company would assess its operations and investment in Russia illustrates the process. Using Chase's model, the firm first identifies the issue as Russia's economic chaos during its change to a market economy after decades of communism and questions whether the company's long-range potential there is worth the risk. Second, it determines the policy of the U.S. government about American investment in Russia, the attitude of Russians toward its product, and the actions of other corporations. Third, it sets priorities on the options available to it and the financial impact of each. Fourth, it decides on an action program. The fifth step, of course, would be to evaluate the company's decision and the reaction to it.

A corporation's relationship with the environment, both in the products it makes and the properties it owns, is a major issue of the 1990s. Astute managements are beginning to take the initiative to clean up operations vulnerable to criticism from environmental groups. Others try to ignore the issue and hope they won't get caught—a dangerously short-sighted policy.

A REFERENCE LIST

The 11 principal areas in which public relations professionals work are the following:

- Reputation—protection and enhancement
     Corporate identity programming
- Information service
     Media relations
- Marketing communications
     Product publicity
- Investor relations
     Stockholder communications
- Financial relations
- Community relations
- Employee relations
- Special events management
- Public affairs
     Governmental relations
- Issues management
- Fund-raising

The 11 types of public relations activity just described also take place, in varying degrees, within other types of organizations. This work is described in greater detail in Part Four.

NONPROFIT ORGANIZATIONS

Significant among the communication channels that tie contemporary society together are organizations made up of individuals or separate businesses sharing strong common interests—financial, professional, social, cultural, or intellectual. Usually, these organizations advance the collective interests of their members. Public relations is essential to their success, for without public understanding and support, goals and objectives will not be realized. Five major types of associations are trade groups, labor unions, membership organizations, professional and cultural societies, and "cause" organizations.

TRADE ASSOCIATIONS

A _trade association_ consists of member companies that produce the same type of product or provide similar services. Although they may compete for the consumer's dollar as individual businesses, they band together in an association to further common interests. Their association promotes or opposes legislation, informs the public about the industry, and undertakes statistical and other types of research for the benefit of its members. Examples of powerful trade associations are the National Association of Manufacturers, the Tobacco Institute, American Bankers Association, and the Pharmaceutical Manufacturers Association.

The food industry provides examples of how trade groups work together to promote a generic product. The California Milk Advisory Board carried out an extensive public relations campaign to convince customers that real butter is "100 percent natural" and lower in fat content than most health-conscious Americans believe. The objective, of course, was to woo consumers away from margarine, which has seriously eroded the butter market.

Another trade group, the Washington State Apple Commission, along with apple growers in other states, faced a crisis when the National Resources Defense Council (NRDC), a private group, asserted that Alar, a chemical used in some orchards to improve apple growth, was carcinogenic. It said that children were more likely than adults to be harmed by such pesticides.

In a Senate hearing, actress Meryl Streep emotionally condemned Alar and other pesticides. Frightened mothers stopped giving their children apples. New York, San Francisco, Los Angeles, and other school districts quit serving the fruit; the Los Angeles cutoff alone involved 5 million apples a year. A serious slump in national sales followed. Apple growers called the surge of bad publicity "unfair."

They soon received support from the federal government. Three agencies—the Food and Drug Administration, the Environmental Protection Agency, and the Department of Agriculture—jointly disputed the NRDC claim and declared apples safe to eat. The Washington State Association, representing a primary growing area, quickly followed with a $1.7 million public relations campaign that switched the focus away from an emphasis on taste by promoting the health value of apples. Other grower groups fought back similarly. These campaigns helped to diminish the public's fear, and sales increased. The use of Alar, already in decline when the fuss began, dwindled still further. The episode showed how volatile public opinion can be. (See Chapter 15 for a description of rival public relations efforts in this controversy.)

LABOR UNIONS

To serve members and build favorable public recognition, labor organizations must rely on public relations extensively. Union leadership administers pension plans, insurance programs, and the like; the members must be kept informed about how these programs may benefit them. Grievance procedures must be explained. New members must be sought and new locals formed. Before contract negotiations, union leadership must learn what the members desire and in turn keep them informed about negotiating strategy. Just as in corporate structures, two-way communication is essential.

If a breakdown in negotiations leads to a strike, or threatens to do so, unions must outline their positions and enlist public support. Since the public often is inconvenienced by strikes, unions must find ways to explain the justness of their cause. When agreement is reached, union leadership must present the contract provisions to the members in order to obtain ratification.

Labor organizations participate heavily in political affairs, from the federal to the local level, by endorsing and financing candidates and taking strong positions on issues. Union leadership urges members to vote according to its recommendations. Less evident, but continuous, is the task of developing and publicizing activities for members and their families, and of participating in community affairs as part of the union's efforts to be a constructive organizational citizen. Political participation and community affairs both require a wide variety of public relations activities. A major problem for unions in the 1990s is to recruit and retain membership, which has been falling. (See Chapter 17 for a detailed discussion.)

MEMBERSHIP ORGANIZATIONS

Millions of adults and youths belong to nonprofit organizations that provide them with services, training, recreation, advice, and education. Prominent among national organizations of this type are the American Association of Retired People (AARP), the Boy Scouts of America, and the American Automobile Association.

PROFESSIONAL AND CULTURAL SOCIETIES

Members of a profession band together in associations for their mutual benefit, including the exchange of information, just as trade associations do. The public relations work of professional societies includes (1) legislative campaigns, (2) advocacy of professional standards, (3) publication of information at both the skilled professional and general readership levels, (4) membership recruitment, and (5) general work to

Celebrities often draw attention to events, especially in travel, entertainment, and charitable publicity work. Liza Minelli poses on the bridge of the M.V. Royal Majesty as the cruise ship's "godmother" at its christening. Captain Petros Maratos watches. In return for her participation, Public Communications, Inc., arranged for a multi-year contribution by Majestic Cruise Lines to a charity she selected.

strengthen the profession's stature in the public mind. Associations of health professionals such as the American Medical Association and the American Dental Association, for instance, conduct vigorous campaigns to promote good health practices. Other representative professional societies are the American Bar Association and the American Chemical Society.

Cultural societies resemble professional groups, except that the common bond of members is interest in a cultural activity rather than career development and stature in the profession. The Metropolitan Museum of Art, Chicago Historical Society, and San Francisco Symphony Orchestra are examples. All use public relations personnel to (1) publicize their programs, (2) produce publications, (3) arrange speaking engagements and event openings, (4) recruit new members, (5) foster community participation and support, and (6) raise funds.

"CAUSE" ORGANIZATIONS

Still another group of organizations consists of those seeking to influence the public and generate support for their points of view on a variety of issues. Representative of this category are the National Safety Council, National Wildlife Federation, Sierra Club, American Association of Retired Persons, American Civil Liberties Union, Mothers Against Drunk Driving (MADD), the National Organization for Women (NOW), and Greenpeace.

Because raising public awareness is the first task, cause groups often stage events to generate media coverage. The demonstration in Washington by AIDS victims and their supporters during the early months of the Clinton administration is an example of this method. Arrests often follow, but so do media publicity and public awareness, some of it antagonistic.

FIGURE 2.1
Both the Greenpeace stamp promoting its dolphin campaign
and the logo of the World Wildlife Fund symbolize the
significant role environmental organizations play in public
relations work.

SOCIAL, HEALTH, AND RELIGIOUS AGENCIES

Nonprofit organizations that serve social welfare, health, and religious needs call extensively on their staffs of public relations specialists to publicize their work and to raise money. As a group, these agencies enjoy public support for the work they do, but increasing scrutiny is being focused on their management. Rivalry for attention sometimes exists among them, as evidenced by the maneuvering of medical groups to influence the shape of the Clinton administration's national health plan.

Social service and religious agencies have four areas in which public relations techniques are essential:

1. Role promotion—stimulating public awareness of their work and demonstrating what can be accomplished through their services

2. Client services—making these services known to the public and convincing individuals to use them

3. Fund-raising

4. Enlistment of volunteers

The Salvation Army and Goodwill Industries are examples of social service agencies. So are the American Red Cross and the Visiting Nurse Association. On a different level are such health organizations as the American Heart Association and the American Cancer Society, which warn the public about the dangers of the diseases they combat (see Figure 2.2). Hospital public relations is a rapidly expanding field as these institutions enlarge their work in preventive medicine and add ancillary services.

FIGURE 2.2
This advertisement by the American Cancer Society urging proper nutrition was published as a public service by 15 magazines with combined circulation of 10.5 million. (Paramount Pictures allowed the Society to use the Spock photograph without charge.) (Courtesy of the American Cancer Society, Inc.)

Religious organizations on state and national levels use public relations practices in much the same way that social services do. Their concerns are to increase the role of religion in contemporary life and to provide related social services. Some church groups also take active roles in such social issues as abortion and alcoholism.

ENTERTAINMENT, SPORTS, AND TRAVEL

Publicizing individuals and promoting entertainment constitute the aspect of contemporary public relations practice that comes closest to the traditional mantle of *press agentry*. This work requires intense contact with the media, by telephone and mail and in person. Name recognition is its primary goal.

The impact of television on the field of personality promotion is immense. An unknown person who appears on a nationally distributed television show may become an almost instant celebrity. Public relations firms specializing in personality buildup have staffs that book clients—show-business people, politicians, sports figures, and authors of promotional-type books in particular—in a highly organized manner for TV and radio talk shows. Distribution of news items about personalities to print media columnists and electronic media commentators, and the scheduling of interviews with newspapers and magazines, also are major functions. So are public relations tours by film and television stars.

Promotion of entertainment events is a many-faceted activity, intensely competitive because many events compete for the consumer's time and money. Exposure in the print and electronic media is fundamental. The success of theatrical engagements, fairs and exhibitions, and entertainment centers such as Disney World depends on their public relations and publicity programs.

Professional and big-time college sports is another category in which energetic public relations efforts are necessary. Every professional team has its public relations specialist, and athletic departments of large universities have their sports information directors.

Closely related to entertainment and sports is travel public relations, because the travel industry also is competing for the public's recreation dollars.

PUBLIC AFFAIRS, THE MILITARY, AND POLITICS

Many men and women pursue public relations careers by working for government agencies, the military services, and political figures.

The massive administrative and legislative structure of federal, state, and local governments needs to explain its work to the taxpayers who support it and to help them obtain the services it provides. This work is done by thousands of specialists, usually called *public information officers* or *public affairs officers*. Best known of these is the presidential press secretary at the White House, who has a sizable staff of assistants. Every government department and agency in Washington has its public information office. Similar but less elaborate establishments do the same work for state governments, large municipalities, and assorted other agencies such as regional water authorities.

The military services have an elaborate public information service network. Its principal functions are to (1) provide information about military policies and operations, (2) encourage recruiting, (3) maintain good relationships between military installations and their surrounding communities, and (4) distribute news about individuals in the service. The way in which the U.S. military forces presented and distributed information about the Persian Gulf War between the allied coalition and Iraq is a graphic example of government public affairs in operation. The carefully designed content of the military briefings and the manner in which military commanders limited reporting by media correspondents strongly influenced the picture of war operations received by the public.

Since the end of the Cold War and the Persian Gulf conflict, with the resultant drastic reduction in the U.S. armed forces, military affairs officers have faced a new challenge. They must explain the closing of military bases, which creates economic problems in nearby communities, and the missions and operations of the much smaller armed forces.

Political leaders frequently have personal public relations aides, although the functions of these assistants may be obscured by a title such as "administrative assistant." Personal image-building is a constant preoccupation of politicians. When a politician runs for major office, the press secretary is a key figure on the candidate's staff. Often a candidate hires a public relations firm that specializes in political campaigns to help plan strategy.

EDUCATION

Public relations programs are essential to the well-being of universities and colleges. Practitioners on campus either conduct or assist in several important functions that further the school's cause among students, alumni, and the public. In large universities, the public relations staffs needed to perform these functions are substantial in size.

In Utah, for example, Brigham Young University mounted an extensive public relations campaign to publicize its "Ramses II: The Pharaoh and His Time" exhibit on loan from the Egyptian government. Public relations staff created visual and printed materials for the event, organized the opening ceremonies and VIP ("very important person") activities, and reached 125,000 university alumni in a direct mail campaign. As a result, 520,000 people visited the exhibition.

Among the areas in which collegiate public relations practitioners may be involved are:

1. News releases—distribution to the news media of information about campus events, research, and faculty/student achievements

2. Publications—preparation of periodicals, brochures, and catalogues

3. Alumni contact work—various activities, including campus tours for returning alumni and other visitors

4. Relations with federal, state, and local governments

5. Fund-raising—solicitation of donations from foundations, alumni, federal and state governments, and special-interest groups. This work is vital to privately operated universities and colleges and also of great importance to tax-supported institutions.

6. Student recruitment

7. Internal public relations with faculty, staff, and student body

In urban areas, elementary and high school districts frequently have public relations officers to assist the news media and to work with parents and school groups. (More information on educational public relations may be found in Chapter 19.)

CASE PROBLEM

Teddy Bear, Inc., is a toy manufacturer located in Columbus, Ohio. Its specialty, "Fred Bear," can play back ten recorded messages at the touch of a button on its back. In its beginning years, the company emphasized product publicity. Now a large national company, it wishes to expand its public relations activities.

You are hired to be vice president of corporate communications and are asked to propose a project in each of the 11 principal areas of public relations outlined in this chapter. What project would you recommend for each area?

QUESTIONS FOR REVIEW AND DISCUSSION

1. Protecting and enhancing a corporation's reputation is an important role for a public relations practitioner. Name three aspects of this function.

2. Some public relations people substitute the term *corporate identity* for *image-building*. Why?

3. What do people in marketing communications do in addition to writing news releases and brochures?

4. What is the difference between *investor relations* and *financial relations?*

5. What kinds of activities are performed by public relations personnel in employee relations?

6. What kinds of publics are usually addressed in public affairs?

7. What are the five basic processes in *issues management?*

8. Describe the principal functions of a trade association.

9. How did the apple industry fight back against charges that the fruit might cause cancer in children?

10. Why do labor unions need public relations programs?

SUGGESTED READINGS

Cantor, Bill. *Experts in Action.* New York: Longman, 1989. Chapters by various authors that highlight the variety of public relations activity.

Carlson, Peter. "The Image Makers." Washington *Post* magazine, February 11, 1990, pp. 12–17, 30–35. Public relations in Washington, DC.

Davids, Meryl. "How Now, IR?" *Public Relations Journal,* April 1989, pp. 15–19. The field of investor relations.

Eilts, Catherine M. "High-Tech Public Relations: An Upstart Matures." *Public Relations Journal,* February 1990, pp. 22–27.

"Financial Services PR: Booming New Area." *Communication World,* September 1987, pp. 31–33.

Foehrenbach, Julie, and Goldfarb, Steve. "Employee Communication in the 1990s." *Communication World,* May–June 1990, pp. 101–106.

Lewton, Kathleen Larey. "Health Care: Critical Conditions." *Public Relations Journal,* December 1989, pp. 18–22. Health-care public relations.

Lowengard, Mary. "Community Relations: New Approaches to Building Consensus." *Public Relations Journal.* October 1989, pp. 24–30.

CHAPTER

The Evolution of Public Relations

PREVIEW   The objective of this chapter is to make students aware of the significant events and personalities that have helped shape today's public relations practices, to place these in context from ancient times, and to define current trends.

Topics covered in the chapter include:

- The roots of public relations
- The evolving functions—press agentry, publicity, counseling
- Early leaders—Ivy Ledbetter Lee, Edward L. Bernays, Doris Fleischman, others
- World Wars I and II
- Trends since World War II
- Growth of international practice

Public relations is a twentieth-century phenomenon whose roots extend deep into history; in a sense it is as old as human communication itself. In succeeding civilizations, such as those of Babylonia, Greece, and Rome, people were persuaded to accept the authority of government and religion through techniques that are still used: interpersonal communication, speeches, art, literature, staged events, publicity, and other such devices. None of these endeavors was called public relations, of course, but their purpose and their effect were the same as those of similar activities today.

The following remarks of Peter G. Osgood, president of Carl Byoir & Associates, provide a few examples of the early practice of the art of public relations:

The art has many roots. For example, the practice of dispatching teams to prepare the way for a traveling dignitary or politician was not invented by Harry Truman or Richard Nixon. Their political ancestors in Babylonia, Greece, and Rome were quite adept at it.

St. John the Baptist himself did superb advance work for Jesus of Nazareth.

Publicity, community relations, speech writing, positioning, government relations, issues analysis, employee relations, even investor relations: when you think about these activities in terms of the skills needed to practice them, it's plain they have deep historical roots.

Generating publicity for the Olympics in ancient Athens, for example, demanded the same skills as [it did in 1984] in Los Angeles.

Speech writing in Plato's time meant the same thing as it does today at Byoir: you must know the composition of your audience, never talk down to them, and impart information that will enlighten their ignorance, change their opinion, or confirm their own good judgments.

Businesses in the Republic of Venice in the latter half of the Fifteenth Century practiced as fine an art of investor relations as IBM does in the United States in the latter half of the Twentieth Century: perhaps even finer since it was practiced one-on-one, face-to-face, every day on the Rialto, just as it was under the spreading elm tree on Wall Street in the early days of the Stock Exchange.

Other examples abound. In the eleventh century, throughout the far-flung hierarchy of the Roman Catholic Church, Pope Urban II persuaded thousands of followers to serve God and gain forgiveness of their sins by engaging in the Holy Crusades against the Muslims. Six centuries later, the church was among the first to use the word *propaganda,* with the establishment by Pope Gregory XV of the College of Propaganda to supervise foreign missions and train priests to propagate the faith. (See Chapter 11.)

The stories that Spanish explorers publicized of the never-discovered Seven Cities of Gold, and even the fabled Fountain of Youth, induced others to travel to the New World. Some of the explorers probably believed those stories themselves. Two more blatant deceptions—examples of actions unacceptable to public relations people today—occurred when Eric the Red, in A.D. 1000, discovered a land of ice and rock and, to attract settlers, named it Greenland; and when Sir Walter Raleigh in 1584 sent back glowing accounts of what was actually a swamp-filled Roanoke Island, to persuade other settlers to travel to America.

It is clear, then, that the idea of using all forms of human communication—drama and storytelling among them—to influence the behavior of other people is nothing new.

An excellent way to understand what public relations is all about today is to examine the evolution of its principal functions—press agentry, publicity, and counseling—along with the methods used to carry out those functions.

PRESS AGENTRY

"Hyping"—the promotion of movie and television stars, books, magazines, and so on through shrewd use of the media and other devices—is an increasingly lively phenomenon in today's public relations world. At the center of hyping is the press agent, whom the *American College Dictionary* defines as "a person employed to attend to the advertising of a theater, performer, etc., through advertisements and notices to the press."

Press agentry is simply an extension of the activities of those who, in ancient civilizations, promoted athletic events such as the Olympic games and built an aura of myth around emperors and heroes. Its modern expression may be found in the press agentry that, during the nineteenth century in America, promoted circuses and exhibitions; glorified Davy Crockett as a frontier hero in order to draw political support from Andrew Jackson; attracted thousands to the touring shows of Buffalo Bill and sharpshooter Annie Oakley; made a legend of frontiersman Daniel Boone; and promoted hundreds of other personalities, politicians, and theatrical performers with remarkable success.

The oldtime press agents and the show people they most often represented played on the credulity of the public in its longing to be entertained, whether deceived or not. Advertisements and press releases were exaggerated to the point of being outright lies. Doing advance work for an attraction, the press agent dropped a sheaf of tickets on the desk of a newspaper city editor along with the announcements. Voluminous publicity generally resulted, and reporters, editors, and their families flocked to their free entertainment with scant regard for the ethical constraints that largely prohibit such practices today.

Small wonder then that today's public relations practitioner, exercising the highly sophisticated skills of evaluation, counseling, communication, and influencing management policies, shudders at the suggestion that public relations grew out of press agentry. And yet some aspects of modern public relations have their roots in the practice.

Phineas T. Barnum, the great American showman of the nineteenth century, for example, was the master of the *pseudoevent,* the planned happening that occurs primarily for the purpose of being reported—a part of today's public relations activities.

Barnum, who was born in Connecticut in 1810, was also a hardheaded businessman, devoted to his family, a generous contributor to charities, a nondrinker, an accumulator of property, imaginative and energetic, a man whose primary love in staging his circus performances was to make children smile. Beyond that, however, most of today's public relations people would like to part company—for Barnum used deception, hoax, and humbuggery in his operations and in his advertising and publicity. Even so, a public hungry for entertainment accepted his exaggerations, perhaps because they were audacious. Spectators thrilled to the wonders that he presented:

■ Joice Heath was a slave who said she was 161 years old and claimed to have been George Washington's nurse. Barnum even produced a stained birth certificate, but an autopsy disclosed she was far younger.

- Tom Thumb became one of the sensations of the century. Barnum discovered Charles S. Stratton in Connecticut when Stratton was 5 years old, only an inch over 2 feet in stature and weighing 15 pounds. Barnum made a public relations event of "General" Tom Thumb's marriage to another midget. After triumphal tours of the United States, where Tom Thumb entertained audiences with singing, dancing, and comedy monologues, Barnum took his attraction to England. A tiny carriage and ponies helped to attract attention to the midget, but Barnum decided that the best way to get public acceptance was first to involve the opinion leaders. Consequently, he invited London society leaders to his townhouse, where they met the quick-witted Tom Thumb. This meeting resulted in an invitation to the palace. Having entertained royalty, Tom Thumb drew full houses every night. Barnum, even in his day, knew the value of third-party endorsement.

- Jenny Lind, the "Swedish Nightingale," was one of Europe's most famous singers but was virtually unknown in the United States. Consequently, Barnum launched an unprecedented press campaign to acquaint the American public with her well-loved voice. He obtained full houses on opening nights in each community by donating part of the proceeds to charity. As a civic activity, the event attracted many of the town's opinion leaders, whereupon the general public flocked to attend succeeding performances—a device still employed today. Barnum also capitalized on the idea, current at the time, that anything from Europe must be culturally superior.

- Jumbo, the world's largest elephant, was brought by Barnum from England with enormous publicity. Posters and pamphlets featuring exaggerated woodcuts and inflated prose trumpeted the animal's size.

- The Barnum & Bailey Circus, with its 3 rings, 2 stands, and 800 employees, was proclaimed "The Greatest Show on Earth." Neil Harris, in his book *Humbug: The Art of P. T. Barnum,* describes the circus as the showman's "one enduring monument to fame; the legacy lies in his name left for the future."

Barnum owed much of his success to a corps of press agents headed by Richard F. "Tody" Hamilton. A famous circus clown, "Uncle" Bob Sherwood, described Hamilton as a verbal conjurer whose language was so polysyllabic that "an Oxford professor would have found it difficult to understand."

Upon Barnum's death in 1891, the London *Times* joined in almost universal acclaim of his life with the eulogy: "His death removes an almost classic figure, and his name is a proverb already, and a proverb it will continue until mankind has ceased to find pleasure in the comedy of the showman and his patrons—the comedy of the harmless deceiver and the willingly deceived."

PUBLICITY

Early Development Publicity, which consists mainly of the issuing of news releases to the media about the activities of an organization or an individual, is one of the earliest forms of public relations. It has been used for virtually every purpose. Signs such as "Vote for Cicero. He is a good man." have been found by archaeologists in ruins of

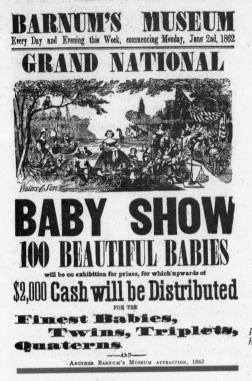

BARNUM'S MUSEUM

Every Day and Evening this Week, commencing Monday, June 2nd, 1862

GRAND NATIONAL

Waters & Son

BABY SHOW
100 BEAUTIFUL BABIES

will be on exhibition for prizes, for which upwards of

$2,000 Cash will be Distributed

FOR THE

Finest Babies, Twins, Triplets, Quaterns

AND

ANOTHER BARNUM'S MUSEUM ATTRACTION, 1862

Phineas T. Barnum, a master of "hype," created pseudoevents such as the beautiful baby show promoted by this poster. Notice how it appeals to two human instincts: the desires to win money and to look at a human oddity, quaterns (called quadruplets in modern usage).

ancient civilizations. In 59 B.C. Julius Caesar ordered the posting of a news sheet, *Acta Diurna,* outside the Forum to inform citizens of actions of Roman legislators; Caesar's *Commentaries* were published largely to aggrandize the achievements of the emperor.

The Colonial Era   In 1620, broadsides were distributed in Europe by the Virginia Company offering 50 acres of free land to those bringing settlers to America by 1625. In 1641, Harvard College published a fund-raising brochure, and in 1758, Kings College (now Columbia University) issued its first press release, announcing commencement exercises.

Mainly through the use of newspapers and pamphlets, a staged event (the Boston Tea Party), and wide publicity accorded the so-called Boston Massacre, fiery Samuel Adams and the Boston Radicals achieved a propaganda triumph in helping persuade the American colonists to revolt against Great Britain. Also highly instrumental in bringing lukewarm citizens into the Revolutionary movement was Tom Paine's *Common Sense;* more than 120,000 copies of the pamphlet were sold in three months. Influencing public opinion both in the colonies and in England were the *Federalist Papers,* comprised of 85 letters written by Alexander Hamilton, James Madison, and John Jay, and a series of articles by John Dickinson titled "Letters from a Farmer in Pennsylvania." The most frequently cited female propagandists of the era included Mercy Otis Warren, Abigail Adams, and Sarah Bache, daughter of Benjamin Franklin, who lent his journalistic skills to the American cause, too.

Nineteenth Century Public affairs were controlled mainly by the aristocratic, propertied class until the revolt of the so-called common man placed rough-hewn Andrew Jackson in the White House in 1828. Amos Kendall, a former Kentucky newspaper editor, became an intimate member of Jackson's "kitchen cabinet" and probably the first presidential press secretary. The appointment demonstrated for the first time that public relations is integral to political policy-making and management.

Jackson's campaign and presidency represented the first attempt in American political life to gain broad-based support for a presidential candidate. Kendall sampled public opinion on issues, advised Jackson, and skillfully interpreted his rough ideas, putting them into presentable form as speeches and news releases. He served as Jackson's advance agent on trips, wrote glowing articles that he sent to supportive newspapers, and was probably the first to use newspaper reprints in public relations; almost every complimentary news story or editorial about Jackson was reprinted and circulated.

After the Jacksonian era, American politicians increasingly used press releases, pamphlets, posters, and emblems to win favor. The effort reached a nineteenth-century crescendo during the presidential campaigns of William Jennings Bryan and William McKinley in 1896.

Throughout the century, publicity techniques helped populate western land. Newly sprung-up villages competed to attract printers, whose newspaper copies and pamphlets describing almost every community as "the garden spot of the West" were sent back East to induce increased settlement. Many settlers were lured to Illinois, for example, by gazettes that extolled the fertile land. Henry W. Ellsworth's *Valley of the Upper Wabash,* published in the 1830s, and another publication, *Illinois in 1837,* were subsidized by speculators seeking to lure land buyers. One critic of the time called these gazettes downright puffery, "full of exaggerated statements, and high-wrought and false-colored descriptions."

In addition, the supporters of such causes as antislavery, antivivisectionism, women's rights, and prohibition employed publicity to maximum effect throughout the century. One of the most influential publicity ventures for the abolition of slavery was the publication of Harriet Beecher Stowe's *Uncle Tom's Cabin.* Stowe was among a number of women who, although they were not public relations people, extensively used some of the techniques of public relations to promote their causes. Sarah J. Hale, editor from 1836 to 1877 of *Godey's Ladies Book,* a best-selling magazine with 150,000 circulation, ardently promoted women's rights. After a women's rights convention in Seneca Falls, New York, in 1845, Amelia Bloomer became famous. Now associated with the loose-fitting trousers she wore in protest of the corset, she edited *The Lily,* a women's rights publication. Noted temperance crusader Susan B. Anthony was business manager of *The Revolution,* which advocated a variety of radical causes. The American Woman Suffrage Association was formed in 1869 with Lucy Stone as editor of its weekly, *The Woman's Journal.* While adoption of the Nineteenth Amendment to the U.S. Constitution in 1920 gave women the right to vote, the movement ended without ensuring women greater property rights.

Professor Carolyn M. Byerly of Radford University argued in a 1993 research study that such campaigns for social reform qualify as public relations operations and deserve a place in the history of the field. She cited a 1989 doctoral dissertation by Genevieve Gardner McBride which pointed out that in Wisconsin the support for a constitutional amendment giving women the right to vote began with a few interested individuals and was carried out through carefully managed informational campaigns that included "publicity, press agentry, publications, petition drives, advertising, merchandising, lobbying, membership recruitment and training, special events, fundraising . . . and issues management, or 'crisis PR.'"

A wave of industrialization, mechanization, and urbanization swept the nation after the Civil War. Concentrations of wealth developed throughout manufacturing and trade. Amid the questioning of business practices, the Mutual Life Insurance Company in 1888 hired journalist Charles J. Smith to write press releases designed to improve its image. In 1889 Westinghouse Corporation established what is said to be the first in-house publicity department, with a former newspaper reporter, E. H. Heinrichs, as manager. In 1897 the term *public relations* was used by the Association of American Railroads in a company listing.

Twentieth Century   As the use of publicity gained increased acceptance, the first publicity agency, known as the Publicity Bureau, was established in Boston in 1900. Harvard College was its most prestigious client. George F. Parker and Ivy Ledbetter Lee opened a publicity office in New York City in 1904. Parker remained in the publicity field, but Lee became an adviser to companies and individuals (as will be discussed in the section that follows). In Washington, D.C., William Wolf Smith established a firm to influence legislators through publicity.

A second Boston publicity business was opened in 1906 by James D. Ellsworth, who later joined the staff of the American Telephone & Telegraph Company. Theodore N. Vail greatly expanded the press and customer relations operations at AT&T after becoming its president in 1907. In 1909 another pioneer, Pendleton Dudley, established a public relations office in New York.

The Santa Fe Railway, at the beginning of the twentieth century, commissioned dozens of painters and photographers to depict scenes in the then little-known Southwest. The paintings unabashedly prettified the American Indian, and the photographs, colored by hand, showed the Indians weaving, grinding corn, and dancing. This corporate image-making attracted hundreds of tourists and contributed to the romanticizing of the Indian and the West.

The Chicago Edison Company broke new ground in public relations techniques under the skillful leadership of its president, Samuel Insull. Well aware of the special need of a public utility to maintain a sound relationship with its customers, Insull created a variety of techniques—he established an external magazine, *Chicago, The Electric City,* in 1903; used press releases extensively; was the first in business to use films for public relations purposes, in 1909; and started the "bill stuffer" idea in 1912 by inserting company information into customer bills.

Henry Ford probably was the first major industrialist to utilize thoroughly two basic public relations concepts. The first was the notion of *positioning*—the idea that credit and publicity always go to those who do something first—and the second idea was ready accessibility to the press. Joseph Epstein, author of *Ambition,* says, "He may have been an even greater publicist than mechanic."

In 1900 Ford obtained coverage of the prototype Model T by demonstrating it to a reporter from the Detroit *Tribune.* By 1903 Ford achieved widespread publicity by racing his cars—a practice that is still carried out today by automakers. Ford hired Barney

The Kid in Upper 4

It is 3:42 a.m. on a troop train.

Men wrapped in blankets are breathing heavily.

Two in every lower berth. One in every upper.

This is no ordinary trip. It may be their last in the U.S.A. till the end of the war. Tomorrow they will be on the high seas.

One is wide awake . . . listening . . . staring into the blackness.

It is the kid in Upper 4.

☆   ☆   ☆

Tonight, he knows, he is leaving behind a lot of little things—and big ones.

The taste of hamburgers and pop . . . the feel of driving a roadster over a six-lane highway . . . a dog named Shucks, or Spot, or Barnacle Bill.

The pretty girl who writes so often . . . that gray-haired man, so proud and awkward at the station . . . the mother who knit the socks he'll wear soon.

Tonight he's thinking them over.

There's a lump in his throat. And maybe —a tear fills his eye. *It doesn't matter, Kid.* Nobody will see . . . it's too dark.

☆   ☆   ☆

A couple of thousand miles away, where he's going, they don't know him very well.

But people all over the world are waiting, praying for him to come.

And he will come, this kid in Upper 4. With new hope, peace and freedom for a tired, bleeding world.

. . . . train, remember

American trains were jammed during World War II with soldiers being carried to ports of embarkation for shipping overseas into combat. Many civilians complained that because of military crowding they could not find seats or sleeping berths on the trains. The New Haven Railroad tried to placate the protesters with an emotional appeal to their patriotism and sympathy.

Oldfield, a champion bicycle racer and a popular personality, to drive a Ford car at a record speed of 1 minute and 6 seconds per mile, or a bit less than 60 miles per hour. The publicity from these speed runs gave Ford financial backing and a ready market for the regular production of cars.

Ford also positioned himself as the champion of the common person and was the first automaker to envision that a car should be affordable for everyone. To this end, he produced his first Model T in 1908 for $850 and, by 1915–1916, was able to reduce its selling price to $360. Such price reductions made Ford dominant in the auto industry and on the front pages of the nation's newspapers. He garnered further publicity and became the hero of working men and women by being the first automaker to double his workers' wages to $5 per day.

Ford became a household word because he was willing to be interviewed by the press on almost any subject, including the gold standard, evolution, alcohol, foreign affairs, and even capital punishment. A populist by nature, he once said, "Business is a service, not a bonanza," an idea reiterated by many of today's top corporate executives who believe business has a social responsibility.

Although Ford was the first major industrialist to hire blacks in large numbers, he also wrote a number of anti-Semitic articles. In the 1930s, his earlier image as the champion of the working class was shattered by his resistance to organized labor, which led to several violent confrontations as the United Automobile Workers attempted to organize Ford workers.

In politics, President Theodore Roosevelt proved himself a master in generating publicity. Roosevelt was the first president to make extensive use of news conferences and interviews in drumming up support for his projects. He knew the value of the presidential tour for publicity purposes. For example, on a trip to what became Yosemite, designed to publicize the idea of national parks, Roosevelt was accompanied by a bevy of reporters and photographers who wrote glowing articles about the need to preserve the area for public recreational use.

Not-for-profit organizations joined the publicity bandwagon in the century's first decade. The American Red Cross and the National Tuberculosis Association began extensive publicity programs soon after their formation in 1908. Two other nonprofit organizations, the Knights of Columbus and the National Lutheran Council, opened press offices in 1918.

COUNSELING

Industrialists and Muckrakers In the latter part of the nineteenth century, the United States was transformed by mighty economic and social forces. Industrialization moved forward on a major scale; cities swelled with even more immigrants; production was rapidly being mechanized; and business firms grew through the use of vastly improved transportation and communication facilities, along with new interlocking corporate structures and financing methods.

It was the era of the so-called robber barons, exploiters of natural resources and labor, known in less accusatory terms as founders of great American industries. Heavy concentrations of power were held by John D. Rockefeller, Sr., in oil; Andrew Carnegie in steel; J. Pierpont Morgan, Cornelius Vanderbilt, and Jay Gould in finance; Leland Stanford, Collis P. Huntington, James J. Hill, and George Pullman in railroading; Gustavus F. Swift and Philip D. Armour in meat packing; and other industrial leaders. Labor strife intensified, and the government, upon the urging of populist and progressive forces, began to challenge big business with the enactment of such measures as the Interstate Commerce Act and the Sherman Antitrust Act.

Within the dozen years after 1900, several magazines developed a literature of exposure that Theodore Roosevelt called the work of "muckrakers." He was comparing the more sensational writers to the Man with the Muckrake in the seventeenth-century work *Pilgrim's Progress*—a character who did not look up to see the celestial crown but continued to rake the filth. Led by Ida M. Tarbell, these writers posed a serious threat to business. Tarbell wrote a series of articles published by *McClure's* in 1903 titled "History of the Standard Oil Company," an attack on the corruption and unfair practices of the Rockefeller oil monopoly. Other noted muckrakers included Upton

Sinclair, who exposed unsanitary and fraudulent practices of the meat packers in his 1906 book *The Jungle*.

The First Public Relations Counsel The combination of stubborn management attitudes and improper actions, labor strife, and widespread public criticism produced the first public relations counselor, Ivy Ledbetter Lee. Although, as previously noted, this Princeton graduate and former business reporter for the New York *World* began his private practice as a publicist, he shortly expanded that role to become the first public relations counsel.

The emergence of modern public relations can be dated from 1906, when Lee was hired by the anthracite coal industry, then embroiled in a strike. Lee discovered that, although the miners' leader, John Mitchell, was supplying reporters with all the facts they requested, by contrast the leader of the coal proprietors, George F. Baer, had refused to talk to the press or even to President Theodore Roosevelt, who was seeking to arbitrate the dispute. Lee persuaded Baer and his associates to change their policy. He issued a press notice signed by Baer and the other leading proprietors that began: "The anthracite coal operators, realizing the general public interest in conditions in the mining regions, have arranged to supply the press with all possible information. . . ."

Lee issued a "Declaration of Principles," which signaled the end of the "public-be-damned" attitude of business and the beginning of the "public-be-informed" era. Eric Goldman said the declaration "marks the emergence of a second stage of public relations. The public was no longer to be ignored, in the traditional manner of business, nor fooled, in the continuing manner of the press agent." The declaration reads:

This is not a secret press bureau. All our work is done in the open. We aim to supply news. This is not an advertising agency; if you think any of our matter ought properly to go to your business office, do not use it. Our matter is accurate. Further details on any subject treated will be supplied

Ivy Ledbetter Lee was recognized early in the twentieth century as the first public relations counsel.

promptly, and any editor will be assisted most cheerfully in verifying directly any statement of fact. . . . In brief, our plan is, frankly and openly, in behalf of business concerns and public institutions, to supply to the press and the public of the United States prompt and accurate information concerning subjects which it is of value and interest of the public to know about.

The continuance of Lee's policy of providing accurate information about corporate and institutional activities has saved American news media millions of dollars in reporter salaries during the intervening nine decades. Despite misleading information given out by some public relations people, news releases quickly became extremely valuable—even a necessity—to the media.

Railroads at the time also were seeking to operate secretly in their dealings with the press. Retained by the Pennsylvania Railroad Company to handle press relations after a major rail disaster, Lee persuaded the president to alter his policy. Lee provided press facilities, released all available information, and enabled reporters to view the disaster scene. Although such action appeared to the conservative railway directors to constitute reckless indiscretion, they later acknowledged that the company had received fairer press comment than on any previous such occasion.

In 1914, John D. Rockefeller, Jr., hired Lee in the wake of the vicious strike-breaking activities known as the Ludlow Massacre at the Rockefeller family's Colorado Fuel and Iron Company plant. Lee went to Colorado and talked to both sides. He also persuaded Rockefeller to talk with the miners and their families. Lee made sure that the press was there to record Rockefeller's eating in the workers' dining hall, swinging a pick ax in the mine, and having a beer with the workers after hours. The press portrayed Rockefeller as seriously concerned about the plight of the workers, thus increasing his popularity with the striking miners. Meanwhile, Lee distributed a factsheet giving management's view of the strike and even convinced the governor of Colorado to write an article supporting the position taken by the company.

Rockefeller's visits with the miners led to policy changes and more worker benefits, but the company also prevented the United Mine Workers from gaining a foothold. George McGovern, former Democratic Party candidate for President, wrote his doctoral dissertation on the Ludlow Massacre. "It was the first time in any American labor struggle where you had an organized effort to use what has become modern public relations to sell one side of a strike to the American people."

Lee's success in transforming a labor dispute into a positive situation (and public image) for the Rockefeller family was based on the fact, according to Gordon M. Sears, president of T. J. Ross and Associates, that "Lee tried to solve the problem or at least establish the proper course toward solution before turning to communications." Lee's achievement led the Rockefeller family to hire him for a full-scale renovation of the Rockefeller name, badly damaged by the muckrakers who often pictured John D. Rockefeller, Sr., as an exploiter and the king of the greedy capitalists. Lee advised the Rockefellers to announce publicly the millions of dollars that they gave to charitable institutions. He also convinced John, Sr., to allow reporters and photographers to record his golf playing and socializing with family and friends. When John, Sr., died in 1937, he was mourned worldwide as a kindly old man and a great humanitarian and philanthropist.

Lee's public relations firm became Lee, Harris, and Lee in 1916. Three years later he was joined by Thomas J. Ross in the firm of Ivy Lee and T. J. Ross and Associates. Among other counseling activities, Lee advised the American Tobacco Company to

John D. Rockefeller, Sr., often was photographed giving dimes to children during the 1920s. His public relations counselor, Ivy Ledbetter Lee, has been credited with suggesting that Rockefeller do so to improve his image, but Lee says he merely convinced Rockefeller to let news photographers show what he had been doing for years. Rockefeller gave millions to charity. Here he presents a dime to William Gebele, Jr., at Lakewood, New Jersey. (AP/Wide World Photos)

initiate a profit-sharing plan, the Pennsylvania Railroad to beautify its stations, and the movie industry to stop inflated advertising and form a voluntary code of censorship.

Lee lost a measure of public trust by advocating diplomatic recognition and trade with the Bolsheviks in the 1920s. He defended his stand by arguing that such action was necessary to resolve differences between the United States and the Soviet Union. His reputation was damaged more severely when a congressional hearing disclosed that he was working for the Hitler government while being paid by Germany's I.G. Farben chemical firm as a subterfuge in the early 1930s. Lee said he opposed Hitler and counseled the firm as a means of obtaining goodwill and product sales in the United States. The secret relationship caused Congress to pass the Foreign Agents Registration Act (see Chapter 15).

Lee died in 1934. He is remembered for four important contributions to public relations: (1) advancing the concept that business and industry should align themselves with the public interest, and not vice versa; (2) dealing with top executives and carrying out no program unless it had the active support and personal contribution of management; (3) maintaining open communication with the news media; and (4) emphasizing the necessity of humanizing business and bringing its public relations down to the community level of employees, customers, and neighbors.

Wartime Counsel to Government Both world wars saw a tremendous upsurge in the role of public relations on behalf of the government—especially the Creel Committee during World War I and the Office of War Information during World War II.

The Creel Committee. "Literally public relations counselors to the United States Government" during World War I is the description given to members of the

PUBLIC RELATIONS ROOTS IN GERMANY, GREAT BRITAIN, AND AUSTRALIA

Germany As the Industrial Revolution swept through Europe, few owners, as in the United States, sensed a need to communicate with the public about their operations. In Germany, however, railroad companies and at least one share-holding corporation began publicity efforts as far back as the mid-nineteenth century. Alfred Krupp, founder of the Krupp Company, which became the premier industrial firm in Germany and the base of the Nazi war power, wrote to a financial adviser in 1866:

> We think . . . it is time that authoritative reports concerning factory matters in accordance with the facts should be propagated on a regular basis through newspaper reports which serve the enlightened public. We can supply the material for this purpose, and should qualified experts at times be unavailable, it is our wish to contact responsible newspaper editors ourselves.

Company documents reveal that Krupp was unable to find a qualified person to assist him in the effort. However, his son, Friedrich Alfred Krupp, hired Adolf Lauter in 1893 to establish a news bureau, and the department was integrated into the firm's operations in 1901.

As the Krupp public relations efforts expanded internationally, other major industries followed suit. Ivy Lee's involvement in 1933 with the I. G. Farben cartel, through its German Dye Trust, was mentioned previously.

Great Britain The industrial and communication systems of Great Britain were already developed in 1910, when the Marconi Company established a department to distribute news releases about its achievements in wireless telegraphy.

Professional public relations counseling was introduced in the country in 1924, when Sir Basil Clarke, a former government press officer, established Editorial Services Ltd. in London. For his first client, a dairy group, he promoted the idea of milk pasteurization, an innovation that had met with some resistance from the public.

The first public relations officer so styled in Britain was Sir John Elliott, appointed in 1925 by the Southern Railway Company.

Beginning in the mid-nineteenth century, the government enjoyed a close working relationship with the Reuters news agency for almost 100 years. Paul Julius Reuter, agency

---

Committee on Public Information by James O. Mock and Cedric Larson in their book *Words That Won the War.* President Wilson called on George Creel, a former newspaper reporter, to organize a comprehensive public relations effort to advise him and his cabinet, to carry out programs, and to influence United States and world opinion. Wrote Mock and Larson:

Mr. Creel assembled as brilliant and talented a group of journalists, scholars, press agents, editors, artists, and other manipulators of the symbols of public opinion as America had ever seen united for a single purpose. It was a gargantuan advertising agency, the like of which the country had never known, and the breathtaking scope of its activities was not to be equalled until the rise of the totalitarian dictatorship after the war. George Creel, Carl Byoir, Edgar Sisson, Harvey O'Higgins, Guy Stanton Ford, and their famous associates were literally public relations coun-

owner, was granted use of cables linking the empire's outposts; in return, agency dispatches did much to further the nation's commercial and political interests, and there is little doubt that the news service was careful to say at crucial points what the British government wished it to say. With such an arrangement, historians have noted, government propaganda was particularly effective in bringing the United States to its side in World War I. Today, Reuters operates with scant if any government influence.

In 1911 the first government public relations campaign was carried out when, at the instigation of Prime Minister David Lloyd George, the Insurance Commission explained the benefits of the National Insurance Act, an unpopular measure that had attracted much adverse publicity. The Air Ministry appointed the first government press officer in 1919, and a year later the Ministry of Health selected Sir Basil Clarke, a former Reuters correspondent, as director of information.

Government public relations was substantially enlarged after World War II. The offices now are organized into three sections: press relations, publicity and inquiry, and intelligence. During recent extended freedom-of-information debates, however, the system was labeled the most secretive in the world (an obvious exaggeration), and demands were made that the service be disbanded and its work turned over to regular administrators.

Via shortwave, the British Broadcasting Company (BBC), chartered in 1922, carries a British point of view in its news dispatches and commentary to an estimated 75 million adults around the world each week. In the early 1990s the BBC greatly expanded its World TV Service.

Australia Public relations in Australia largely consisted of publicity efforts until after World War II. When U.S. General Douglas MacArthur arrived in Australia after his escape from Corregidor in 1942, he introduced the term *public relations* and, with a highly skilled staff, demonstrated numerous ways of promoting his image and war policy.

The industry grew steadily, and, in 1960, the Public Relations Institute of Australia (PRIA) was formed. It now includes more than 1500 practitioners throughout the country. Women, today comprising about one-third of the nation's public relations specialists, were among its founders.

Notable practitioners include George Fitzpatrick, credited with being the first Australian to conduct public relations, and Eric White, who, a Hill and Knowlton official said, "virtually created the public relations industry" in Australia. As early as the 1960s White oversaw extensions of his firm in six Pacific Rim countries.

selors to the United States Government, carrying first to the citizens of this country and then to those in distant lands, the ideas which gave motive power to the stupendous undertaking of 1917–1918.

Among numerous other activities, the committee persuaded newspapers and magazines to contribute volumes of news and advertising space to encourage Americans to save food and to invest heavily in Liberty Bonds, which more than 10 million people purchased. Thousands of businesses set up their own groups of publicity people to expand the effort. Wilson accepted Creel's advice that hatred of the Germans should be played down and loyalty and confidence in the government should be emphasized. The committee publicized the war aims and ideals of Woodrow Wilson—to make the world safe for democracy and to make World War I the war to end all wars. The American Red

Cross, operating in cooperation with the committee, enrolled more than 19 million new members and received more than $400 million in contributions during the period.

The massive effort had a profound effect on the development of public relations by demonstrating the success of these full-blown techniques. It also awakened an awareness in Americans of the power of persuasive approaches. This, coupled with postwar analysis of British propaganda devices alleged to have helped get the nation into the war, resulted in a number of scholarly books and college courses on the subject. Among the books was Walter Lippmann's classic *Public Opinion*, in which he pointed out how people are moved to action by "the pictures in our minds."

Another legacy was the training received by the noted public relations practitioners Carl Byoir, associate chairman of the committee, and Edward L. Bernays. Byoir in 1930 founded a company that for more than a half century was one of the largest public relations firms in the United States. Bernays's contributions to public relations will be discussed shortly.

Office of War Information (OWI).   To head the vital war information operation during World War II, President Franklin Roosevelt turned to Elmer Davis, an Indiana-born journalist and a Rhodes Scholar. Davis had spent 15 years as a novelist and freelance writer, 10 years as a New York *Times* reporter, and 3 years as a radio commentator for the Columbia Broadcasting System.

Profiting by knowledge of the techniques so successful in World War I, Davis orchestrated an even larger public relations effort during World War II. His job was exceptionally difficult because his office had to coordinate information from the military and numerous government agencies, wrestle for funds each year with a Congress suspicious that the OWI would become Roosevelt's personal propaganda vehicle, and overcome opposition from a large segment of the press that resented having to do business with an official spokesperson.

As in World War I, the OWI's campaigns were extremely successful in promoting the sale of war bonds and in obtaining press and broadcast support for other wartime necessities. These included food, clothing, and gasoline rationing; more "victory gardens"; higher productivity and less absenteeism; and secrecy regarding troop movements and weaponry development.

The OWI news bureau had 250 full-time employees, and 300 reporters and correspondents used its facilities. Davis established a Domestic Branch, which, according to the director, "did not withhold news because we did not like it, nor delay it to produce a greater effect." His Overseas Branch also provided news to foreign peoples but with selective timing and emphasis. The OWI worked harmoniously and effectively with the Office of Censorship.

Of the domestic operation, Davis declared: "It is the job of OWI not only to tell the American people how the war is going, but where it is going and where it came from—its nature and origins, how our government is conducting it, and what (besides national survival) our government hopes to get out of victory."

The Voice of America, established by the Department of State in 1942, carried news of the war to all parts of the world. The film industry provided support through such means as Frank Capra's documentary film for the U.S. Signal Corps, designed to build patriotism; bond-selling tours by film stars; and the production of commercial movies glorifying U.S. fighting forces.

Howard Chandler Christy's poster stimulated recruiting during
World War I long before women could join the U.S. Navy.

The OWI was the forerunner of the U.S. Information Agency, established in 1953 under President Eisenhower to "tell America's story abroad." A number of the people who worked with Davis became public relations leaders during the ensuing decades.

Further Development of the Counseling Function The role of the public relations practitioner as an adviser to corporate and institutional managements grew in significance as the American economy expanded during the 1920s. The persons most responsible for defining this function and drawing public attention to it were Edward L. Bernays and his wife and partner Doris E. Fleischman. Fleischman was a talented writer, ardent feminist, and former assistant women's page and assistant Sunday editor of the New York *Tribune.* Married in 1922, they became equal partners in the firm of Edward L. Bernays, Counsel on Public Relations. The partnership continued until Fleischman's death in 1980.

Fleischman, indeed, was an equal partner in the work of the firm, interviewing clients, writing news releases, editing the company's newsletter, and writing and editing books and magazine articles, among other duties. As a contributor to a 1989 book, *Women in Mass Communication: Challenging Gender Values,* edited by Pamela J. Creedon, historian Susan Henry, a professor of journalism at California State University, Northridge, says that Bernays called Fleischman "the brightest woman I'd ever met in my life" and "the balance wheel of our operation." At one point Bernays

Edward L. Bernays, a legendary figure in public relations with a career spanning about three-quarters of a century, celebrated his 100th birthday in 1991. He was honored at a dinner by the Boston chapter of the Public Relations Society of America.

*Doris Fleischman was the partner and wife of
Edward L. Bernays in their pioneer public relations
counseling firm.*

recalled that, "I used to say to her, 'It's great to have a George Gallup right in the house.'"

The gender value system of the time, however, did not allow Fleischman to represent the firm to its clients or even to be included in the firm's title. Other historians have credited to Bernays both his own and their shared public relations achievements, included in the list of early examples of counseling that follows shortly.

The Concept Explained   "In writing this book I have tried to set down the broad principles that govern the new profession of public relations counsel." With this opening sentence of *Crystallizing Public Opinion,* published in 1923, Bernays coined a term to describe a function that was to become the core of public relations. He illuminated the scope and function, methods and techniques, and social responsibilities of public relations. Following by a year Walter Lippmann's insightful treatise on public opinion, the book attracted much attention, and Bernays was invited by New York University to offer the first public relations course in the nation.

Even so, the name and definition that Bernays gave to the scope and function of public relations failed for years to gain acceptance by editors and scholars, most of whom equated the new business with press agentry. Stanley Walker, famed city editor of the New York *Herald Tribune,* wrote later:

Bernays has taken the sideshow barker and given him a philosophy and a new and awesome language. . . . He is no primitive drum-beater. . . . He is devoid of swank and does not visit newspaper offices [as did the circus advance agents]; and yet, the more thoughtful newspaper editors, who have their own moments of worry about the mass mind and commercialism, regard Bernays as a possible menace, and warn their colleagues of his machinations.

This antipathy toward public relations still lingers among many journalists.

In 1955 Bernays refined his approach to public relations and, in a book titled *The Engineering of Consent,* he gave the field a new description. To many people, the word *engineering* implied manipulation through propaganda and other devices. Bernays, who himself later railed at use of the word *image* to mean reputation-building, defended his terminology and concept:

> The term engineering was used advisedly. In our society, with its myriad of group interests, interest groups, and media, only an engineering approach to the problems of adjustment, information, and persuasion could bring effective results. . . .
>
> Public relations practiced as a profession is an art applied to a science, in which the public interest and not pecuniary motivation is the primary consideration. The engineering of consent in this sense assumes a constructive social role. Regrettably, public relations, like other professions, can be abused and used for anti-social purposes. I have tried to make the profession socially responsible as well as economically viable.

Early Examples of Counseling   The following examples illustrate how effectively Bernays performed his public relations work:

- When, in the 1910s, the actor Richard Bennett wanted to produce *Damaged Goods,* a play about sex education, Bernays blunted the anticipated criticism of moralists, and possibly avoided a police raid, by organizing the Sociological Fund of the *Medical Review of Reviews* journal, with contributors paying $4 each to attend the play as an educational event.

- To help Procter & Gamble sell Ivory soap, Bernays attracted the attention of children and their parents to cleanliness by developing a nationwide interest in soap sculpture.

- In an effort to humanize President Calvin Coolidge, described by the writer Dorothy Parker as "weaned on a pickle," Bernays arranged a breakfast at the White House during which Al Jolson, the Dolly Sisters, and other celebrities performed. The unprecedented event brought nationwide publicity.

- At a time when public opinion and some legislation kept women from smoking in public, Bernays was hired by George Washington Hill, president of the American Tobacco Company, to expand sales of Lucky Strike cigarettes. Bernays consulted a psychoanalyst, who told him that cigarettes might be perceived as "torches of freedom" by women seeking equality with men. Bernays helped break the barrier by inducing ten debutantes to "light up" while strolling in New York City's traditional Easter parade.

- Later, when research showed that sales of Lucky Strike cigarettes to women were down because many felt that the green package clashed with their clothes, Bernays tried to persuade Hill to change the color. Unsuccessful in the effort, Bernays made green fashionable by arranging a prestigious socialites' ball with that color scheme; getting makers of accessories to promote green shoes, hosiery, and gloves; and arranging for green fashion displays on the covers of *Harper's Bazaar* and *Vogue* on the date of the ball. (Only during World War II, when an ingredient in the color became an industrial scarcity, did Hill relent, nevertheless reaping continued sales with the slogan, "Lucky Strike Green Has Gone to War.")

■ When the short-hair fashion introduced by dancer Irene Castle sharply reduced the sale of hairnets, Bernays, working for the Venida Company, emphasized the use of hairnets as a safety measure for women working with machinery, and laws were passed requiring the protective devices. The sanitary aspect of hairnets worn by cooks and waitresses also was heralded.

Perhaps the most spectacular example of Bernays's skill took place in 1929. To celebrate the fiftieth anniversary of Thomas Edison's invention of the electric light bulb, Bernays arranged the worldwide-attention-getting Light's Golden Jubilee. On October 21, many of the world's utilities shut off their power all at one time, for one minute, in honor of Edison. President Herbert Hoover and many other dignitaries attended a banquet climaxing the celebration. The event achieved such fame that the U.S. Post Office, on its own, issued a commemorative two-cent postage stamp.

Sociologist Leonard W. Doob described the jubilee as "one of the most lavish pieces of propaganda ever engineered in this country during peace time." Bernays, wrote Doob, was working "not for Edison or for Henry Ford, but for very important interests [General Electric and Westinghouse had hired Bernays] which saw this historic anniversary as an opportunity to publicize the uses of the electric light."

Light's Golden Jubilee is considered one of Bernays's major accomplishments. It showed, in 1929, the potential of effective public relations. And when television commentator Bill Moyers interviewed Bernays in 1984 on a Public Broadcasting Service program about the early beginnings of public relations, Moyers said: "You know, you got Thomas Edison, Henry Ford, Herbert Hoover, and masses of Americans to do what you wanted them to do. You got the whole world to turn off its lights at the same time. You got American women to smoke in public. That's not influence. That's power."

Replied Bernays: "But you see, I never thought of it as power. I never treated it as power. People want to go where they want to be led."

Although he retired from full-time consulting in 1962, Bernays continued to write, give interviews, and lecture about his favorite theme of public relations as a profession and an applied social science. He is widely acknowledged as the founder of modern public relations; one historian has even described him as "the first and doubtless the leading ideologist of public relations." Sigmund Freud, founder of psychoanalysis, must have been proud of his nephew. In 1990 *Life* magazine cited Bernays as one of the 100 most important Americans of the twentieth century. He died in 1995.

Other Public Relations Pioneers   Benjamin Sonnenberg, Rex Harlow, and Leone Baxter loom large in the list of other early, influential public relations counselors.

Benjamin Sonnenberg.   It was Sonnenberg who suggested that the Texaco Company sponsor performances of the Metropolitan Opera Company on national radio. Sponsorship of the Saturday afternoon series, which began in 1940, still continues. Sonnenberg, who believed that a brief mention of a client in the right context is better than a long-winded piece of flattery, proposed Texaco's sponsorship after some segments of the American public criticized the company for negotiating with Adolf

Hitler on an oil deal in the mid-1930s. With time, Texaco emerged as a patron of the arts, and critics forgot about the dealings with Hitler before the outbreak of World War II.

Rex Harlow.   Harlow, known as "the father of public relations research," was probably the first full-time public relations educator. As a professor in Stanford University's School of Education, Harlow began teaching a public relations course on a regular basis in 1939. In that same year he founded the American Council on Public Relations (which eventually became the Public Relations Society of America), serving as its president for eight years. He criss-crossed the country giving workshops and seminars for practitioners that continued for about 20 years. It is estimated that 10,000 people received their first formal instruction in public relations from this educator.

In 1952, Harlow founded the *Social Science Reporter,* one of the first newsletters in the field. In it he actively sought to show practitioners and top management how social science research findings benefit the practice of public relations. Harlow, a prolific writer, produced many articles and seven books on public relations. He died in 1993 at age 100.

Leone Baxter.   A partner for more than 25 years with Clem Whitaker in the firms of Whitaker & Baxter, Campaigns Incorporated, W&B Advertising, and California Feature Service, Leone Baxter has headed Whitaker & Baxter International since her partner's death in 1961. As president, she counsels clients in the United States and abroad, formulates plans, and directs the staff that carries them out.

The firm is credited with being the first professional political campaign management organization in the United States, setting the pace for many thousands today. The firm orchestrated the advertisements, front groups, and movie shorts that distorted and challenged Upton Sinclair, the muckraking author of *The Jungle* and other exposés of American capitalism's seamy underside, when Sinclair ran for governor of California in 1934. The story of tactics employed in the campaign, which Sinclair lost, is related in Greg Mitchell's 1993 book, *The Campaign of the Century.*

Some Whitaker & Baxter guidelines became standard political campaign tenets:

- Attempt to create actual news instead of merely sending out publicity.

- More Americans like corn than caviar.

- "The average American doesn't want to be educated, doesn't want to improve his mind, doesn't want to work, consciously, at being a good citizen. But most every American likes to be entertained. . . . So, if you can't fight, *put on a show!*"

- Never wage a campaign defensively! "The only successful defense is a spectacular, hard-hitting, crushing offensive."

Baxter has won the Gold Anvil, PRSA's highest personal award, for her distinguished career and for ethical contributions to the public relations profession. Her philosophy, often expressed—and not always popular—emphasizes that "the public assessment of our profession in the final analysis must hinge very largely on the profession's candid assessment of itself, on its standards and its own efforts to create and maintain a highly capable, ethical, and responsible profession."

*Leone Baxter, with Clem Whitaker, founded the first pro-
fessional political campaign management firm in the
United States in 1933. The firm conducted campaigns for
a number of California governors including Earl Warren
and gained national attention in General Dwight
Eisenhower's presidential campaign of 1952. Whitaker
died in 1961. Baxter, headquartering in San Francisco,
heads Whitaker and Baxter International, counselors in
national and international public affairs.*

Among the most widely known advocates of social causes in the twentieth century
who effectively used some of the techniques of public relations were Margaret Sanger,
founder of the Planned Parenthood Federation of America; singer Kate Smith, who sold
thousands of dollars in U.S. bonds during World War II while making Irving Berlin's
"God Bless America" almost the national anthem; Dorothy Day, founder of the widely
respected *Catholic Worker* magazine in 1933 and its editor until 1980, an active pacifist
and worker for the nonviolent achievement of social justice; Gloria Steinem, cofounder
with Patricia Carbine of *Ms.* magazine, chronicler of the feminist movement for more
than two decades; and Betty Friedan, originator of the National Organization of Women
(NOW) in 1966, who promoted numerous women's causes and whose accomplishments
included the adoption of a pro-choice plank at the NOW convention in 1967.

Serving on the Management Team   Public relations counseling is at its best when it
functions at the very top level of management. American corporate executives have
been slow to accept this viewpoint. Its recognition in recent years has resulted mostly
from the experiences of companies whose leaders understood much of what public
relations is all about.

Arthur Page, who became vice president of the American Telephone & Telegraph
Company in 1927, helped shape today's practice by advocating the philosophy that public relations is a management function and that it should have an active voice in management. He also expressed the belief that a company's performance, not press agentry,
comprises its basis for public approval.

Alfred P. Sloan, then president of General Motors Corporation, also was among the
first executives to place great trust in public relations. In 1931, during the early years of

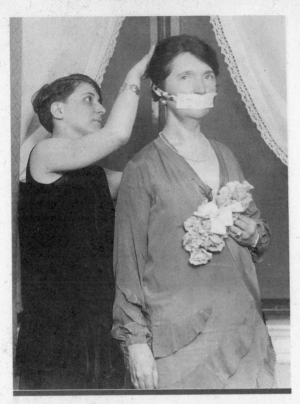

Margaret Sanger's battle for public acceptance of birth control was a public relations campaign in the early 1900s, using speeches, writings, demonstrations, and confrontations with the law. When Boston authorities refused her permission to speak in 1929, she had her mouth taped shut symbolically for news photographs. Later she said, "As a propagandist, I see immense advantages in being gagged. It silences me, but it makes millions of others talk and think the cause in which I live."

the Great Depression when business was attacked widely for its failures, Sloan hired Paul W. Garrett as his first public relations employee.

Garrett was charged with ascertaining public attitudes and executing a program to bring the company full public approval. For one thing, the board of directors felt that favor might be gained by making the billion-dollar corporation appear small. Garrett considered that approach neither reasonable nor possible. Instead, he informed management that it must interpret itself by words and deeds that had meaning to those outside the company, that it must put the broad interests of the public first, that it must develop sound internal relationships with its employees, and that it must be frank and honest and explain the company's policies clearly and simply through every possible medium.

Garrett's program proved highly effective, and his speechmaking and other activities during a 25-year career with General Motors broadened the understanding of leaders of many other major organizations about the full-fledged public relations function. *Fortune* magazine, in a series of articles in 1938 and 1939, praised the GM program, along with those of Chrysler, Ford, and AT&T, and also lauded public relations itself as a valuable economic, social, and political function.

Another example of high-level management counseling that won wide attention was that provided by Earl Newsom for Henry Ford II. When Ford took over the reins of

FOUR MODELS OF PUBLIC RELATIONS

To aid in understanding the history of formal public relations as well as its practice today, Professors James E. Grunig of the University of Maryland and Todd Hunt of Rutgers: The State University of New Jersey have constructed four models of public relations. All four models are practiced today, but the "ideal" one—that in increasing use—is the two-way symmetric model. They explain the models in their 1984 book *Managing Public Relations:*

Press Agentry/Publicity   Propaganda is the purpose, sought through one-way communication that is often incomplete, distorted, or only partially true. The model is source → receiver. Communication is viewed as telling, not listening, and little if any research is undertaken. P. T. Barnum was the leading historical figure during this model's heyday from 1850 to 1900. Sports, theater, and product promotion are the main fields of practice today.

Public Information   Dissemination of information, not necessarily with a persuasive intent, is the purpose. The model is source → receiver. Research, if any, is likely to be confined to readability tests or readership studies. Ivy Lee is the leading historical figure during this model's early development period from about 1900 into the 1920s. Government, nonprofit associations, and business are primary fields of practice today.

Two-way Asymmetric   Scientific persuasion is the purpose, and communication is two-way, with imbalanced effects. The model is source → receiver, with feedback (←) to the source. Research is both formative, helping to plan an activity and to choose objectives, and evaluative, finding if the objective has been met. Ivy Lee is the leading historical figure during the model's period beginning in the 1920s. Competitive business and public relations firms are the primary places of practice today.

Two-way Symmetric   Gaining mutual understanding is the purpose, and communication is two-way with balanced effects. The model is group → group with feedback (←). Formative research is used mainly both to learn how the public perceives the organization and to determine what consequences the organization has for the public, resulting in the counseling of management about policies. Evaluative research is used to measure whether a public relations effort has improved both the understanding publics have of the organization and that which management has of its publics.

Edward L. Bernays, educators, and professional leaders have been the main historical figures of the two-way symmetric model, followed by some organizations since the 1960s and 1970s.

the company, he was relatively unknown, because Edsel Ford had been groomed as the heir apparent. There was widespread conjecture as to whether Henry Ford II could lead the company properly. The grandson of the pioneer automobile maker employed Newsom in 1945 to advise him during a strike by the United Automobile Workers. Planning was Newsom's forte: he issued no news releases and held no news conferences. By preparing five major speeches for Ford II before major, influential audiences, Newsom achieved both public and press recognition for Ford's ability, along with much quotable copy.

	Model			
	One-Way		Two-Way	
ROLE	Press Agentry/ Publicity	Public Information	Two-Way Asymmetrical	Two-Way Symmetrical
Purpose	Propaganda	Dissemination of information	Scientific persuasion	Mutual understanding
Organizational contribution	Advocacy	Dissemination of information	Advocacy	Mediation
Nature of communication	One-way; complete truth not essential	One-way; truth important	Two-way; imbalanced effects	Two-way; balanced effects
Communication model	Source → Rec.*	Source → Rec.	Source → Rec. ← feedback	Group → Group ← feedback ←
Nature of research	Little; "counting house"	Little; readability, readership	Formative; evaluative of attitudes	Formative; evaluative of understanding

Note. Adapted from J. Grunig (1987, p. 9).

* "Rec." is abbreviation for "Receiver."

Characteristics of Four Models of Public Relations

PUBLIC RELATIONS COMES OF AGE

AFTER WORLD WAR II

The booming economy after World War II produced rapid growth in all areas of public relations. Companies opened public relations departments or expanded existing ones. Government staffs increased in size, as did those of nonprofit organizations such as educational institutions and health and welfare agencies. Television emerged in the late 1940s as a new challenge for public relations expertise. New firms sprang up in cities throughout the country, many discovering that they were required not only to sell their own services to potential clients but first to educate many managers on the value of public relations itself.

By 1950 an estimated 17,000 men and 2,000 women were employed as practitioners in public relations and publicity. Typical of the public relations programs of large corporations at midcentury was that of the Aluminum Company of America. Heading the operation was a vice president for public relations–advertising, aided by an assistant public relations director and an advertising manager. Departments included community relations, product publicity, motion pictures and exhibits, employee publications, news bureau, and industrial economics (speechwriting and educational relations). *Alcoa News* magazine was published for all employees, as well as separate publications for those in 20 plants. The main broadcast effort was sponsorship of Edward R. Murrow's "See It Now" television program.

A British scholar, J. A. R. Pimlott, wrote in 1951: "Public relations is not a peculiarly American phenomenon, but it has nowhere flourished as in the United States. Nowhere else is it so widely practiced, so lucrative, so pretentious, so respectable and disreputable, so widely suspected and so extravagantly extolled."

Census-takers in 1960 counted 23,870 men and 7,271 women engaged in public relations, although some observers put the total figure at approximately 35,000. Since 1960, the number of public relations practitioners has dramatically increased, as stated in Chapter 1. In 1986 women, for the first time, comprised more than 50 percent of public relations personnel. Recent surveys show that four out of five large companies and trade organizations now have public relations departments. Additionally, there are more than 6000 public relations firms.

Journalism and mass communications schools also have felt the impact of public relations majors. In 1994 an estimated 190 colleges and universities offered degrees or sequences in public relations—about 50 percent of the total number of institutions offering journalism and mass communications programs.

WHY PUBLIC RELATIONS IS GROWING

Ronald B. Millman, a partner of the Financial Relations Board, Inc., of Chicago and president of that city's PRSA chapter, says public relations "came of age" during the 1980s. Citing the increasing number of practitioners and the rise in billings by the top ten U.S. public relations firms (to more than $910 million in 1990, more than seven times that of 1980), Millman offers seven reasons for the growth:

■ *PR is cost-efficient.* An annual public relations campaign costs less than the production of most television commercials.

■ *PR has won over management.* With issues such as ecology, civil rights, equal rights, and consumerism commanding increased attention, management has come to realize the value of its public relations operation.

■ *The penalties of poor PR are viewed each night on the 10 o'clock news.* With the Exxon oil disaster as an example, good managers realize they must prepare for crises as though they were part of the year's business plan.

■ *PR is no longer measured by the ink (or time) it produces.* Measurement tools are now far more sophisticated.

■ *PR is becoming more specialized.* Many public relations firms now concentrate their efforts solely in one area, such as finance, consumer marketing, crisis communications, employee communications, and politics.

■ *PR tools are becoming more complex.* For example, video news releases are a basic ingredient of almost every marketing public relations program, and faxing releases is an accepted means of distributing news not only to the media but also to the business community.

■ *Markets are going international.* The stakes of competing in the global marketplace have increased along with the obstacles, such as different languages, cultures, and approaches. Public relations is the technique of choice as a global communication tool.

The popularity of public relations as a major field of study is reflected in annual statistics gathered by the Association for Education in Journalism and Mass Communication (AEJMC). As early as 1987, Professor Paul Peterson of Ohio State University, who conducted the annual AEJMC survey for many years, declared, "Indications are clear that the areas of advertising and public relations are the leaders in attracting student interests." Professor Lee Becker, who now conducts the survey, estimates that almost 22,000 majors are studying public relations in 190 American colleges and universities. This figure does not include many public relations sequences in departments and schools of communication. Reports from Australia, Singapore, England, and Germany also show major increases in public relations enrollments.

The Public Relations Student Society of America, founded in 1968, provides important professional training on campus (see Chapter 4). The International Association of Business Communicators (IABC) also has individual student members and some student chapters, but no national student organization.

Public Relations Literature   A measurement of the growth of public relations in the twentieth century also may be found in its literature. From 1900 to 1928, only two books with "public relations" in their titles were listed in the catalogue *Books in Print.* Landmark publications include the following:

- 1902: "What Is Publicity?" by H. C. Adams, in the *American Review.* Perhaps the first magazine article dealing with public relations as a topic.

- 1915: *Publicity and Progress,* by H. H. Smith.

- 1920: *Winning the Public,* by S. M. Kennedy.

- 1922: *Getting Your Name in Print,* by Funk & Wagnalls, the dictionary publisher.

- 1923: *Crystallizing Public Opinion,* by Edward L. Bernays. The first book to reach a wide audience about how public relations can be used to shape public opinion.

- 1924: *Public Relations: A Handbook of Publicity,* by John C. Long.

- 1944: Founding of *Public Relations Journal,* the monthly magazine of the Public Relations Society of America.

- 1947: *Practical Public Relations,* by Rex Harlow and Marvin Black. Perhaps the first regular public relations textbook.

- 1949: *Public Relations in Management,* by J. Handly Wright and Byron H. Christian. The first attempt to link public relations with management.

- 1952: *Effective Public Relations,* by Scott Cutlip and Allen Center. The best-known basic textbook for many years.

- *Social Science Reporter,* founded by Rex F. Harlow. The first newsletter in the field to emphasize the relationship between public relations and applied social science theory.

- 1955: Founding of *Public Relations Quarterly.*

- *Social Science in Public Relations,* by Rex F. Harlow. The first book applying social science theory to public relations.

- 1970: Founding of *IABC Communication World,* monthly magazine of the International Association of Business Communicators.

- 1974: Founding of *Public Relations Review,* first quarterly refereed journal in public relations. By the Foundation for Public Relations Education and Research.

- 1976: Founding of *IPRA Review,* first magazine devoted to international public relations. By the International Public Relations Association.

- 1989: Founding of *Public Relations Research Annual,* edited by James E. Grunig and Larissa A. Grunig.

- 1992: *Excellence in Public Relations and Communication Management,* edited by James E. Grunig. The results of a massive research study sponsored by IABC that lays out a general theory of contemporary public relations.

Each year hundreds of articles and numerous books are published about public relations and related fields; a wide selection of the most current titles is listed in the bibliography at the end of this book. The body of knowledge about the field has been abstracted and codified by PRSA and is available on computer diskette.

Public Relations Growth   Public relations has become essential in modern life because of a multiplicity of reasons, including the following: heavy, continuing population growth, especially in cities where individual citizens have scant direct contact with Big Business, Big Labor, Big Government, Big Institutions, and other powerful organizations influencing their lives; scientific and technological advances, including automation and computerization; the communications revolution; mergers and consolidations, with bottom-line financial considerations often replacing the more personalized decision making of previous, more genteel times; and the increased interdependence of a complex world society.

Many citizens feel alienated, bewildered by such rapid change, cut off from the sense of community that characterized the lives of previous generations. They seek power through innumerable pressure groups, focusing on causes such as environmentalism, human rights, and antinuclear campaigns. Public opinion, registered through continual polling, has become an increasingly powerful force in combatting or effecting change.

Both physically and psychologically separated from their publics, American business and industry have turned increasingly to public relations specialists for audience analysis, strategic planning, and issues management, among other functions. Corporate social responsibility has become the norm and the expectation. One of the most important tasks of these specialists is that of environmental surveillance—serving, in effect, much like the periscope of a submarine. The continued growth of companies, if not survival itself, depends in large part on the skills of public relations people.

Research has assumed an importance never before known. Back in 1853, Theodore N. Vail, founder of the American Telephone & Telegraph Company, had sensed its importance, sending letters to his customers seeking their opinions. In 1912, public relations-wise Henry Ford had asked 1000 customers why they had purchased his Model T car. These were among the forerunners of the social science research techniques that were developed after World War I. In the 1930s, George Gallup, Elmo Roper, Claude Robinson, and others began to conduct modern public opinion and marketing surveys. They provided a tool by which public relations specialists and others could evaluate public attitudes quantitatively and obtain objective measurements to supplement personal estimates of public opinion.

COMMUNICATIONS IN THE 1990S

As the 1990s began, communications leaders outlined major issues that public relations people and management executives should anticipate confronting during the decade—issues such as global competition, the environment, and government regulation (all to be reviewed later in this section).

One-third of the way through the decade, *PR Reporter* summarized actions that forward-looking organizations seemed to be taking in managing their public relations programs. The overriding trend, according to the newsletter, is *seeking to change the behaviors of publics,* not merely communicating with them. Some advice stemming from these current directions includes:

Inez Kaiser was the first black practitioner to handle national accounts

- Replace much of the advertising and other media operations with direct, personal contacts, exchanging opinions and forming coalitions with power leaders.

- Use definitive research methods to guide practitioners in their efforts to motivate behavior.

- Minimize risk-taking by anticipating changes.

- Refine feedback systems.

- Seek real culture change, not with gimmicks, but by continuous open communication that leads to solid working relationships.

- Go direct to your publics through access-entertainment media.

- Keep a low profile: mass communications activates competitors and opponents as well as supporters.

- View employees as your No. 1 public. Expect them to keep informed and be accountable.

- Promote employee teamwork through lateral communication—department-to-department, worker-to-worker. Minimize up-and-down direction.

- Integrate all aspects of your communications (advertising, public relations, marketing, direct mail, promotion) so they will work in tandem to achieve overall objectives.

Issues helping shape the nature of public relations during the 1990s, as envisioned by communications leaders and management executives, include the following:

A Global Economy   Every national economy and every business is part of an integrated global economy. The internationalization of business means that companies and public relations people must learn a great deal about foreign cultures, business practices, and languages. Accompanying this globalization thrust, the wealth of the world has largely shifted from the West to the Pacific Rim, especially to Japan, Taiwan, Singapore, and Korea. Of the largest 25 companies in the world, 19 are Japanese and one is European.

J. F. Coates, coauthor of a recent book titled *What Futurists Believe,* writes: "The primary challenge to American business is for better design, higher quality, more sure and speedy service, durable performance, and general reliability in schedules, claims, and effectiveness." And Daniel W. Bellack, chairman of TFB/BBDO Business Communications, Inc., says: "Global strategy really means localizing. . . . Be sure you understand each local market, culture, and, of course, language."

Quality of the Environment   Concern for the environment is now a widespread issue, and people in many countries believe that protecting it is so important that no requirements and standards can be too high. Environmental issues also translate as a "quality of life" issue: people are concerned about their health and perceive a direct self-interest in such issues as the "greenhouse effect," acid rain, pollution, toxic wastes, and the spread of AIDS. Because such issues are transnational in scope, international dialogue and cooperation are prerequisites for effective solutions.

Corporations in the 1990s must be more sensitive to environmental concerns than in the past and show diverse publics that they are part of the solution, not the problem. At the same time, says C. J. Silas, chairman of Phillips Petroleum Company, "The challenge for industry and government will be to balance the two good, but seemingly paradoxical, objectives of environmental protection and economic growth and development."

Increased Management Role for Public Relations   Impediments to sales success such as environmental concerns require that public relations play a major role in the strategic planning and policy formulations of companies. John L. Clendenin, chairman of BellSouth Corporation, says, "I can't imagine any institution being able to operate successfully in today's environment without effective and proactive public relations management."

James A. Burke, former chairman of Johnson & Johnson, adds, "The CEO must have an understanding of how essential it is for public relations to be an intimate part of the decision-making process." Robert E. Allen, chairman of AT&T, puts it quite simply: "I need PR at my side, not in my wake." This means that in the 1990s "Public relations professionals had better be prepared to think and perform like senior-level managers," says Lawrence G. Foster, vice president of public relations for Johnson & Johnson.

New Emphasis on Issues Management   Many countries are seeking to cope with a flood of public policy issues. Governments as well as corporations are turning to experts skilled in problem analysis and conflict resolution to deal with the tough problems facing society and the planet Earth. Because of these pressures, John D. Francis, president of the Canadian Public Relations Society, says, "Issues management—improving the potential for controlling situations by understanding the attitudes of the public, the media, and opinion leaders and planning accordingly—will also be increasingly important in the 1990s." (See Chapter 14.)

Increased Government Regulation and Intervention   The resurgence of popular movements and activist groups will place more pressure on governments to make sure that corporations and other institutions are socially and environmentally responsible. The public also will demand "right to know" laws giving them access to full and complete information that corporations now consider proprietary. On another level, government will expect corporations to provide more financial resources (taxes) to clean up the environment.

Proliferation of Publics   The splintering of mass markets into hundreds of smaller markets, begun mainly in the 1980s, will continue through the 1990s. Public relations personnel will use microdemographics (closely defining target audiences by age, sex, educational level, and the like) to reach multiple publics with tailored information. In addition to traditional publics such as consumers, stockholders, employees, and the community, audiences also will be fragmented into special-interest groups mobilized around specific issues.

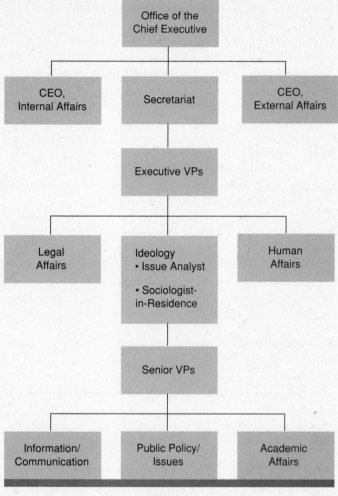

PROJECTED MANAGEMENT
STRUCTURE IN THE YEAR 2000

FIGURE 3.1
The organization chart of a future corporate structure in public
relations, designed by veteran counselor John F. Budd, Jr.
(Copyright 1989, John Budd, Jr.)

Robert L. Dilenschneider, former president and CEO of Hill and Knowlton, says the special-interest environmental groups with large membership that largely comprise the "green movement" will demonstrate their power in public affairs and public discussion.

Decline of Mass Media   The fragmentation of publics also means the decline of mass media as vehicles with which to reach audiences. The big four media—newspapers, magazines, radio, and television (except cable)—will not be truly major players in public relations communication. Technology will provide an infinite number of avenues for transmitting messages to specific audiences; the key terms will be *niche programming* and *narrowcasting*.

Cynthia Pharr, president of Tracy-Locke Pharr Public Relations, puts it this way: "With mass media rapidly giving way to specialized vehicles of communication, it is essential to tailor messages to narrow, well-defined audiences." This means identifying and understanding particular interest groups, working effectively with the media those groups trust, and developing a variety of messages to reach different audiences. The "one-size-fits-all" news release, she contends, is dead. "Targeting demands multiple releases, each featuring an element or angle that appeals to the audience it hopes to capture," Pharr adds. (See Chapter 12.)

Advent of New Media Technologies "The challenge of the nineties for the communicator is to catch up with, and master, the exploding field of high-tech communication tools," says John Armstrong, a veteran counselor and professor at the University of Portland, Oregon. (Technology is discussed in Chapter 21.) Futurist Joseph Coates adds: "Information technology, by the end of the century, will put every worker in the global corporation in easy communication with any other worker in the global corporation, as well as with any customer, constituent, client, vendor, or regulator." For example, an international network permits General Electric Company employees to communicate worldwide, using voice, video, and computer data, by simply dialing seven digits on the telephone. In sum, such a large number of communication vehicles will undercut the influence of the mass media.

International Media Relations Worldwide announcements of new ventures will become the norm during the 1990s. Satellite transmission of press conferences and simultaneous briefings by teams of public relations professionals in various countries will increase. Corporations will maintain decentralized public relations offices in Asia and Africa, says Ann Wilkinson, manager of worldwide public relations for National Semiconductor. Corporations will publish customer and employee newsletters in a variety of languages. Her company, for example, now publishes a consumer newsletter in six.

Higher Priority on Employee Communications Employee relations and communications will be a priority for a number of reasons. First, because the wave of mergers and acquisitions, generally resulting in the discharge of some employees (downsizing), is likely to continue through the 1990s, employee loyalty and trust of their employers will remain at an all-time low. Says James H. Dowling, president of Burson-Marsteller Public Relations: "The development of employee commitment to the venture—in the face of increased employee distrust of institutions and their leadership—may be the ultimate public relations challenge in the 1990s."

Second, the composition of the American work force is rapidly changing to include more women, minorities, and foreign-born persons. This will require management activity in job and literacy training, and in child care. Communicating to a multiethnic work force will be a major public relations challenge, and the issues will be complex.

Increased Research and Surveys Public relations people, according to Dilenschneider, will spend much more time analyzing information on a continuing basis. He adds, "Public relations people will become masters of sampling and surveying, of focused research and intricate problem-solving." In employee communications, greater use will be made of attitude surveys and reader-viewer studies to measure the results of communications.

The Skilled Practitioner For the global corporation of the 1990s, public relations personnel will require training and professional experience in marketing, international business, finance, and government. They must be able to perform like senior-level managers, thinking, visualizing, and implementing strategies.

Richard G. Charlton, vice president of corporate communications for Parker Hanifin Corporation, believes the 1990s will mark the rise of the generalist in public relations. "In the public relations department of the '90s," he explains, "there will likely be more flexible staffing, so that a public relations generalist can cover a story for the corporate newsletter or video news program and at the same time prepare an external news release." In addition, the public relations professional will provide increased coaching for middle managers to make them effective speakers and small-group discussion leaders.

CASE PROBLEM 1

The latter part of this chapter lists a number of national and global trends predicted to shape the practice of public relations during the 1990s. Select one of these issues and do some additional research. Write a short paper from the standpoint of what a public relations person should know about this issue and how it may affect working in public relations.

CASE PROBLEM 2

The 100th anniversary of a U.S. global soft drinks company is approaching.

As head of the company's public relations department, you are directed to develop a program that will call the event—and the product—to the attention of people around the world.

It's a mammoth undertaking but you have an almost unlimited budget.

Outline some of the actions that you and your colleagues would take. How can the company's history be used?

QUESTIONS FOR REVIEW AND DISCUSSION

1. The roots of public relations extend deep into history. What are some of the early antecedents of today's public relations practice?

2. What is meant by "hyping"?

3. Which practices of press agent Phineas T. Barnum should modern practitioners use? Which should they reject?

4. Describe briefly the publicity practices used by Henry Ford and by Theodore Roosevelt.

5. Ivy Lee made four important contributions to public relations. Can you identify them?

6. What effect did the Creel Committee of World War I have on the development of public relations?

7. Who was Doris E. Fleischman? Name at least three other women who used public relations techniques in pursuit of their causes.

8. Identify three of the successful public relations campaigns conducted by Edward L. Bernays.

9. What are some of the aspects of current American social and business life that make public relations essential?

10. What major national and global issues confront public relations practitioners today?

SUGGESTED READINGS

Badaracco, Claire. "Publicity and Modern Influence." *Public Relations Review,* Fall 1990, pp. 5–18. The history of publicity in American life.

Budd, John F. "PR Sages See Growth." *Communication World,* May–June 1990, pp. 95–98. Trends in public relations.

Chesler, Ellen. *Woman of Valor: Margaret Sanger and the Birth Control Movement in America.* New York: Simon & Schuster, 1992.

Coates, Joseph F. "Business Communication in Millenium III." *Communication World,* May–June 1990, pp. 129–134. Trends in public relations.

Corrigan, Dennis. "The Number One Issue for Professional Communicators: Building Management Support." *Communication World,* September 1992, pp. 13–17.

Creedon, Pamela J. "Public Relations History Misses 'Her' Story." *Journalism Educator,* Autumn 1989, pp. 26–36. Portrayal of women in histories of public relations.

Cutlip, Scott M. "Pioneering Public Relations for Foreign Governments." *Public Relations Review,* Spring 1987, pp. 13–34.

Fuhrman, Candice Jacobson. *Publicity Stunt: Great Staged Events That Made the News.* San Francisco: Chronicle Books, 1989.

Fullerton, Ronald A. "Art of Public Relations: U.S. Department Stores, 1876–1923." *Public Relations Review,* Fall 1990, pp. 68–79.

Gibson, Dirk. "The Making of the Hoover Myth: A Critical Analysis of FBI Public Relations." *Public Relations Quarterly,* Winter 1988–1989, pp. 7–15.

Grates, Gary F. "Competing in the '90s: What Business Wants and Needs from Public Relations Professionals." *Public Relations Quarterly,* Summer 1993, pp. 20–23.

Leahigh, Alan K. "The History of—Quote, Unquote—Public Relations." *Public Relations Quarterly,* Fall 1993, pp. 24–25. Quotes about public relations through the centuries.

Mitchell, Greg. *The Campaign of the Century: Upton Sinclair's Race for Governor of California and the Birth of Media Politics.* New York: Random House, 1992. Beginnings of American political public relations.

Nagy, Alex. "Word Wars at Home: U.S. Response to World War II Propaganda." *Journalism Quarterly,* Spring 1990, pp. 207–213.

Olasky, Marvin. "Engineering Social Change: Triumphs of Abortion Public Relations from the Thirties Through the Sixties." *Public Relations Quarterly,* Winter 1988–1989, pp. 17–21.

O'Neil, Kathleen. "U.S. Public Relations Evolves to Meet Society's Needs." *Public Relations Journal,* November 1991, pp. 28–30. Brief history of U.S. public relations.

Pearson, Ron. "Perspectives on Public Relations History." *Public Relations Review,* Fall 1990, pp. 27–38.

"Public Relations in the Year 2000." *Public Relations Journal,* January 1990. Entire issue devoted to series of articles exploring multiple trends in public relations.

Saxon, A. H. *P.T. Barnum: The Legend and the Man.* New York: Columbia University Press, 1990.

"Twelve Trends That Are Steering Public Relations Practice." *PR Reporter,* March 15, 1993, pp. 1–4.

The Individual in Public Relations

P R E V I E W   The objective of this chapter is to give the student a personal perspective on public relations work—how the individual fits into public relations practice and the rewards and challenges for a practitioner.

Topics covered in the chapter include:

- The difference between public relations and journalism

- Personal qualifications and attitudes

- Professional organizations providing support

- Internships

- Women and minorities in a diversified work force

- Salaries in public relations

HOW PUBLIC RELATIONS DIFFERS FROM JOURNALISM

As explained in Chapter 1, a basic difference exists between public relations and journalism. Although they may need many of the same skills as news reporters—writing ability, skill at synthesizing large amounts of information, interviewing ability—public relations practitioners have an entirely different mission. The goal of reporters is to uncover the facts, to the fullest extent possible, and to keep watch on society's institutions. Ideally, reporters practice objectivity and have no causes to promote or protect.

Public relations representatives, on the other hand, are by definition advocates. Their mission is to help their employer or client accomplish organizational goals and objectives. They do this by informing and educating the public, as reporters do, but the objective is to influence the public in a favorable way. Public relations people do as much listening as communicating, and they often implement preventative strategies. If they know that their employers or clients are vulnerable to criticism for certain policies and decisions, they suggest ways to remove the vulnerability by changing the policy or positioning a decision in a more favorable light.

A CHANGING FOCUS IN PUBLIC RELATIONS

Traditionally, it was widely held that public relations practitioners should if possible have experience as reporters, to polish their writing skills and to learn firsthand how the media function. In an earlier era, a large percentage of public relations people did have newspaper or broadcast experience. This is no longer true for several reasons, however.

The field of public relations has broadened far beyond working with the mass media. Writing skill and knowledge of the media are vital, but so is training in management, logistics, and planning—skills not usually acquired on a reporter's beat. In fact, former newspaper reporters often fail at public relations because they don't perceive the work as more than writing news releases and don't understand the multiple special publics a public relations program should reach. Some former reporters also have trouble conforming as corporation-oriented team players who must use comprehensive communication strategies.

Another factor limiting the number of graduates who acquire reporting experience before beginning public relations careers is the limited number of newspaper jobs. There are more corporations and institutions with public relations departments than there are daily and weekly newspapers. Movement of well-educated graduates direct from the classroom into public relations jobs is well accepted today, and a *PR Reporter* survey showed that there are now just as many practitioners in the field without newspaper experience as there are with such experience.

Part of the reason for this, no doubt, is the major growth of public relations sequences and programs at the undergraduate level in American universities. Professor Paul Peterson of Ohio State University in a recent study found almost 10,000 majors in public relations. Actually, Peterson's survey probably underestimates the number of students planning careers in public relations since an unknown number of journalism majors also go into public relations, as well as students who study public relations in

JOB LEVELS IN PUBLIC RELATIONS

Entry-Level Technician
Use of technical "craft" skills to disseminate information, persuade, gather data, or solicit feedback.

Supervisor
Supervises projects, including planning, scheduling, budgeting, organizing, leading, controlling, and problem-solving.

Manager
Constituency and issue-trend analysis; departmental management, including organizing, budgeting, leading, controlling, evaluating, and problem solving.

Director
Constituency and issue-trend analysis; communication and operational planning at departmental level, including planning, organizing, leading, controlling, evaluating, and problem solving.

Executive
Organizational leadership and management skills, including developing the organizational vision, corporate mission, strategic objectives, annual goals, businesses, broad strategies, policies, and systems.

Source: Adapted from the *Public Relations Professional Career Guide,* Public Relations Society of America, 33 Irving Place, New York, NY 10003.

departments of speech communication and business. Increasing numbers of these students go directly into public relations careers after graduation.

Many graduates choose public relations because they find the work at times to be stimulating and challenging, providing variety along with the routine. One day the young practitioner may prepare a news release; the next, work on a slide presentation; and the following, organize a conference. On a typical day, the practitioner may answer press inquiries, compile lists for mailing and for media contacts, escort visitors, read proof, write a brochure, scan incoming publications, help produce displays, select photographs, or compile questionnaires.

PERSONAL QUALIFICATIONS AND ATTITUDES

ATTRIBUTES FOR SUCCESS

Any attempt to define a single public relations type of personality is pointless, because the field is so diverse that it needs people of differing personalities. Some practitioners deal with clients and the public in person on a frequent basis; others work primarily at desks, planning, writing, and researching. Many do both.

A few basic personal attributes are evident in all successful practitioners, however, no matter what their specific assignments. These include:

1. Ability with words, written or spoken

2. Analytical skill, to identify and define problems

3. Creative ability, to develop fresh, effective solutions to problems

4. An instinct for persuasion

Bill Cantor, writing in the Public Relations Student Society of America's *Forum*, emphasizes the importance of curiosity and persistence.

The public relations professional should have an inquiring mind, should want to learn everything possible about the product, service, client or organization, and the competition.

Because public relations is not an exact science, frequently the public relations person must try a number of approaches in order to solve a problem, some of which might not work. If and when they don't work, the professional does not regard them as personal blunders, but as learning experiences. Problems are solved by persistence and intelligence.

Veteran public relations executives responsible for hiring staff members emphasize that normal personalities possessing the required skills are better suited for most public relations jobs than the brash "glad hand" type, a cliché some people erroneously associate with public relations work.

FOUR ESSENTIAL ABILITIES

Those who plan careers in public relations should develop four basic abilities, no matter what area of work they enter. These are writing skill, research ability, planning expertise, and problem-solving ability.

1. *Writing skill.* The ability to put information and ideas onto paper clearly and concisely is essential. Good grammar and good spelling are vital, not only to convey thoughts precisely but to make a favorable impression on those who receive written material. Misspelled words and sloppy sentence structure look amateurish. The importance of writing skill is emphasized in a career advice column in *Working Woman:* "I changed careers, choosing public relations as having the best potential, but found it difficult to persuade employers that my *writing and interpersonal skills* were sufficient for an entry-level job in the profession."

2. *Research ability.* Arguments for causes must have factual support instead of generalities. A person must have the persistence and ability to gather information from a variety of sources, as well as to conduct original research by designing and implementing opinion polls or audits. Too many public relations programs fail because the organization does not do its homework by assessing audience needs and perceptions. Skillful use of computer databases for acquiring information is an important element of research work, as is the ability to interpret survey results.

3. *Planning expertise.* A public relations program involves a number of communication tools and activities that must be carefully planned and coordinated. A person needs to be a good planner to make certain that materials are distributed in a timely manner,

PUBLIC RELATIONS PERSONALITY CHECKLIST

This checklist, based on careful evaluation, can measure the effectiveness of your personality in terms of the public relations profession.

Rate each item "yes" or "no." Each "yes" counts for 4 points. A "no" doesn't count. Anything below 60 is a poor score. A score between 60 and 80 suggests you should analyze your weak areas and take steps to correct them. Scores above 80 indicate an effective public relations personality.

_____ Good sense of humor	_____ Enjoy listening
_____ Positive and optimistic	_____ Enjoy helping other people resolve problems
_____ Friendly, meet people easily	_____ Curious about many things
_____ Can keep a conversation going with anybody	_____ Enjoy reading in diverse areas
_____ Take frustration and rejection in stride	_____ Determined to complete projects
_____ Able to persuade others easily	_____ High energy level
_____ Well-groomed, businesslike appearance	_____ Can cope with sudden emergencies
_____ Flair for showmanship	_____ See mistakes as learning experiences
_____ Strong creative urge	_____ Factual and objective
_____ Considerate and tactful	_____ Respect other people's viewpoints
_____ Adept in use of words	_____ Perceptive and sensitive
_____ Able to gain management's confidence	_____ Quickly absorb and retain information
_____ Enjoy being with people	

_____

Source: PRSSA Forum, Spring 1990.

events occur without problems, and budgets are not exceeded. Public relations people must be highly organized, detail-oriented, able to see the big picture.

4. *Problem-solving ability.* Innovative ideas and fresh approaches are needed to solve complex problems or to make a public relations program unique and memorable. Although many public relations people plod along and continue to handle new situations in a routine, unimaginative way, their results are rarely the kind that merit increased salaries and promotions. If a public relations person shows top management how to solve problems creatively, that person becomes a key part of the organization. Technicians who just do what they are told, however, can be easily replaced.

Three typical help-wanted advertisements illustrate how a public relations career may develop. The first is for an entry-level position of a routine nature, the second for a middle-level position requiring a few years of experience, and the third for a high-level director who does strategic planning, directs a staff, and serves as the institution's spokesperson.

SKILLS FOR THE 1990S

What kind of public relations staff person is needed in the late 1990s? AT&T has compiled a list of skills and personal characteristics that it looks for in potential employees:

Professional Experience/Acquired Skills

■ Polished, versatile communications skills
   —at the core, public relations writing
   —interpersonal (oral and aural skills, including public speaking)
   —visual (including print and electronic media)

■ Strategic PR thinking, problem solving, planning
   —results orientation

■ Providing PR counsel and support to management
   —special emphasis on marketing, finance, international business, employee relations, constituency and governmental relations

■ Understanding, working effectively with mass media

■ Understanding, effectively using organizational communications

■ Enthusiasm for and ability to explain technological change

■ PR evaluation; survey research

■ Special events management

■ Managing, supervising and developing subordinates in a creative professional environment

■ External focus, involvement with outside publics and process of social change

■ Understanding corporate social responsibility and relationships to governmental and nonprofit sectors.

Desired Personal Characteristics

■ Intellectual curiosity

■ Results orientation

■ Creativity

■ Flexibility

■ Energy

■ Initiative

■ Integrity

■ Ability to meet deadlines

■ Broad interests (e.g., with regard to political, social, economic issues)

■ Foreign language fluency

Source: AT&T.

STAFF AIDE

Credit union seeks public relations aide to write and edit monthly newsletter, design and write brochure, and plan a variety of promotions for each quarter. Successful applicant must maintain rapport with members through publications as well as telephone and personal contact and assist various departments with public relations/promotion activities. Degree in public relations or journalism required. Candidate should be a self-starter with initiative to work independently, be able to work under pressure to meet deadlines, and accept constructive criticism without being offended.

EVENTS PLANNING COORDINATOR

Publishing company located in New York City is seeking an events planning coordinator to execute corporate special events. Must have 3–5 years experience in public relations, corporate affairs and/or special events. Position requires strong writing, planning, and organization skills.

UNIVERSITY DIRECTOR OF PUBLIC AFFAIRS

The university seeks an individual to create, direct, and manage a comprehensive and integrated public affairs program in support of the university's mission and goals on a national, regional, and community level. This entails developing communication and public affairs strategies and programs in conjunction with the president and other officers and academic leaders.

Serving as the principal spokesperson for the university, specific responsibilities include directing the dissemination of information within the university itself, to the media and to the many publics involved with the university, promoting special events, enhancing the university's visibility and identifying areas within the community that could benefit from university resources and facilities.

Systematic research shows that there is a hierarchy of roles in public relations practice. In several studies, Professors Glen Broom and David Dozier of San Diego State University have found four empirically grounded organizational roles. They describe the roles as follows:

Communication Managers. Practitioners playing this role are perceived by others as the organization's public relations experts. They make communication policy decisions and are held accountable by others and themselves for the success or failure of communication programs. They follow a systematic planning process.

Communication Liaisons. Practitioners playing this role represent the organization at public meetings and create opportunities for management to hear the views of priority publics. Predominantly communication facilitators, these practitioners also identify alternative solutions to organizational problems. Similar to communication managers in many respects, communication liaisons do not make policy decisions and are not held accountable for program success or failure.

Media Relations Specialists. Practitioners playing this role actively seek to place messages about the organization in the mass media. At the same time, they keep others in the organization informed of what is being said about the organization (and about issues important to the organization) in the media. They do not make policy, nor are they accountable for program outcomes.

Communication Technicians. Practitioners playing this role are responsible for producing communication products, implementing decisions made by others. They take photographs, assemble graphics; write brochures, pamphlets and news releases; and handle all aspects of production. They do not participate in policy decision-making, nor are they responsible for outcomes.

The San Diego research indicates that practitioners, as well as employers, rate the communication manager at the top of the hierarchy in terms of prestige and salary levels.

QUALITIES FOR A SUCCESSFUL CAREER

Art Stevens, president of Lobsenz-Stevens, Inc., in New York City and author of *The Persuasion Explosion,* has formulated what it takes to become successful in public relations. The individual . . .

1. Must be an excellent writer capable of writing client reports, effective article themes to editors, news releases, captions, annual reports, feature stories, and the like. His or her writing must require little editing and supervision.

2. Must be able to do short- and long-range planning, conceive and execute a full public relations plan for each account, and adhere strictly to deadlines.

3. Must be innovative and imaginative, not bound by trite, traditional ideas. Must be willing to keep an open mind to new ideas, to researching better ways.

4. Must be well informed about a client's business and continue to keep abreast of all developments in business and government that have an effect on the client's or company's business. Must function as a counselor as well as a communicator.

5. Must be results-oriented, whether the task is the placement of major stories about a client in important publications or the successful execution of a special event. Must be a doer, a self-starter. Must know what follow-up means, and have a solid respect for timetables and deadlines.

6. Must be thorough "pro," skilled in all the techniques used in the practice of public relations: writing and distribution of news releases, producing press kits, running press conferences, and so on. Must be familiar with feature writers, magazine contributors, and hot current subjects being written about.

7. Must know how to create publicity by conceiving a meaningful idea and carrying it through to its conclusion. Must know how to create sundry ideas where none are evident and must know where to take them.

8. Must know what it takes to establish and maintain acquaintanceship with key media people, since editorial contact is one of the primary functions of the public relations professional. The public relations professional must know how to deal with the media and understand their need for quick and responsive answers.

9. Must be able to learn and grow as new situations and client needs arise. Must draw upon prior experiences in the public relations field to move into new situations effortlessly and effectively.

10. Must be a good manager, capable of organizing and arranging his or her workload for maximum results. Must be capable of carrying many assignments at the same time, and be in control of each one.

11. Finally, the public relations professional must not be a yes man/woman. Public relations has outgrown the caricature of second-class professionalism by producing individuals who speak their minds confidently to top management of major corporations and make valuable recommendations to these executives. So long as the public relations professional earns the respect and confidence of the chief executive officer, public relations will grow as a profession and will contribute to the broad communications goal of companies and institutions across the United States.

Source: Newsletter of the PRSA Counselors Academy.

Although this hierarchy of roles can serve as a career ladder for aspiring public relations professionals, many practitioners continue to play lower-level organizational roles (technician or media relations specialist) even after years of professional experience.

NEEDED: AN UNDERSTANDING OF ECONOMICS

In preparing themselves for public relations careers, students should obtain as solid a grounding in economics as possible. Once they are employed as professionals, they should study the financial aspects of their employers or clients. More and more, public relations involves distribution and interpretation of financial information. To handle this material well, the practitioner first must understand it.

After a few years of work, some public relations people return to the classroom to earn advanced degrees. The Master of Business Administration degree, commonly called the MBA, probably is the most frequently sought, but the list of master's and Ph.D. degrees held by public relations specialists ranges over many fields.

Students who plan to do corporate public relations work should remember the fundamental fact about American business: every company was created to earn a profit for those who risked their money to start it. Businesses can continue to exist only as long as they are profitable. The task of public relations in the business world is to help companies prosper. Unfortunately, many college students believe that American business makes excessive profits. This belief arises from a lack of comprehension of free enterprise economics. Typical of this general attitude is a survey of public relations majors in 18 universities nationwide. Professor Richard Piland of Miami University (Ohio) analyzed the responses of 1052 public relations majors to a survey questionnaire. He found a disturbing concept that business profits are far higher than they actually are and a belief among many students that most companies could easily raise wages without raising prices.

Many progressive companies use a *triangle* concept, representing three basic elements in their business. Customers, shareholders, and employees form the three sides. The management goal is to keep the sides of the triangle in balance, satisfying all three. Public relations has an important role in achieving this balance through effective communication with the three groups.

SPECIALIZED FIELDS

Developing expertise in a special field is an excellent way for public relations practitioners to advance their careers. The area of public relations with the highest median salary in the 1993 Public Relations Society of America survey was investor relations, which requires detailed financial knowledge. International public relations (languages and customs) was second, and environmental affairs (science and law) was third. Scientific knowledge is a valuable asset, because the ability to explain developments in science, medicine, and electronic technology so ordinary citizens can understand them is a sought-after talent.

Intensified public concern about protecting the environment makes public relations work in that field a swiftly growing specialty. Major newspapers and some television stations assign reporters to the "earth watch." Aware that they are vulnerable to bad publicity about their pollution problems, corporations are trying to clean up their offenses and present a "green" image. Consumers increasingly judge companies and organizations by the "dirty" and "clean" images they present. This has created an opportunity for public relations specialists qualified to speak with authority about the often complex environmental issues society faces.

PROFESSIONAL SUPPORT SERVICES

ORGANIZATIONS AND SOCIETIES

Public relations groups at the local, state, national, and international levels provide an important channel of communication for practitioners in all areas of the profession. Some of the better-known organizations include the Council for the Advancement and Support of Education (CASE), the National Investor Relations Institute (NIRI), and the International Public Relations Association (IPRA).

The largest national group is the Public Relations Society of America, with about 15,000 members and more than 101 chapters. PRSA was organized in 1948 with the merger of two groups, the National Association of Public Relations Counsel and the American Council on Public Relations, and in 1951 was joined by the American Public Relations Association. The society has 14 special interest sections, a national professional development and awards program, and publishes the monthly magazine *Public Relations Journal*. PRSA also operates an Information Center, which provides answers to members' research requests from its extensive library and from the Nexis and Dialog databases. The society distributes issue papers that help recipients plan strategies. It is the parent organization of the Public Relations Student Society of America (discussed in the next section).

The second largest organization of communication and public relations professionals is the International Association of Business Communicators (IABC), with more than 11,000 members in more than 35 countries. Members are predominantly in the United States. Canada is second, and about 4 percent are spread around the world with the largest chapters in the United Kingdom and Hong Kong. Although its membership has diversified somewhat in recent years, a large percentage of IABC members are involved in employee communications. Two-thirds of the respondents in a recent Profile study, for example, said employees were their primary audience. The organization publishes the monthly magazine *Communication World*.

PRSA and IABC investigated the possibility of merging during the late 1980s but decided against doing so. They continue to cooperate on a number of issues, such as ethics and professionalism.

INTERNSHIPS

Internships are extremely popular in the communications industry, and a student whose resume includes practical work experience along with an academic record has an important advantage. Obtaining an internship offered by a public relations firm, company department, or charitable agency is among the best ways to get this desired experience.

FIGURE 4.1
Shown here are the logos of the Public Relations Society of
America (PRSA), the Public Relations Student Society of
America (PRSSA), the International Association of Business
Communicators (IABC), and the International Public Relations
Association (IPRA).

The intern, in most cases, earns academic credit and gets firsthand knowledge of work in the professional field.

Although internships offer an advantage in getting a first job, the practice by some companies of using unpaid interns has drawn increasing criticism because it puts downward pressure on wages in fields where internships proliferate. The contention is that when students or recent graduates work for nothing, aspiring professionals will accept low beginning salaries. A trend is growing among colleges and universities, and employers as well, to advocate paid internships. The brightest students are insisting on payment for their work, and employers find that students are more productive when treated like actual employees.

Another way for students to get exposure and experience is through membership in the Public Relations Student Society of America (PRSSA). The society has chapters at about 175 universities and a national membership of 6,000. Many students participate in a national case study competition or carry out projects on local campuses as part of a corporate collegiate program. Many chapters also have student-run firms that implement programs for local and campus organizations. A university must offer five courses in public relations before a PRSSA chapter can be established on its campus.

A DIVERSIFIED WORK FORCE

More than half the public relations practitioners in the United States are women, an increasing number of whom hold high-level management positions. Thus the public relations industry provides a healthy diversity of gender perspective as it prepares and delivers its messages.

Public relations falls seriously short, however, in developing a work force rich in racial diversity. As the industry faces the challenge of addressing the abundance of target audiences in the increasingly multiracial, multicultural American population, its composition remains overwhelmingly white.

MINORITIES

More than 25 percent of the U.S. population in the mid-1990s consists of racial minorities—primarily African Americans, Hispanics, Asians and Pacific Islanders, and Native Americans. The number of minority workers in public relations falls far short of equaling that population percentage.

In its 1993 salary survey of members, the Public Relations Society of America found that 95 percent of respondents were white, 2 percent black, 2 percent Hispanic, and 1 percent Asian. Because the questionnaire went only to PRSA members, it does not necessarily represent the total public relations work force.

Some public relations firms say that they have difficulty hiring minority staff members because they receive so few applications from minority aspirants. Seeking to improve the situation, PRSA has taken several significant steps to stimulate recruitment of minorities. It has a national task force to promote minorities in public relations, a program of seminars and a speakers bureau to identify and encourage candidates, a list of minority candidates available, and a scholarship fund to place minority students in intern programs.

Various explanations have been offered for the shortage of minorities in public relations. Among them are inadequate school counseling to steer minority students toward public relations careers, a fear among some young people—usually unfounded—that they will not be accepted by coworkers; a dislike of being paraded as "token" minorities and assigned only to minority clients; and, in some instances, actual discrimination by public relations offices and/or clients.

Some minority men and women take the route into "mainstream" departments and firms. Others join local and regional minority-owned firms. These firms, usually small, earn much of their income by representing minority clients or working in the minority marketplace on behalf of large general firms such as fast-food companies and financial institutions.

African American Kim Hunted, president of LaGrande Communications in Los Angeles, pointed out at a PRSA meeting that a "minority market" as such does not exist, because the diverse and segmented audiences within the spectrum of minority populations respond to different messages.

As public relations practice becomes more and more internationalized with the growth of global corporations, public relations firms entering the world market have an especially strong need for diversified ethnic staffs. With constant communication between their U.S. offices and firms abroad, they need staff members with language skills, personal knowledge of other countries, and sensibility to the customs and attitudes of others. Knowledge of Spanish and the Asian languages is especially valuable because so much market potential exists in the Spanish-speaking and Pacific Rim countries.

WOMEN

As more and more young women entered the public relations field during the 1980s, the percentage of female workers rose swiftly. In February 1987, the U.S. Bureau of Labor Statistics for the first time showed women in the majority, at 51.7 percent. Five years later, in 1992, the bureau reported that women's portion of the work force had risen to 58.5 percent. The percentage of women in other fields has increased similarly. By 1993, according to the *Wall Street Journal,* one in three young lawyers was female, one in four young doctors, and one in five young dentists.

Denise A. Gray-Felder, a rising national leader in public relations, is a division manager in corporate communications at AT&T's headquarters in New Jersey. A former national president of Women in Communications, Gray-Felder was instrumental in setting up PRSA's Minority Scholarship Program. She is a life member of the NAACP and active in a number of voluntary organizations.

Statistical surveys have shown that the percentages of women workers are much higher in the lower and middle levels of public relations work than in the top command positions. A recent *PR Reporter* survey showed that women represent nearly 77 percent of practitioners under age 24 and 66 percent of those age 30 to 34, but at age 40 and up men predominate. This has led to charges of a "glass ceiling" that subtly prevents women from obtaining the highest positions of authority in the field.

Others, both women and men, deny that such a restraint exists. They point to numerous women holding top positions in their firms and departments. High-level positions go to persons who are prepared by experience to hold them, they point out, and as the younger women become senior in experience, more will achieve the highest positions. The trend is inevitable, if uneven.

This group of high-ranking executives exemplifies the rise of women to senior positions in public relations at large corporations and counseling firms. From left to right, top row: Lynda J. Stewart, ABC, Director of Communications and Employee Relations, Cox Enterprises, Inc.; Sharon A. Paul, Executive Vice President of Public Affairs, Labatt Breweries of Canada; Joyce Hergenhan, Vice President of Public Relations, General Electric; Marilyn Laurie, Senior Vice President/Public Relations, AT&T. From left to right, bottom row: Karen Bachman, Vice President of Communications, Honeywell, Inc.; Ann H. Barkelew, APR, Vice President of Corporate Public Relations, Dayton-Hudson Corporation; Linda Baker, Senior Vice President, Visa International Corporate Relations; Sunshine Overkamp, Vice President, Membership, Marketing, and Communication, Council on Foundations.

Women Receive Lower Pay   Despite the numerical superiority of women in public relations, studies show that from top to bottom men earn more money than women do. The longtime gap in male vs. female salary scales remains entrenched, although narrowing at some levels.

The 1993 salary survey of PRSA members showed that among practitioners with less than five years of experience, male respondents received a median salary 16 percent higher than female respondents. The gap widened as experience grew, until at the top level, more than 20 years of experience, the male median salary was 37 percent higher than the female. As a group, the male respondents at this level were older and had more experience than the women.

An exception was the next highest bracket, 15 to 19 years of experience, where the gap narrowed to 18 percent. Optimists find hope in this figure, since it covers women who entered public relations work in the 1970s and are reaching the time in their careers where they are prepared to hold top management positions now held primarily by men approaching retirement.

A fact influencing the salary gap is that corporate/industrial public relations work, traditionally dominated by men, pays the highest salaries, while the public sector and nonprofit organizations, in which women dominate, are among the lowest.

Other social and economic explanations for this discrepancy are advanced, many of them involving conflicting pressures on a woman's time by job demands and child-bearing. Some pessimists worry that the large number of women in the field will result in a "velvet ghetto" in public relations with lower prestige and pay than in fields requiring comparable education and skill. Optimists, on the other hand, believe that equality in pay will be achieved eventually.

WHAT KINDS OF SALARIES?

Public relations work pays relatively well. This is true from the entry level to the top, where a few senior executives receive between $300,000 and $400,000 in various forms of annual compensation, including bonuses and stock options. At the bottom of the ladder, college graduates hunting jobs find that beginning public relations positions pay higher average salaries than those in advertising, newspapers, and broadcasting.

A 1993 national survey of 1992 college graduates with bachelor's degrees, taken by Ohio State University, showed a median weekly salary of $350 for those with full-time jobs in journalism and mass communications. The breakdown by type of employment:

Public relations	$375
Advertising	356
Daily newspapers	350
Weekly newspapers	300
Television	300
Radio	289

The 1993 PRSA survey reported a median annual salary of $46,204 for all society members who responded. Indicative of the male-female pay difference just discussed, this overall figure was derived from a $58,477 median for men and a $39,542 median for women.

This table, compiled from the survey, shows the salary advancement achieved as practitioners acquire experience. These are median figures including all types of public relations work.

Experience	Men	Women
1–4 years	$30,117	$25,886
5–9 years	44,399	37,509
10–14 years	60,190	46,242
15–19 years	65,690	55,893
20 years or more	79,915	58,487

The box titled "Public Relations Salaries" shows median salaries in a number of areas of public relations practice.

PUBLIC RELATIONS SALARIES

Area	Median	%Men	%Women
Industrial/manufacturing	$62,303	57	43
Public relations counseling firm	53,728	50	50
Utility	52,672	49	51
Financial/insurance	49,602	43	57
Media/communications	49,473	42	58
Miscellaneous services	47,915	37	63
Scientific/technical	44,351	38	62
Government	44,019	51	49
Association/foundation	43,388	46	54
Solo practitioner	43,101	42	58
Transportation/hotels/resorts/entertainment	41,843	31	69
Health care	41,550	30	70
Advertising agency	41,066	36	64
Education	41,008	42	58
Religious/charitable	35,545	34	66

Source: Public Relations Journal survey of members, 1993

CASE PROBLEM

Research has shown that at least five basic factors determine how satisfied a person is in a particular job. They are (1) autonomy, (2) creativity, (3) income, (4) power, and (5) prestige. When Margaret DeFleur, a doctoral candidate at Syracuse University, applied these factors to people working in mass media industries, she found respondents most satisfied with the "prestige" of their jobs. Following in descending order of satisfaction were creativity, autonomy, power, and income. Rank these five elements in order of importance, to show what you believe would give you the most satisfaction in a public relations job. Explain your rationale.

QUESTIONS FOR REVIEW AND DISCUSSION

1. In what ways does a job in public relations differ from one in news reporting?

2. Why do some former newspaper reporters fail in public relations work?

3. Those who plan careers in public relations should develop four basic abilities. What are they?

4. What kinds of jobs are available in public relations?

5. What basic economic fact should students who enter corporate public relations work always keep in mind?

6. Glen Broom and David Dozier say there is a hierarchy of roles in public relations. What are they?

7. What is the largest national organization of public relations professionals? The second largest?

8. Why is it important for a student to complete an internship while in college?

9. How do you explain the fact that women in public relations are paid less than men?

10. What are three other factors in addition to compensation that public relations practitioners consider when looking for a job?

SUGGESTED READINGS

Becker, Lee B., and Kosicki, Gerald M.   "Annual Census of Enrollment Records Fewer Undergrads." *Journalism Educator,* Autumn 1993, pp. 55–65.

Belz, Andrew, and others.   "Using Role Theory to Study Cross Perceptions of Journalists and Public Relations Practitioners." *Public Relations Research Annual,* vol.

1, ed. James and Larissa Grunig. Hillsdale, NJ: Lawrence Erlbaum Associates, 1989, pp. 125–140.

Bovet, Susan L. "Firms Use Internships to Test Entry-Level Job Seekers." *Public Relations Journal,* September 1992, pp. 26–28.

Condino, Joan. "The Young and the Restless." *Public Relations Journal,* June 1987, pp. 18–22. Recent college graduates making careers in public relations.

DeFleur, Margaret. "Foundations of Job Satisfaction in the Media Industries." *Journalism Educator,* Spring 1992, pp. 3–14. Jobs in public relations rank high in overall job satisfaction.

Goldman, Elaine. "Developing a Personal Career Blueprint." *Public Relations Journal,* August 1993, pp. 31–32.

Gross, Howard. "Business Educators See the Light." *Communication World,* March 1993, pp. 21–25. The need for business graduates to master communication skills.

Kern-Foxworth, Marilyn. "Minorities: The Shape of Things to Come." *Public Relations Journal,* August 1989, pp. 14–22. Minorities in the public relations field.

Kern-Foxworth, Marilyn. "African-American Achievements in Public Relations." *Public Relations Journal,* February 1991, pp. 18–19.

Newman, Judith. "Thinking of a Career Switch? Try PR." *Cosmopolitan,* May 1992, pp. 96, 98.

Olson, Laury Masher. "Job Satisfaction of Journalists and PR Personnel." *Public Relations Review,* Winter 1989, pp. 37–45.

Redeker, Lauren. "Internships Provide Invaluable Job Preparation." *Public Relations Journal,* September 1992, pp. 20–21.

Rentner, Terry Lyn, and Bissland, James H. "Job Satisfaction and Its Correlates Among Public Relations Workers." *Journalism Quarterly,* Winter 1990, pp. 950–955.

"PR Pros Vote 59%–28% for PR vs. Liberal Arts Major." *O'Dwyer's PR Services Report,* July 1993, pp. 1, 5, 15.

Schuler, Joseph F. "Trivet! Kak u Tebya? As Global Economy Heats Up, Demand for Multilingual Practitioner Grows." *Public Relations Journal,* November 1990, pp. 10, 16.

Schwartz, Donald, Yarbrough, J. Paul, and Shakra, Therese. "Does Public Relations Education Make the Grade?" *Public Relations Journal,* September 1992, pp. 18–19. Includes survey of practitioners on what skills students should master while in college.

Tortorello, Nicholas J., and Wilheim, Elizabeth. "Salary Survey: Salary Growth Stalls but Firms and Women Gain." *Public Relations Journal,* July 1993, pp. 10–19. Eighth annual survey of salaries in public relations.

Toth, Elizabeth L., and Grunig, Larissa A. "The Missing Story of Women in Public Relations," *Journal of Public Relations Research,* vol. 5, no. 3, 1993, pp. 153–175. Research study on women as managers and technicians in public relations.

Wakefield, Gay, and Cottone, Laura. "Knowledge and Skills Required by Public Relations Employers." *Public Relations Review,* Fall 1987, pp. 24–32.

CHAPTER

Public Relations Departments
and Firms

P R E V I E W   The objective of this chapter is to explain what top managements expect from their public relations departments and to give students an understanding of how departments and public relations firms operate.

Topics covered in the chapter include:

- The role of public relations departments

- Organization of departments

- Line and staff functions

- Public relations firms

- Advertising and public relations mergers

- Work in a public relations firm

- Fees and charges

PUBLIC RELATIONS DEPARTMENTS

ROLE

For a century, public relations departments have served companies and organizations. George Westinghouse is reported to have created the first corporate department in 1889 when he hired two men to publicize his pet project, alternating current (AC) electricity. Their work was relatively simple when compared to the melange of physical, sociological, and psychological elements that contemporary departments employ. Eventually Westinghouse won out over Thomas A. Edison's direct current system, and his method became the standard in the United States. Westinghouse's public relations department concept has also grown into a basic part of today's electronic world.

Today, public relations is expanding from its traditional functions, enlarged over the years as explained in Chapter 3, to exercise its influence in the highest levels of management.

Importance in the 1990s In a changing environment, and faced with the variety of pressures previously described, executives increasingly see public relations not as publicity and one-way communication, but as a process of negotiation and compromise, with a number of key publics. James Grunig, professor of public relations at the University of Maryland, calls the new approach "building good relationships with strategic publics," which will require public relations executives to be "strategic communication managers rather than communication technicians."

Grunig, head of a six-year, IABC Foundation research study on *Excellence in Public Relations and Communications Management,* continues:

When public relations helps that organization build relationships, it saves the organization money by reducing the costs of litigation, regulation, legislation, pressure campaign boycotts, or lost revenue that result from bad relationships with publics—publics that become activist groups when relationships are bad. It also helps the organization make money by cultivating relationships with donors, customers, shareholders and legislators.

The results of the IABC study seem to indicate that chief executive officers (CEOs) consider public relations a good investment. A survey of 200 organizations showed that CEOs gave public relations operations a 184 percent return on investment (ROI), a figure just below that of customer service and sales/marketing.

Professional public relations people, ideally, assist top management in developing policy and communicating with various groups. Indeed, the IABC study emphasizes that CEOs want communication that is strategic, based on research, and involves two-way communication with key publics.

Dudley H. Hafner, executive vice president of the American Heart Association (AHA), echoed these thoughts:

In the non-profit business sector, as well as in the for-profit businesses of America, leadership needs to pay close attention to what our audiences (supporters or customers as well as the general public) want, what they need, what their attitudes are, and what is happening in organizations similar to ours. Seeking, interpreting, and communicating this type of critical information is the role of the communications professional.

Research indicates, however, that the role of public relations in an organization often depends on the type of organization, the perceptions of top management, and even the capabilities of the public relations executive.

Research studies by Professor Larissa Grunig at the University of Maryland and Mark McElreath at Towson State University, among others, show that large, complex organizations have a greater tendency than do smaller firms to include public relations in the policy-making process. Companies such as IBM and General Motors, which operate in a highly competitive environment, are more sensitive than many others to policy issues and public attitudes, and to establishing a solid corporate identity. Consequently, they place more emphasis on news conferences, formal contact with the media, writing executive speeches, and counseling management about issues that could potentially affect the corporate bottom line.

In such organizations, classified as mixed organic/mechanical by management theorists, the authority and power of the public relations department are quite high. Public relations is part of what is called the "dominant coalition" and has a great deal of autonomy.

In contrast, a small-scale organization of low complexity, with a standardized product or service, feels few public pressures and little governmental regulatory interest. It has scant public relations activity, and staff members are relegated to such technician roles as producing the company newsletter and issuing routine news releases. Public relations in what is called the traditional organization has little or no input into management decisions and policy formation.

Research also indicates that the type of organization involved may be less significant in predicting the role of its public relations department than are the perceptions and expectations of its top management. In many organizations top-level management perceives public relations as primarily a journalistic and technical function—media relations and publicity. In large-scale mechanical organizations of low complexity, there also is a tendency to think of public relations as only a support function of the marketing department.

Such perceptions by top management severely limit the role of the public relations department as well as its power to take part in management decision making and solve problems. Instead, public relations staff members are relegated to being technicians who simply prepare messages without input on what should be communicated.

A third dimension influencing the role and function of a public relations department is the background and capabilities of its staff. As the IABC Foundation research has pointed out, CEOs want strategic communication managers; yet a large number of public relations managers, many of them journalists by training, self-select technician roles because they lack a knowledge base in research, environmental scanning, problem solving, and managing total communication strategies.

Instead, they continue to be preoccupied with one-way communication to the mass media even though, as the IABC research points out, the mass media "generally are not the most effective way of communicating with strategic publics—especially at the stage of building relationships rather than responding to issues."

Florida Power & Light's carefully prepared crisis management plan received a severe test when Hurricane Andrew struck south of Miami in 1992; 20,000 homes were made uninhabitable and 1.4 million homes lost electricity. The company's public relations department handled 1600 media calls during the ensuing month and distributed 66 press releases and background information sheets.

According to Dena Winokur and Robert Kinkead, writing in the *Public Relations Journal,* CEOs increasingly will view public relations as a strategic management tool. They write:

CEOs in the '90s and beyond will demand communication counselors who can analyze corporate cultures and understand how to influence their evolution. These counselors must be as comfortable in the board room as they are at the computer keyboard. They must be able to handle a crisis, write a speech, and devise a corporate strategy with equal ease.

THE ENVIRONMENT FOR EXCELLENT PUBLIC RELATIONS

The role and function of public relations departments often depend on the organizational environment. The following are attributes of organizational excellence that foster excellence in public relations:

1. *Human resources.* People are given autonomy and empowered to make decisions. There is interdependence and teamwork.

2. *Organic structure.* Bureaucracy is eliminated and decisions are made on a decentralized basis. Organic organizations are more innovative and generate more job satisfaction.

3. *Intrapreneurship.* Innovation is rewarded.

4. *Symmetrical communication systems.* There is two-way communication and dialogue. Listening, negotiation, and conflict resolution are favored over orders and persuasion.

5. *Leadership.* Management by walking around. Delegation versus authoritative models.

6. *Strong, participative cultures.* People are actively involved in making decisions.

7. *Strategic planning.* The bottom line is maximized by identifying important environmental opportunities. Strategic planning is done through environmental scanning and selection of issues.

8. *Social responsibility.* Organization balances self-interest with public interest.

9. *Support for women and minorities.* There is active effort to recruit and promote representatives from these groups.

10. *Quality as a priority.* There are internal quality control programs and an emphasis on monitoring customer feedback.

11. *Effective operational systems.* Management does research on how the organization does its business and how productivity can be increased.

12. *Collaborative societal culture.* Participation is a hallmark of organization.

EXPECTATIONS OF MANAGEMENT

In today's environment, every organization must be cognizant of many factors that can affect its success. Modern management recognizes that public relations is a tool for problem solving as well as attention-getting, and has several expectations.

1. *Information analysis.* Public relations staff members should function as information analysts and information brokers, communicating both outward from management and inward to management with the views of the public and employees.

2. *Issues management.* The public relations staff should monitor trends in society and pinpoint public concerns before they erupt into full-fledged controversies. Indeed, as a PRSA Task Force on the Stature and Role of Public Relations pointed out:

the greatest value of the public relations professional is in anticipating and shaping what is happening, not in reporting or coping with what has already been determined. By the time an organization is confronted with attitudes of its publics, it is usually too late for public relations thinking to have an effect on them. Dealing with existing attitudes is important, but helping to shape and direct future attitudes is far more valuable.

3. *Training.* Public relations personnel must counsel management on how to communicate the organization's position to the public effectively. Because of societal pressures, top management increasingly is spending more time on public affairs and in speaking to a variety of audiences. Peter Drucker, a management expert, estimates that top executives now spend up to 75 percent of their time on public affairs. Top executives also are less hesitant than previously to appear on television talk shows.

4. *Management expertise.* Public relations personnel—at least those who aspire to key positions in the organization—must master the techniques of management and strategic planning. They must understand such concepts as Management by Objective (MBO), allocation of resources, supervision of personnel, and use of cost-effective

communication tools. Robert H. Hood, president of the Douglas Aircraft Company of McDonnell Douglas Corporation, says:

> The way public relations can have the most value is to make it an integral component of the management team. That means being in the room when key decisions are made and strategies developed.

DEPARTMENT ORGANIZATION

The head executive of a public relations or similarly named department usually has one of three titles—manager, director, or vice president. A vice president of corporate communications may have direct responsibility for the additional activities of advertising and marketing communications.

A department usually is divided into specialized sections that have a coordinator or manager. Common sections found in a large corporation are media relations, investor relations, consumer affairs, governmental relations, community relations, marketing communications, and employee communications.

A typical organizational chart for a public relations department is shown in Figure 5.1.

One of the world's largest corporations, General Motors, has more than 300 public relations personnel and a wide range of job titles based on geography and operating divisions. Each division, such as Buick or the Saginaw Steering Gear Division, has its own director of public relations. General Electric, another corporate giant, has several hundred persons in various public relations functions.

These examples should not mislead the reader about the size and budget of public relations departments. Multimillion-dollar corporations often have small departments. A Conference Board survey of 150 major U.S. corporations found that the typical department has nine professionals. The typical department budget, the survey noted, was about $3.5 million.

Public relations personnel also may be dispersed throughout an organization in such a manner that an observer has difficulty in ascertaining the extent of public relations activity. Some may be housed under marketing communications in the marketing department. Others may be assigned to the personnel department as communication specialists producing newsletters and brochures. Still others may be in marketing, working exclusively on product publicity. Decentralization of the public relations function, and the frictions it causes, will be discussed later in this chapter.

LINE AND STAFF FUNCTIONS

Traditional management theory divides an organization into *line* and *staff* functions. A line manager, such as a vice president of manufacturing, can delegate authority, set production goals, hire employees, and directly influence the work of others. Staff people, in contrast, have little or no direct authority. Instead, they indirectly influence the work of others through suggestions, recommendations, and advice.

According to accepted management theory, public relations is a staff function. Public relations people are experts in communication; line managers, including the chief executive officer, rely on them to use their skills in preparing and processing data, making recommendations, and executing communication programs to implement the organization's policies.

Public relations staff members, for example, may find through a community survey that people have only a vague understanding of what the company manufactures. In order to improve community comprehension and create greater rapport, the public relations department may recommend to top management that a community open house be held at which product demonstrations, tours, and entertainment would be featured.

Notice that the department *recommends* this action. It would have no direct authority to decide arbitrarily on an open house and to order various departments within the company to cooperate. If top management approves the proposal, the department may

FIGURE 5.1

This chart explaining the organization of Visa International's corporate relations division shows the diversity of activities carried out under the direction of the senior vice president for corporate relations.

Visa International Corporate Relations

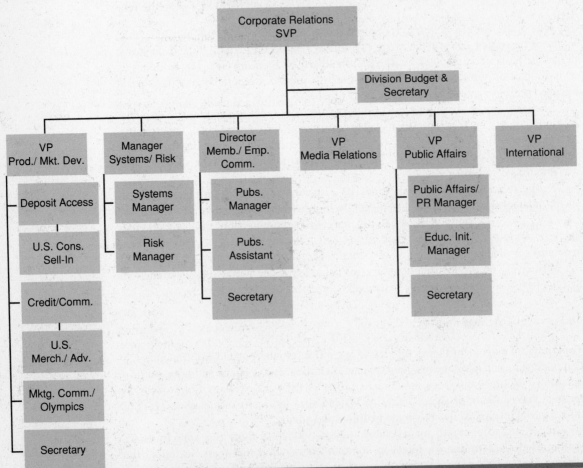

take responsibility for organizing the event. Top management, as line managers, has the authority to direct all departments to cooperate in the activity.

Although public relations departments can function only with the approval of top management, there are varying levels of influence that departments may exert. These levels will be discussed shortly.

Access to Management The power and influence of a public relations department usually result from access to top management, which uses advice and recommendations to formulate policy. That is why public relations, as well as other staff functions, is located high in the organizational chart and is called upon by top management to make reports and recommendations on issues affecting the entire company. In today's environment, public acceptance or nonacceptance of a proposed policy is an important factor in decision making—as important as costing and technological ability. This is why the former president of RJR Nabisco, F. Ross Johnson, told the *Wall Street Journal* in an interview that his senior public relations aide was "Numero Uno" and quipped, "He is the only one who has an unlimited budget and exceeds it every year."

The organizational chart of General Motors, for example, also shows public relations as a policy group reporting directly to the executive committee, consisting of the GM president and key board members. Other policy groups with the same status as public relations include engineering, marketing, personnel, and research—all of which have functions that affect every area of the corporation.

Levels of Influence Management experts state that staff functions in an organization operate at various levels of influence and authority. On the lowest level, the staff function may be only *advisory:* line management has no obligation to take recommendations or even request them.

When public relations is purely advisory, often it is not effective. A good example is the Alaska oil-spill crisis (see Chapter 9). Exxon generated a great deal of public, legislative, and media criticism because public relations was relegated to a low level and was, for all practical purposes, nonexistent.

Johnson & Johnson, on the other hand, gives its public relations staff function higher status. The Tylenol crisis, in which seven persons died after taking capsules containing cyanide, clearly showed that the company based much of its reaction and quick recall of the product on the advice of public relations staff. In this case, public relations was in a *compulsory-advisory* position (see the case study on Tylenol in Chapter 9).

Under the compulsory-advisory concept, organization policy requires that line managers (top management) at least listen to the appropriate staff experts before deciding on a strategy. Don Hellriegel and John Slocum, authors of the textbook *Management,* state: "Although such a procedure does not limit the manager's decision-making discretion, it ensures that the manager has made use of the specialized talents of the appropriate staff agency."

Another level of advisory relationship within an organization is called *concurring authority.* For instance, an operating division wishing to publish a brochure cannot do so unless the public relations department approves the copy and layout. If differences arise, the parties must agree before work can proceed. Many firms use this mode to prevent departments and divisions from disseminating materials not in conformity with company standards. In addition, the company must ascertain that its trademarks are used correctly to ensure continued protection (see Chapter 13).

Concurring authority, however, also may limit the freedom of the public relations department. Many companies have a policy that all employee magazine articles and external news releases must be reviewed by the legal staff before publication. The material cannot be disseminated until legal and public relations personnel have agreed upon what will be said. The situation is even more limiting on public relations when the legal department has *command authority* to change a news release with or without the consent of public relations. This is one reason that newspaper editors find some news releases so filled with "legalese" as to be almost unreadable.

SOURCES OF FRICTION

Ideally, public relations is part of the managerial subsystem. It is, say professors James and Larissa Grunig at the University of Maryland, "the management of communication between an organization and its publics."

A CORPORATE CAMPAIGN FOR THE UNITED WAY

The corporate relations department of the Panhandle Eastern Corporation, headquartered in Houston, played a key role in a program to revitalize employee participation in the local United Way campaign.

Background   A scandal, involving the national office of the United Way of America in Alexandria, Virginia, generated extensive news coverage and prompted many Americans to rethink their contributions to the United Way. This factor, coupled with a weak economy, threatened the success of Panhandle Eastern's 1992 campaign among its employees. (See Chapter 18.)

The Plan   The corporate relations department approached the situation from two directions. First, it decided to inform all company employees about the scandal and how the company was responding to it. Second, the public relations staff decided on a "family" theme that demonstrated United Way needs on the Texas Gulf Coast and how they related to the employees. Before the campaign began, the department had to reach 2000 Houston employees and 3000 industrial employees in 29 states.

Communications Strategy   The department prepared a Q&A brochure addressing the scandal. In addition, it prepared written and oral communications, including testimonials, that told employees how their contributions were wisely used by the local United Way and what had been done nationally to assure the integrity of the organization. Special events, displays, team tracking boards, competitions for donated prizes, a campaign newspaper, and speeches rounded out the communications activity during the campaign.

Evaluation   The company's 1992 contributions increased 6 percent from the previous year and raised $1 million for the local United Way, which was the highest level in company history. In a postcampaign survey, most respondents were aware that the United Way Texas Gulf Coast and United Way of America are distinct groups that responded appropriately to the scandal.

However, other staff functions also are involved in the communication process with internal and external publics. And, almost invariably, friction occurs. The four areas of possible friction are legal, human resources, advertising, and marketing.

Legal   The legal staff is concerned about the possible effect of any public statement on current or potential litigation. Consequently, lawyers often frustrate public relations personnel by taking the attitude that any public statement can potentially be used against the organization in a lawsuit. Conflicts over what to release and when often have a paralyzing effect on decision making, causing the organization to seem unresponsive to public concerns. This is particularly true in a crisis, when the public demands information immediately.

Human Resources   The traditional personnel department has now evolved into the expanded role of "human resources," and there are often turf battles over who is responsible for employee communications. Human resources personnel believe they should control the flow of information. Public relations administrators counter that satisfactory external communications cannot be achieved unless effective employee relations are conducted simultaneously. Layoffs, for example, not only affect employees but community and investor relations.

Advertising   Advertising and public relations departments often collide because they compete for funds to communicate with external audiences. During the recession of the early 1990s, for example, the Conference Board reported that corporations increased public relations spending while advertising departments topped the list of budget cuts.

Philosophical differences also arise. Advertising's approach to communications is, "Will it increase sales?" Public relations asks, "Will it make friends?" These differing orientations frequently cause breakdowns in coordination of overall strategy.

Marketing   Marketing, like advertising, tends to think only of customers or potential buyers as key publics. Public relations, on the other hand, defines "publics" in a broader way—any group that can have an impact on the operations of the organization. These publics include governmental agencies, environmental groups, neighborhood groups, and a host of other "publics" that marketing would not consider "customers."

The friction between marketing and public relations people reached a new height in the early 1990s when marketing departments began to advocate the concept of "integrated marketing communications." Many public relations people interpreted this to mean that "marketing imperialism" was on the march to take over and control the public relations function.

Some public relations people thought this trend would mean a loss of autonomy for them and that public relations would lose its counseling role to top management. Others were concerned that marketing-directed public relations would reduce professionals to the role of technicians working to support marketing objectives and functions. Historically, this work has been to handle product publicity.

Another argument was that public relations should do more than get people to buy goods and services. Marketing, by definition, is persuasive in intent. On the other hand, IABC's excellence study concludes that the ideal of public relations is symmetrical communication—the building of mutual understanding and communication between the organization and its various publics.

> ### INTEGRATED COMMUNICATIONS: A SUCCESS STORY
>
> All too often, integrated marketing communications means a second-class role for public relations. Marketing or advertising departments make all the decisions and only involve public relations professionals at the stage when product news releases are to be written.
>
> Nissan took a different approach for the successful American introduction of its new luxury car, the Infiniti J30.
>
> The company, at the very beginning, formed a team of representatives from the advertising, marketing, and public relations departments who worked together to create a coordinated communication strategy. Everyone had a legitimate role and voice in determining the positioning of the new car. Greg Elliott, Infiniti's public relations manager, readily admits, "In the past, public relations didn't have this strong a role."
>
> Elliott, interviewed by *Public Relations Journal,* said, "This was a really good integration team. Its members acknowledged and appreciated the role of public relations. Oftentimes, there is a lack of understanding—in marketing, sales, or training—of what public relations can or can't do. But with these folks, we were seen as a legitimate marketing partner."

All this has led James Grunig, editor of the IABC study, to conclude, "We believe, then, that public relations must emerge as a discipline distinct from marketing and that it must be practiced separately from marketing in the organization."

Turf battles, competition for resources, and arguments about who integrates communication strategies no doubt will continue to cause friction during the remainder of the 1990s. Logic dictates, however, that an organization needs a coordinated and integrated approach to communications strategy. Indeed, the Conference Board also found in its survey that CEOs increasingly want "business-related results," and all departments need to align their activities with their organization's overall strategic goals.

The following suggestions may help achieve this goal:

1. Representatives of departments should serve together on key committees to exchange information on how various programs can complement each other to achieve overall organizational objectives.

2. Heads of departments should be equals in job title. In this way, the autonomy of one department is not subverted by another.

3. All department heads should report to the same superior, so that all viewpoints can be considered before an appropriate strategy is formulated.

4. Informal, regular contacts with representatives of other departments help dispel mindsets and create understanding and respect for each other's viewpoint.

5. Written policies should be established to spell out the responsibilities of each department. Such policies are helpful in settling disputes over which department has authority to communicate with employees or alter a news release.

Some organizational charts for public relations and other departments are shown in Figure 5.2.

ADVANTAGES AND DISADVANTAGES OF WORKING IN A DEPARTMENT

Work in a public relations department can be invigorating and can offer staff members a sense of accomplishment as they help the organization achieve its objectives. The advantages of employment in a corporate setting are (1) generally good salaries, (2) extensive health and insurance benefits, (3) the opportunity to work with a group of professional peers, and (4) extensive resources. The disadvantages can be (1) a laborious approval process before production or dissemination of information, (2) lack of understanding by management of the public relations function, (3) lack of advancement opportunities in a small department, and (4) involvement in routine activities that change little over a period of time.

Although the general trend is for public relations to expand its role and influence in the corporation, it is also true that corporate downsizing and mergers are resulting in public relations staff cutbacks. Most RCA corporate public relations people, for exam-

FIGURE 5.2
This chart depicts three examples of corporate management
organization, showing the important position of public relations.

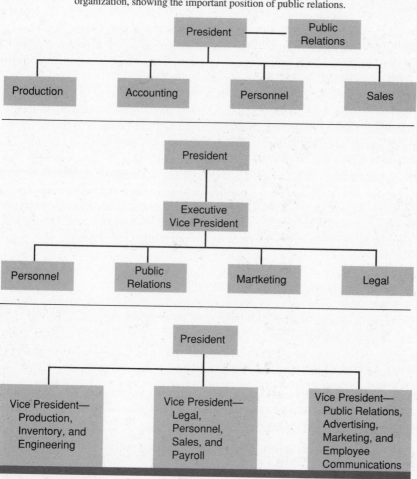

ple, lost their jobs when their company merged with the General Electric Company. And when Mobil Corporation moved its headquarters to Fairfax, Virginia, it closed its public relations office in New York. Only 28 of the 66 staff members followed the company to Virginia.

Public relations firms are the major beneficiaries of corporate retrenchment, and the major growth area in public relations employment is in this area.

PUBLIC RELATIONS FIRMS

In size, public relations firms range from one- or two-person operations to worldwide giants such as Burson-Marsteller, which employs more than 2000 people. The scope of services provided to clients varies accordingly. Big or small, each has an identical purpose: to give counsel and, to the extent a client wishes, perform the technical services required to carry out an agreed-upon program. The counseling firm may operate as an adjunct to an organization's public relations department or, if no department exists, conduct the entire public relations effort.

These firms have proliferated in proportion to the growth of the global economy. As American companies expanded after World War II into booming domestic and worldwide markets, many corporations felt a need for public relations firms that could provide them with professional expertise in communications.

Stimulating the growth of public relations firms were increased urbanization, expansion of government bureaucracy and regulation, more sophisticated mass media systems, the rise of consumerism, international trade, and the demand for more information. Professionals were needed to maintain lines of communication in an increasingly complicated world and to provide much of the material to be distributed. Some experts, who point out that public relations services seem to grow best in an atmosphere of conflict, say that the number of firms multiplied as the American public placed less trust in large corporations and demanded more corporate responsibility in environmental and consumer matters. Whatever the reason, American Business Lists of Omaha has compiled a list of 6644 public relations firms operating in the United States.

THE SERVICES THEY PROVIDE

Counseling firms today offer services far more extensive than those provided by the nation's first firm, the Publicity Bureau, founded in 1900 in Boston. Today, public relations firms provide a wide variety of services:

- ■ *Marketing communications.* Promotion of products and services. Such tools as news releases, feature stories, special events, brochures, and media tours are used.

- ■ *Executive speech training.* Top executives are coached on public affairs activities, including personal appearances.

- ■ *Research and evaluation.* Scientific surveys to measure public attitudes and perceptions are conducted.

THE TEN LARGEST PUBLIC RELATIONS FIRMS

Name	Fee Income	Employees
Burson-Marsteller (A)	$203.7 million	2071
Shandwick	$166.1 million	1857
Hill and Knowlton (A)	$149.1 million	1577
Omnicom PR Network (A)	$ 65.6 million	987
Edelman Public Relations Worldwide	$ 59.8 million	684
Fleishman-Hillard	$ 58.6 million	638
Ketchum Public Relations (A)	$ 45.6 million	396
The Rowland Co. (A)	$ 44.0 million	490
Ogilvy Adams & Rinehart (A)	$ 36.1 million	338
Manning, Selvage & Lee (A)	$ 31.4 million	320

"A" denotes adverising agency subsidiary.

Source: *O'Dwyer's PR Services Report,* May 1993, p. 18. Copyright 1993 by the J.R. O'Dwyer Company, Inc.

■ *Crisis communication.* Management is counseled on what to say and do in an emergency such as an oil spill or recall of an unsafe product.

■ *Media analysis.* Appropriate media are examined for targeting specific messages to key audiences.

■ *Community relations.* Management is counseled on ways to achieve official and public support for such projects as building or expanding a factory.

■ *Events management.* News conferences, anniversary celebrations, rallies, symposiums, and national conferences are planned and conducted.

■ *Public affairs.* Materials and testimony are prepared for government hearings and regulatory bodies, and background briefings are prepared.

■ *Employee communications.* Ways to motivate employees and raise productivity are discussed with management.

■ *Positioning a company.* Advice is given on corporate identity programs that establish a place in the market for the company and its products.

■ *Financial relations.* Management is counseled on ways to avoid takeover by another firm and effectively communicate with stockholders, security analysts and institutional investors.

Increasingly, public relations firms emphasize the counseling aspect of their services, and a number of executives object to the idea that they operate public relations "agencies." They say that public relations is a management consulting function and cannot be delegated to others, as the term *agent* implies. In fact, public relations *consultancy* is the favored term in the United Kingdom and other British Commonwealth nations. Advertising firms, in contrast, are properly called agencies because they serve as agents buying time or space on behalf of a client.

We approach public relations as a management and counseling function and, consequently, use the term *public relations firm* throughout the book. At the same time, we realize that a number of public relations "agencies" do exist because they simply act as agents preparing and distributing publicity materials on behalf of clients.

GLOBAL REACH

Public relations firms, large and small, tend to cluster in major metropolitan areas. On an international level, the firms and their affiliates are found in most major world cities. Burson-Marsteller, headquartered in New York, claims to have the most extensive wholly owned worldwide operations with offices in 52 cities and 29 nations. Some of the major cities having Burson-Marsteller offices include Bangkok, Barcelona, Beijing, Berlin, Bombay, Brussels, Budapest, Canberra, Copenhagen, Hong Kong, Kuala Lumpur, London, Los Angeles, Paris, Prague, Rome, San Francisco, Sao Paulo, Singapore, Sydney, Taipei, Tokyo, Toronto, Vienna, Warsaw, Washington, D.C., and Zurich.

The importance of international operations is reflected in the fact that about half of Burson-Marsteller's revenues are generated by its offices outside the United States. In 1992, for example, U.S. operations accounted for $99 million in revenues while European operations posted $70 million. Asia accounted for almost $20 million and Latin America almost $5 million.

Shandwick, headquartered in London, also has global reach with 800 of its 1857 employees located in North America. It has 85 offices in North America, the United Kingdom, continental Europe, and Asia Pacific. Unlike Burson-Marsteller, Shandwick is a holding company and its various offices throughout the world operate under a variety of local names. Some Shandwick U.S. properties include Golin/Harris Communications, Miller Communications, Dorf & Stanton, and Rogers & Cowan.

Hill and Knowlton, based in New York, has a similar list of worldwide offices, 57 in 27 nations. Daniel Edelman Public Relations Worldwide, New York, has 27 offices in 15 nations. Fleishman-Hillard, St. Louis, has 22 offices in 11 nations.

International work isn't only for the large firms. Small and medium-sized firms also are establishing bases abroad through networks of affiliated public relations firms. For example, about 60 firms around the world have established an affiliate network called Worldcom Group, Inc., that boasts of more than 100 offices on six continents. Another network of affiliated firms, Pinnacle Worldwide, has a combined size of 45 offices in 23 countries. Omnicom PR Network, formed as a holding company by a group of public relations and advertising companies, has 58 member firms and 52 affiliates in 48 countries.

The future will not be the past.

1992

The economic unification
of Europe
•
Barcelona Olympics
•
Seville World's Fair

1996

U.S. Elections
•
Summer Olympics

1997

Repatriation of Hong Kong

2000

U.S. Elections
•
The next millenium

If any of these dates will impact
your business, discuss them with

Burson·Marsteller

FIGURE 5.3
With an eye to the future, Burson-Marsteller emphasizes the
international aspect of public relations in this advertisement
listing major events of this decade in which the firm is
involved.

Essentially, firms in an affiliation cooperate with each other to service clients with international needs. A firm in India may call its affiliate in Los Angeles to handle the details of a news conference for a visiting Indian trade delegation. This approach gives small firms with limited resources an opportunity to offer the same kinds of services as the largest firms.

The large international firms, as well as various affiliated groups, have been well established in Western Europe for several years. A new area of expansion is the major cities of Eastern Europe and the former Soviet Union. Another area of new business is Latin America as free market economies become the rule rather than the exception. Asia, particularly China with its large population, also presents new opportunities. To date, however, international firms have not expanded their operations on the African continent. (See Chapter 16.)

ADVERTISING AND PUBLIC RELATIONS MERGERS

Until the 1970s, the largest public relations firms were independently owned by their principal officers or, in some cases, by employee stockholders. A significant change began in 1973 when Carl Byoir & Associates, then the third largest U.S. firm, was purchased by the advertising firm of Foote, Cone & Belding.

In rapid succession, Burson-Marsteller became part of Young & Rubicam advertising conglomerate; Manning, Selvage & Lee was absorbed into Benton & Bowles; Doremus & Company joined BBDO-Inc. advertising; and Hill and Knowlton became part of J. Walter Thompson, Inc.

Although ownerships have changed over the years, seven of the ten largest public relations firms still are related to advertising agencies or their holding companies (see the "top ten" table on p. 107). The WPP Group, London, includes Hill and Knowlton and Ogilvy Adams & Rinehart; Young & Rubicam still owns Burson-Marsteller and Cohn & Wolfe; Saatchi & Saatchi, London, has The Rowland Company; and Grey Advertising includes the GCI Group.

Initially, supporters of mergers between advertising agencies and public relations firms believed that it was only the natural evolution of integrating various communication disciplines into "total communications networks." They maintained that no single-function agency was really equipped with personnel and resources to handle complex, often global, marketing functions in an efficient way for a client. On a more practical level, joint public relations and advertising endeavors would both increase the pool of potential new clients and expand the number of geographical locations.

Although the premise was logical, the complexities of the marketplace have made total communications networks less than effective. In many cases, corporations bypassed the concept of "one-stop shopping" from a megafirm and preferred, instead, to use the services of independent, specialized firms. For example, of the 40 largest firms after the "big ten," less than one-fourth are owned by advertising companies. Other clients resisted because they perceived a possible conflict of interest if a subsidiary of a megafirm had the account of a business competitor. As a result, the advertising agency and the public relations firm owned by the same company often don't collaborate much and, more often than not, have their own client lists.

Acquisitions of public relations firms by advertising agencies have slowed considerably in the 1990s, but the idea of offering clients total communication networks has not gone away. Large advertising firms are advocating the concept of "integrated marketing communications." This means, in simple terms, that agencies are now offering clients more than advertising services. "Integrated" programs include advertising, direct mail, sales promotion, and public relations.

Public relations firms also are repositioning themselves as offering expertise in "strategic" marketing communications services. President David Drobis of Ketchum Public Relations calls it "convergent communications." As part of this trend, a number of firms are dropping the term *public relations* from their official titles and using such words as *communications* to indicate that they offer more than "public relations services," which is often interpreted as only product publicity. Most public relations firms, however, still don't offer advertising services to clients.

Another trend is for large public relations firms to grow by acquiring other firms. The most common method of expansion into a new geographic or practice area is to buy an existing firm. Shandwick, for example, rapidly expanded its operations by going on a three-year international buying spree of 38 public relations and related firms between 1986 and 1989.

STRUCTURE OF A COUNSELING FIRM

A small public relations firm may consist only of the owner (president) and an assistant (vice president), supported by a secretary. Larger firms have a hierarchy something like this:

- President
- Executive vice president
- Vice president
- Account supervisor
- Account executive
- Assistant account executive
- Secretarial/clerical staff

The chart of Ketchum Public Relations/San Francisco is fairly typical. The president is based in the New York office of Ketchum Public Relations, so the executive vice president is the on-site director in San Francisco. A senior vice president is associate director of operations. Next in line are several vice presidents who primarily do account supervision or special projects.

An *account supervisor* is in charge of one major account or several smaller ones. An *account executive,* who reports to the supervisor, is in direct contact with the client and handles most of the day-to-day activity. At the bottom of the list is the *assistant account executive,* who does routine maintenance work compiling media lists, gathering information, and writing rough drafts of news releases.

Recent college graduates usually start as assistant account executives. Once they learn the firm's procedures and show ability, promotion to account executive may occur within 6 to 18 months. After two or three years, it is not uncommon for an account executive to become an account supervisor.

Executives at or above the vice presidential level usually are heavily involved in selling their firm's services. In order to prosper, a firm must continually seek new business and sell additional services to current clients. Consequently, the upper management of the firm calls on prospective clients, prepares proposals, and makes new business presentations. In this very competitive field, a firm not adept at selling itself frequently fails.

Firms frequently organize account teams, especially to serve a client whose program is multifaceted. One member of the team, for example, may set up a nationwide media tour in which an organization representative is booked on television talk shows. Another may supervise all materials going to the print media, including news stories, feature articles, background kits, and artwork. A third may concentrate on the trade press or perhaps arrange special events.

WORKING IN A PUBLIC RELATIONS FIRM

To many, work in a public relations firm sounds glamorous. A person associates with a number of highly intelligent, creative people, and there is the stimulation of working on several exciting projects at any one time. One day may find the account executive at the opening of a plush restaurant, while the next finds the intrepid executive flying to New York or London to set up a press conference. Of course, there are the proverbial cocktail parties and the pleasure of learning that a well-written feature article has been picked up by 180 daily newspapers.

Although all these happenings do occur in public relations, they are less routine than one would suspect. On many days, an account person may sit in a small cubicle writing a standard news release about a new diesel engine and having a Big Mac for lunch. On other days, the person may spend fruitless hours on the phone trying to book a client's representative for radio and television interviews. It is not very exciting to write a brochure about the services of an engineering firm or to have a masterpiece of prose reduced to alphabet soup by a client's penchant for complex sentences.

The Frustrations and the Rewards   Working for a public relations firm can be a source of both frustrations and rewards. Individuals often cite the following frustrations:

1.   *Lack of privacy.* For their staff, most firms provide cubicles that are small, open at the top, and without doors. As one employee points out, "You have to think and work in a fishbowl."

2.   *Constant documentation of work.* Great emphasis is placed on productivity, and account executives are expected to have 80 to 90 percent of their working hours billable to a client. Time sheets, accurate to the nearest 15 minutes and describing each activity in detail, must be recorded so that the firm may prepare the proper billings.

3.   *Many demands on time.* An account executive usually works on several projects, and it is difficult to give each client the undivided attention that is often demanded.

4.   *Client relationships.* Few clients have a good understanding of what public relations can or cannot accomplish. A firm's personnel must constantly educate clients about public relations.

5.   *Extended workdays.* Many times an account person must attend night functions or work overtime to meet a deadline.

Despite these frustrations, many people thrive in a public relations firm. They enjoy the constant challenge of coming up with creative ideas—the psychic reward of observing their idea for a slogan become a household term or a planned special event achieve international publicity. Those who leave a public relations firm for jobs with corporations often miss the diversity of assignments.

What It Takes   What, then, does it take to work in a public relations firm? Harold Burson, chairman of Burson-Marsteller, once told a national convention of the Public Relations Student Society of America (PRSSA) about the characteristics he seeks in a prospective employee.

First he asks a job applicant, "What do you read?" Burson wants individuals who are aware of the complex world around them. "If you want to pursue a career in public relations, learn to read—everything," he exhorts. Burson has the feeling that those who don't read can't write. And, he points out, in order to succeed in public relations a person must perfect his or her writing skills.

Burson also searches for people who have strong self-discipline. He says:

You are, to some considerable degree, able to do what you want to do and at your own pace. You can turn out a major feature article that sparkles or you can, in the same time frame, deliver up eight mundane news releases written to formula. You can go for a placement on the "Today" show or with the local town daily. You can take a day doing it—or two days. In most cases, you won't get much supervision. You're on your own for a lot of the work you do—almost regardless of who employs you.

Other public relations executives echo what Burson says about reading, writing, and self-discipline. They add such characteristics as the ability to (1) organize and plan, (2) juggle several projects at once without getting rattled, (3) give good, persuasive presentations, and (4) work well with others.

PROS AND CONS OF USING A PUBLIC RELATIONS FIRM

Because public relations is a service industry, a firm's major asset is the quality of its people. Potential clients thinking about hiring a public relations firm usually base their decisions on that fact, according to a survey of Fortune 500 corporate vice presidents.

Consultant Alfred Geduldig, who conducted the survey, also found that (1) quality of presentation, (2) possible conflicts, and (3) the writing ability of the firm's personnel also were important—more so than costs, size of client list, or even "full service" capability. He also found that projects accounted for 70 percent of the work assigned to public relations firms. Financial, product, and corporate positioning projects were popular assignments.

Advantages   Public relations firms offer many services and capabilities:

■ *Objectivity.* The firm can analyze a client's needs or problems from a new perspective and offer fresh insights.

■ *Variety of skills and expertise.* The firm has specialists, whether in speechwriting, trade magazine placement, or helping with proxy battles.

■ *Extensive resources.* The firm has abundant media contacts and works regularly with numerous suppliers of products and services. It has research materials, including data information banks, and experience in similar fields.

■ *Offices throughout the country.* A national public relations program requires coordination in major cities. Large firms have on-site staffs or affiliate firms in many cities and even around the world.

■ *Special problem solving.* A firm may have extensive experience and a solid reputation in desired areas. For example, Burson-Marsteller is well known for expertise in crisis communications, health and medical issues, and international coordination of special projects. Hill and Knowlton is known for expertise in public affairs, and Ketchum Public Relations is the expert in consumer marketing.

- *Credibility.* A successful public relations firm has a solid reputation for professional, ethical work. If represented by such a firm, a client likely will get more attention among opinion leaders in mass media, government, and the financial community.

A SAMPLE OF PROGRAMS

Public relations firms, throughout the world, handle a variety of assignments. Here are some examples that have received a "Golden World Award" from the International Public Relations Association (IPRA):

- *Strategic Objectives, Inc. (Canada).* Conducted a program to launch a new product line of skin and hair-care products for mothers-to-be and babies on behalf of Body Shop. The bilingual (English and French) campaign included a media kit of feature releases on such matters as mother/baby lore, baby massage, father-baby bonding, and product information.

- *Burson-Marsteller (Brazil).* Helped 100 McDonald's outlets in the country to communicate that the company was cutting prices and that the price reduction would not affect quality or the size of servings.

- *Ogilvy Adams & Rinehart (Chicago).* Conducted a campaign to increase the consumption of oatmeal by positioning the Quaker Oats Company as a source of consumer information about nutrition issues. The public relations firm developed a "Quaker Oats 'Feeling Good' Challenge" survey that helped consumers assess their health habits.

- *Paragan Communications, Inc. (United Kingdom).* When quota restrictions led to price increases on England's favorite types of fish, the industry engaged the public relations firm to conduct a campaign that encouraged consumers to eat alternative species, rather than switch to nonfish foods.

- *Turnbull Fox Phillips (Australia).* Deregulation of the telephone system promoted Telecom Australia to hire the public relations firm to explain new service options to the public. As a result, the company lost only 2.3 percent of its market share.

- *Perceptions, Inc. (Philippines).* Johnson & Johnson, a manufacturer of health-care products, hired the public relations firm to publicize its cooperation with UNICEF's Child Survival Program. Johnson & Johnson provided money and helped with the preparation of pamphlets on health care. The company's involvement created goodwill among government officials, health workers, and medical professionals.

- *Kibao Communications (South Africa).* This firm helped the Durban City Council communicate a new culture of racial tolerance and understanding after it integrated its beaches in 1989 and abolished "beach apartheid." A major vehicle was a street-theater show based on the principle that if people can laugh and do so with each other, they can co-exist on the beaches.

- *Roger Pereira Communications (India).* The firm, with the help of a major industrialist, produced a television soap opera that sought to improve attitudes toward women by discouraging forced marriages and promoting such subjects as health education and population control. Called "Humraahi" (Come Along with Me), the program was a serial telecast in prime time.

- *Golin/Harris Communications (Philadelphia).* The Pennsylvania Department of Environmental Resources increased its community recycling programs more than fourfold in a three-year promotion effort by the firm. The program included a mix of publicity, special events, educational literature, and paid advertising.

On the Minus Side   Despite many successes, not everything goes smoothly between a firm and its client. There are several "complaints" about public relations firms:

- *Superficial grasp of a client's unique problems.* While objectivity is gained from an outsider's perspective, there is often a disadvantage in the public relations firm's not thoroughly understanding the client's business or needs.

- *Lack of full-time commitment.* A public relations firm has many clients to service. Therefore, no single client can monopolize its personnel and other resources.

- *Need for prolonged briefing period.* Some companies become frustrated because time and money are needed for a public relations firm to research the organization and make recommendations. Consequently, the actual start of a public relations program may take weeks or months.

- *Resentment of internal staff.* The public relations staff members of a client organization may resent the use of outside counsel because they think it implies that they lack the ability to do the job.

- *Need for strong direction by top management.* High-level executives must take the time to brief outside counsel on specific objectives sought.

- *Need for full information and confidence.* A client must be willing to share its information, including the skeletons in the closet, with outside counsel.

- *Costs.* Outside counsel is expensive. In many situations, routine public relations work can be handled at lower cost by internal staff.

The problems often are two-way. Personnel in counseling firms complain at times that they cannot do a highly effective job for clients because (1) top corporate executives do not take time to define objectives and clarify what they want a public relations program to accomplish; (2) the clients fail to provide the information needed to tailor a program to the specific problem; and (3) clients often are penny-wise and pound-foolish in terms of not approving expenditures for key items.

Counselors also complain that clients often think of public relations as some sort of magical cure-all that can accomplish miracles. By the time counsel is called in, they say, the crisis has already occurred—and there really isn't much a public relations program can do. Public relations counsel must continually tell clients that they cannot (1) guarantee specified results, (2) change public perceptions or attitudes overnight, and (3) make any organization something that it is not.

FEES AND CHARGES

The Three Methods of Charging   A public relations firm charges for its services in several ways. The three most common methods are as follows:

1. *Basic hourly fee, plus out-of-pocket expenses.* The number of hours spent on a client's account is tabulated each month and billed to the client. Work by personnel in the counseling firm is billed at various hourly rates—for example, a secretary typing envelopes at $20 an hour and an account executive working at $85 an hour. Out-of-pocket expenses, such as cab fares, car rentals, airline tickets, and meals, also are billed to the client.

2. *Retainer fee.* A basic monthly charge billed to the client covers ordinary administrative and overhead expenses for maintaining the account and being "on call." Many retainer fees also specify the number of hours the counseling firm will spend on the account each month. Additional work is billed at normal hourly rates. Out-of-pocket expenses normally are billed separately.

3. *Fixed project fee.* The public relations firm agrees to do a specific project, such as an annual report, a newsletter, or a special event, for a fixed fee. For example, a counseling firm may write and produce a quarterly newsletter for $30,000 annually. The fixed fee is the least popular of the three methods because it is difficult to estimate accurately all work and expenses in advance.

The primary basis for all three methods is to estimate the number of hours that a particular project will take to plan, execute, and evaluate. The first method—the basic hourly fee—is the most flexible and most widely used among large firms. It is preferred by public relations people because they are paid for the exact number of hours spent on a project and because it is the only sound way that a fee can be determined intelligently. The retainer fee and the fixed project fee are based on an estimate of how many hours it will take to counsel a client.

How Estimates Are Made   A number of variables are considered when a public relations firm estimates the cost of a program. These may include the size and duration, geographical locations involved, the number of personnel to be assigned to the project, and even the nature of the client. A major variable, of course, is billing the use of the firm's personnel to a client at the proper hourly rate.

The hourly billing rate of employees depends on their experience, title, and salary level. An account executive who earns $32,000 annually would be making $20 per hour, based on an average work year of 1600 hours after deducting vacation, holidays, illness, and personal time off. The firm's management must also include such overhead expenses as office space, equipment, utilities, phone, insurance benefits, and pension plans. Another factor is the percentage of profit after all the bills are paid. In general, public relations firms try to operate on a profit level of between 18 and 22 percent.

Usually a public relations firm bills clients at three to five times a staff person's base hourly salary. The account executive in the example just cited would cost a client between $60 and $100 per hour. At this rate, the account executive should generate between $96,000 and $160,000 of billable income for the firm on an annual basis. Meeting these standards of productivity and profitability is an important criterion for a person's career advancement in the firm. The principals of a counseling firm, because of their much higher salaries, often command $150 to $500 an hour depending on the size and capabilities of the firm.

The primary income of a public relations firm comes from the selling of staff time, but some additional income results from mark-ups on all production costs, such as printing, photography, and art work that the firm facilitates and supervises. The standard in the trade is between 15 and 20 percent of costs. Out-of-pocket expenses are billed to clients at net cost.

Billing on the Basis of Placement   As already noted, the industry standard for public relations firms, like law or management consulting firms, is to charge clients an amount based on the number of hours spent on a project.

A few firms, however, charge on the basis of actual media placements. Primetime, for example, has a price list for various media. Typical charges are $42,800 for placing a piece on CBS-TV's *60 Minutes,* $21,135 for a story in *People* magazine, and $11,875 for an article in the New York *Times.*

Payment for actual placement, however, has some complications. Does a client pay for a placement if the article also contains negative information or material about competitors? Does the client pay for multiple placements of the same story? Payment for placement also stirs up media hostility because there's an assumption that the media can be "bought."

Jack O'Dwyer, publisher of an industry newsletter, summed up the attitude of most public relations professionals. He told *Columbia Journalism Review,* "PR people don't like publicity sold by the pound. They feel it is immoral, illogical. It puts a price tag on media copy, which isn't supposed to be for sale." Joseph F. Awad, retired director of public relations for Reynolds Metals Company, states an additional objection. Payment for placement, he says, "focuses attention on publicity almost as a value itself, and away from the practice of public relations."

Consequently, most professional public relations firms avoid payment for placement or even making arrangements with clients for a percentage of sales that might result from marketing communications efforts. There are two practical reasons:

1.   Committing staff time and resources is risky because of numerous variables and unpredictable developments. Even with outstanding work, media coverage can never be assumed or guaranteed.

2.   A financial interest by a public relations firm in the success of a product or service can lead to overzealous and even unethical tactics in order to get favorable publicity and sales results.

Chapter 6 discusses professionalism and ethical standards in greater detail. Guaranteeing media placements and working on commission, for example, are against the professional code of conduct for the Public Relations Society of America (PRSA).

CAPITALIZING ON NEW YEAR'S RESOLUTIONS

Consumer research, use of product spokespeople, promotions, and speaker training are extensively used by public relations firms to help clients boost sales.

A good example is the campaign the San Francisco firm of Hi-Tech Public Relations and its division, Access Public Relations, did for Quicken, the world's best-selling personal finance software.

Background   Intuit, Inc., publisher of Quicken, wanted to reach the vast but largely untapped market of women. Research showed that women handled the bookkeeping chores in most U.S. homes, but relatively few women read personal computer publications, in which Intuit and Quicken had received wide coverage for many years.

The Plan   Hi-Tech did an audit of woman's magazines and found that editors had little knowledge or interest in personal computers or related topics. In addition, a quick scan of Intuit's sales data revealed that the company's best sales were between Christmas and New Year's. This led to the idea that a campaign could be structured around New Year's resolutions.

Hi-Tech commissioned a Gallup Poll to find out what Americans were resolving to do in the New Year. The survey showed that controlling personal finances was the top resolution, followed by losing weight and quitting smoking. Gary W. Thompson, president of Hi-Tech, explains: "This gave us our news hook. Americans need help keeping their New Year's resolutions, and today's personal computer software can provide that help."

Communications Strategy   Quicken teamed with a pair of noncompeting software products—a weight-loss package and a stop-smoking package—to lessen the commercial nature of the message. Information about all three products was included in press materials.

An expert spokesperson was engaged. Instead of a computer expert, Hi-Tech used a professor of clinical psychology who had studied New Year's resolutions. Under his guidance, a brochure was created titled "Quicken's Guide to Helping You Keep Your Resolutions." A press kit was produced on how to make and keep resolutions.

The professor also was given speaker training and booked on a media tour. In three days, he generated nine television appearances, including CNN, *The Today Show* and *The Home Show;* 12 radio broadcasts; two national newspaper articles; three nationally syndicated columns; and extensive local coverage in three major cities.

Evaluation   The final tally was 100 million media impressions. All media tour coverage mentioned Quicken's ease of use and its potential to help people save time and money, key copy points that the professor was trained to include when answering media questions. Quicken also received more than 1000 telephone requests for the brochure. Because of this campaign, the company estimates that five copies of Quicken were sold at the retail level for each call it received.

CASE PROBLEM

You will graduate from college in several months and plan a career in public relations. After several interviews, you receive two job offers. One is with a large paint manufacturer in the state capital, 100 miles away. The public relations staff numbers about 20, and it is customary for beginning staff members to start in employee relations. Later, with more experience, you might be assigned to product press relations, investor relations, or community affairs.

The second job offer is from a small local public relations firm in which you would be an assistant account executive on several current accounts, including a resort hotel and a dry-cleaning chain. The jobs pay about the same, but the corporation offers better overall employee benefits.

What factors would you consider before choosing either job? What job would you take? Explain your reasons.

QUESTIONS FOR REVIEW AND DISCUSSION

1. How have the role and function of public relations departments changed in recent years?

2. In what ways do the structure and external environment of a corporation affect the role and influence of the public relations department?

3. What three types of service does management expect from a public relations department?

4. What is the difference between a line and a staff function? To which function does public relations belong, and why?

5. Why is a compulsory-advisory role within an organization a good one for a public relations department to have?

6. What are two advantages and disadvantages of working in a corporate public relations department?

7. In your opinion, should public relations or human resources be responsible for employee communications?

8. Public relations firms offer many services to their clients. List and describe five of these.

9. What are the three largest public relations firms in the world?

10. What reasons are given for keeping public relations and marketing as separate departments in an organization? Do you feel these reasons are justified? Why or why not?

11. Use of integrated marketing communications seems to be a major trend in the 1990s. How can various departments in an organization work together to implement overall communication strategies?

12. What are some reasons why a company hires a public relations firm? What "complaints" do companies have about public relations firms?

13. What are the standard methods used by a public relations firm to charge for its services?

Bovet, Susan Fry. "Trends in the 'New' Europe." *Public Relations Journal,* September 1993, pp. 18–24. Public relations trends in Europe and a list of public relations firms that have offices on the continent.

Campbell, Catherine B. "Does Public Relations Affect the Bottom Line? CEOs Think So." *Public Relations Journal,* October 1993, pp. 14–17.

Coronna, David M. "Add Public Policy to Marketing Portfolio." *Public Relations Journal,* September 1993, pp. 12–14. Marketing must consider impact of public issues on product promotion.

Dilenschneider, Robert L. *Power and Influence: Mastering the Art of Persuasion.* New York: Prentice Hall Press, 1990. A personal account by the former president of Hill and Knowlton public relations firm.

Grunig, James E., editor. *Excellence in Public Relations and Communication Management.* Hillsdale, NJ: Lawrence Erlbaum, 1992.

Grunig, Larissa A. "Power in the Public Relations Department." Chapter 5 of *Public Relations Research Annual,* Vol. 2, ed. James and Larissa Grunig. Hillsdale NJ: Lawrence Erlbaum Associates, 1990, pp. 115–156.

Hauss, Deborah. "Global Communications Come of Age." *Public Relations Journal,* August 1993, pp. 22–26. Case studies on how various companies are communicating worldwide.

Josephs, Ray. "Japan Booms with Public Relations Ventures." *Public Relations Journal,* December 1990, pp. 18–25. American firms forge links with Japanese counterparts.

Lauzen, Martha M. "When Marketing Involvement Matters at the Manager Level." *Public Relations Review,* Fall 1993, pp. 247–259. The relationship between the marketing and public relations departments in an organization.

Nager, Norman R., and Truitt, Richard H. *Strategic Public Relations Counseling.* New York: Longman, 1987.

"Profiles of the Top 25 PR Firms," *O'Dwyer's PR Services Report,* May 1993, pp. 49–66.

Reisman, Joan. "Taking on the World." *Public Relations Journal,* March 1990, pp. 18–24. Global outreach of public relations firms.

Ritchie, Eugene, and Spector, Shelley. "Making a Marriage Last: What Qualities Strengthen Client-Firm Bonds?" *Public Relations Journal,* October 1990, pp. 16–21.

Ryan, Michael. "Organizational Constraints on Corporate Public Relations Practitioners." *Journalism Quarterly,* Summer–Fall, 1987, pp. 473–482.

Schultz, Don E., Tannenbaum, Stanley I., and Lauterborn, Robert F. *Integrated Marketing Communications.* Chicago: NTC Books, 1993.

Thompson, Gary W. "Consumer PR Techniques in the High Tech Arena." *Public Relations Quarterly,* Winter 1992–1993, pp. 21–23.

"Who's Who in the Pacific." *Inside PR,* December 1992, pp. 19–23. Profiles of public relations firms.

Wilmot, Richard E. "How to Build Credibility with Senior Management." *Communication World,* June 1989, pp. 32–37.

Winokur, Dena, and Kinkead, Robert W. "How Public Relations Fits into Corporate Strategy." *Public Relations Journal,* May 1993, pp. 16–23.

CHAPTER

Ethics and Professionalism

P R E V I E W   The goal of this chapter is to give students an understanding of the ethical standards and professionalism required of public relations practitioners today, and to help them identify their own standards as public relations professionals.

The topics covered in this chapter include:

- Definition
- Codes of ethics
- Professionalism, licensing, and accreditation
- Ethics in individual practice
- Ethical dealings with news media
- Business, government, and ethics

Ethics refers to the value system by which a person determines what is right or wrong, fair or unfair, just or unjust. It is expressed through moral behavior in specific situations. An individual's conduct is measured not only against his or her conscience but also against some norm of acceptability that has been societally, professionally, or organizationally determined. The difficulty in ascertaining whether an act is ethical lies in the fact that individuals have different standards and perceptions of what is "right" and "wrong." Often the situation is not black or white, but falls into the gray area.

A person's philosophical orientation can also determine how he or she acts in a specific situation. Philosophers say the three basic value orientations are (1) absolutist, (2) existentialist, and (3) situationalist. The absolutist believes every decision is either "right" or "wrong," regardless of the consequences. The existentialist, whose choices are made without a prescribed value system, decides on the basis of immediate rational choice. The situationalist's decisions are based on what would cause the least harm or most good.

Most people, depending on the actual situation, probably choose a course of action somewhere along the continuum of the three types. They make decisions on the building blocks of truth-telling, promise-keeping, loyalty, and commitment.

Public relations professionals have the added dilemma of making decisions that satisfy (1) the public interest, (2) the employer, (3) the professional organization's code of ethics, and (4) their personal values. In the ideal world, the four would not conflict. In reality, however, they often do.

CODES OF ETHICS

Most professional organizations and many businesses have codes of ethics. These documents, also called *codes of professional conduct,* are supposed to set acceptable norms of behavior for working professionals and employees. The Public Relations Society of America and the International Association of Business Communicators both have such codes for their members, to be discussed in the following pages. The PRSA code is emphasized because of its age (dating back to 1950) and its enforcement process, unique among communications organizations.

THE PRSA CODE OF PROFESSIONAL STANDARDS

When the Public Relations Society of America was founded in 1948, one of its first concerns, according to the late Rea W. Smith, former executive vice president, was "the development of an ethical code so that (1) its members would have behavioral guidelines, (2) managements would have a clear understanding of standards, and (3) professionals in public relations would be distinguished from shady promoters and ballyhoo advance men who, unfortunately, had been quick to appropriate the words 'public relations' to describe their operations."

The PRSA Code of Professional Standards for the Practice of Public Relations was adopted in 1950 and strengthened by revisions in 1959, 1963, 1977, 1983, and 1988. The PRSA Assembly approved the latest revision in order (1) to make the language clearer and more understandable—hence easier to apply and to follow and (2) to help advance the unification of the public relations profession—part of PRSA's mission. No substantive changes were made.

The 1988 revision was based on the Code of the North American Public Relations Council (NAPRC), an organization of 13 member groups, including PRSA. At the time of the revision 8 of the 13 had revised their own codes in accordance with the NAPRC code, actions considered important steps toward unification. See the current PRSA "Declaration of Principles" and "Code of Professional Standards for the Practice of Public Relations," reprinted here.

PRSA'S DECLARATION OF PRINCIPLES

Members of the Public Relations Society of America base their professional principles on the fundamental value and dignity of the individual, holding that the free exercise of human rights, especially freedom of speech, freedom of assembly, and freedom of the press, is essential to the practice of public relations.

In serving the interests of clients and employers, we dedicate ourselves to the goals of better communication, understanding, and cooperation among the diverse individuals, groups, and institutions of society, and of equal opportunity of employment in the public relations profession.

We Pledge:

■ To conduct ourselves professionally, with truth, accuracy, fairness, and responsibility to the public;

■ To improve our individual competence and advance the knowledge and proficiency of the profession through continuing research and education;

■ And to adhere to the articles of the Code of Professional Standards for the Practice of Public Relations as adopted by the governing Assembly of the Society.

PRSA'S CODE ENFORCEMENT

The PRSA has a Board of Ethical and Professional Standards to receive, initiate, and review complaints about members. If a complaint has merit, the case is sent to district-level grievance boards charged with gathering testimony and making a recommendation to the board.

The findings are reviewed and a final decision made by the society's board of directors. PRSA may *expel, suspend, censure,* or *reprimand* a member if he or she is found in violation of the code. If a person is expelled from PRSA—the highest sanction—it simply means he or she cannot be a member. PRSA has no legal authority to prohibit an expelled member from continuing to practice public relations.

The threat of condemnation by one's professional peers, however, is a strong incentive for following the code. The bylaws do permit public announcement of actions taken against a member, but this usually is done through insertion of a short item in the society's internal newsletters, and no general news release is made.

The PRSA can discipline only its own members; it has no legal right to condemn nonmembers for incompetent practice. Since only about 10 percent of the estimated 157,000 public relations people in the United States are members of PRSA, code enforcement provisions possibly are less important than the existence of the code itself.

As Donald B. McCammond, a former ethics board chairman, once said, "The board of ethics is more interested in compliance with the code than in recrimination and headlines."

ETHICAL DILEMMAS IN PUBLIC RELATIONS PRACTICE

How would you respond to the following situations? Consider your answers. Then, turn the page to see how your responses correspond with interpretations of the PRSA Code.

1. The company president asks you to write a news release claiming that a new product is four times better than the competition and that it represents a "revolutionary" breakthrough in technology.

2. You're a student intern at a public relations firm. One of your assignments is to call corporations and say you're a student doing a class project. You would like to know what kinds of outside public relations services would be most helpful to the company.

3. An American company wants to increase its visibility and market share in Eastern Europe. As director of public relations, you invite a group of German business editors to visit the firm's headquarters with all expenses paid.

4. Your company, in order to improve the quality and media acceptance of news releases, hires the local daily's business editor on a retainer fee for periodic advice and counsel.

5. Your company, as part of its Christmas tradition, gives journalists who regularly cover it an expensive gift. Last year, it was a weekend at a local resort.

6. You are asked by your employer to establish a "citizens' task force" for the purpose of writing state legislators opposing an environmental bill that negatively affects the company.

7. Your public relations firm is competing for an account with two other firms. As a sales point, you say, "We can get you coverage in the *Wall Street Journal*."

8. You're looking for a job in public relations, and a tobacco company offers you the highest salary.

9. You work for a public relations firm. A printing company representative contacts you with the following proposal: If you refer clients that result in new business, the representative will pay you a $250 "finder's fee."

Types of Complaints A compilation by the Foundation for Public Relations Research and Education (now called the Institute for Public Relations Research & Education) found that in a 33-year period the ethics board received or initiated 165 complaints about code violations by PRSA members. Of that total, the board determined that 65 percent merited investigation.

ANSWERS TO ETHICAL DILEMMAS IN PUBLIC RELATIONS PRACTICE

1. Making extravagant claims about a product, which cannot be substantiated, should be avoided. Article 4 says a member shall adhere to the highest standards of truth and accuracy. Article 5 also says that a member shall not knowingly disseminate false and misleading information.

2. Although you're a student, you are acting as an agent of the public relations firm. Consequently, you are not representing yourself with honesty and integrity (Article 2), and you are serving the undisclosed interest (Article 8) of the public relations firm that is seeking the information for marketing and direct mail purposes.

3. Inviting German editors to headquarters, all expenses paid, is permissible under Article 6, which is concerned about corrupting the channels of communication. It can be argued that the visit has legitimate news value, and it furthers press understanding of the company's operations. Article 6 would be violated, however, if the all-expense-paid trip were simply a pleasant holiday.

4. Hiring an editor to be a consultant violates Article 6 about the corruption of communication channels because there is a strong indication that such an arrangement is designed to gain preferential or guaranteed news coverage. Article 6, however, would not necessarily be violated if there were full public disclosure and the editor's employer approved.

5. Article 6 does not forbid gifts of nominal value to the media, especially if the gift is a sample of the company's product. Major gifts, however, raise serious questions about expectations of favorable media coverage in return—and thus could corrupt the channels of communication.

6. The establishment of "citizen task forces" violates Article 8, especially if the intent is to portray the group as independent or unbiased—yet serving the undisclosed interest of the company organizing and funding its activities. This is not in accord with the public interest (Article 1), nor is the practitioner dealing fairly with the public (Article 3).

7. Promising an employer or client that you can get coverage in a specific publication is a violation of Article 9, which says a member shall not guarantee the achievement of specified results beyond the member's direct control. A person can guarantee the quality of work, but not the decisions of editors.

8. The decision to work for a tobacco company is a personal choice. Article 11, however, says that a member should not place himself or herself in a position where the member's personal interest is in conflict with an employer or client. Therefore, if you oppose smoking and believe it is hazardous to health, it would be difficult to fulfill your obligations to your employer.

9. Accepting a "finder's fee" from a printing representative violates Article 12, which states that such fees should not be accepted unless the employer or client is told and gives consent. Accepting a "finder's fee" places the practitioner in a conflict-of-interest situation (Article 10) because he or she may not act in the best interests of the client or employer.

Many cases involve several articles of the code. The articles most frequently cited in complaints were, in descending order of frequency:

- Article 3: Fair dealing with clients, employers, and the public

- Article 5: Intentional communication of false and misleading information

- Article 1: Conducting professional life in accordance with the public interest

- Article 4: Adherence to standards of accuracy and truth

- Article 6: Engaging in practices that corrupt the channels of communication or processes of government

Eventually, 32 of the 165 complaints were forwarded to judicial panels, and ten individuals ultimately were disciplined by the society. Two were expelled, two suspended, three censured, and three reprimanded. In the remaining 22 cases, the charges were dismissed for lack of evidence or the member resigned while the case was in progress.

PRSA'S CODE OF PROFESSIONAL STANDARDS FOR THE PRACTICE OF PUBLIC RELATIONS

These articles have been adopted by the Public Relations Society of America to promote and maintain high standards of public service and ethical conduct among its members.

1. A member shall conduct his or her professional life in accord with the *public interest.*

2. A member shall exemplify high standards of *honesty and integrity* while carrying out dual obligations to a client or employer and to the democratic process.

3. A member shall *deal fairly* with the public, with past or present clients or employers, and with fellow practitioners, giving due respect to the ideal of free inquiry and to the opinions of others.

4. A member shall adhere to the highest standards of *accuracy and truth,* avoiding extravagant claims or unfair comparisons and giving credit for ideas and words borrowed from others.

5. A member shall not knowingly disseminate *false or misleading information* and shall act promptly to correct erroneous communications for which he or she is responsible.

6. A member shall not engage in any practice which has the purpose of *corrupting* the integrity of channels of communications or the processes of government.

7. A member shall be prepared to *identify publicly* the name of the client or employer on whose behalf any public communication is made.

8. A member shall not use any individual or organization professing to serve or represent an announced cause, or professing to be independent or unbiased, but actually serving another or *undisclosed interest.*

9. A member shall not *guarantee the achievement* of specified results beyond the member's direct control.

10. A member shall *not represent conflicting* or competing interests without the express consent of those concerned, given after a full disclosure of the facts.

11. A member shall not place himself or herself in a position where the member's *personal interest is or may be in conflict* with an obligation to an employer or client, or others, without full disclosure of such interests to all involved.

12. A member shall *not accept fees, commissions, gifts or any other consideration* from anyone except clients or employers for whom services are performed without their express consent, given after full disclosure of the facts.

13. A member shall scrupulously safeguard the *confidences and privacy rights* of present, former, and prospective clients or employers.

14. A member shall not intentionally *damage the professional reputation* or practice of another practitioner.

15. If a member has evidence that another member has been guilty of unethical, illegal, or unfair practices, including those in violation of this Code, the member is obligated to present the information promptly to the proper authorities of the Society for action in accordance with the procedure set forth in Article XII of the Bylaws.

16. A member called as a witness in a proceeding for enforcement of this Code is obligated to appear, unless excused for sufficient reason by the judicial panel.

17. A member shall, as soon as possible, sever relations with any organization or individual if such relationship requires conduct contrary to the articles of this Code.

Critics complain that ten disciplinary cases in 33 years doesn't speak particularly well for code enforcement. Others, more positive, see the scarcity of "convictions" as evidence of high ethical standards among PRSA members.

The critics must remember that PRSA is a voluntary membership society, and the organization doesn't have a legal mandate to be a court of law, which can subpoena witnesses, order the presentation of evidence, or even fine individuals for refusing to cooperate. On the other hand, the optimists often underestimate the perception among many practitioners that it is "unprofessional" to question or criticize the activities of fellow members in the "club."

For example, when some members criticized the public relations department of Firestone Tire Company for disseminating false and misleading information about the safety of the tiremaker's radial tires, they themselves were criticized as being "unprofessional" by people such as Denny Griswold, owner and editor of *PR News*.

Some PRSA members contend that Article 14—stating that a member shall not intentionally damage the professional reputation or practice of another practitioner—means that one should remain silent about the performance of his or her peers. PRSA's interpretation carries no such connotation, however. It simply says that a practitioner should not solicit clients by demeaning the quality or ability of the competition. In sum, the concept of "professionalism" means that there should be a healthy, frank discussion of contemporary practice.

An example of how the board of ethics is most effective occurred when a PRSA member scheduled a press conference and several speeches for an "independent" British scientist who had tested a new medical product. A reporter discovered that the scientist was, in fact, an employee of the manufacturer. An inquiry from the board resulted in an immediate response from the member, who enclosed a letter to the client resigning from the account while citing Article 17. The client wanted to communicate false and misleading information, which is contrary to the code.

OTHER CODES

The PRSA code of professional standards, despite some flaws of enforcement, is unique in the communications field in having a highly structured grievance procedure and a history of actually censuring or expelling members of the organization.

The International Association of Business Communicators (IABC) has the ability to suspend members for up to one year after the third violation (see next section), but professional advertising and journalism groups have so far declined to undertake the disciplining of their individual members. Organizations such as the Business/Professional Advertising Association, the American Society of Newspaper Editors (ASNE), and the Society of Professional Journalists (SPJ) have canons or codes of professional conduct, but their function primarily is informational and educational—enunciating standards of conduct rather than enforcing them.

SPJ, for example, took this approach in 1987 after a lengthy and bitter controversy about a statement in its code that, "Journalists should actively try to prevent violation of these standards. . . ." Convention delegates voted to eliminate the clause, primarily because of fears that enacting any punishment would open the society to costly lawsuits, concerns about First Amendment rights of journalists, and the difficulty of establishing a workable method of enforcement. The SPJ code now states in part that, "This society shall, by programs of education and other means, encourage individual journalists to adhere to these tenets. . . ."

SPJ thus followed the lead of ASNE. In the 1920s that organization considered expelling, suspending, or censuring its members for ethical violations. In 1932 ASNE amended its canons to permit such action, but no effort to censure its members has been undertaken.

IABC's Code of Ethics   The International Association of Business Communicators adopted a code of standards in 1976, superseded by a code of ethics approved in 1985. The IABC code contains only 7 provisions, as compared with 14 in the PRSA code. Like the PRSA code, IABC encourages its members to (1) be truthful and accurate, (2) obey the law, (3) treat employer or client information with confidentiality, and (4) uphold the organization's standards. The code also encourages members to get permission before using printed materials from other organizations.

IABC places primary emphasis on information and education about the code rather than actual enforcement. An ethics committee answers inquiries from members and works with the national professional development committee to assure that ethics is discussed in chapter, district, and national meetings. For example, IABC bylaws require that at least one article about ethics shall appear annually in the organization's magazine, *Communication World,* and at least one session on ethics be conducted at the international conference. IABC, as well as PRSA, also distributes copies of the code to all members and includes a pledge to support the code in all membership application forms.

Sanctions against a member found in violation of the code primarily consist of warnings that IABC considers to be "informative and educational." It is only after the third warning that, if the individual shows no serious commitment to improvement and the situation is a "flagrant" violation, the IABC executive board can suspend a member for up to one year.

IABC headquarters receives inquiries every month about the code, mostly involving questions about copyright, plagiarism, and invasion of privacy. An example is an

---

IABC'S CODE OF ETHICS

Communication and Information Dissemination

1. Communication professionals will uphold the credibility and dignity of their profession by encouraging the practice of honest, candid and timely communication.

> The highest standards of professionalism will be upheld in all communication. Communicators should encourage frequent communication and messages that are honest in their content, candid, accurate and appropriate to the needs of the organization and its audiences.

2. Professional communicators will not use any information that has been generated or appropriately acquired by a business for another business without permission. Further, communicators should attempt to identify the source of information to be used.

> When one is changing employers, information developed at the previous position will not be used without permission from that employer. Acts of plagiarism and copyright infringement are illegal acts; material in the public domain should have its source attributed, if possible. If an organization grants permission to use its information and requests public acknowledgement, it will be made in a place appropriate to the material used. The material will be used only for the purpose for which permission was granted.

Standards of Conduct

3. Communication professionals will abide by the spirit and letter of all laws and regulations governing their professional activities.

> All international, national and local laws and regulations must be observed, with particular attention to those pertaining to communication, such as copyright law. Industry and organizational regulations will also be observed.

4. Communication professionals will not condone any illegal or unethical act related to their professional activity, their organization and its business or the public environment in which it operates.

inquiry whether it is all right to use a published article, with minor changes, without getting permission (it isn't). Between 1985 and 1990, however, only two formal complaints were filed. One involved a case of possible embezzlement of funds from a chapter treasury, which was turned over to the police, and the other a case of plagiarism, which was resolved by talking to the individual. To date, no member has been suspended because of code violations.

In general, legal counsel for membership organizations such as IABC, ASNE, and SPJ caution against establishing quasi-legal mechanisms to discipline members, primarily because of possible lawsuit. A member censured or expelled by such an organization, for example, might sue, claiming defamation and libel, or that the organization's

It is the personal responsibility of professional communicators to act honestly, fairly and with integrity at all times in all professional activities. Looking the other way while others act illegally tacitly condones such acts whether or not the communicator has committed them. The communicator should speak with the individual involved, his or her supervisor or appropriate authorities—depending on the context of the situation and one's own ethical judgment.

Confidentiality/Disclosure

5. Communication professionals will respect the confidentiality and right-to-privacy of all individuals, employers, clients and customers.

Communicators must determine the ethical balance between right-to-privacy and need-to-know. Unless the situation involves illegal or grossly unethical acts, confidences should be maintained. If there is a conflict between right-to-privacy and need-to-know, a communicator should first talk with the source and negotiate the need for the information to be communicated.

6. Communication professionals will not use any confidential information gained as a result of professional activity for personal benefit or for that of others.

Confidential information cannot be used to give inside advantage to stock transactions, gain favors from outsiders, assist a competing company for whom one is going to work, assist companies in developing a marketing advantage, achieve a publishing advantage or otherwise act to the detriment of an organization. Such information must remain confidential during and after one's employment period.

Professionalism

7. Communication professionals should uphold IABC's standards for ethical conduct in all professional activity, and should use IABC and its designation of accreditation (ABC) only for purposes that are authorized and fairly represent the organization and its professional standards.

IABC recognizes the need for professional integrity within any organization, including the association. Members should acknowledge that their actions reflect on themselves, their organizations and their professions.

censure deprived him or her of getting a job in the communications field. Also, it is expensive for an organization to "prosecute" ethics cases. Reportedly, PRSA spent more than $100,000 on staff time and legal counsel to investigate allegations of ethics violations by Tony Franco, a case discussed at the end of this chapter.

Video News Release Code   *TV Guide* published a cover story about video news releases (VNRs) in a February 1992 issue, calling them "Fake News." VNR producers called the article a "hatchet job." Six video news producers, members of the Public Relations Service Council in New York, then drew up a Code of Good Practice and pointed out that a seal bearing the code's insignia would reassure news directors that the release contained accurate information and was clearly labeled as coming from a corporate sponsor.

In its March 6–12, 1993, issue *TV Guide* pointed out that a survey had shown that almost half of TV station news directors failed to identify the source of VNRs on news shows. The survey was conducted by Nielsen Media Research for Medialink, one of the VNR production firms.

Bob Kimmel, senior vice president for the News/Broadcast Network, told *O'Dwyer's PR Services Report* that the survey proves ethical guidelines are needed for VNR handling. "We are doing everything we can by putting the source of the material on the VNR. We can't control what happens at the news level, however." Many stations pass off the VNRs as products of their own staffs. (See Chapter 24.)

This photograph released by General Motors shows two puffs of smoke under the Chevrolet pickup truck being "tested" by NBC on its Dateline program. The automaker demonstrated that the smoke came from rocket engines installed under the truck. NBC was forced to make an immediate settlement with GM. (Reuters/Bettmann)

CODE OF GOOD PRACTICE

The objective of a VNR is to present information, pictures, and sound that television journalists can use and rely on for quality, accuracy, and perspective.

Information contained in a VNR must be accurate and reliable. Intentionally false and
misleading information must be avoided.

A video news release must be clearly identified as such, both on the video's opening
slate and on any advisory material and scripts that precede or accompany tape distribution.

The sponsor of the video news release must be clearly identified on a video slate and on
the VNR tape. Name and phone number of a responsible party must be provided on the
video for journalists to contact for further information.

Persons interviewed in the VNR must be accurately identified by name, title, and affiliation on the video.

PROFESSIONALISM, LICENSING, AND ACCREDITATION

PROFESSIONALISM

Among public relations practitioners there are considerable differences of opinion about
whether public relations is a craft, a skill, or a developing profession. Certainly, at its present level, public relations does not qualify as a profession in the same sense that medicine and law do. Public relations does not have prescribed standards of educational
preparation, a mandatory period of apprenticeship, or state laws that govern admission.

Adding to the confusion about professionalism is the difficulty of ascertaining what
constitutes public relations practice. John F. Budd, Jr., a veteran counselor, wrote in
Public Relations Quarterly: "We *act* as publicists, yet we *talk* of counseling. We *perform* as technologists in communication but we *aspire* to be decision-makers dealing in
policy."

On the other hand, there is an increasing body of literature about public relations—
including this text and many others in the field. PRSA has compiled a Body of
Knowledge abstract that contains more than 1000 references, available on computer
disk or hard copy. Substantial progress also is being made in developing theories of public relations, conducting research, and publishing scholarly journals.

There is also the idea, advanced by many professionals and PRSA itself, that the
most important thing is for the individual to *act like a professional* in the field. This
means that a practitioner should have:

1. A sense of independence.

2. A sense of responsibility to society and the public interest.

3. Manifest concern for the competence and honor of the profession as a whole.

4. A higher loyalty to the standards of the profession and fellow professionals than to
the employer of the moment. The reference point in all public relations activity must be
the standards of the profession and not those of the client or the employer.

Unfortunately, a major barrier to professionalism is the attitude that many practitioners themselves have toward their work. As James Grunig and Todd Hunt state in their text *Managing Public Relations,* practitioners tend to hold more "careerist" values than professional values. In other words, they place higher importance on job security, prestige in the organization, salary level, and recognition from superiors than on the values listed above. For example, 47 percent of the respondents in a survey of IABC members gave a neutral or highly negative answer when asked if they would quit their jobs rather than act against their ethical values. And 55 percent considered it "somewhat ethical" to present oneself misleadingly as the only means of achieving an objective. Almost all agreed, however, that ethics is an important matter, worthy of further study.

On another level, many practitioners are limited in their professionalism by what might be termed a "technician mentality." These people narrowly define professionalism as the ability to do a competent job of executing the mechanics of communicating (preparing news releases, brochures, newsletters, etc.) even if the information provided by management or a client is in bad taste, is misleading, lacks documentation, or is just plain wrong.

The *Wall Street Journal* several years ago highlighted the pitfalls of the technician mentality. The story described how Jartran, Inc., used the services of the Daniel J. Edelman, Inc., public relations firm to distribute a press packet to the media. The packet included a letter offering information about wheels falling off trucks owned by U-Haul, its archrival. When the newspaper reporter asked about the ethics of this approach, an Edelman junior account executive was quoted as saying, "It was their idea. We're merely the PR firm that represents them."

In other words, readers may get the impression that the public relations expertise of a firm is available to the highest bidder, regardless of professional values, fair play, and ultimately, the public interest. When public relations firms and departments take no responsibility for what is communicated—only *how* it is communicated in terms of techniques—they reinforce the perception that public relations is more flackery than profession.

Some practitioners defend the technician mentality, however, arguing that public relations people are like lawyers in the court of public opinion. Everyone is entitled to his or her viewpoint and, whether the public relations person agrees or not, the client or employer has a right to be heard. Thus, a public relations representative is a paid advocate, just as a lawyer is. The only flaw in this argument is that public relations people are not lawyers, nor are they in a court of law where judicial concepts determine the role of defendant and plaintiff. In addition, lawyers have been known to turn down clients or resign from a case because they doubted the client's story.

In Chapter 13, which concerns legal aspects of public relations, it is pointed out that courts increasingly are holding public relations firms accountable for information disseminated on behalf of a client. Thus, it is no longer acceptable to say, "The client told me to do it."

LICENSING

Proposals that public relations practitioners be licensed were discussed before PRSA was founded. One proponent, Edward L. Bernays, who was instrumental in formulating the modern concept of public relations (see Chapter 3), believed that licensing would protect the profession and the public from incompetent, shoddy opportunists who do not have the knowledge, talent, or ethics required.

The problem is stated by PRSA's task force on demonstrating professionalism:

Pick up any metropolitan newspaper and scan the employment ads. Under the "public relations" classification, you are likely to find opportunities for door-to-door salespersons, receptionists, used-car salesmen, singles bar hostesses and others of less savory reputation. The front pages of the newspapers are full of stories about former government employees peddling influence and calling it public relations.

Thus, under the licensing approach, only those individuals who pass rigid examinations and tests of personal integrity could call themselves "public relations" counselors. Those not licensed would have to call themselves "publicists" or adopt some other designation.

Several arguments for mandatory licensing and registration with legal sanctions exist:

1. It would define the practice of public relations.

2. It would establish uniform educational curricula.

3. It would set uniform ethical and professional standards.

4. It would provide for decertification of violators of ethical standards.

5. It would protect the consumer of public relations services (clients and employers) from impostors and charlatans.

6. It would protect qualified practitioners from unfair competition from the unethical and unqualified.

7. It would raise the credibility of public relations practitioners.

8. Since licensing would not control anyone's right to deal with the media, government, or public, or to speak out in any way, no infringement of First Amendment rights would be involved.

Several arguments against licensing and in favor of continued reliance on a voluntary approach to public relations ethics also exist:

1. Any licensing in the communications field is an infringement on the First Amendment.

2. It is difficult to define public relations.

3. Too much emphasis would be placed on education.

4. Voluntary accreditation is sufficient to establish standards.

5. Civil and criminal laws already exist to deal with malpractice.

6. Legislatures show little or no interest in licensing public relations since the health and welfare of the general public are not at stake.

7. Licensing would be a state function, and public relations people often work on a national and international basis.

8. Licensing assures only minimum competence and professional standards; it doesn't necessarily assure high ethical behavior.

9. The credibility and status of an occupation are not necessarily assured through licensing. Attorneys, for example, don't particularly enjoy high public status and prestige because they are licensed. Nor do licensed practical nurses.

10. The machinery required for government to license and police all public relations practitioners in this country would be elaborate and very costly to the American taxpayer.

A PRSA study group on licensing and registration bluntly reported:

There is an almost universal disdain for licensing and a sharp dislike for any type of government oversight of public relations practice. It is our judgment . . . that the ethical code and sense of public and professional morality that must be maintained by public relations professionals cannot be delegated to government. The process of morality, while personal, is democratic and cannot be legislated. It can best be sustained through peer-imposed discipline based on a common code of ethics and consistently maintained levels of professional excellence in practice.

ACCREDITATION

The major effort to improve standards and professionalism in public relations has been related to establishing accreditation programs. PRSA, for example, began its accreditation program in 1965.

To become an accredited member of the society, with the designation *APR,* a person must have at least five years' experience in public relations practice or teaching, must have two sponsors who will testify as to integrity and ability, and must pass a one-day written examination and an oral exam as well. To date, about a third of PRSA's 15,000 members have earned the *APR* designation.

Since *APR* is trademarked by PRSA, a person is prohibited from using *APR* if he or she isn't a current member of the society.

In 1989 the PRSA Assembly adopted a requirement that, in order to maintain accreditation, *APR*s must accumulate ten points every three years in the areas of education, professionalism, or service. The system went into effect in 1991. PRSA is the only group of U.S. professional communicators to have such a requirement.

In 1990 PRSA established a College of Fellows in order to recognize accredited members who for 20 years or more have demonstrated superior capability as practitioners, whose personal and professional qualities have served as role models for other practitioners, and who have advanced the state of public relations. Eighty-five of the society's members were the first Fellows elected.

In recent years the society has also launched an information campaign to make the general public and potential employers aware of what the *APR* designation means. In this way, it is hoped that such a "seal of approval" will separate public relations professionals from those less qualified. It is a slow process, however, because many senior public relations practitioners do not feel the need to prove themselves through a "test." Another major obstacle is that few employers require accreditation as a prerequisite for top-level positions in public relations.

The International Association of Business Communicators also has an accreditation program for its membership. A member may use the designation *ABC (Accredited Business Communicator)* after submitting a portfolio for evaluation and passing written and oral examinations. At present, fewer than 5 percent of IABC's more than 11,000 members have an *ABC* designation.

In the United Kingdom persons wishing to join the 4000 full members of the Institute of Public Relations not only must have four years of experience at an executive level but also hold a public relations degree from one of seven recognized university programs or from the Communications, Advertising and Marketing Foundation, an industry examining body. Full members are accorded the MIPR designation.

Requiring members of a professional organization to fulfill academic standards "certainly makes sense," said Dr. Larissa Grunig, associate professor of public relations at the University of Maryland College of Journalism. "I'm envious the British can enforce such a requirement."

OTHER STEPS TOWARD PROFESSIONALISM

PRSA, IABC, and the Public Relations Division of the Association for Education in Journalism and Mass Communication (AEJMC) have worked to improve and standardize the curricula for programs of public relations at the bachelor's and master's degree level. The 1987 Commission on Undergraduate Public Relations Education set the new standard that a public relations sequence should have a minimum of five core courses covering the following public relations topics: (1) principles and theory, (2) writing and publicity techniques, (3) research for planning and evaluation, (4) case studies on strategy and implementation, and (5) supervised internship. This core curriculum has been endorsed by PRSA, IABC, the Public Relations Division of AEJMC, and the public relations section of the International Communication Association.

The educational and professional community generally agrees that preparation for public relations work requires a specialized course of study with strong emphasis on a broad liberal arts education coupled with a minor in economics or a business area. Highly traditional schools and departments of journalism, however, continue to insist that a journalism curriculum is the best preparation for a public relations career.

The Institute for Public Relations Research & Education (PRSA) and the IABC Foundation also work to expand the body of knowledge about public relations. Both advance professionalism through sponsorship of books and monographs, symposiums, scholarships, and grants for research studies. A major project of the IABC Foundation, for example, has been a six-year, $400,000 study to investigate "Excellence in Public Relations and Communication Management" through a series of surveys and the testing of organizational communication models. Findings of the project are discussed in Chapter 5.

In 1990 PRSA established its own foundation to fund a number of special projects. One is a $50,000 National Minority Scholarship program to encourage more minority students to select public relations as a career. The foundation also funds the Body of Knowledge project, previously described in this chapter.

ETHICS IN INDIVIDUAL PRACTICE

Despite codes of professional practice and formalized accreditation, ethics in public relations boils down to deeply troubling questions for the individual practitioner: Will I lie for my employer? Will I rig a doorprize drawing so a favorite client can win? Will I deceive in order to gain information about another agency's clients? Will I cover up a hazardous condition? Will I issue a news release presenting only half the truth? Will I seek to bribe a reporter or a legislator? Will I withhold some information in a news conference, and provide it only if a reporter asks a specific question? Will I quit my job rather than cooperate in a questionable activity? In other words, to what extent, if any, will I compromise my personal beliefs?

These and similar questions plague the lives of many public relations people, although a number hold such strong personal beliefs and/or work for such highly principled employers that they seldom need to compromise their personal values. If employers make a suggestion that involves questionable ethics, the public relations person often can talk them out of the idea by citing the possible consequences of such an action—adverse media publicity, for example.

"To thine own self be true," advised New York public relations executive Chester Burger at an IABC conference. A fellow panelist, Canadian politician and radio commentator Stephen Lewis, commented: "There is a tremendous jaundice on the part of the public about the way things are communicated. People have elevated superficiality to an art form. Look at the substance of what you have to convey, and the honesty used in conveying it." With the audience contributing suggestions, the panelists formulated the following list of commendable practices:

- Be honest at all times.

- Convey a sense of business ethics based on your own standards and those of society.

- Respect the integrity and position of your opponents and audiences.

- Develop trust by emphasizing substance over triviality.

- Present all sides of an issue.

- Strive for a balance between loyalty to the organization and duty to the public.

- Don't sacrifice long-term objectives for short-term gains.

Adherence to professional standards of conduct—being truly independent—is the chief measure of a public relations person. Faced with such personal problems as a mortgage and children to educate, practitioners may be strongly tempted to become yes men (or yes women) and decline to express their views forcefully to an employer, or to resign. J. Kenneth Clark, vice president of corporate communications, Duke Power Company, Charlotte, North Carolina, gave the following advice to an IABC audience:

If the boss says newspapers are no damn good, the yes man agrees.

If the boss says to tell a reporter "no comment," the yes man agrees.

If the boss says the company's employees get a paycheck and don't really need to be informed about anything else, the yes man agrees.

If the boss says the public has no right to pry into what's going on inside a company—even though that company is publicly held and is dependent upon public support and public sales—the yes man nods his head agreeably and starts work on the corporate version of a Berlin Wall.

The fate of the yes man is as inevitable as it is painful. Although your boss may think you're the greatest guy in the world for a while, you're going to lose your internal credibility because you never really state your professional opinions. And you're talking to a person who dotes on strong opinions and does not think highly of people who fail to offer them.

Allen H. Center, a professor at San Diego State University and a long-time corporate public relations executive, has written: "Public relations has emerged more as an echo of an employer's standards and interests than that of a professional discipline applied to the employer's problems." Yet many a practitioner has resigned rather than submit to a compromising situation.

Told that his job at a company was "to turn excrement into applesauce" (the official used a less elegant word than *excrement*), one public relations man resigned. He pointed out later that "the attitude exemplified two things—the reality of the company at the top level, where policy is made, and the perception at that level of the role of public relations."

In some cases practitioners have been arbitrarily fired for refusing to write news releases that are false and misleading. This happened to an accredited PRSA member in the San Francisco Bay area. The company president wanted him, among other things, to write and send a news release giving a list of company clients when, in fact, none of the companies had signed a contract for services. When the practitioner refused, on the grounds that the PRSA code would be violated, he was fired. In turn, the practitioner sued the company for unlawful dismissal and received almost $100,000 in an out-of-court settlement.

Tommy Ross, pioneer public relations practitioner and partner of Ivy Lee before founding T. J. Ross and Associates, once told a *Fortune* magazine interviewer: "Unless you are willing to resign an account or a job over a matter of principle, it is no use to call yourself a member of the world's newest profession—for you are already a member of the world's oldest."

Thus, it can be readily seen that ethics in public relations really begins with the individual—and is directly related to his or her own value system as well as to the good of society. Although it is important to show loyalty to an employer, practitioners must never allow a client or an employer to rob them of their sense of self-esteem.

The most practical consideration facing a public relations specialist in his or her deal-ings with the news media is that anything less than total honesty will destroy credibility and, with it, the practitioner's usefulness to an employer. The news media depend on public relations sources for much of the information they convey to readers and listen-ers. Although a number of public relations releases are used simply as tips on which to develop stories, many reporters and editors know that they can rely on the accuracy and thoroughness of much public relations copy and use it with little change.

Achieving trust is the aim of all practitioners, and it can be achieved only through highly professional and ethical performance. It is for this reason that providing junkets with doubtful news value, extravagant parties, expensive gifts, and personal favors for media representatives should never be done. On occasion, an unethical journalist will ask favors, but the public relations professional will decline such requests tactfully.

Newspeople and public relations executives alike questioned the propriety of Coca-Cola USA's sending sample cans of Coke Classic stuffed with $5 bills to 200 consumer and trade reporters and editors. The attention-getting gimmick was part of the compa-ny's "Magic Summer '90" promotion in which 750,000 cans of the soft drink were to be distributed nationwide containing up to $200 cash and prize vouchers for trips and tick-ets to vacation and entertainment destinations. The cans were devised so that the cash or a voucher would pop up when what looked like an ordinary container was opened.

When some cans malfunctioned and a few purchasers drank the slightly noxious liquid, Coca-Cola USA launched an advertising campaign urging consumers to "take a good look" and not to drink the liquid. It then cancelled the promotion. The public rela-tions newsletter *Bulldog Reporter* quoted a number of newspeople and public relations executives who, for the most part, pointed out that the sending of cash to news sources raised the question of a conflict of interest whether a bribe was intended or not. (Ethical aspects of media relations are discussed further in Chapter 23.)

AUTOS: SHADES OF GRAY

Although it is fairly obvious that expensive gifts and bribes are unethical by almost any-body's standard of professionalism, the most difficult ethical situations are those that are neither black nor white, but differing shades of gray.

Relationships between automotive journalists and car manufacturers are question-able, according to an article in the *Wall Street Journal*. It is not unusual, for example, for an editor at *Car and Driver* to write reviews for autos made by a manufacturing firm that also employs the journalist as a consultant. As the article writer says, "Welcome to the world of automotive enthusiast journalism where the barriers that separate advertisers from journalists are porous enough for paychecks to pass through."

PRSA's Article 6 forbids "corrupting the channels of communication" by placing journalists on the payroll, but this stricture doesn't seem to mean much in the world of "buff" magazines such as *Car and Driver, Motor Trend,* and *Road & Track.* The jour-nalists say they are professionals and would never let their consulting relationships

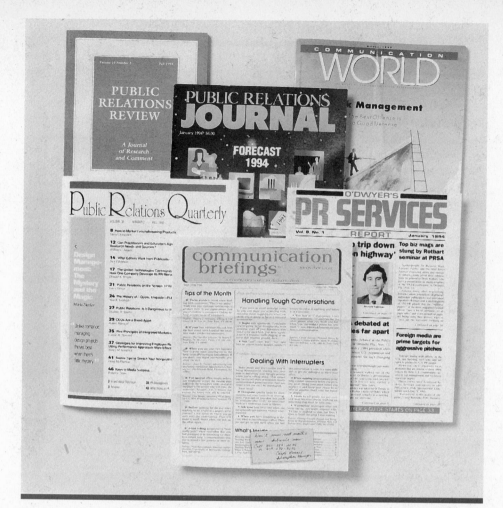

FIGURE 6.1
Magazines and newsletters edited for public relations profes-
sionals—among them *Bulldog Reporter*—provide a forum for
discussion of current issues. Also shown here are the *Public
Relations Review,* the *Public Relations Journal,
Communication World, International Public Relations, PR
Reporter, PR News, Jack O'Dwyer's Newsletter,* and
Communication Briefings.

interfere with their writing independence, but the public is left wondering about the
integrity of such statements. At the same time, if hiring editors to be consultants is
standard operating procedure, how does the public relations person for an auto company reconcile this "reality" with the standards of his or her profession? Ethical issues in
the travel industry are discussed in Chapter 20. Some other aspects of public relations–news media ethical relationships are examined in "The Press Party" section of
Chapter 23.

Public relations executives and lobbyists were heavily embroiled in the top-level business and government scandals of the 1980s and early 1990s involving Wall Street securities firms, defense industries, the savings and loan industry, and the Iran–Contra affair. Ironically, the revelations followed a period when hundreds of business firms adopted codes of ethics and required employees to attend ethics seminars and sign annual affidavits that they were following company policy. The Ethics Resource Center reported that, whereas only three of every four of the 1500 largest corporations had written codes of ethics in 1984, by 1990 virtually all had them. Companies conducting extensive ethics training programs for employees included Martin Marietta, McDonnell Douglas, and General Dynamics.

According to the Ethics Resource Center, the following matters are addressed most often in the codes of business corporations:

- A general statement of company philosophy and commitment to ethical conduct

- Compliance with all applicable laws and regulations

- Prohibition of bribery and kickbacks

- Conflicts of interest

- Gifts, gratuities, and entertainment

- Confidential and proprietary information

- Accurate books, records, and financial reports

- Proper use of corporate assets

- Proper relationships with dealers, agents, suppliers, competitors, customers, and government representatives

- Honesty in communication

- Political activities and relationships with foreign governments

- Social responsibility of the company

- Industrial integrity and adherence to high standards of personal morality

Said Don Bates, APR, president of the Bates Company, in a speech at Northern Illinois University: "Often, the public relations practitioner drafts the code to begin with, assisted by top management and corporate counsel. Regardless, he [or she] has a crucial role in promoting its existence and significance to employees, suppliers, and others."

ETHICS AND LAWS CONCERNING FINANCIAL NEWS

Public relations personnel working for publicly held companies have not only an ethical but also a legal obligation to promptly release news about dividends, earnings, new

GUIDELINES FOR FAIR DEALING

Ketchum Public Relations has established guidelines for its employees on how to deal fairly with clients.

The code deals with (1) truth and accuracy in communications, (2) confidential information, (3) purchasing, (4) gifts and excessive entertainment and other payments, (5) industry groups, (6) union agreements, (7) suppliers to the agency and clients, (8) services for competitors, (9) use of inside information, and (10) misuse of businesss opportunities.

"We will deal with clients in a fair and businesslike fashion, providing unbiased, professional recommendations to move their business ahead," the code promises.

"We will safeguard their proprietary information and help protect their financial assets."

Many other public relations firms have similar codes.

products, mergers, and any other developments that might affect security values or influence investment decisions of stockholders or the public. As noted on the preceding pages, news must not be delayed so that insiders can derive financial benefit. The Securities and Exchange Commission (SEC), described in Chapter 13, strictly enforces these requirements.

Corporations are also prohibited from using "hype" in connection with the sale of new securities or from being overly optimistic about the financial health of the companies. Public relations staff members and outside counsel increasingly are being held responsible by the SEC, and they also run the risk of violating PRSA's guidelines for financial public relations. These tell practitioners to find out for themselves if management gives them questionable information to disseminate. The rule states: "Where members have any reason to doubt that projections have an adequate basis in fact, they shall satisfy themselves as to the adequacy of the projections prior to disseminating them." Practitioners are put on notice that they can't simply plead, "This is what management told me to say."

A more troublesome ethical dilemma is how and when to release information regarding mergers and acquisitions. Such negotiations between companies are very sensitive; untimely release of information may adversely affect a company's bargaining position. Secrecy of negotiations is essential in business but, at the same time, the SEC requires public release of information. The problem is what and how much to disclose at any given time. If negotiations are just starting, for example, is it all right to be evasive so investors don't misinterpret the information? The SEC definition of "material information" is somewhat elastic and subject to a number of court interpretations.

Public relations personnel also must be well aware of Federal Trade Commission (FTC) regulations regarding the promotion of a product or service. A company can get into trouble for such things as unsubstantiated claims, fraudulent testimonials, deceptive pricing, surveys that are not really independent, and rigged contests. Again, the public relations professional has the responsibility to ascertain the facts rather than to take the word of the marketing or advertising director.

The Food and Drug Administration (FDA) also has a list of regulations concerning the promotion and advertising of medicines and drugs.

CASE STUDY 1:
HILL AND KNOWLTON'S CAMPAIGN FOR A FREE KUWAIT

The activities of Hill and Knowlton, one of the largest public relations firms, in promoting U.S. entry into the Persian Gulf War produced a barrage of criticism from print and broadcast sources and in the public relations trade press as well.

The reports charged that Hill and Knowlton, working for the Citizens for a Free Kuwait, misled the American public about atrocities committed by Iraqi soldiers in order to "sell" the war. Precipitating the reports on CBS-TV's *60 Minutes* and ABC-TV's *20/20* was a New York *Times* op-ed piece by John MacArthur, publisher of *Harper's* magazine. MacArthur revealed that the tearful 15-year-old girl who testified about the atrocities before the Congressional Human Rights Caucus, identified only as Nayirah, actually was the daughter of the Kuwait ambassador to the United States, Saud Nasir Al-Sabah. (See Chapter 15.)

Neither of the television programs, nor Amnesty International, could find confirmation of Nayirah's claim that hundreds of babies had been taken from their incubators by Iraqi soldiers and left on the floor to die. Hill and Knowlton was criticized by *60 Minutes* for allegedly showing that "war can be marketed, just like soft drinks and toothpaste."

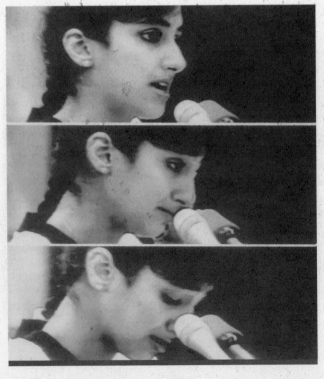

After a 15-year-old Kuwaiti girl indentified only as "Nayirah" told a Congressional committee a horror story of how Iraqi invaders had mistreated Kuwaiti babies in a hospital during the Persian Gulf War, it was disclosed that she actually was the daughter of the Kuwaiti ambassador to the United States.

CBS reported that a video news release of Nayirah's statement was distributed to promote the war. Six senators cited the "babies" story, and the war was approved by a margin of five senators, CBS noted.

Lauri Fitz-Pegado, representing the firm on the programs, said she believed Nayirah was telling the truth. She told CBS she did not know that $11.8 million of the funds for the Citizens for a Free Kuwait account came from the Kuwaiti government and only $17,861 from 78 citizens.

Thomas E. Eidson, president and CEO of Hill and Knowlton, strongly defended the firm's actions. He said Nayirah's identity had been disclosed to the Congressional Human Rights Caucus, which decided, at the request of her father, not to make her identity known in fear of reprisal against those left behind in Kuwait.

Eidson said the firm had been "fully vindicated" by a report from Kroll Associates that confirmed the deaths of at least seven babies removed from their incubators.

"Hill and Knowlton's representation of Citizens for a Free Kuwait was conducted with the highest of professional and ethical standards," Eidson said. He assailed journalists for committing "the unconscionable journalistic crimes of not checking facts" and failing to present both sides of the story.

Several public relations executives, questioned by *O'Dwyer's PR Services Report,* said H&K had violated the PRSA code article relating to "honesty and integrity" and the article forbidding use of an individual "professing to be independent but actually serving another undisclosed interest." Chicago counselor Philip Lesley said the concealment was a "direct breach" of Article 8 of the code outlawing "fronts." He was quoted as adding that the "overwhelming quest for ever higher profits and volume" has caused firms to "lose sight of ethics."

Some counselors declined to criticize H&K, citing Article 14 of the PRSA code, which says, "A member shall not intentionally damage the professional reputation or practice of another practitioner." Others called for the PRSA board to investigate the situation to show that the society "can keep its own house clean." The board issued a statement saying, in part: "The role of PR is to help organizations—even individuals and governments—exercise fully, however controversial the subject might be, their basic right of free speech." It added that members must adhere to the PRSA code, which emphasizes "truth, accuracy, fairness, and responsibility to the public."

Eidson said public relations firms "are now faced with a real and frightening dilemma when it comes to decisions about whether to take on controversial clients. It is my fear that under the abusive media assault the distinction between controversial and contemptible clients will be blurred, and that firms like H&K will shy away from controversial clients. I want to have the right to represent controversial clients."

QUESTIONS FOR DISCUSSION

■ In view of the sensational nature of Nayirah's testimony, should H&K have investigated its factual basis? Should H&K have foreseen the media repercussions of not frankly stating her connection to the Kuwaiti government?

■ Should H&K have disclosed publicly the source of funds supporting Citizens for a Free Kuwait? Is the use of a "front" organization such as Citizens for a Free Kuwait deceptive and a breach of the PRSA code of ethics?

■ In the interest of protecting the reputation of public relations practitioners, should other firms refrain from criticizing them?

■ Should public relations firms accept controversial clients? Where would you draw the line?

■ Did the news media treat H&K fairly in this case?

CASE STUDY 2:
HILL AND KNOWLTON'S ANTI-ABORTION CAMPAIGN

A lively controversy with multiple ethical aspects erupted in 1990 when Hill and Knowlton agreed to conduct an anti-abortion campaign for U.S. Roman Catholic bishops. The bishops also hired the Worthlin Group, a leading Republican polling operation that served Ronald Reagan in his campaign for the White House and during his presidency. The aim of the bishops' campaign, costing $3–$5 million over a three- to five-year period, was to persuade both Catholics and non-Catholics to oppose abortion.

Many Hill and Knowlton employees publicly criticized the decision; two resigned, and the firm lost at least one client. President Robert L. Dilenschneider said any employee could refrain from working on the account with impunity.

"Some organizations have lost sight of fundamental values, such as the sanctity of human life, or they have tried to convince America that the main issue in the abortion debate is the right to choose rather than, as it really is, what is being chosen," said Cardinal John J. O'Connor, archbishop of New York and chairman of the Committee for Pro-Life Activities of the U.S. Catholic Conference. Noting that abortion-rights groups have hired pollsters and media advisers to help them, O'Connor added: "Given the stakes—life itself—we can do no less."

Critics branded the campaign as a waste of church resources and a violation of the constitutional separation of church and state. Charged Kate Michelman, president of the National Abortion Rights Action League: "They're not just trying to deliver a message, they're trying to interject their religious and moral views into politics."

Jerry Dalton, PRSA president, said in a letter to the New York *Times* that the bishops have a First Amendment right to use public relations counsel to help them shape arguments against abortion.

"However controversial or unpopular a cause, advocates—or opponents—have the right to seek professional PR counsel to help them shape and communicate persuasive arguments," Dalton wrote. "That's what the First Amendment is all about." Other corporate executives, interviewed by the *Public Relations Journal,* echoed Dalton's opinion.

A former priest, Eugene Kennedy, professor of psychology at Loyola University, wrote in the New York *Times* that the bishops had chosen a strategy "that is manipulative at best and numbingly amoral at worst."

"Good shepherds do not invite wolves to help them tend flocks. . . . You call in PR operatives when the truth won't do. . . . Humans cannot be manipulated into moral positions."

A story in *National Catholic Reporter* titled "What Does H&K Sell?" provided the answer: "Anything the customer is prepared to pay for."

Dilenschneider responded to both attacks: "We do not shy away from controversy but we will not misrepresent a client's position. And if cash were the determinant for representation of a client, we would certainly not have turned away, as we have, representation of Muammar al-Qaddafi, General Noriega, Ferdinand Marcos. South Africa (in its previous posture), Guatemala, and the Colombian drug lords."

In a letter to the New York *Times,* Dilenschneider wrote that Hill and Knowlton has a long record of representing those whom others shun, sometimes at personal risk, as in the civil rights struggle in the 1960s.

Pickets march outside the Hill and Knowlton office in New York to protest the public relations firm's decision to conduct an anti-abortion campaign for U.S. Roman Catholic bishops.

Other criticisms of the firm's acceptance of the Catholic account included the following:

1. The firm violated Article 10 of the PRSA code: "A member shall not represent conflicting or competing interests without the express consent of those concerned, given after a full disclosure of the facts." The *Bulldog Reporter* newsletter raised the issue, pointing out that among Hill and Knowlton's hundreds of clients are the Church of Scientology; DNS, a gene-splicing bioengineering firm; Wyeth-Ayerst, makers of contraceptive devices; and Playboy Enterprises, which supports abortion rights. The newsletter said representatives of the Bishops Committee in both New York and Washington said they were unaware of Hill and Knowlton's ties to Playboy.

    Asked about a possible conflict of interest, according to the newsletter Dilenschneider replied: "We will not resign any business we currently have."

2. Hill and Knowlton responded slowly in handling the firm's internal communications problem. Staff members complained that they first heard of H&K's agreeing to work for the bishops from newspaper reports. No backup spokesperson was appointed to respond to innumerable press inquiries after the story broke, according to some accounts.

3. The firm should not accept "an assignment whose ultimate goal is to limit our fundamental rights," according to a petition signed by 160 staff members in the company's New York office. Davia Tenin, vice president for marketing at the Wertheim Schroder investment banking firm, said the decision "says to me that it is going to sacrifice women's rights for the pocketbook."

4. Acceptance of the account reinforced with some people the image of public relations professionals as being simply "hired guns" (the accusation of Frances Kissling, president of Catholics for a Free Choice). Other published statements included the stereotypical charge that "PR people don't care whose side they are on so long as the pay is good" and Kennedy's statement, "You call in public relations operatives when the truth won't do."

In 1993, priests in thousands of Catholic churches handed out 5 million postal cards, asking people to sign and send them to Washington, D.C. The cards voiced opposition to the Freedom of Choice Act, a bill that would prohibit states from restricting abortion.

Many Catholics who support abortion rights called the church's efforts intimidating. "Catholics . . . resent the bishops using the Mass and the pulpit to pursue this agenda," said Frances Kissling of Catholics for a Free Choice.

Said John Walsh, spokesman for the Archdiocese of Boston: "This is not in our view the imposition of a narrow sectarian religious agenda. It gets to the question of what kind of society are we going to have."

QUESTIONS FOR DISCUSSION

The Hill and Knowlton controversy raises a number of questions for discussion. Some of them involve ethics, while others are operational in nature:

- Should Hill and Knowlton have accepted the Catholic bishops' account, or should it have adopted Burson-Marsteller's policy of not handling religious or political accounts?

- Do the bishops have a constitutional right to use a public relations firm to develop new strategies?

- Was the principle of separation of church and state violated?

- Did Hill and Knowlton violate an article of the PRSA Code of Professional Standards for the Practice of Public Relations?

- Did the firm follow the precepts of a public relations communications crisis plan?

CASE STUDY 3: THE FRANCO AFFAIR

The public relations profession was jolted in late 1986 when it was disclosed that Anthony "Tony" M. Franco, then national president of the Public Relations Society of America, had been charged by the Securities and Exchange Commission with insider trading.

In a civil action suit, the SEC alleged that Franco had violated Section 10(b) and rule 10b-5 of the Securities Exchange Act of 1934, which prohibits use of inside information to buy or sell shares of stock in a company. The act also requires insiders to make immediate public disclosure of any information that materially affects the price of a stock.

Franco, chairman and chief executive officer of his own public relations firm in Detroit, Anthony M. Franco, Inc., was charged with using confidential information from a client, Crowley, Milner and Company, in 1985. The company had hired Franco to prepare a news release about its proposed acquisition by Oakland Holding Company with a stock offer of $50 per share.

The SEC suit charged that Franco used this confidential information, before any public disclosure was made, to have his broker purchase 3000 shares of Crowley, then listed on the American Stock Exchange at $41 a share. The purchase of so many shares, on a stock relatively inactive on the market, triggered the American Stock Exchange to inform the Crowley company that Franco was the purchaser.

According to the SEC complaint, Franco denied he was responsible for the trade. Later that day, however, Franco allegedly telephoned his broker and directed him to rescind the trade. Franco did not deny that the stock purchase had been made, but maintained that his broker had acted without his authorization, and the purchase of the stock a day before public announcement of an acquisition was an unfortunate coincidence.

The SEC notified Franco that it was investigating the incident, which resulted in Franco's being named a defendant in a civil suit filed in the U.S. District Court for the District of Columbia. On January 1, 1986, Franco became the new national president of PRSA.

The Franco case became public knowledge on August 27, 1986, when the *Wall Street Journal* and the Associated Press carried the news that Franco had signed a consent decree with the SEC. In a consent decree, the defendant neither denies nor admits any of the allegations but promises to obey the law in the future.

The knowledge that Franco had signed a consent decree generated a storm of criticism in the public relations community. Many practitioners saw it, in the words of several, as a real "tragedy," "a terrible stigma for PR people," and "a stupid mistake by someone who is supposed to stand for everything that is right about PR."

The board of directors of the large Chicago PRSA chapter immediately called for Franco's resignation as president of PRSA. Charles Werle, chapter president, said: "Regardless of the legal ramifications of the SEC consent decree, our decision was based on the fact that Franco accepted the national presidency of PRSA knowing that there was a possibility of a damaging SEC action involving him personally that could reflect negatively on PRSA during his term of office. Withholding such information could easily be interpreted as a violation of the PRSA code of ethics."

On August 28, Franco did resign. He said that his resignation was in the best interest of PRSA and that the widespread criticism of his actions made it impossible to do his job effectively. He did, however, retain his membership and requested a hearing before the PRSA Board of Ethics.

The PRSA ethics board finally met on September 19 to hear testimony from Franco and his lawyer. On October 4, the society's board of directors met to hear the recommendations of the ethics board and to determine what disciplinary actions, if any, to take. While the board of directors was in executive session, Franco sent word that he was resigning his membership, effective immediately. Since the society can discipline only members, Franco had removed himself from PRSA code enforcement procedures. Code violations being considered by the board at the moment of Franco's resignation from membership were:

■ A member shall deal fairly with clients, employers, fellow practitioners, and the public.

■ A member shall safeguard confidences of present and former clients, as well as others who have disclosed confidences to a member in the context of communications relating to an anticipated professional relationship.

■ A member shall not intentionally communicate false or misleading information, and is obligated to use care to avoid communicating false or misleading information.

In the aftermath of the Franco affair, PRSA initiated new rules and regulations. Candidates for national office are now required to sign a disclosure statement that they are not involved in anything that might reflect adversely on the society. And new bylaws now permit the society to continue investigating a code violation for up to 90 days after a member has resigned membership. A member can also be temporarily suspended from membership if he or she has been named a defendant in a criminal case.

CASE PROBLEM

Prism Computer Corporation, a manufacturer of personal computers, has developed a new laser printer that is cheaper and more efficient than those produced by competitors. Although prototype models have been built, actual production of the new printer has been stalled up to three months by manufacturing problems.

Despite these difficulties, Prism's top management believes it is important from a marketing standpoint to announce that the new laser printer is now available. Consequently, they ask you as the product information specialist to write and distribute a new product release about the laser printer and its features.

You are told that no mention should be made in the news release that the product won't be available for another three months. What would you do in this situation? Does the situation violate professional ethics in any way? Why or why not?

QUESTIONS FOR REVIEW AND DISCUSSION

1. Sound ethical practice is essential in public relations work. What is meant by *ethics,* and how is it that two individuals can disagree about what constitutes an ethical dilemma?

2. What do you consider the most important points in the PRSA and IABC codes? How do the standards serve the interest of (1) the organizations' members and (2) the public? Can you find any loopholes that might hinder full-fledged enforcement?

3. What are some of the principal problems involved in enforcing the codes?

4. What does the PRSA code say about giving gifts and free trips to representatives of the media? Is it all right to buy drinks or dinner for a news reporter?

5. Under what circumstances should public relations practitioners (1) criticize each other and (2) not criticize each other?

6. To what four standards should a practitioner adhere in acting like a professional?

7. Should public relations practitioners be licensed? What are some of the reasons pro and con?

8. What special ethical and legal obligations are involved in the handling of financial news? What agencies enforce the legal requirements?

9. Is the use of a "front" organization deceptive?

10. What portion of the PRSA code, if any, did Hill and Knowlton violate when it accepted the Catholic bishops' anti-abortion account?

11. Review the Tony Franco case study. Do you think Franco should have been expelled from PRSA? Why or why not?

Baker, Lee W.   *The Credibility Factor: Putting Ethics to Work in Public Relations.* Burr Ridge, IL: Irwin, 1993.

Bivins, Thomas H.   "A Systems Model for Ethical Decision Making in Public Relations." *Public Relations Review,* Winter 1992, pp. 365–384.

Bivins, Thomas H.   "A Theory-Based Approach to Public Relations Ethics." *Journalism Educator,* Winter 1991, pp. 39–41.

Bovet, Susan Fry.   "The Burning Question of Ethics: The Profession Fights for Better Business Practices." *Public Relations Journal,* November 1993, pp. 24–25, 29.

Drummond, Joan.   "Ethics vs. the Economy: Video News Releases Flood the Marketplace." *Quill,* May 1993, pp. 35–37.

Edelman, Daniel J.   "Ethical Behavior Is Key to Field's Future." *Public Relations Journal,* November 1992, pp. 31–32.

Heger, Kyle.   "One Communicator's Gold Star Is Another's Scarlet Letter." *Communication World,* September 1989, pp. 34–36. Ethics and professional practice.

Hiebert, Ray E.,   editor. "Public Relations Ethics." *Public Relations Review,* Spring 1993, pp. 1–91. Series of articles on ethics in this special issue.

"H&K Defends Credibility After Baby Story Expose." *O'Dwyer's PR Services Report,* February 1992, pp. 1, 8–11.

"H&K Sees Vindication in Report on Kuwait Babies." *O'Dwyer's PR Services Report,* August 1992, pp. 1, 7–10.

"H&K Chief Warns Firms About Press." *Public Relations Journal,* June 1993, pp. 7, 11. Public relations firm responds to media criticism of Kuwait account.

Holmes, Paul.   "Why Good Public Relations Is More Important Than Ethics." *Inside PR,* February 1993, pp. 14–17. Proper application of public relations theory is better than programs in business ethics.

Kennedy, Eugene.   "Catholic Bishops' Big PR Blunder." New York *Times,* April 19, 1990. Article on opposite editorial page.

Lesly, Philip, and others.   "Licensing Public Relations." *Public Relations Review,* Winter 1986. Entire issue devoted to the pros and cons of licensing.

Lipman, Joanne.   "PR Firm Faces New Assault over Tactics." *Wall Street Journal,* January 7, 1992, p. B3. Hill and Knowlton controversy over Citizens for Kuwait account.

MacArthur, John R.   "Remember Nayirah, Witness for Kuwait?" New York *Times,* January 6, 1992, p. A11. Op-ed article attacking Hill and Knowlton for distortion of facts.

McCauley, Kevin.   "H&K Keeps Pro-Life Account Despite Heavy Opposition." *O'Dwyer's PR Services* magazine, June 1990, pp. 1, 8, 31–35.

McElreath, Mark P. "Insider Trading." *Communication World,* December 1993, pp. 34–37. Ethics of insider trading.

McElreath, Mark P. "When the Press Comes Knocking: Balancing the Public's Need to Know with the Customer's Right to Privacy." *Communication World,* October 1993, pp. 33–35.

McElreath, Mark P. "Going One-on-One: Where Most Ethical Dilemmas and Solutions Occur." *Communication World,* August 1993, pp. 17–19.

McElreath, Mark P. "Dealing with Ethical Dilemmas." *Communication World,* March 1993, pp. 11–15.

McElreath, Mark P. "Who Cares if You Violate the IABC Code of Ethics?" *Communication World,* April 1993, pp. 10–14.

Pratt, Cornelius B. "Critique of the Classical Theory of Situational Ethics in U.S. Public Relations." *Public Relations Review,* Fall 1993, pp. 219–234.

Pratt, Cornelius B. "PRSA Members' Perceptions of Public Relations Ethics." *Public Relations Review,* Summer 1991, pp. 145–159.

Seligman, Mac. "Travel Writers' Expenses: Who Should Pay?" *Public Relations Journal,* May 1990, pp. 27–28, 34.

Shamir, Jacob, Reed, Barbara Strauss, and Connell, Steven. "Individual Differences in Ethical Values of Public Relations Practitioners." *Journalism Quarterly,* Winter 1990, pp. 956–963.

Spicer, Christopher H. "Images of Public Relations in Print Media." *Journal of Public Relations Research,* vol. 5, no. 1, 1993, pp. 47–61.

Truitt, Richard, and Young, Davis. "What's Right?" *Public Relations Journal,* July 1991, pp. 27–28. Several case problems in ethics.

Templin, Neal. "Car Magazines Signal End to Auto Maker's Freebies." *Wall Street Journal,* February 5, 1991, p. B1. The ethics of reporters accepting gifts and consulting fees from auto manufacturers.

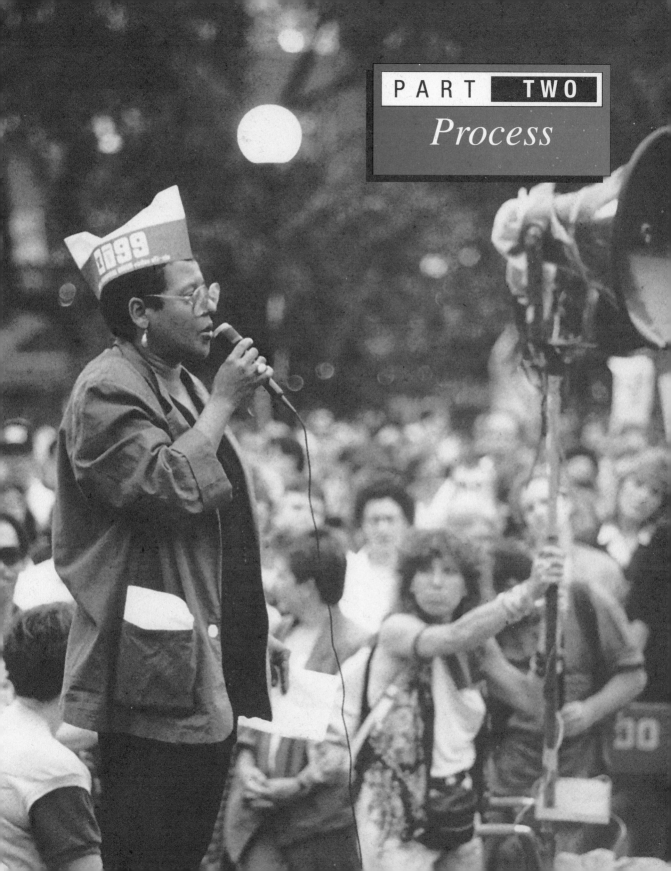

Research

PREVIEW   The objective of this chapter is to demonstrate the necessity for research as a basic element in public relations programs, and to give students an understanding of techniques and applications in informal and formal research.

Topics covered in the chapter include:

- The importance of research

- Informal research methods

- Use of databases

- Formal research: random sampling

- Questionnaire design

- Ways of reaching respondents

Effective public relations is a process, and the essential first step is research. Today, research is widely accepted by most public relations professionals as a necessary and integral part of the planning, program development, and evaluation process.

In basic terms, research is a form of listening. Professors Glen Broom and David Dozier of San Diego State University, in their book *Using Research in Public Relations,* say simply, "Research is the controlled, objective, and systematic gathering of information for the purpose of describing and understanding."

Before any public relations program can be undertaken, information must be gathered, data collected, and interpretation done. Only by performing this first step can an organization begin to map out policy decisions and strategies for effective communication programs.

Broom and Dozier quote a number of public relations executives on the importance of research. Among them is Blair C. Jackson, senior vice president of Rogers & Cowan, Inc., in New York:

The most compelling reason for using research is to make sure that your program is the best it can be—that what you are doing is as "right on" as it can be. You will be confident that you are addressing the right audiences, that you are using the right messages, and that you are focusing on the right perceptions or attitudes. Evaluation research will tell you whether or not it works.

E. William Brody and Gerald Stone, in their book *Public Relations Research,* are more blunt. They simply say, "Those whose practices do not include research are doomed to the fate of dinosaurs because they are operating in an aggressive, rapidly changing environment with yesterday's tools."

WHY RESEARCH IS NECESSARY

Research is necessary in today's complex society for at least six reasons. One is the increasing fragmentation of audiences into groups that have specific interests and concerns. One research firm, for example, has classified 240,000 neighborhoods in the United States into 40 different lifestyle groups. To communicate effectively, it is necessary to have a detailed knowledge of audiences. A practitioner who understands these audiences—their attitudes, hopes, fears, concerns, frustrations—will be better able to formulate messages that appeal specifically to them. In addition, self-interest is a strong motivating force. If communication can be tailored to the self-interest of audiences, there is a much greater chance of reaching them.

A second reason is the increasing isolation of top management from personal contact with the public. Top management and those in specialized professions tend to associate only with each other. Rarely does an executive, for example, get a chance to exchange views with an assembly-line worker or talk with customers in a department store. Systematic and periodic research about employees and customers can help bridge this gap and give executives vital feedback.

Third, research can prevent organizations from wasting time, effort, and money in attacking perceived image problems that are not readily solved by extensive public relations programs.

Much money and energy also are spent on public relations activities that do not interest the public. More than a few organizations, for example, continue to flood the media with information about routine staff promotions. A systematic monitoring of whether such information is used would, no doubt, eliminate much of this material.

Fourth, research can provide the facts on which a public relations program is based. A good example is an extensive communications audit that Ketchum Public Relations did for a U.S. pharmaceutical company about the information needs of selected medical practitioners in six countries.

Data were collected in three ways. One method was to hold four focus group sessions with medical personnel in three nations. The second was to conduct in-depth interviews with a small group of "elite" physicians, including specialists at medical schools. Third, telephone interviews were conducted with a larger group of physicians representing various medical special ties. On the basis of this research, Ketchum was able to recommend a detailed marketing communications plan for the client.

Fifth, surveys can generate publicity through dissemination of results. Indeed, many research surveys are designed to attract media coverage by providing entertaining pieces of information.

Simplesse, maker of Simple Pleasures frozen dessert, did a survey showing that 44 percent of the people who eat a large amount of ice cream are more likely to take a tub bath. And Kiwi Brands, a shoe polish company, obtained extensive media coverage about a survey it commissioned that showed a high correlation between ambition and shiny shoes. The study found that 97 percent of self-described "ambitious" young men believe polished shoes are important.

A sixth reason for doing research is to establish a baseline for determining the success of a program. This is particularly relevant in a public awareness campaign.

The American Iron and Steel Institute, wanted to raise public awareness about the steel industry's recycling efforts and the fact that steel cans are 100 percent recyclable. Pre-program research through focus groups, telephone interviews, and mail questionnaires determined the consumer awareness level. This information then became the benchmark to measure public awareness after a public information program.

Post-program research in three of six markets showed major increases in public awareness of steel recycling. In Sacramento, for example, public awareness rose from 40 percent to 63 percent. Benchmark studies are discussed in Chapter 10.

WHAT RESEARCH CAN ACCOMPLISH

Research, or fact-gathering, can accomplish a number of objectives:

1. Help probe basic attitudes of groups so that pertinent messages can be structured.

2. Measure true opinions of various groups. A vocal minority may not represent the group's genuine feelings or beliefs.

3. Identify opinion leaders who can influence target publics.

4. Reduce costs by concentrating on valid objectives and key audiences.

5. Help pretest messages and proposed communication channels on a pilot basis before implementing an entire program.

6. Help determine the timing of a public relations program to take advantage of current public interests and concerns.

7. Achieve two-way communication. Feedback from audiences can fine-tune messages and generate mutual understanding.

8. Reveal trouble spots and public concerns before they become page-one news. Problems seldom just happen; they often begin as minor nuisances and then develop into full-scale explosions.

9. Achieve credibility with top management. Executives want facts, not guesses and hunches. The participation of public relations personnel in management decision making is strongly correlated with the ability to do research and relate findings to the organization's objectives.

Various kinds of research can be used to accomplish an organization's objectives and need for information. It really depends on the subject and the situation. Time and budget are important considerations, as well as the perceived importance of the situation. Consequently, many questions should be asked before formulating a research design, such as:

1. What is the problem? *task ~ what do you need to know?*

2. What kind of information is needed? *~*

3. How will the results of the research be used?

4. What specific public (or publics) should be researched?

5. Should the organization do the research or hire an outside consultant?

6. How will the research data be analyzed, reported, and applied?

7. How soon are the results needed?

8. How much will it cost?

These questions will help the public relations person determine the extent and nature of the research needed. Only informal research may be required; a number of approaches are given in the following pages. Scientific survey sampling is explained later in this chapter.

INFORMAL RESEARCH METHODS

Research does not consist necessarily of formal methods such as scientific surveys and statistical tabulations. In fact, Walter K. Lindenmann, senior vice president and director of research for Ketchum Public Relations, New York, found in a survey that almost three-fourths of the respondents described public relations research as casual and informal, rather than scientific and precise.

Gael Walker, a lecturer in public relations at the University of Technology in Sydney, found similar results when she surveyed 980 Australian public relations executives. The following describes briefly the most common informal research techniques.

Surveys of public opinion, often taken by researchers on the street or in shopping malls, help public relations practitioners define target audiences they wish to reach and to shape their messages.

ORGANIZATIONAL MATERIALS

Robert Kendall, in his book *Public Relations Campaign Strategies,* calls this *archival research.* Essentially, it means that all pertinent data "on record" should be collected. The material may include the organization's policy statements, business records, marketing studies, annual financial reports, speeches by key executives, reports on past public relations efforts, pamphlets, newsletters, news releases, and press clippings.

The purpose of gathering such materials is to achieve a better understanding of the organization. Kendall says, "Archives thus provide a repository of basic detailed facts about the organization that are more precise than people's memory; archives provide the resources for background research, which is the essential first step in most other research techniques." Archival research also is a major component in most audits whose objective is to determine how the organization communicates to its internal and external publics.

LIBRARY RESEARCH

Reference books, other scholarly publications, and books and journals about particular subjects should be consulted. Old Stone Bank of Providence, Rhode Island, and its public relations counsel, for example, did research in the Library of Congress to develop a community relations program that promoted literacy and reading by children.

Government documents offer a variety of demographic information about various kinds of publics. One popular source is the *Statistical Abstract of the United States,* compiled from census data. Another source is the U.S. Commerce Department, which does studies analyzing consumer buying habits and trends in various industries. One survey on consumer book-buying, for example, reported that Austin, Texas, leads the nation in book purchases ($196 per household).

Valuable information can also be found in various national polls and trend newsletters. The *Gallup Poll* and the *Gallup Report* give an index of public opinion on a variety of issues; this information often helps organizations understand better the opinions of the public without having to do original research. Corporations have duly noted national polls showing widespread public concern for the quality of the environment. An example of a trend newsletter is the *Yankelovich Monitor,* which measures how Americans spend their leisure time.

Finding material in a library is getting much easier, thanks to CD-ROM technology. Two such indexes are *ABI/INFORM,* which indexes more than 300 business journals, and *INFOTRAC,* which indexes 960 periodicals, journals, and major newspapers. By typing key words into a computer terminal, a researcher can quickly locate pertinent information.

ON-LINE DATABASES

Although the library offers numerous sources of information, the information revolution has made it possible for working professionals to do much of this research in their office through on-line databases.

Literature searches, which are the most often used form of informal research in public relations, can be done by using a computer and a modem to extract information from an estimated 1500 electronic databases that store an enormous amount of current and historical information.

In fact, a survey of IABC members disclosed that more than three-fourths of the respondents regularly used a modem in their work. Another survey, by PRSA/Mead Data Central, found that public relations offices spent at least $1000 annually on electronic information services. Use of on-line databases also saves time. NEXIS, in sales literature about its on-line system, says an average search takes only 38 minutes compared to 105 minutes needed through manual methods.

Public relations departments and firms use on-line databases in several ways:

■ Researching facts and figures to support a proposed project or campaign that requires top management approval.

■ Keeping up-to-date with news about clients and their competitors.

■ Tracking the media campaigns of an organization and the press announcements of its competitors.

■ Finding a special quotation or impressive statistic for a speech or report.

■ Tracking the press and business reaction to an organization's latest actions.

■ Finding an expert for advice on an issue or a possible strategy.

■ Keeping top management apprised of current business trends and issues.

■ Learning the demographics and attitudes of target publics.

On-line databases are available on a subscription basis and usually charge by the minute in the same way that a telephone company charges for long-distance calls.

According to BiblioData, publisher of an annual directory titled *Fulltext Sources On-line,* almost 4000 periodicals, newspapers, newswires and TV/radio transcripts are available. Here are some of the databases commonly used in public relations:

Burrelle's Broadcast Database   This contains the full-text transcripts of radio and television programs within 24 hours after they are transmitted. Sources include ABC, CBS, NBC, National Public Radio, and selected syndicated programs.

GEMS FROM DATABASE RESEARCH

Databases contain masses of information available to assist public relations practitioners on difficult assignments who need answers to obscure questions. Specialists trained in database research usually can find the answers, often in a surprisingly short time.

    Writing in *Communication World,* Hank Bachrach gave this sampling of questions database researchers have been requested to answer:

- What is the state-by-state tally of sheep slaughtered in the past year?

- How much underwear is produced in Malaysia?

- What is the heartbeat of an elephant? of a mouse?

- How many bottle caps are produced in the United States?

- What are the thermodynamic properties of potassium?

- How is a wife in a harem defined for tax purposes?

Drawing by Curt Hopkins in *Communication World.* (Reprinted courtesy of *Communication World.*)

CompuServe Considered the nation's largest vendor of computer services, it has a subscriber base of more than 200,000 and offers a number of specialized electronic bulletin boards, including those for advertising, marketing, and public relations.

Datatimes Contains more than 1400 local, regional, national, and international sources, including newspapers, industry journals, magazines, news services, business newsletters, news releases, and broadcast transcripts.

Dialog This service, now combined with Vu/Text Information Services, provides access to full text and abstracts of articles from a variety of sources. Its 400 databases, updated daily, cover all areas of business, current affairs, science, technology, medicine, and social sciences.

Dow Jones News/Retrieval A source of business information, it provides the full text of the *Wall Street Journal,* access to 185 other business and financial publications, profiles of 5000 companies, and Dun & Bradstreet reports on company credit ratings.

Nexis This includes 8 million full-text articles from more than 125 magazines, newspapers, newsletters, and news services. Contains full text from the New York *Times* and Washington *Post,* abstracts from leading international publications. There also is an advertising and marketing intelligence database.

The Source Similar to CompuServe, it provides news, games, numerous types of information, and electronic mail.

DATABASE RESEARCH DEPENDS ON KEY WORDS

On-line database research is based on providing key words for which the computer program searches in thousands of articles.

The Delahaye Group, a news coverage analysis firm, had some fun with key words during the 1992 presidential election. It used the NEXIS/LEXIS on-line database to find the number of times "Bill Clinton" and "George Bush" appeared in news stories within ten words of another designated keyword. Here is a partial summary of the results:

Key word	Bill Clinton	George Bush
Saxophone	462	17
Taxes	3635	768
Change	3611	898
Sex	115	24
Madonna	42	12
Love	401	130
Education	1247	242
Environment	609	230

June 1990

ALPHA LIST

of sources available in NEXIS®

and related services

Ad Day
Advanced Manufacturing Technology
Advantage*
Advertising Age®
ADWEEK
Aerospace America
Aerospace Daily®
AI Expert*
Air Force Magazine
Air Transport World*
Airports®
Alaska Business Monthly*
Alaska Journal of Commerce*
ALERT[1]
   —Archive
   —Update
Almanac of American Politics, The
American Banker
American Family Physician
American Federationist*
American Hospital Formulary Service
Drug Information 1987, The

Arthritis & Rheumatism
Asahi News Service
Asia Pacific Business*
Asian Wall Street Journal Weekly**
Associated Banks of Europe
   Corporation
Associated Press, The (AP)
   —Campaign News
   —Candidate Biographies
   —News
Atlanta Business Chronicle*
Atlantic, The*
Austin Business Journal*
Automation*
Automotive Engineering*
Automotive Industries*
Automotive Marketing*
Automotive News®
AutoWeek®
Aviation Daily®
Aviation Week & Space Technology

Boston Globe, The
Boulder County Business Report*
British Journal of Surgery
Broadcasting*
Bulletin on the Rheumatic Diseases
Business & Commercial Aviation*
Business America*
Business Asia***
Business Atlanta*
Business China***
Business Digest of Southeastern
   Massachusetts*
Business Digest of the Cape &
   Islands*
Business Eastern Europe***
Business Europe***
Business First-Buffalo*
Business First-Columbus*
Business First-Louisville*
Business for Central New Jersey*
Business Insurance®

San Fransisco Business Times*
San Fransisco Chronicle, The
Sarasota Magazine*
Saskatchewan Business*
Saturday Evening Post*
Scientific American*
Screen Finance
Seattle Business*
Seattle Times, The
Securities Regulation & Law Report
Securities Week
Seminars in Arthritis & Rheumatism
Seminars in Hematology

Technology Review*
Telecommunications*
Telephony*
Texas Secretary of State Corporate
   Information
Texas Secretary of State Sales and
   Use Tax
Texas Secretary of State Uniform
   Commercial Code
Time
Times and The Sunday Times, The
Toledo Business Journal*
Transportation & Distribution*

Wall Street Journal**
Ward's Auto World*
Washington Business Journal*
Washington Monthly*
Washington Post, The
Washington Post Biographical Stories,
   The
Washington Quarterly, The
Washington Times, The
Weekly of Business Aviation™ The
Westchester County Business Journal,
   The*
Which Computer?*

FIGURE 7.2
This small sample indicates the extent and variety of database
sources available to users of Nexis © and related services.

Government Databases A number of government databases are available, either directly from the federal government or through commercial databases that package the information for resale to subscribers. Data from the U.S. Census Bureau, particularly valuable for demographic and economic information, can be purchased on computer tapes and diskettes.

A California charity, for example, employed census facts to determine areas of the state with households earning more than $20,000 and thus more likely to make contributions. And the public relations department of a large corporation used census data to determine the size of the Spanish-speaking audience in major cities in which the company had plant sites.

The Environmental Protection Agency operates an on-line issues information file, open to the public. The file contains material on the background, current status, impact, and implications of key environmental issues. A public relations person assigned to write a speech for a client on an environmental issue can quickly tap up-to-date information.

The government, primarily the National Science Foundation, also supplies large amounts of information on Internet, essentially a giant information network that links millions of computers around the world.

Internet, however, isn't really owned by anyone or even operated by any one entity. There isn't even a complete, unified list of all the databases available. Consequently, the most common use of Internet so far has consisted of electronic mail among scientists, academics, and government employees.

CONTENT ANALYSIS

This research method can be relatively informal or quite scientific in terms of random sampling and establishing specific subject categories. It is often applied to news stories about an organization. At a basic level, a researcher can assemble news clips in a scrapbook and count the number of column inches.

In general, Kendall says content analysis involves ". . . systematic analysis of any of several aspects of what a communication contains, from key words or concept references, such as company name or product; to topics, such as issues confronting the organization; to reading ease, of company publications; or to all elements of a company video production."

A good example of content analysis is the way a company evaluated press coverage of its publicity campaign to celebrate its 100th anniversary. According to Walter Lindenmann of Ketchum Public Relations: "A low-budget content of analysis was carried out on 427 newspaper, magazine, radio, and television placements referring both to the client and its product. The research found that the client's principal themes and copy points were referred to in most of the media coverage the company had received."

Another use of content analysis is to determine if a need exists for additional public relations efforts. Faneuil Hall Marketplace in Boston stepped up its public relations activities after it was found that the number of travel articles about it had decreased. An anniversary celebration of the Marketplace helped generate increased coverage.

Content analysis can be applied also to letters and phone calls. They provide good feedback about problems with the organization's policies and services. A pattern of letters and phone calls pointing out a problem is evidence that something should be done. Content analysis is discussed further in Chapter 10 on evaluation.

INTERVIEWING

As in content analysis, there are several levels of interviewing. Almost everyone, on a daily basis, talks to colleagues and calls other organizations to gather information.

Public relations personnel, faced with solving a particular problem, often "interview" other public relations professionals for ideas and suggestions.

If research is needed on public opinion and attitudes, many public relations firms conduct short interviews with people in a shopping mall or at a meeting. This kind of research is called *intercept* interviews, because people literally are intercepted in public places and asked their opinion.

The intercept interview is not scientific in terms of sampling method, but it does give an organization a sense of current thinking or exposure to certain key messages. A health group wanted to find out if the public was actually receiving its message and retaining crucial aspects of the message. To gather such information, shopping center or "mall" intercept interviews were conducted with 300 adults at six malls. Both unaided and aided-recall questions were asked to assess overall publicity impact.

In another example, intercept interviews helped a fast-food restaurant chain determine customer attitudes about a city law regarding the recycling of the packaging in retail food establishments. Interviewers intercepted patrons at ten different fast-food restaurants and got useful information about consumer perceptions and behavior patterns relating to the issue.

Intercept interviews last only two to five minutes. At other times, the best approach is to do in-depth interviews to get more comprehensive information. Major fund-raising projects by charitable groups, for example, often require in-depth interviewing of community and business opinion leaders. The success of any major fund drive seeking $500,000 or more is the support of key leaders and wealthy individuals.

Interviews with influential people in a community are needed to obtain their reactions to the proposed drive and, more important, to secure their financial support. In such a situation, interviewing the average homemaker or person in the street will not generate the type of information or financial support needed to determine the feasibility of the project.

This approach is called *purposive interviewing* because the interviewees are carefully selected for their expertise, influence, or leadership. The Greater Durham, North Carolina, Chamber of Commerce interviewed 50 "movers and shakers" in the community to determine support for an extensive image-building and economic development program.

FOCUS GROUPS

A good alternative to individual interviewing is the focus group. The technique is widely used in advertising, marketing, and public relations to help identify attitudes and motivations of important publics. Another purpose of focus groups is to formulate or pretest message themes and communications strategies before launching a full campaign.

The Paging Services Council used six focus groups in three major cities to plan a public relations campaign that would help consumers understand that "beepers" were more than little, black boxes worn only by doctors and drug dealers. The focus groups helped the council and its public relations firm (1) define target audiences, (2) test program messages, (3) explore consumer attitudes about paging, and (4) evaluate product positioning statements. In another situation, the U.S. Office of Disease Prevention and Health Promotion conducted 12 focus groups with senior citizens to determine how receptive they were to health-related information, and to ascertain the kinds of information that people wanted.

Focus groups usually consist of 8 to 12 people representing the characteristics of the target audience, such as employees, consumers, or community residents. The Paging Services Council used baby boomers and users of pagers.

A trained facilitator uses nondirective interviewing techniques that encourage group members to talk freely about a topic or give candid reactions to suggested message themes. The setting is usually a conference room and the discussion is informal. A focus group may last one or two hours, depending on interaction and subject matter.

A focus group, by definition, is an informal research procedure that develops qualitative information instead of hard data. Results cannot be summarized by percentages or even projected onto an entire population. Nevertheless, focus groups are useful in

---

INFORMAL VS. FORMAL RESEARCH

Informal methods of finding and compiling information are often called *qualitative* research, while more formal, scientific methods are called *quantitative* research. Here is a summary of the differences between the two approaches:

Informal (Qualitative)	**Formal (Quantitative)**
"Soft" data	"Hard" data
Usually open-ended free response, unstructured	Usually closed-ended, forced choice, highly structured
"Exploratory," probing, fishing expedition type of research	"Descriptive" or "explanatory" type of research
Usually "valid," but not reliable	Usually "valid" and reliable
Rarely "projectable" to larger audiences	Usually very "projectable" to larger audiences
Generally uses nonrandom samples	Generally uses random samples
Examples	**Examples**
Focus groups	Telephone polls
One-on-one, depth interviews	Mail surveys
Observation, participation, role-playing studies	Mall intercept studies
Convenience polling	Face-to-face interview studies
	Shared cost or omnibus studies
	Panel studies

Source: Walter K. Lindenmann, *A Guide to Public Relations Research,* Copyright 1993 Ketchum Public Relations.

identifying the range of attitudes and opinions in the participants. Such insights can help an organization structure its messages or, on another level, formulate hypotheses and questions in a quantitative research survey.

COPY-TESTING

All too often, organizations fail to communicate effectively because they produce and distribute materials that the target audience can't understand. In many cases, the material is written above the educational level of the audience.

Consequently, representatives of the target audience should be asked to read or view the material in draft form before it is mass-produced and distributed. This can be done on a one-to-one basis or in a small group setting.

A brochure about employee medical benefits or pension plans, for example, should be pretested with rank-and-file employees for readability and comprehension. Executives and lawyers who must approve the copy may understand the material, but a worker with a high school education might find it difficult to follow.

Another approach is to determine the degree of difficulty by applying a readability formula to the draft copy. Fog, Flesch, and similar techniques have formulas that relate the number of words and syllables per sentence or passage to reading level. Highly complex sentences and multisyllable words require an audience with a college education.

FORMAL RESEARCH: RANDOM SAMPLING

The informal approaches to research just mentioned can provide good insight to public relations staff members and help them formulate effective programs. Practitioners must be sure, however, that the feedback is representative, so that decisions are made on the basis of information typical of general trends or majority views.

The numbers and types of people interviewed are critical factors. If not enough people are questioned, or they don't represent target publics, the results of the survey may be distorted. When public relations people want more dependable, precise responses, they often use a more quantitative approach that includes scientific sampling methods. Such sampling is based on two important factors, randomness and the use of large numbers of interviewees.

RANDOM-SAMPLING PROCEDURES

For best results, a *random* sample is taken. In statistics, this means that everyone in the targeted audience (as defined by the researcher) has an equal chance of being selected for the survey. This is also called a *probability* sample.

In contrast, a *nonprobability* survey is not random at all. Mall-intercept interviews, for example, are usually restricted only to shoppers in the mall at the time interviewers are working. A number of factors affect exactly who is interviewed, including the time of day and the location of the intercept interviews. Researchers doing interviews in the morning may have a disproportionate number of homemakers while interviews after 5 P.M. may include more high school students and office workers. Also, if the researcher stands outside a record store or athletic shoe outlet, the age of those interviewed may be much younger than that of the general population.

A random sampling could be accomplished much better if researchers were present at all hours and conducted interviews throughout the mall. This would ensure a more representative sampling of mall shoppers, particularly if large numbers were interviewed.

Researchers must be careful, however, about projecting results to represent an entire city's population. Market surveys show that the demographic characteristics of shoppers vary from mall to mall. In other words, the selection of malls for random intercept interviewing often depends on how the researcher defines the target audience.

A survey sponsored by American Express and the French government shows how selection of a sample can distort the results. The survey found that the stereotype about the French being unfriendly was untrue. However, the sample consisted of 1000 Americans who had visited France more than once over the past two years. This select group would seem to be already favorably disposed to France because they have made return visits. Perhaps the survey results would be different if a random sample of first-time U.S. visitors to France were used.

The most precise random sampling is usually done from lists that give the name of everyone in the targeted audience. This is relatively simple when doing a random survey of an organization's employees or members because the researcher can randomly select, for example, every 25th name on a list.

Another common method to ensure representation is to draw a random sample that matches the characteristics of the audience. This is called *quota sampling*. Human resource departments usually have breakdowns of employees by job classification, and it is relatively easy to proportion a sample accordingly. If 42 percent of the employees work on the assembly line, for instance, then 42 percent of the sample should be assembly-line workers. A quota sample can be drawn on any number of demographic factors—age, sex, religion, race, income—depending on the purpose of the survey.

Random sampling becomes more difficult when there are no comprehensive lists. In that case, researchers surveying the general population often use telephone directories or customer lists to select respondents at random.

A travel company used a nationwide telephone survey of 1000 adult Americans to determine if the hurricane that devastated the island of Kauai affected vacation plans to visit the other Hawaiian islands not struck by the hurricane. On the basis of the results, the travel company restructured its advertising and public relations messages to emphasize that resorts on the other islands were open for business as usual.

THE SIZE OF THE SAMPLE

In any probability study, there is always the question of sample size. National polling firms usually sample 1200 to 2000 persons and get a highly accurate idea of what the U.S. adult population is thinking. The average national poll samples 1500 people, and the margin of error is within three percentage points 95 percent of the time. In other words, 19 out of 20 times that the same questionnaire is administered, the results should be within the same three percentage points and reflect the whole population accurately.

The three-percentage-point variance in poll results is important in predicting the outcome of an election. If 48 percent of the voters say they will support Candidate A and 52 percent endorse Candidate B, the election is too close to call. What the three-point variance means is that Candidate A may actually receive 45 to 51 percent of the vote. Candidate B, on the other hand, may gather 49 to 55 percent of the vote. This means that, given the statistical accuracy of polls, either candidate could win.

In public relations the primary purpose of poll data is to get indications of attitudes and opinions, not to predict elections. Therefore, it is not usually necessary or practical to do a scientific sampling of 1500 people. A sample of 250 to 500 will give relatively accurate data—with a 5 or 6 percent variance—that will help determine general public attitudes and opinions. A sample of about 100 people, accurately drawn according to probability guidelines, will include about a 10 percent margin of error.

This percentage of error would be acceptable if a public relations person, for example, asked employees what they want to read in the company magazine. Sixty percent may indicate that they would like to see more news about opportunities for promotion. If only 100 employees were properly surveyed, it really doesn't matter if the actual percentage is 50 or 70 percent. The large percentage, in either case, would be sufficient to justify an increase in news stories about advancement opportunities.

This is also true in ascertaining community attitudes. If a survey of 100 or fewer citizens indicates that only 25 percent believe the organization is a good community citizen, it really doesn't matter whether the result is 15 or 40 percent. The main point is that the organization must take immediate steps to improve its image.

QUESTIONNAIRE DESIGN

Although correct sampling is important in gaining accurate results, pollsters generally acknowledge that sampling error may be far less important than the errors that result from poor question selection.

BIAS IN QUESTIONS

The wording of questions on a questionnaire is a time-consuming process; every attempt should be made to ensure that a question does not bias the respondent's answer. There is a difference between one question, "Is it a good idea to limit handguns?" and another, "Do you think registration of handguns will curtail crime?" On first glance, they seem to be asking the same thing. On closer examination, however, one can realize that a respondent could easily answer "yes" to the first question and "no" to the second.

The first question asks if the limiting of handguns is a good idea. The second asks if people think it will curtail crime. A third question that might elicit a different response would be, "Do you think laws curtailing the use of handguns would work?" Thus, the questions emphasize three different aspects of the problem. The first stresses the value of an idea, the second explores a possible effect, and the third examines the practicality of a proposed solution. Research shows that people often think something is a good idea, but do not think it would work. Another related problem is how respondents might interpret the words *limit* and *curtail*. To some, they may refer to a total ban on handguns, while others may think the words suggest that all guns should be kept away from people with criminal records.

Questionnaires also should avoid leading questions that set up a behavioral context. An example of a leading question was one asked by the disposable-diaper industry: "It is estimated that disposable diapers account for less than 2 percent of the trash in today's landfills. In contrast, beverage containers, third-class mail, and yard wastes are estimated to account for about 21 percent of the trash in landfills. Given this, in your opinion, would it be fair to ban disposable diapers?" Not surprisingly, 84 percent of the respondents said "no."

A loaded question uses highly charged words to elicit a certain response. Such words are italicized in this example from U.S. English, Inc., a group advocating English as the official language of the United States. It asked: "Do you think American taxpayers should be *forced* to pay for special voter registration drives for those who *insist* on or want to vote in a language other than English?"

Industry surveys often use leading words to elicit a certain response. One survey of newspaper editors asked: "By which method listed below do you prefer to receive *critical* information?" Not surprisingly, fax was the number one choice. However, perhaps the survey results would be different if the question simply asked, "By what method do you prefer to receive information?"

COURTESY BIAS

Some survey questionnaires do not generate accurate answers because respondents do not want to offend the researcher or give an answer that doesn't represent perceived popular opinion. They choose the "correct" answer instead of the one that accurately reflects their feelings. Surveys, for example, show that 80 percent of Americans are environmentalists. However, as skeptics point out, would anyone admit to a researcher that he or she was not concerned about the environment?

Surveys of public relations practitioners about the value of research also show a degree of "courtesy bias" in choosing the correct answer. Almost 90 percent agreed that research is a necessary and integral part of public relations work. However, almost the same percentage agrees that, in actual fact, research is still talked about much more than it is actually done.

Those conducting employee surveys also fall into the "courtesy" trap by posing such questions as "How much of each newsletter do you read?" or "How well do you like the column by the president?" Employees may never read the newsletter or may think the president's column is ridiculous, but they know the "correct" answer should be that they read the "entire issue" and that the column is "excellent."

Less of this *courtesy bias* is obtained if the respondents are reasonably assured that their answers are confidential, that there is a mechanism for questionnaires to be filled out in such a way that no one (including the surveyor) will know who completed which questionnaire. Because employees usually consider the public relations department a part of management, many companies seeking candid feedback from employees hire an outside research firm to interview employees or process questionnaires. In any case, a survey of employee attitudes should guarantee anonymity to the respondent.

Answer categories can skew a questionnaire. It is important that answer choices are provided to cover a range of opinions. A national polling organization several years ago asked the question "How much confidence do you have in business corporations?" but provided only the following answer categories: (*a*) a great deal, (*b*) only some, and (*c*) none at all. A large gap exists between "a great deal" and the next category, "only some." Such categories invariably skew the results to show very little confidence in business. A better list of answers might have been (*a*) a great deal, (*b*) quite a lot, (*c*) some, (*d*) very little, and (*e*) none. Perhaps an even better approach would be to provide the answer categories (*a*) above average, (*b*) average, and (*c*) below average. The psychological distance between the three choices is equal, and there is less room for respondent interpretation of what "quite a lot" means.

In general, "yes-or-no" questions are not very good for examining respondents' perceptions and attitudes. A "yes" or "no" answer provides little feedback on the strength or weakness of a respondent's opinion. A question such as "Do you agree with the company's policy of requiring drug testing for all new employees?" can be answered by "yes" or "no," but more useful information would be obtained by setting up a Likert-type scale—(*a*) Strongly agree, (*b*) Agree, (*c*) Undecided, (*d*) Disagree, (*e*) Strongly disagree. These types of answers enable the surveyor to probe the depth of feeling among respondents, and may serve as guidelines for management in making major changes or just fine-tuning the existing policy.

Another way of designing a numerical scale in order to pinpoint a respondent's beliefs or attitudes is to use, for example, a 5-point scale. Such a scale might look like this:

Question: How would you evaluate the company's efforts to keep you informed about job benefits? Please circle one of the following numbers ("1" being a low rating and "5" being a high rating).

Answer: 1   2   3   4   5

The advantage of numerical scales is that medians and means can be easily calculated. In the example above, the average from all respondents might be 4.25, which indicates that employees think the company does keep them informed about job benefits but that there is still room for communication improvement.

Another way to get at perceptions is to use the *semantic differential technique.* Essentially, this is a list of bipolar words; the respondent places a mark along a continuum. A semantic scale might look like this:

Question: How would you evaluate the company magazine on the following criteria?

Unbiased	____	____	____	____	____	Biased
Trustworthy	____	____	____	____	____	Untrustworthy
Valuable	____	____	____	____	____	Worthless
Fair	____	____	____	____	____	Unfair
Interesting	____	____	____	____	____	Uninteresting

QUESTIONNAIRE GUIDELINES

Here are some general guidelines for the construction of questionnaires:

1. Decide what kinds of information are needed and in what detail.

2. State the objectives of the survey in writing.

3. Decide which group will receive the questionnaire.

4. Decide on the size of the sample.

5. State the purpose of the survey and guarantee anonymity.

6. Use closed-end (multiple-choice) answers as much as possible. Respondents find it easier and less time-consuming to check answers than compose them in an open-end (essay) questionnaire.

7. Design the questionnaire in such a way that answers can be easily coded for statistical analysis.

8. Strive to make the questionnaire no more than 25 questions. Long questionnaires "put off" people and reduce the number of responses.

9. Use categories when asking questions about education, age, and income. People are more willing to answer when a category or range is used. For example, what category best describes your age? (*a*) Under 25, (*b*) 26 to 40, etc.

10. Use simple, familiar words. Readability should be appropriate for the group being sampled. At the same time, don't "talk down" to respondents.

11. Avoid ambiguous words and phrases that may confuse the respondent.

12. Edit out leading questions that suggest a specific response or bias an answer.

13. Remember context and placement of questions. One question close to another can influence response to the later question.

14. Provide space at the end of the questionnaire for respondents' comments and observations. This allows them to provide additional information or elaboration that may not have been covered in the main body of the questionnaire.

15. Pretest the questions for understanding and possible bias. Representatives of the proposed sampling group should read the questionnaire and make comments for possible improvement.

WAYS OF REACHING RESPONDENTS

MAIL QUESTIONNAIRES

Questionnaires may be used in a variety of settings. They may be handed out at a manufacturing plant, at a county fair, or even in a bank lobby. Most survey questionnaires, however, are mailed to respondents. There are several reasons for this:

FULL INFORMATION, NOT HYPE, NEEDED FOR REPORTING SURVEY RESULTS

Disraeli, one of England's greatest prime ministers, once said, "There are three kinds of lies: lies, damn lies, and statistics." Indeed, in today's society, there is a proliferation of questionable research studies that are labeled "advocacy research" because the results are skewed by vested interests to promote a cause or product.

For example, Chrysler sponsored a study that showed Americans overwhelmingly preferred a Chrysler to a Toyota. And a Levi Strauss study found that 90 percent of college students think Levi 501 jeans are the most "in" clothing. However, a closer look at these studies shows some problems in sampling and even questionnaire design. Chrysler surveyed only 100 Americans in each of two tests, and none of them owned a foreign car. In the Levi study, its jeans were the only ones on the list.

Part of the problem is sloppy media reporting. It, however, is compounded by marketing departments, lobbyists, and public relations firms that publicize the results of surveys and fail to give full information about how the study was conducted.

The American Association for Public Opinion Research (AAPOR) has established professional and ethical guidelines for the conduct and reporting of research studies. The following is a selection of guidelines from the code concerning the reporting of research findings in news releases and other publicity materials:

1. Identify who sponsored the survey.

2. Give exact wording of the questions asked.

3. Define the population actually sampled.

4. Give size of sample. This should include the number of questionnaires mailed out and the number returned.

5. Tell what allowance should be made for sampling error.

6. Tell what results are based on parts of the sample, rather than the whole sample.

7. Indiciate whether interviewing was done personally, by telephone, or mail; at home or on street corners.

8. Give time of the interviews in relation to relevant events.

Source: Adapted from the code of professional ethics and practices, American Association for Public Opinion Research, Box 17, Princeton, NJ 08540.

1. Because the researchers have better control as to who receives the questionnaire, they can make sure the survey is representative.

2. Large geographical areas can be covered economically.

3. It is less expensive to administer them than to hire an interviewer to conduct personal interviews.

4. Large numbers of people can be included at minimal cost.

Mail questionnaires have some disadvantages. The biggest is a low response rate. A mail questionnaire by a commercial firm to the general public usually produces a response rate of 1 to 2 percent. If the survey concerns issues affecting the general public, the response rate might be 5 to 20 percent. A much better response rate would be generated, however, if the questionnaire were mailed by an organization to its members. In this case, the response rate may be 30 to 80 percent. The more closely people identify with the organization and the questions, the better the response.

The response rate to a mail questionnaire can be increased, say the experts, if all the guidelines of questionnaire construction are followed. In addition, a researcher should keep the following suggestions in mind:

1.   Include a stamped, self-addressed return envelope and a personally signed letter explaining the importance of participation.

2.   Provide an incentive. Commercial firms often encourage people to fill out questionnaires by including a token amount of money or a discount coupon. Other researchers promise to share the results of the survey with the respondent.

3.   Mail questionnaires by first-class mail. Some research shows that placing special issue stamps on the envelope attracts greater interest than simply using a postage meter.

4.   Mail a reminder postcard three or four days later.

5.   Do a second mailing (either to nonrespondents or to the entire sample) two or three weeks after the first mailing. Again, enclose a stamped, self-addressed return envelope and a cover letter explaining the crucial need for the recipient's participation.

TELEPHONE SURVEYS

Surveys by telephone, particularly if the survey is locally based, are extensively used by research firms. The telephone survey has several advantages:

1.   There is an immediate response or nonresponse. A researcher doesn't have to wait several weeks for responses to arrive by mail.

2.   A telephone call is personal. It is effective communication, and it is much cheaper than a personal interview.

3.   A phone call is less intrusive than going door-to-door and interviewing people. Surveys show that many people are willing to talk on the phone for up to 45 minutes but will not stand at a door for more than 5 or 10 minutes and are less willing to admit strangers to their homes.

4.   The response rate, if the survey is properly composed and phone interviewers trained, can reach 80 to 90 percent.

One major disadvantage of phone interviews is the difficulty in getting access to everyone's telephone number. In some cities, up to a third of households have unlisted telephone numbers. Although researchers can utilize a "reverse" telephone book that lists numbers according to street address, this method is not as effective as actually knowing who is being called. Another disadvantage is the negative connotation of a phone interview because so many salespeople have attempted to sell goods by posing as researchers.

PERSONAL INTERVIEWS

The personal interview is the most expensive form of research because it requires trained staff and travel. If travel within a city is involved, a trained interviewer often can interview only eight or ten people a day—and salaries and transportation costs make it expensive. There is also the need for considerable advance work in arranging interviews and appointments and, as previously pointed out, researchers encounter reluctance by residents to admit strangers to their homes.

Personal interviews, on the other hand, can be cost-effective and can generate a wealth of information if the setting is controlled. Many research firms conduct personal interviews at national conventions or trade shows, where there is a concentration of people with similar interests. An equipment company, for example, may hire a research firm to interview potential customers at a national trade show.

THE PIGGYBACK SURVEY

An alternative method of reaching respondents is the piggyback method. This is also known as the omnibus approach, which Kendall defines as ". . . a survey in which two or more clients participate by buying space in the interview instrument or in segments of the questionnaire as administered in a single survey."

For example, an airline may place one or two questions in a national poll asking respondents about how they perceive the reputation of the airline for dependable service. In the same survey, a national health organization may have several questions on how the public feels about sporting events sponsored by tobacco companies.

The method is attractive to public relations people for two reasons. One is cost. The expense of a national piggyback poll is a fraction of the cost for an organization if it conducted its own survey. There are limitations, however. Kendall explains, ". . . the researcher is limited to a small number of questions and the population must be the same, usually the general public, for all those cooperating in the project."

A second reason is that the logistics and details of conducting formal research are handled by polling firms, such as Gallup or Harris, that have the expertise to do them properly. Many current public relations practitioners have not been trained in social science research methods, and they are not predisposed or competent to do systematic, formal research.

Indeed, a number of surveys have documented the hypothesis that the more sophisticated the research, the less compatible practitioners will find it. This explains the point made earlier that today's public relations personnel, for the most part, are likely to use informal research methods similar to journalistic newsgathering techniques. It is expected, however, that more sophisticated research methods will be used increasingly by tomorrow's professionals, who will have completed college courses in research and statistics.

CASE PROBLEM

Universal Manufacturing Coporation is located in a midwestern city of 500,000 people. Its 6000 employees make it one of the largest employers in the country, and the company has been in its present location for the past 50 years. Despite this record, management believes that the company doesn't have a strong identity and visibility in the community.

The director of public relations is asked to prepare a new public relations plan for the coming fiscal year. She recommends that the company first do research to determine exactly what its image is in the community.

If you were the public relations director, what informal methods of research would you use? What more formal research methods could be used? What kinds of information about the company's image should be researched?

QUESTIONS FOR REVIEW AND DISCUSSION

1. Name four reasons why research is necessary in today's complex society.

2. What kinds of objectives can be accomplished through public relations research?

3. How can survey research data be used as a publicity tool?

4. What questions should you ask before formulating a research study?

5. Name at least five informal research methods.

6. Do public relations practitioners use more informal research methods, or more formal, scientific methods to do research?

7. What are on-line databases and how are they used?

8. What is an intercept interview?

9. What is the procedure for organizing and conducting a focus group?

10. What is the difference between probability (random) and nonprobability samples?

11. What percentage margin of error is associated with various sample sizes? What size samples are usually adequate for public relations research?

12. Name at least five guidelines that should be followed when preparing a survey questionnaire.

13. What is a Likert-type scale? How is it different from semantic differential?

14. Compile a list of pros and cons of mail questionnaires, telephone surveys, personal interviews, and piggyback surveys.

15. Discuss the concept of "advocacy research." Do you think it is an acceptable practice in public relations? Why or why not?

Broom, Glen, and Dozier, David. *Using Public Relations Research.* Englewood Cliffs, NJ: Prentice Hall, 1990.

Brody, E. W., and Stone, Gerald. *Public Relations Research.* New York: Praeger, 1989.

Crossen, Cynthia. "Studies Galore Support Products and Positions, but Are They Reliable?" *Wall Street Journal,* November 14, 1991, p. 1A, 8A.

Dozier, David M., and Repper, Fred C. "Research Firms and Public Relations Practices," in *Excellence in Public Relations and Communication Management,* ed. James E. Grunig. Hillsdale, NJ: Lawrence Erlbaum Associates, 1992, pp. 185–215.

Grunig, Larissa A. "Using Focus Group Research in Public Relations." *Public Relations Review,* Summer 1990, pp. 36–49.

Kendall, Robert. *Public Relations Campaign Strategies.* New York: HarperCollins, 1992, pp. 33–131. Four chapters describe types of survey research.

Lindenmann, Walter. *A Guide to Public Relations Research.* Ketchum Public Relations, 1133 Avenue of the Americas, New York, NY 10036. A 70-page booklet available for $10. Copyright 1993.

Masterton, John. "Discovering Databases." *Public Relations Journal,* November 1992, pp. 12–19. On-line services and their capabilities.

Patton, Michael Quinn. *Qualitative Evaluation and Research Methods,* 2nd ed. Newbury Park, CA: Sage, 1990.

"A Revolution in Search of Revolutionaries." *Communication World,* March 1991, pp. 15–24. A roundtable discussion on the use of on-line databases.

Ryan, Michael, and Martinson, David L. "Social Science Research, Professionalism and Public Relations Practitioners." *Journalism Quarterly,* Summer 1990, pp. 377–390.

Shaffer, Jim. "The Maxi Communication Audit: A Precision Instrument for Change." *Communication World,* January–February 1993, pp. 20–23.

Simpson, Andrea L. "Ten Rules of Research: Meaningful, Cost-Effective Research for PR Programs." *Public Relations Quarterly,* Summer 1992, pp. 27–28.

Stempel, Guido, and Westley, Bruce. *Research Methods in Mass Communications.* Englewood Cliffs, NJ: Prentice Hall, 1989.

Stoltz, Eric, and Torobin, Jack. "Public Relations by the Numbers." *American Demographics,* January 1991, pp. 42–46. Research methods.

Planning the Action

P R E V I E W   This chapter describes how to organize and execute a well-planned public relations campaign, step-by-step, and how the procedure is applied specifically to the forward-looking technique called issues management.

Topics covered in the chapter include:

- Management by objective
- Define the problem
- Set objectives
- Define the audiences
- Execute the program
- Assess the results
- Issues management

The concept of *management by objectives (MBO)* increasingly is being applied to public relations planning. Once the situation has been researched (previous chapter), it is now necessary to plan a program of action. Norman R. Nager and T. Harrell Allen, in their book *Public Relations Management by Objectives* (Longman), discuss nine basic MBO steps, whether a practitioner is writing a single news release or putting together a multi-faceted communications program. The steps, adapted from their book, are as follows:

1. *Client/employer objectives.* What is the purpose of the communication, and how does it help promote or achieve the objectives of the organization? Specific objectives such as "to position the product as the leading one in the market" are more meaningful than "to make people aware of the product."

2. *Audience/publics.* Who exactly should be reached with the message, and how can that audience help achieve the organization's objectives? What are the characteristics of the audience, and how can demographic information be used to structure the message?

3. *Audience objectives.* What is it that the audience wants to know, and how can the message be tailored to audience self-interest?

4. *Media channels.* What is the appropriate channel for reaching the audience, and how can multiple channels (news media, brochures, special events, direct mail, etc.) reinforce the message among key publics?

5. *Media channel objectives.* What is the media gatekeeper looking for in a news angle, and why would a particular publication be interested in the information?

6. *Sources and questions.* What primary and secondary sources of information are required to provide a factual base for the message? What experts should be interviewed? What database searches should be conducted?

7. *Communication strategies.* What environmental factors will affect the dissemination and acceptance of the message? Are the target publics hostile or favorably disposed to the essence of the message? What other events or pieces of information negate or reinforce the message?

8. *Essence of message.* What is the planned communications impact on the audience? Is the message designed merely to inform, or is it designed to change attitudes and behavioral patterns? Are organizational expectations realistic?

9. *Nonverbal support.* How can photographs, graphs, films, artwork, and so forth clarify and add interest to the written message?

Nager and Allen make the case that MBO techniques can do much to help a public relations person work through a systematic process of determining exactly what must be done and why. MBO provides focus and direction for producing effective program plans and public relations materials. In the pages that follow, additional discussion is provided about defining the problem, setting objectives, selecting audiences, choosing communication strategies, establishing time lines, and assessing the results.

THE STEPS IN DETAIL

DEFINE THE PROBLEM

The initial step in formulating a public relations program is to determine the nature of the problem the practioner is called on to solve.

Recognition of public relations problems sometimes is more difficult than might be assumed. All too frequently a chief executive, deeply immersed in the immediate pressure of making the company return a satisfactory profit, is unaware that a public relations problem exists in the organization—a problem that in the long run may seriously threaten the very profitability for which the chief executive is striving. The same dulled awareness of trouble may exist in nonprofit and social service organizations.

Using sensitive antennae developed to detect the moods of both the public and employees, a public relations director and/or a counseling firm should recognize a problem as it develops. Then the specialist must demonstrate to top management that a problem is emerging that requires prompt attention. Unless this attention-calling function is carried out successfully, the necessary funds for attacking the problem will not be forthcoming from management.

If an unexpected crisis occurs, the problem is urgently and painfully evident to everyone. When seven persons in Chicago died after taking capsules of Tylenol laced with cyanide, top management at Johnson & Johnson, makers of the headache remedy, instantly recognized a public relations crisis. The question was not "Should we do something?" but "What can we do right now?" (A discussion of the Tylenol crisis appears in Chapter 9.)

When no dramatic event occurs to raise a danger flag, a public relations problem may be less readily recognized. The problem may be insidious, sneaking up over a long time or concealed beneath the surface of routine corporate or organizational life.

So numerous and so varied are the problems addressed by public relations practitioners that listing them all is impossible. They may be grouped, however, into three general categories. Each must be approached in a different way.

1. *Overcoming a negative perception of an organization or product.* Usually such perceptions develop slowly. A specific occurrence may jar management into recognizing the unfavorable trend and precipitate action. Here are a few examples of negative perceptions:

   a. Resistance by the public to company products on the basis of price, quality, or company behavior—for example, a word-of-mouth assertion that a local manufacturing company is damaging the environment by secretly dumping toxic waste material in nearby hills.

   b. Belief expressed by security analysts that a manufacturing company's production equipment has become outdated, making the firm lose ground competitively

   c. Evidence that employees believe their company lacks concern for their interests

   d. Complaints from patients about what they perceive as excessively high hospital bills

   e. A decline in membership of a professional association

2. *Conducting a specific one-time project.* On most public relations assignments in this category the practitioner starts from a neutral position. No obvious negative perceptions exist to be overcome. If they do exist, they will come to light later in the program. Conversely, latent support for the program probably exists but has not been developed. The specialist given such an assignment is in the same position as a baseball hitter stepping up to the plate: no balls or strikes have yet been called on the batter. To make a hit, the batter must study the pitcher's movements and "stuff"—that is, define the problem being faced. Here are typical problems in the one-time project category that a public relations specialist must define and attempt to solve:

a. Organize a citizens' campaign demanding that the city council adopt an ordinance banning smoking in public buildings and restaurants.
b. Introduce a new product.
c. Conduct a fund drive for a hospital expansion.
d. Enlist employee input and support for a major revision of company medical benefits.
e. Obtain shareholder approval for acquisition of another company.

3. *Developing or expanding a continuing program.* Much public relations work is of an ongoing nature—the necessity to create or maintain a favorable situation. Although lacking the urgency of a crisis or the clearly drawn needs of a one-time project, this work is vital. It also contains the inherent danger of slipping into stagnant routine and losing effectiveness. The practitioner should watch for fresh techniques, especially the rapidly expanding use of computer technology, and should review the entire program periodically to determine whether it needs redefining. The following are common examples of continuing program objectives:

a. Maintain community confidence that a company is a good corporate citizen with a sense of social responsibility.
b. Satisfy employees that the company is a good place to work. Retention of trained employees is a constant management problem.
c. Convince householders that their city's recycling program is achieving significant results and encourage them to increase their contributions to it.
d. Raise funds on an annual basis to keep human welfare programs like those of the American Red Cross or American Heart Association functioning.
e. Supply the media with a steady flow of newsworthy information about the employer and answer their requests promptly and openly.

To summarize, a public relations program usually is designed to correct a negative situation; achieve a well-defined, one-time objective; or maintain and improve an existing positive situation.

SET OBJECTIVES

To conduct successful campaigns, practitioners should ask, "Precisely what do we wish to accomplish?" The more specifically they answer that question, the better is the prospect for success and the greater the potential for measuring results. A vague goal such as, "To get publicity for our new product," is relatively meaningless. The objective might be better stated: "To make people aware of our new product and induce them to buy it." The significant target is the number of units sold, not the size of the press clipping file.

It is particularly important that public relations objectives complement and reinforce the organization's objectives. Professor David Dozier of San Diego State University expressed the point well in a *Public Relations Review* article, saying: "The prudent and strategic selection of public relations goals and objectives linked to organizational survival and growth serves to justify the public relations program as a viable management activity."

The Two Types of Objectives Objectives are of two types—*informational* and *motivational.*

An *informational objective* may be to tell people about an event, introduce a product, or seek to enhance the perception of a company. One difficulty with informational campaigns occurs in measuring how well the objective has been achieved, because public awareness is somewhat abstract and difficult to quantify.

GOALS, OBJECTIVES, AND STRATEGIES

Confusion sometimes arises concerning the actual meaning of these three words, widely used in public relations programming. A practical illustration can be found in the campaign to revive interest in the Six Flags Great Adventure theme park in New Jersey and promote its giant new roller coaster.

Goal Gain widespread media coverage of the park to increase slumping attendance by emphasizing fun and safety.

Objectives

■ Create a positive image of the park to overcome public worry about injuries suffered by park visitors.

■ Introduce the spectacular new roller coaster, "The Great American Scream Machine."

Strategies

■ Bozell PR, hired for $150,000 to conduct the campaign, held a fun/educational kickoff event in nearby Philadelphia to highlight safety improvements at the park. This included musicians, live safari animals, performers, and a video of the new coaster. Takeaway informational packets and souvenirs were distributed.

■ A comprehensive publicity kit and video were sent to the media.

■ A grand opening of the Great American Scream Machine was held.

The grand opening received coverage by network news programs, newspapers such as the New York *Times* and *USA Today,* and magazines including *Fortune* and *Money.* More than 100 stories ran in regional media.

Park attendance increased 20 percent. More than 1.3 million individuals rode on the Great American Scream Machine. The campaign won a PRSA Silver Anvil award.

Although difficult to accomplish, *motivational objectives* are easier to measure. They should be stated as succinctly as possible, such as, "Increase attendance at this year's concert by 25 percent," "Convince voters to approve the bond issue for the new municipal stadium," or "Improve the employees' understanding of the company's retirement program." (Evaluation of public relations campaigns is discussed in Chapter 10.)

If well planned and conducted, public relations projects can accomplish much, but they cannot achieve impractical goals. Objectives must be realistic. They should be placed high, so participants must stretch to reach them, but not at an impossible level. If a goal is unattainable, despite determined and ingenious efforts to achieve it, the failure may cause frustration and disenchantment among those who work on a campaign. This creates a negative attitude toward future projects. If a public fund-raising goal is impossibly high and the drive fails by a wide margin, the campaign force is embarrassed, and public support for the project may dwindle.

Budget Considerations   In setting objectives, practitioners must consider the amount of money available. Budget and achievement are not always directly related, of course. Under some circumstances a small budget judiciously spent may attain remarkable success. Nevertheless, large expenditures increase the prospect of success because they make possible the use of more extensive methods and staff. If the cost of a campaign exceeds the value of its objective, however, the effort cannot be called a success. When a charitable organization spends so much to conduct a fund drive that operating costs absorb an excessive portion of the donations, it is properly open to public criticism. (A discussion of fund raising appears in Chapter 18.) No matter how much money is spent and how much effort is made, a program cannot succeed if the product is poor or the objective unacceptable to the audience.

A management decision must be made, either to establish a large objective or a set of objectives and supply sufficient funds to permit success, or to allot a limited amount of money and set an objective attainable with such a sum. The public relations specialist should supply top management with well-informed opinions about what its money might achieve.

The Time Factor   Time is another factor to be considered in setting an objective. The amount of time to be spent on a campaign depends on its purpose and its nature. Some programs should be quick, hard-driving, and completed within a relatively brief, specified period. Other projects—for instance, publicity for an event such as an exhibition—have a built-in time limit; by the close of the show they have either succeeded or failed. When a project is designed to correct a negative perception or to develop public acceptance of a new concept, a long period of time may be required. *Negative attitudes change slowly.* There is no quick fix for an unfavorable public perception. Objectives for such projects should be determined with this in mind; one-, two-, and three-year goals may be appropriate. Interim measurements of progress can be made, but everyone involved in creating the program must recognize the need for patience.

The Written Statement   Before planning a program, the practitioner should state its objective, or objectives, in writing. This helps to focus individual thinking and to prevent later misunderstanding with management. Depending on the complexity of the program, the goal can be summarized in two or three sentences, perhaps in one. Many social service and other nonprofit organizations have a basic "mission statement" defining their purpose; any specific public relations program should be checked against this for consistency.

Take the case of a small women's college in financial trouble because its enrollment has fallen. It could achieve financial security by admitting men, but its student body and faculty want it to remain all-female. It decides, therefore, to mount a major campaign among alumnae for contributions. Its objective might be summarized as follows:

Conduct a $75 million endowment campaign among alumnae to preserve the college's 100-year tradition of providing its female student body with a unique academic and social atmosphere

DEFINE THE AUDIENCES

Once the objective has been set, the practitioner should define the audience or audiences at which the campaign will be aimed. Precisely whom is the campaign intended to inform or motivate? The purpose of specifying an audience is simply to avoid wasted effort and dollars. Some campaigns can be aimed at the general public. Other campaigns should be directed at a smaller, more focused audience. Spending large sums of money to educate the public at large on issues in which it has no stake is nonproductive. Targeting the message to the appropriate audience is more likely to produce significant results.

Public relations programs fall into three general categories, aimed at these groups: (1) *a broad general audience,* (2) *an external target audience,* and (3) *an internal audience.*

Entire Public   In a broad-based project aimed at the *entire public,* the practitioner seeks to register as many impressions as possible on as many individuals as possible. The American Cancer Society, for example, uses a number of methods to warn every person it can reach about the seven danger signs of cancer. The more often that individuals read or hear about those signs, the more likely they are to check their bodies for symptoms. On a local level, sponsors of a citywide July 4 ethnic festival in a midwestern city, trying to attract as many people as possible to the event, spread the word through newspaper stories, radio and television shows, publicity photographs in newspapers of exotic foods to be sold, club meeting announcements, personal solicitation of ethnic groups to operate booths, and as many other methods as they had the time and money to employ.

External Target Audience   In a campaign aimed at an external *target audience,* selection of public relations methods is more restricted. Impressions made upon individuals not concerned with an issue are wasted. Broadside use of radio and television, in particular, might be of scant value—if, indeed, the practitioners could convince news directors and program directors to use their material.

How is a target audience campaign conducted? As an example, consider the campaign run by motorcycle enthusiasts seeking repeal of a state law that requires them to wear helmets while riding. The issue is of minimal interest to the general public. The campaign must be aimed at two special audiences—state legislators, who will vote on the repeal proposal, and motorcycle users, whose opinions pro and con will influence their decision. Since the issue is nonpartisan and involves no expenditure of state money, two common concerns of legislators—party loyalty and the budget—are not involved.

Sharp differences of opinion exist among motorcyclists as to the wisdom of the repeal effort. Those who favor repeal maintain that the government has no right to tell them as citizens how they should dress—an emotional argument—and that helmets impair their peripheral vision—a physical one. They agree that the use of helmets reduces the danger of head injuries but argue that they should have freedom of choice about wearing them. Supporters of the law contend that helmets save lives and that the government has a duty to protect those motorcyclists who would be foolhardy enough to ride bareheaded unless forbidden by law.

The perimeters of the two target audiences are easily defined. There is a known number of legislators, approximately 100. The names and addresses of registered motorcycle owners and licensed riders can be obtained from the Department of Motor Vehicles. Motorcycle sales agencies, equipment stores, and repair shops are natural channels of repeal communication. So are motorcycle clubs.

The proponents of repeal ask club members to write to their legislators, using sample letters provided for them. Clubs are urged to adopt formal resolutions to be sent to the legislature. Repeal advocates testify before legislative committee hearings on the bill and hold face-to-face discussions with individual legislators, pressing their cause. They distribute pamphlets and information sheets urging repeal. They hand out stickers with a catchy repeal slogan to their members and place piles of them in motorcycle shops for free distribution. They submit feature stories favoring repeal to motorcycle publications and request supporting editorials.

Safety organizations and motorcyclists who want the helmet law retained also mount a campaign, but with less fervor and money. They cite instances in which a motorcyclist's life was saved by a helmet and show the legislators graphs depicting the rise in motorcycle fatalities in states that have repealed the helmet law. However, their arguments are overpowered by the pile of letters, petitions, and resolutions favoring repeal that arrive on legislators' desks. Convinced that a majority of motorcyclists desire repeal, the legislators shrug, "If they want to risk their necks, let them," and pass the bill repealing the law.

The general public, meanwhile, hears little about the dispute, except for a few news stories by legislative reporters, a smattering of letters to newspaper editors, and passing glimpses of stickers. Its awareness of the intense, tightly focused public relations campaign is almost nonexistent. Its concern about the outcome is negligible.

Internal Audience   The third type of campaign is aimed at an *internal audience*. This might be the employees of a company or members of a professional organization. This kind of campaign also relies upon specific types of public relations tools.

If a company plans to revise the stock-purchase plan it offers to employees, for instance, management should explain the changes and the reasons for them to employees. Failure to do so may produce confusion, rumors, and suspicious grumbling that management is attempting a trick that will harm employees financially. It is axiomatic that in any large group some people will resist change and suspect the motives for it. Although the issue is of intense concern to employees, the general public probably knows (or cares) nothing about it and has no influence in shaping the outcome. Thus distribution of the company's message to the public is pointless.

To tell its story to employees, management uses brochures illustrated with simple graphs and charts explaining how the revised plan will operate and how it will benefit the work force. These are distributed at in-plant meetings or mailed to employees' homes. Top management officials address groups of employees, give audiovisual presentations, and answer questions. One issue of the employee magazine concentrates on the plan. If the company's plants are situated in several cities, the chief executive officer may use a videoconference to address the staffs of all the plants simultaneously. Or, the top official may make a videotape, copies of which are distributed systemwide. These actions constitute an intensive internal communications project, yet the only information the public may learn about it is from a news story on the financial pages reporting the proposal.

That is how public relations programs are planned for carefully analyzed audiences. A good program is designed to fit the need as carefully as a tailor measures a customer for an expensive suit.

PLAN THE PROGRAM

As indicated in the discussion of the ways in which audiences should be defined and addressed, a practitioner has numerous options available when planning the program. A list is provided of principal ways in which public relations messages can be delivered. Subsequent chapters will examine each of these three methods in detail: written tactics (Chapter 22), spoken tactics (Chapter 23), and visual tactics (Chapter 24).

Written Methods

- News releases
- Factsheets
- Newspaper and magazine feature articles
- Newsletters
- Brochures and handbooks
- Company periodicals
- Annual reports
- Corporate advertising
- Books
- Facsimile releases
- Electronic bulletin boards

Visual Methods

- Television newscasts
- Television appearances
- Videotapes
- Motion pictures
- Slides and filmstrips
- Transparencies
- Still photographs
- Teleconferencing
- Charts and graphs
- Other graphics (cartoons, paintings, logos)
- Billboards
- Video news releases

Spoken Methods

- Face-to-face discussions
- Speeches
- Radio newscasts
- News conferences
- Press parties
- Interviews, printed and broadcast
- Meetings
- Word-of-mouth (the "grapevine")
- Audiotapes

The three types of methods truly provide a smorgasbord from which to choose! In most cases, an integrated program using several of these methods in a coordinated manner is best. Under certain circumstances, however, the practitioner might find it desirable or necessary to use only a single carefully chosen medium.

EXECUTE THE PROGRAM

Conducting a public relations project requires preparation time, efficient administration, and sufficient trained personnel. Temporary additions to the staff may be needed, along with the services of outside specialists.

An example of a well-run program occurred in Minnesota, where a civic organization named Our Fair Carousel raised $1 million to save the picturesque, 75-year-old Minnesota State Fair carousel, which was to have been sold horse-by-horse at a New York auction.

The civic group pledged to repay the City of St. Paul for a $1.3 million emergency loan it obtained to keep the carousel. It generated concern for the carousel by several techniques: telephone interviews with opinion leaders; a newsletter distributed in Minnesota and to members of the National Carousel Association; displays of carousel horses; and media publicity stressing nostalgia and the economic value of the carousel.

During a year-long drive, Our Fair Carousel raised $1 million from individuals and foundations, plus a $500,000 pledge from a corporation that agreed to prepare a new site for the carousel and provide a $350,000 interest-free loan to repay the balance of the city's loan. Our Fair Carousel received a PRSA Silver Anvil award for this public service.

When a crisis arises, a program in response must be executed quickly. Having a contingency plan ready for use in a foreseeable crisis speeds the response time, but some crises take unexpected forms. In most projects, however, crisis urgency is not involved. Sufficient time usually is available to prepare the materials and make the physical arrangements before the kickoff date. A program that starts, then bogs down because necessary materials are not ready or speakers are not available, is headed for failure.

The director and staff of a campaign must take several steps in order to execute the program efficiently:

■ Create a program calendar and maintain a checklist of progress. This prevents the possibility of deadlines being missed or of some aspects being overlooked.

■ Write the printed material and scripts.

■ Obtain management approval of program material.

■ Order the printing, after obtaining price bids and having specialists prepare attractive layouts.

■ Write the speeches to be delivered. These may include the "pattern" speech, a basic presentation that various speakers may adapt appropriately to fit individual situations.

■ Train the speakers and brief them thoroughly.

■ Arrange meeting dates and places, and schedule speakers.

■ Make contact with editors to propose feature stories in newspapers and magazines and supporting editorials if the campaign objective justifies them.

■ Offer articulate representatives for appearances on radio and television shows.

■ Send out invitations to news conferences, press parties, and meetings.

The press tour checklist used by Hewlett-Packard Company managers in planning introductions of major new products, reproduced on page 197, shows the meticulous detail with which a major corporation prepares a public relations program.

PREPARING A PROGRAM PLAN

Writing a plan for a public relations activity is nothing more than preparing a blueprint of what is to be done and how it will be accomplished. By preparing such a plan, either as a brief outline or an extensive document, the practitioner can make sure that all elements have been properly considered and that everybody involved knows what the procedure is. Ketchum Public Relations, San Francisco, uses the following outline in preparing program plans for clients:

1. *Define the problem.* Valid objectives cannot be set without a clear understanding of the problem. To understand the problem, (1) discuss it with the client to find what the public relations effort is expected to accomplish, (2) do some initial research, and (3) evaluate ideas in the broader perspective of the client's long-term goals.

2. *Identify objectives.* Once the problem is understood, it should be easy to define the objective. A stated objective should be evaluated by asking, (1) does it really solve the problem? (2) is it realistic and achievable? and (3) can success be measured in terms meaningful to the client?

3. *Identify audience.* Identify, as precisely as possible, the group of people who comprise the primary audience for the message. If there are several groups, list them according to what group would be most important in achieving the client's primary objectives.

4. *Develop strategy.* The strategy describes how, in concept, the objective is to be achieved. Strategy is a plan of action that provides guidelines and themes for the overall effort. There is usually one, and often several, strategies for each target audience. Strategies may be broad or narrow, depending on the objective and the audience.

5. *Specify tactics.* This is the body of the plan that describes, in sequence, the specific activities proposed to achieve each objective. In selecting communication tools—news releases, brochures, radio anouncements, videotapes, special events, etc.—make sure the communication tools are appropriate for the designated audience.

6. *Develop calendar.* It is important to have a timetable, usually in chart form, that shows the start and completion of each project within the framework of the total program. Using a calendar enables practitioners to make sure that projects—such as brochures, slide presentations, newsletters, and invitations—are ready when they are needed.

7. *Ascertain budget.* How much will it cost to implement the public relations plan? Outline, in sequence, the exact costs of all activities. Budgets should include such details as postage, car mileage, labor to stuff envelopes, typesetting, office supplies, telephone, etc. About 10 percent of the budget should be allocated for contingencies.

8. *Specify evaluation procedures.* Determine what criteria will be used to evaluate the success of the public relations program. Evaluation criteria should be realistic, credible, specific, and in line with client expectations. When determining objectives, make sure that each of them can be adequately evaluated at the end of the program.

ASSESS THE RESULTS

Every public relations campaign is an educational experience for those who conduct it as well as for those to whom it is directed. Assessment of the program's results, like the fact-finding step taken before it is planned, should be a time for candor and self-examination.

The results of some projects are easily determined. A fund drive either meets its announced goal or it does not. A campaign for passage of certain legislation either succeeds or fails. The crowds attending a state fair can be counted at the turnstiles. However, measuring the effectiveness of campaigns with more abstract goals, such as reversing a negative perception, is more difficult because no obvious statistics are available as benchmarks.

In summary, many resources are needed to design a public relations plan for a company or a client. These resources—public relations, marketing, editorial, financial, and research—draw from a large set of tools, some of which are shown in Figure 8.2. Turning a public relations idea into an effective program involves following a well-

FIGURE 8.1

A timetable for the Koosh Kins public relations program conducted by Ketchum Public Relations, San Francisco, showing the steps to be taken week by week over a four-month period.

	W1	W2	W3	W4	W5	W6	W7	W8	W9	W10	W11	W12	W13	W14	W15	W16
-- Book meetings								xxx	xxx	xxx	xxx					
-- Production/Execution												xxx				
-- Follow up														xxx	xxx	
TOP 40 NEWSPAPER/SYNDICATE MAILING																
-- Revise/review mailing lists	xxx	xxx														
-- Develop creative mailing concepts	xxx	xxx														
-- Customize/update press materials					xxx	xxx										
-- Issue for client approval			xxx	xxx												
-- Reproduce photos				xxx	xxx											
-- Draft pitch letter			xxx													
-- Production/execution					xxx	xxx	xxx									
-- Follow up							xxx	xxx	xxx	xxx	xxx	xxx	xxx			
TOP 20 MARKETS/NATIONAL TV MORNING SHOWS																
-- Revise/review mailing lists							xxx	xxx								
-- Customize/update press materials							xxx	xxx								
-- Develop personalized mailing							xxx	xxx								
-- Issue for client approval							xxx									
-- Draft pitch letter							xxx	xxx								
-- Production/execution								xxx	xxx							
-- Follow up													xxx	xxx	xxx	xxx
4th QUARTER MEDIA OPPORTUNITIES/INQUIRIES	xxx	xxx	xxx	xxx	xxx	xxx	xxx	xxx	xxx	xxx	xxx	xxx	xxx	xxx	xxx	xxx
SUNDAY SUPPLEMENTS																
-- Develop media list				xxx	xxx	xxx										
-- Coordinate mailing list				xxx	xxx	xxx										
-- Follow-up phone calls							xxx	xxx								

2622K p. 1

FIGURE 8.2
Some of the tools needed to design a public relations plan
are shown here.

structured pattern. The practitioner moves logically, first defining the problem, then progressing through subsequent steps that include setting an objective, identifying the audiences to be reached, planning the program, creating a timetable and budget, and executing the program. When carried out efficiently, these steps should produce a cohesive, workable public relations program that obtains results.

ISSUES MANAGEMENT

We have been discussing the step-by-step progression to be followed in all types of public relations programs. Now we will see how these principles are applied in an area of practice critical to progressive corporations and of significance to social and health organizations as well. It is *issues management*.

Corporations do not exist in a vacuum. They are an integral part of society, and what they do, or don't do, affects a broad range of publics and institutions. In today's world, the success of a corporation involves more than producing goods and services at a profit. A corporation's policies and actions are shaped and developed in reaction to political, economic, social, and technological forces.

A corporation must consider numerous publics and institutions in developing its policies and strategies. Among these are the general public, media, activist groups, government officials, regulatory agencies, and local, state, and national laws. Any one of these can have a major effect on the future and success of the corporation. Corporations also operate in an environment where *social responsibility* is not only expected but required.

The interaction of corporations with various elements of society has led to the emergence of issues management as an important part of effective public relations and strategic corporate planning. Essentially, issues management is a proactive and systematic approach to identifying issues and concerns that currently face a corporation or that will emerge in the next 12 to 36 months. Issues management and corporate policymaking require sophisticated understanding of the various publics and pressures that affect decisions. Figure 8.3 shows the interactive nature of the process.

FIGURE 8.3
This model shows the interactive nature of the public policy model.

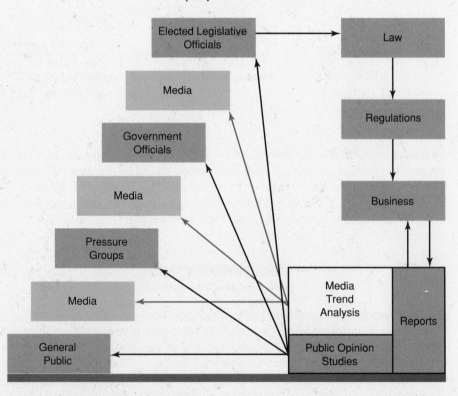

Public Relations Journal defines issues management thus: "Issues management is the management process whose goal is to help preserve markets, reduce risk, create opportunities, and manage image as an organizational asset for the benefit of both the organization and its primary shareholders."

Ideally, strategic planning allows a corporation to analyze issues, formulate policy, and take action before the emerging issues become subjects of newspaper headlines and part of the public agenda. In reality, many companies have the difficult task of managing an issue after it has reached the public debate stage.

Public relations counselors W. Howard Chase and Barrie L. Jones were among the first practitioners to specialize in issues management. They define the process as (1) identification of the issues, (2) systematic analysis, (3) strategy options, (4) action plan, and (5) evaluation of results. PPG Industries perceives the process along the same lines but identifies the steps as (1) issue identification, (2) impact assessment, (3) position formulation, (4) action-plan development and implementation, and (5) communications. Inherent in either process, however, is the idea that issues management involves input from all levels of the corporation and must have the complete commitment of top management.

Perhaps the best way to illustrate issues management is to show how Dow Chemical Company used the concept to improve its credibility and reputation among key publics.

Issue Identification   Dow Chemical, as the second-largest chemical manufacturer in America, was a major supplier of Agent Orange to the U.S. government during the war in Vietnam. The defoliant contained a tiny amount of a by-product called Dioxin that was later alleged to cause a form of cancer. Complaints and damage suits focused primarily on the company, and Dow suffered a critical loss of credibility and reputation as the charges and lawsuits were being settled.

Issue Analysis   Top management formed an internal task force that included employees from public relations, public affairs, and marketing research to study the company's public policy approach and to identify Dow's key audiences. The task force interviewed employees and managers to get their opinions, and an independent survey was commissioned to obtain the attitudes of community leaders, media executives, and government officials. They were asked about Dow's environmental performance, concern for employees, and corporate citizenship. The survey findings, according to Richard Long, director of corporate communications, depicted Dow as "an insular and sometimes arrogant company that shunned compromise—a reputation which a modern company can ill afford."

Strategy Options   The internal task force and top management, not wishing to perpetuate the negative image of Dow among key publics, decided that the best objective was to "make Dow a more highly regarded company among the people who can influence its future." Top management agreed on the following strategies: (1) company "practices" must change before "perceptions" can improve, (2) communications must improve with public interest groups, (3) philanthropic efforts would be coordinated with public affairs to reach key audiences, (4) new substantive and symbolic programs would be created to show Dow's changed policies, and (5) a long-range approach to public policy would be implemented, because company reputations are not formed overnight.

Action Plan   The tactics for accomplishing Dow's strategies included the following:

■ To improve media relations, a 24-hour-a-day toll-free 800 number was established and advertised in journalism periodicals to let newspeople know that Dow was accessible to answer any inquiries.

■ Every executive who might have media contacts was taught the concepts of effective media relations and how to field reporters' questions.

■ Dow, assisted by other corporations, established and funded a science-writing center at the University of Missouri School of Journalism. It features science-writing courses for working journalists and a reference library to help reporters become better informed about the chemical industry.

■ Dow scientists are sent regularly to various cities for interviews with local media on such topics as environmental standards, hazardous waste management, and chemical plant safety.

■ Dow has established coalitions with such groups as the League of Women Voters and the National Resources Defense Council to communicate the dangers of hazardous household wastes and ways to preserve the environment.

■ An extensive speakers' program has been established in which Dow executives talk to civic and environmental groups.

■ Local plant managers in 65 locations across the United States have been given resources and advice from corporate headquarters on how to conduct plant tours and organize volunteer efforts.

■ "Public interest reports," published by Dow about a number of economic and political issues, are regularly mailed to 60,000 opinion leaders.

■ Dow contributes more than $1 million annually to a national education program that publicizes the importance of organ transplants and the need for organ donors.

■ A national nonproduct advertising campaign focuses on the benefits of Dow's research and the ways company employees work to benefit other people.

Evaluation   After two years of effort, an independent survey showed highly favorable attitudes toward Dow on the part of customers, scientists, and employees. There also was a 60 percent gain in favorable media opinion, and the *Washington Journalism Review* found that Dow's public relations efforts were better than those of any other chemical company on the Fortune 500 list.

A PRESS TOUR CHECKLIST

This summary of planning for a press tour by Hewlett-Packard officials illustrates the time and care the corporation uses to assure a smooth and effective trip.

- **Stage 1** Four months ahead of release date:
  Establish objectives of tour, prepare detailed cost estimates, determine makeup of tour party, set dates

- **Stage 2** Three months ahead of press-release date:
  Develop written pitch for editor/market analyst telephone calls; make appointments by telephone, plan schedule in order of cities to be visited, emphasizing cities with most publications; make hotel arrangements

- **Stage 3** Three weeks ahead of tour start:
  Prepare complete agenda including summary page and timing for each day, prepare overhead and 35mm slides, videotape; dry run all speakers and visuals at least twice, prepare information package to give to each group visited

- **Stage 4** Seven days ahead of tour start:
  Practice packing and unpacking products, phone each journal to confirm appointments, tour leader make special book with chapters on each publication, including personal quirks of editors; make certain tour leader has plenty of credit in credit-card accounts and ample cash

- **Stage 5** Departure of tour:
  Secretary calls each editor/market analyst to confirm HP visit the day before the HP crew arrives

- **Stage 6** On the road:
  Public relations check with desk clerk on arrival to see that everything is in order, during morning reconfirm flights and make notes for special discussions, check catering for refreshments, take notes on meetings with editors for managers

- **Stage 7** Week following tour:
  Write letter to main editor contact at each publication and send a copy to other editors at same site. Personalize your thanks, ask if editor needs additional information or photographs

- **Stage 8** Four weeks following tour:
  Create book with all printed data, letters, schedules from the tour to be used as a reference for next tour of your division group

Action Time	Clock Time	Elapsed Time	Event Movement
00:00	08:55:00	00:00	Arrival
00:15	08:55:15	00:15	Greeting at Door
00:30	08:55:45	00:45	Movement to Meeting
01:00	08:56:45	01:45	Pool Spray
06:00	09:02:45	07:45	Briefing
00:30	09:03:15	08:15	Private exit photo w/ POTUS/VPOTUS/CEO
00:40	09:03:55	08:55	Movement to 2nd Floor Demo Area
03:00	09:06:55	11:55	Demo #1: Architecture (Rebuilding L.A.)
03:00	09:09:55	14:55	Demo #2: Education (Aircraft Maintenance)
03:00	09:12:55	17:55	Demo #3: Pharmaceutical design/surgery
01:00	09:13:55	18:55	Movement to Cafeteria
00:30	09:14:25	19:25	Hold backstage
01:15	09:15:40	20:40	Video Presentation
00:20	09:16:00	21:00	Ken Coleman Intro of McCracken, POTUS, VPOTUS
00:30	09:16:30	21:30	Movement to Stage
00:50	09:17:20	22:20	Welcome by Ed McCracken
00:30	09:17:50	22:50	Introduction of The Vice President
09:30	09:27:20	32:20	Remarks by The Vice President
00:30	09:27:50	32:50	Introduction of the President
10:00	09:37:50	42:50	Remarks by The President
01:00	09:38:50	43:50	Opening overview from Ed McCracken
00:20	09:39:10	44:10	Segue into Engineering
01:00	09:40:10	45:10	One Minute Presentation: Engineering
00:20	09:40:30	45:30	Segue into Manufacturing
01:00	09:41:30	46:30	One Minute Presentation: Manufacturing
00:20	09:41:50	46:50	Segue into Human Resources
01:00	09:42:50	47:50	One Minute Presentation: Human Resources
00:20	09:43:10	48:10	Segue into Sales & Marketing
01:00	09:44:10	49:10	One Minute Presentation: Sales & Marketing
00:20	09:44:30	49:30	Segue into Power Challenge Team
01:00	09:45:30	50:30	One Minute Presentation: Power Challenge Team
00:30	09:46:00	51:00	Invitation to Open Discussion by Ed McCracken
23:15	10:09:15	74:15	Discussion with the President and Vice President
			ANY LOST TIME WILL BE MADE UP HERE!!!
00:30	10:09:45	74:45	Close of Discussion
01:00	10:10:45	75:45	Closing Remarks by The Vice President
01:30	10:12:15	77:15	Closing Remarks by The President
00:30	10:12:45	77:45	Goodbye by Ed McCracken
00:15	10:13:00	78:00	Exit, Stage Left, with Music and Video
02:00	10:15:00	80:00	Rope Line to Holding Room
00:00	10:15:00	80:00	Holding Room
00:00	10:15:00	80:00	Depart

FIGURE 8.4
A public appearance by a President involves intricate timing.
This schedule covering a visit by President Clinton (called
POTUS in the listing) and Vice President Gore (VPOTUS) to
Silicon Graphics Corporation at Mountain View, California,
illustrates the extremely detailed planning required to make the
event run smoothly and protect the President's safety.

	Movement
	Notes
	Tom Jermoluk and Ken coleman prepositioned in McCracken
	Pool heads upstairs
	Tour Guide: Jim White/ Computer Operator: Michael Jones
	Tour Guide: John Kidd/ Computer Operator: Mark Daly
	Tour Guide: Tom Davis/ Computer Operator Michael Wills
	Pool move to cafeteria cutaway/ Meanwhile Coleman briefs audience, intros VIPS
	HOUSE LIGHTS DOWN
	POTUS and VPOTUS view from backstage
	HOUSE LIGHTS UP
	Coleman exits STAGE LEFT, takes seat.
	POTUS and VPOTUS flank McCracken
	McCracken
	VP Gore Introduces
	M.C.: Ed McCracken
	Marc Hannah, Chief Scientist
	M.C.: Ed McCracken
	Steve Goggiano, Gen Mgr., Engineering (Remote Live)
	M.C.: Ed McCracken
	Leilani Gayles, VP, Human Resources
	M.C.: Ed McCracken
	Dave Bagshaw, VP, Corporate Marketing
	M.C.: Ed McCracken
	John Brennan (Power Challenge, an Interdisciplinary project combining the areas)
	Audience consists totally of employees from these live areas of Silicon Graphics
	POTUS and VPOTUS may remark on what they've seen, ask follow up, get feedback
	ANY TIME LOST WILL BE MADE UP HERE!!!
	M.C.: Ed McCracken
	Moving STAGE LEFT to STAGE RIGHT via front-of-stage buffer zone to holding room

CASE PROBLEM 1

Alpha Corporation's large manufacturing facility in Knoxville employs 15,000 people. The corporation's manufacturing facilities in five other Tennessee towns employ another 3,000 people. Recent research shows little public awareness of the company's contributions to the state economy and its charitable activities in the communities where it operates.

Top management decides that this situation must be corrected. One decision is to produce a brochure that will create more awareness of the corporation among key publics. You are assigned to write the brochure.

Before writing anything, use the MBO guidelines at the beginning of the chapter (adapted from the Nager-Allen text) to outline the brochure's objectives in the context of the nine guidelines mentioned.

CASE PROBLEM 2

The Wonderlawn Company, a client of your public relations firm, has developed an exciting garden tool, the Laserzapper, whose laser beams destroy weeds in lawns without damaging the grass. It plans both to introduce the product nationally with heavy media coverage and to develop a marketing program focused on the peak potential sales periods of the year.

The Laserzapper helps the environment because it uses no poisonous chemicals. The user walks around the lawn, holding the three-foot-long wand horizontally and waist-high while its laser beams flash down on the weeds.

Although the Laserzapper will be offered first to home gardeners, Wonderlawn sees future uses in agriculture to control weeds in fields.

Using the eight-point method described in this chapter, prepare a public relations program for introducing the Laserzapper. Develop a set of public relations objectives, identify groups of potential purchasers, decide which promotional techniques will be most effective, create a timetable, develop a defensive strategy against anticipated attacks from the chemical companies, and write a catchy promotional slogan.

QUESTIONS FOR REVIEW AND DISCUSSION

1. Name the first step in every successful public relations program.

2. Negative perceptions often develop about an organization. What are some danger signals for which a public relations director should watch?

3. List three examples of specific one-time projects a public relations specialist might be asked to conduct.

4. If assigned to research the reasons why a certain brand of bicycle sells poorly, what important questions would you ask?

5. Describe how you would try to determine why the number of volunteer workers at a hospital is decreasing and list ways to recruit new volunteers.

6. Why should the goal of a public fund drive be set at an attainable level?

7. Public relations objectives should be stated in writing. Prepare a one-sentence statement of objectives for a campaign to convince local residents that the local factory of a national company is a good community citizen.

8. What public relations methods are often used to reach an internal audience?

9. List five visual methods for delivering public relations messages.

10. A program calendar is a basic tool in a public campaign. Why is it so important?

11. What does a company seek to accomplish by using issues management?

SUGGESTED READINGS

Blankinship, Steve. "Issues Management." *Communication World,* August 1993, pp. 24–27.

Hainsworth, Brad. "How Corporations Define Issue Management." *Public Relations Review,* Winter 1988, pp. 18–30.

Heath, Robert L. "Corporate Issues Management: Theoretical Underpinnings and Research Foundations." *Public Relations Research Annual,* Vol. 2, ed. James and Larissa Grunig. Hillsdale, NJ, Lawrence Erlbaum, 1990, pp. 29–66.

Heath, Robert L., and Nelson, Richard. *Issues Management.* Newbury Park, CA: Sage Publications, 1986.

"Issues Management in Public Relations." *Public Relations Review,* Spring 1990, pp. 1–62. Series of articles and research studies on issues management.

Kendall, Robert. *Public Relations Campaign Strategies.* New York: HarperCollins, 1992.

Nager, Norman R., and Allen, T. Harrell. *Public Relations Management by Objectives.* New York: Longman, 1983.

Pearson, Ron. "Public Relations Writing Methods by Objectives." *Public Relations Review,* Summer 1987, pp. 14–26.

Pollare, Frank L. "Surviving the Budgeting Game." *Public Relations Journal,* March 1990, pp. 29–30.

Ramsey, Shirley A. "Issues Management and the Use of Technologies in Public Relations." *Public Relations Review,* Fall 1993, pp. 261–275.

Reid, Sheryll. "How to Develop a Strategic Plan." *Public Relations Journal,* August 1987, p. 31.

Simmons, Robert E. *Communication Campaign Management.* New York: Longman, 1990.

Tucker, Kerry, and Trumpfheller, Bill. "Building an Issues Management System." *Public Relations Journal,* November 1993, pp. 36–37.

Tucker, Kerry, and Broom, Glen. "Managing Issues as Bridge to Strategic Planning." *Public Relations Journal,* November 1993, pp. 38–40.

CHAPTER

9

Communication

P R E V I E W   In this chapter, the objective is to explain the basic process of communication, the theories that underlie it, and its techniques, in order to help students formulate and disseminate effective messages.

Topics covered in this chapter include:

- A public relations perspective

- Paying attention to the message

- Understanding the message

- Believing the message

- Remembering the message

- Acting on the message

- Crisis communication, with case studies

- Risk communication

The third step in the public relations process, after research and planning, is communication. This step is the one most prominently associated with public relations work.

In a public relations program plan, as pointed out in Chapter 8, communication is the *implementation of a decision.* In other words, communication is the process and means by which objectives are achieved. It may take the form of news releases, news conferences, special events, brochures, speeches, bumper stickers, newsletters, parades, posters, and the like. In a program plan, this stage is referred to as *strategies and tactics;* it is also known as *outbound communication.*

The goals of the communication process are to inform, persuade, motivate, or achieve mutual understanding. To be an effective communicator, a person must have basic knowledge of what constitutes communication and how people receive messages. Also needed is an understanding of the way people process information and possibly modify their attitudes, opinions, and actions.

A PUBLIC RELATIONS PERSPECTIVE

The professional communicator considers a host of variables when planning a message on behalf of an employer or client.

Patrick Jackson, editor of *PR Reporter* and a public relations counselor, says communicators should ask themselves a series of questions before preparing any communication materials:

1. Is it appropriate?
   a. For the sender?
   b. For the recipient?

2. Is it meaningful?
   a. Does it stick to the subject?
   b. Is it geared to the recipient's interest, not the sender's?

3. Is it memorable?
   a. In phraseology or metaphor?
   b. Through the use of visual or aural devices?

4. Is it understandable?
   a. In both denotative and connotative language?
   b. Graphically or aurally?

5. Is it believable?
   a. Does the audience trust the spokesperson?
   b. Does the communication exhibit expertise in the subject matter?

"Many a wrongly directed or unnecessary communication has been corrected or dropped by using a screen like this," Jackson says.

In addition to examining the proposed content, a communicator should determine exactly what objective is sought through the communication. James Grunig, professor of public relations at the University of Maryland, lists five possible objectives for a communicator:

1. *Message exposure.* Public relations personnel provide materials to the mass media and disseminate other messages through controlled media such as newsletters and brochures. Intended audiences are exposed to the message in various forms.

2. *Accurate dissemination of the message.* The intended audience acknowledges the message and retains all or part of it.

3. *Acceptance of the message.* Based on its view of reality, the audience not only retains the message but accepts it as valid.

4. *Attitude change.* The audience not only believes the message but makes a verbal or mental commitment to change behavior as a result of the message.

5. *Change in overt behavior.* Members of the audience actually change their current behavior or begin a new behavior.

Grunig says that most public relations experts usually aim at the first two objectives, exposure to the message and accurate dissemination. The last three objectives depend in large part on a mix of variables—predisposition to the message, peer reinforcement, feasibility of the suggested action, and environmental context, to name a few. The first two objectives are easier to evaluate than attitude change (see Chapter 10).

Although the communicator cannot always control the outcome of a message, researchers recognize that effective dissemination is the beginning of the process that leads to opinion change and adoption of products or services. Therefore, it is important to review all components of the communication process.

David Therkelsen, director of public relations for the American Red Cross in St. Paul, Minnesota, succinctly outlines the process:

To be successful, a message must be *received* by the intended individual or audience. It must get the audience's *attention.* It must be *understood.* It must be *believed.* It must be *remembered.* And ultimately, in some fashion, it must be *acted upon.* Failure to accomplish *any* of these tasks means the entire message fails.

Therkelsen appropriately places the emphasis on the audience and what it does with the message. The following sections elaborate on the six elements he enumerates.

RECEIVING THE MESSAGE

Several communication models explain how a message moves from the sender to the recipient. Some are quite complex, attempting to incorporate an almost infinite number of events, ideas, objects, and people that interact on the message, channel, and receiver.

Most communication models, however, incorporate four basic elements. David K. Berlo's model is an example. It has *sender/source (encoder), message, channel,* and

EFFECTIVE COMMUNICATIONS

Philip Lesly, president of the Philip Lesly Company, outlined some guidelines for effective communications. Lesly made his remarks during a lecture, sponsored by the Ball Corporation, at Ball State University. His points are summarized here.

- Approach everything from the viewpoint of the audience's interest—what is on their minds, what is in it for them.

- Give the audience a sense of involvement in the communication process and in what is going on. Get them involved and you get their interest.

- Make the subject matter part of the atmosphere the audience lives with—what they talk about, what they hear from others. That means getting the material adopted in their channels of communication.

- Communicate with people, not at them. Communication that approaches the audience as a target makes people put their defenses up against it.

- Localize—get the message conveyed as close to the individual's own milieu as possible.

- Use a number of channels of communications, not just one or two. The impact is far greater when it reaches people in a number of different forms.

- Maintain consistency—so what is said on the subject is the same no matter which audience it's directed to or what the context is. Still, tailor-make each message for the specific audience as much as possible.

- Don't propagandize but make sure that you make your point. When a communicator draws conclusions in his [or her] summation of information, it is more effective than depending on the audience to draw its own conclusions.

- Maintain credibility—which is essential for all these points to be effective.

receiver (decoder). A fifth element, *feedback* from the receiver to the sender, is now incorporated in modern models of communication.

Mass media researcher Wilbur Schramm's early models (see Figure 9.1) started with a simple communication model (top), but he later expanded the process to include the concept of "shared experience" (middle diagram). In other words, little or no communication is achieved unless the sender and the receiver share a common language and even an overlapping cultural or educational background. The importance of "shared experience" becomes apparent when a highly technical news release about a new computer system causes a local business editor to shake his or her head in bewilderment.

Schramm's third model (bottom) incorporates the idea of continuous feedback. Both the sender and the receiver continually encode, interpret, decode, transmit, and receive information. The loop process also is integral to all models showing the public relations process of research, planning, communication, and evaluation. This concept was illustrated in Chapter 1, which showed public relations as a cyclical process. Communication to internal and external audiences produces feedback that is taken into consideration during research, the first step, and evaluation, the fourth step. In this way, the structure and dissemination of messages are continuously refined for maximum effectiveness.

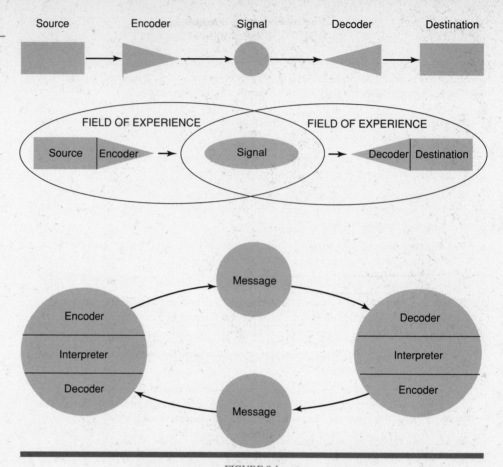

FIGURE 9.1

Three of Wilbur Schramm's communication models, with the
latter two showing the importance of "shared experience" and
the feedback loop process.

THE IMPORTANCE OF TWO-WAY COMMUNICATION

Another way to think of feedback is two-way communication. One-way communication, from sender to receiver, only disseminates information. Such a monologue is less effective than two-way communication, which establishes a dialogue between sender and receiver.

Grunig goes even further to postulate that the ideal public relations model is two-way symmetrical communication. That is, communication is balanced between the sender and the receiver. He says: "In the symmetric model, understanding is the principal objective of public relations, rather than persuasion."

In reality, research shows most organizations have mixed motives when they engage in two-way communication with targeted audiences. Although they may employ dialogue to obtain a better sense of how they can adjust to the needs of an audience, their

A HIERARCHY OF COMMUNICATION CHANNELS

The effectiveness of a message often depends on the channel used. Frederic Volkmann, director of public relations for Washington University, St. Louis, gives the following list in descending order of effectiveness:

1. One-to-one, face-to-face conversation

2. Small group discussion, meeting

3. Speaking before a large group

4. Phone conversation

5. Handwritten, personal note

6. Typewritten or word-processed personal letter

7. Mass-produced, nonpersonal letter

8. Brochure or pamphlet sent as direct mail piece

9. Article in an organizational newsletter

10. News carried in the popular press

11. Advertising in the mass media

12. Billboards, skywriting, and the like

Volkmann believes that "it is the responsibility of an effective public relations plan to force communication up the ladder of effectiveness, striving constantly to narrow the audience to a manageable size, and to deliver the message on a one-to-one basis."

Source: PR Reporter, August 26, 1991, p. 4.

---

motive often is asymmetrical—to convince the audience of their point of view through dialogue. As Grunig states: "Practitioners of the two-way symmetrical model are not completely altruistic; they also want to defend the interests of their employers—they have mixed motives."

The most effective two-way communication, of course, is two people talking to each other. Small-group discussion is also effective. In both forms the message is fortified by gestures, facial expressions, intimacy, tone of voice, and the opportunity for instant feedback. If the listener asks a question or appears puzzled, the speaker has an instant cue and can rephrase the information or amplify a point.

Barriers to communication tend to mount as one advances to large-group meetings and, ultimately, to the mass media. Organizational materials can reach thousands and, through the mass media, even millions of people at the same time, but the psychological and physical distance between sender and receiver is considerably lengthened. Communication is less effective because the audience no longer is involved with the source. No immediate feedback is possible, and the message may undergo distortion as it passes through mass-media gatekeepers.

A BEHAVIORAL COMMUNICATION MODEL

Awareness	→	Latent readiness	→	Triggering event	→	Behavior

The above behavioral communication model, suggests *PR Reporter*, is better than traditional communication models because it forces practitioners to think in terms of what behaviors they are trying to motivate in target publics, rather than what information is being communicated. The process is described as follows:

1. *Awareness.* Salience or relevance is the key to reaching awareness. The purpose of communication here is to create awareness, which is the start of any behavioral process.

2. *Latent readiness.* Either positive or negative readiness to behave in a certain way starts to form, often subconsciously (latently). People get ready to act by accumulating and developing experience, information, word-of-mouth, beliefs, opinions, and emotions.

3. *Triggering event.* The triggering event step gives people a chance to act on their latent readiness. Triggering events may be an election day, a store sale, distribution of a company's annual report, or even a news release announcing a new product or service. Public relations people should build triggering events into their planning: this moves the emphasis from communication to behavior motivation.

4. *Behavior.* Although the ultimate goal is to motivate people to buy something or act in a certain way, they may adopt intermediate behaviors such as requesting more literature, visiting a showroom, or trying the product or idea experimentally.

Models of communication emphasize the importance of feedback as an integral component of the process. As they implement communication strategies, public relations personnel need to give it careful attention.

Although it is impractical, indeed nearly impossible, to disseminate messages widely on a one-to-one basis, Chapters 7 and 10 show how pretesting of messages, focus-group meetings, and systematic evaluation can help bridge the gap. Another approach is to build opportunities for feedback into the communication process. This can be accomplished, for example, by providing toll-free 800 telephone numbers the public can call with comments and telling people whom they can contact directly with questions.

PAYING ATTENTION TO THE MESSAGE

Sociologist Harold Lasswell, in the 1940s, defined the act of communication as "Who, says what, in which channel, to whom, with what effect?"

Although in public relations much emphasis is given to the formation and dissemination of messages, this effort is wasted if the audience pays no attention. It is therefore important to remember the axiom of Walt Seifert, professor emeritus of public relations at Ohio State University. He says: "Dissemination does not equal publication, and publication does not equal absorption and action." In other words, "All who receive it won't publish it, and all who read or hear won't understand or act upon it."

Seifert and social psychologists recognize that the majority of an audience at any given time is not particularly interested in a message or in adopting an idea. This doesn't mean, however, that audiences are merely passive receivers of information. Werner Severin and James Tankard, in their text *Communication Theories,* quote one researcher as saying:

The communicator's audience is not a passive recipient—it cannot be regarded as a lump of clay to be molded by the master propagandist. Rather, the audience is made up of individuals who demand something from the communication to which they are exposed, and who select those that are likely to be useful to them.

This is called the *media uses and gratification theory* of communication. Its basic premise is that the communication process is interactive. The communicator wants to inform and even persuade; the recipient wants to be entertained, informed, or alerted to opportunities that can fulfill individual needs.

In other words, audiences come to messages for very different reasons. People use mass media for such purposes as (1) surveillance of the environment to find out what is happening, locally or even globally, that has some impact on them, (2) entertainment and diversion, (3) reinforcement of their opinions and predispositions, and (4) decision making about buying a product or service.

Uses and gratification theory assumes that people make highly intelligent choices about which messages require their attention and fulfill their needs. If this is true, as research indicates it is, the public relations communicator must tailor messages that focus on getting the audience's attention.

One approach is to understand the mental state of the intended audience. Grunig and Hunt, in *Managing Public Relations,* suggest that communication strategies be designed to attract the attention of two kinds of audiences, those who actively seek information and those who passively process information.

Passive audiences may initially pay attention to a message only because it is entertaining and offers a diversion. They can be made aware of the message through brief encounters—with a billboard glimpsed on the way to work, a radio announcement heard in the car, a television advertisement broadcast before a show begins, and information available in a doctor's waiting room. In other words, they use communication channels that can be utilized while they are doing little else.

For this reason, passive audiences need messages that have style and creativity. The person must be lured by photos, illustrations, and catchy slogans into processing information. Press agentry, the dramatic picture, the use of "beefcake" or "cheesecake" models, radio and television announcements, and events featuring entertainment can make passive audiences aware of a message. The objectives of a communication, therefore, are simply exposure to and accurate dissemination of a message. In most public relations campaigns, communications are designed to reach primarily passive audiences.

A communicator's approach to audiences that actively seek information is different. These people are already at the *interest* stage of the adoption process (discussed later) and seek more sophisticated supplemental information. The tools may include brochures, in-depth newspaper and magazine articles, slide presentations, videotape presentations, symposiums and conferences, major speeches before key groups, and demonstrations at trade shows.

At any given time, of course, the intended audience has passive and active information-seekers in it. It is important, therefore, that multiple messages and a variety of communication tools be used in a full-fledged information campaign.

Public relations personnel have two ways by which to determine strategies. First, research into audience attitudes can give insight into the extent of group interest in, or apathy toward, a new product or idea. Second, more efficient communication can be achieved if the intended audience is segmented as much as possible. After dividing an audience into segments, a practitioner can select the appropriate communication tools.

OTHER ATTENTION-GETTING CONCEPTS

Communicators should think in terms of the five senses—sight, hearing, smell, touch, and taste. Television and film or videotape are the most effective methods of communication because they engage an audience's senses of sight and hearing. In addition are their attractions of color and movement. Radio, on the other hand, relies on only the sense of hearing. Print media, although capable of communicating a large amount of information in great detail, rely only on sight.

Individuals learn through all five senses, but psychologists estimate that 83 percent of learning is accomplished through sight. Hearing accounts for 11 percent. Fifty percent of what individuals retain consists of what they see and hear. For this reason speakers often use visual aids.

These figures have obvious implications for the public relations practitioner. Any communication strategy should, if possible, include vehicles of communication designed to tap the senses of sight or hearing, or a combination of the two. In other words, a variety of communication tools is needed, including news releases, publicity photos, slide presentations, videotapes, billboards, newsletters, radio announcements, video news releases, media interviews, and news conferences. This multiple approach not only assists learning and retention, discussed later, but provides repetition of a message in a variety of forms that accommodate audience needs.

Other research suggests that audience attention can be generated if the communicator raises a "need" level first. The idea is to "hook" an audience's attention by beginning the message with something that will make its members' lives easier or benefit them in some way. An example is a message from the Internal Revenue Service. It could begin with a reminder about the necessity of filing tax returns on time, but it would get far more audience attention if it opened by urging people to take all the exemptions for which they were eligible. The prospect of paying less tax would be alluring to most people.

Public relations writers also should be aware that audience attention is highest at the beginning of a message. Thus it is wise to state the major point at the beginning, give details in the middle, and end with a summary of the message.

Another technique to garner audience attention is to begin a message with a statement that reflects audience values and predispositions. This is called *channeling*. (See

Chapter 11.) According to social science research, people pay attention to messages that reinforce their predispositions.

Prior knowledge and interest also make people pay more attention to messages. If a message taps current events or issues of public concern already in the news, there is an increased chance that the audience will pay attention.

UNDERSTANDING THE MESSAGE

Communication is the act of transmitting information, ideas, and attitudes from one person to another. Communication can take place, however, only if the sender and receiver have a common understanding of the symbols being used.

Words are the most common symbols. The degree to which two people understand each other is heavily dependent on their common knowledge of word symbols. Anyone who has traveled abroad can readily attest that very little communication occurs between two people who speak different languages. Even signs translated into English for tourists often lead to some confusing and amusing messages. A brochure for a Japanese hotel, for example, said, "In our hotel, you will be well fed and agreeably drunk. In every room there is a large window offering delightful prospects."

Even if the sender and receiver speak the same language and live in the same country, the effectiveness of their communication depends on such factors as education, social class, regional differences, nationality, and cultural background.

Employee communication specialists are particularly aware of such differences as a multicultural work force becomes the norm for most organizations. One major factor is the impact of a global economy in which organizations have operations and employees in many countries. A second factor is the increasing multicultural composition of the American work force. One study says that 85 percent of new entries in the work force by the year 2000 will be white women, immigrants, African Americans, Hispanics, and Asians. For many of these workers, English will be a second language.

These statistics will require communicators to be better informed about cultural differences and conflicting values in order to find common ground and build bridges between various groups. At the same time, a major task will be to communicate in clear and simple terms. A national survey by the Educational Testing Service found that 42 million American adults fall within the lowest category of literacy. Other studies show that one in eight employees reads at no better than fourth-grade level.

WRITING FOR CLARITY

The nature of the audience and its literacy level are important considerations for any communicator. The key is to produce messages that match, in content and structure, the characteristics of the audience.

The Illinois Public Health Department had the right idea when it commissioned a song in rap-music style as one way to inform low-income, poorly educated groups about the dangers of AIDS. The words and music of the "Condom Rag," however, were offensive to elected officials, who cancelled the song.

This example poses the classic dilemma for the expert communicator. Should the message be produced for supervisors, who may be totally different in background and education from the intended audience, or should it be produced with the audience in mind? The obvious answer is the latter, but it is often difficult to convince management of this. One solution is to copy-test all public relations materials on a target audience. This helps convince management—and communicators—that what they like isn't necessarily what the audience wants, needs, or understands.

Another approach is to apply readability and comprehension formulas to materials before they are produced and disseminated. Learning theory makes the case: the simpler the piece of writing, the easier it will be for audiences to understand.

The most widely known readability formula is one by Rudolph Flesch. Another is by Farr, Jenkins, and Peterson. Both are based on average sentence length and the number of one-syllable words per 100 words. In general, Flesch recommends that news release sentences should average 19 words. This doesn't mean that all sentences should be this length. Some variety is desired, but long, complex sentences reduce comprehension.

Another formula, proposed by Dale and Chall, involves average sentence length and the percentage of words used that are outside Dale's list of 3000 easy words. Its advantage is its ability to predict reading comprehension.

The *Cloze* procedure, developed by William Taylor, also tests comprehension. The concept comes from the idea of closure, the human tendency to complete a familiar but incomplete pattern. In the *Cloze* procedure, copy is tested for comprehension and redundancy by having test subjects read passages in which every fifth or ninth word is removed. Their ability to fill in the missing words determines whether the pattern of words is familiar and people can understand the message.

Audience understanding and comprehension can also be increased by following some of the following concepts.

Use Symbols, Acronyms, and Slogans Clarity and simplicity of message are enhanced by these devices. Each is a form of shorthand that quickly conceptualizes ideas and travels through extended lines of communication.

The world is full of symbols, such as the Christian cross, the Star of David, and the crusading sword of the American Cancer Society. Corporate symbols such as the Mercedes Benz star, the General Electric logo, and the multicolored apple of Apple Computer are known throughout the world. On a national level, one of the most successful symbols ever used by the U.S. government is Smokey the Bear, which has reminded several generations of Americans about the danger of forest fires.

A symbol should be unique, memorable, widely recognized, and appropriate. Organizations spend considerable time and energy searching for unique symbols that convey the essence of what they are or hope to be. Considerable amounts of money are then spent on publicizing the symbols and creating meanings for them.

Acronyms also are shorthand for conveying information. An acronym is a word formed from the initial letters of other words. The Group Against Smokers' Pollution goes by the acronym GASP; Juvenile Opportunities in Business becomes JOB. The National Organization for Women has the acronym NOW, which says a great deal about its political priorities.

FIGURE 9.3
Smokey the Bear has become so well known as a
symbol of the fight against forest fires that this poster
delivers its message effectively by implication.

In many cases, the acronym—because it is short and simple—becomes the common name. The mass media continually use the term AIDS instead of "acquired immune deficiency syndrome." And "UNESCO" is easier to write and say than United Nations Educational, Scientific, and Cultural Organization. During the debate on the North American Free Trade Agreement, the media and the public simply referred to it as NAFTA.

Public relations personnel, when involved in naming an organization, committee, or special event, should consider a title that provides a good acronym, especially if the official name is quite long. It will aid in audience understanding and comprehension.

Slogans help condense a concept. Massive advertising and promotion have made "Don't Leave Home Without It" readily identified with American Express. "The Ultimate Driving Machine" is strongly identified with BMW, an acronym for Bavarian Motor Works.

Avoid Jargon   One source of blocked communication is technical and bureaucratic jargon. When delivered to a general audience, it is called *semantic noise* by social scientists. Jargon interferes with the message and impedes the receiver's ability to understand it. An example of a useless news release is the following, which was actually sent to business editors of daily newspapers. This is how it began:

Versatec, a Xerox Company, has introduced the Graphics Network Processor-SNA (Model 451). The processor, operating as a 377x RJE station, sends and receives EBCDIC or binary data in IMB System Network Architecture (SNA) networks using Synchronous Data Link Control (SDLC) protocol. . . .

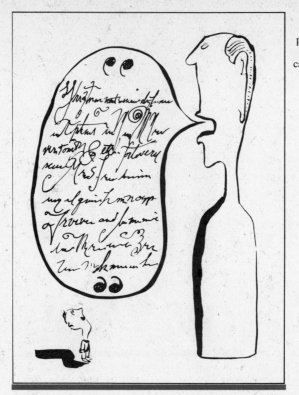

FIGURE 9.4
Miscommunication caused when one party uses jargon not understandable to the other is a common difficulty. This cartoon exemplifies the bewilderment of a listener exposed to such specialized "in" talk.

This news release may be perfectly appropriate for an engineering publication serving a particular industry, but the information needs to be written in simple terms for the readers of a daily newspaper. A failure to understand the audience means a failure in communication.

Avoid Clichés and Hype Words   Highly charged words with connotative meanings can pose problems, and overuse of clichés and hype words can seriously undermine the credibility of the message.

The *Wall Street Journal,* for example, mocked the business of high-technology public relations with a story titled, "High-Tech Hype Reaches New Heights." A reporter analyzed 201 news releases and compiled a "Hype Hit Parade" which included the 11 most overused and ineffective words. They were *leading, enhanced, unique, significant, solution, integrated, powerful, innovative, advanced, high performance,* and *sophisticated.*

Similar surveys have uncovered overused words in business and public relations. A New York firm, John Rost Associates, compiled a list of words and phrases used excessively in business letters and reports. The list includes: *agenda, proactive, interface, networking, finalize, done deals, impact, bottom-line, vis-à-vis, world class, state-of-the-art, user-friendly, competitive edge, know-how, win-win, breakthrough, fast track, hands-on, input, dialogue,* and *no-brainer.*

A survey of corporate annual reports also reveals the constant use of certain words. Robert K. Otterbourg, president of a company that does annual reports for corporations, says the most overused words include *challenge, opportunity, fundamental achievements, pioneering efforts,* and *state-of-the-art.*

When words are overused, their special meaning becomes devalued. As the *Wall Street Journal* implies, if every product is "unique" and "sophisticated," the words simply become meaningless hype that impresses neither the media gatekeeper nor the public.

Avoid Euphemisms   A euphemism, according to *Webster's New World Dictionary,* is "the use of a less expressive or direct word or phrase for one considered distasteful or offensive."

Public relations personnel should use positive, favorable words to convey a message, but they have an ethical responsibility not to use words that hide information or mislead. Probably little danger exists in substituting positive words such as *alcohol misuse* for *alcohol abuse,* which has a negative connotation. Nor is it improper to say that someone *has a disability* rather than use the more negative word *handicapped.*

In today's society, some euphemisms cause more amusement than concern. Stockbrokers, after the stock market crash of 1987 (referred to on Wall Street as "a major technical correction"), are now called "account executives" and "financial consultants." Car mechanics are "automotive internists" and grocery store checkout clerks "associate scanning professionals." Used luxury cars are "preowned."

More dangerous are the euphemisms that actually alter the meaning or impact of a precise word. Writers call this *doublespeak*—words that pretend to communicate but really don't. Governments are famous for doublespeak. For example, in World War II, Winston Churchill spoke of "dehousing" the civilian population of Germany, which really meant full-scale bombing of cities. In Vietnam, "resource control programs" were really efforts to poison vegetation and the water supply. And in the 1980s, the U.S. State Department decided to eliminate *killing* from its human rights reports and call it "unlawful or arbitrary deprivation of life." In the Persian Gulf War, U.S. military briefing officers described civilian casualties and destruction caused by bombs that missed their military targets as "collateral damage."

Corporations also use euphemisms and doublespeak to hide unfavorable news. Reducing the number of employees, for example, is often called "right-sizing," "skill mix adjustment," or "career assignment and relocation." An airline once called the crash of a plane "the involuntary conversion of a 727."

Use of euphemisms to hide or mislead obviously is contrary to professional public relations standards and the public interest. As William Lutz writes in *Public Relations Quarterly,* "Such language breeds suspicion, cynicism, distrust, and, ultimately, hostility."

Avoid Discriminatory Language   In today's world, effective communication also means *nondiscriminatory* communication. Public relations personnel should double-check every message to eliminate undesirable gender, racial, and ethnic connotations.

In regard to gender, it is unnecessary to write about something as being *man-made* when a word like *synthetic* or *artificial* is just as good. Companies no longer have *manpower* but *employees, personnel,* and *workers.* Most civic organizations have *chairpersons* now, and cities have *fire fighters* instead of *firemen,* and *police officers* instead of *policemen.* Airlines, of course, have *flight attendants* instead of *stewardesses.* Although much progress has been made in desexing language, some changes remain awkward.

For example, the terms *businessperson* and *congressperson* are resisted by many writers as being too stilted.

Careless writing and editing, or lack of sensitivity, also can cause a company trouble. The city of San Francisco, feeling the pressure of its powerful gay lobby, threatened to cancel a $500,000 contract with General Motors for vehicles after it was learned that a GM internal video contained a reference to a foreign competitor's product as "that little faggot truck."

In a letter of apology to the city, GM explained that the "faggot" reference was unintentional and made by a customer being interviewed for the video on why he preferred Chevrolet products to foreign models. The company also added a new directive to its antidiscrimination policy: "Abuse of the dignity of anyone through slurs or other derogatory or objectionable conduct, including that based on sexual orientation, is offensive employee behavior. . . ."

Writers also should be careful about descriptive phrases for women. *Bulldog Reporter,* a West Coast public relations newsletter, has given several "fireplug" awards to public relations firms for the way they have described women in news releases. One Chicago firm, for example, spoke of a company president: "A tall, attractive blonde who could easily turn heads on Main Street is instead turning heads on Wall Street."

In *Bulldog*'s opinion, the prize for capitalizing on racist, sexist stereotypes goes to a Los Angeles public relations firm's news release about the appointment of a female to head a Japanese company's consumer electronics division. It said, in part, "Demure, naturally pretty and conservative in her dress and manner, Miho Suda could easily pass as a college student." *Bulldog* saw this kind of writing as "a desperate and ignorant pitch that completely overlooked Ms. Suda's qualifications and achievements. It practically positions her as the corporate geisha."

Nor is it appropriate in professional settings to say that a woman is the wife of someone also well known. A female vice president of a public relations firm cried foul when a local newsletter described her as the wife of a prominent journalist. The newsletter editor apologized in the next issue.

Messages should avoid any ethnic designations. It is unacceptable to say, for example, "Juan Hernandez, a Latino, is employed. . . ." Persons using any racial reference should always ask whether the same sentence would sound awkward if the word *white* or *Anglo-Saxon* were substituted for *black, Latino, Asian,* and so on. (Chapter 13 discusses the possible legal consequences of racial slurs.)

BELIEVING THE MESSAGE

One key variable in the communication process, discussed further in Chapter 11, is *source credibility.* Do members of the audience perceive the source as knowledgeable and expert on the subject? Do they perceive the source as honest and objective or just representing a special interest? Audiences, for example, ascribe lower credibility to statements in an advertisement than to the same information contained in a news article because news articles are selected by media gatekeepers.

Source credibility is a problem for any spokesperson for an organization because of perceived bias. Even organization executives, whom the media rate as the most knowledgeable sources within an organization, get low ratings.

In a survey of 1000 adults conducted by Porter/Novelli public relations, only 9 percent of the respondents thought organization executives were believable in a crisis situation. Public relations personnel don't fare much better as being credible spokespersons. In fact, a New York firm once did a survey asking journalists to name an animal most like a public relations person; 81 percent of the respondents named the weasel. On the positive side, 71 percent of the journalists responding thought public relations personnel were needed to get an organization's message disseminated.

The problem of source credibility is the main reason that organizations, whenever possible, use respected outside experts or celebrities as representatives to convey their messages.

The *sleeper effect* also influences source credibility. This concept was developed by Carl Hovland, who stated: "There is decreased tendency over time to reject the material presented by an untrustworthy source." His finding grew out of studies in the 1940s in which test subjects registered a greater amount of opinion change after nine weeks than they did after only several days of being exposed to a message. One possible explanation was that people tend to forget the source of information over time.

In other words, even if organizations are perceived initially as not being very credible sources, people may retain the information and eventually separate the source from the opinion. On the other hand, studies show that audiences register more constant opinion change if they perceive the source to be highly credible in the first place.

A second variable in believability is the *context* of the message. Action (performance) speaks louder than a stack of news releases. A bank may spend thousands of dollars on a promotion campaign with the slogan, "Your Friendly Bank—Where Service Counts," but the effort is wasted if employees are not trained to be friendly and courteous. An industrial firm can position itself as deeply concerned about chemical wastes, but all the executive speeches in the world mean nothing if the company makes headlines after dumping toxic wastes into the local river.

Incompatible rhetoric and actions can be somewhat amusing at times. At a press briefing about the importance of "buying American," the U.S. Chamber of Commerce passed out commemorative coffee mugs marked in small print on the bottom, "Made in China."

Another barrier to the believability of messages is the audience's predispositions. This problem brings to mind the old saying, "Don't confuse me with the facts, my mind is already made up."

In this case, Leon Festinger's theory of *cognitive dissonance* should be understood. In essence, it says that people will not believe a message contrary to their predispositions unless the communicator can introduce information that causes them to question their beliefs.

Creating dissonance can be done in at least three ways. First, make the target audience aware that circumstances have changed. "In other words," says Patrick Jackson of *PR Reporter,* "they needn't rationalize any longer; it's safe and OK to change because the situation has changed." Second, give information about new developments or discoveries. This is an unthreatening way to break through a person's opinions. Third, use an unexpected spokesperson. The Clinton administration, on the health reform issue, sought to overcome the opposition of conservatives by getting the endorsement of several respected Republican senators.

REMEMBERING THE MESSAGE

Many messages prepared by public relations personnel are repeated extensively, for several reasons:

- Repetition is necessary because all members of a target audience don't see or hear the message at the same time. Not everyone reads the newspaper on a particular day or watches the same television news program.

- Repetition reminds the audience, so there is less chance of a failure to remember the message. If a source has high credibility, repetition prevents erosion of opinion change.

- Repetition helps the audience remember the message itself. Studies have shown that advertising is quickly forgotten if not repeated constantly.

- Repetition can lead to improved learning and increase the chance of penetrating audience indifference or resistance.

Researchers say that repetition, or redundancy, also is necessary to offset the "noise" surrounding a message. People often hear or see messages in an environment filled with distractions—a baby crying, the conversations of family members or office staff, a barking dog, or even the receiver daydreaming or thinking of other things.

THE DECLINE OF MESSAGE UNDERSTANDING

Messages tend to disintegrate as they pass through various levels of an organizational structure. E. Scannell, author of *Communication for Leadership* (McGraw-Hill, 1970), developed the following chart. It shows, in numerical terms, how much of the original message remains as it travels down the corporate hierarchy:

100 percent	Top management's understanding
66 percent	Vice president's understanding
56 percent	General supervisor's understanding
40 percent	Plant manager's understanding
30 percent	Foreman's understanding
20 percent	Production line worker's understanding

Message entropy, coupled with various barriers to effective communication, is a problem that every professional communicator must overcome.

Consequently, communicators often build repetition into a message. Key points may be mentioned at the beginning and then summarized at the end. If the source is asking the receiver to call for more information or write for a brochure, the telephone number or address is repeated several times. Such precautions also fight *entropy,* which means that messages continually lose information as media channels and people process the information and pass it on to others.

The key to effective communication and retention of the message is to convey information in a variety of ways, using multiple communication channels. This helps people remember the message as they receive it through different media and extends the message to both passive and active audiences.

A good example of using multiple communication tools is a campaign to get a bond issue passed for Macomb Community College in Michigan. The message was quite simple: Vote "Yes." A nonprofit citizens group used 13 communication tools to put the message across: *news releases, media interviews, news conferences, rallies, debates, campaign buttons, speaker's bureau, posters, direct mail, flyers, newsletters, phone calls to registered voters,* and *an essay contest.* The bond issue passed.

ACTING ON THE MESSAGE

The ultimate purpose of any message is to have an effect on the recipient. Public relations personnel communicate messages on behalf of organizations to change perceptions, attitudes, opinions, or behavior in some way. Marketing communications, in particular, has the objective of convincing people to buy goods and services.

THE FIVE-STAGE ADOPTION PROCESS

Getting people to act on a message is not a simple process. In fact, research shows that it can be a somewhat lengthy and complex procedure that depends on a number of intervening influences. One key to understanding how people accept new ideas or products is to analyze the adoption process. The five stages are summarized as follows:

1. *Awareness.* A person becomes aware of an idea or a new product, often by means of an advertisement or a news story.

2. *Interest.* The individual seeks more information about the idea or the product, perhaps by ordering a brochure, picking up a pamphlet, or reading an in-depth article in a newspaper or magazine.

3. *Evaluation.* The person evaluates the idea or the product on the basis of how it meets specific needs and wants. Feedback from friends and family is part of this process.

4. *Trial.* Next, the person tries the product or the idea on an experimental basis, by using a sample, witnessing a demonstration, or making qualifying statements such as, "I read. . . " or "Senator Dole says. . . "

5. *Adoption.* The individual begins to use the product on a regular basis or integrates the idea into his or her belief system. The "Senator Dole says. . . " becomes "I think. . . " if peers provide support and reinforcement of the idea.

It is important to realize that a person does not necessarily go through all five stages with any given idea or product. The process may be terminated after any step. In fact, the process is like a large funnel. Although many are made aware of an idea or a product, only a few will ultimately adopt it.

This is because a number of factors affect the adoption process. Everett Rogers, author of *Diffusion of Innovation,* lists at least five:

- *Relative advantage.* The degree to which an innovation is perceived as better than the idea it replaces.

- *Compatibility.* The degree to which an innovation is perceived as being consistent with the existing values, experiences, and needs of potential adopters.

- *Complexity.* The degree to which an innovation is perceived as difficult to understand and use.

- *Trialability.* The degree to which an innovation may be experienced on a limited basis.

- *Observability.* The degree to which the results of an innovation are visible to others.

FIGURE 9.5

This graph shows the steps through which an individual or other decision-making unit goes in the innovation-decision process from first knowledge of an innovation to decision to adopt it, followed by implementation of the new idea and confirmation of the decision.

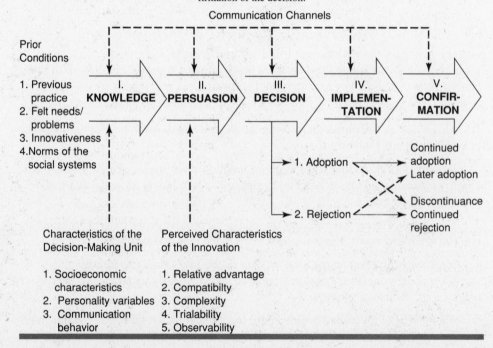

Polltaker George Gallup also has compiled a list of factors that can influence adoption of a message: (1) complexity of the idea, (2) difference from accustomed patterns, (3) competition with prevailing ideas, (4) necessity of demonstration and proof, (5) strength of vested interests, (6) failure to meet a felt need, and (7) frequency of reminders.

The communicator should be aware of these factors and attempt to implement communication strategies that will overcome as many of them as possible. Repeating a message in various ways, reducing its complexity, taking into account competing messages, and structuring the message to meet the needs of the audience are ways to do this.

THE TIME FACTOR

Another aspect that confuses people is the amount of time needed to adopt a new idea or product. Depending on the individual and situation, the entire adoption process can take place almost instantly if the result is of minor consequence or requires low-level commitment. Buying a new brand of soft drink or a bar of soap is relatively inexpensive and often done on impulse. On the other hand, deciding to buy a new car or vote for a particular candidate may involve an adoption process that takes several weeks or months.

Rogers's, research shows that people approach innovation in different ways, depending on their personality traits and the risk involved. "Innovators" are venturesome and eager to try new ideas, while "Laggards" are traditional and the last to adopt anything. Between the two extremes are "Early Adopters," who are opinion leaders; "Early Majority," who take the deliberate approach; and "Late Majority," who are often skeptical but bow to peer pressure.

Psychographics, discussed in Chapter 11, can often help communicators segment audiences that have "Innovator" or "Early Adopter" characteristics and would be predisposed to adopting new ideas.

HOW DECISIONS ARE INFLUENCED

Of particular interest to public relations people is the primary source of information at each step in the adoption process. Mass media vehicles such as advertising, short news articles, feature stories, and radio and television news announcements are most influential at the *awareness* stage of the adoption process. A news article or a television announcement makes people aware of an idea, event, or new product. They also are made aware through such vehicles as direct mail, office memos, and simple brochures.

Individuals at the *interest* stage also rely on mass media vehicles, but they are actively seeking information and pay attention to longer, in-depth articles. They rely more on detailed brochures, specialized publications, small-group seminars, and meetings to provide details. At the *evaluation, trial,* and *adoption* stages, group norms and opinions are the most influential. Feedback, negative or positive, from friends and peers may determine adoption. If a person's friends generally disapprove of the candidate, the movie, or the automobile brand, it is unlikely that the individual will complete the adoption process even if he or she is highly sold on the idea. If a person does make a commitment, mass media vehicles become reinforcing mechanisms. Studies show, for example, that owners of a new car are the most avid readers of that car's advertising.

The complexities of the adoption process show that public relations communicators need to think about the entire communication process—from the formulation of the message to the ways in which receivers ultimately process the information and make decisions. By doing so, communicators can form more effective message strategies and develop realistic objectives for what can actually be accomplished.

A special kind of communication problem comes up when an organization faces a crisis. The following section gives some tips and case studies on how to communicate in such a situation.

CRISIS COMMUNICATIONS

The communication process, difficult in the best of times, is severely tested in crisis situations when there is a high degree of uncertainty. At such times verifiable information to confirm or substantiate what is happening or has happened may be lacking.

This causes people actively to seek information and become, as research suggests, more dependent on media for information that will satisfy the human desire for closure. A crisis situation, in other words, puts a great deal of pressure on organizations to provide accurate, complete information to the mass media and the public as quickly as possible.

There are many dimensions of what constitutes a crisis for an organization. Pacific Telesis, the parent company of Pacific Bell, defines a crisis as "an extraordinary event or series of events that adversely affects the integrity of the product; the reputation or financial stability of the organization; or the health or well-being of employees, the community, or the public-at-large."

Here is a sampling of major crises that have hit various organizations:

■ The safety of Dow-Corning's silicone gel breast implants came under fire from both the medical community and thousands of women who claimed that they were harmed by the product.

■ Sears was charged by consumer agencies in several states with defrauding customers and making unnecessary repairs at its auto centers. (See Chapter 14.)

■ An outbreak of food poisoning, leading to the death of a 2-year-old, was traced to contaminated beef served by Jack-In-The-Box restaurants in Washington State.

■ United Way of America was rocked by the disclosure that its chief executive used organization funds to support a lavish personal lifestyle. (See Chapter 18.)

■ An activist environmental group claimed that the pesticide Alar used on apples is a health hazard to children. The claim was featured on *60 Minutes,* causing a major drop in apple sales, affecting thousands of apple growers.

■ A Florida man claimed that his wife's fatal brain tumor was caused by her frequent use of a cellular phone. He filed a lawsuit and received national exposure with an appearance on *Larry King Live.*

Such situations, including disasters in which people are injured and killed, constitute major crises because the reputation of a company, industry, product, or service is in jeopardy. Economic survival is often at stake. A company can lose millions of dollars overnight if the public perceives that a serious problem exists.

Johnson & Johnson, manufacturer of Tylenol, saw the brand's market share shrink from 37 percent to barely 6 percent in a matter of days after capsules laced with cyanide killed seven people in Chicago. By the time it was established that someone had tampered with the product after it had reached store shelves, the ordeal had cost the company $50 million to recall the product and test all its manufacturing processes.

During times of crisis, the media play an important role in the communication process. As previously mentioned, people become more media-dependent as they actively seek information to confirm what has happened and learn the reasons for the problem. They use the media as a *surveillance* mechanism to determine whether they should stop using a product, donating to a particular nonprofit organization, or supporting a political candidate.

The mass media, responding to heightened public interest, also demand more information from the organization involved. In many cases, it is the public relations spokesperson who must handle a barrage of requests for information within a matter of hours. He or she also faces an uphill battle, because audiences usually ascribe low credibility to organizational spokespersons in times of crisis. Here are some guidelines for communicating effectively and establishing credibility with the press:

- Never say "No comment." A survey by Porter/Novelli found that nearly two-thirds of the public feel that "no comment" almost always means that the organization is guilty of wrongdoing.

- Always try to be helpful. Too many executives are so guarded in media interviews that they miss opportunities to get their own case across.

- Be familiar with print and broadcast deadlines. Calling a news conference on or after a deadline may hurt the organization's chance to get fair or full treatment.

- Establish good rapport and credibility with the media before a crisis hits. If journalists know from past experience that the organization communicates in a credible way, they will be more inclined to believe the organization's side of the story.

FIGURE 9.6
This poll result confirms what astute public relations people know from experience: a "no comment" response from a corporate spokesperson tends to increase suspicion of misconduct.

Americans Say "No Comment" = Guilty

When asked if they agree that when a company spokesperson declines to comment, it almost always means the company is guilty of wrongdoing, 65% said yes.

35%

65%

Source: Porter/Novelli

The key to successful communications with the media and the public during a crisis is to become a credible source of information. There are numerous lists about how to accomplish this, and the guidelines of *PR Newswire* are fairly typical:

- ■ Appoint a spokesperson whom the media can trust and who has authority to speak for the organization. It also is a good idea to designate one central spokesperson so that the organization speaks with one voice.

- ■ Set up a central media information center where reporters can obtain updated information and work on stories. Telephone lines, modular jacks for reporter computers, fax machines, and word processors are usually provided.

- ■ Provide a constant flow of information, even if the situation is unchanged or negative. An organization builds credibility by addressing bad news quickly; when information is withheld, the cover-up becomes the story.

- ■ Be accessible by providing after-hours phone numbers or carrying a cellular phone at all times.

- ■ Keep a log of media calls, and return calls as promptly as possible. A log can help track issues being raised by reporters and give a record of which media showed the most interest in the story.

- ■ Be honest. Don't exaggerate, and don't obscure facts. If the organization is not sure of something, or doesn't have the answer, it should say so. If the information can't be provided, an explanation should be given.

These guidelines reflect common sense, but when a crisis hits, it is surprising how many organizations become defensive. How organizations approach a crisis and deal with it from a communications standpoint, research has indicated, often depends on the philosophy of top management. Dow-Corning, for example, had considerable negative coverage because management perceived the media as enemies.

Corporate spokespeople accused the media of reporting only the "sensationalistic, anecdotal side of the breast implant story, which has unnecessarily frightened women across the country." At a news conference, the head of Dow's health-care business continued the attack by telling the assembled reporters that they took "memos out of context and distorted reality." It would be an understatement to say that this is a poor way to establish credibility with the press, which already was labeling Dow-Corning's defense a "cover-up." In the Porter/Novelli survey, 95 percent of the respondents said they are more offended by a company's lying about a crisis than by the actual crisis.

Jack-In-The-Box also violated the tenets of crisis communications in the first days of the reported food poisonings. The company initially said "no comment" and then waited three days to hold a news conference at which the company president tried to shift the blame onto the meat packing company. And again, the Porter/Novelli survey tells how this kind of action is perceived. Seventy-five percent of the respondents said companies refuse to take responsibility for crises.

David Vogel, a business professor at the University of California in Berkeley, says: "There are two principles: accept responsibility and take action." Even if the organization is not directly at fault, it should take responsibility for its product and the public safety.

The principles of crisis management and communications can best be illustrated by two situations that have now entered the literature as classics. One is Johnson & Johnson's 1982 handling of the Tylenol poisonings in Chicago. It illustrates how an organization can effectively deal with a crisis that threatens a major product. The second case is Exxon's 1989 oil spill in Valdez, Alaska. It illustrates the pitfalls of not having an effective crisis communications plan.

TYLENOL: THE RIGHT WAY

Johnson & Johnson was galvanized into action as soon as news reports reached it about seven persons dying in Chicago from cyanide contained in Tylenol capsules.

Lawrence G. Foster, vice president for public relations, immediately sent an associate to Chicago aboard a company jet to collect firsthand information. He also set up a large bank of telephones to handle the mass of media inquiries he knew would come. To answer the phones, Foster brought to headquarters in New Brunswick, New Jersey, 50 public relations staff members from Johnson & Johnson's subsidiaries. This quick action enabled reporters to reach the company without frustrating delays.

Open Policy   Without hesitation, during the first hours of the crisis, top management put into operation an open information policy. This was in keeping with the long-established written corporate credo, which declared that the company's first responsibility is to "those who use our products and services." The credo stated, "In a business society, every act of business has social consequences and may arouse public interest. Every time business hires, builds, sells, or buys, it is acting for the . . . people as well as for itself, and it must be prepared to accept full responsibility."

The company immediately halted Tylenol production, stopped distribution, and recalled supplies from retailers. To recover the capsules from consumers' homes, the company issued coupons with which consumers could exchange containers of capsules for an equal amount of Tylenol tablets, which were not subject to cyanide tampering. Later, the company announced a toll-free number individuals could telephone to request a $2.50 coupon for purchase of safe replacement Tylenol. Altogether, the company recalled 22 million bottles of Tylenol capsules.

The public relations department was besieged with inquiries from the media—1411 telephone calls during the first ten days, a figure that rose to 2500 before the story died down. A seven-member management committee, of which the public relations director was a member, met twice daily at the height of the crisis to evaluate the situation. To unify management's response to the public, the president of the McNeil subsidiary served as the principal spokesman.

From the first, the company cooperated fully with federal investigators, never waiting for them to pressure it to act. It offered a $100,000 reward for capture of the perpetrator. After testing 8 million recalled capsules, investigators determined that the cyanide had not entered the fatal capsules during the manufacturing process, but on the store shelves. In fact, the exhaustive and costly testing found only eight tampered-with bottles, in which 75 capsules contained cyanide.

While conducting the recall and debating a future course, Johnson & Johnson took numerous public opinion surveys. These showed, among other things, that because of the intensive news coverage more than 90 percent of the public knew after the first week not to take Tylenol capsules. By the second week, more than 90 percent knew that Johnson & Johnson was not to blame. Although the company was absolved of blame, numerous marketing experts asserted that Tylenol as a brand name was dead; that if the company decided to resume selling such a medication, it must change the brand name and image.

Ignoring the doomsayers, Johnson & Johnson decided to gamble on restoring Tylenol to public acceptance. Much of the public appeared to know that the product was safe and the tampering had been an isolated incident.

Recovery Campaign   Thus began the second phase of the Tylenol story, the comeback campaign.

To prevent a recurrence, Johnson & Johnson designed a tamper-resistant container for Tylenol capsules. It strongly endorsed federal legislation making tampering a felony and regulations requiring tamper-resistant packaging for a wide range of over-the-counter drugs. Company representatives visited the offices of more than 160 members of Congress to gain support for the regulations and legislation.

The public phase of Tylenol's recovery campaign opened with a 30-city video teleconference from New York six weeks after the deaths occurred; more than 500 media representatives attended. During the 90-minute teleconference, James E. Burke, chief executive officer, and other company officials spoke, the new packaging was shown, and the audience heard a videotaped statement by the head of the Food and Drug Administration. Samples of the safety packaging were distributed.

To induce the public to overcome its lingering psychological resistance, Burke announced two attractive offers. Former users who had thrown away their capsules were invited to call a toll-free number and request a free bottle in the new packaging. No proof of previous ownership was required. Advertisements in Sunday newspapers with 40 million combined circulation contained coupons entitling the bearer to a $2.50 discount on the purchase of any Tylenol product. This permitted consumers to obtain smaller Tylenol packages free. The headline of the advertisement was "Thank you, America." Use of the toll-free numbers by the public to obtain information and free bottles was immense; more than 325,000 calls were made.

Burke also used the teleconference to thank the news media for the fair, responsible way in which they reported the cyanide deaths—the kind of public compliments reporters and editors rarely hear. Restoration of public confidence was so successful that six months after the death story broke, Tylenol had recaptured about 32 of the 37 percent of the market it had previously held, despite vigorous advertising efforts by its competitors.

Lessons of the Tylenol Story   Open communication was one key to Johnson & Johnson's success. The other key was the company's adherence to its longtime policy that the safety of its customers comes first.

Several specific steps were especially helpful. Establishment of additional telephone lines and expansion of the public relations staff gave reporters quick access to company representatives. Selection of a skillful principal spokesman provided the firm's statements with consistency. The company's close cooperation with government investigators encouraged public confidence.

Another less tangible but significant factor was evident in Johnson & Johnson's previous record of friendly dealing with the media. When the crunch came, Johnson & Johnson benefited from its adherence to a longtime constructive relationship with the media.

EXXON: THE WRONG WAY

Riding low in the water with its load of crude oil from the Alaska pipeline, the huge tanker *Exxon Valdez* plowed south from the port of Valdez, Alaska, in a drizzle shortly after midnight of March 24, 1989. Suddenly it ran onto a reef, split open, and spilled masses of oil into the sea. Thus began one of history's worst environmental accidents—and a public relations performance so bungled that the public perceived the Exxon Corporation as a cold, uncaring company more concerned about escaping responsibility than about the damage it had caused.

The Facts   Shortly after the *Exxon Valdez* sailed from the terminal into Prince William Sound, Captain Joseph J. Hazelwood turned over command of the vessel to Third Mate Gregory Cousins, who was not legally licensed to pilot a ship in those waters. Concerned about floating ice, the captain instructed Cousins to steer the ship out of the normal southbound shipping channel to a certain point, then turn back into its normal course. The return was not made in time and the ship hit Bligh Reef, where rocks tore eight holes in its bottom.

Nearly 11 million tons of oil—240,000 barrels—spread across the remote, austerely scenic sound, fouling some 1100 miles of shoreline. Immense numbers of fish died, and Alaska's fishing industry was critically damaged. More than 30,000 dead birds and about 1,000 dead sea otters were counted.

By the end of summer 1989, Exxon had spent more than $1 billion on cleanup work, yet the job was far from finished, and the company's reputation had suffered an extreme blow. The company fired Captain Hazelwood, who later was acquitted of operating a ship while intoxicated.

Exxon's Public Relations Actions   During the hours just after the accident, as the public began to comprehend the enormity of the spill, Lawrence G. Rawl, Exxon's chairman, made two public relations mistakes that he later regretted.

■ He elected to stay at New York headquarters rather than fly to the oil spill scene and take charge of the cleanup in person. Instead, he sent lower-level officials. This was widely interpreted as indifference on his part.

■ He decided that all information about the spill and cleanup efforts should be released at Valdez, on the scene. This remote port of 3000 people had only limited telephone lines and other facilities, so reporters who flew to Alaska had trouble getting out their stories. Exxon officials in New York refused to talk for nearly a week, creating an impression that Exxon was not seriously concerned and was trying to restrict coverage.

Rawl himself made no public comment until six days after the accident and didn't meet reporters until April 18. Three weeks had passed after the spill before he went to Alaska.

Ten days after the spill, Exxon published a full-page newspaper advertisement in the form of an open letter from Rawl. In it he said, "I want to tell you how sorry I am that this accident took place." He failed to state, however, that Exxon accepted responsibility for the spill, an omission that was widely noticed.

Quarrel with Alaska and U.S. Coast Guard   Soon after this, Exxon got into a public quarrel with the state of Alaska and U.S. Coast Guard officials over delays in the cleanup effort, and tried to shift the blame for this from itself to them. This led Governor Steve Cowper to accuse Exxon of making false statements.

Exxon claimed that it could have minimized the damage had it been permitted to use chemical dispersants quickly after the spill, but was prevented from doing so by the state and the Coast Guard. State officials called this claim false; they said that Exxon had not sought permission for general use of dispersants. Cowper called the Exxon assertion a "systematic effort to mislead the public." Exxon's claim about dispersants apparently was a legal maneuver for use in defense of anticipated lawsuits, but it added to the public image of a belligerent, uncooperative company.

Public Reaction   Response by the public to these events was strongly against Exxon, both for letting the spill occur and for the way it handled the cleanup. More than 18,000 customers mailed their credit cards back to the company. Talk of a boycott was heard; an Exxon statement called such action unjust. Late-night TV talk-show hosts aimed their barbs at Exxon. Congressional committees did the same. Company officials were summoned to the White House and told that cleanup efforts were inadequate. Corporate profits fell, and stockholders gave Rawl a bad time at the annual meeting. In the same time period, Exxon dropped from 8th to 110th on *Fortune*'s list of most admired companies in America.

Press coverage, portraying the oil spill as a major environmental disaster, was intense in the year following the accident. The Associated Press, for example, moved more than 2000 stories on it. Professor William J. Small of Fordham University, who has researched the press coverage of the spill, wrote: "Probably no other company ever got a more damaging portrayal in the mass media."

Aftermath   More than two years after the disaster, Exxon entered a guilty plea in federal court and agreed to pay the U.S. and Alaskan governments $1.1 billion to settle criminal and civil cases against it. Then in 1994 a federal jury ordered Exxon to pay $5 billion in damages to fishers and some 10,000 other persons in a civil class action suit. The corporation said it had spent another $3 billion on cleanup work. The *Exxon Valdez,* the source of all that followed, was repaired and renamed the *Exxon Mediterranean;* it sails only in foreign waters.

Exxon still is associated with oil spills and environmental disasters. The Porter/Novelli survey asked respondents what corporate crises they could recall. More than 50 percent named the *Exxon Valdez* oil spill without any prompting. The more recent Sears crisis about unnecessary auto repairs (1992) was recalled by 23 percent. In contrast, only 11 percent could recall the Tylenol tampering crisis.

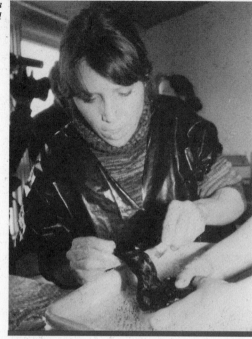

Using a toothbrush and soapy water, Dr. Jessica Porter cleans the oil off a sea bird at the animal rescue center in Valdez, Alaska, in March 1989. Thousands of birds were covered with oil that leaked from the tanker Exxon Valdez in an environmental disaster.

Perhaps more sobering for Exxon is the survey result that a large majority said an organization's wrongdoings affect their purchase of its products. Another survey by the Michael Peters Group reported that 77 percent of Americans consider a company's environmental reputation when they buy products and services.

With these attitudes in mind, Exxon began a campaign in late 1993 to clear its name. The target audience was the scientific community. Through research studies, the company tried to dispel the widespread belief that Alaska's Prince William Sound suffered long-term environmental damage from the 1989 spill.

Lessons of the Exxon Case Careful study shows four major shortcomings in Exxon's public relations operation during the oil spill:

1. Failure of the company's top official to establish clear public command of the problem from the start, by going to the scene.

2. Failure to provide an open flow of information to the media, with ample facilities for its distribution.

3. Creation of an adversarial relationship with state and federal governments. This led to a perception that the company was belligerent and uncooperative.

4. Failure to have an adequate crisis plan ready to handle such an oil spill emergency. The company had publicly belittled the possibility of an Alaskan oil spill and became complacent.

In an review with *Fortune,* Rawl, when invited to give advice to other chief executive officers on handling such a crisis, answered, "You'd better prethink which way you are going to jump from a public affairs standpoint before you have any kind of problem. You ought to always have a public affairs plan, even though it's kind of hard to force yourself to think in terms of a chemical plant blowing up or spilling all that oil in Prince William Sound."

Few companies have ever had such a costly lesson in public relations.

RISK COMMUNICATION

During the past decade, public concern for the environment has caused the development of something called *risk communication.* In essence, this is defined as any verbal or written exchange that attempts to communicate information regarding risk to public health and the environment.

Organizations, including large corporations, increasingly engage in risk communication to inform the public of risks associated with the ingredients of products and in trying to control, eliminate, and clean up potential hazards. These issues are subject to expensive lawsuits, governmental legislation, and consumer boycotts if organizations fail to communicate with the public on complex environmental matters.

Risk communication usually involves communication with hostile, uninformed, or concerned audiences. Some concepts that guide it are:

■ Risks voluntarily encountered tend to be accepted better than risks involuntarily encountered.

■ The more control individuals have over a situation, the less risk they perceive.

■ The more complex a situation is, the higher the perception of risk.

■ Familiarity breeds confidence.

■ Perception of risk increases when the messages of experts conflict.

■ The severity of consequences affects risk perception.

Risk communication requires interaction between an organization and its publics. Emphasis is on mutual understanding and cooperation, not merely trying to persuade a skeptical public that the organization is doing the right thing.

Jeffrey P. Julin, writing in IABC's *Communication World,* outlined some approaches that public relations practitioners should take in risk communication:

■ Understand the public's concerns.

■ Simplify and clarify technical messages.

■ Go to the public, meet on its turf.

■ Develop ongoing dialogue.

Tools of Public Relations

*E*xperts in public relations use many methods to deliver their messages, from simple devices such as news releases to campaigns requiring numerous tools. This color section presents a sampling of those tools in graphic from. The ways in which public relations methods are applied in professional practice are described throughout the textbook.

CREATED EVENT An estimated 6000 bikers parade to County Stadium in Milwaukee to celebrate the 90th birthday of the Harley-Davidson motocycle. The event was created by the manufacturing company and organized through a network of owner groups.

VIDEO NEW RELEASE *When some customers claimed they had found syringes in Pepsi cans, the company distributed a video news release (VNR) showing that intrusion of its high-speed bottling process was virtually impossible. The claims proved to be a hoax.*

COMPANY MANUAL *Visa used specially created cartoons of the comic strip character Cathy to give a light touch to its "Credit Cards: An Owner's Manual." The manual discussed the wise use of credit.*

PERSONAL APPEARANCE *President Clinton plays the saxophone for U.S. soldiers as part of a campaign to strengthen his image as a vigorous chief executive who shares the interests of young Americans.*

PRODUCT PUBLICITY *Cucumbers received national publicity from this photograph of a young man spreading them in an 11-foot-deep wooden tank at Hausback Pickle Company in Saginaw, Michigan. Publicists can draw attention even to unexciting products by creating unusual photographs like this one.*

NEWSLETTER Distribution of a newsletter such as this one by the Mt. Diablo Medical Center in northern California is an effective method of communication from an organization to its membership or to an entire community.

INVESTOR IMFORMATION Keeping investors informed about their company's financial condition and activities is an essentail part of corporate public relations. This Southern Company newsletter is an attractive example of how companies reach their stockholders.

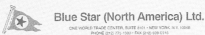

Blue Star PACE Ltd.

701 SUTTER STREET, 5TH FLOOR • SAN FRANCISCO, CA 94109
(415) 808-2026 • FAX (415) 673-0365

**BLUE STAR RESCUES
STRANDED HONOLULU CARGO**

HONOLULU -- (February 14, 1992) -- Some 30 containers stuffed with food,
clothing, bedding and construction materials, as well as earth moving equipment -- all
abandoned by a bankrupt shipping line -- will be rescued by Blue Star PACE and shipped
to victims of Hurricane Val in Western and American Samoa, the company announced.

Dick Hanft, vice president, Western Region for Blue Star PACE, said the company
has diverted one of its vessels -- the California Star -- to make a special delivery of the
stranded cargo at the Port of Pago Pago.

The containers, some destined for Tonga and Tahiti, were abandoned at dockside
Feb. 6 when Hawaii-Pacific Lines Ltd. ceased operations. The company had provided the
only shipping link between Hawaii and the Samoas, Tonga, the Cook Islands and
Christmas Island.

The California Star, the closest Blue Star vessel to the stranded cargo, arrives
Honolulu Monday to pick up the cargo.

"The extra port calls aren't out of the ordinary," Hanft said. "Blue Star always steps
in to contribute when people need help."

Both the Samoas are recovering from Hurricane Val, which tore through the
Samoas in December, causing an estimated $100 million in damage.

Blue Star PACE provides direct shipping service to ports in Australia, New
Zealand, and several South Pacific Islands from the East, West and Gulf coasts of North
America.

Besides relief aid materials, the abandoned containers contain soft drinks,
household appliances, automotive parts and consumer electronics. A cement truck and
fuel truck were also stranded at the Port of Honolulu. Whene said that Blue Star will
evaluate whether to expand permanently its American Samoa scheduled service.

more

TELEGRAM: "BLUESTARLI" • TELEX: 184926 BLUE STAR SFO

Blue Star (North America) Ltd.

ONE WORLD TRADE CENTER, SUITE 8101 • NEW YORK, N.Y. 10048
PHONE (212) 775-1500 • FAX (212) 938-0316

**BLUE STAR LINE TO CALL MEXICO
FROM AUSTRALIA AND NEW ZEALAND**

NEW YORK -- Blue Star Line (BSL) will make direct calls to the Port of Lazaro
Cardenas, Mexico, effective with the Aug. 7 sailing of the M/V Washington Star from New
Zealand, the company announced this week.

BSL's Lazaro Cardenas call is the first direct liner service from Australia/New Zealand to
the west coast of Mexico. Northbound calls will serve the growing and changing trade from
Australia and New Zealand to Mexico, with sailings every three weeks and a 16-day transit time.

"Blue Star Line has long been the principal northbound carrier into Mexico through our
transshipment services," said BSL president Ray Tilley. "This new direct service is further
evidence of our longstanding commitment to the Mexican trade."

Tilley said that direct service will be supported with three additional transshipment
opportunities to Lazaro Cardenas on the west coast, and to Vera Cruz on the east coast.

BSL already provides the most complete shipping service available between North America
and the Pacific Basin. With more than 80 sailings per year in both directions, BSL handles
refrigerated containers, dry containers, breakbulk and heavylift cargoes.

Tilley said that meat exporters "were excited and encouraged" about the new direct calls.
"The new service is an extremely positive development, and we have every expectation of its
success," Tilley said.

In addition to beef, goat, mutton, veal and lamb, Australian and New Zealand exporters
send a variety of dairy products, wool and processed foods to Mexico.

Rates and booking information can be obtained through any Blue Star Line office or agent,
or through the company's New York headquarters at 212-775-1500.

# # #

23 July 1992

Contact: Kevin Plagman
             Communications West
             1426 Eighteenth Street
             San Francisco, CA 94107
             415-863-7220

ITT 422914 W.U. TELEX: 12-6115 TWX: 710-581-4102

NEWS RELEASE *An organization's announcement of news about itself in the form of a
ready-to-publish news release is a basic tool of public relations. This release by an international shipping line is concise, factural, and clearly written.*

*NEWS CONFERENCE News
and background information
often is distributed to the media
by an organization's spokesperson at a news conference for
reporters and editors. Gary
Phillips, director of Victoria
magazine, left, and Kim Waller
of Town and Country.*

CORPORATE ANNUAL REPORT *An eye-catching cover on its corporate annual report drives home Polygram's message, "Creativity is our business." This innovative approach appeals to the record company's youthful audience. Most annual reports are far more conservative. (See Figure 22.5 in chapter 22, p.582)*

PolyGram
Annual Report 199

BEST WESTERN LOGOS 1947-1991

1947 · 1962 · 1964 · 1966

1974 · 1982 · 1985 · 1991

ORGANIZATION LOGOS
Companies sometimes revise their identifying symbols to reflect changes in art styles and their business. The Best Western motel chain changed its logo several times between 1947 and 1993 as it evolved from a Western states regional operation into an international firm.

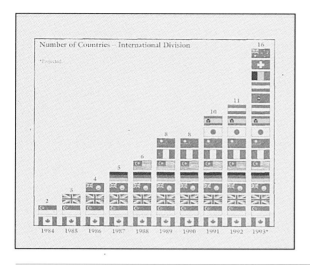

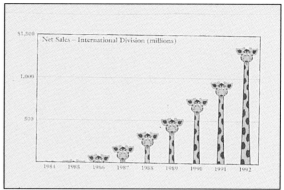

DISTINCTIVE GRAPHICS *Instead of using plain lines in the bar charts of its annual report, Toys "R" Us caught the readers' attention by employing clever graphics.*

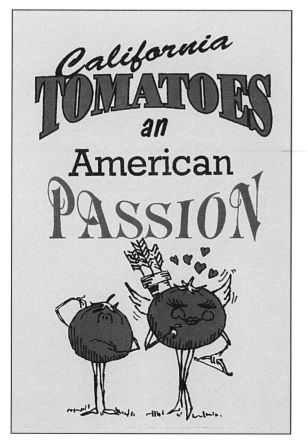

CONSUMER BROCHURE *This whimsical cover sets the tone for a brochure the tomato industry distributed at fairs and festivals. A brochure is a standard tool for delivering basic infromation about an organization or product in easily understood form.*

More Fun. More Friends. More Life.

For more enjoyment, greater popularity
and a more healthful life, be a nonsmoker.

SURGEON GENERAL'S WARNING: Smoking By
Pregnant Women May Result in Fetal Injury,
Premature Birth, And Low Birth Weight.

♥ American Heart Association

POSTER *An effective poster delivers a simple message in few words and includes a striking illustration. This poster by the American Heart Association urging youths not to smoke is a good example.*

CORPORATE SPONSORSHIP *Many corporations draw attention to their products by sponsoring sporting events and competitors. Name recognition of products, vital in marketing, is enhanced by such exposure. This Kodak film race car is a high-speed traveling billboard.*

SYRINGE HOAX VICTIMIZES PEPSI

A hoax of nationwide proportions against the makers of Pepsi-Cola created an intense but short-lived crisis for the soft-drink company.

A man in Tacoma, Washington, claimed in 1993 that he had found a syringe inside a can of Diet Pepsi. As the news spread, men and women across the country made similar claims of finding foreign objects in Pepsi cans—a broken sewing needle, a screw, a bullet, even a narcotics vial.

Pepsico faced a potentially catastrophic situation. The medical implications of contaminated drink cans were frightening. Some of the media drew comparisons to the Tylenol deaths. Demands for a recall of all Pepsi products arose.

Company officials were confident that insertion of foreign objects into cans on their high-speed, closely controlled bottling lines was virtually impossible. Their urgent problem was to convince the public that this was true, and that the foreign objects had been inserted after the cans were opened. In their ultimately successful public relations campaign, they used some of the methods the makers of Tylenol found so helpful.

Three steps by Pepsi were especially important:

1. The company immediately cooperated with the U.S. Food and Drug Administration. Commissioner David Kessler advised them that no recall of Pepsi was necessary. He publicly supported Pepsi's decision against a recall.

2. Pepsi president Craig E. Weathrup immediately made numerous appearances on national television programs and gave newspaper interviews to state the company's case that its bottling lines were secure. Kessler made a joint appearance with him on ABC's *Nightline*.

3. To provide visual evidence, Pepsi distributed video news releases nationwide by satellite for three days. These showed pictures of a bottling line moving at nearly 2000 cans a minute, so fast that tampering with a can before it was sealed appeared impossible. The first of these VNRs, at the peak of the panic, was seen by a record 183 million viewers, according to a Nielsen survey.

A week after the scare began, Pepsi ran full-page advertisements with the headline, "Pepsi is pleased to announce . . . nothing." It stated, "As America now knows, those stories about Diet Pesi were a hoax. . . " Then getting double mileage, the advertisement announced Pepsi's summer promotion plans.

Meanwhile, law enforcement investigators forced numerous claimants to admit that they had made up their stories. Eventually, 39 people in 20 states were arrested; eight pleaded guilty and others faced legal action.

Looking back, Rebecca Madeira, Pepsi-Cola vice president for public affairs, told *Public Relations Journal,* "A crisis can only be in your control if you cooperate with the media, invite them in, and furnish them with facts. Your only defense when your company is on trial is to be a participant in that trial."

Pepsi is pleased
to announce...

...nothing.

As America now knows, those stories about Diet Pepsi were a hoax. Plain and simple, not true. Hundreds of investigators have found no evidence to support a single claim.

As for the many, many thousands of people who work at Pepsi-Cola, we feel great that it's over. And we're ready to get on with making and bringing you what we believe is the best-tasting diet cola in America.

There's not much more we can say. Except that most importantly, we won't let this hoax change our exciting plans for this summer.

We've set up special offers so you can enjoy our great quality products at prices that will save you money all summer long. It all starts on July 4th weekend and we hope you'll stock up with a little extra, just to make up for what you might have missed last week.

That's it. Just one last word of thanks to the millions of you who have stood with us.

Drink All The Diet Pepsi You Want.
Uh Huh.

This message is brought to you by the Pepsi-Cola Company 4242 E. Raymond, Phoenix, Arizona

---

FIGURE 9.7
After proof emerged that claims of finding syringes and other foreign objects in Pepsi soft drink cans were false, PepsiCola management published a full-page newspaper advertisement with an eye-catching headline.

■ Be inclusive, friends and foes, and listen to both.

■ Build coalitions.

■ Power-share, give the public opportunities to help make decisions.

Risk communication, as an integral part of public relations practice, is predicted to increase in importance.

CASE PROBLEM

Extensive information campaigns are being mounted throughout the world to inform people about the dangers of acquired immune deficiency syndrome (AIDS). Information specialists must utilize a variety of communication strategies and tactics to create public awareness and cause changes in individual behavior patterns.

At the same time, the communication process is very complex because a number of variables must be considered. Using this chapter as a guide, how would you apply the various communication concepts and theories to the task of informing people about AIDS?

QUESTIONS FOR REVIEW AND DISCUSSION

1. What kinds of questions, according to Patrick Jackson, should a communicator ask before preparing any communication materials?

2. James Grunig says there are at least five possible objectives for a communicator. What are they? What two objectives do most public relations campaigns try to achieve?

3. What are the five basic elements of a communication model?

4. Why is two-way communication (feedback) an important aspect of effective communication?

5. What are the advantages and disadvantages, from a communication standpoint, of reaching the audience through mass media channels?

6. Explain the behavioral communication model. What is the importance of the "triggering event"?

7. What is the premise of the media uses and gratification theory?

8. What kinds of messages and communication channels would you use for a passive audience? An active information-seeking audience?

9. Why is it necessary to use a variety of messages and communication channels in a public relations program?

10. Why is it important to write with clarity and simplicity? How can symbols, acronyms, and slogans help?

11. Explain the concept behind readability formulas.

12. What kinds of things should be avoided when writing public relations messages?

13. Why is it important to build repetition into a message?

14. Explain the five steps in the adoption process. What are some of the factors that affect the adoption of an idea or product?

15. What basic guidelines should be used in conducting crisis communications?

16. What is *risk communication?*

SUGGESTED READINGS

"Assessing the Damage: Practitioner Perspectives on the Valdez Disaster." *Public Relations Journal,* October 1989, pp. 40–45.

"Behavioral Model Replacing Communications Model as Basic Theoretical Understanding of PR Practice." *PR Reporter,* July 30, 1990, pp. 1–3. The importance of "triggering events" in creating opinion change.

Berzok, Robert M. "Recipe for Effective Communication: Substitute Emotion for B.S." *Communication World,* October 1993, pp. 23–25.

Carney, Ann, and Jorden, Amy. "Prepare for Business-Related Crises." *Public Relations Journal,* August 1993, pp. 34–36.

Cipalla, Rita. "Coping with Crisis: What the Textbooks Don't Tell You." *Communication World,* August 1993, pp. 28–29.

DeFleur, Melvin, and Ball-Rokeach, Sandra. *Theories of Mass Communication.* New York: Longman, 1989.

Dyer, Samuel Coad, Miller, Mark M., and Boone, Jeff. "Wire Service Coverage of the Exxon Valdez Crisis." *Public Relations Review,* Spring 1991, pp. 27–36.

Feder, Barnaby J. "PR Mistakes Seen in Breast-Implant Case." New York *Times,* January 29, 1992, p. C1–C2.

"In a Crisis, What You Say Isn't Always What the Public Hears." *Public Relations Journal,* September 1993, pp. 10–11. Results of Porter/Novelli survey on how public perceives corporate crises.

Julin, Jeffrey P. "Is PR a Risk to Effective Risk Communication?" *Communication World,* October 1993, pp. 14–16. Part of eight-page section on risk management.

McCarthy, Michael J. "Pepsi Faces Problem in Trying to Contain Syringe Scare." *Wall Street Journal,* June 17, 1993, pp. B1, B6.

"Pepsi's Big Scare." *Public Relations Journal,* August 1993, pp. 6–7, 13. The company's communication strategy to combat reports of syringes in Pepsi cans.

Patterson, Bill. "Crises Impact on Reputation Management." *Public Relations Journal,* November 1993, pp. 47–48. Includes media relations checklist.

Read, Nat B. "Sears PR Debacle Shows How Not to Handle a Crisis." *Wall Street Journal,* January 11, 1993, p. A4.

Rumptz, Mark. "A Public Relations Nightmare: Dow-Corning Offers Too Little, Too Late." *Public Relations Quarterly,* Summer 1992, pp. 30–32.

Sen, Falguni, and Egelhoff, William G. "Six Years and Counting: Learning from Crisis Management at Bhopal." *Public Relations Review,* Spring 1991, pp. 69–84.

Severin, Werner, J. and Tankard, James W. *Communication Theories: Origins, Methods, and Use.* White Plains, NY: Longman, 1992.

Small, William J. "Exxon Valdez: How to Spend Billions and Still Get a Black Eye." *Public Relations Review,* Spring 1991, pp. 9–26.

Therkelsen, David. "A Model for Moving from Message to Desired Action." *PR Reporter,* September 14, 1992, p. 1. Guidelines for strategies in each step of the communication process.

Vendrell, Ignasi B. "Oil Spills Show Lessons Still Not Learned." *Public Relations Journal.* December 1993, pp. 40, 38–39.

Evaluation

P R E V I E W   In this chapter the objectives are to explain the critical role of evaluation in public relations, to describe the advantages and disadvantages of various evaluation methods, and to help students select the ones most suitable for specific programs.

Topics covered in the chapter include:

- The purpose of evaluation
- Objectives: A prerequisite for evaluation
- Current status of measurement and evaluation
- Measurement of production
- Message exposure
- Audience comprehension
- Audience change and action
- Supplemental activities

The fourth step of the public relations process is evaluation. It is the measurement of results against established objectives set during the planning process discussed in Chapter 8.

Evaluation is well described by Prof_____ nd of Bowling Green State University. He defines it as "th_____ rogram and its results. It is a means for practitioner_____ nd to themselves."

Results and accoun_____ s Glen Broom and David Dozier of San Diego Stat_____ *arch in Public Relations,* they state, "Your program_____ ct—to change or maintain something about a situ_____ research to measure and document program effects._____

Professor Frank Wylie, _____ e University in Long Beach, summarizes:

We are talking about an orderly e_____ specific objectives of our public relations plan. We are_____ d wrong, how much progress we've made and, most imp_____ e.

The desire to do a better job_____ ating public relations efforts, but another equally_____ adoption of the management-by-objectives system_____ lations personnel. They want to know if the mone_____ c relations are well spent and contribute to the reali_____ such as attendance at an open house, product sale_____ prevent the spread of AIDS.

OBJECTIVES: A PRERE_____ _____TION

Before any public relations program can be properly evaluated, it is important to have a clearly established set of measurable objectives. These should be part of the program plan (discussed in Chapter 8), but some points need reviewing.

First, public relations personnel and management should agree on the criteria that will be used to evaluate success in attaining objectives. A Ketchum Public Relations monograph simply states, "Write the most precise, most results-oriented objectives you can that are realistic, credible, measurable, and compatible with the client's demands on public relations."

Second, don't wait until the end of the public relations program to determine how it will be evaluated. Albert L. Schweitzer at Fleishman-Hillard public relations in St. Louis, makes the point: "Evaluating impact/results starts in the planning stage. You break down the problem into measurable goals and objectives, then after implementing the program, you measure the results against goals."

If an objective is informational, measurement techniques must show how successfully information was communicated to target audiences. Such techniques fall under the rubric of "message dissemination" and "audience exposure," but they do not measure the effect on attitudes or overt behavior and action.

Motivational objectives are more difficult to accomplish. If the objective is to increase sales or market share, it is important to show that public relations efforts caused the increase rather than advertising or other marketing strategies. Or, if the objective is to change attitudes or opinions, research should be done before and after the public relations activity to measure the percentage of change.

Although objectives may vary, the following checklist contains the basic evaluation questions that any practitioner should ask:

1. Was the activity or program adequately planned?

2. Did recipients of the message understand it?

3. How could the program strategy have been more effective?

4. Were all primary and secondary audiences reached?

5. Was the desired organizational objective achieved?

6. What unforeseen circumstances affected the success of the program or activity?

7. Did the program or activity fall within the budget set for it?

8. What steps can be taken to improve the success of similar future activities?

CURRENT STATUS OF MEASUREMENT AND EVALUATION

During the past decade, public relations professionals have made considerable progress in evaluation research and the ability to tell clients and employers exactly what has been accomplished. More sophisticated techniques than previously are being used, including computerized news clip analysis, survey sampling, and attempts to correlate efforts directly with sales.

Deborah Hauss, writing in the *Public Relations Journal,* notes, "The latest technological advances, computer software programs and other state-of-the-art applications in public relations research and evaluation have added a vital twist to the age-old media clip book."

In fact, Hauss declares, "The days of mainly clipping articles for the decision maker to review are gone." This is not to say, however, that counting news clips by the inch has disappeared. It only means that there is increasing recognition in the industry that, as Dozier puts it, "The outcome of a successful public relations program is not a hefty stack of news stories. . . . Communication is important only in the *effects* it achieves among publics."

Indeed, the emphasis on media coverage as an evaluation method is reinforced by a comparative analysis of winning programs in PRSA's national award program. Bissland found that 79 percent of the winning programs in 1988–1989 used media coverage as an

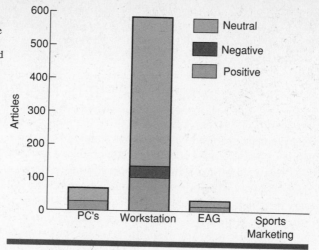

FIGURE 10.1
An analysis of clippings received by Hewlett-Packard concerning the different categories of its work shows the total in each category and how many were positive, negative, and neutral in tone. (Copyright © 1989 The Delahaye Group, Inc.)

evaluation component. He also found increased use of other evaluation methods to supplement media coverage. There was a trend for more documentation of (1) actual audiences reached, (2) audience feedback, (3) behavioral science measurements, (4) inferred achievement, and (5) substantiated achievement.

Today, the trend toward more systematic evaluation has accelerated for a number of reasons. One primary reason, according to a poll of *Public Relations Journal* readers, is that management demands more measurable, bottom-line results and accountability.

Other reasons that have influenced the trend are (1) more expertise by public relations practitioners who have studied social science research methods as part of their college education, (2) user-friendly computer software programs, and (3) the need for solid data to make public relations programs more cost-effective and an integral part of the organization's communications strategy.

Despite advances in evaluation techniques, there are still those who say public relations is not an exact science and is extremely difficult to measure. To an extent, they are right. However, Walter K. Lindenmann, senior vice president and director of research of Ketchum Public Relations, takes a more optimistic view. He wrote in *Public Relations Quarterly:* "Let's get something straight right off the bat. First, it is possible to measure public relations effectiveness. . . . Second, measuring public relations effectiveness does not have to be either unbelievably expensive or laboriously time-consuming."

Lindenmann suggests that public relations personnel use a mix of evaluation techniques, many borrowed from advertising and marketing, to provide more complete evaluation. In addition, he notes that there are at least three levels of measurement and evaluation.

On the most basic level are compilations of message distribution and media placements. The second level, which requires more sophisticated techniques, deals with the measurement of audience awareness, comprehension, and retention of the message. The most advanced level is the measurement of changes in attitudes, opinions, and behavior.

The following sections outline the most widely used methods for evaluating public relations efforts, including measurement of production, message exposure, audience comprehension, attitude change, and audience action. In addition, supplemental activities such as communication audits, readability tests, event evaluation, and split messages are discussed.

MEASUREMENT OF PRODUCTION

One elementary form of evaluation is simply to count how many news releases, feature stories, photos, letters, and the like are produced in a given period of time.

This kind of evaluation is supposed to give management an idea of a staff's productivity. Public relations professionals, however, do not believe that this evaluation is very meaningful because it emphasizes quantity instead of quality. It may be more cost-effective to write fewer news releases and spend more time on the few that really are newsworthy. It may, for example, be more important for a staff person to spend five weeks working on an article for the *Wall Street Journal* or *Fortune* than to write 29 routine personnel releases.

Another side of the production approach is to specify what the public relations person should accomplish in obtaining media coverage. One state trade association evaluated its director of media relations on the expectation that (1) four feature stories would be run in any of the 11 largest newspapers in the state and (2) news releases would be used by at least 20 newspapers, including 5 or more among the 50 largest.

Such evaluation criteria not only are unrealistic but almost impossible to guarantee because media gatekeepers—not the public relations person—make such decisions. Management may argue, however, that such placement goals provide incentive to the public relations staff and are tangible criteria in employee performance evaluation.

Closely allied to the production of publicity materials is their distribution. Thus a public relations department might report, for instance, that a total of 756 news releases were sent to 819 daily newspapers, 250 weeklies, and 137 trade magazines within one year, or that 110,000 copies of the annual report were distributed to stockholders, security analysts, and business editors. Although such figures may be useful in evaluating how widely a particular piece of publicity was distributed, they do not answer the question of readership or, more important, of attitude change.

MEASUREMENT OF MESSAGE EXPOSURE

The most widely practiced form of evaluating public relations programs is the compilation of press clippings and radio-television mentions. Public relations firms and company departments working primarily on a local basis often have a secretary or intern clip the area newspapers. Large companies with regional, national, or even international outreach usually hire clipping services to scan large numbers of publications. It also is possible to have "electronic" clipping services monitor and tape major radio and television programs on a contractual basis. Burrelle's, for example, monitors nearly 400 local TV stations in 150 cities.

The public relations firm of GCI Group used news clips as one measure of its program to publicize the opening of the $67 million Liberty Science Center, an interactive science and technology facility in New Jersey designed to improve science education. According to its report:

Print coverage included more than 1300 placements in four months, including the New York *Times, New York,* Associated Press, *Ladies' Home Journal, Time, Weekly Reader, Continental Profiles, Travel & Leisure, Business Week,* and more. Television coverage totaled 225 minutes. *Good Morning America* produced a four-minute feature two weeks before the opening. The other 37 television placements included repeated features on CNN, WABC-TV, WCBS-TV, and NJ Network.

This kind of compilation measures the media's acceptance of the story and shows that the client got extensive coverage. It also shows that the project accomplished the first stage of the adoption process by making people aware of the Liberty Science Center.

MEDIA IMPRESSIONS

In addition to the number of media placements, public relations departments and firms report how many people may have been exposed to the message. These numbers are described as *media impressions,* the potential audience reached by a periodical or a broadcast program.

If, for example, a story about an organization appears in the local daily with a circulation of 130,000, the media impressions are 130,000. If another story is published the next day, this counts for 130,000 more impressions. Estimated audiences for radio and television programs, certified by auditing organizations, also are used to compile media impressions.

A regional or national news story can generate millions of impressions by the simple multiplication of each placement times the circulation or audience of each medium. Some examples:

■ Stories about Earth Train, a program by Gateway Pacific Foundation to advance the understanding of environmental issues among youth, generated 155 million impressions. (See Chapter 17.)

■ Media coverage of Dole Food Company's nutrition education campaign to create public awareness about the health benefits of eating fruits and vegetables generated 60 million media impressions.

■ A Coors event promoting the beer producer's commitment to a $40 million adult literacy program generated 64.5 million media impressions.

Media impressions are commonly used in advertising to illustrate the penetration of a particular message. Such figures give a rough estimate of how many people are exposed to a message. They don't, however, disclose how many people actually read or heard the stories and, more important, how many absorbed or acted on the information. Other techniques needed for this kind of evaluation are discussed later in this chapter.

DOLLAR VALUE

Another approach is to calculate the value of message exposure. This is done by converting publicity stories in the regular news columns or on the air into equivalent advertising costs. For example, if a 5-inch article about an organization appeared in a publication that charges $100 per column inch for advertising, a public relations person might report to management that the article was worth $500 in media exposure.

Dollar value, as an evaluation component, was used in several programs that received PRSA's 1993 Silver Anvil Awards:

- General Motors, when it introduced its new credit card that offered a 5 percent rebate on a new car, reported, "Total audience readership/viewership topped 330 million with an ad equivalency in excess of $900 million."

- Vail Valley in Colorado, after a three-year public relations effort to promote the ski resort as a summer destination, reported, "Equivalent ad value of publicity achieved was $5,362,209 with gross impressions of more than 200 million."

Although such results graphically show top management the value of publicity efforts, the technique is a bit like comparing apples and oranges. Advertising copy is directly controlled by the organization and can be oriented to specific objectives. The organization also controls the size and placement of the message. News mentions, on the other hand, are determined by media gatekeepers and can be negative, neutral, or positive. In addition, a news release can be edited to the point that key corporate messages are deleted. In other words, the organization can't control size, placement, or content.

It becomes a question of what is being measured. Should an article be counted as equivalent advertising space if it is negative? It is also questionable whether a 15-inch article that mentions the organization only once among six other organizations is comparable to 15 column-inches of advertising space. And the numbers game doesn't take into account that a 4-inch article in the *Wall Street Journal* may be more valuable in reaching key publics than a 20-inch article in the Denver *Post*. Others argue that news mentions have even more value than comparable advertising because they have higher credibility with the public.

In summary, the dollar-value approach to measuring publicity effectiveness is somewhat suspect, and there has been a rapid decline of such statistics in PRSA award entries. The equating of publicity with advertising rates for comparable space does not engender good media relations. The technique reinforces the opinion of many media gatekeepers that all news releases are just attempts to get "free advertising."

SYSTEMATIC TRACKING

As noted earlier, message exposure traditionally has been measured by sheer bulk. New advances in computer software and databases, however, now make it possible to track media placements in a more sophisticated way.

Computer databases can analyze the content of media placements to determine such variables as market penetration, type of publication, tone of coverage, sources quoted, and mention of key copy points. Ketchum Public Relations, for example, can build up to 40 variables into its computer program, including the tracking of reporter bylines to determine if a journalist is predisposed negatively or positively to the client's key messages.

Ketchum, Burson-Marsteller, CARMA International, The Delahaye Group, PR Data Systems, and other firms do content analysis by studying news stories from Dialog and Mead Data Central's NEXIS/LEXIS databases, which include the contents of hundreds of publications. Many firms can also extrapolate details by cross-tabulating geographic coverage, favorableness, circulation reports, and reporters' attitudes or biases.

The value of systematic tracking is manifested in several ways. One is immediate feedback regarding media use of the message—which media used it and whether key copy points were mentioned. Xerox Corporation, for example, held a press conference for its latest new products in New York City. By 9 A.M. the next day, the public relations staff already knew the fruits of their labors. A summary report, gleaned from media databases by its public relations firm, Burson-Marsteller, listed the major media outlets that had covered the Xerox event. In addition, it contained an analysis of whether the coverage was positive, neutral, or unfavorable.

Database analysis also helped EDS, another firm, determine that the 530 articles about the company during its two-year campaign to increase corporate visibility did appear in targeted thought-leader media, including the New York *Times,* the *Economist, Fortune,* and the *Wall Street Journal.* In addition, 88 percent carried the corporation's desired messages. One key message was the continued growth and strength of the company after the 1986 departure of H. Ross Perot, its president.

Content analysis also can help an organization focus its media strategy more effectively. If 40 percent of its news releases consist of management and personnel stories, but account for only 5 percent of the stories published, it seems logical that fewer news releases about personnel need to be prepared. On another level, systematic tracking can determine which media are actually using the organization's materials. If only half the publications on a company's mailing list have a record of ever having used company-provided materials, it might be wise and cost-effective to cull the mailing list.

REQUESTS AND "800" NUMBERS

Another measure of media exposure is to compile the number of requests for more information. A story in a newspaper or an appearance of a company spokesperson on a broadcast often provides information as to where people can get more information about a subject.

In many cases, a toll-free 800 number is provided. Dayton Hudson Corporation, owner of several department store chains, used a toll-free hotline number as part of its "Child Care Aware" program to help educate parents about quality child care and how to get it. In a six-month period, 19,000 calls were received seeking advice and copies of a brochure. Dole Food Company, through its toll-free 800 number, got requests for more than 100,000 copies of its brochure titled, "Fun with Fruits and Vegetables: Kid's Cookbook."

On another level, many trade and specialized magazines contain cards on which readers may request more information about a specific product or service by circling a number. If such information is disseminated in a newsletter or brochure, a self-addressed postcard often is enclosed so that more information can be requested.

Requests for speakers and experts also can show the effectiveness of a public relations program. An information campaign by a group of actuarial societies to demonstrate the importance of their work in helping formulate public policy was judged a success, in part because requests for its representatives to testify before Congress and regulatory bodies increased 34 percent. In addition, requests for speakers to appear before business, trade, and professional organizations increased 41 percent.

COST PER PERSON

Another way to evaluate exposure to the message is to find out how much it costs to reach each member of the audience—the *cost per person.*

The technique is commonly used in advertising in order to place costs in perspective. Although a 30-second commercial during the 1993 Super Bowl telecast cost $850,000 ($28,000 per second), advertisers felt it was well worth the price because an audience of more than 100 million people was reached for about eight-tenths of a cent each—a relatively good bargain even if several million viewers probably visited the refrigerator while the commercial was playing.

Cost-effectiveness, as this technique is known, is also used in public relations. A campaign by the Virginia Department of Tourism to attract Canadian visitors, for example, cost $5,500 but generated 90,000 consumer inquiries. This made the cost per inquiry only six cents. In addition, the campaign gave a very good return on investment (ROI) because it was credited with generating $75 million in Canadian tourism for the state.

Collateral materials such as films, brochures, and newsletters can also be evaluated on a cost-per-person basis. A sports video produced by Nike may cost $50,000 but reach 150,000 high school students during its distribution period. It thus costs Nike 33 cents to reach each student. Cost-effectiveness, of course, is increased if the video is shown to additional teenagers.

Determining cost-effectiveness of public relations materials is important, and it can help professionals control the price of message exposure. One organization, for example, had only 500 employees and was spending $3500 on a monthly magazine—$7 per person. It quickly decided on a newspaper format that cost only $2 per employee to produce and distribute.

AUDIENCE ATTENDANCE

Counting audience attendance is a relatively simple way of evaluating the effectiveness of pre-event publicity. Sail Boston, a week-long celebration of the Grand Regatta Columbus '92 Quincentenary, attracted 7 million visitors, according to the Greater Boston Convention and Visitors Bureau.

On a smaller scale, the public relations effort by the city of Columbia, South Carolina, was credited with outstanding attendance at various events for the 50th anniversary reunion of Doolittle's Raiders, a World War II group. The reunion was judged a success because 2500 attended a dedication ceremony, 1500 toured a museum display, and 800 went to the dinner dance.

Poor attendance at a meeting or event can indicate inadequate publicity and promotion. Another major cause is lack of public interest, even when people are aware that a meeting or event is taking place. Low attendance usually results in considerable finger-pointing; thus an objective evaluation of exactly what happened—or didn't happen—is a good policy.

MEASUREMENT OF AUDIENCE COMPREHENSION

So far, techniques of measuring audience exposure and accurate dissemination of the message have been discussed. A higher level of evaluation is to determine whether the audience actually understood the message and retained it.

Walter Lindenmann calls this the second level of public relations evaluation. He notes:

At this level, public relations practitioners measure whether target audience groups actually *received* the messages directed at them: whether they paid *attention* to those messages, whether they *understood* the messages, and whether they have *retained* those messages in any shape or form.

The tools of survey research are needed to answer such questions. Members of the target audience must be asked about the message and what they remember about it. General Motors, for example, conducted a tracking study two weeks after the launch of its new credit card and found that 53 percent of the consumer respondents were aware of the new card and remembered the 5 percent rebate toward the purchase of a new car. Sixty-four percent said they learned of the GM card from either print or broadcast media.

Another way of measuring audience awareness and comprehension is the day-after recall. Under this method, participants are asked to view a specific television program or read a particular news story; then they are interviewed to learn which messages they remembered.

Ketchum Public Relations, on behalf of the California Prune Board, used this technique to determine if a 15-city media tour was conveying the key message that prunes are a high-fiber food source. Forty women in Detroit considered likely to watch daytime television shows were asked to view a program on which a Prune Board spokesperson would appear. The day after the program, Ketchum asked the women questions about the show, including their knowledge of the fiber content of prunes. Ninety-three percent remembered the Prune Board spokesperson and 65 percent, on an unaided basis, named prunes as a source of high fiber.

Another dimension of audience comprehension and retention is acceptance of the message. A person may easily understand the message that Mobil Corporation is the sponsor of *Masterpiece Theater* on public television but may or may not agree that Mobil is a company that practices a high degree of social responsibility—the real message that Mobil wants to communicate through its sponsorship.

Again, surveys or interviews can be used to discover whether audiences agree with opinion statements. As noted in Chapter 7, the most commonly used method is a Likert-type scale, in which respondents can indicate the extent of their agreement with an opinion statement. For example:

Mobil makes significant contributions to the arts in America and is a socially responsible company.

_____ Strongly agree (5)
_____ Agree (4)
_____ Undecided (3)
_____ Disagree (2)
_____ Strongly disagree (1)

Depending on the results of such a survey, Mobil may decide that more public relations efforts are needed in order to gain acceptance of its message among the American public. Or, if people do agree with the statement, only reinforcement of the message is needed.

MEASUREMENT OF AUDIENCE CHANGE

Closely related to audience comprehension of a message are changes in an audience's perceptions and attitudes.

A major technique to determine such changes is the *benchmark study*. Basically, it is a measurement of audience attitudes and opinions before, during, and after a public relations campaign. Benchmark studies, also called baseline studies, graphically show the percentage difference in attitudes and opinions as a result of increased information and publicity. A number of possible intervening variables may account for changes in attitude, of course, but statistical analysis of variance can help pinpoint to what degree the change is attributed to public relations efforts.

EDS, a leading computer services company, used a benchmark survey to determine its image. It found, among other things, that many business executives thought Ross Perot was still company president. The survey also found that 83 percent of the executives polled did not name EDS when asked about information technology providers, even though it was a $6 billion corporation.

The survey findings caused EDS to launch the communications plan mentioned earlier (p. 243). At the end of the campaign, a new benchmark study showed that unaided company awareness among business executives had jumped from 17 to 25 percent. In addition, a survey of journalists showed that 60 percent of the respondents now thought EDS was the industry leader in the global technology information market.

The American Iron and Steel Institute also did a benchmark survey to determine the effectiveness of its campaign to inform the public about the industry's recycling efforts. Before the program only 52 percent of the respondents in Columbus, Ohio, were aware that steel cans are recyclable. After the campaign, the percentage had risen to 64 percent.

The value of the benchmark survey is underscored by Frank R. Stansberry, manager of guest affairs for Coca-Cola. He told the *Public Relations Journal:* "The only way to determine if communications are making an impact is by pre- and posttest research. The first survey measures the status quo. The second one will demonstrate any change and the direction of that change."

MEASUREMENT OF AUDIENCE ACTION

The ultimate objective of any public relations effort is to make something happen. This takes us back to the beginning of the chapter, which pointed out that the purpose of public relations activity is to accomplish organizational objectives.

The objective of the amateur theater group is not to get media publicity; the objective is to sell tickets. The objective of an environmental organization such as Greenpeace is not to get editorials written in favor of whales, but to motivate the public to (1) write elected officials, (2) send donations for its preservation efforts, and (3) get protective legislation passed. The objective of a company is to sell its products and services, not get 200 million media impressions. In all cases, the tools and activities of public relations are a means, not an end.

Thus it can be seen that public relations efforts are ultimately evaluated on how they help an organization achieve its objectives. Here are some bottom-line examples:

- The Illinois Department of Public Aid doubled applications for child support enforcement after a media campaign encouraged parents to call for assistance in collecting delinquent child support payments.

- Friskies PetCare Company, as the result of sponsoring a national canine frisbee competition, increased sales in each of the seven target markets.

- Black & Decker boosted sales of power drills by 22 percent, or about a $10 million sales increase, after it sponsored the 75th anniversary celebration of the patenting of the first pistol-grip, trigger-switch drill.

- Sail Boston, the celebration featuring sailing ships from around the world, caused a 6 percent rise in tourism for the year.

- Vail Valley's hotel/lodging unit night revenues increased 30 percent during the summer months after its extensive public relations campaign.

- A proposal on the Ohio ballot requiring cancer warnings on thousands of products from peanut butter to plywood was defeated after an extensive grass-roots campaign by a coalition of citizen groups and business organizations.

In all these cases, target audiences received information, understood it, and acted on it—by visiting a tourist site, filling out an application, buying a product or service, or voting in an election.

Other changes in behavior can be ascertained through surveys to determine if people have altered their personal patterns. Have they quit smoking? Did they get an annu-

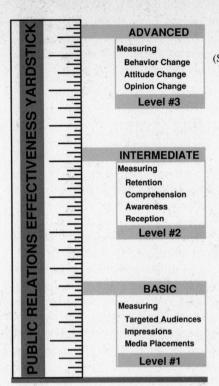

FIGURE 10.2
Evaluation goals for public programs can be grouped at
three levels of measurement, as shown in this chart.
(Source: Ketchum Public Relations, New York; published in
Public Relations Quarterly)

al physical checkup? Are they driving more carefully? How people answer often depends on the previous public relations efforts of organizations and groups.

MEASUREMENT OF SUPPLEMENTAL ACTIVITIES

COMMUNICATION AUDIT

The entire communication activity of an organization should be evaluated at least once a year to make sure that every primary and secondary public is receiving appropriate messages.

David Hilton-Barber, past president of the Public Relations Institute of South Africa, has written:

The most important reasons for an audit are to help establish communication goals and objectives, to evaluate long-term programs, to identify strengths and weaknesses, and to point up any areas which require increased activity.

. . . A communications audit can be useful at any time, but is especially appropriate when a company changes direction—changes product/service emphasis, goes public, merges or acquires—or when there is a change in management. The audit is also useful when management senses that something is wrong with its communications efforts and wants to find out what it is—or when a communications function is being created or restructured.

A communication audit, as an assessment of an organization's entire communication program, could include the following:

1. Analysis of all communication activities—newsletters, memos, policy statements, brochures, annual reports, position papers, mailing lists, media contacts, personnel forms, graphics, logos, advertising, receptionist contacts, waiting lounges for visitors, and so on

2. Informal interviews with rank-and-file employees and middle management and top executives

3. Informal interviews with community leaders, media gatekeepers, consumers, distributors, and other influential persons in the industry

A number of research techniques, as outlined in Chapter 7, can be utilized during a communication audit—including mail and telephone surveys, focus groups, and so forth. The important point is that the communications of an organization should be analyzed from every possible angle, with the input of as many publics as possible. Security analysts may have something to say about the quality of the company's financial information; municipal leaders are best qualified to evaluate the company's efforts in community relations. Consumers, if given a chance, will make suggestions about quality of sales personnel and product instruction booklets.

PILOT TESTS AND SPLIT MESSAGES

Evaluation is important even before a public relations effort is launched. If exposure to a message is to be maximized, it is wise to pretest it with a sample group from the targeted audience. Do its members easily understand the message? Do they accept the message? Does the message motivate them to adopt a new idea or product?

A variation of pretesting is the *pilot test*. Before going national with a public relations message, companies often test the message and key copy points in selected cities to learn how the media accept the message and how the public reacts. This approach is quite common in product marketing because it limits the costs and enables the company to revamp or fine-tune the message for maximum exposure. It also allows the company to switch channels of dissemination if original media channels are not exposing the message to the proper audiences.

The *split-message approach* is common in direct mail publicity campaigns. Two or three different appeals may be prepared by a charitable organization and sent to different audiences. The response rate is then monitored (perhaps the amount of donations is totaled) to learn what message and graphics seemed to be the most effective.

A variation of the split message can even be done in community relations. A company may select two comparable communities and target one of them for an extensive community relations program while the second community remains untouched. After one year, a survey will indicate if the residents of the targeted community have improved their opinions of the company. These results should be compared to those found in a follow-up survey in the community where nothing special was done.

It has already been pointed out that meetings can be evaluated to some degree by the level of attendance. Such data provide information about the number of people exposed to a message, but still don't answer the more crucial question of what they thought about the meeting.

Public relations people often get an informal sense of an audience's attitudes by its behavior. A standing ovation, spontaneous applause, complimentary remarks as people leave, and even the expressions on people's faces provide clues as to how a meeting was received. On the other hand, if people are not responsive, if they ask questions about subjects supposedly explained, if they express doubts or antagonism, the meeting can be considered only partly successful.

Public relations practitioners use a number of information methods to evaluate the success of a meeting, but they also employ more systematic methods. The most common technique is an evaluation sheet that participants fill out at the end of the meeting.

A simple form asking people to rate such items as location, costs, facilities, and program on a 1-to-5 scale (1 being the best) can be used. Other forms may ask people to rate aspects of a conference or meeting as (1) excellent, (2) good, (3) average, and (4) could be better.

Evaluation forms also can ask how people heard about the program and what suggestions they would make for future meetings.

The systematic gathering of such information enables meeting planners to pinpoint problem areas and to recognize which aspects of the program went especially well. A better meeting then can be planned next time. The evaluation thus is not just an analysis of a past event but the start of planning for future activities.

NEWSLETTERS

Editors of newsletters should evaluate readership annually. Such an evaluation can help ascertain (1) reader perceptions, (2) the degree to which stories are balanced, (3) kinds of stories that have high reader interest, (4) additional topics that should be covered, (5) credibility of the publication, and (6) the extent to which it is meeting organizational objectives.

Systematic evaluation, it should be emphasized, is not based on whether all the copies are distributed or picked up. This information doesn't tell the editor what the audience actually read, retained, or acted upon. A newsletter, newspaper, or even a brochure can be evaluated in a number of ways. The methods include (1) content analysis, (2) readership interest surveys, (3) readership recall of articles actually read, (4) application of readability formulas, and (5) use of advisory boards.

Content Analysis From a representative sample of past issues, stories may be categorized under general headings such as (1) management announcements, (2) new product developments, (3) new personnel and retirements, (4) features about employees, (5) corporate finances, (6) news of departments and divisions, and (7) job-related information.

Such a systematic analysis will show what percentage of the publication is devoted to each category. It may be found that one division rarely is covered in the employee newsletter or that management pronouncements tend to dominate the entire publication. Given the content-analysis findings, editors may wish to shift the content somewhat.

Readership Interest Surveys   The purpose of these surveys is to get feedback about the types of stories employees are most interested in reading.

The most common method is simply to provide a long list of generic story topics and have employees rate each as (1) important, (2) somewhat important, or (3) not important. The International Association of Business Communicators (IABC) conducted such a survey on behalf of several dozen companies and found that readers were not very interested in "personals" about other employees (birthdays, anniversaries, and the like).

A readership interest survey becomes even more valuable when it is compared with the content analysis of a publication. Substantial differences signal a possible need for changes in the editorial content.

Article Recall   The best kind of readership survey occurs when trained interviewers ask a sampling of employees what they have read in the latest issue of the publication.

Employees are shown the publication page by page and asked to indicate which articles they have read. As a check on the tendency of employees to report that they have read everything, interviewers also ask them (1) how much of each article they have read and (2) what the articles were about. The results are then content-analyzed to determine which kinds of articles have the most readership.

A variation of the readership recall technique involves individual evaluation of selected articles for accuracy and clarity. For example, an article about a new production process may be sent before or after publication to the head of production for evaluation. On a form with a rating scale of excellent, good, fair, and deficient, the person may be asked to evaluate the article on the basis of such factors as (1) technical data provided, (2) organization, (3) length, (4) clarity of technical points, and (5) quality of illustrations.

Advisory Boards   Periodic feedback and evaluation can be provided by organizing an employee advisory board that meets several times a year to discuss the direction and content of the publication. This is a useful technique because it expands the editor's feedback network and elicits comments that employees might be hesitant to tell the editor face-to-face.

A variation of the advisory board method is periodically to invite a sampling of employees to meet to discuss the publication. This approach is more systematic than just soliciting comments from employees in the hallway or cafeteria.

CASE PROBLEM

The Ohio Department of Transportation, with 17 rideshare groups, is planning a Rideshare Week. The objective is to increase participation in car-pooling and use of mass transit during this special week. A long-term objective, of course, is to increase the number of people who use car pools or mass transit on a regular basis.

Your public relations firm is retained to promote Ohio Rideshare Week. Your campaign will include a news conference with the governor encouraging participation, press kits, news releases, interviews on broadcast talk shows, special events, and distribution of Rideshare information booklets at major businesses.

What methods would you use to evaluate the effectiveness of your public relations efforts on behalf of Ohio Rideshare Week?

QUESTIONS FOR REVIEW AND DISCUSSION

1. What is the role of stated objectives in evaluating public relations programs?

2. What primary method of evaluation do public relations people use? Is there any evidence that other methods are increasingly being used?

3. What are some general types of evaluation questions that a person should ask about a program?

4. Name four ways by which publicity activity is evaluated. What, if any, are the drawbacks to each one?

5. Do you think news stories about a product or service should be evaluated in terms of comparable advertising costs? Why or why not?

6. What are the advantages of systematic tracking and content analysis of news clippings?

7. How are pilot tests and split messages used to determine the suitability of a message?

8. How does measurement of message exposure differ from measurement of audience comprehension of the message?

9. How are benchmark studies used in evaluation of public relations programs?

10. What is a communication audit?

11. What methods of evaluation can be done for a company newsletter or magazine?

SUGGESTED READINGS

Bissland, James. "Accountability Gap: Evaluation Practices Show Improvement." *Public Relations Review,* Summer 1990, pp. 25–35.

Broom, Glen, and Dozier, David. *Using Research in Public Relations.* Englewood Cliffs, NJ: Prentice Hall, 1990. Chapter 4, "Using Research to Evaluate Programs."

Deveny, Kathleen. "In Weighing Impact of Super Bowl Ads, Marketers Have Trouble Keeping Score." *Wall Street Journal,* January 26, 1993, p. B1. The difficulty of evaluating cost-effectiveness.

Hauss, Deborah. "Measuring the Impact of Public Relations." *Public Relations Journal,* February 1993, pp. 14–21. New electronic research methods improve campaign evaluation.

Holloway, Deborah. "How to Select a Measurement System That's Right for You." *Public Relations Quarterly,* Fall 1992, pp. 15–18. Pros and cons of various evaluation methods.

Kendall, Robert. *Public Relations Campaign Strategies.* New York: HarperCollins, 1992. Part 5, "Evaluation."

Lindenmann, Walter K. "An Effectiveness Yardstick to Measure Public Relations Success." *Public Relations Quarterly,* Spring 1993, pp. 7–9.

Lindenmann, Walter K. "Research, Evaluation and Measurement: A National Perspective." *Public Relations Review,* Summer 1990, pp. 3–16.

Lindenmann, Walter K. "Beyond the Clipbook." *Public Relations Journal,* December 1988, pp. 22–26.

Lipman, Joanne. "Study Suggests Cost of PR Is on the Rise." *Wall Street Journal,* September 9, 1991, p. B4. The issue of equating publicity and advertising.

Piekos, Jennie, and Einsiedel, Edna. "Roles and Program Evaluation: Techniques Among Canadian Public Relations Practitioners." *Public Relations Research Annual,* Vol. 2, ed. by James and Larissa Grunig. Hillsdale, NJ: Lawrence Erlbaum Associates, 1990, pp. 95–114.

Simmons, Robert E. *Communication Campaign Management.* White Plains, NY: Longman, 1990. Chapter 10 on "Evaluating Campaign Results."

Skutski, Karl J. "Conducting a Total Quality Communications Audit." *Public Relations Journal,* April 1992, pp. 32, 29, 30–31.

Tortorello, Nicholas, and Dowgiallo, Ed. "Evaluating the Impact of Public Relations." *Public Relations Journal,* November 1990, pp. 34, 36–37.

Wiesendanger, Betsy. "Electronic Delivery and Feedback Systems Come of Age." *Public Relations Journal,* January 1993, pp. 10–14. Computer analysis of press clippings.

PART THREE
Strategy

Public Opinion and Persuasion

P R E V I E W   The objectives of this chapter are to explain what constitutes public opinion and how it is formed, and to guide students in selecting the appropriate techniques for public relations situations.

Topics covered in the chapter include:

- What is public opinion?
- Opinion leaders as catalysts
- The media's role
- Persuasion: pervasive in our lives
- Factors in persuasive communication
- Propaganda
- Persuasion and manipulation
- The ethics of persuasion

WHAT IS PUBLIC OPINION?

Americans talk about public opinion as if it were a monolithic entity overshadowing the entire landscape. Editorial cartoonists, in contrast, humanize it in the form of John Q. or Jane Publics, characters who symbolize what people think about any given issue. The reality is that public opinion is somewhat elusive and extremely difficult to measure at any given moment.

In fact, to continue the metaphor, public opinion is a number of monoliths and John and Jane Q. Publics all existing at the same time. Few issues create unanimity of thought among the population, and public opinion on any issue is split in several directions. It may also come as a surprise to note that only a small number of people, at any given time, take part in public opinion formation on a specific issue.

There are two reasons for this. First, psychologists have found that the public tends to be passive. Few issues generate an opinion or feeling on the part of an entire citizenry. It is often assumed that a small, vocal group represents the attitude of the public when, in reality, it is more accurate to say that the majority of the people—because the issue doesn't interest or affect them—are apathetic. Thus, "public" opposition to nuclear power plants is really the view of a small, but significant, number of Americans who are concerned about the issue.

Second, one issue may engage the attention of one part of the population, while another arouses the interest of another segment. Parents in a community, for example, may form public opinion on the need for improved secondary education, while senior citizens constitute the bulk of public opinion on the need for increased Social Security benefits.

These two examples illustrate the most common definition of public opinion: "Public opinion is the sum of individual opinions on an issue *affecting* those individuals." Another popular definition states: "Public opinion is a collection of views held by persons *interested* in the subject." Thus a person unaffected by or uninterested in (and perhaps unaware of) an issue does not contribute to public opinion on the subject.

Inherent in these definitions is the concept of *self-interest*. The following statements appear in the literature of public opinion:

1. Public opinion is the collective expression of opinion of many individuals bound into a group by common aims, aspirations, needs, and ideals.

2. People who are interested or who have a vested or *self-interest* in an issue—or who can be affected by the outcome of the issue—form public opinion on that particular item.

3. Psychologically, opinion basically is determined by *self-interest*. Events, words, or any other stimuli affect opinion only insofar as their relationship to *self-interest* or a general concern is apparent.

4. Opinion does not remain aroused for any long period of time unless people feel their *self-interest* is acutely involved or unless opinion—aroused by words—is sustained by events.

5. Once *self-interest* is involved, opinion is not easily changed.

How practitioners utilize the concept of self-interest in focusing their message to fit the audience is discussed under "Appeal to Self-Interest," later in this chapter.

The literature also emphasizes the importance of *events* in the formation of public opinion. Social scientists, for example, have made the following generalizations:

1. Opinion is highly sensitive to *events* that have an impact on the public at large or a particular segment of the public.

2. By and large, public opinion does not anticipate *events*. It only reacts to them.

3. *Events* trigger formation of public opinion. Unless people are aware of an issue, they are not likely to be concerned or have an opinion. Awareness and discussion lead to crystallizing of opinions and often a consensus among the public.

4. *Events* of unusual magnitude are likely to swing public opinion temporarily from one extreme to another. Opinion does not stabilize until the implication of the event is seen with some perspective.

An example of an event that triggered formation of public opinion—and caused people to swing from apathy to outrage—was the Exxon oil spill in Alaska. During the first month after the spill, media coverage was intense, and polls showed rapid growth in the public's support for environmental causes. Memberships in environmental organizations soared; there were many calls for legislation to prevent future spills. As the months went by and media coverage thinned, polls showed that Americans had considerably moderated their initial feelings. However, public opinion experts believe that the event set in motion political forces that in the long run will lead to tougher environmental legislation. (Exxon is discussed in detail in Chapter 9.)

It also has been found that people have more opinions and are able to form opinions more easily with respect to goals than with the methods necessary to reach those goals. Thus there is fairly strong public opinion, according to polls, in favor of improving the quality of the nation's schools. There is not much agreement, however, on how this goal should be accomplished. One group advocates higher salaries for "master" teachers, while another equally vocal group endorses substantial tax increases for school operations. A third group thinks more rigorous standards will solve the problem. All three groups, plus assorted other ones with still other solutions, make up public opinion on the subject.

OPINION LEADERS AS CATALYSTS

Public opinion on an issue may have its roots in self-interest or in events, but the primary catalyst is public discussion. Only in this way does opinion begin to crystallize, and pollsters can measure it.

Serving as catalysts for the formation of public opinion are people who are knowledgeable and articulate about specific issues. They are called *opinion leaders*. Soci-

THE LIFE CYCLE OF PUBLIC OPINION

Public opinion and persuasion are important catalysts in the formation of a public issue and its ultimate resolution. The natural evolution of an issue involves five stages:

Definition of the Issue   Activist and special interest groups raise an issue, perhaps a protest against scenic areas being threatened by logging or strip mining. These groups have no formal power but serve as "agenda stimuli" for the media that cover controversy and conflict. Visual opportunities for television coverage occur when activists hold rallies and demonstrations.

Involvement of Opinion Leaders   Through media coverage, the issue is put on the public agenda and people become aware of it. Opinion leaders begin to discuss the issue and perhaps see it as symbolic of broader environmental issues.

Public Awareness   As public awareness grows, the issue becomes a matter of public discussion and debate, with extensive media coverage. Complexity of the issue is simplified by the media into a "them vs. us" issue. Suggested solutions tend to be at either end of the spectrum.

Government/Regulatory Involvement   Public consensus begins to build for a resolution as government/regulatory involvement occurs. Large groups identify with some side of the issue. Demand grows for government to act.

Resolution   The resolution stage begins as people with power and authority (elected officials) draft legislation or interpret existing rules and regulations to make a statement. A decision is made to protect the scenic areas, or to reach a compromise with advocates of development. If some groups are unhappy with the outcome, however, the cycle may repeat itself.

ologists describe them as (1) highly interested in the subject or issue, (2) better informed on the issue than the average person, (3) avid consumers of mass media, (4) early adopters of new ideas, and (5) good organizers who can get other people to take action.

TYPES OF LEADERS

Sociologists traditionally have defined two types of leaders. First are the *formal opinion leaders*, so called because of their positions as elected officials, presidents of companies, or heads of membership groups. Often news reporters ask them for statements when a specific issue relates to their areas of responsibility or concern. People in formal leadership positions also are called *power leaders*.

Second are the *informal opinion leaders*, who have clout with peers because of some special characteristic. They may be *role models* who are admired and emulated, or opinion leaders because they can exert peer pressure on others to go along with something. In general, informal opinion leaders exert considerable influence on their peer groups by being highly informed, articulate, and credible on particular issues.

Regis McKenna, a marketing communications expert in the high technology industry, likes to think of opinion leaders as *luminaries* because "there are only about 20 to 30 key people in every industry who have major influence on trends, standards, and an organization's reputation." He successfully used these luminaries to launch Apple Computer's Macintosh by cultivating and briefing them on the new product before any public announcement was made.

McKenna knew that journalists contact key opinion leaders in an industry whenever a new product is introduced. Positive statements to the press from key opinion leaders, obtained in advance, provided important third-party endorsement for the new Macintosh. This is a form of two-step information flow, discussed next.

THE FLOW OF OPINION

Many public relations campaigns, particularly those in the public affairs area, concentrate on identifying and reaching key opinion leaders who are pivotal to the success or failure of an idea or project. Sociologists Elihu Katz and Paul Lazarsfeld in the 1940s discovered the importance of opinion leaders during a study of how people chose candidates in an election. They found that the mass media had minimal influence on electoral choices, but voters did rely on person-to-person communication with formal and informal opinion leaders.

These findings became known as the *two-step flow theory of communication.* Although later research confirmed that it really was a multiple-step flow, the basic idea remained intact. Public opinion is really formed by the views of people who have taken the time to sift information, evaluate it, and form an opinion that is expressed to others.

The *multiple-step flow model* is graphically illustrated by a series of concentric circles. In the epicenter of action are opinion makers. They derive large amounts of information from the mass media and other sources, and share that information with people in the adjoining concentric circle, who are labeled the "attentive public." These latter are interested in the issue but rely on opinion leaders to provide synthesized information and interpretation. The outer ring consists of the "inattentive public." They are unaware of or uninterested in the issue and remain outside the opinion-formation process. The multiple-step flow theory, however, means that some will eventually become interested in, or at least aware of, the issue.

THE MEDIA'S ROLE

The mass media, of course, pervade all three of the circles, but opinion leaders are the most active in consuming information. An opinion leader on local politics, for example, avidly reads stories and editorial comment about the affairs of the city, while a member of the inattentive public may skip such reading in favor of the sports page. It should be noted, however, that the devoted sports-page reader may be an informal opinion leader among his or her friends about who is the best player in the league.

Communication researchers disagree on a unified theory that explains the effects of mass media, but some findings are now generally accepted. A common one is the contention by Lazarsfeld and Katz that the influence of the mass media is limited to agen-

PROFILE OF AN OPINION LEADER

A survey of 20,000 Americans by the Roper Organization found that 10 to 12 percent of the general public are opinion leaders. These "influentials," those whom other people seek out for advice, are described as follows:

■ *Activity.* They have done three or more of the following the past year: attended a public meeting, written a legislator, served as an officer or committee member of a local organization, attended a political speech or rally, written a letter to the editor, worked for a political party, worked for an activist group, written an article, held or run for political office.

■ *Income.* Almost 30 percent earn $50,000 or more while almost another third earn less than $30,000 annually.

■ *Age.* The majority are between 30 and 49. Another third are at least 50 years old.

■ *Education.* Three-fourths have gone to college; 11 percent have attended graduate school.

■ *Media usage.* Reading is the preferred way to get news and information. Nine of ten read newspapers regularly, but few watch television. Most prefer reading books or going to movies.

■ *Marital status.* Most are married and live in two-income households where their children are reared.

■ *Topics of importance.* They are slightly more brand-loyal than other consumers and are looking for ways to manage time more effectively. A high percentage of them call spending time with their families a high priority.

■ *Recreation.* They are more likely than the general population to participate in sports such as swimming and bicycling on a regular basis. They are more interested in the arts than in professional sports.

■ *Environmentalism.* They are more apt than others to be concerned about recycling and the environmental movement.

Source: Adapted from *PR Reporter,* "Opinion Leaders: New Study Outlines How to Reach Them," October 5, 1992.

da setting. Media tell the public, through selection of stories and headlines, what to think *about*—but not what to think. Social scientist Joseph Klapper calls this the "limited effects" model of mass media. He postulates, "Mass media ordinarily does not serve as a necessary and sufficient cause for audience effects, but rather functions among and through a nexus of mediating factors and influences." Such factors may include the way in which a person filters information and is influenced by peers.

Although this understanding of mass media influence is generally regarded as valid, other research indicates that mass media can have a "moderate" or even "powerful" effect on the formation of opinions and attitudes. When people have no prior information or attitude disposition regarding a subject, the mass media do play a role in telling people what to think. Psychologist Carl Hovland says people tend to change their perceptions if the information or opinion provided (by mass media and other sources) is not ego-involving or contradictory to previous experiences. Thus a person who doesn't know much about the state budget tends to accept the newspaper's headline, "School Officials Call Budget a Disaster."

Mass media effects also are increased when people cannot verify information through personal experience and knowledge. They are highly dependent on the mass media for information, and they tend to accept a definition of a situation presented to them by television or other media. Professors Sandra Ball-Rokeach and Melvin DeFleur, authors of *Theories of Mass Communication,* contend that the greater the dependency on media in connection with a particular message, the greater the possibility that the message will change audience knowledge, feelings, and behaviors.

This concept of media dependency, coupled with the idea expressed in Chapter 9 that the media create awareness of an issue or topic, indicates that public relations professionals should understand that using mass media can be an important element in the formation of public opinion.

Professor Oscar H. Gandy, Jr., of the University of Pennsylvania, for example, says public relations people are major players in forming public opinion because they often provide the mass media with the information. This, in turn, determines the framework and agenda for public discussion. According to Gandy, up to 50 percent of what the media carry comes from public relations sources in the form of what he describes as "information subsidies."

This opinion of the influential role of public relations personnel, via the mass media, is echoed by Elizabeth L. Toth and Richard L. Heath, authors of *Rhetorical and Critical Approaches to Public Relations.* They say, "Few professions have so many skilled and talented individuals contributing to the thoughts, actions, and politics of our nation."

PERSUASION: PERVASIVE IN OUR LIVES

Persuasion has been around since the dawn of human history. It was formalized as a concept more than 2000 years ago by the Greeks, who made *rhetoric,* the art of using language effectively and persuasively, part of their educational system. Aristotle was the first to set down the ideas of *ethos, logos,* and *pathos,* which roughly translate as "source credibility," "logical argument," and "emotional appeal."

More recent scholars, such as Winston Brembeck and William Howell, describe *persuasion* as "communication to influence choices." Another definition treats persuasion as "a process that changes attitudes, beliefs, opinions, and behaviors."

Such definitions are consistent with the role of public relations professionals in today's society. Indeed, Heath says:

. . . public relations professionals are influential rhetors. They design, place, and repeat messages on behalf of sponsors on an array of topics that shape views of government, charitable organizations, institutions of public education, products and consumerism, capitalism, labor, health, and leisure. These professionals speak, write, and use visual images to discuss topics and take stances on public policies at the local, state, and federal levels.

The dominant public view of public relations, in fact, is one of persuasive communication actions performed on behalf of clients, according to Professors Dean Kruckeberg at the University of Northern Iowa and Ken Starck at the University of Iowa. Gandy adds that ". . . the primary role of public relations is one of purposeful, self-interested communications." And Charles Steinberg even called public relations the "engineering" of consent to create "a favorable and positive climate of opinion toward the individual, product, institution or idea which is represented."

To accomplish this goal, public relations personnel use a variety of techniques to reach and influence their audiences. At the same time, persuasion or rhetoric should be considered more than a one-way flow of information, argument, and influence. In the best sense, Toth and Heath say persuasion should be a dialogue between points of view in the marketplace of public opinion, where any number of persuaders are hawking their wares.

Indeed, persuasion is an integral part of democratic society. It is the freedom of speech used by every individual and organization to influence opinion, understanding, judgment, and action.

USES OF PERSUASION

Persuasion is used to (1) change or neutralize hostile opinions, (2) crystallize latent opinions and positive attitudes, and (3) conserve favorable opinions.

The most difficult persuasive task is to turn hostile opinions into favorable ones. There is much truth to the adage "Don't confuse me with the facts; my mind is made

---

A SAMPLER ON PERSUASION

A number of research studies have contributed to a basic understanding of persuasion concepts. Here are some basic ideas from the text *Public Communication Campaigns,* edited by Ronald E. Rice and William J. Paisley (Sage, 1982):

- Positive appeals generally are more effective than negative appeals for retention of the message and actual compliance.

- Radio and television messages tend to be more persuasive than print but, if the message is complex, better comprehension is achieved through print media.

- Strong emotional appeals and fear arousal are most effective when the audience has minimal concern about or interest in the topic.

- High fear appeals are only effective when a readily available action can be taken to eliminate the threat.

- Logical appeals, using facts and figures, are better for highly educated, sophisticated audiences than strong emotional appeals.

- Altruistic need, like self-interest, can be a strong motivator. Men are willing to get a physical check-up more to protect their families than themselves.

- A celebrity or an attractive model is most effective when the audience has low involvement, the theme is simple, and broadcast channels are used. An exciting spokesperson attracts attention to a message that would otherwise be ignored.

up." Once people have decided, for instance, that oil companies are making excessive profits or that a nonprofit agency is wasting public donations, they tend to ignore or disbelieve any contradictory information. Everyone, as Walter Lippmann has described, has pictures in his or her head based on an individual perception of reality. People generalize from personal experience and what peers tell them. For example, if a person has an encounter with a rude clerk, the inclination is to generalize that the entire department store chain is not very good. The self-perception of the audience is a barrier to communication that will be discussed later in this chapter.

Persuasion is much easier if the message is compatible with a person's general disposition toward a subject. If a person tends to identify Toyota as a company with a good reputation, he or she may express this feeling by purchasing one of its cars. Nonprofit agencies usually crystallize the public's latent inclination to aid the less fortunate by asking for a donation. Both examples illustrate the reason that organizations strive to have a good reputation—it is translated into sales and donations. The concept of message channeling will be discussed in more detail later in the chapter.

The easiest form of persuasion is communication that reinforces favorable opinions. Public relations people, by providing a steady stream of reinforcing messages, keep the reservoir of goodwill in sound condition. More than one organization has survived a major problem because public esteem for it tended to minimize current difficulties. Continual efforts to maintain the reservoir of goodwill is called *preventive public relations*—the most effective of all.

FACTORS IN PERSUASIVE COMMUNICATION

A number of factors are involved in persuasive communication, and the public relations practitioner should be knowledgeable about each one. The following is a brief discussion of (1) audience analysis, (2) source credibility, (3) appeal to self-interest, (4) clarity of message, (5) timing and context, (6) audience participation, (7) suggestions for action, (8) content and structure of messages, and (9) persuasive speaking.

AUDIENCE ANALYSIS

Knowledge of audience characteristics such as beliefs, attitudes, concerns, and lifestyles is an essential part of persuasion. It helps the communicator tailor messages that are salient, answer a felt need, and provide a logical course of action.

Basic demographic information, readily available through census data, can help determine an audience's gender, income level, education, ethnic background, and age groupings. Other data, often prepared for marketing departments, give information on a group's buying habits, disposable income, and ways of spending leisure time.

Polling and surveys, discussed in Chapter 7, tap a target audience's attitudes, opinions, and concerns. Such research tells about the public's resistance to some ideas, as well as its predisposition to support other ideas. Recycling programs in the United States, for example, made a slow start in the 1980s because the public was resistant. People were accustomed to throwing away used newspapers, bottles, and cans without a thought about the environmental consequences. In an affluent, disposable-oriented society, convenience was king.

Another tool of audience analysis is use of *psychographics.* This method attempts to classify people by lifestyle, attitudes, and beliefs. The Values and Lifestyle Program, popularly known as VALS, was developed by SRI International, a research organization in Menlo Park, California, in the mid-1970s.

VALS is now routinely used in public relations to help communicators structure persuasive messages to different elements of the population. A good illustration is the way Burson-Marsteller used VALS for its client, the National Turkey Foundation. The problem was simple: how to encourage turkey consumption throughout the year, not just at Thanksgiving and Christmas.

One element of the public was called Sustainers and Survivors; VALS identifies them as low-income, poorly educated, often elderly people who ate at erratic hours, consumed inexpensive foods, and seldom ate out. Another element was the Belongers, who were highly family-oriented and served foods in traditional ways. The Achievers, on the other hand, were more innovative and willing to try new foods.

Burson-Marsteller tailored a strategy for each group. For Survivors and Sustainers, the message stressed bargain cuts of turkey that could be stretched into a full meal. The message for Belongers focused on cuts that signaled turkey, such as drumsticks. Achievers, better educated and at higher income levels, received the message about gourmet cuts and new, innovative recipes.

This segmentation of the consumer public into various VALS lifestyles enabled Burson-Marsteller to select appropriate media for specific story ideas. An article placed in *True Experience,* a publication reaching the demographic characteristics of Survivors and Sustainers, was headlined "A Terrific Budget-Stretching Meal." *Better Homes and Gardens* was used to reach Belongers with such titles as "Streamlined Summer Classics" and stories about barbecued turkey on the Fourth of July. Articles for Achievers in *Food and Wine* magazine and *Gourmet* included recipes for turkey salad and turkey tetrazzini.

Such audience analysis, coupled with suitably tailored messages in the appropriate media outlets, is the technique of *channeling.* Persuasive messages are more effective when they take into account the audience's lifestyles, beliefs, and concerns.

SOURCE CREDIBILITY

A message is more believable to the intended audience if the source has *credibility.* This was Aristotle's concept of *ethos,* mentioned earlier, and it explains why organizations use a variety of spokespeople, depending upon the message and the audience.

The California Strawberry Advisory Board, for example, arranges for a home economist to appear on television talk shows to discuss nutrition and to demonstrate easy-to-follow strawberry recipes. The audience for these programs, primarily homemakers, not only identifies with the representative but perceives her as highly credible. By the same token, a manufacturer of sunscreen lotion uses a professor of pharmacology who is past president of the State Pharmacy Board to discuss the scientific merits of sunscreen versus suntan lotions.

The Three Factors Source credibility is based on three factors. One is *expertise.* Does the audience perceive the person as an expert on the subject? Companies, for example, use engineers and scientists to answer news conference questions about how an engineering process works or whether an ingredient in the manufacturing process of a product presents a potential hazard.

The second component is *sincerity.* Does the person come across as believing what he or she is saying? Bill Cosby may not be an expert on all the products he endorses, but he does get high ratings for sincerity.

The third component, even more elusive, is *charisma.* Is the individual attractive, self-assured, and articulate, projecting an image of competence and leadership?

Ideally, a source will exhibit all three attributes. Lee Iacocca, former chairman of the Chrysler Corporation, is a good example. He was highly credible as an expert on Chrysler products. In countless advertisements and speeches, he came across as a candid, no-nonsense individual who sincerely believed that Chrysler products were the best on the market. Iacocca also had charisma; he was self-assured, confident, and articulate.

Not every organization, however, has a Lee Iacocca for its president. Depending on the message and the audience, various spokespersons can be used and quoted for source credibility. A news release for a new product, for example, might quote the director of research and development (R&D) for the company. If the information is about an organization's financial picture, the most credible person would be the chief executive officer (CEO) or the vice president of finance, primarily because of perceived expertise.

Expertise is less important than sincerity and charisma if celebrities are used as spokespersons. Their primary purpose is to call attention to the product or service. Another purpose is to associate the celebrity's popularity with the product. This technique is called *transfer,* mentioned later in this chapter as a propaganda device.

Candice Bergen, for example, was ranked by Video Storyboard Tests in 1993 as the nation's most appealing product endorser, the first woman to occupy the top spot. Bergen, star of the *Murphy Brown* TV comedy, is the spokesperson for Sprint. Using celebrities such as Bergen, Michael Jordan, or Madonna is not without its problems, however.

One problem is the increasing clutter of endorsements, to the point that the public cannot remember who endorses which product. This is particularly true in the athletic shoe business, in which Nike, L.A. Gear, and Reebok use multiple sports figures. A second problem is overexposure of a celebrity such as Bill Cosby who endorses many products. With overexposure, credibility with the public tends to fall, especially when news stories report how much money the celebrity is paid for the endorsements.

The third problem occurs when an endorser's actions undercut the product or service. Actress Cybill Shepherd, who starred in commercials for beef, caused considerable anguish in the cattle industry when she was quoted in a magazine as saying that she rarely ate beef. Florida orange juice producers immediately cancelled Burt Reynolds as a spokesperson because of his bitter break-up with Loni Anderson. The producers thought his marital problem was at odds with the image of orange juice as a healthful, happy, family product.

Problems with celebrities have caused many companies to use cartoon figures as a way to attract audience interest. McDonald's uses "The Little Mermaid," and a battery company has its "Energizer bunny." As one advertising agency executive says, "They're much more controllable than a real live celebrity." And like live celebrities, people dressed in costume representing the cartoon character can go on media tours and attend special events. A troupe of California dancing raisins made several national media tours.

In summary, the use of various sources for credibility depends, in large part, on the type of audience being reached. That is why audience analysis is the first step in formulating persuasive messages.

APPEAL TO SELF-INTEREST

Self-interest was described during earlier discussion about the formation of public opinion. Publics become involved in issues or pay attention to messages that appeal to their psychic or economic needs.

Self-interest is also manifested by the individual or organization that disseminates persuasive messages. Heath writes:

> A rhetoric paradigm for the study of public relations is made meaningful by acknowledging that it assumes the assertion of self-interest. People and the organization for which they work use rhetoric to achieve compliance, good will, understanding, appreciation, and action. They use rhetoric to create images and manage reputations.

The focus here, however, is on the organization's efforts to tailor its messages to the self-interests of the audience.

Publicity for a personal computer can serve as an example. A news release to the trade press serving the computer industry might focus on the technical proficiency of the equipment. The audience, of course, consists of engineers and computer programmers interested in the hardware. A brochure prepared for the public, however, may emphasize how the computer can (1) help people keep track of personal finances, (2) assist youngsters in becoming better students, (3) fit into a small space, and (4) offer good value. Consumers are less interested in technical details than in how the personal computer can make life easier for them.

Charitable organizations don't sell products, but they do need volunteers and donations. This is accomplished by careful structuring of messages that appeal to self-interest. This is not to say that altruism is dead. Thousands of people give freely of their time and money to charitable organizations, but they do receive something in return or they would not do it. The "something in return" may be (1) self-esteem, (2) the opportunity to make a contribution to society, (3) recognition from peers and the community, (4) a sense of belonging, (5) ego gratification, or even (6) a tax deduction. Public relations people understand psychic needs and rewards, and that is why there is constant recognition of volunteers in newsletters and at award banquets. (Further discussion of volunteerism appears in Chapter 18.)

Sociologist Harold Lasswell says people are motivated by eight basic appeals. They are power, respect, well-being, affection, wealth, skill, enlightenment, and physical and mental vitality. Psychologist Abraham Maslow, in turn, says any appeal to self-interest must be based on a *hierarchy of needs*. The first and lowest level involves basic needs such as food, water, shelter, and even transportation to and from work. The second level consists of security needs. People need to feel secure in their jobs, safe in their homes, and confident about their retirement. At the third level are "belonging" needs—people seek association with others. This is why individuals join organizations.

"Love" needs comprise the fourth level in the hierarchy. Humans have a need to be wanted and loved—fulfilling the desire for self-esteem. At the fifth and highest level in

Pump prices and tax collectors – VI

Autumn is here, and with it—effective October 1—the higher federal tax on gasoline. Part of the recently passed 1993 federal budget plan, the 4.3 cents per gallon tax is expected to generate almost $5 billion in new revenues for the government.

We're not arguing that gasoline shouldn't be taxed. That's up to voters and their legislators to decide. But from time to time we like to point out that we're not the only ones making money from sales of our products.

We thought we'd use this space to show the impact of the tax increase in places around the country. In fact, a sizeable chunk of what motorists pay at the pump goes directly to tax collectors—federal, state and local.

The chart below lists major markets where Mobil does most of its business and the range of federal, state and local taxes that goes into the price at the pump. Looking at the numbers, effective October 1, 1993, the average tax per gallon for the metropolitan areas listed is 44.1 cents. If the national average is close to that number, it means that at current demand levels gasoline users are now paying $50 billion a year in direct taxes.

Gasoline taxes in cents per gallon in some key locations:

METROPOLITAN AREA	FEDERAL TAX*	STATE EXCISE TAX	OTHER STATE AND LOCAL TAXES**	TOTAL
Chicago	18.63	19.00	21.66	59.29
Long Island, NY	18.63	8.00	26.49	53.12
New Haven, CT	18.63	29.00	5.28	52.91
Buffalo, NY	18.63	8.00	25.79	52.42
Albany, NY	18.63	8.00	25.79	52.42
Los Angeles	18.63	17.00	11.84	47.47
Providence, RI	18.63	28.00	0	46.63
Tampa	18.63	4.00	21.17	43.80
Miami	18.63	4.00	20.17	42.80
Baltimore	18.63	23.50	0	42.13
Philadelphia	18.63	12.00	10.35	40.98
Boston	18.63	21.00	.50	40.13
Fairfax, VA	18.63	17.50	3.13	39.26
Detroit	18.63	15.00	5.61	39.24
Dallas	18.63	20.00	.59	39.22
Phoenix	18.63	18.00	1.00	37.63
Newark, NJ	18.63	10.50	4.04	33.17
St. Louis	18.63	13.00	0	31.63

AVERAGE OF THESE AREAS: 44.13

* Includes federal excise taxes, the federal underground storage tank tax and a recovery of the Superfund tax on petroleum.
** Includes sales taxes, gross receipts taxes, local government excise taxes, underground storage tank taxes, and other non-income taxes.
(Sales taxes, expressed in cents per gallon, assume a pre-tax dealer price of $1 per gallon.)

Mobil®

FIGURE 11.1
Mobil Corporation has achieved wide attention with its persuasive advertisements on issues, often sharply worded. This typical one, published after new federal taxes were imposed in 1993, shows how much of the per-gallon gasoline price at the pump goes to pay taxes. (© 1993 Mobil Corporation, printed with permission)

APPEALS THAT MOVE PEOPLE TO ACT

Persuasive messages often include information that appeals to an audience's self-interest. Here is a list of persuasive message themes:

- Make money
- Save money
- Save time
- Avoid effort
- More comfort
- Better health
- Cleaner
- Escape pain
- Gain praise
- Be popular
- Be loved/accepted
- Keep possessions
- More enjoyment

- Satisfy curiosity
- Protect family
- Be stylish
- Have beautiful things
- Satisfy appetite
- Be like others
- Avoid trouble
- Avoid criticism
- Be individual
- Protect reputation
- Be safe
- Make work easier
- Be secure

Source: Charles Marsh, "Fly Too Close to the Sun," *Communication World,* September 1992, p. 24.

Maslow's hierarchy are self-actualization needs. Once the first four needs are met, Maslow says, people are free to achieve maximum personal potential; for example, through traveling extensively or perhaps becoming experts on orchids.

Maslow's hierarchy helps explain why some public information campaigns have difficulty getting the message across to people classified in the VALS lifestyle categories as "survivors" and "sustainers." Efforts to inform minorities and low-income groups about AIDS provide an example of this problem. For these groups, the potential danger of AIDS is less compelling than the day-to-day problems of poverty and satisfying the basic needs of food and shelter.

The challenge for public relations personnel, as creators of persuasive messages, is how to tailor information to fill or reduce a need. More than one social scientist has said that success in persuasion largely depends on the ability to assess audience needs and self-interests accurately.

CLARITY OF MESSAGE

Many messages fail because the audience finds the message unnecessarily complex in content or language. The most persuasive messages are direct, are simply expressed, and contain only one primary idea. Peter Drucker, a management expert, once said, "An innovation, to be effective, has to be simple and it has to be focused. It should do only one thing, otherwise it confuses." The same can be said for the content of any message.

Public relations personnel should always ask two questions: "What do I want the audience to do with the message?" and "Will the audience understand the message?" Although persuasion theory says people retain information better and form stronger opinions when they are asked to draw their own conclusions, this doesn't negate the importance of explicitly stating what action an audience should take. Is it to buy the product, visit a showroom, write a member of Congress, make a $10 donation, or what?

If an explicit request for action is not part of the message, members of the audience may not understand what is expected of them. Public relations firms, when making a presentation to a potential client, always ask for the account at the end of the presentation.

TIMING AND CONTEXT

A message is more persuasive if environmental factors support the message or if the message is received within the context of other messages and situations with which the individual is familiar. These factors are called timing and context.

Information from a utility on how to conserve energy is more salient if the consumer has just received the January heating bill. A pamphlet on a new stock offering is more effective if it accompanies an investor's dividend check. A citizens' group lobbying for a stoplight gets more attention if a major accident has just occurred at the intersection.

Political candidates are aware of public concerns and avidly read polls to learn what issues are most salient with voters. If the polls indicate that high interest rates and high-quality secondary education are key issues, the candidate begins to use these issues—and to offer his or her proposals—in the campaign.

Timing and context also play an important role in achieving publicity in the mass media. Public relations personnel, as pointed out earlier, should read newspapers and watch television news programs to find out what media gatekeepers consider newsworthy. A manufacturer of a locking device for computer files got extensive media coverage about its product simply because its release followed a rash of news stories about thieves' gaining access to bank accounts through computers. Media gatekeepers, ordinarily uninterested in security devices for computers, found the product newsworthy within the context of actual news events.

The value of information and its newsworthiness are based on timing and context. Public relations professionals disseminate information at the time it is most highly valued.

AUDIENCE PARTICIPATION

A change in attitude or reinforcement of beliefs is enhanced by *audience involvement and participation.*

An organization, for example, may have employees discuss productivity in a quality-control circle. Management may already have figured out what is needed, but if workers are involved in the problem solving, they often come up with the same solution or even a better one. And, from a persuasion standpoint, the employees are more committed to making the solution work because it came from them—not as a policy or order handed down by higher management.

Participation can also take the form of samples. Many companies distribute product samples so the consumer can conveniently try them without expense. A consumer who samples the product and makes a judgment about its quality is more likely to purchase it.

Activist groups use participation as a way of helping people actualize their beliefs. Not only do rallies and demonstrations give people a sense of belonging, but the act of participation reinforces their beliefs. Asking people to do something—conserve energy, collect donations, or picket—activates a form of self-persuasion and commitment.

SUGGESTIONS FOR ACTION

A principle of persuasion is that people endorse ideas only if they are accompanied by a proposed action from the sponsor.

Recommendations for action must be clear. Public relations practitioners must not only ask people to conserve energy, for instance, but also furnish detailed data and ideas on how to do it.

A campaign conducted by Pacific Gas & Electric Company provides an example. The utility inaugurated a Zero Interest Program (ZIP) to offer customers a way to implement energy-saving ideas. The program involved several components:

- *Energy kit.* A telephone hotline was established and widely publicized so interested customers could order an energy kit detailing what the average homeowner could do to reduce energy use.

- *Service bureau.* The company, at no charge, sent representatives to homes to check the efficiency of water heaters and furnaces, measure the amount of insulation, and check doors and windows for drafts.

- *ZIP.* The cost of making a home more energy-efficient was funded by zero-interest loans to any qualified customer.

CONTENT AND STRUCTURE OF MESSAGES

A number of techniques can make a message more persuasive. Writers throughout history have emphasized some information while downplaying or omitting other pieces of information. Thus they addressed both the *content and structure of messages.*

Expert communicators continue to use a number of devices, including (1) drama, (2) statistics, (3) surveys and polls, (4) examples, (5) testimonials, (6) mass media endorsements, and (7) emotional appeals.

Drama   Because everyone likes a good story, the first task of a communicator is to get audience attention. This is often accomplished by graphically illustrating an event or situation. Newspapers often dramatize a story to get reader interest in an issue. Thus we read about the family evicted from its home as part of a story on the increase in bankruptcies; the old man who is starving because of red tape in the welfare office; or the worker who is now disabled because of toxic waste. In newsrooms, this is called *humanizing an issue.*

Dramatizing is also used in public relations. Relief organizations, in particular, attempt to galvanize public concern and donations through drama as shown in Figures

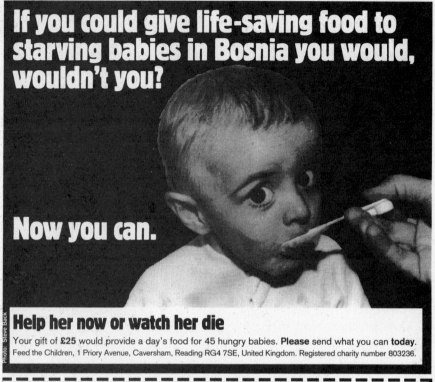

FIGURE 11.2
Emotional appeals involving children are used frequently by
charitable organizations to stimulate fund-raising. This appeal
by the Feed the Children organization is similar to those used
by American organizations.

11.2 and 11.3. The UNICEF fund-raising letter's description of a child dying of malnutrition, like the stark black-and-white photographs used by other relief organizations,
creates powerful imagery, emotion, and drama.

A more mundane use of dramatizing is the so-called *application story,* sent to the
trade press. This is sometimes called the *case study technique,* in which a manufacturer
prepares an article on how an individual or a company is using the product. Apple

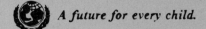

Dear Friend:

In the ten seconds it took you to open and begin to read this letter,
three children died from the effects of malnutrition somewhere in the
world.
No statistic can express what it's like to see even one child die that
way ... to see a mother sitting hour after hour, leaning her child's
body against her own ... to watch the small, feeble head movements
that expend all the energy a youngster has left ... to see the panic
in a dying tot's innocent eyes ... and then to know in a monent that
life is gone.

But I'm not writing this letter simply to describe an all-too-common
tragedy.

> I'm writing because, after decades of hard
> work, <u>UNICEF</u> -- the United Nations Children's
> Fund -- has <u>identified</u> <u>four</u> <u>simple</u>, low-cost
> techniques which, <u>if</u> <u>applied</u>, have the <u>potential</u>
> <u>to</u> <u>cut</u> <u>the</u> <u>yearly</u> <u>child</u> <u>mortality</u> <u>rate</u> <u>in</u> <u>half</u>.

These methods don't depend on solving large-scale problems like
increasing food supply or cleaning up contaminated water. They can be
put into effect before a single additional bushel of wheat is grown,
or before a single new well is dug.

They do depend on <u>what</u> <u>you</u> <u>decide</u> <u>to</u> <u>do</u> by the time you finish reading
this letter. You see, putting these simple techniques to work
requires the support of UNICEF's projects by people around the world.
In our country, it means helping the U.S. Committee for UNICEF
contribute to that vital work.

FIGURE 11.3
Successful persuasion by direct mail depends heavily on an
eye-catching opening that persuades the recipient to read on
rather than toss the letter aside. Letters such as this UNICEF
appeal often stir the reader's sense of guilt, then suggest how
the reader can contribute to ease the problem.

Computer, for example, provides a number of application stories about the unique ways in which its product is being used.

Statistics   It is often said that people are impressed by statistics. Use of numbers can convey objectivity, size, and importance in a credible way. The Pharmaceutical Manufacturers Association, responding to President Clinton's criticism of the high cost of prescription drugs, used facts and numbers to rebut the charges in a series of advertisements. One ad, which focused on drugs for ulcer patients, used the theme that drugs actually reduce health-care costs. It stated:

In 1976, the year before the introduction of the first modern anti-ulcer drug, there were 155,000 ulcer operations. By 1987, the number had dropped to under 19,000. And today, while ulcer drug therapy costs a sizable $1000 a year, it is far less expensive than surgery, which averages $25,000, resulting in an estimated savings of $3 billion a year.

Surveys and Polls   Airlines and auto manufacturers, in particular, use the results of *surveys and polls* to show that they are first in "customer satisfaction," "service," and even "leg room" or "cargo space." The most credible surveys are those conducted by independent research organizations, but readers still should read the fine print to see what is being compared and rated. Is an American-made auto, for example, being compared only with other U.S. cars or with foreign cars as well? Also there is the selected publicizing of results. An airline may be highly rated in cabin service but be at the bottom of the list for on-time arrivals and departures.

Examples   A statement of opinion can be more persuasive if some *examples* are given. A school board often can get support for a bond issue by citing examples of how the present facilities are inadequate for student needs. Environmental groups give examples of how other communities have successfully established greenbelts when requesting a local city council to do the same. Auto manufacturers often attest to the durability of their vehicles by citing their performance on a test track or in a cross-country road race.

Testimonials   A form of source credibility, *testimonials* can be either explicit or implied. A campaign to curtail alcohol and drug abuse may feature a pop singer as a spokesperson, or have a young woman talk about being paralyzed and disfigured as the victim of a drunk driver. Implied testimonials also can be effective. Proclamations by mayors and governors establishing Red Cross Day or Library Week are implied testimonials. The testimonial as a propaganda device is discussed later in the chapter.

Endorsements   *Endorsements* can be made by individuals, organizations, or media outlets. In addition to endorsements by celebrities, as discussed earlier, products and services benefit from endorsements by experts. A well-known medical specialist may publicly state that a particular brand of exercise equipment is best for general conditioning. Organizations such as the American Dental Association and the National Safety Council also endorse products and services.

Media endorsements come through editorials and surveys that rate products and services. Daily newspapers regularly endorse political candidates and community efforts such as the United Way campaign. Another type of endorsement is a newspaper or magazine survey or ranking of the best restaurants, shopping malls, bookstores, and so on in an area. Manufacturers constantly tout the fact that one of their models was named "car of the year" or "best-in-class" by *Car and Driver* or other car buff magazines.

Emotional Appeals   Fund-raising letters from nonprofit groups, in particular, use this persuasive device. Amnesty International, an organization dedicated to human rights and fighting state terrorism, began one direct-mail letter with the following message in large red type:

"We Are God in Here . . . "
   . . . That's what the guards taunted the prisoner with as they applied electrical shocks to her body while she lay handcuffed to the springs of a metal bed. Her cries were echoed by the screams of other victims and the laughter of their torturers.

Such emotional appeals can do much to galvanize the public into action, but they also can backfire. Such appeals raise ego defenses, and people don't like to be told that in some way they are responsible. A description of suffering makes many people uncomfortable, and, rather than take action, they may tune out the message. A relief organization runs full-page advertisements in magazines with the headline "You Can Help Maria Get Enough to Eat . . . Or You Can Turn the Page." Researchers say that most people, their ego defenses raised, turn the page and mentally refuse to acknowl-

---

KEYS TO PERSUASION: MULTIPLE TOOLS AND LONG-TERM ACTIVITY

The public's attitudes and behavior can be changed through information campaigns if multiple tools of communication are utilized over a long period of time.

Stanford University conducted a five-year information campaign to improve the health of people living in Monterey and Salinas by bombarding them with health promotion messages. Messages were delivered through newspapers, radio, television, pamphlets, classes, contests, on-the-job education, advice stuffed in grocery bags, tips for school children, and a weekly medical column. During the campaign, researchers estimate that every adult was hit with a campaign message about twice a week.

After five years, surveys showed that citizens of these two cities had a 13 percent drop in smoking, and changes in blood pressure and cholesterol were better than those found in two control cities not exposed to the information campaign. The researchers estimate that the information campaign saved hundreds of people from dying of heart attacks and cancer. Monterey County is estimated to have saved $38 million in medical costs, while the information campaign only cost $340,000 per year.

Research studies show that most public information campaigns fail because they are short-term and generally use only public service advertising. Mass media campaigns succeed only if they (1) address an issue of ongoing public concern, (2) incorporate multiple tools of communication, (3) utilize the principles of behavior change, and (4) continue long enough to achieve total saturation of the messages.

THE FORMULA FOR WRITING THAT SELLS AND PERSUADES

James F. Fox, owner of a public relations firm in New York City, says persuasive writing begins with determining the audience's attitudes and identifying with them. The formula for persuasive writing, he says, is this:

1. Get attention.

2. Show a need.

3. Satisfy that need.

4. Point out benefits.

5. Request action.

Source: PR Reporter, November 18, 1985.

---

edge that they even saw the ad. In sum, emotional appeals that attempt to lay a guilt trip on the audience are not very successful.

Strong fear arousals also can cause people to tune out, especially if they feel that they can't do anything about the problem anyway. Research indicates, however, that a moderate fear arousal, accompanied by a relatively easy solution, is effective. A moderate fear arousal is: "What would happen if your child were thrown through the windshield in an accident?" The message concludes with the suggestion that a baby, for protection and safety, should be placed in a secured infant seat.

Psychologists say the most effective emotional appeal is one coupled with facts and figures. The emotional appeal attracts audience interest, but logical arguments also are needed.

PERSUASIVE SPEAKING

Psychologists have found that successful speakers (and salespeople) use several persuasion techniques:

1. *Yes–yes.* Start with points with which the audience agrees, to develop a pattern of "yes" answers. Getting agreement to a basic premise often means that the receiver will agree to the logically developed conclusion.

2. *Offer structured choice.* Give structured choices that require the audience to choose between A and B. Political candidates or cause-oriented organizations often use this technique. President Clinton framed the debate on national health-care reform by asking simply, "Should Americans have health security or should they not?"

3. *Seek partial commitment.* Get a commitment for some action on the part of the receiver. This leaves the door open for commitment to other parts of the proposal at a later date. "You don't need to decide on the new insurance plan now, but please attend the employee orientation program on Thursday."

4. *Ask for more/settle for less.* Submit a complete public relations program to management, but be prepared to compromise by dropping certain parts of the program. It has become almost a cliché that a department asks for a larger budget than it expects to receive. Or, to put it another way, the entire sales field is built on the notion of setting prices that can be marked down.

A persuasive speech can either be one-sided or give several sides of an issue, depending on the audience. A series of studies by Hovland and his associates determined that one-sided speeches were most effective with persons favorable to the message, while two-sided speeches were most effective with audiences that might be opposed to the message.

By mentioning all sides of the argument, the speaker accomplishes three objectives. First, he or she is perceived as having objectivity. This translates into increased credibility and makes the audience less suspicious of motives. Second, by giving all sides, the speaker is treating the audience as mature, intelligent adults. Third, including counterarguments allows the speaker to control how these arguments are structured. It also deflates opponents in the audience who might challenge the speaker by saying, "But you didn't consider. . . ."

Panel discussions and debates present other problems. Psychologists say the last person on a panel to talk probably will be most effective in changing audience attitudes—or at least be longer remembered by the audience. But it has also been shown that the first speaker sets the standard and tone for the remainder of the discussion. Being first or last is better positioning than being between two presentations.

PROPAGANDA

No discussion of persuasion would be complete without mentioning propaganda and the techniques associated with it.

Webster's New World Dictionary defines *propaganda* as "the systematic, widespread promotion of a certain set of ideas, doctrines, etc. to further one's own cause." Its roots go back to the seventeenth century, when the Roman Catholic Church set up the *congregatio de propaganda* (congregation for propagating the faith). The word took on extremely negative connotations in the twentieth century.

In World Wars I and II, propaganda was associated with the information activities of the enemy. Germany and Japan were sending out "propaganda" while the United States and its allies were disseminating "truth." Today, propaganda connotes falsehood, lies, deceit, disinformation, and duplicity—practices that opposing groups and governments accuse each other of employing.

Some have even argued that propaganda, in the broadest sense of the word, also includes the advertising and public relations activity of such diverse entities as Exxon and the Sierra Club. Social scientists, however, say that the word *propaganda* should be used only to denote activity that sells a belief system or constitutes political or ideological dogma.

Advertising and public relations messages for commercial purposes, however, do use several techniques commonly associated with propaganda. The most common are the following:

1. *Plain folks.* An approach often used by individuals to show humble beginnings and empathy with the average citizen. President Clinton, for example, likes to remind people of his boyhood in rural Arkansas.

2. *Testimonial.* A frequently used device to achieve credibility, as discussed earlier. A well-known expert, popular celebrity, or average citizen gives testimony about the value of a product or the wisdom of a decision.

3. *Bandwagon.* The implication or direct statement that everyone wants the product or that the idea has overwhelming support. "Millions of Americans support a ban on abortion" or "Every leading expert believes. . . ."

4. *Card-stacking.* The selection of facts and data to build an overwhelming case on one side of the issue, while concealing the other side. The advertising industry, for example, says a ban on beer advertising would lead to enormous reductions in network sports programming, and a ban on cigarette advertising would kill several hundred magazines.

5. *Transfer.* The technique of associating the person, product, or organization with something that has high or low credibility, depending on the intention of the message. Rolex watches are associated with high performance athletes, or a product used by NASA astronauts is associated with high reliability. On the negative side, opponents of a politician may attempt to link the person with drug lords or individuals reputed to be corrupt.

6. *Glittering generalities.* The technique of associating a cause, product, or idea with favorable abstractions such as freedom, justice, democracy, and the American way. Las Vegas bills itself as "The American Way to Play," and American oil companies argue for off-shore drilling to keep "America energy-independent."

A student of public relations should be aware of these techniques, if only to make certain that he or she doesn't intentionally use them to deceive and mislead the public. Ethical responsibilities exist in every form of persuasive communication; guidelines are discussed at the end of the chapter.

PERSUASION AND MANIPULATION

The discussion on previous pages examined ways in which an individual can formulate persuasive messages. The ability to use these persuasive techniques often leads to charges that public relations practitioners have great power to influence and manipulate people.

In reality, the effectiveness of persuasive techniques is greatly exaggerated. Persuasion is not an exact science, and no sure-fire way exists to predict that people will be persuaded to believe a message or act on it. If persuasive techniques were as refined as the critics say, all people might be driving the same make of automobile, using the same soap, and voting for the same political candidate.

This doesn't happen because several variables intervene in the flow of persuasive messages. Katz says the two major intervening variables are selectivity and interpersonal relations; these are consistent with the "limited effects" model of mass communications.

For purposes of discussion, the limitations on effective persuasive messages can be listed as (1) lack of message penetration, (2) competing messages, (3) selective exposure, and (4) selective perception.

LACK OF MESSAGE PENETRATION

The diffusion of messages, despite modern communication technologies, is not pervasive. Not everyone, of course, listens to the same television program or reads the same newspapers and magazines. Not everyone receives the same mail or attends the same meetings. Everyone the communicator wants to reach will not be in the audience eventually reached, despite advances in audience segmentation techniques. There also is the problem of messages being distorted as they pass through media gatekeepers. Key message points often are left out or the context of the message is changed.

COMPETING MESSAGES

In the 1930s, before much was known about the complex process of communication, it was believed that people received information directly without any intervening variable. This was called the *bullet theory* or the *hypodermic needle theory of communication.*

Today, communication experts realize that no message is received in a vacuum. Messages are filtered through a receiver's entire social structure and belief system. Nationality, race, religion, gender, cultural patterns, family, and friends are among the variables that filter and dilute persuasive messages. In addition, people receive countless competing and conflicting messages daily from the mass media and their peers. Social scientists say a person usually conforms to the standards of his or her family and friends. Consequently, most people do not believe or act on messages that are contrary to group norms.

SELF-SELECTION

The people most wanted in an audience are often the least likely to be there. As any minister attests, sinners don't go to church on a regular basis. Vehement supporters or loyalists frequently ignore information by the other side. They do so by being selective in the messages that they want to hear. They read books, newspaper editorials, and magazine articles, and view television programs that support their predispositions. This is why social scientists say that the media are more effective in reinforcing existing attitudes than in changing them.

> ### "DON'T CROSS THE ETHICAL LINE"
>
> Michael Levine in his book *Guerilla PR* discusses persuasion and ethics in sternly realistic terms:
>
> Ethics is more than a simple matter of right and wrong. You will truly hurt yourself if you behave unethically. For one, you can't get away with falsehoods, with backstabbing, with intentional and malicious manipulation of people and media outlets. The folks out there are far too smart to be taken in. The only result will be the complete discrediting of you and your project. So if you're one of those people who has no moral problem with unethical behavior, think of such a stance as bad for business. You can take the morality right out of the equation. But I hope you could see it as more than just a business decision.
>
> Ethical behavior is important in all aspects of life. I cringe when I see a decent person justifying abhorrent business practices simply because "that's the way it's done." There's no excuse for that. Maybe powerful people—including powerful publicists—can get away with it. So walk the straight and narrow. Do what you can to aggressively pursue your PR objectives, but don't cross the ethical line. You'll sleep better at night.
>
> ——————————
>
> Michael Levine *Guerilla PR*. New York: Harper Business.
>
> Excerpted in *Communication World,* March 199?, p. 993.

SELF-PERCEPTION

Self-perception is the channel through which messages are interpreted. People will perceive the same information differently, depending on predispositions and already formulated opinions. *Inside PR* newsletter describes how people react to news stories: "If they believe something to be true and see a story affirming that belief, their belief is strengthened. If they believe something to be true and see a story challenging that belief, they assume the story is biased or just plain wrong."

Thus, depending on a person's views, an action by an organization may be considered a "great contribution to the community" or a "self-serving gimmick." A good example of how self-perceptions influence messages was the divided public opinion about the North American Free Trade Agreement (NAFTA). Although the Clinton administration used economic experts, who cited graphs and statistics about how the agreement would create major economic benefits for the United States, many labor and environmental groups remained convinced that thousands of American jobs would be lost as companies rushed across the border to take advantage of cheap Mexican labor.

THE ETHICS OF PERSUASION

Public relations people by definition are advocates of clients and employers. The emphasis is on persuasive communication to influence a particular public in some way. At the same time, as Chapter 6 pointed out, public relations practitioners must conduct their activities in an ethical manner.

The use of persuasive techniques, therefore, calls for some additional guidelines. Professor Richard L. Johannesen of Northern Illinois University, writing in *Persuasion,* a text by Charles Larson, lists the following ethical criteria for using persuasive devices that should be kept in mind by every public relations professional:

1. Do not use false, fabricated, misrepresented, distorted, or irrelevant evidence to support arguments or claims.

2. Do not intentionally use specious, unsupported, or illogical reasoning.

3. Do not represent yourself as informed or as an "expert" on a subject when you are not.

4. Do not use irrelevant appeals to divert attention or scrutiny from the issue at hand. Among the appeals that commonly serve such a purpose are "smear" attacks on an opponent's character, appeals to hatred and bigotry, innuendo, and "God" or "devil" terms that cause intense but unreflective positive or negative reactions.

5. Do not ask your audience to link your idea or proposal to emotion-laden values, motives, or goals to which it actually is not related.

6. Do not deceive your audience by concealing your real purpose, your self-interest, the group you represent, or your position as an advocate of a viewpoint.

7. Do not distort, hide, or misrepresent the number, scope, intensity, or undesirable features of consequences.

8. Do not use emotional appeals that lack a supporting basis of evidence or reasoning or that would not be accepted if the audience had time and opportunity to examine the subject itself.

9. Do not oversimplify complex situations into simplistic, two-valued, either/or, polar views or choices.

10. Do not pretend certainty when tentativeness and degrees of probability would be more accurate.

11. Do not advocate something in which you do not believe yourself.

It is clear from the preceding list that a public relations professional should be more than a technician or a "hired gun." This raises the issue that public relations personnel often lack the technical and legal expertise to know whether information provided to them by the client or employer is accurate.

Heath makes it clear that this doesn't excuse public relations professionals from ethical responsibility. He writes:

The problem of reporting information that they cannot personally verify does not excuse them from being responsible communicators. Their responsibility is to demand that the most accurate information be provided and the evaluation be the best available.

Persuasive messages require truth, honesty, and candor for two practical reasons. First, Heath says that a message already is suspect because it is advanced on behalf of a client or organization. Second, half-truths and misleading information do not serve the interests of the publics the organization is trying to persuade.

CASE PROBLEM

The school system of a major city wants to draw attention to the need for more volunteer adult tutors in the city's 200 public schools. Budget cutbacks in teaching staff and other resources have made it a vital necessity to recruit volunteers who would work with students on an individual basis to improve reading and math skills.

Your public relations firm has volunteered to organize a public information campaign. Explain what you would do in each of the following categories that relate to the structure and content of persuasive messages: drama, statistics, examples, testimonials, endorsements, and emotional appeals.

QUESTIONS FOR REVIEW AND DISCUSSION

1. Public opinion is highly influenced by self-interest and events. What are these concepts?

2. What is the importance of opinion leaders in the formation of public opinion?

3. What is the role of mass media in opinion formation?

4. What are the stages of public opinion in the life cycle of an issue?

5. Name the three objectives of persuasion in public relations work. What objective is the most difficult to accomplish?

6. Can you name and describe the nine factors involved in persuasive communication?

7. What are three factors involved in source credibility?

8. What are the pros and cons of using celebrities for product endorsements?

9. What are the levels of Maslow's hierarchy of needs? Why is it important for public relations people to understand the basic needs of people?

10. Why is audience involvement and participation important in persuasion?

11. What kinds of techniques can a person use to write persuasive messages?

12. Name several propaganda techniques. Should they be used by public relations people?

13. What are some ethical responsibilities of a person who uses persuasion techniques to influence others?

Bartel, Richard D. "A Widening Expert/Public Opinion Gap: An Interview with Daniel Yankelovitch." *Challenge,* May–June 1992, pp. 20–28.

DeFleur, Melvin L., and Ball-Rokeach, Sandra. *Theories of Mass Communication.* White Plains, NY: Longman, 1989.

Gandy, Oscar H., Jr. "Public Relations and Public Policy: The Structuration of Dominance in the Information Age." In *Rhetorical and Critical Approaches to Public Relations,* ed. Elizabeth L. Toth and Richard L. Heath. Hillsdale, NJ: Erlbaum Associates, 1992, pp. 131–165.

Heath, Richard L. "The Wrangle in the Marketplace: A Rhetorical Perspective of Public Relations." In *Rhetorical and Critical Approaches to Public Relations,* ed. Elizabeth L. Toth and Richard L. Heath. Hillsdale, NJ: Erlbaum Associates, 1992, pp. 17–36.

Larson, Charles U. *Persuasion: Reception and Responsibility,* 6th ed. Belmont, CA: Wadsworth, 1992.

Myers, Wendy S. "Money Isn't Everything: How to Motivate People for Results." *Women in Business,* November–December 1992, pp. 30–32.

Nagy, Alex. "Word Wars at Home: U.S. Response to World War II Propaganda." *Journalism Quarterly,* Spring 1990, pp. 207–213.

Pollay, Richard W. "Propaganda, Puffing and the Public Interest." *Public Relations Review,* Fall 1990, pp. 39–54. Hill and Knowlton's work for the tobacco industry in the 1950s.

Reardon, Kathleen K. *Persuasion in Practice.* Newbury Park, CA: Sage, 1991.

Smith, Ronald D. "Psychological Type and Public Relations: Theory, Research, and Applications." *Journal of Public Relations Research,* vol. 5, no. 3, 1993, pp. 177–199.

Tucker, Kerry, and McNerney, Sharon Long. "Building Coalitions to Initiate Change." *Public Relations Journal,* January 1992, pp. 28–31.

Severin, Werner, and Tankard, James. *Communication Theories.* New York: Longman, 1992.

Yankelovitch, Daniel. "How Public Opinion Works." *Fortune,* October 5, 1992, pp. 102–106.

The Audience and How to Reach It

P R E V I E W   The objective of this chapter is to explain the characteristics of the audiences public relations people seek to address and how the various media can be used to reach them.

Topics covered in the chapter include:

- ■ Nature of the public relations audience

- ■ Two special audiences: seniors and minorities

- ■ Matching audience and media

- ■ Newspapers

- ■ Created events: making news happen

- ■ Magazines and books

- ■ Radio

- ■ Television and films

THE NATURE OF THE PUBLIC RELATIONS AUDIENCE

If the audience on which public relations practitioners focus their messages were a monolithic whole, their work would be far easier—and far less stimulating. The audience, in fact, is just the opposite: a complex intermingling of groups with diverse cultural, ethnic, religious, and economic attributes whose interests coincide at times and conflict at others.

For the public relations professional, knowledge of these shifting audience dynamics is essential. A successful campaign must be aimed at those segments of the mass audience that are most desirable for its particular purpose and must employ those media most effective in reaching them. Some of these segments are easily identifiable and reachable, a category that Zoe McCathrin of Kent State University calls "prepackaged publics." These are well-organized groups whose members have banded together in a common interest; they constitute ready-made targets for practitioners who have projects of concern to them. Examples of such prepackaged publics are businesspeople in Rotary Clubs, animal lovers in the Humane Society, and educationally involved members of the Parent-Teachers Association.

Diversity is the most significant aspect of the mass audience in the United States. Differences in geography, history, and economy among regions of the sprawling country are marked; ranchers in Montana have different attitudes from those found in the heavily populated Eastern seaboard cities. Yet people in the two areas have national interests in common. Ethnic cultures also shape the audience segments public relations practitioners address.

SENIOR AND ETHNIC MARKETS

As the demographic makeup changes dramatically in the United States, two major target audiences have emerged that deserve special attention. One is the *seniors*. This group frequently is defined as men and women 65 years or older, although some sociologists and marketing experts include everyone over age 50. The other group consists of *ethnic minorities,* who differ from the traditional mainstream citizenry in race, language, and customs.

Similar audiences are developing to various degrees in other countries.

SENIORS

Medical advances have improved life expectancy so much that by the year 2000 almost 35 million Americans will be 65 or older, according to the U.S. Bureau of the Census. These older citizens form an important opinion group and a consumer market with special interests.

When appealing to seniors, public relations people should try to ignore the stereotypes of "old folks" so often depicted in the movies and television. Some 80-year-old women sit in rocking chairs, knitting or snoozing, but others cheer and boo ardently while watching professional basketball on TV. Nor are all grandfathers crotchety complainers with quavering voices or kindly patriarchs who fly kites with their grandsons. As many differences in personality, interest, financial status, and living styles exist in the older audience as among their young adult grandchildren.

Public relations practitioners should bear in mind these special characteristics of seniors:

■ With the perspective of long experience, they are often less easily convinced than young adults, demand value in the things they buy, and pay little attention to fads.

■ They vote in greater numbers than their juniors and are more intense readers of newspapers.

■ They form an excellent source of volunteers for social, health, and cultural organizations because they have time and often are looking for something to do.

■ They are extremely health conscious, out of self-interest, and want to know about medical developments. A Census Bureau study showed that most people past 65 say they are in good health; not until their mid-80s do they frequently need assistance in daily living.

Financially, the elderly are better off than the stereotypes suggest. The poverty rate among older Americans is slightly below that of the population at large. The Census Bureau found that people aged 65 to 74 have more discretionary income than any other group. In many instances their homes are completely paid for. While they are poor customers for household goods, they eat out frequently and do much gift buying. They travel frequently. In fact, seniors account for about 80 percent of commercial vacation travel, especially cruises.

MINORITIES

Historically, the United States has welcomed millions of immigrants and assimilated them into the cultural mainstream. They bring a bubbling mixture of personal values, habits, and perceptions that are absorbed slowly, sometimes reluctantly. The questions of assimilation—how much, how little?—also exist with two longtime indigenous minorities, African Americans and Native Americans. This diversity is a great strength of the United States but also a source of friction and misunderstandings. The techniques of public relations can be invaluable in improving these relationships.

Recently the easily identifiable minority groups—primarily Hispanics, African Americans, Asians, and Native Americans—as a whole have been growing five times faster than the general population. The U.S. Census Bureau predicted that by the year 2010 Hispanics and African Americans each will make up 13 percent of the U.S. population, a total of 26 percent, while Anglos will be 58 percent. Asian Americans and Native Americans will provide the remaining percentage. Even greater changes will occur by 2050, the Census Bureau predicted. See Figure 12.1.

A basic point to remember is that the minority population forms *many* target audiences, not a massive monolithic group whose interests are identical. Asians in San Francisco have different cultures and concerns than Hispanics in Miami. Indeed, some of the sharpest racial tensions in the country exist between minority groups; for exam-

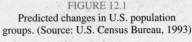

FIGURE 12.1
Predicted changes in U.S. population
groups. (Source: U.S. Census Bureau, 1993)

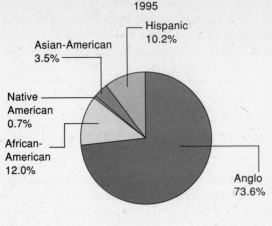

1995

Hispanic
10.2%

Asian-American
3.5%

Native
American
0.7%

African-
American
12.0%

Anglo
73.6%

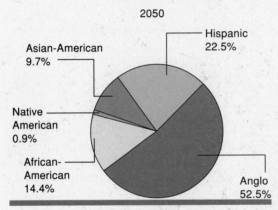

2050

Hispanic
22.5%

Asian-American
9.7%

Native
American
0.9%

African-
American
14.4%

Anglo
52.5%

ple, between African Americans and Korean shopkeepers during the 1992 Los Angeles riot. Thus the practitioner must define the audience with particular care and sensitivity.

Expanding populations have been accompanied by an increase in the number and strength of the minority media through which messages can be delivered. The National Newspaper Publishers Association, representing the African American press, lists nearly 200 member publications, and the 1993 *Gale Directory of Publications and Broadcast Media* lists 199 Hispanic publications. Spanish and African American radio stations have increased correspondingly. Two Spanish-language TV networks, Univision and Telemundo, serve millions of viewers. The Black Entertainment Television Network has a large national audience. Thus a substantial number of outlets exist through which practitioners can deliver audio, visual, and printed messages.

Business Wire, a major distributor of public relations messages, recognizes diversity of interest among the minority groups by operating separate Hispanic, African American, and Asian media circuits within the United States. As further indication of diversity, the Gale directory lists ethnic publications in 45 foreign languages.

Public relations people should give particular attention to the sensitivities of minority audiences. For example, the familiar figure of Aunt Jemima on packages of Quaker Oats food products was widely regarded in the black community as a patronizing stereotype. To change this perception, Quaker Oats cooperated with the National Council of Negro Women to honor outstanding African American women in local communities, who then competed for a national award. At the local award breakfasts, all food served was Aunt Jemima brands, and Quaker Oats officials participated in the programs. The project generated an atmosphere of mutual understanding.

CHARACTERISTICS OF THE AUDIENCE

Human drives have changed little over the centuries. Near the close of the twentieth century we continue to love, hate, worship, work for food and shelter, protect our families, and respond to our neighbors' needs much as our ancestors did three hundred years ago. Knowing how to appeal to these basic emotions is a fundamental need for men and women in public relations.

Even with these drives constant, specific aspects and attitudes of the audience change. In numerous respects, audience trends of the 1990s differ from those of the 1930s, for example, in ways significant to the public relations practitioner:

1. *The public is increasingly visually oriented.* The enormous impact of television on daily life is largely responsible for an increased visual orientation. Many people obtain virtually all their news from the TV screen; that news is told primarily in pictures presented briefly, at a swiftly changing pace. Such exposure leads to a shortened attention span so that, for example, political leaders' policies reach the public largely in ten-second "sound bites." Television also serves as a potent communicator of manners and mores.

Never has a country had as much information available to its citizens as the United States has today—yet the rate of illiteracy is disgracefully high.

Nevertheless, those who cannot read or write, or who do so at a child's level, are part of the public relations audience. How can messages reach them? A challenge for the practitioner!

2. *Fervent support is generated for single issues.* Many individuals become so zealously involved in promoting or opposing a single favorite issue that they lose the social and political balance so needed in a country. Such vehement behavior may create severe public relations problems for the objects of their attacks.

3. *Heavy emphasis is placed on personality and "celebrity."* Sports stars, television and movie actors, and rock music performers are virtually worshiped by some fans. When stars embrace causes, many people blindly follow them. More and more, we see them being used as spokespersons for both commercial and social purposes. Their power as fund-raisers is impressive.

4. *Strong distrust of authority and suspicion of conspiracy exist.* People have been so inundated with exaggerated political promises, seen so much financial chicanery, and been exposed to so many misleading television advertisements that many of them distrust what they read and hear. They suspect evil motives and tend to believe rumors. An extreme example of this tendency is found in a recent New York *Times*/CBS poll which showed that 29 percent of the New York City black citizens questioned believed or thought it possible that the U.S. government created the AIDS virus in a laboratory to infect black people. The need for public relations programs to develop an atmosphere of justifiable, rational trust is obvious.

5. *The international audience for public relations is expanding swiftly.* Growth of huge global corporations and expanded foreign marketing by smaller firms open many opportunities. Increased foreign ownership of U.S. companies, especially in the media field, also creates new relationships and public relations problems.

MATCHING AUDIENCE AND MEDIA

This chapter explains each of the major media—how it functions and ways in which it can be used for public relations purposes. With such an array of printed, spoken, and visual communication methods available, practitioners must make choices in order to use their time and budgets efficiently.

Before we look at each of the media in some detail, some general guidelines exist for matching audience and media:

- Print media are the most effective for delivering a message that requires absorption of details and contemplation by the receiver. Printed matter can be read repeatedly and kept for reference. Newspapers are the fastest with the most widespread impact. Magazines, while slower, are better directed to special-interest audiences such as trade and professional groups. Books take even longer but can generate strong impact.

- Television has the strongest emotional impact of all media. Its visual power makes situations seem close to the viewer. The personality of the TV communicator creates an influence that print media cannot match.

- Radio's greatest advantages are flexibility and the ability to reach specific target audiences. Messages can be prepared for and broadcast on radio more rapidly than on television, at much lower cost. Because there are nine times as many radio stations as TV stations, audience exposure is easier to obtain.

In some campaigns the most cost-effective results come from use of a single medium. Other campaigns work best when several types of media are used. Wise selection of media, based on the audience sought and the money available, is an important skill for public relations practitioners to develop.

MEDIA RELATIONS

Before examining the print, electronic, and film media individually, we need to look at the basic relationship between the media and public relations practitioners. Unless public relations people understand this sometimes sensitive interplay, they cannot be fully effective.

Public Relations
150 Alhambra Circle
Coral Gables, FL 33134
305-529-4504

TEXACO

News from
TEXACO

LA GIRA LATINOAMERICANA TEXACO DE LA SINFONICA DEL NUEVO MUNDO

A INICIARSE EL 4 DE AGOSTO EN LA ARGENTINA

La Sinfónica del Nuevo Mundo Actuará en
Buenos Aires y Montevideo

CORAL GABLES -- El Teatro Colón en Buenos Aires y el Teatro

Solís en Montevideo, dos de los salones de concierto de mayor

renombre en todo el mundo, se encontrarán colmados de la música

de la Sinfónica del Nuevo Mundo durante la Gira Texaco que dicha

orquesta realizará por la América Latina.

La Sinfónica del Nuevo Mundo tocará en tres conciertos,

vendidos ya a capacidad, en el Teatro Colón, recientemente

renovado, antes de volar a Montevideo, donde tocará para un

público numeroso en el Teatro Solís.

Gracias en parte a una generosa donación de la Fundación

Filantrópica Texaco, la orquesta partirá en su gira hacia la

Argentina el 1 de agosto.

FIGURE 12.2
To reach ethnic audiences in the United States and audiences
in other countries, some organizations distribute news releases
in languages other than English. This Texaco release in
Spanish is an example.

Editors and reporters on the one hand, and public relations people on the other, need each other. The media must have material and ideas from public relations sources, and practitioners must have the media as a place to display their stories.

Public relations people need to remember several things about editors and reporters:

1. They are busy. When you approach them with a story idea, either verbally or on paper, make your sales pitch succinctly and objectively.

2. Editors pride themselves on making their own decisions about what stories to run and how to run them. That is their job. Excessive hype of a story often turns them against it. An aggressive demand that editors *must* run a story will make them bristle and will lead to rejection.

3. Able editors and competent public relations people respect each other and work well together. If editors discover, however, that they have been misled or fed false information, they will never again fully trust the offending practitioner and will look negatively on future submissions from that source.

Practitioners also need to remember several things about themselves when dealing with the media:

1. Your job is important in keeping the public informed. You are performing a service, not asking a favor, when you submit a story idea or a news release.

2. You should assume that your story will be judged on its merits, as seen by the editor, and should not demean yourself by begging an editor to use it.

3. Your role continues after the story or idea has been accepted. You cannot control the tone of the story that appears, but you can influence it by providing favorable story angles and additional information. A public relations person's helpful, pleasant personality does influence most writers, at least subtly.

THE PRINT MEDIA

NEWSPAPERS

Every edition of a newspaper contains hundreds of news stories and pieces of information, in much greater number than the largest news staff can gather by itself. More than most readers realize, and many editors care to admit, newspapers depend upon information brought to them voluntarily.

The *Columbia Journalism Review* noted, for example, that in one edition the *Wall Street Journal* had obtained 45 percent of its 188 news items from news releases. Because of its specialized nature, the *Journal*'s use of news releases may be higher than that of general-interest daily newspapers. Public relations generates about 50 percent of the stories in New York City newspapers, according to Albert Scardino, press secretary for former Mayor David L. Dinkins.

Approximately 1570 daily newspapers and 7600 weekly newspapers are published in the United States. Most cities today have only one daily newspaper, although competition between two newspapers, or more, exists in the metropolitan centers and in a few smaller cities. While some metropolitan newspapers have circulations of more than a million copies a day, approximately two-thirds of the daily newspapers have circulations of 20,000 or less.

Newspapers published for distribution in the late afternoon, called evening or P.M. papers, outnumber morning (A.M.) papers approximately three to one. Especially in larger cities, however, a substantial trend toward morning publication is in progress. Some cities have 24-hour newspapers; these publish several editions around the clock. Knowledge of a newspaper's hours of publication and the deadlines it enforces for submission of copy is essential for everyone who supplies material to the paper.

Approximately three-quarters of American daily newspapers are owned by newspaper groups. The publishers and editors of a group-owned newspaper have broad local autonomy but must adhere to certain operating standards and procedures laid down by the group headquarters.

A Commercial Institution   In dealing with a newspaper, public relations people should remember that it is a commercial institution, created to earn a profit as a purveyor of news and advertising. Although newspapers often are so deeply rooted in a community that they seem like public institutions, they are not. Their publishers and editors as a whole seek to serve the public interest, and often succeed admirably in doing so. Like any other business, however, a newspaper that does not earn a profit soon disappears. Therefore, in the long run and sometimes in the short run as well, management decisions about what appears in a newspaper must be made with the balance sheet in mind.

Newspapers receive about 70 percent of their income from advertising and about 30 percent from circulation sales. They cannot afford to publish press releases that are nothing more than commercial advertising; to do so would cut into their largest source

MEDIA DIRECTORIES

Accurate, up-to-date mailing lists and files of personal contacts are essential in public relations programs. Media directories are a primary source in preparing such lists.

Numerous directories exist, some of them quite specialized. The following major ones are widely used:

- *Gale's Directory of Publications and Broadcast Media* (Detroit: Gale Research, Inc.). Lists newspapers, magazines, journals, related publications, and radio and television stations. Annual.

- *Broadcasting/Cablecasting Yearbook* (Washington: Broadcast Publications, Inc.). Lists radio and television stations and cable TV systems.

- *Editor & Publisher International Year Book* (New York: *Editor & Publisher*). Detailed information about newspapers, their associations, and agencies that serve them.

- *SRDS Special Issues* (Wilmette, IL: Standard Rate & Data Service). Six issues a year provide editorial profiles of more than 5000 major print media.

- *Working Press of the Nation* (Chicago: National Research Bureau). Lists more than 30,000 publicity outlets in the print and electronic media.

- *Bacon's PR and Media Information Systems* (Chicago). Covers magazines, newspapers, radio, and television.

Several firms offer mailing lists designed to reach target audiences. They handle distribution of a client's news releases by mail, wire, or satellite. Among the major ones are PR Newswire (New York), Business Wire (New York), Media Distribution Services (New York), Burrelle's Information Services (Livingston, NJ), and North American Precis Syndicate, Inc. (New York).

of income. To be published, a release submitted to a newspaper must contain information that an editor regards as news of interest to a substantial number of readers.

Since newspapers are protected by the First Amendment to the Constitution, they cannot be forced to publish any material, including news releases, nor need they receive permission from the government or anyone else to publish whatever they desire. Editors resist pressure on them to suppress material they consider to be newsworthy and, conversely, to print material they believe to be unnewsworthy. However, the definitions of newsworthiness are abstract and fluctuating. What one newspaper considers to be news, another will not.

Nevertheless, editors do not enjoy the unfettered privilege of publishing whatever they desire. Two severe limitations hang over their decisions:

1. *The laws of libel and invasion of privacy.* Publication of material that, if challenged in court, is ruled to be libelous or an unreasonable invasion of privacy can cost a newspaper extremely heavy judgments and legal expenses. The newspaper management is legally responsible for everything a newspaper publishes, including material submitted by outsiders. Even letters to the editor are covered by the law of libel.

2. *The interests and desires of their readers.* If a newspaper fails to publish news and features that readers find to be valuable or entertaining, its circulation will dwindle and it will perish. Alert editors, therefore, are receptive to fresh ideas. They recognize the need for community service and look for ways in which their newspapers can perform this function. Their doors are open to public relations representatives who supply ideas and information that help the papers to please and inform their readers and to carry out the newspapers' social responsibility.

Organization of a Newspaper   Those who work with newspapers in any aspect of public relations should know how a newspaper staff is organized, so they can take story ideas or policy problems to the proper person. In the usual table of organization, the publisher is the director of all financial, mechanical, and administrative operations. Frequently the publisher also has ultimate responsibility for news and editorial matters; in many instances he or she carries the title of editor and publisher.

THREE CARDINAL RULES FOR NEWS RELEASES TO NEWSPAPERS

A news release submitted to a newspaper should . . .

1.   Contain information that is newsworthy in that newspaper's circulation area.

2.   Be addressed to the city editor if it is of general interest, or to the appropriate section editor if it contains special-interest material such as sports news.

3.   Be delivered to the newspaper well in advance of the desired publication date, to provide time for processing.

The editor heads the news and editorial department. The associate editor conducts the editorial and commentary pages and deals with the public concerning their content. The managing editor is the head of news operations, to whom the city editor and the editors of sections such as sports, business, entertainment, and family living answer. Some newspapers have an executive editor above the managing editor. The city editor directs the local news staff of reporters. Some members of the city staff cover beats such as police and city hall; others are on general assignment, meaning that they are sent to cover any type of story the city editor deems to be potentially newsworthy. (Submission of news releases to editors is discussed in Chapter 22.)

Weekly newspapers have a different focus from that of daily newspapers, and much smaller staffs. The weekly concentrates exclusively on its own community. Its target zone may be no more than one segment of a metropolitan area. Weekly editors need the help of much volunteered material. Although weekly newspapers often are overlooked in public relations programs, they can be effective outlets for those who study how to meet their needs. The circulation for each weekly newspaper may be small because of its limited distribution area, but the intensity of readership is high and story exposure is good.

Large daily newspapers, to demonstrate editorial independence, often have a rule against publishing a news release exactly as received. Relatively few weekly newspapers have the staffs to enforce such a policy.

PUBLIC RELATIONS OPPORTUNITIES IN NEWSPAPERS

Material for a newspaper should be submitted either as a news release ready for publication or as a factsheet from which a reporter can develop a feature story or interview. When an invitation to a news conference is sent to a newspaper, it should include a factsheet containing basic information. Frequently, the reporter to whom an editor assigns a news release for processing rewrites and expands it, developing additional story angles and background. When a public relations representative presents an important story idea in factsheet form rather than as a news release for publication, a personal conversation with the appropriate editor, if it can be arranged, helps to sell the concept and expand its potential. *Such personal calls on editors should last no longer than is necessary to explain the idea adequately.* Although some practitioners make a follow-up phone call shortly after the factsheet has arrived, this practice irritates many editors. They dislike being interrupted. (Preparations of news releases and factsheets is discussed in Chapter 22).

Emphasizing contemporary living styles, newspapers often publish special sections on home improvement, fashion and beauty, business, sports, and recreation. This trend creates additional opportunities for practitioners, because editors seek story ideas and well-developed releases for these sections.

A public relations representative wishing to discuss a large-scale project such as a communitywide fund drive should do so by appointment with the managing editor or city editor after the deadline hour has passed. A cooperative plan of publicity can be developed at such a session. A newspaper is more likely to give a major project sympathetic treatment if its editors receive background information before the first stories break. This allows them time to think about the ramifications of the project and plan coverage.

Contact:	Brad Hennig	Contact:	Ann Morley Wool
	VISA International		Susan Donnelly
	(415) 358-2435		Edelman Public Relations
			(212)704-8118/8166

VISA OLYMPICS OF THE IMAGINATION

FACT SHEET

WHO: Ten children from the U.S. will win spots on an international team of student artists traveling to the Olympic Winter Games in Norway in February 1994.

Ten children from Norway and five from Canada will also be part of the 25-person team.

WHAT: VISA and ten major U.S. newspapers are challenging youngsters, ages 11 to 13, to draw or paint a picture depicting their vision of what the Olympic Games will look like 100 years from now.

One winner will be awarded the grand prize by each of the following participating newspapers:

The Atlanta Journal-Constitution	Boston Herald
Chicago Tribune	The Denver Post
Fort Worth Star-Telegram	Houston Chronicle
Los Angeles Times	The New York Times
San Francisco Chronicle	The Seattle Times

NEWSPAPER PARTNERS

The Atlanta Journal-Constitution

Boston Herald

Chicago Tribune

The Denver Post

Fort Worth Star-Telegram

Houston Chronicle

Los Angeles Times

The New York Times

San Francisco Chronicle

The Seattle Times

WHEN: September 1, 1993 -- Nationwide contest kick-off
October 15, 1993 -- Contest entry deadline
December 7, 1993 -- Winners announced
February 11 - 16, 1994 -- Trip to Olympic Winter Games

WHY: The contest marks the 100th anniversary of the founding of the Olympic movement.

HOW: Entry forms, announcements and rules will appear regularly in each newspaper during the contest period, and contest kits will be distributed directly to schools in the readership area. Additionally, newspapers will select a local panel of judges to nominate the finalists and winners.

VISA INTERNATIONAL   Post Office Box 8999   San Francisco   California   94128

FIGURE 12.3

A basic step in obtaining good coverage in the media is to provide them with key information in advance, so they can assign reporters and photographers. Distribution of a factsheet, such as this one from Visa Olympics of the Imagination, is an efficient method.

At times, an organization's representative or other individual needs to discuss a policy issue with the newspaper management—a complaint against perceived mistreatment by the newspaper, for example, or an attempt to obtain editorial support. Usually this is done by appointment with the editor or associate editor or, in the case of a news story, with the managing editor. Often problems arise from misunderstanding rather than from intent.

NEWS

FOR IMMEDIATE RELEASE   CONTACT: Dave Gundersen
                                                    (612) 883-8512

FASCINATING SHOPS, DESIGNED FOR BROWSING AND BUYING,
ADD TO THE ALL-FAMILY FUN AT KNOTT'S CAMP SNOOPY

BLOOMINGTON, MN -- Snoopy's Boutique, a shop devoted exclusively to Peanuts merchandise, is just one of seven unique shopping opportunities awaiting guests at Knott's Camp Snoopy.

Throughout the $70 million indoor family theme Park at the heart of Mall of America, specialty stores and shops add to the family fun. The shelves at Snoopy's Boutique are filled with thoughtfully selected wares: toys, clothing, games and collectibles, featuring Snoopy, Charlie Brown, Lucy, Linus and the entire cast of lovable Peanuts characters.

Dropping by the Park's Knott's Berry Market evokes the nostalgic sights and sounds and smells of Mrs. Knott's own kitchen. For the first time outside Southern California, the Market offers a complete selection of Knott's Berry Farm's world-famous jams, jellies, preserves and more good things to eat.

The mail order counter packs and ships Knott's famous gift baskets and boxes. A cozy coffee/cappuccino bar, and fudge and peanut butter-making are also at the Market.

-more-

Knott's Camp Snoopy • Mall of America • 5000 Center Court • Bloomington, MN 55425-5550
(612) 883-8500

KNOTT'S CAMP SNOOPY
2-2-2

The rustic, bustling Crafts Barn is sure to intrigue visitors. Talented craftspeople in residence hand-make and sell one-of-a-kind craft items, reflecting the rich folk heritage of Minnesota and the upper Midwest.

Walking through the door and into Camp Snoopy Toys is like a step back in time. Designed to evoke images of an old-fashioned toy factory, the shop offers a large stock of toys, games, books and videos. Sports fans enjoy Good Sports, offering official sports team logo merchandise, plus colorful Snoopy-themed sportswear. One-of-a-kind collectibles of famous teams and athletes are also on display and for sale.

If the latest, hottest fashions in tee-shirts, sweatshirts and caps are on your shopping list, head directly to Joe Cool's Hot Shop, a place with its own, "cool" attitude. At Geodes, mineralogists use a diamond-tipped saw to cut open nature's fascinating "hollow rocks" to reveal the sparkling, 65 million year-old crystallization inside.

The air at Peppermint Patty's Candy is perpetually perfumed with sweet smells as fresh fudge and caramel corn are prepared to the enjoyment of guests watching. The shop offers a huge variety of candy, plus chocolates by the piece or box.

Browsing and shopping at Knott's Camp Snoopy is a unique experience in itself, carefully planned to enhance and expand the magic of the most delightful seven acres anywhere.

-KNOTT'S CAMP SNOOPY-

051192

FIGURE 12.4
A news release such as this one, from Knott's Camp Snoopy,
an indoor family theme park in a Minnesota shopping mall, can
be published exactly as received, if an editor chooses, or can
serve as the basis for stories prepared by reporters.

To cite an actual example, in a city with three hospitals, directors of the smallest institution believed that the city's newspaper was ignoring it. They were upset because no story had been published about enlargement of the hospital's outpatient treatment facilities. When a director discussed the problem with the newspaper's associate editor, however, the fact emerged that the hospital administrator had failed to notify the paper about the construction. He had assumed wrongly that the editors knew about it.

The lesson here is clear: when you have news to announce, tell the media; don't wait for them to come to you.

CREATED EVENTS: MAKING NEWS HAPPEN

Some news stories *happen*. Other stories must be *created*. Successful public relations practitioners must do more than produce competent, accurate news releases about routine occurrences in the affairs of their clients or employers. They must use ingenuity and organizing ability to create events that attract coverage in the news media. Historian Daniel Boorstin calls these projects "pseudoevents." This extra dimension of creativity is the difference between acting to make news and merely reacting to news that happens. We are not speaking here of feeding phony stories to the media or doing anything else unethical. We are talking about causing something to occur.

Such created events vary in scope from the huge anti- and pro-abortion marches in Washington, staged by ardent advocates of opposite positions, to small, clever publicity promotions that draw media coverage because they are unusual, involve prominent people, or are just plain fun.

The two following events took place only because public relations persons conceived the ideas. Both received wide news coverage and achieved their objectives.

■ The small Stevens Aviation Company found that Southwest Airlines was using a slogan Stevens had created. It might have filed a lawsuit to stop the practice. Instead, at the suggestion of a public relations firm, Stevens chairman Kurt Herwald challenged Southwest chairman Herb Kelleher to a winner-take-all arm-wrestling match.

After a lively advance buildup, the match was held in a professional wrestling arena in Dallas, before television cameras. Herwald won but announced that Stevens Aviation would allow Southwest to use the slogan, anyway. The three national TV networks covered the match, CNN gave it strong play, and hundreds of newspapers carried news service accounts.

During the six months after the match, Stevens's business volume increased 30 percent.

■ Participation in a longtime volunteer tutor program in the New York City public schools lagged dangerously. So a public relations firm created a two-week Read Aloud event in conjunction with the program's thirty-fifth birthday.

Hundreds of prominent people, including President Bush's wife Barbara, read aloud to students in various schools. Advance media coverage and daily stories about the celebrity appearances were so effective that the campaign created a 22 percent increase in volunteers. Also important, it let children meet stimulating role models.

Every one of the events in the accompanying list represents a legitimate news story that the local newspaper and other media might cover. But these stories exist only because a public relations adviser convinced the company to sponsor or conduct them. Once this decision is made, the practitioner must produce a flow of news releases with fresh angles, as well as use other techniques to build public interest.

Openings of stores and shopping centers, as well as groundbreakings, happen so frequently that the ingenuity of public relations representatives is challenged. Newspapers are weary of the traditional, rigidly posed group of men in dark business suits and incongruous hardhats lined up behind one man with a shovel. The same is true of ribbon-cuttings. Some newspapers refuse to publish these photographic clichés. However, fresh approaches can be found, especially if a little humor is employed.

MAGAZINES

Magazines differ markedly from newspapers in content, time frame, and methods of operation. Therefore, they present different opportunities and problems to the public relations practitioner. In contrast to the daily newspaper with its hurry-up deadlines, magazines are published weekly, monthly, or sometimes quarterly. Because these publications usually deal with subjects in greater depth than newspapers do, magazine editors may allot months for the development of an article. Those who seek to supply subject ideas or ready-to-publish material to them must plan much further ahead than is

TRUCKLOAD OF BROCCOLI FOR BUSH

Quick thinking by a group of packers and growers at a vegetable packing shed in Guadalupe, California, created an entertaining news event that held international attention for a week.

One Monday morning, a packing executive mentioned to the group at work a little TV news story that President Bush had banned broccoli from the menu on Air Force One, his private plane, because he disliked the rugged green vegetable.

"Let's send him a case of broccoli," someone said. "No, let's send a whole truckload so they'll really notice it," another replied.

The next evening a big rig carrying nearly 10 tons of broccoli hit the road on a 3000-mile haul to Washington, D.C. Growers told the media what was happening. They hoped to give some cases to the White House and planned to donate the remainder to Washington food charities.

Would the anti-broccoli president accept the gift? Humorous speculation kept the story going.

On Friday the White House staff phoned to say that Mrs. Bush would receive the broccoli donation on the White House lawn on Monday morning. As cameras rolled and reporters sniffed the homely but wholesome vegetable, Mrs. Bush was presented with three cases of broccoli, a broccoli bouquet, and a recipe book. The TV networks featured the story tongue-in-cheek. Back at the packing shed, orders for broccoli rolled in.

"We could have spent $50,000 on ads in trade journals and not had anything like the impact we're getting," a packing house executive said. Thinking big and acting quickly made the idea succeed.

Barbara Bush, representing her husband, holds up her hands in mock surrender when presented with boxes of broccoli. California growers won national attention by sending a truckload of the vegetable to the White House after President Bush banned broccoli from Air Force One because he disliked it.

necessary with newspapers. Ideas for Christmas season stories, for example, should be submitted by July.

A newspaper is designed for family reading, with something for men, women, and children; its material is aimed at an audience of varying educational and economic levels. Its editors fire buckshot, to hit the reading interests of as many persons as possible. Magazine editors, on the other hand, in most instances aim carefully at special-interest audiences. They fire rifle bullets at limited, well-defined readership groups.

The more than 12,000 periodicals published in the United States may be classified in several ways. For purposes of this discussion, periodicals are grouped into two broad categories, those for the public at large and those for specific audiences. Each is in turn broken down into several subdivisions.

Periodicals for the Public at Large   Among the types in this category are the following:

General Interest.   Only a few national magazines with across-the-board appeal exist today. Prominent among them are *Reader's Digest,* enormously successful worldwide;

THIRTY-TWO WAYS TO CREATE NEWS FOR YOUR ORGANIZATION

1. Tie in with news events of the day.
2. Work with another publicity person.
3. Tie in with a newspaper or other medium on a mutual project.
4. Conduct a poll or survey.
5. Issue a report.
6. Arrange an interview with a celebrity.
7. Take part in a controversy.
8. Arrange for a testimonial.
9. Arrange for a speech.
10. Make an analysis or prediction.
11. Form and announce names for committees.
12. Hold an election.
13. Announce an appointment.
14. Celebrate an anniversary.
15. Issue a summary of facts.
16. Tie in with a holiday.
17. Make a trip.
18. Make an award.
19. Hold a contest.
20. Pass a resolution.
21. Appear before public bodies.
22. Stage a special event.
23. Write a letter.
24. Release a letter you have received.
25. Adapt national reports and surveys for local use.
26. Stage a debate.
27. Tie into a well-known week or day.
28. Honor an institution.
29. Organize a tour.
30. Inspect a project.
31. Issue a commendation.
32. Issue a protest.

People, which capitalizes on the contemporary interest in personalities; and *National Geographic.*

News Magazines.   High-circulation weekly news magazines report and interpret the news, adding background that daily newspapers lack time to develop. The biggest periodicals of this type are *Time, Newsweek,* and *U.S. News & World Report.*

Women's Interest.   Magazines designed for women have a very large audience. They publish articles about fashions and beauty, cooking, home decorating, self-improvement, work and leisure, and personal relationships. Prominent in this group are *Ladies' Home Journal, Cosmopolitan, Working Woman, Better Homes and Gardens, Good Housekeeping,* and *Family Circle.*

Men's Interest.   Growing participation of women in athletics has increased female readership of traditionally male sports magazines. *Sports Illustrated* and *Field and Stream* are perhaps the best known of these magazines. With their emphasis on sex, *Playboy* and *Penthouse* aim primarily at the male audience but also draw substantial female readership.

The Senior Market.   *Modern Maturity,* published by the American Association of Retired Persons (AARP), has the largest magazine circulation in the United States, more than 22 million. Maturity News Service sells feature stories of particular interest to older readers. Many monthly publications for seniors, usually distributed free in places where retirees live (such as mobile-home parks) are excellent outlets for public relations material at the local level. In general, older citizens read magazines and newspapers more than young people do; retirees in particular are heavy watchers of television as well.

The categories of magazines just listed offer public relations opportunities that pay large rewards in readership when successful. They are difficult markets to hit, however, except by highly experienced specialists well acquainted with the magazines' operating methods. Far more abundant opportunities for placing public relations material exist with the other periodicals, those aimed at more specific audiences.

Periodicals for Specific Audiences   The specific-interest group includes a wide array of publications, including the following:

Special-Audience Magazines.   Hundreds of these prosper because they are carefully edited on single themes. Each attracts an audience with strong interest in its particular topic; this audience in turn draws advertisers whose products are especially relevant to these readers. A glance at the magazine rack in a supermarket gives an indication of the diversity of special-interest magazines—only an indication, however, because such periodicals are far too numerous for over-the-counter sale. Many are distributed primarily by subscription.

A few examples include *Dog World, Backpacker, Stereo Review, Car Craft, Skin Diver, Surfing, Ski, International Photographer,* and *World Oil.* Broader in appeal than many of these are magazines about business, including *Fortune, Business Week, Forbes,* and *Barron's.*

Trade Journals.   Each of the special-audience magazines listed above appeals to a portion of the public that cares about its particular topic mostly as a hobby or a sport. Trade journals, on the other hand, are designed for persons who read them for business and professional reasons, not recreational ones. While virtually unknown to the public, these periodicals are vital channels of communication within various industries and professions. In their pages, readers learn about the activities of their competitors, new products and trends in their field of work, and the movement of individuals from one job to another. Often trade journals have the same intimacy in their respective fields as weekly newspapers do in their communities.

The following small sampling of trade journals indicates the extremely specialized nature of their contents: *American Christmas Tree Journal, Mini-Micro Systems, Fleet Owner, The Indian Trader, Insulation Outlook, Progressive Grocer, Wire Journal International.*

Placement of material in trade journals is an essential assignment for many public relations representatives. A story about a new product published in an appropriate trade journal may be more valuable to the manufacturer of that product than a story about it in a large newspaper, because the information reaches a target audience containing potential purchasers. Products and specialized services offered by companies often are not publicized to a general audience, because it neither needs nor cares about them. If a manufacturer of coin-operated machines has a new product ready for release, for example, its public relations representative should concentrate on placing announcement stories in such trade journals as *American Coin-Op, Play Meter Magazine,* and *Vending Times.*

Practitioners handling specialized products or services should scrutinize pertinent trade journals, to be certain that they are supplying these publications with effective news releases, story ideas, and illustrations. A one-year analysis of these journals will show how well a client and its competitors fared. With this analysis in hand, the publicist might find it desirable to submit more stories about large orders received by the client, for example, or stories about unusual uses of a product.

Company and Organizational Magazines.   There are two types of company and organizational magazines:

1. *Internal,* designed for and distributed primarily to employees, retirees, influential outsiders who may have some interest in the organization, and often stockholders of the firm. (These are discussed in Chapter 22.)

2. *External,* distributed to selected portions of the public. Published by companies and organizations to promote public appreciation of the sponsor, and to form a psychological tie between sponsor and recipient, these usually are circulated among customers, stockholders, and users of the sponsor's services. The editorial content appearing in such external periodicals has general appeal—articles on travel, personalities, self-help, food, and the like—plus material about the issuing company. The magazines that airline travelers find in the seat pockets in front of them, such as *American Way* (American Airlines) and *TWA Ambassador* (Trans World Airlines), are prime examples of this group. Such external magazines offer a good target for the public relations specialist. Their audiences tend to be relatively affluent.

A study of the annual *Writer's Market* and the monthly periodicals *Writer's Digest* and *The Writer* will provide abundant information about individual magazines and the kind of material each publishes. Every magazine has its special formula.

Operating with much smaller staffs than newspapers have, magazines are heavily dependent on material submitted from outside their offices. Some, especially the smaller ones, are almost entirely staff-written. The staffs create ideas and cover some stories; they also process public relations material submitted to them. The more carefully the submitted material is tailored to the particular periodical's audience and written in a style preferred by the editor, the more likely it is to be published, with or without rewriting by the staff. Many magazines purchase part, or almost all, of their material from freelance writers on a fee basis. An editor may buy a submitted article for publication if it fits the magazine's formula, or the editor may commission a writer to develop an idea into an article along specified lines.

Editors are always looking for ideas. Many magazine articles had their origins in suggestions submitted by public relations practitioners. An article in a women's magazine on preventing sunburn, for example, may have resulted from a letter and a press kit sent to an editor by a sunscreen manufacturer or by the manufacturer's public relations firm.

A public relations practitioner has four principal approaches for getting material into a periodical:

1. Submit a story idea that would promote the practitioner's cause either directly or subtly, and urge the editor to have a writer, freelance or staff, develop the story on assignment.

2. Send a written query to the editor outlining an article idea and offering to submit the article in publishable form if the editor approves the idea.

3. Submit a completed article, written either by the practitioner or by an independent writer under contract, and hope that the editor will accept it for publication. In this and the two previously mentioned instances, however, the editor should be made fully aware of the source of the suggestion or article. As pointed out in Chapter 6, allowing a freelance writer to place what presumably is an "independent" article is a violation of Article 9 of the PRSA Code of Professional Standards, which forbids using third parties who are purported to be independent but serve the special interests of the employer or client.

4. For trade journals and other periodicals that use such material, submit news releases in ready-to-publish form.

The size and nature of each magazine determines its content. Most common is a formula of several major articles, one or two short articles, and special departments. These may be personal commentary, a compilation of news items in a specific category (short items about new products in a trade journal, for example), or chitchat about personalities. Special departments offer excellent public relations opportunities. A favorable item in one of them need not be long to be effective.

When a magazine has a by-lined columnist and the publicist has material suitable for that column, it may be sent directly to the columnist. The risk is that if the columnist rejects the item, he or she may throw it in the wastebasket when in fact it might be usable elsewhere in the magazine. When there is doubt, it is safer to submit such material to the editor. Examination of a magazine's masthead will show the name of the proper editor to address.

BOOKS

Because their writing and publication is a time-consuming process, often involving years from the conception of an idea until appearance of the volume, books are not popularly recognized as public relations tools. Yet they can be. A book, especially a hardcover one, has stature in the minds of readers. They read it with respect and give attention to the message it carries.

Books are promulgators of ideas. As channels of communication, they reach thoughtful audiences, including opinion leaders. Often publication of a book starts a trend or focuses national discussion on an issue.

The standard method of book publishing is for an author and publisher to sign a contract describing the material the author will deliver to the publisher and the conditions under which the publisher will issue and sell the book. The publisher pays the cost of production and marketing. The author receives a royalty fee on each copy sold, perhaps 10 to 15 percent of the retail price. Publishers often make advance payments to authors against the royalties their books are expected to earn.

A book published in hardcover often requires a year from acceptance of the manuscript to publication. Thus, a public relations effort made through publication of a hardcover book must be long range in nature and aimed at the broad-stroke influencing of public opinion. The hardcover book is not the tool for stirring up a new hula-hoop fad or publicizing a video game.

The tremendous growth of paperback publishing has opened new avenues for use of books as public relations vehicles. Hundreds of titles ranging from classical literature to how-to-do-it books on gardening, plumbing, and sex are on sale. An examination of nonfiction titles on the paperback shelves will show the range of opportunity that exists to promote products, ideological movements, personalities, and fads.

The traditional royalty system of hardcover books is also used for paperback books, but various forms of fee payments to authors are employed as well.

Literary agents have an influential role in the creation of books. An agent represents the author in dealings with publishers, urging a publishing house to accept a manuscript and negotiating contracts that include provisions for subsidiary rights, film rights, and other sources of income. For this assistance, the agent ordinarily receives 10 percent of the author's income from the literary property involved. Unless he or she is well acquainted with the publishing industry, a public relations representative seeking to publicize a client's cause through publication of a book is well advised to work through an agent rather than make a personal round of publishing houses. Competent agents know the financial angles and offer shrewd editorial advice as well.

Although the fact is seldom mentioned publicly, companies and nonprofit organizations sometimes pay subsidies to both hardcover and paperback publishers to help defray production costs of a book they wish to see published. The subsidy may take the form of a guarantee to purchase a specific number of copies. A corporation, for example, might wish to commemorate its centennial with a company history or to publicize its chief executive officer in a book, and may desire the prestige of a prominent publishing house behind it. Yet sales experience indicates that the book will not sell enough copies for the publisher to break even. So a quiet subsidy arrangement is made. A handsome book results; it receives favorable reviews, the corporation gains prestige, the publisher makes some money, and the public's fund of knowledge is increased. The book must be an honest one, however, not a blatant "puff" job. It must report the bad with the good. If not, everyone involved loses respect instead of gaining it.

The idea for a beautifully illustrated book on New England, to cite an example, might come from a state travel agency, which approaches the publisher either directly or through an author. The state agency pays part of the publisher's cost, knowing that the book will draw visitors to the area.

Another recently developed form of subsidized book has been created by Whittle Publications L. P. Books in the series are underwritten by major advertisers and cover important business and social topics. Each book contains full-page color advertisements for the sponsor's service or product interspersed throughout the text. Copies are sent free to managers and policymakers in business and the public sector.

Typical of such subsidized books published by Whittle is *Life After Television* by George Gilder, which contains 18 full-page advertisements for Federal Express.

PUBLIC RELATIONS OPPORTUNITIES IN BOOKS

As indicated above, books as public relations tools, both hardcover and paperback, usually are best suited to promote ideas and create a favorable state of mind. Political movements often are publicized through books by proponents. On a more mundane level, every book published about gardening indirectly helps the sale of garden tools. Although a specific brand of tools is not mentioned in such a book, it benefits from the book's existence. The manufacturer's public relations representative can help the company's cause by assisting the author in assembling material for the book. Public relations efforts need not be overt to be effective. Also, public relations benefits may occur without being planned. The cookbook *The Complete Dairy Foods Cookbook,* by E. Annie Proues and Lew Nichols, inevitably helped promote use of dairy products, while *The Joy of Chocolate,* by Judith Olney, must have made chocolate manufacturers happy.

From the point of view of publishers, publicity for books and their authors is an important public relations function. The public relations departments of publishing houses use news releases, prepublication endorsements, interviews, and other standard techniques to create awareness of a forthcoming book. A writer may be taken on a tour of major cities for interviews and autograph parties, or speak to reviewers nationwide by satellite.

THE SPOKEN AND VISUAL MEDIA

RADIO

Speed and mobility are the special attributes that make radio unique among the major media of communication. If urgency justifies such action, messages can be placed on the air by radio almost instantly upon their receipt at a radio station. They need not be delayed by the time-consuming production processes of print. Since radio programming is more loosely structured than television programming, interruption of a program for an urgent announcement can be done with less internal decision making. Although most public relations material does not involve such urgency, moments of crisis do occur when quick on-the-air action helps a company or other organization get information to the public swiftly.

Radio benefits, too, from its ability to go almost anywhere. Reporters working from mobile trucks can be broadcasting from the scene of a large fire within minutes after it has been discovered. They can hurry from a press conference to a luncheon speech, carrying only a small amount of equipment. A disc jockey can broadcast an afternoon program from a table in a neighborhood shopping center. Flexibility is ever-present.

So is flexibility among listeners. Radios in automobiles reach captive audiences, enhancing the popularity of drive-time disc jockeys. The tiny transistor or mini earphone-type radio brings programs to mail carriers on their routes, carpenters on construction sites, homeowners pulling weeds in their gardens.

More than 11,000 radio stations are on the air in the United States, ranging from low-powered outlets operated by a handful of staff members to large metropolitan stations audible for hundreds of miles. Slightly less than half of these stations are of the amplitude modulation (AM) type; the others use frequency modulation (FM), which has shorter range but generally clearer reception. Some AM stations aim at general audiences, using middle-of-the-road music, while others appeal to special listener interests. FM stations, with restricted listening areas, usually seek target audiences. Both AM and FM stations attempt to develop distinctive "sounds" by specializing in one kind of music or talk format. A public relations practitioner should study each station's format and submit material suitable to it. Don't send information about senior citizen recreational programs to the news director of a hard-rock station with an audience primarily of teenagers.

A radio station operates under license, renewable every seven years, from the Federal Communications Commission. After several decades of strict FCC regulation, the radio industry was partially deregulated in 1981, thus obtaining greater flexibility in programming. No longer must a station devote part of its air time to nonentertainment programming or restrict the number of minutes in each hour devoted to commercials. Even with these restrictions removed, a station may encounter license renewal trouble if it cannot demonstrate reasonably well under challenge that it operates in the public interest, necessity, and convenience. All programs are subject to the laws of libel.

PUBLIC RELATIONS OPPORTUNITIES IN RADIO

Commercial radio is highly promotional in nature and provides innumerable opportunities for public relations specialists to further their causes. Radio programs may be divided into two general categories, news and entertainment. A station's news director is responsible for the former, the program director for the latter. At least eight possible targets exist in radio:

1. *Newscasts.* Many stations have frequent newscasts, of which the five-minute variety is the most common. If the station has a network affiliation, some newscasts it carries are national in content. Of much more interest to the public relations practitioner are the local newscasts. News releases sent to a radio station should cover the same newsworthy topics as those sent to a newspaper; they should follow identical rules of

accuracy and timeliness. The practitioner cannot expect to hear extended versions of these releases on the air. Brevity is fundamental on radio. A story that runs 400 words in a newspaper may be told in 50 words or fewer on radio. Lengthy news releases for radio stations are unnecessary, indeed unwise.

2.   *Community calendars.* Stations broadcast a daily program called the "Community Bulletin Board" or a similar title. This listing of coming events is an excellent place to circulate information about a program the practitioner is handling.

3.   *Actualities.* Radio news directors brighten their newscasts by including *actualities.* These are brief reports from scenes of action, either live or on tape. Public relations representatives may supply stations with actualities to be used on newscasts. If a high executive of a practitioner's client speaks at a luncheon, a brief taped highlight from that speech, if sent to a radio station, may find a place on a local newscast. So might a taped highlight from the dedication ceremony for a manufacturing plant. Radio stations tend to have small news staffs and cannot cover as many events as they desire. They welcome assistance if it is provided in an objective manner.

4.   *Talk shows.* Another goal is the radio talk show, on which a moderator and guests discuss issues. Placement of a client on a talk show provides exposure for the individual and for the cause being espoused. Talk shows may be news-oriented, such as a discussion of a controversial issue, and produced by the news director. Or they may be enter-

Radio talk show hosts broadcast from the White House by invitation of President Clinton as part of his promotion campaign for his health care program. Donna Shalala, director of the Health, Education, and Welfare Department, explains the plan to a Connecticut broadcaster.

tainment-oriented, controlled by the program director and handled by a staff producer. Midmorning homemaker hours have numerous spots for guest appearances.

Talk shows have become so important in forming public opinion that President Clinton and his wife Hillary brought about 150 radio talk-show hosts to the White House for a briefing on the Clinton health-care plan a day before the President unveiled it before Congress in a nationally televised speech. The Clintons' hope was that the talk-show hosts, thus briefed, would give a favorable "spin" to their on-air discussions of the program.

5.   *Editorials.* Powerful radio stations often broadcast editorials, comparable to newspaper editorials, usually delivered by the station manager. Public relations specialists may be able to persuade a station to carry an editorial of endorsement for their cause. They should stay alert, too, for editorials that condemn a cause they espouse. The representative should request equal time on the air for a rebuttal, usually given by a leading executive of the organization or cause under attack. Hundreds of smaller stations, however, do not carry editorials.

6.   *Disc jockey shows.* On the entertainment side, disc jockeys in their programs of music and chitchat frequently air material provided by public relations sources. The DJs conduct on-the-air contests and promotions, give away tickets to shows, discuss coming local events, offer trivia quizzes—whatever they can think of to make their programs distinctive and lively. A disc jockey talking on the air several hours a day devours large amounts of material. After studying a program's style, an able practitioner can supply items and ideas that the DJ welcomes, and thus promote the causes of public relations clients.

7.   *Community events.* At times, radio stations sponsor community events such as outdoor concerts or long-distance runs. Repeated mention of such an event on the air for days or weeks usually turns out large crowds. Here, too, is an opportunity for the public relations person, either to convince a station to sponsor such an event or to develop tie-ins with it.

8.   *Public service announcements.* These commercials promoting public causes such as health-care and civic programs are run free of charge by stations, usually in unsold time slots during scheduled commercial breaks. PSA scripts should be written to run 20, 30, or 60 seconds. Use of celebrity voices is common.

A close relationship exists between radio stations and the recording industry. Recording companies depend on the stations to play their new releases; the stations in turn use those companies as the primary source for the music they play. This relationship has created a highly specialized form of public relations work by representatives of the record companies.

TELEVISION

Our lives feel the impact of television more than that of any other communications medium. More than 1500 television stations are in operation, projecting over-the-air visual programming. According to estimates provided by the A. C. Nielsen Company, the major rating firm for national programming, more than 88 million American households own television sets. According to Nielsen statistics, the average American family watches television about 7 hours a day.

Little wonder that public relations specialists look upon television as an enormous arena in which to tell their stories!

The fundamental factor that differentiates television from the other media and gives it such pervasive impact is the visual element. Producers of entertainment shows, newscasts, and commercials regard movement on the screen as essential. Something must happen to hold the viewer's attention. Persons talking on the screen for more than a brief time without movement, or at least a change of camera angle, are belittled as "talking heads."

Because of this visual impact, television emphasizes personality. Entertainment programs are built around stars. Only on television do news reporters achieve "star quality." When public relations people plan material for television, they should remember the importance of visual impact and personality.

Television shows live and die by their ratings. A scorecard mentality dominates the selection of programs and program content, especially on the networks. The viewing habits of a few thousand Americans, recorded by the Nielsen, Arbitron, and other rating services, determine what programs all TV watchers can see. The explanation is money. Networks and local stations determine the prices they charge to show commercials by the estimated size of the audience watching a program when the commercial is shown. Thus the larger the audience, the higher the price for commercial time and the higher the profit. Even nonprofit television stations keep a close watch on the size of their audiences, because their income in part comes from the grants corporations give them to show certain programs.

A tremendous battle for admission to the home viewer's screen has developed among cable TV, video, and the traditional over-the-air stations and networks. In the mid-1970s, the three basic commercial networks were viewed by 92 percent of the audience during prime-time evening hours. This figure had fallen into the low 60 percent range in the early 1990s and continued to fall as the total television audience was fragmented.

This turmoil opened enormous new programming potential and a consequent increase in public relations opportunities. When a cable system offers 100 or more channels, as some are technically capable of doing, the demand for program material is voracious.

Although most television stations are on the air for 18 hours or more a day, only a few hours of programming originate in their studios—mostly newscasts, local talk shows, and midmorning homemaker programs. Much of the day's programming consists of network "feeds," if the station has a network affiliation. Development of satellite transmission (discussed in Chapter 21) has created numerous smaller networks that provide entertainment, news, and sports shows, giving independent stations new sources of programming.

Cable Television Because television networks and individual stations, especially those in major cities, gear their programming to large audiences, public relations practitioners have difficulty in obtaining air time for projects lacking mass appeal. Cable television, however, often presents valuable opportunities.

More than 56 million U.S. households were wired for cable TV in the mid-1990s. However, the number of viewers for a cable channel usually is relatively small, because the total TV audience is fragmented among the numerous competing channels. On the plus side, the public relations specialist faces fewer editing and management barriers in getting a program or short segment broadcast.

The Cable Communications Policy Act of 1984 gives local authorities the right to demand that cable systems to which they grant operating franchises include an *access channel* for public, educational, or government programming, without advertising. Public relations directors for cultural, social, and other nonprofit agencies—and even for commercial interests—can use these so-called PEG channels effectively to promote public-service causes by creating interesting programs.

Some cable systems also produce *local origination* (LO) programming. LO programs may carry advertising. They offer an outlet for public relations material that provides substantial information without being obviously commercial in tone. Video news releases of various lengths are a good possibility for local origination programs.

PUBLIC RELATIONS OPPORTUNITIES IN TELEVISION

The possibilities for the public relations specialist to use television are so numerous that they are worth examining on two levels, network and local.

The Network Level   There are six principal methods commonly used:

1. *Guest appearances on news and talk shows.* Placement of clients on such programs as the *Tonight* and *Today* shows allows them to give plugs to new products, books, films, and plays, and to advocate their causes. For entertainment personalities in particular, these interviews provide a setting in which to display their skills. National leaders are interviewed in depth on the Sunday discussion panel shows such as *Meet the Press*. Guests on network interview shows must be articulate and poised, so they won't freeze up before the camera. Consequently, they are carefully screened by show production staffs before being granted an appearance. Nationally syndicated talk programs such as the *Phil Donahue Show* and *Oprah Winfrey Show* which are sold to individual stations, provide excellent showcases.

  Public relations people wishing to place guests on these programs should apply to the producers of the shows.

2. *News releases and story proposals to network news departments.* This process is identical to that followed with radio stations. If a story or an idea is accepted, the assignment editor gives it to a reporter for visual development. Letters like the one in Figure 12.5 often are sent directly to popular TV personalities, suggesting stories for them to do. When a client is criticized in a controversial news situation or editorial, a representative should submit the client's response and urge that it be used on the air. If the response is submitted in concise videotape form, the likelihood of a quick airing is increased.

3. *Video news releases,* commonly called VNRs. These are ready-to-broadcast tapes or background footage for use in news programs. News programs will use VNRs in

*Vice President Al Gore and political challenger Ross Perot
debated the North American Free Trade Agreement (NAFTA)
in an aggressive television confrontation hosted by Larry King.
Perot vigorously opposed the NAFTA treaty, which Congress
later approved.*

some form if they are well done and avoid delivering an obvious commercial message. (VNRs are discussed in Chapter 24.)

4. *Program ideas.* The representative of an important cause may propose to a network that it build an episode in a dramatic or situation comedy series around this cause. The public relations person can assist the program producer by supplying technical information. Such programs do not make overt sales pitches for the treatment organizations, but the message is inherent in the story line.

Activist groups apply considerable pressure on television producers and the networks to include social issues such as environmental cleanups, drunk driving, and AIDS in their program scripts. Characters in situation comedies or dramas quite frequently take strong advocacy positions in the plot line, thus delivering a message to viewers.

5. *Silent publicity.* There are almost subliminal impacts in entertainment programs that quietly publicize a representative's cause. In a private detective show, for example, the star may be shown chasing the villain through an airport terminal past a TWA sign. Or the automobiles used by the lead characters may be Ford products exclusively. Sometimes a program's credits include a mention such as, "Transportation provided by American Airlines." Another way to generate silent publicity, especially valuable for the tourist industry, is to convince network show producers to shoot their programs in a client's city or region, showing the scenery there. The network series *Miami Vice, The*

California Milk Advisory Board

400 Oyster Point Boulevard
Suite 214
South San Francisco, CA 94080
(415) 871-6455
FAX (415) 583-7328

October 26, 1990

Mr. Willard Scott
Today Show
NBC Television Network
30 Rockefeller Plaza
New York, NY 10112-0100

Dear Mr. Scott:

As all of the men in America know, you're our fashion plate.
Well, you ought to know that consumers nationwide are "having a cow" over a
California Milk Advisory Board-sanctioned line of clothing that bears the
markings of the Holstein cow. As the story goes, inspiration for the clothing
came straight from the pasture.

> There once was a black and white bovine
> Who thought her coat so de-vine
> She made clothing to wear
> Put them on if you dare
> And be cool in your cow-like de-sign
>
> Now these clothes have unusual charm
> And they don't only belong in the barn
> So put on the cow garb
> Watch the cattle come charge
> You'll be the hottest Holstein on the farm

Any questions, please call 415/871-6455

Sincerely,

Adri G. Boudewyn
Director of Communications Services

Under the Authority of the Director of Food and Agriculture, State of California

FIGURE 12.5

Pitch letters to broadcasters and editors, intended to stimulate their
interest in a story idea, are an essential public relations tool. They are
often written cleverly to catch the recipient's attention in a crowded
mailing, as is this one to a prominent national television figure known
for doing offbeat things on the air.

Streets of San Francisco, and *Cheers* (set in Boston) provided those localities with
immeasurable publicity.

6. *Public service announcements.* These are run occasionally by stations nationwide
as public relations gestures. The Advertising Council prepares material for national
nonprofit organizations as a public service.

The Local Station Level The methods listed for network public relations apply just as effectively on the local level—indeed, even more so in some instances, because competition for time on local stations often is less intense. The more intimate nature of local programming increases public relations opportunities. Even a diaper-changing contest at a shopping mall can gain air time.

There are four most frequently used techniques:

1. *Guest appearances on local talk shows.* Visiting experts in such fields as home-making crafts, sponsored by companies and trade associations, demonstrate their skills for moderator and audience. National public relations firms send such clients around well-established circuits of local television and radio shows in each city they visit.

2. *Protest demonstrations.* Filmed demonstrations are such a staple on some television stations in large cities as to be a visual cliché. A group supporting or opposing a cause notifies a station that it will march at a certain time and place. Carrying placards, the marchers parade before the camera and a representative is shown explaining their

---

HOW TO PLACE A CLIENT ON A TV TALK SHOW

Television stations are looking for interesting, articulate guests for their talk shows. The larger the station, the more stringent are its requirements for accepting a guest. This summary of needs and procedures for *AM/San Francisco,* the morning show on KGO-TV, the ABC network outlet in San Francisco, is typical of those for metropolitan stations. The information is from an article published in *Bulldog,* a West Coast public relations newsletter.

The station wants guests "who will provide information that will help our viewers to save money and save time, helpful hints around the house, consumer-type things." The station also uses guests from the business community who can comment on money, taxes, the stock market, and similar topics.

KGO-TV defines the audience for this show as primarily nonworking women, 18 to 49, married, with at least one child. The show also attracts working viewers before they leave for their jobs.

Segments on the one-hour show run from 6 to 10 minutes. The usual pattern is to open with a celebrity-entertainer, then offer two segments on consumer topics. Segments 4, 5, and 6 cover "more serious subjects."

The production staff normally will consider for appearance only those who have appeared on television previously. Usually it asks to see a video clip of a prior TV appearance; an effective clip is an important way to gain acceptance.

"TV is a visual medium and a lot of our audience isn't just sitting there watching. They're folding clothes or ironing, so we need a voice that will grab their attention."

The public relations practitioner should submit a brief written query to the show's producer—"a 1-page letter getting straight to the basics: whom you're offering, what their experience is, exactly what their topic would be, what shows they've been on previously, a bio (biographical statement) and all other information available on the person, as well as clippings, copies of articles on the person or topic."

Staff members try to answer queries in about a week, perhaps sooner. The show is booked at least a week in advance but sometimes has last-minute openings.

cause. Although, for fairness, stations should put on an advocate for the other side in the same sequence, some stations neglect this responsibility, and so the marching group's point of view dominates. Many group demonstrations are so much alike, however, that their impact is minimized. Stations use them primarily because they involve movement.

3. *Videotapes for news shows.* Smaller TV stations, in particular, lack enough staff to cover all potentially newsworthy events in their areas. Practitioners can fill the gaps by delivering videotapes of events they handle, for inclusion in newscasts. Excerpts from a local speech by a prominent client may be incorporated in an evening news show. Arrival or departure at the local airport of a client in the news might be used, too, if the person says something newsworthy on camera.

4. *General-interest films.* Local cable channels sometimes will show films of 15- or 20-minute duration produced by corporations in which the direct commercial message is nonexistent or muted. The purpose of such films is to strengthen a company's image as a good community citizen. Films explaining large civic programs by nonprofit organizations also may be used.

MOTION PICTURES

Mention of motion pictures brings to mind, first and inevitably, the commercial entertainment film turned out by that nebulous place called Hollywood. From a public relations point of view, possibilities for influencing the content of commercial motion pictures for client purposes are relatively limited. Practitioners who know their way through the labyrinth of Hollywood financing and production can make deals for silent publicity through use of brand-name merchandise; and in a broad sense, causes sometimes get a helping hand from the thrust of a plotline, perhaps inadvertently.

Some producers charge from $10,000 to $60,000 for a commercial mention in their films, depending on the amount of exposure.

Public relations counselors and corporate departments serve occasionally as advisers on films that involve their areas of expertise. Filmmakers seek this advice to prevent embarrassing technical errors on the screen and to protect themselves from inadvertently angering a group that might retaliate by denouncing the picture. In terms of specific public relations results similar to those obtainable from the other mass media, however, commercial films are a minor channel.

SPONSORED FILMS

In other forms, the motion picture is an important public relations tool.

Corporations and nonprofit organizations use motion pictures and videotapes for internal purposes as part of audiovisual programs to train and inform their employees, or for external purposes to inform and influence the public and the financial community.

When, for example, Levi Strauss & Co. needed to explain to its employees a new personnel management program called Teamwork, it prepared a video for them. This was built around an a cappella singing group, which demonstrated the importance of individuals working together. Virtually all employees who saw it called the unusual approach beneficial. Like some other corporations, San Diego Gas & Electric Company produces a periodic Employee Video News Magazine. The topics covered range from the company's annual meeting to an employees' campaign against graffiti.

A second significant use of the motion picture in public relations is directly promotional. Although avoiding frontal-attack sales messages such as those in television commercials, these films seek to whet the interest of audience members who are potential purchasers of the sponsor's product or contributors to the sponsor's cause. For example, a travel agency shows members of an invited audience a film about a Caribbean cruise. Colorful photography with voice-over narration depicts the scenery cruise passengers will see. Shipboard activities, including a few humorous touches, are shown. So are the luxurious accommodations and the enormous buffet tables from which travelers select their meals (no passenger ever is seasick in such films, of course).

Similarly, a university president at a dinner meeting of alumni shows a film of the campus as it is today. The film is a carefully contrived balance of nostalgia and progress, with scenes of football games and students at work in the new science building. Having rekindled alumni interest in the old school, the film closes with a recital of the university's plans and aspirations. Usually these include the need for a new building, the funds for which the alumni are invited to contribute.

A discussion of filmmaking appears in Chapter 24.

CASE PROBLEM

Cygna Labs, a medium-sized pharmaceutical firm located in Salt Lake City, has developed a sunscreen lotion. The product, Sun-Cure, joins a number of similar products on store shelves. Independent laboratory testing shows that Sun-Cure is particularly effective in blocking UVB rays, which cause burning and even premature aging of the skin. It is a good product and gets high ratings from dermatologists.

Unfortunately, the public still shows confusion about the differences between sunscreens and suntan lotions, as well as the merits of competing brands. Your public relations firm is retained to develop a product publicity program for Sun-Cure that would reach daily newspapers, selected magazines, radio, and television. What communication strategies would you develop for getting coverage in each medium?

QUESTIONS FOR REVIEW AND DISCUSSION

1. Why is the senior audience so important in the United States, and what are some of its characteristics?

2. On what basis do newspaper editors select the news releases they publish?

3. A good public relations person knows how to create news events. Why is this important?

4. What significant differences between magazines and newspapers must a public relations practitioner keep in mind when submitting material to them?

5. Why are special-audience magazines and trade journals such important targets for many public relations people?

6. For what purpose can books be used effectively as public relations outlets?

7. What two special attributes make radio distinctive among the major media of mass communication?

8. Do local radio newscasts have a good potential as an outlet for news releases? If so, why?

9. Ratings determine which television programs survive and which die. Why do ratings have such power?

10. How should public relations representatives go about trying to place their clients on television interview shows?

SUGGESTED READINGS

Claudill, James. "Working with Editorial Boards." *Public Relations Journal,* March 1989, pp. 31–32.

Dahmen, Jerry. "Ten Commandments You Don't Want to Break!" *Communication World,* August 1992, pp. 16–17. Radio news director gives tips on media relations.

Dilenschneider, Robert L. "Use Ingenuity in Media Relations." *Public Relations Quarterly,* Summer 1992, pp. 13–15.

DuPont, Stephen. "The Personal Touch: A Guide to Media Relations Angling." *Communication World,* January 1990, pp. 20–22.

Elfenbein, Dick. "What Editors Want from Publicists—and When." *Public Relations Quarterly,* Fall 1993, pp. 14–16.

Feder, Barnaby J. "PR Mistakes Seen in Breast-Implant Case." New York *Times,* January 29, 1992, pp. C1–C2. Product recall.

Fischer, Rick. "Media Lists: Let Your Computer Do the Searching." *Public Relations Quarterly,* Summer 1990, pp. 15–21.

Gerlin, Andrea. "Radio Stations Gain by Going After Hispanics." *Wall Street Journal,* July 14, 1993, pp. B1, 8.

Grabowski, Gene. "The Seven Deadly Sins of Media Relations." *Public Relations Quarterly,* Spring 1992, pp. 37–39.

Graham, Barbara M. "Two Dozen Ways to Guarantee Failure in Media Relations." *Public Relations Quarterly,* Summer 1992, p. 23.

Kenworthey, Charles W. "Enjoying News Media." *Communication World,* May–June 1992, pp. 18–19.

LoDestro, Michele. "Why Editors Put the Fear of God in Publicists." *IABC Communication World,* July 1990, pp. 16–19.

Matera, Fran. "Dealing with 'Tabloid' Broadcasters." *Public Relations Journal,* May 1990, pp. 32–33.

Sabolik, Mary. "Print Media Placement Strategies for the New Segmentation." *Public Relations Journal,* November 1989, pp. 15–19.

Shell, Adam. "Perot, Talk Shows and the New Media." *Public Relations Journal,* September 1992, pp. 8, 13.

Stone, Robert J. "Keys to Media Success." *Public Relations Quarterly,* Fall 1993, pp. 46–47.

Wester, Natalie Y. "Build Confidence with Media Training." *Public Relations Journal,* February 1992, pp. 26–28.

Weiner, Richard. *New World Dictionary of Media and Communications.* Englewood Cliffs, NJ: Prentice Hall, 1990.

Winter, Grant. "Improving Broadcast News Conferences." *Public Relations Journal,* July 1990, pp. 25–26.

Public Relations and the Law

P R E V I E W   In this chapter the objective is to provide a general understanding of legal considerations involved in public relations and to show students specifically how laws on copyright, trademarks, and the preparation and distribution of messages affect public relations practice.

Topics covered in this chapter include:

- A sampling of legal problems
- Libel and slander
- Rights of employees
- Photo releases
- Ownership of ideas and copyright
- Trademarks
- Misappropriation of personality
- Federal Trade Commission
- Securities and Exchange Commission
- Meeting rooms, plant tours, and open houses

A SAMPLING OF LEGAL PROBLEMS

The law and its many ramifications are somewhat abstract to the average person. Many people may have difficulty imagining exactly how public relations personnel can run afoul of the law, or generate a suit, by simply communicating information.

To bring things down to earth, and to make this chapter more meaningful, we provide here a sampling of recent government regulatory agency cases and lawsuits that involved public relations materials and the work of practitioners.

■ The Princeton Dental Resource Center paid a $25,000 settlement after the New York attorney general's office charged the organization with making false and misleading claims. Its newsletter, produced by a public relations firm, had reported that eating chocolate inhibited tooth decay.

■ Labtest International, a New Jersey firm, was ordered by a U.S. District Court to pay $111,000 to Washington Business Information, Inc., for copyright infringement. It had illegally photocopied the company's weekly *Product Safety Letter.*

■ The Church of Scientology filed a libel suit against the vice president of corporate affairs for Eli Lilly & Co. after he called the church a "commercial enterprise" in an article that appeared in *USA Today.*

■ General Electric was forced to change the promotion of its "Energy Choice" light bulbs and pay a $165,000 settlement after the Federal Trade Commission (FTC) charged GE with failing to disclose that the bulbs were more energy-efficient only because they provided less light than the standard product.

■ The Securities and Exchange Commission (SEC) stopped the mailing of 45,000 prospectuses from Krupp Securities of Boston because the company had attached a sales brochure to the prospectus, a violation of SEC guidelines.

■ Joe Montana, former star quarterback of the San Francisco 49ers, sued the San Jose *Mercury News* for invasion of privacy and "misappropriation of personality" after the newspaper printed and sold posters of him without his consent.

■ The estate of the late children's author, Dr. Seuss, won a $1.5 million judgment against a Los Angeles T-shirt maker for infringement of copyright. The manufacturer portrayed a parody of Dr. Seuss's Cat in the Hat character smoking marijuana and giving the peace sign.

■ The North Carolina attorney general's office launched an investigation of a BellSouth Corporation subsidiary, alleging that the corporation coerced employees to write misleading letters to the state utilities commission.

■ An artist sued American Family Association (AFA) for copyright infringement after the association used portions of his work in a mass mailing.

■ The SEC suspended stock sales of ATI, Inc., after the company made the misleading claim in a news release that one of its disinfectants was "newly developed" and was able to kill one kind of herpes virus.

- The Jos. Schlitz Brewing Company and its public relations firm were sued for $3.5 million by three former company executives who maintained that a news release had libeled them.

- A news release by Getty Oil about an impending merger with Pennzoil became a significant document in the court case charging Texaco with illegally interfering with Pennzoil's move to purchase Getty. The result was a $3 billion judgment against Texaco.

- Hill and Knowlton filed a lawsuit against three former H&K employees, claiming that they had violated their employment contracts by recruiting H&K clients and staff for their new firm, Capitoline International Group.

- Mr. Coffee, Inc., signed a settlement with the Federal Trade Commission (FTC) after the agency charged the company with making false and misleading claims about its coffee filters being "chlorine free" and made from recycled paper.

These examples provide some idea of the legal pitfalls that a public relations person may encounter in preparing materials for a client or employer. In many cases the suits are eventually dismissed or settled out of court, but the organization still pays dearly for the adverse publicity generated and the expense of defending itself.

Public relations personnel and firms must also be aware that they can be held legally liable if they provide advice or tacitly support an illegal activity of a client or employer. This area of liability is called *conspiracy*. A public relations person can be named as a co-conspirator with other company officials if he or she . . .

1. Participates in an illegal action such as bribing a government official or covering up information of vital interest to the public health and safety.

2. Counsels and guides the policy behind an illegal action.

3. Takes a major personal part in the illegal action.

4. Helps establish a "front group" whereby the connection to the public relations firm or its client is kept hidden.

5. Cooperates in any other way to further an illegal action.

LIBEL AND SLANDER

Public relations professionals should be thoroughly familiar with the concepts of libel and defamation. Such knowledge is crucial if an organization's internal and external communications are to meet legal and regulatory standards with a minimum of legal complications. At the same time, a knowledgeable public relations staff can help monitor the media and other sources to spot potentially libelous statements about the client or employer.

Defamation includes libel and slander. Historically, libel referred to written defamation, while slander was spoken. As a practical matter today, says attorney Gerhart L. Klein, there is little difference. The courts have come to treat broadcast defamation as libel.

LAWSUITS AGAINST A COMPANY

There isn't much investigative reporting in public relations work, but libel and slander suits are filed against company officials when they send out news releases or make false statements that injure someone's reputation. More than one executive has been sorry that he or she lost control during a news conference and called the leaders of a labor union "a bunch of crooks and compulsive liars." Suits have also been filed for calling a news reporter "a pimp for all environmental groups" or charging that a dissident stockholder is "a closet communist."

Although news releases rarely are involved in libel suits, a 1987 ruling supports the idea that a company can use the same standards of defense as does a media organization that prints the story. The ruling was made by a justice of the New York Supreme Court, who dismissed a $20 million libel suit against J. Walter Thompson advertising agency. The case involved a former employee who claimed she was libeled by a news release from the firm announcing that she had been dismissed because of financial irregularities in the department she headed. The New York justice ruled that the plaintiff had not proved a "preponderance of evidence that the publisher acted in a grossly irresponsible manner without due consideration for the standard of information gathering and dissemination ordinarily followed by responsible parties."

The situation just described is the major reason why organizations often say an employee left for "personal reasons" instead of spelling out the exact circumstances. To say otherwise, unless the person is convicted in a court of law, is to invite charges of libel and damage to a person's professional reputation.

Don Sneed, Tim Wulfemeyer, and Harry Stonecipher, in a *Public Relations Review* article, suggest that (1) opinion statements be accompanied by the facts upon which the opinions are based, (2) statements of opinion be clearly labeled as such, and (3) the context of the language surrounding the expressions of opinion is reviewed for possible legal implications.

LAWSUITS FILED BY A COMPANY

Litigation can always happen, but that doesn't mean that an organization must avoid statements of opinion in public relations materials. Truth is a traditional defense against libel charges, but opinions also have a degree of legal protection through the First Amendment guarantee of freedom of speech.

In one case, the owner of the New York Yankees was sued for libel by a baseball umpire when a team news release called him a "scab" who "has had it in" for the Yankees and had "misjudged" plays. A lower court awarded damages, but the New York Supreme Court overturned the judgment by ruling that the comments in the news release constituted protected statements of opinion under the fair comment concept.

DEFAMATION SUIT EXPLODES NBC'S CREDIBILITY

General Motors filed a multimillion-dollar defamation suit against the National Broadcasting Company early in 1993 after its TV network's *Dateline* news program carried a story about gas tanks on GM pick-up trucks exploding in side-impact collisions.

The auto company accused the network of using toy rocket engines as "igniters" in its staged crashes, significantly understating vehicle speed at the moment of impact, and wrongly saying that a fuel tank ruptured in one of the crashes.

GM's general counsel, in a news conference, meticulously documented the case against NBC with hundreds of enlarged photos, footage of the NBC film, home videos of a fireman at the scene, excerpts from interviews with witnesses, and exhibits of how small rocket engines are ignited.

NBC, a unit of General Electric Co., made a settlement with GM within 24 hours. GM dropped the suit for a 9-minute retraction on the news program and $2 million to cover the costs of its investigation. In the aftermath of the incident, NBC fired three *Dateline* producers and pressured NBC News President Michael Gartner to resign.

GM, clearly the victor, reported a favorable upswing in public opinion polls regarding the company and its trucks.

Executives are often incensed when an environmental group includes their corporation on its annual list of "dirty dozen" polluters or on similar lists. A corporate reputation can be damaged, but the defamation is difficult to prove in a court of law. The company must show beyond all doubt that the damaging words were not true, and that the statements actually caused a drop in sales and/or public esteem.

For the most part, corporations and organizations are subject to the legal concept of *fair comment and criticism.* This is the same defense used by theater and music critics when they lambaste a play or concert. The term means that companies and individuals who voluntarily display their wares to the public for sale or consumption are subject to "fair comment," whether good or bad. Thus, an individual or corporation criticizing another corporate entity for shoddy products or poor service usually is protected, provided it is done with honest purpose and lack of malicious intent.

A utility in Indiana once tried to sue a citizen who wrote a letter to a newspaper criticizing the utility for seeking a rate hike. The judge threw the suit out of court, stating that the rate increase was a "matter of public interest and concern" even if the letter writer didn't have all the facts straight.

THE "PUBLIC FIGURE" CONCEPT

The other concept that public relations personnel should know about, from the standpoint of answering press inquiries, is what constitutes a *public figure.* Does the press, for example, have a right to publish information about the activities of the company chief executive officer? Does a newspaper have a right to make judgments about the management decisions of a company executive? Can an executive who is the subject of such a newspaper article sue for invasion of privacy? The answers tend to vary somewhat depending upon how the courts continue to define "public figure." Recent court decisions are somewhat contradictory on the matter.

Such persons as political candidates, government officeholders, actors, athletes, and business figures such as Donald Trump or Lee Iacocca usually are considered public figures and thus have trouble winning suits for libel, slander, and invasion of privacy. On the other hand, a corporate executive who has not sought the limelight is more likely to be considered a private citizen, with better odds for winning such a suit. The U.S. Supreme Court, however, in 1986 ruled that private individuals who sue for libel must prove, not simply claim, that a news account was false.

Public relations counselors have an obligation to keep up with the changing standard of what constitutes a public figure. They must also advise top executives that some of their immunity to press criticism and investigative reporting dissipates if they voluntarily step into debates on controversial issues. Immunity also is lessened if the company is involved in a major news event, such as the Tylenol poisonings.

RIGHTS OF EMPLOYEES

EMPLOYEE COMMUNICATIONS

The concepts of libel, defamation, and invasion of privacy must be kept in mind as public relations personnel write and edit materials that involve employees.

It is no longer true, if it ever was, that an organization has an unlimited right to publicize the activities of its employees. In fact, Morton J. Simon, a Philadelphia lawyer and author of *Public Relations Law* (1969), said, "It should not be assumed that a person's status as an employee waives his right to privacy." Simon correctly points out that a company newsletter or magazine does not enjoy the same First Amendment protection that the news media enjoy when they claim "newsworthiness" and "public interest." A number of court cases, he says, show that company newsletters are considered commercial tools of trade.

This distinction does not impede the effectiveness of newsletters, but it does indicate that they should try to keep employee stories organization-oriented. Indeed, most lawsuits and complaints are generated by "personals columns" that may invade privacy by telling everyone that Joe Doaks honeymooned in Hawaii or that Mary Worth is now a great-grandmother. This information in itself may not constitute an invasion of privacy, but it is often compounded into possible defamation by "cutesy" editorial asides that are in poor taste.

An employee publication also must be careful to avoid stereotypical or racial comments. An employee can file a lawsuit or a complaint to the Equal Employment Opportunity Commission based on the way he or she is portrayed. For example, it would be poor practice to do a feature story about the organization's only black manager and write, "John, a black with amazing leadership abilities, is going places." This implies that blacks generally lack leadership abilities. Women are also stereotyped. A woman in the accounting department with an MBA degree doesn't like being described as "a beautiful redhead with laughing eyes who hides her petite figure behind a charcoal-gray business suit. . . ."

In sum, one should avoid anything that might subject an employee to ridicule by fellow employees. It is expensive and unpleasant for an organization to deal with a lawsuit of any kind, even one with no merit.

Here are some guidelines to remember when writing about employee activities:

1. Keep the focus on organization-related activities.

2. Have employees submit "personals" in writing.

3. Double-check all information for accuracy.

4. Ask, "Will this embarrass anyone or cause someone to be the butt of jokes?"

5. Have employees initial a draft copy of the story in which they are named.

6. Don't rely on secondhand information; confirm the facts with the person involved.

7. When photographing or writing about employees, tell them what the purpose of the photo or story is and how it will be used.

8. Have employees sign a blanket release that the organization may publicize their work activity in newsletters and news releases.

ADVERTISING CONSIDERATIONS

The information just given applies to employee newsletters and news releases. If an employee's photograph or comments are used in an advertisement or sales brochure, however, it is essential that a signed release be on file. As an added precaution it is better to give some financial compensation to make a more binding legal agreement.

Chemical Bank of New York unfortunately learned this lesson the hard way. The bank used pictures of 39 employees in various advertisements designed to "humanize" the bank's image, but the employees maintained that no one had requested permission to use their photos in advertisements. Another problem was that the pictures had been taken up to five years before they began appearing in the series of advertisements.

An attorney for the employees, who sued for $600,000 in damages, said, "The bank took the individuality of these employees and used that individuality to make a profit."

COMBATTING SEXUAL HARASSMENT

The issue of sexual harassment has legal and public relations implications for an organization. It is important for organizations to have clear policies; it also is important for these policies to be clearly communicated to employees.

Expensive and time-consuming lawsuits, employee turnover, absenteeism, and loss of productivity can be reduced if the organization uses a variety of communication tools to tell employees about grievance procedures and their rights. Hill and Knowlton suggests a variety of techniques for disseminating information, including bulletin boards, memos, personnel manuals, videos, and small discussion groups.

The judge agreed and ruled that the bank had violated New York's privacy law. The action is called *misappropriation of personality,* which is discussed later in this chapter. Jerry Della Femina, an advertising executive, succinctly makes the point: get permission. "If I used my mother in an ad," he said, "I'd get her permission—and I almost trust her 100 percent."

Written permission should also be obtained if the employee's photograph is to appear in sales brochures or even in the corporate annual report. (In the case of outsiders, the same rule applies. If, for example, a corporation wants to show customers dining in one of its chain restaurants, permission must be given in writing.) To avoid any possible lawsuits, many companies use professional models as "customers."

PRESS INQUIRIES

Because press inquiries have the potential of invading an employee's right of privacy, public relations personnel should follow basic guidelines as to what information will be provided in the employee's behalf.

In general, employers should give a news reporter only basic information. This may include (1) confirmation that the person is an employee, (2) the person's title and job description, and (3) date of beginning employment, or, if applicable, date of termination.

Unless it is specified by law or permission is given by the employee, a public relations person should avoid providing information about an employee's (1) salary, (2) home address, (3) marital status, (4) number of children, (5) organizational memberships, and (6) job performance.

If a reporter does seek any of this information, because of the nature of the story, several methods may be followed.

First, a public relations person can volunteer to contact the employee and have the person speak directly with the reporter. What the employee chooses to tell the reporter is not then a company's responsibility. Second, many organizations do provide additional information to a reporter if it is included on an optional biographical sheet that the employee has filled out. In most cases, the form clearly states that the organization may use any of the information in answering press inquiries or writing its own news releases. A typical biographical form may have sections in which the employee can list his or her (1) honors and awards, (2) professional memberships, (3) marital status and names of any children, (4) previous employers, (5) educational background, and (6) hobbies or interests. This sheet should not be confused with the person's official employment application, which must remain confidential.

If an organization uses biographical sheets, it is important that they be dated and kept current. A sheet compiled by an employee five years previously may be hopelessly out of date. This is also true of *file photographs* taken at the time of a person's employment (see the section "Photo Releases").

INFORMATION ABOUT EMPLOYEE BENEFITS

Recently enacted federal and state legislation makes it easier for employees to know what benefits they are entitled to. For one thing, regulations require that pension and insurance plans be written in such a way that employees can understand them. The rationale is that an employee should not be deprived of benefits simply because no one in the organization explained them in basic English. Suits can be filed against employers who have not complied with the law. Furthermore, employers must post information about health and safety regulations, workers' compensation guidelines, and so on. In 1988, a congressional bill requiring employers to give 60 days' notice of plant closings and mass layoffs became law.

EMPLOYEE FREEDOM OF SPEECH

Public relations executives, as well as high-level managers, must work to ensure that employees are not arbitrarily denied promotion or fired simply because they have criticized the organization. Employees, as citizens, have a right to express a point of view. Thus, many employee newsletters now carry "letters to the editor" from employees who question company policy. This not only breeds a healthy atmosphere of two-way communication but makes employee publications more credible.

Unfortunately too many executives still perceive employee questions and criticism as "disloyalty." Public relations personnel can do much to dispel this perception by educating managers about employee rights. A number of state and federal laws already protect the job rights of "whistle-blowers," and this area is rapidly expanding to prevent employees from being dismissed just because they express views not popular with the boss.

On another level, companies have a legal right to prevent employees and former staff members from disclosing confidential information and trade secrets obtained on the job.

PHOTO RELEASES

A public relations department should have a central photographic file containing readily available information: (1) source of the picture and date taken, (2) copyright information, and (3) signed releases from subjects in photos.

Such information will ensure the proper use of photos and substantially reduce the threat of lawsuits. A notation of the date taken, for example, will help eliminate the use of pictures that are no longer appropriate for news releases or company brochures. It is embarrassing to publish a picture of a person who died three years ago, or to show in a new brochure a picture of a manufacturing facility that was sold last year.

Permission statements indicate whether the photo may be used in company brochures and advertising or whether it is strictly a file photo for use in the employee magazine. The copyrighting of a picture by a freelance photographer may mean that the organization cannot use it again unless the photographer gives permission or receives payment. A photo release is important if a person protests that his or her picture was used without permission.

Ordinarily a public relations practitioner doesn't need to worry about getting a signed release if the person gives "implied consent" by posing for the picture and is told how it will be used. This is particularly true for "news" pictures to be published in internal newsletters or for materials accompanying a news release.

If it is not known in what specific ways the photo will ultimately be used, however, the best solution is to get a written release. Public relations personnel often accompany a photographer to (1) ensure that the names of all persons in a picture are properly recorded and (2) to have each sign a release.

Here is a Lockheed release form:

The undersigned, having previously consented to being photographed, does hereby authorize Lockheed Aircraft Corporation and Lockheed Missiles & Space Company, Inc., to use and reproduce the said photograph and copy for Lockheed publicity and promotional purposes.

OWNERSHIP OF IDEAS

The word *idea* conveys many meanings; ownership often is difficult to prove unless the "idea" is expressed in some tangible form. Organizations, however, solicit ideas and also receive a number of unsolicited ones. Because of this, public relations staffs need to know some basic legal concepts about the handling and ownership of ideas.

Employee Ideas   Many organizations regularly encourage employees to submit ideas on how to conserve energy, make the workplace safer, or even produce a better product. More thought must be given to the process, however, than simply installing suggestion boxes. The organization must clearly spell out the conditions under which an idea will be accepted and the extent of compensation that will be paid for an implemented idea. This information is best conveyed on the suggestion forms that the employee uses to present his or her idea.

If cash awards are to be made for good ideas, it is best to specify the maximum amount that will be paid. This tends to limit the organization's liability, but court cases can still result if an employee is not given a reasonable amount for an idea that saves a company millions of dollars.

Solicited Proposals   Public relations firms and advertising agencies often are asked by an organization to present proposals for communications programs. And, in a competitive situation, a winning proposal is selected. What is less clear, however, is whether the organization can implement any of the ideas proposed by the losing firms. The courts have generally ruled that if the idea is original and in concrete form (the slogan of an advertising campaign, for example, or a novel idea for a sponsored event), there is an implied contract that the company should provide reasonable compensation. To protect themselves further, a number of public relations firms are now copyrighting their proposals. (Copyright protection is discussed in the next section.)

Unsolicited Public Ideas   Businesses often receive unsolicited advice on how to develop new products or improve existing ones, and the public relations department is frequently responsible for keeping track of these suggestions. It is important, then, to establish policies for handling submitted ideas.

Some companies totally reject all unsolicited ideas and have the public relations department return the communication with a polite letter. Others will consider an idea if the sender signs a release form that (1) the company is the sole arbiter of how much the idea is worth, (2) no compensation whatsoever will be given, or (3) a specific maximum amount (perhaps $100 to $500) will be awarded if the idea is used. The latter, however, may not prevent a lawsuit if the value of the idea is worth more than a token amount of money.

The worth of an idea, of course, is determined by how detailed and specific it is. A scribbled note suggesting that the company have a scholarship program for minority students is less valuable, obviously, than a detailed plan outlining how such a program would be set up and funded.

USE OF COPYRIGHT

Should a news release be copyrighted? How about a corporate annual report? Can a *New Yorker* cartoon be used in the company magazine without permission? What about reprinting an article from *Fortune* magazine and distributing it to the company's sales staff? Are government reports copyrighted? What constitutes copyright infringement?

These are some of the bothersome questions that a public relations professional should be able to answer. Knowledge of copyright law is important from two perspectives: (1) what organizational materials should be copyrighted and (2) how correctly to utilize the copyrighted materials of others.

Before going into these areas, however, it is important to know what copyright means. In very simple terms, *copyright* means protection of a creative work from unauthorized use. A section of the U.S. copyright law of 1978 states: "Copyright protection subsists . . . in the original works of authorship fixed in any tangible medium of expression now known or later developed." The word *authorship* is defined in seven categories: (1) literary works; (2) musical works; (3) dramatic works; (4) pantomimes and choreographic works; (5) pictorial, graphic, or sculptural works; (6) motion pictures; and (7) sound recordings. The word *fixed* means that the work is sufficiently permanent or stable to permit it to be perceived, reproduced, or otherwise communicated.

The shield of copyright protection was reduced somewhat in 1991 when the Supreme Court ruled unanimously that directories, computer databases, and other compilations of facts may be copied and republished unless they display "some minimum degree of creativity." The court stated, "Raw facts may be copied at will."

Thus a copyright does not protect ideas, but only the specific ways in which those ideas are expressed. An idea for promoting a product, for example, cannot be copyrighted—but brochures, drawings, news features, animated cartoons, display booths, photographs, recordings, videotapes, corporate symbols, slogans, and the like that express a particular idea can be copyrighted.

Because much money, effort, time, and creative talent are spent on organizational materials, copyright protection is important. By copyrighting materials, a company can prevent competitors from capitalizing on its creative work or producing a facsimile brochure that tends to mislead the public. A manufacturer of personal computers would be in serious legal difficulties if it began distributing sales brochures that tended to look just like ones from Apple Computer. (The concept of trademark infringement [such as copying the Apple logo with slight changes] will be discussed in the section titled "Trademarks.")

The 1978 law, in a major change from the previous one, presumes that material produced in some tangible form is copyrighted from the moment it is created. This is particularly true if the material bears a copyright notice. One of the following methods may be employed:

1. Using the letter "c" in a circle (©), followed by the word *copyright*.

2. Citing the year of copyright and the name of the owner.

This presumption of copyright is often sufficient to discourage unauthorized use, and the writer or creator of the material has some legal protection if he or she can prove that the material was created before another person claims it.

A more formal step, providing full legal protection, is official registration of the copyrighted work within three months after creation. This is done by depositing two copies of the manuscript (it is not necessary that it has been published), recording, or artwork with the Copyright Office, Library of Congress, Washington, DC 20559. Copyright registration forms are available from U.S. post offices. Registration is not a condition of copyright protection, but it is a prerequisite to an infringement action against unauthorized use by others.

Copyright protection of a work lasts for the life of the author plus 50 years, and no longer. Material copyrighted by a business or organization is protected for 75 years from the time the material is published. When a public relations writer creates materials as part of regular employment for an organization, the employer owns the material and has right of copyright. In legal terms, this situation is known as "work made for hire."

PHOTOGRAPHY AND ARTWORK

The copyright law makes it clear that freelance and commercial photographers retain ownership of their work. In other words, a customer who buys a copyrighted photo owns the item itself, but not the right to make additional copies. That right remains with the photographer unless transferred in writing.

In a further extension of this right, the duplication of copyrighted photos also is illegal. This was established in a 1990 U.S. Federal District Court case in which the Professional Photographers of America (PP of A) sued a nationwide photofinishing firm for ignoring copyright notices on pictures sent for additional copies.

Freelance photographers generally charge for a picture on the basis of its use. If it is used only once, perhaps for an employee newsletter, the fee is low. If, however, the company wants to use the picture in the corporate annual report or on the company calendar, the fee may be considerably higher. Consequently it is important for a public relations person to tell the photographer exactly how the picture will be used. Arrangements and fees then can be determined for (1) one-time use, (2) unlimited use, or (3) the payment of royalties every time the picture is used.

In practice there is much slippage in honoring a photographer's copyright—either because the client is unfamiliar with the copyright law or the photographer doesn't pursue the letter of the law. Nevertheless, responsible public relations practitioners strive to give adequate compensation and recognition for a photographer's creative work.

The guidelines discussed for photography also apply to created artwork and even variations of a famous theme. Saul Steinberg, who created the famous "New Yorker's View of the World" for the *New Yorker* magazine, successfully sued Columbia Pictures for using a facsimile of the copyrighted artwork to promote the film *Moscow on the Hudson.* The judge ruled that a promotional poster for the movie "meticulously imitated" Steinberg's artwork and violated copyright law. In other words, slightly changing a copyrighted photo or a piece of artwork can be considered a violation of copyright if the intent is to capitalize on widespread recognition of the original work.

RIGHTS OF FREELANCE WRITERS

Although the rights of freelance photographers have been established for some years, it was only recently that freelance writers gained more control over the ownership of their work.

In the now famous Reid Case (*Community for Creative Nonviolence* v. *Reid*), the U.S. Supreme Court in 1989 ruled that writers retained ownership of their work and that purchasers of it simply gained a "license" to reproduce the copyrighted work.

Prior to this ruling, the common practice was to assume that commissioned articles were "work for hire" and the purchaser owned the copyright. In other words, a magazine could reproduce the article in any number of ways and even sell it to another publication without the writer's permission.

Under the new interpretation, ownership of a writer's work is subject to negotiation and contractual agreement. Writers may agree to assign all copyright rights to the work they have been hired to do, or they may give permission only for a specific one-time use.

Public relations firms and corporate public relations departments are responsible for ensuring compliance with the copyright law. This means that all agreements with a freelance writer must be in writing, and the use of the material must be clearly stated. Ideally, public relations personnel should negotiate multiple rights and even complete ownership of the copyright.

FAIR USE VERSUS INFRINGEMENT

Public relations people are in the business of gathering information from a variety of sources, so it is important to know where *fair use* ends and *infringement* begins.

Fair use means that part of a copyrighted article may be quoted directly, but the quoted material must be brief in relation to the length of the original work. It may be, for example, only one paragraph in a 750-word article and up to 300 words in a long article or book chapter. Complete attribution of the source must be given regardless of the length of the quotation. If the passage is quoted verbatim, quote marks must be used.

It is important to note, however, that the concept of fair use has distinct limitations if part of the copyrighted material is to be used in advertisements and promotional brochures. In this case, permission is required. It also is important for the original source to approve the context in which the quote is used. A quote out of context often runs into legal trouble if it implies endorsement of a product or service.

The copyright law does allow limited copying of a work for fair use such as criticism, comment, or research. However, in recent years, the courts have considerably narrowed the concept of "fair use" when multiple copies of a copyrighted work are involved.

A landmark case was a successful lawsuit in 1991 by book publishers against Kinko's, a national chain of photocopying stores. The chain was charged with copyright infringement because it reproduced excerpts from books without permission and sold them in anthologies to college students. Although Kinko's argued "fair use" for educational purposes, the court rejected this defense. The court settlement cost Kinko's $500,000 in damages and almost $1.5 million in legal fees.

Even the unauthorized photocopying of newsletters and published articles can cost the organization large sums of money. Texaco, for example, lost a lawsuit filed by publishers of scientific journals who claimed that the company violated the copyright law by permitting scientists on a routing list to photocopy articles for future research.

It also is considered infringement if an organization photocopies an article for distribution to employees or outside publics. Quantity reprints should always be ordered directly from the publication, which charges a fee.

The same concept applies to videotaping television shows or news programs. The Supreme Court has ruled that it is "fair use" to make a videotape of a television show for later personal viewing, but a public relations staff must get permission from the television producer if widespread use of the videotape is planned. Adolph A. Coors Company paid $40,000 to CBS-TV for the right to show a videotape throughout the country of a *60 Minutes* segment about the company.

Government documents (city, county, state, and federal) are in the public domain and cannot be copyrighted. Public relations personnel, under the fair use doctrine, can freely use quotations and statistics from a government document, but care must be exercised to ensure that the material is in context and not misleading. The most common problem occurs when an organization uses a government report as a form of endorsement for its services or products. An airline, for example, might cite a government study showing that it provides the most service to customers, but neglects to state the basis of comparison or other factors.

DINOSAURS AMBUSHED IN *JURASSIC PARK*

Although the book and film of *Jurassic Park* are protected by copyright, the dinosaurs aren't.

According to the *Wall Street Journal,* companies spent tens of millions of dollars in advertising and promotion to be part of the dinosaur frenzy but sidestepped paying for an expensive official tie-in with the popular movie. This, in the advertising industry, is called ambush marketing.

Manor Care's Choice Hotels, for example, created a Choiceasaurus for a guest contest and even echoed *Jurassic Park*'s "65 million years in the making" tagline, assuring families that "offers like this happen every 60 million years."

Universal Studios set up a hotline (1-800 DINO COP) in a search for companies that may have violated the movie's copyright. However, the studio was handicapped by the fact that it has no ownership rights to dinosaurs in general, which are in the public domain.

COPYRIGHT GUIDELINES

A number of points have been discussed about copyright. A public relations person should keep the following in mind:

1. Ideas cannot be copyrighted, but the expression of those ideas can be.

2. Major public relations materials (brochures, annual reports, videotapes, motion pictures, position papers, and the like) should be copyrighted if only to prevent unauthorized use by competitors.

3. Although there is a concept of *fair use,* any copyrighted material intended directly to advance the sales and profits of an organization should not be used unless permission is given.

4. Copyrighted material should not be taken out of context, particularly if it implies endorsement of the organization's services or products.

5. Quantity reprints of an article should be ordered from the publisher.

6. Permission is required to use segments of television programs or motion pictures.

7. Permission must be obtained to use segments of popular songs (written verses or sound recordings) from a recording company.

8. Photographers retain rights to negatives and permission must be received to reprint photos for other uses than originally agreed upon.

9. Photographs of current celebrities or those who are now deceased cannot be used for promotion and publicity purposes without permission.

10. Permission is required to reprint cartoon characters such as Snoopy or Garfield. In addition, cartoons and other artwork or illustrations in a publication are copyrighted.

11. Government documents are not copyrighted, but caution is necessary if the material is used in a way that implies endorsement of products or services.

12. Private letters, or excerpts from them, cannot be published or used in sales and publicity materials without the permission of the letter writer.

TRADEMARKS

What do Reebok, IBM, Sony, Porsche, and McDonald's have in common? Their names are registered trademarks protected by law and should be capitalized any time they are used.

This section will discuss trademarks and the role that a public relations department plays in (1) selecting trademarks, (2) safeguarding their use, and (3) avoiding improper use of other registered trademarks. It also will briefly explain the significance of generic names.

According to the Trademark Law Revision Act of 1988, a *trademark* is "any word, name, symbol, or device, or any combination thereof, (1) used by a person, or (2) which a person has a bona fide intention to use in commerce and applies to register on the principal register established by the Act, to identify and distinguish his or her goods. . . ."

Or, to put it more simply, a trademark is "a name, symbol, or other device identifying a product, officially registered and legally restricted to the use of the owner or manufacturer" *(American Heritage Dictionary)*.

SELECTING TRADEMARKS

To protect a trademark by law, a company registers its name, logo (identifying symbol), and product names. The registered trademark symbol is a superscript, small capital "R" in a circle—®. "Registered in U.S. Patent and Trademark Office" and "Reg. U.S. Pat. Off." also may be used. A "TM" in small capital letters indicates a trademark that isn't registered. It represents a company's common-law claim to a right of trademark, or a trademark for which registration is pending.

A service mark is like a trademark, but it designates a service rather than a product, or is a logo. An "SM" in small capitals in a circle—Ⓢⓜ—is the symbol for a registered service mark. If registration is pending, the "SM" should be used without the circle.

Businesses and industrial firms spend millions of dollars each year in the search for a distinctive name, slogan, or logo that can be used to symbolize the company in the minds of the American consumer. Research indicates that 53 percent of Americans claim brand quality takes precedence over price considerations so, quite literally, a famous trademark is worth millions of dollars. Additional millions are spent advertising and publicizing the trademark (see Figure 13.1).

FIGURE 13.1
Protection of trademarks requires corporate diligence. Some
companies deliver warning messages through advertisements in
trade magazines. Xerox Corporation explains the proper use of
its name.

XEROX

You can't Xerox
a Xerox
on a Xerox.

But we don't mind at all if you copy a copy on a Xerox copier.

In fact, we prefer it. Because the Xerox trademark should only identify products made by us. Like Xerox copiers and Xerox printing systems.

As a trademark, the term Xerox should always be used as an adjective, followed by a noun. And it's never used as a verb.

© 1991 XEROX CORPORATION. XEROX® is a trademark of XEROX CORPORATION.

Of course, helping us protect our trademark also helps you. Because you'll continue to get what you're actually asking for.

And not an inferior copy.

XEROX
The Document Company

SAFEGUARDING TRADEMARKS

A public relations practitioner must be thoroughly familiar with the registered trademarks of his or her employer so that the trademarks can be used correctly in news releases, brochures, background kits, videotapes, and so on. A registered trademark name, for example, is always capitalized. Failure to do so in company materials can lead to a loss of trademark status; if so, the word becomes generic, available for anyone's use.

The public relations department and legal counsel work to safeguard an organization's trademarks in several ways. They are:

1. Ensuring that company trademarks are capitalized in all organizational literature and graphics.

2. Using trademarks as proper adjectives followed by generic terms. Some examples of proper usage are Kleenex tissues, Kodak film, Life Savers candy, and Vaseline petroleum jelly.

3. Never using trademarks as verbs. It is proper to say "Make six copies on the Xerox copier," but not "Xerox the report."

4. Ensuring that any graphics of the logo or phrases ("Reach Out and Touch Someone") indicate that they are trademarked by using, ®, TM, Ⓢ, or SM next to the logo or phrase.

5. Distributing trademark manuals and brochures to editors and reporters and placing advertisements in trade publications, designating names to be capitalized.

6. Educating employees as to what the company's trademarks are and how to use them correctly.

7. Monitoring publications—newspapers, trade magazines, newsletters—to ensure that trademarks are capitalized. If not, a gentle reminder is sent.

8. Monitoring publications to ensure that other organizations are not infringing on a registered trademark. If they are, the legal department pursues the situation with letters and threats of injunctions or lawsuits.

9. Placing advertisements in journalism magazines and reviews reminding readers of trademark names. Johnson & Johnson does this for Band-Aids, Xerox reminds the press that there is no such thing as a "xerox"—only a Xerox copier—and Coca-Cola is adamant that *Coke* is always capitalized.

10. Making sure the trademark is actually being used. A 1988 revision of the Trademark Act no longer permits an organization to hold a name in reserve.

AVOIDING IMPROPER USE OF OTHER REGISTERED TRADEMARKS

Public relations personnel often work with the legal department and outside design consultants to come up with names, slogans, and logos for an organization. The first step is to conduct a brainstorming session for ideas, but the second step is to research a potential trademark to be sure it isn't already being used. This is usually done by specialty trademark search firms that make extensive use of the computer.

news release

INTEL CORPORATION
3065 Bowers Avenue
P.O. Box 58065
Santa Clara, CA 95052-8065

CONTACT: Paula Zimmerman
             (609) 936-7615

                                   FOR IMMEDIATE RELEASE

             AUTHORING SYSTEM DEVELOPED
             FOR INTEL'S DVI TECHNOLOGY

LAS VEGAS, Nev., November 13, 1989 -- Intel Corporation's

Princeton Operation today announced a new software authoring

package designed exclusively for Intel's DVI™ Technology

called Authology*: MultiMedia. The program was created by

CEIT Systems, Inc., a developer of software tools for

multimedia and interactive video authoring, located in San

Jose, California.

     Authology: MultiMedia authoring software enables DVI

Page 4
Intel/IU-631

*DVI is a trademark of Intel Corporations.
*Authology is a registered trademark of CEIT Systems, Inc.
*Comdex is a registered trademark of Interface Group, Inc.
*Lumena is a trademark of Time Arts, Inc.

FIGURE 13.2
This news release contained trademarked names, so the Intel
Corporation, which issued it, lists the registered trademarks at
the end of the release. This common practice helps to protect
the trademarks and emphasizes to the media recipients that the
names should be capitalized.

Today, when there are thousands of businesses and organizations, finding a name trademark not already in use is extremely difficult. The task is even more frustrating if a company wants to use a trademark on an international level.

It is not uncommon for a company to start with 150 possible names and, after a trademark search, be left with only two or three possible designations. The other choice a company has is to purchase rights to a name. First Interstate Bank, in 11 western states, had to pay a small, rural Vermont bank $1 million because that bank owned the name First Inter-State Bank. By purchasing the name, the bank's holding corporation now has its name registered in all 50 states.

The complexity of finding new names, coupled with the attempt of many to capitalize on an already known trade name, has invariably spawned a number of lawsuits claiming trademark infringement. Here are some examples:

- Levi Strauss & Co. asked Jordache to drop its "101" mark because it infringed on Levi's "501" trademark for its jeans. Jordache, in turn, filed suit asking the U.S. Patent and Trademark Office to cancel Levi's "501" trademark status.

- The New York *Times* asked a Washington, D.C., public relations firm to stop using the slogan, "All the News (Releases) Fit to Print." The newspaper claimed it infringed on its registered trademark, "All the News That's Fit to Print."

- Anheuser-Busch filed a trademark infringement suit against a University of North Carolina student after he designed and sold T-shirts saying "Nag Head, N.C.—King of Beaches." On the back the shirt said, "This beach is for you." After four years of litigation, a federal appeals court found that his parodies couldn't possibly be confused with company trademarks.

- The U.S. Olympic Committee filed suit against the March of Dimes for trademark infringement because the charity sponsored the "Reading Olympics," which rewarded children for reading books. Under federal statute, no one can use the word "Olympic" or related words and symbols without the U.S. Olympic Committee's consent. The March of Dimes, to avoid a lengthy court battle, changed the name of its program to "Reading Champions."

NIKE STUBS TRADEMARK TOE AT OLYMPICS

A trademarked name registered more than 60 years ago by a Barcelona sock company kept Nike, Inc., out of the 1992 Olympics.

The athletic shoe manufacturer had paid millions to be an official sponsor of the Olympics and to have its name on the U.S. and Algerian track and field uniforms. It was also using the Olympics as a venue to introduce a new line of sports clothing. However, a Spanish high court ruled the Beaverton, Oregon, firm's trademark infringed on the trademark of the Barcelona sock company. The court barred Nike from selling or advertising its sports apparel in Spain.

Nike estimated potential marketing losses at $20 million in Spain and several times that figure worldwide. The snafu, however, did give Nike a place in the Olympic marketing fiasco competition.

In all these cases organizations claimed that their registered trademarks were being improperly exploited for commercial or organizational purposes. Some guidelines used by courts to determine if there has been trademark infringement are as follows:

1. Has the defendant used a name as a way of capitalizing on the reputation of another organization's trademark—and does the defendant benefit from the original organization's investment in popularizing its trademark?

2. Is there an intent (real or otherwise) to create confusion in the public mind? Is there an intent to imply a connection between the defendant's product and the item identified by trademark?

3. How similar are the two organizations? Are they providing the same kinds of products or services?

4. Has the original organization actively protected the trademark by publicizing it and by actually continuing to use it in connection with its products or services?

5. Is the trademark unique? A company with a trademark that merely describes a common product might be in trouble.

MISAPPROPRIATION OF PERSONALITY

A form of trademark infringement also can result from the unauthorized use of well-known entertainers and professional athletes in an organization's publicity and promotion materials. A photo of Tom Cruise may make a company's advertising campaign more interesting, but the courts call it "misappropriation of personality" if permission and licensing fees have not been negotiated.

Bette Midler, for example, won a $400,000 judgment against Young & Rubicam (later confirmed by the Supreme Court on appeal) after the advertising agency used another singer to do a "sound-alike" of her singing style and rendition of the song, "Do You Wanna Dance?" for a Ford auto commercial.

The court ruled, "When a distinctive voice of a professional singer is widely known and is deliberately imitated in order to sell a product, the sellers have appropriated what is not theirs."

Companies and advertising firms also have encountered legal trouble by using "look-alikes" of famous personalities to sell goods. Woody Allen has used the law to stop ads featuring actors who resemble him, and game-show hostess Vanna White successfully sued a manufacturer over an advertisement that showed a glamorously dressed robot ready to turn a letter as she does on *Wheel of Fortune.*

The Supreme Court let stand a ruling by a federal appeals court in California (*Samsung* v. *White*) that decreed, "the law protects the celebrity's sole right to exploit this value of a celebrity identity . . . whether the celebrity has achieved this fame out of rare ability, dumb luck or a combination thereof."

Deceased celebrities also are protected. In order to use a likeness of a famous person, or to imitate a particular voice or singing style, the user must pay a licensing fee to an agent representing the families, studios, or estates of the deceased.

Companies want to publicize their trademarks to the point that they become household names, but there is a danger in doing so. A U.S. court of appeals has stated: "When the public takes unto itself a trade name word and substitutes it for the commodity, the manufacturer loses the exclusive right to the name."

Some trade names that have become generic through general use include *aspirin, thermos, corn flakes, nylon, cellophane, shredded wheat,* and *mimeograph.* This essentially means that any company can use these names to describe a product.

When a trade name becomes generic, the company suffers a tremendous loss; that is why corporations zealously guard the trademark from incorrect use. Coca-Cola, it is said, has a battery of 200 lawyers constantly monitoring how restaurants and the media use the name *Coke.* If a person orders a Coke in a restaurant and is served another kind of cola, Coca-Cola lawyers immediately file suit. Xerox spends several hundred thousand dollars annually making sure the public understands that *Xerox copy* and *photocopy* are not interchangeable words.

On occasion, a company attempts to trademark a common word and is rebuffed by the U.S. Patent and Trademark Office. Microsoft Corporation attempted to gain a trademark on the word *Windows.* Although the company said the term *Windows* had become synonymous with its products, the government sided with Microsoft's competitors, who claimed that it was a generic term in the computer industry long before the Microsoft product of the same name arrived on the scene.

FEDERAL TRADE COMMISSION

It is well known that the Federal Trade Commission (FTC) has jurisdiction over advertisements to determine that they are not deceptive or misleading, but public relations personnel should know that the commission also has jurisdiction over product news releases and product photography.

In the eyes of the FTC both advertisements and product publicity materials are vehicles of commercial trade—and therefore subject to regulation. Thus, a company cannot claim "freedom of speech" when the FTC moves to curb news releases that are misleading or making deceptive claims.

The FTC, for example, filed an administrative complaint against Campbell Soup Company for claiming that its soups were low in fat and cholesterol and thus helpful in fighting heart disease. The agency charged that the claim was deceptive because publicity and advertisements didn't disclose that the soups also were high in sodium, a fact that increases the risk of heart disease.

Although the FTC kept a somewhat low profile during the laissez-faire Reagan years, the agency has taken a more active stance in the 1990s, especially in regard to health and environmental claims for products. Traditionally, the agency filed a complaint against the manufacturer of the product. Recent cases, however, show a tendency to prosecute advertising agencies and production companies that script and produce the commercials.

In general, the FTC monitors advertising and publicity by assigning one of the following labels to materials it considers misleading:

1. Unsubstantiated claims

2. Ambiguous claims

3. Fraudulent testimonials

4. Puffery and exaggerated claims

5. Deceptive demonstrations

6. Deceptive pricing

7. Defamation of the competition

8. Fraudulent contests

9. Misuse of the word *free*

10. "Bait and switch" tactics

FTC investigators are usually on the lookout for unsubstantiated claims. Some of the words in promotional materials that trigger FTC interest are: authentic, certified, cure, custom-made, germ-free, natural, unbreakable, perfect, first-class, exclusive, and reliable.

Public relations practitioners must be cognizant of FTC guidelines when writing product publicity. Section 43(a) of the Lanham Act subjects anyone to liability who participates in the making or dissemination of a false or misleading representation in any advertising or promotional material. This includes advertisements, product news releases, videos, and brochures.

The following guidelines should be taken into account when writing product publicity materials:

1. Make sure the information in the release is accurate and can be substantiated.

2. Don't make flat statements that are difficult to prove. Stick to the facts. Don't "hype" the product or service by using flowery, nonspecific adjectives.

3. Make sure that celebrities who endorse a product actually use it. They should not say anything about the product's properties that cannot be substantiated.

4. Don't use testimonials from satisfied consumers for publicity purposes unless the individuals give written permission.

5. Watch the language. Don't say "independent research study" when the research was done by the organization's staff.

6. If government findings are quoted, provide proper context. Government agencies do not endorse products.

7. Describe tests and surveys in sufficient detail so the consumer understands what was tested and under what conditions.

8. Describe prizes and awards accurately.

9. Remember that a product is not "new" if only the packaging has been changed or the product is more than six months old.

Companies found in violation of FTC guidelines usually are given the opportunity to sign a consent decree. This means that the company admits no wrongdoing but agrees to change its advertising and publicity claims.

Companies also may be fined by the FTC or ordered to engage in corrective advertising and publicity.

SECURITIES AND EXCHANGE COMMISSION

The megamergers of the 1980s, coupled with insider trading scandals on Wall Street, made the Securities and Exchange Commission (SEC) practically household words in the business world. This federal agency closely monitors the financial affairs of publicly traded companies and protects the interests of stockholders and potential investors.

SEC guidelines on public disclosure and insider trading are particularly relevant to corporate public relations staff members who play a key role in meeting disclosure requirements. The distribution of misleading information or failure to make a timely disclosure of material information may be the basis of liability under the SEC code. A company may even be liable if it satisfies regulations by getting information out, but decreases the likelihood of use in the media by presenting crucial information in a vague manner or by burying it deep in the news release.

In addition, the courts are increasingly applying the "mosaic doctrine" to financial information. Maureen Rubin, an attorney writing in *Public Relations Journal,* explained that a court may examine *all* information released by a company, including press releases, to determine whether, taken as a whole, they combine to create an "overall misleading" impression.

It is no wonder that specialists in investor and financial relations are highly paid. They must not only be fully aware of SEC regulations and the laws of other governmental agencies, but they must constantly monitor new interpretations and court decisions that can affect their clients and employers. Equipped with such knowledge, these experts must make judgments every day on the release of information.

The SEC has three basic guidelines:

1. Full information must be given on anything that might materially affect the company's stock.

2. Timely disclosure is essential. A company must act promptly to dispel or confirm rumors that result in unusual market activity or market variations.

3. Insider trading is illegal. Company officials, including public relations staffs and outside counsel, cannot use inside information to buy and sell company stock. (See the Anthony M. Franco case in Chapter 6.)

Through the years there have been a number of cases in which companies have been heavily fined for not adhering to these guidelines. The major case setting the pattern for illegal insider trading occurred in 1965 involving Texas Gulf Sulphur. Company executives used inside information about an ore strike in Canada to buy up stock while at the same time issuing a news release tending to deny that a rich strike had been found.

Some recent court cases have included the following:

- *Staffin* v. *Greenberg (1982).* A public disclosure must not only be accurate but also sufficiently complete so as not to be misleading. There is no obligation to disclose every material fact, but the information released must be complete enough so as not to mislead.

- *Apple Computer Inc. (1984).* A group of stockholders filed a lawsuit against company executives, claiming that they sold 2.1 million shares of stock and received proceeds of $84.1 million by making "positive public statements" about the expected success of the Lisa when the executives knew about slow sales and production difficulties.

- *Cytryn* v. *Cook (1990).* A U.S. District Court used the concept of "mosaic doctrine" to rule that the proper test of a company's adequate financial disclosure was not the literal truth or the materiality of each positive statement, but the overall misleading impression that it combined to create in the eyes of potential investors.

These examples should make it clear that public relations staff and counsel are responsible for the full, accurate, and prompt disclosure of financial data. A public relations person is often privy to information affecting the price of stock before the press and the public know about it.

Most corporations have developed policies to handle financial rumors and also to adhere to SEC and other regulatory guidelines. For example, to avoid any hint of possible insider trading, many corporations have a policy that earnings reports are released to the media before company executives and employees are informed.

OTHER REGULATORY AGENCIES

Although the SEC and FTC are the major federal agencies concerned with the content of advertising and publicity materials, the Food and Drug Administration (FDA) and the Bureau of Alcohol, Tobacco and Firearms (BATF) also have established guidelines.

The FDA oversees the advertising and promotion of prescription drugs, over-the-counter medicines, and cosmetics. Under the Federal Food, Drug, and Cosmetic Act, any person (which includes advertising and public relations firms) who misbrands or "causes the misbranding" of labeling or advertising may be liable under the law. Misbranding can occur when a company's staff, or its advertising and public relations firm, prepares or disseminates false or misleading information about a product.

The Federal Alcohol Administration Act also is concerned about misbranding and the dissemination of false or misleading information. Wineries, for example, have problems with BATF by implying the health benefits of drinking wine. Geyser Peak winery was requested to pull advertisements that included the statement, "As age enhances wine, wine enhances age." Even if this statement could be proven, the BATF takes the attitude that such claims for alcoholic products cannot be allowed.

The BATF is also modest. It rejected a design for a wine label that featured a bare-breasted mermaid drawn by Art Deco master Erte. The bureau cited a rule barring "any statement, design, device or representation which is obscene or indecent."

SEC DISCLOSURE REQUIREMENTS

The Securities and Exchange Commission (SEC) requires public relations personnel to disclose the following information about a company in a timely fashion:

- Dividends or their deletion
- Annual and quarterly earnings
- Preliminary, but unaudited, interim earnings
- Annual reports
- Stock splits
- Mergers or takeovers
- Major management changes
- Major product developments
- Expansion plans
- Change of business purpose
- Defaults
- Proxy materials
- Disposition of major assets
- Purchase of own stock
- Announcements of major contracts or orders

To be avoided are the following:

- Unrealistic sales and earnings reports
- Glowing descriptions of products in the experimental stage
- Announcements of possible mergers or takeovers that are only in the speculation stage
- Junkets for business reporters or offers of stock to financial analysts and columnists
- Omission of unfavorable news and developments
- Leaking of information to selected outsiders and financial columnists

Another federal agency, the Environmental Protection Agency (EPA), has been considering strict guidelines for environmental communications. Under one proposed EPA requirement, glass bottle users would have to include a 32-word statement about recycling containers in their advertisements. The advertising industry lobbied against such restrictions.

Summary A public relations firm and its writers need to know regulatory guidelines and keep up with changes in the law. Court cases have established that advertising and public relations firms can be liable under the law for disseminating false and misleading information on behalf of a client. As one attorney says, an outside firm should be careful about the type of information and documentation supplied by its client.

CORPORATE FREE SPEECH

FTC and SEC regulations, coupled with Supreme Court decisions, have made it quite clear that commercial speech (advertising and product publicity) is not fully protected by the First Amendment. Commercial speech can be regulated and even restricted if standards of disclosure, truth, and accuracy are violated. A more difficult question is whether advertising of a legal consumer product can be banned on the basis of health considerations. A major legal battle is being fought as numerous public groups continue to seek the banning of cigarette advertising.

On another level, however, the Supreme Court has upheld the right of corporations to express their views on matters of public policy and interest.

A series of court cases has supported the concept of corporate free speech. Some landmark cases are as follows:

■ *First National Bank of Boston (1978).* The Supreme Court struck down a Massachusetts law that prohibited corporations from publicizing their views on issues subject to the ballot box. The ruling essentially gave corporations the same status as an individual under the First Amendment.

■ *Consolidated Edison (1980).* The Supreme Court ruled that a New York Public Utilities Commission regulation prohibiting utilities from making statements on matters of public policy and controversy was unconstitutional.

■ *Pacific Gas & Electric (1986).* The Supreme Court ruled that the California Public Utilities Commission could not require PG&E to include messages from activist consumer groups in its mailings to customers. The utility argued that inclusion of such messages impaired the company's right to communicate its own messages.

Although corporations can speak out on public issues in the context of First Amendment rights, a 1990 decision by the Supreme Court seems to indicate that this "free speech" right doesn't extend to endorsement of political candidates.

In a 6–3 decision in *Austin* v. *Michigan Chamber of Commerce,* the Court said a Michigan law that prohibits corporations from buying newspaper advertisements on behalf of a political candidate did not violate the chamber's right to free speech. The Michigan legislation, which applies to all incorporated bodies (even the Sierra Club and the American Civil Liberties Union) is part of a campaign finance law.

MEETING ROOMS, PLANT TOURS, AND OPEN HOUSES

What is the responsibility of a firm if meeting rooms are made available to community groups? What about the legal ramifications of having plant tours or a community open house?

These are not idle questions to the public relations staff, who are often responsible for such activities. Providing a meeting room, having an open house, or giving a plant tour is part of community relations.

MEETING ROOMS

Every firm or organization that makes a meeting room available to community groups should have an established policy in writing that specifies what types of groups qualify. Some companies specify that only nonprofit groups associated with the United Way may use facilities. Other firms allow religious organizations, hobby clubs, and senior citizen groups if an employee of the company sponsors them.

Groups should submit a written request and perhaps sign a standard form that outlines their responsibilities in using the room. The standard form might clearly state that the company in no way officially endorses the activities of the group. Furthermore, standard agreement forms enable the organization to keep track of which groups have booked the room for which date. Also, from a legal standpoint, the company is less liable if the community group has formally requested such use.

Here are some other points to remember:

1. The room must be clean and well maintained so that there are no safety hazards such as worn rugs, frayed electrical cords, or flimsy chairs.

2. Instructions on how to operate the coffee maker or other electrical equipment must be clearly posted.

3. An employee of the company should be on the premises during the meeting in case of emergency.

4. Parking lots must be well lighted and easily accessible.

5. Icy sidewalks and other possible danger areas must be made safe before the meeting.

It is only good community relations to ensure that a community meeting room creates goodwill for the company, not antagonisms or even possible lawsuits because of negligence.

PLANT TOURS AND OPEN HOUSES

Plant tours should not be undertaken lightly. They require detailed planning by the public relations staff to guarantee the safety and comfort of visitors. Consideration must be given to such factors as (1) logistics, (2) possible work disruptions as groups pass through the plant, (3) safety, and (4) amount of staffing required.

A well-marked tour route is essential; it is equally important to have trained escort staff and tour guides. Guides should be well versed in company history and operations, and their comments should be somewhat standardized to make sure that key facts are conveyed. In addition, guides should be trained in first aid and thoroughly briefed on what to do in case of an accident or heart attack. At the beginning the guide should outline to the visitors what they will see, the amount of walking involved, the time required, and the number of stairs. This warning tells visitors with heart conditions or other physical handicaps what they can expect.

Many of the points about plant tours are applicable to open houses. The additional problem is having large numbers of people on the plant site at the same time. Such an event calls for special logistical planning by the public relations staff, possibly including the following measures: (1) arranging for extra liability insurance, (2) hiring off-duty police for security and traffic control, (3) arranging to have paramedics and an ambulance on site, and (4) making contractual agreements with vendors selling food or souvenirs.

Such precautions will generate goodwill and limit the company's liability. It should be noted, however, that a plaintiff can still collect if negligence on the part of the company can be proved.

PUBLIC RELATIONS AND LEGAL COUNSEL

Public relations and legal counsel are often at odds, as is pointed out in Chapter 4, but this is not an ideal situation.

A better relationship consists of a strong rapport between the two staffs so that their individual stores of expertise can complement each other. Public relations personnel are not lawyers, and they often need assistance in choosing the proper course of action about a matter that has clear legal ramifications. On the other hand, lawyers need to understand how important the court of public opinion is in determining the future of an organization. Respect and credibility must be maintained by both sides.

A number of steps can be taken by a company or organization to ensure that the public relations and legal staffs have a cordial, mutually supportive relationship:

1. The public relations and legal staffs should report to the same top executive, who can effectively listen to the viewpoints of both sides and decide on a course of action.

2. The organization should draft a clearly defined statement of responsibilities for each staff and its relationship to the other. Neither should dominate.

3. Both functions should be represented on key committees.

4. Public relations personnel and legal staff should get to know each other personally so a trusting relationship can be built.

5. Periodic consultations should be held during which materials and programs are reviewed.

6. The legal staff, as part of its duties, should brief public relations personnel on impending developments in litigation, so press inquiries can be answered in an appropriate manner.

Admittedly, the list is idealistic. As laws and government regulations become more complex, however, it is essential that public relations and legal counsel work as equal partners in achieving organizational objectives.

CASE PROBLEM

Russian River Vineyards is a large winery located near Healdsburg, north of San Francisco. As director of public relations for the winery, you are charged with increasing public awareness of the vineyard's wines and instituting an employee and community relations program.

Some of your ideas include (1) public tours through the winery, (2) a grape harvest festival every fall at which local musicians would perform and local artists would display their works, (3) advertisements quoting a government study about the high percentage of varietal grapes in Russian River wines, (4) photocopying magazine articles that mention the winery favorably and mailing them to wine consumers, (5) a "folksy" newsletter for employees of the winery, (6) employment of a freelance photographer to take pictures of employees and winery guests for possible use in future product publicity, and (7) release of an "independent" survey quoting wine experts about the quality of the vineyard's products.

Each of these activities involves an understanding of the law and various governmental regulations. What legal aspects should be considered in each project?

QUESTIONS FOR REVIEW AND DISCUSSION

1. What are the five situations in which a public relations person, as the representative of an organization, can be named a co-conspirator with other company officials?

2. In what ways do libel and slander considerations affect the work of a public relations person?

3. What is the concept of *fair comment and criticism,* and what are the limitations?

4. What are some guidelines to follow in employee communications to avoid lawsuits?

5. What are some guidelines to follow if a news reporter inquires about an employee?

6. What is the concept of *implied consent* in the taking of photographs?

7. What legal precautions should an organization take if it actively solicits suggestions from employees and the public?

8. What are the basic guidelines of the 1978 copyright law about which public relations personnel should be familiar?

9. What constitutes "infringement" of copyrighted materials?

10. Why is it important for public relations personnel to know about trademarks?

11. What constitutes "misappropriation of personality"?

12. Name at least five guidelines of the Federal Trade Commission that affect the way products can be publicized.

13. In what ways does the Securities and Exchange Commission regulate financial public relations activity? What kinds of information must be disclosed in a timely fashion?

14. What are some guidelines to remember if an organization is having an open house or a tour of a manufacturing facility?

15. Do corporations have the right of free speech regarding issues of public concern?

16. What should be the relationship between the public relations and legal staffs of an organization?

SUGGESTED READINGS

Ansberry, Clare. "Alterations of Photos Raise Host of Legal, Ethical Issues." *Wall Street Journal,* January 26, 1989, p. B1.

Baron, Ted. "Beware of These Costly Legal Traps." *Public Relations Quarterly,* Summer 1991, pp. 20–21.

Bitter, John. "The Hazards of Success." *Communication World,* September 1990, pp. 36–37. Trademarks.

Bovet, Susan Fry. "Sexual Harassment: What's Happening and How to Deal with It." *Public Relations Journal,* November 1993, pp. 26–29. Ethical and legal guidelines.

Brynes, Sondra J. "Privacy vs. Publicity: Flip Sides of the Same Coin." *Public Relations Review,* Winter 1990, pp. 29–35.

Collins, Erik L., and Cornet, Robert J. "Public Relations and Libel Law." *Public Relations Review,* Winter 1990, pp. 36–47.

Davids, Meryl. "How Now, IR?" *Public Relations Journal,* April 1989, pp. 15–19. SEC disclosure requirements.

Durant, Sandra, and Isaacs, Audrey. "Law, Loyalty, and Communication." *Communication World,* October 1987, pp. 30–31. Laws affecting employee communications.

Egan, William C. "Brand Equity: The Value of a Trademark." *Editor & Publisher,* December 5, 1992, pp. 4T–5T, 26T. Part of a 26-page annual section on trademarks and how to use them.

Hayes, Arthur. "Emerging Multimedia Products Raise Concerns over Copyrights." *Wall Street Journal,* January 27, 1992, p. B3.

Hayes, Arthur. "Computer Message Prompts Libel Suit." *Wall Street Journal,* March 26, 1993, p. B5.

"Judge Says Corporations Must Pay to Reprint Copyrighted Articles." *Chronicle of Higher Education,* July 29, 1992, p. A10.

Lipman, Joanne. "Firms' Outings Pose Liability Dilemma." *Wall Street Journal,* September 14, 1988, p. 35.

Lipman, Joanne. "Soundalike Ads Should Sound Alarms in Wake of Court Ruling." *Wall Street Journal,* March 26, 1992, p. B5.

Marcus, Amy D. "False Impressions Can Spur Libel Suits, Even if News Media Get the Facts Right." *Wall Street Journal,* May 15, 1990, p. B1.

Mattman, Jurg W. "Checklist: Securing and Insuring Special Events." *Public Relations Journal,* March 1987, p. 30.

Miller, Stephen C. "Privacy in E-Mail? Better to Assume It Doesn't Exist." New York *Times,* June 7, 1992, p. F8.

Pratt, Catherine A. "First Amendment Protection for Public Relations Expression: The Application and Limitations of the Commercial and Corporate Speech Models." *Public Relations Research Annual,* Vol. 2, ed. James and Larissa Grunig, Hillsdale, NJ: Lawrence Erlbaum Associates, 1990, pp. 205–218.

Rubin, Maureen. "Threat to Corporate Image Advertising Left Unresolved." *Public Relations Journal,* September 1990, pp. 37–39. Corporate advertising and First Amendment rights.

Saddler, Jeanne. "Green Marketing Guidelines Issued by Federal Agency." *Wall Street Journal,* July 29, 1992, p. B5.

Szeremet, Michael. "Shareholder Activists Move Toward Diplomacy." *Public Relations Journal,* August 1993, pp. 29–30. Changes in SEC rules.

Sneed, Don K., Wulfemeyer, Tim, and Stonecipher, Harry M. "Public Relations News Releases and Libel: Extending First Amendment Protections." *Public Relations Review,* Summer 1991, pp. 131–143.

Weatherington, Richard. "IRS Cracks Down on Employee Misclassification." *Public Relations Journal,* February 1992, pp. 30–32. Rules and regulations regarding contract workers and freelance writers.

Wood, Alden S. "Don't Tread on Trademarks." *Communication World,* March 1991, p. 42.

Corporations

P R E V I E W   The objective of this chapter is to give students a better understanding of public relations in corporations, including the areas of consumerism, the
environment, business-media relations, and employee relations.

Topics covered in the chapter include:

- The corporate role

- The human factor

- Consumerism

- Corporations and the environment

- Marketing public relations

- The business-media relationship

- Financial information

- Sensitivity to minorities

- Employee communications

THE CORPORATE ROLE

This is an era of giantism in American and, indeed, world business. International conglomerates control subsidiary companies that often produce a grab bag of seemingly unrelated products and services under the same corporate banner. These conglomerates must deal with government at many levels. Their operations affect the environment, control the employment of thousands, and have an impact on the financial and social well-being of millions. Truly, they have a compelling influence on contemporary life.

Bigness brings remoteness. The popular phrase "the faceless corporation" may be a cliché, but it represents a genuine distrust in the public mind—a distrust often based on lack of knowledge about a corporation rather than on actual unfavorable experiences.

When an oil company pays more than $13 billion to buy out a competitor, as Standard Oil of California did to purchase the Gulf Corporation, the scope of the deal exceeds the comprehension of most citizens. They feel uneasy about the vast economic power of such a huge enterprise and suspect that it wields enormous backstage political influence. Beyond these broad, vague concerns they also see such a combination in short-range personal perspective: "Will this force me to pay more for a gallon of gasoline?"

Since a corporation's impact on society is felt at so many levels, those who plan and conduct its public relations face a complex task. Even relatively small corporations need public relations programs that show them conducting their affairs, both external and internal, in a socially responsible manner.

Figure 14.1 presents, in schematic form, the way one company—General Electric—categorizes the various concerns it must take into consideration at every step of executive decision making.

THE HUMAN FACTOR

THE PUBLIC PERCEPTION

The fundamental, irreplaceable element of every business is people—those who produce goods and services, those who consume them, and those inside and outside the companies whose lives and attitudes are influenced by how the companies act. What corporations *do* is not enough. The public's perception of their conduct also matters. A corporation may operate in a completely legal, technically sound, and financially efficient manner yet find itself viewed by segments of the public as cold, greedy, and heedless of cherished social values. The public relations practitioner's job is to see that this does not happen. The practitioner must work within the company to foster constructive, socially aware behavior, and outside the company to convince the public that the firm is a worthy, caring corporate citizen.

WHAT CAN HAPPEN WHEN BUSINESSES
OVERLOOK THE HUMAN FACTOR

Businesses sometimes fail to recognize the human factor. They become so engrossed in computer technology, cash-flow charts, and management techniques that they overlook

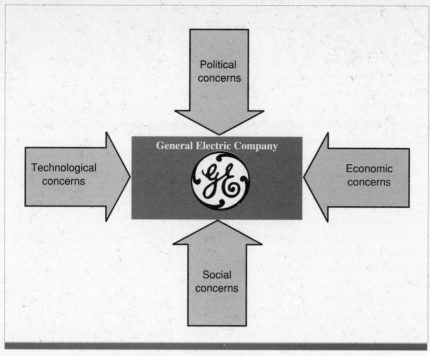

FIGURE 14.1
General Electric Company sees four factors that must be taken into
consideration whenever a management decision is made: (1)
Political—How do government regulations and other pressures affect
the decision? (2) Technological—Do we have the engineering know-
how to accomplish the goal? (3) Social—What is our responsibility to
society? (4) Economic—Will we make a profit?

personal sensitivities. In a public relations blunder, the U.S. Bank of Washington in
Spokane did exactly that, to its regret. A man in shabby clothes parked his pickup truck
in the bank's parking lot, cashed a check, then asked the teller to validate his 60-cent
parking ticket. She refused, claiming that cashing a check wasn't a transaction, as
required for validation. When the man protested, she called a supervisor, who looked
distastefully at the ragged character and also refused.

"Fine," the man replied. "You don't need me and I don't need you." Whereupon he
closed his account and took the $1 million he had on deposit to a competing bank down
the street.

When a corporation lets itself be perceived as a bully, especially against a child, its
stature suffers. The Anheuser-Busch brewery learned just that. Lisa French won a contest at her junior high school in Georgia for her poster against alcohol and drug abuse.
Her design featured a skeleton, a tombstone, a beer can, a dog resembling Spuds
MacKenzie (a canine featured in Anheuser-Busch advertisements) and the slogan
"Drinking is like shaking hands with death." The prize poster was to be displayed on
neighborhood area billboards for a month.

The poster went up on ten billboards. Within days, the dog was blacked out. Shortly
thereafter the posters were removed.

Lisa's parents charged that an Anheuser-Busch distributor pressured the billboard company into removing the posters. The mother said that a brewery official had told her that the posters were offensive to the alcohol industry.

Learning of the incident, the Associated Press (AP) sought comment from the Anheuser-Busch division manager, the company's public relations firm, and the billboard company. All refused to say anything, a fact that the widely distributed AP story pointed out.

Lisa received a lesson in pressures against freedom of speech, and Anheuser-Busch got an embarrassing, self-inflicted black eye.

Perception! In these examples, the bank appeared to be snobbish and prone to judging customers by their appearance. The brewery came across as willing to use corporate might against a 12-year-old girl for expressing an opinion that differed from its own.

The lesson is clear: before a company takes an action affecting the public, its management should attempt to view the move through the eyes of others. Providing management with these outside perceptions is the job of the public relations specialists. Their antennae must be sensitive to changes in public attitudes.

A contrast to these incidents: when thunderstorms knocked out electric service for a prolonged period during a July heat wave, the Baltimore Gas & Electric Company gave 7000 customers free dry ice to preserve their perishable foods. The result was a perception that the company cared about its customers.

Similarly, corporate managements should pay heed to how their actions are perceived by their employees. If employees believe that management is treating them unfairly, their work suffers and internal tensions develop.

A disturbing difference in how a company's top management and its employees perceive the workplace atmosphere sometimes develops, with potentially dangerous consequences. The problem can exist, as well, in large nonprofit organizations.

A survey by *Industry Week* and the Wyatt Company points up this conflict in attitudes. It reported that while 69 percent of senior managers responding believed their organizations' management style encouraged treating employees with respect, only 24 percent of their line managers believed this was true. Moreover, 64 percent of the top management respondants believed their firms encouraged freedom of expression, while only 29 percent of the line supervisors thought so. Since line supervisors are in personal contact with the bulk of the employees, their opinion should be closer to that of the work force than top management's is.

These findings define the challenge for company public relations departments, since they, in conjunction with the human relations department, have the responsibility for communication between management and employees.

COMPUTERS VERSUS HUMANS

As computer wizardry multiplies and increasingly ingenious automated voice equipment comes into service, companies are tempted to substitute this technology for human contact with customers. This should be done with extreme caution. Unwise use of electronic response may alienate the very people the company needs to please. A dissatisfied customer who telephones to protest a billing error or shipping mistake resents being answered by a recording. Far too many consumers have had bad experiences such as this actual example. A newcomer in an area needed information about a telephone installation he had ordered, so he called the customer service number of the phone company. He was answered by a recorded voice, which gave him a choice of numbers to press on his touchtone phone. That produced another recorded answer, which gave him a further set of extension numbers from which to choose. That brought a third recorded answer, stating that all customer service representatives were busy but one would answer him shortly. He was put on hold for nearly 30 minutes. Each minute a recorded voice told him that his call was important to the company and asked him to keep holding. Then he was abruptly disconnected. He had to start again from the beginning. About 40 minutes elapsed before he reached a live voice. The result: an infuriated customer. This from a telephone company that was running TV commercials praising its splendid service! This is an extreme instance, but it illustrates how a company can alienate the public. Similarly, complaining letter-writers dislike receiving a computerized form-letter reply. Nor are customers placated by the cliché answer, "It was a computer error." They know that mistakes on computers almost always result from errors committed by operators of the machines. Here is an area in which corporate public relations practitioners should exercise influence with management to maintain the human touch.

COURTESY PAYS

Too many corporations ignore opportunities to bind customers to them with small gestures such as thank-you letters. Although easily offended if they believe they are taken for granted, customers are impressed if someone in a supposedly remote corporation writes a note of appreciation.

Responding to customer inquiries and complaints is not only good public relations but good business. *Esquire* magazine carried the following item:

In a rare follow-up on complaints and inquiries from customers, Coca-Cola discovered that more than 30 percent of those who said they felt their complaints had not been resolved satisfactorily no longer buy company products and that 17 percent of those whose inquiries were satisfied buy more Coca-Cola products now. A company spokesperson reflected, "This study demonstrates that forward-looking management can turn the corporate response system into a high performance profit center."

CONSUMERISM

The day when business could operate successfully on the Latin precept of *caveat emptor*—"Let the buyer beware"—is long gone. In today's society, sellers are expected to deliver goods and services of safe, acceptable quality on honest terms, without misleading claims and deceptive financing practices. Consumers have rights protected by the federal government and enjoy the assistance of government and private agencies in enforcing those rights. Consumerism is a significant and growing force in the conduct of business. The manner in which public relations practitioners help to guide a company in handling the pressures of consumerism strongly affects the public's attitude toward that company.

DEVELOPMENT OF THE CONSUMER MOVEMENT

The consumer movement developed during the past three decades because far too often business firms were caught either cheating their customers or carelessly giving them inferior products, then making it difficult for them to obtain adjustments. Public trust in business diminished. When the firm of Yankelovich, Skelly and White took a poll in 1967 to measure public trust, the result showed confidence in business at about 70 percent. In a similar poll 14 years later, public confidence had plummeted to 19 percent. The troubles encountered by consumers contributed to this precipitous decline, which paralleled a loss of approval of most public institutions during that period.

Indicative of the public resentment was the creation in newspapers of "Action Line" columns, whose editors publish complaints from badly treated customers and try to solve their problems. In many instances a telephone call from "Action Line" to an offending business, with the implied threat of bad publicity, obtains results that the frustrated customer has been unable to achieve directly. Some television stations have similar consumer-service programs.

The high priest of the consumer movement during its growth stages was Ralph Nader, a youthful attorney in Washington, D.C. His book *Unsafe at Any Speed,* published in 1965, was a searing indictment of automobile safety standards. Nader organized study groups that published generally critical reports on other industries and dwelt heavily upon corporate responsibility to consumers.

Rising consumer protests coincided with a period of rapid expansion in the "watchdog" role of government. The power of federal regulatory agencies over business expanded in numerous directions. The Food and Drug Administration determines what medications can be sold to the public. The Federal Trade Commission regulates truth in advertising, and the Securities and Exchange Commission controls the financial conduct of corporations (see Chapter 13). The National Highway Traffic Safety Administration sets standards for automobile manufacture. The Consumer Product Safety Commission examines other manufactured goods. Other federal and state agencies have consumer-oriented policing powers in their domains.

CONSUMERISM TODAY

Although President Reagan's efforts to limit government regulation of business reduced government's role in several fields during the 1980s, public demand for government protection of consumers remained strong. In a study taken by Louis Harris and Associates, strong sentiment was expressed favoring continued government regulation of safety, health, and truth in advertising, although opposition was voiced to regulation as a general concept.

As citizens have frustrating experiences in obtaining good service and quality, and as they learn about the conviction of many companies and their executives for various forms of cheating, the momentum of consumerism multiplies. Nader said recently, "The '90s will make the '60s pale into insignificance in terms of the reform drive to clean up the fraud, waste, abuse, and crimes of many corporations."

USE OF BOYCOTTS

The *boycott*—refusal to buy the products or services of an offending company—is a widely used tool of the consumer movement, aimed at firms for many different reasons.

A
Consumer Guide
to
Safe Handling
and Preparation
of

GROUND MEAT and GROUND POULTRY

FIGURE 14.2
After news of deaths from consumption of undercooked hamburgers in restaurants created public concern, the Safeway market chain sought to bolster confidence by distributing this pamphlet in its stores. The information came from U.S. government and food industry sources.

At one point during 1993, for example, activist groups were conducting boycotts against Kraft Foods and Nabisco for allegedly selling cigarettes to teens, Levi Strauss for moving plants abroad, Ford Motor Company for discriminating against Catholics in Northern Ireland, Mitsubishi for destruction of rain forests, and Pepsico for company investments in Burma.

Earlier a boycott against Burger King by the Christian Leadership for Responsible Television ended after the fast-food chain published half-page advertisements nationwide stating that it "wishes to go on record as supporting traditional American values on television." The boycott's operators had claimed that the company promoted gratuitous sex and violence by sponsoring certain TV programs.

Boycott groups traditionally figured that they needed five to ten years to succeed in their causes, if they were to succeed; in some recent cases the time period for success has been less than two years.

Todd Hunter, writing in *Business and Society Review,* attributed the speedup to use of such tactics as placing full-page advertisements in newspapers and magazines, distributing videotapes telling the boycotters' story, and focusing their boycott efforts on the companies' images. In response, companies have developed answers to queries that explain their conduct, direct attention to their good actions, and perhaps try to put the boycotters in a negative light.

In the private sector, the nationwide network of Better Business Bureaus provides machinery through which wronged consumers may seek satisfaction. Nader's operations in Washington continue to publicize defective products and services. Other consumer organizations do similar work. *Consumer Reports* is widely read.

Formation of the Society of Consumer Affairs Professionals in Business (SOCAB) provides an avenue for exchange of information among specialists in the field and a method for increasing corporate awareness of what can be accomplished in building goodwill.

Thus business and financial organizations function under extensive legal controls and unofficial pressures designed to give the public safe, reliable merchandise, and honest services. Whether a company meets the demands of consumers willingly or grudgingly—volunteering corrective action when the need is evident or fighting against having to do so—influences the public's perception of it.

PUBLIC ANGER GETS RESULTS

Public anger against a company can develop quickly. When R.J. Reynolds began to test-market a new cigarette aimed at blacks, called Uptown, criticism was vehement for both health and racial reasons. Antismoking groups pointed out that blacks historically have suffered higher rates of cancer than other groups. Dr. Louis W. Sullivan, Health and Human Services Secretary, accused R.J. Reynolds of "promoting a culture of cancer." It retorted that he was promoting paternalism.

Within days the company cancelled the test-marketing, not with an apology but with a grumbling statement that the brand had received "unfair and biased attention" and that the criticism was "a further erosion of the free enterprise system."

Unfortunately, companies with clean records and constructive consumer programs tend to be lumped with the bad ones in the public's mind. Their public relations representatives must work diligently and ingeniously to make the public aware of this commendable performance. The challenge to these practitioners is to remain watchful for any company action that would blemish a good record.

PRODUCT RECALLS

Recall of a defective product from its purchasers is the most visible, and frequently very expensive, form of corporate response to consumer pressure. Millions of automobiles have been called back for correction of defects that might endanger the safety of riders. Some recalls by the automakers are preventive and voluntary. Others have been done by agreement between manufacturer and the federal government. In certain instances, however, car makers have strenuously opposed government recall demands. Reaching the owners of defective automobiles is relatively easy, because of the state car registration laws. When other types of products are involved, especially those often purchased as gifts, the problem is more difficult.

Experience has shown that if a manufacturer recalls a defective product voluntarily, in a gracious manner that offers the owner suitable compensation, the company may generate enough good will to overcome the negative implications of the recall.

The public's perception of a product and its maker at the time the recall notice is issued influences its reaction. When Saturn Corporation voluntarily recalled more than 380,000 compact autos in 1993, in order to repair a wiring flaw that had caused 34 known motor fires but no injuries, the publicity might have damaged the make's image badly. Relatively little complaint was heard, however, because most owners liked their Saturns. A recent independent survey had shown that the Saturn ranked first among all American makes in customer satisfaction, behind only the Japanese luxury makes Lexus and Infiniti.

AUTO REPAIR FRAUD HARMS SEARS

Sears, Roebuck & Company suffered a damaging loss in public confidence when California and New Jersey departments of consumer affairs caught company auto repair shops making unnecessary repairs to customers' automobiles and charging for work that was never done.

After receiving more than 3000 complaints, the California attorney general threatened to close the shops. Sears responded unwisely by calling the charges politically motivated and denying any fraud. This response irritated the public. Anger against the company grew.

After several days Sears published newspaper advertisements in which the corporation chairman admitted that "mistakes may have occurred." He did not, however, cancel the Sears policy of giving its auto mechanics quotas to meet and paying them commissions, a practice widely blamed for stimulating the misconduct.

With public indignation high, nearly a week passed before Sears finally announced abolition of the commission system. Not only had the company been caught cheating customers, but the inept handling of the crisis damaged its reputation even more. Business at Sears auto repair shops dropped off 28 percent in the weeks after the California charges were made public.

When Saturn owners took their cars to the shop for the free repair work, which required about 45 minutes overall, many dealers served them refreshments. Drivers found that their cars had been washed without charge before being returned to them. Dealers extended their hours in some instances and put on extra help to avoid delays. One dealer explained, "We're just doing what we normally do, which is exceed the customers' expectations."

The recall cost the company, a subsidiary of General Motors, about $8 million. Saturn publicity depicted the recall as evidence of the extra effort the company makes to please and protect its customers. Many owners accepted the explanation willingly, despite the inconvenience they suffered, because they liked the way they had been treated previously. Accumulated customer good will paid off.

CORPORATIONS AND THE ENVIRONMENT

Public demand for protection of the environment, born of a growing realization that the earth's resources are limited, places a heavy burden on corporations. Much of the world's pollution, but far from all, has been created by their manufacturing processes and use of their products. The public wants those products but protests against the pollution they have created. In earlier decades, smoking factory smokestacks were applauded as a sign of prosperity. Today they are a badge of corporate dishonor, because medical science has established that air pollution damages health.

Social responsibility requires that companies eliminate, to the best of their ability, the sources of environmental damage they have created. At the same time, corporate managements must protect the interests of their stockholders. This often creates a difficult balancing act. Corporate offenses include dumping toxic waste into waterways, polluting the air with discharges from manufacturing processes, and destroying rain forests and wetlands to obtain materials. Activist groups representing many different clean-up causes focus the public mood by conducting campaigns against individual companies, sometimes in a highly emotional manner. (Environmental groups are discussed in Chapter 17.)

Even the best-intentioned corporations sometimes have difficulty in eliminating their offenses, because the cost can be extremely high and new ways must be found to replace the bad ones.

Alice Rivlin, a noted economist active in the Wilderness Society, summarized the problem many industries face:

It's sometimes difficult for companies to be as environmentally responsible as they'd like to be, because it's costly in the short run. That's part of the general problem of short-term focus in American companies. But I think if they take a long-range view, especially with the rising concern about the environment in the general public, it's clear that long-term profitability will be aided by environmental responsibility.

THE PUBLIC RELATIONS ROLE

Public relations people representing corporations concentrate on three areas concerning the environment:

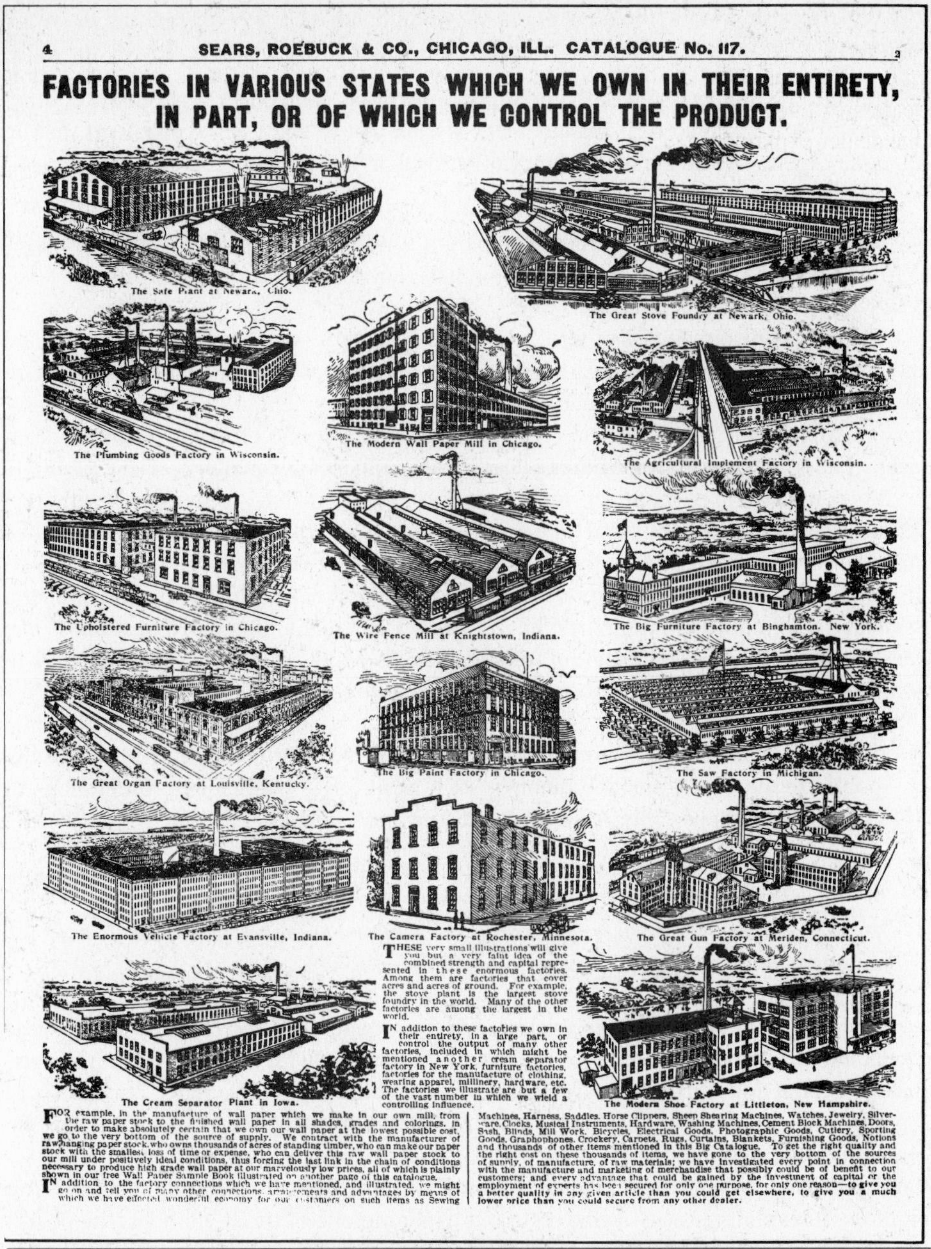

4 SEARS, ROEBUCK & CO., CHICAGO, ILL. CATALOGUE No. 117. 3

FACTORIES IN VARIOUS STATES WHICH WE OWN IN THEIR ENTIRETY, IN PART, OR OF WHICH WE CONTROL THE PRODUCT.

The Safe Plant at Newark, Ohio.

The Great Stove Foundry at Newark, Ohio.

The Plumbing Goods Factory in Wisconsin.

The Modern Wall Paper Mill in Chicago.

The Agricultural Implement Factory in Wisconsin.

The Upholstered Furniture Factory in Chicago.

The Wire Fence Mill at Knightstown, Indiana.

The Big Furniture Factory at Binghamton, New York.

The Great Organ Factory at Louisville, Kentucky.

The Big Paint Factory in Chicago.

The Saw Factory in Michigan.

The Enormous Vehicle Factory at Evansville, Indiana.

The Camera Factory at Rochester, Minnesota.

The Great Gun Factory at Meriden, Connecticut.

The Cream Separator Plant in Iowa.

The Modern Shoe Factory at Littleton, New Hampshire.

THESE very small illustrations will give you but a very faint idea of the combined strength and capital represented in these enormous factories. Among them are factories that cover acres and acres of ground. For example, the stove plant is the largest stove foundry in the world. Many of the other factories are among the largest in the world.

IN addition to these factories we own in their entirety, in a large part, or control the output of many other factories, included in which might be mentioned another cream separator factory in New York, furniture factories, factories for the manufacture of clothing, wearing apparel, millinery, hardware, etc. The factories we illustrate are but a few of the vast number in which we wield a controlling influence.

FOR example, in the manufacture of wall paper which we make in our own mill, from the raw paper stock to the finished wall paper in all shades, grades and colorings, in order to make absolutely certain that we own our wall paper at the lowest possible cost, we go to the very bottom of the source of supply. We contract with the manufacturer of raw hanging paper stock, who owns thousands of acres of standing timber, who can make our paper stock with the smallest loss of time or expense, who can deliver this raw wall paper stock to our mill under positively ideal conditions, thus forging the last link in the chain of conditions necessary to produce high grade wall paper at our marvelously low prices, all of which is plainly shown in our free Wall Paper Sample Book illustrated on another page of this catalogue.

IN addition to the factory connections which we have mentioned, and illustrated, we might go on and tell you of many other connections, arrangements and advantages by means of which we have effected wonderful economy for our customers on such items as Sewing Machines, Harness, Saddles, Horse Clippers, Sheep Shearing Machines, Watches, Jewelry, Silverware, Clocks, Musical Instruments, Hardware, Washing Machines, Cement Block Machines, Doors, Sash, Blinds, Mill Work, Bicycles, Electrical Goods, Photographic Goods, Cutlery, Sporting Goods, Graphophones, Crockery, Carpets, Rugs, Curtains, Blankets, Furnishing Goods, Notions and thousands of other items mentioned in this Big Catalogue. To get the right quality and the right cost on these thousands of items, we have gone to the very bottom of the sources of supply, of manufacture, of raw materials; we have investigated every point in connection with the manufacture and marketing of merchandise that possibly could be of benefit to our customers; and every advantage that could be gained by the investment of capital or the employment of experts has been secured for only one purpose, for only one reason—**to give you a better quality in any given article than you could get elsewhere, to give you a much lower price than you could secure from any other dealer.**

FIGURE 14.3
Smoke pouring from their smokestacks once was advertised by companies as a sign of prosperity. Today it is condemned for polluting the atmosphere. This page from the 1908 Sears Roebuck catalogue illustrates what a radical change has occurred.

1. Present to the public the company's environmental accomplishments, its plans for long-term cleanup, and explanations of the company's problems in achieving its goals.

2. Inform top management of the public's perceptions and concerns about the company's environmental record. If management is reluctant to address the problems, public relations experts should persuade senior officials that they should act to protect the company's reputation.

3. Conduct environmental cleanup campaigns within the company urging employees to follow good environmental practices, such as recycling, on and off the job.

Specialists recommend that as a first step a company should take an environmental audit. This involves a detailed investigation of every aspect of the business for its impact on the environment. An audit by a qualified outsider may be more objective than a self-examination. Next, management should create a long-range cleanup program. Some environmental faults may be overcome quickly and cheaply, others only at high cost and retooling.

A company may need to raise prices of its products to remain profitable. Willingness to spend money and take risks is what Alice Rivlin was talking about. Jobs may be in jeopardy because of these decisions, a painful personnel problem.

Bad news always attracts more attention than good news. Public disclosure that a company is committing an environmental sin automatically gets more headlines than the success of a three-year program to reduce waste paper by 25 percent. Two ways in which a public relations practitioner can respond to this psychological fact are:

■ Search out all the environmentally positive actions the company has taken and publicize them in a creative manner, such as through videotaped presentations to community groups. This projects a "good citizen" image.

■ Have a crisis plan ready in case a company environmental blunder comes to light. Be ready to explain how it came about; why it is difficult to correct, if that is true; and the company's plans to correct it. All defensive words fail, of course, if the company does not act vigorously to solve the problem.

Corporate products and methods viewed as dangerous today often were quite acceptable to society when they were created. Pesticides were hailed as a boon to agricultural production; further research has revealed their danger to humans. Asbestos was regarded as valuable fire insulation material; today it is known to cause cancer, yet removing it from buildings is costly and difficult. Lead was used widely in manufactured products; now medical evidence shows the peril of lead poisoning, especially to children. In explaining why a corporation is violating one of today's taboos, the practitioner can make a valid point by emphasizing the historical perspective. Realistic people recognize that complex solutions take time, but they must be convinced that the company is taking action, not just talking.

THE "GREEN" IMAGE

Green has become the symbolic word for being environmentally clean. Many companies try to wrap themselves in mantles of green for image purposes or to sell "green" products.

Presenting a "green" corporate image is desirable IF it is honest. Some companies that have presented themselves in this light, such as by claiming that their products are biodegradable or nontoxic when they aren't, have been publicly embarrassed by having to retract the claims. Others have been caught doing bad things at the same time they were promoting their good acts. Chevron U.S. published a series of advertisements illustrating how its employees try to protect wildlife. Yet it agreed to pay an $8 million fine for violating the federal Clean Water Act by repeatedly dumping excessive amounts of oil, grease, and other toxic wastes from a drilling platform in the Pacific Ocean off California.

When a corporation comes under attack from an activist environmental group, some senior officials instinctively want to fight back in a combative manner. In some instances, that may be a sensible course. Certain protest groups use extremely emotional, even violent, tactics that invite a hard response. Other companies find a policy of conciliation better; they try to work with the environmental group involved in a joint effort to find a solution. The better a company's overall environmental record is, the more effectively it can respond to attack on a specific offense.

ONE COMPANY'S PROGRAM

The 3M Company, operating in 20 countries worldwide, has won numerous awards for its "Pollution Prevention Pays" program. The manufacturing company calculates that the program has saved it $500 million since its inception in 1975.

Company management decided to concentrate on reducing the air pollution created by its production processes. This involved identifying pollution sources, modifying operations, installing control equipment, changing products, recycling, and encouraging suggestions from employees. More than 2500 projects have been put in operation around the world. These have reduced 3M's air pollutants by 120,000 tons. In the early 1990s, 3M decided to invest another $150 million in air pollution control equipment and renamed the project "3P Plus."

Vital to the program is the public relations department, which is responsible for all environmental communications—internal, to stimulate employee understanding and appreciation, and external, to inform the public about what is happening. For employees the department conducts motivational meetings, shows videotapes, and issues special publications. For external use, it distributes news releases and other material, holds media briefings, and conducts plant tours for community leaders. An environmental communications team within the department answers media and public questions and arranges interviews.

A FEW EXAMPLES

Some actions, big and small, that corporations have taken to improve the environment:

- Many companies recycle their waste paper. Bank of America, for example, recycles nearly 10,000 tons a year. American Airlines uses recycled paper for napkins and tissues. Americans recycle more than 33 million tons of paper a year.

- San Diego Gas & Electric Company pays a contractor $130,000 a year to remove graffiti scrawled on its buildings.

■ A California wine and food company packs its shipments in popcorn instead of plastic foam because popcorn is biodegradable.

■ Procter & Gamble began selling several of its products in bottles made of recycled plastic.

■ McDonald's decided to prepare its french fries in vegetable oil instead of fat and to replace its plastic foam sandwich boxes with paper-based wrapping. Later it announced plans to eliminate at least 80 percent of its garbage.

MARKETING PUBLIC RELATIONS

The tools and techniques of public relations are used extensively to support the marketing and sales objectives of a business. This is called "marketing communications" or "marketing public relations." Personnel who work in this area usually serve in or are closely affiliated with the marketing department.

Intel, for example, has product public relations specialists who report to a marketing vice president instead of the vice president of corporate communications. At Hewlett-Packard, the public relations department has a section called Product Press Relations. General Motors, in 1990, tied its public relations to marketing by creating a new department of "Communications and Marketing."

Thomas L. Harris, former vice chairman of Golin/Harris Communications in New York, in his book *A Marketer's Guide to Public Relations,* says that corporate public relations and marketing public relations will be more highly defined within business organizations. Corporate public relations, he states, will remain a management function supporting overall corporate objectives, while marketing public relations will be a marketing management function.

COMPANIES PLEDGE "DOLPHIN-SAFE" TUNA

Environmentalists achieved a widely publicized victory when the three largest canners of tuna announced that henceforth they would buy only tuna caught by methods that do not endanger dolphins.

The H. J. Heinz Company announced its decision; its two chief competitors followed within hours. So did a large pet food company. This ended a 14-year campaign by the Humane Society of the United States to stop the netting of the playful, intelligent dolphins, which often became entangled in fishing boats' nets and drowned.

A crusade by schoolchildren pressured the tuna companies. So did such actions as having characters in movies and comic strips refuse to eat tuna sandwiches. Some restaurants took tuna off their menus.

While environmentalists celebrated, members of the American Tuna Boat Association feared their livelihoods would be destroyed. They predicted that foreign boats, operating without such restrictions, would harvest most of the tuna and sell the fish to U.S. customers.

Harris defines marketing public relations as "the process of planning, executing and evaluating programs that encourage purchase and consumer satisfaction through credible communication of information and impressions that identify companies and their products with the needs, wants, concerns, and interests of consumers."

The objectives of marketing public relations, often called *marcom* in industry jargon, are accomplished in several ways.

Product Publicity   The cost and clutter of advertising and sales promotion have mounted dramatically, and companies have found that product publicity is a cost-effective way of reaching potential consumers. Products, if presented properly, can be newsworthy and catch the eyes of reporters and editors. Life Savers, for example, generated many news articles about the introduction of Life Saver Holes, pellet candies that represented the "holes" in its regular product.

Other forms of product publicity are found on the food, auto, real estate, business, travel, and sports pages of newspapers as news and feature stories. These cover the development and launching of new products, and even new uses for established products. Radio and television talk shows and consumer programs also contain large amounts of product publicity.

Joan Aho Ryan and George H. Lemmond, writing in the *Public Relations Journal*, make the case for product publicity: "Cynical consumers, zapping commercials and ignoring print ads, are more receptive to the editorial message. The 'third party endorsement' allows advertisers to sell a new product while enveloping the commercial message in a credible environment."

Information Bureaus   Several companies operate information bureaus that help position their products in the marketplace. Quaker's Gatorade has its Sports Science Institute, Reebok has an Aerobic Information Bureau, and Nutri/System operates a Health and Fitness Information Bureau. One primary function of these "information bureaus" is the distribution of news releases and press kits that report research results and give consumer tips on keeping healthy and fit. Of course, the sponsor of the research and the source of the "tips" are mentioned in the resulting news stories.

Polls Bearing a Brand Name   Another form of product publicity that gets good media coverage is polls. The Chlor-Trimeton Allergy Season Index has measured pollen counts since 1984. Philip Morris Company publicized its Merit brand cigarettes by publishing the Merit Report, a public opinion poll on a wide variety of topics. Even the Gallup Poll, which newspapers use regularly, is a product publicity technique for the company to promote its polling services to business and industry.

Public Relations Tours   Company executives can do much to promote products by giving speeches and news conferences. Perhaps the most effective CEO in this respect was Lee Iacocca of Chrysler Corporation, who was the company's top salesman. Early in the 1990s, he made a six-city tour to promote Chrysler's new products and to tell people that the automaker had recovered from an earlier recession. He took his message to 12,000 invited opinion-makers and gave numerous news interviews.

School Promotions   Companies try to instill brand loyalty early by sponsoring special programs in schools. AT&T has an Adventure Club, which includes student newsletters, classroom posters, and teaching guides designed to foster understanding of communications and build AT&T awareness among first-graders. Coca-Cola's Minute Maid unit enhanced the wholesome image of its juice products by sponsoring a literacy program. More than 3.7 million elementary-school children were encouraged to read a book a week during summer vacation and track their progress on a chart provided by the unit. Product coupons were provided with the chart. Nike, Inc., sent 1 million high school students free textbook covers bearing the company's name.

Parent and consumer groups are less than happy about school children being the target of corporate marketing programs, but officials in financially strapped school districts often welcome business support if the program isn't too commercial and serves a legitimate educational function.

Cause-Related Marketing   Companies in highly competitive fields often strive to differentiate themselves by supporting causes that appeal to various market segments. American Express, for example, promised its customers that if they used its credit card for purchases, 1 percent of the bill would be given to the Statue of Liberty restoration campaign. Visa and MasterCard have used the same technique with the Sierra Club and other conservation groups.

Another approach is to underwrite events and information campaigns. Reebok International Ltd. supplied $10 million for a "Human Rights Now!" concert tour, which helped focus the world's attention on human rights abuses. Johnson & Johnson's Personal Products Company underwrote a $1 million campaign to educate the public about the sensitive issue of domestic violence.

Although cause-related marketing doesn't necessarily improve product sales, public relations professionals call it an effective way to communicate a company's values and corporate philosophy. From a marketing perspective, support of a popular cause can foster brand loyalty by consumers who believe in that cause.

Companies usually avoid controversial causes that could lead to a possible boycott by consumers.

Corporate Sponsorships   An estimated 3500 or more companies are spending between $2 and $3 billion annually on sponsorships of all kinds. Growth averaged about 30 to 40 percent during the past decade, and a continued stampede to corporate sponsorship is occurring during the 1990s.

The popularity of sponsored events is due to several reasons. They give companies high visibility among key audiences that can afford and would be interested in a particular product or service. Event sponsorship also generates news coverage, brings out audiences, provides a focal point for marketing efforts and sales campaigns, and often is more cost-effective than an advertising campaign. The tobacco industry became an early leader in sponsorship primarily because its advertising on radio and television was banned by U.S. law.

Sporting Events   Sporting events are extremely popular and are well funded by corporations. The Orange Bowl is now officially the Federal Express Orange Bowl and the Sun Bowl is the John Hancock Sun Bowl, although the media have resisted using these official titles. In fact, a dozen of the 19 annual college football bowl games have title sponsors.

Companies attempting to reach specialized audiences sponsor many sports. Volvo, the Swedish auto maker, and Grundig of West Germany have sponsored the Track and Field Federation of East Germany; the Japanese manufacturer Toshiba is a sponsor of the Tour de France bicycle race. Chrysler Plymouth Division sponsors the U.S. Pro Ski Tour and provides $1 million in prizes. The Kemper Insurance Group has sponsored the Professional Golf Association for more than 20 years.

SELECTION CRITERIA FOR CORPORATE SPONSORSHIPS

Corporations are inundated with requests from organizations to sponsor everything from rock concerts to museum exhibits and sporting events. Consequently, each corporation selects sponsorships that best support its marketing and public relations objectives. A company considering a sponsorship should ask these questions:

■ Can the company afford to fulfill the obligation? The sponsorship fee is just the starting point. Count on doubling it to have an adequate total event budget.

■ Is the event or organization compatible with the company's values and mission statement?

■ Does the event reach the corporation's target audience?

■ Is there enough time before the event to maximize the company's use of the sponsorship?

■ Are the event organizers experienced and professional?

■ Is the event newsworthy enough to provide the company with opportunities for publicity?

■ Will the event be televised?

■ Will the sales force support the event and use it to leverage sales?

■ Does the event give the company a chance to develop new contacts and business opportunities?

■ Can the company live with the event on a long-term basis while its value builds?

■ Is there an opportunity for employee involvement? Corporate sponsorships can be used to build employee morale and teamwork.

■ Is the event compatible with the "personality" of the company's products?

■ Can the company reduce the cash outlay and enhance the marketing appeal by trading off products and in-kind services?

■ Will management support the event? If the answer is yes to the previous questions, the likelihood of management support of the sponsorship is fairly high.

Source: John M. Barr, "Maximizing the Value of Sponsorships," *Public Relations Journal,* April 1993, p. 30.

Manufacturers of products for affluent customers tailor their sponsorships accordingly. Range Rover, the British maker of expensive four-wheel-drive vehicles, underwrites equestrian events and yachting races. Lexus, the luxury car division of Toyota, sponsors polo championships because, an official said, "Involvement in this event allows us to position the Lexus product line in the proper demographic segment."

On an international level, the 1992 Summer Olympic Games in Barcelona, Spain, attracted scores of multinational corporations. Involvement in the Olympics is an effective way of reaching a worldwide audience, but some marketing experts wonder if the numerous sponsorships create so much clutter that audiences tune out most of the messages. Still, promotion and advertising before and after the event place a company in a special niche as an "Olympic sponsor." (Sports publicity is discussed further in Chapter 20.)

Art and Music   General Motors GMC Division, interested in selling pickups, sponsored a 15-city country and western tour featuring Randy Travis and Tammy Wynette. Toyota underwrote performances of the Dallas Opera and the Miami City Ballet. Ford Motor Company, seeking to enhance its image among the affluent and well-educated, sponsored an exhibition of impressionistic paintings in Pittsburgh.

THE BUSINESS-MEDIA RELATIONSHIP

Reporting by the media is a basic source of public information about the performance and objectives of business. Too frequently it generates misunderstanding and irritation between these two essential segments of society, a situation for which both sides are partially responsible. The trouble arises most frequently when a corporate business becomes involved in a communication crisis.

Many business executives regard media stories about their companies as inaccurate, incomplete, and biased, an opinion at odds with the view of many business editors and writers. The pattern emerges in most polls taken on the relationship. A poll by Louis Harris and Associates asked, "Would you rate business journalism positively on being fair, balanced and accurate?" Results showed a striking discrepancy in the percentage of "Yes" responses amoung the four groups polled:

Business executives	27 percent
Writers and editors	84 percent
Business academics	64 percent
Journalism academics	72 percent

A majority of all four categories agreed, however, that the quality of business reporting had improved substantially during the past 25 years.

Corporate managers' principal complaints against media coverage are inaccuracy, incomplete coverage, inadequate research and preparation for interviews, and antibusiness bias.

Business editors and reporters state in response that often they cannot publish or broadcast thorough, evenhanded stories about business because many company executives, uncooperative and wary, erect barriers against them. Writers complain about failing to obtain direct access to decision-making executives and being restricted to using public relations statements that don't contain information they need. Journalists assert, too, that some business leaders don't understand the concept of objectivity and assume that any story involving unfavorable news about their company is intentionally biased.

Public relations practitioners serving business stand in the middle. They must interpret their companies to the media, while showing their chief executive officers and other high officials how open, friendly press relations can serve their interest.

News stories about business leaders and corporations involving deception of the public, fraud, cheating of the government, and theft of funds hit the front pages and newscasts often enough to damage the public's conception of big business. When senior public relations executives at an annual session of the Arthur Page Society in 1993 discussed the problem, 70 percent agreed with the statement that "less trust in business" existed than was the case 15 years earlier. Thus corporate public relations practitioners need to build public confidence in business as a whole as well as represent their own companies.

Environmental reporting, a rapidly expanding field, is an area in which the media, by their own admission, are weak. Reporters assigned to the often-complicated "earth" beat often lack sufficient technical knowledge or skill to tell technical stories in easily understood language. Experienced reporters in the field are wary of news releases from corporations making unsubstantiated "green" claims and from activist groups leveling excessive charges on skimpy evidence.

FINANCIAL INFORMATION

At a time when corporate mergers, takeovers, and financial scandals make headlines almost daily, the role of investor relations is essential in corporate operations. This falls within the general scope of public relations.

The men and women who handle investor relations work are specialists. In large corporations they may function as a separate unit, in smaller companies as part of the public relations department. No matter how the organization chart is designed, cooperation between the general public relations function and this special field should be close. A good public image strengthens a company's financial position, and the other way around.

The two primary targets for a company's financial information are (1) its stockholders and (2) the financial analysts who advise brokers and bankers on the current and probable future financial health of a company. Since large blocks of stock often are held by a single investor, such as a pension fund, special attention must be paid to those investors, as well as to the growing number of foreign stockholders. (Corporate annual reports are discussed in Chapters 13 and 22.)

Annual meetings of corporations commonly are routine and dull, with everything going precisely as management has arranged it. Proxy votes obtained in advance assure management solid control of the voting. Managements often present slide and video-taped shows to illustrate their achievements, serve light refreshments, and in general try to create an atmosphere of competence and geniality. Behind the scenes, many hours of public relations department work have been spent in planning the meetings.

At times abrasive moments of controversy may arise if stockholders challenge management policies. This is done through antimanagement resolutions that must be put to a vote of all stockholders. During the 1990s many of these concern the environment, demanding that the company do something the activists advocate or stop doing something they dislike. During the 1980s resolutions frequently demanded that companies quit doing business in South Africa because of apartheid.

Many resolutions, especially those by environmentalists, seek changes in corporate advertising policy. Both Bristol-Meyers and Gerber Products were confronted by proposals that they stop advertising their baby formula products directly to parents on grounds that the advertising encourages mothers to stop breast-feeding.

Although antimanagement resolutions rarely pass, they obtain publicity and at times gather enough votes to influence management thinking. Sometimes managements negotiate compromises with advocacy groups in exchange for withdrawal of their resolutions.

Financial Analysts   Discussion of a company's condition and prospects with financial analysts is important because the advice they give to traders influences the price of a company's stock. In addition to periodic formal presentations to groups of analysts, investor relations people send them a steady flow of information by computer, fax, and even video.

Investor relations work has no room for publicity hype and verbal sleight-of-hand. Financial analysts are experts, and their questions are searching. When a company's chief executive officer makes a presentation, the public relations department is called on to help him prepare. An effective presentation showing a solid growth pattern and sound financing may win "buy" recommendations and make the stock price rise, thus increasing the company's value.

SENSITIVITY TO MINORITIES

Swift expansion of the minority population in the United States, bringing with it intensified problems of language and cultural differences, demands heightened sensitivity by corporation managements. Traditionally, senior managements have been white males, although female and minority faces are increasingly evident in executive suites. Feedback on attitudes of minority customers and employees collected by public relations departments helps broaden management perspectives.

The racial mixture of work forces sometimes becomes an issue if a large minority group in a community believes that a company fails to hire enough of its members. Communications within a company also can be a problem if some employees speak little or no English. These difficulties can be overcome if management handles them in a sensitive manner.

COMPANY PUBLISHES REPORT CARD ON RACIAL DIVERSITY IN ITS WORK FORCE

Some companies, such as the San Diego Gas & Electric Company, have a policy of periodically announcing the racial mix of their employees in a company publication.

Under the headline, "A diverse work force for a diverse territory," a recent issue of *Inside SDG&E* printed this typical report:

SDG&E Employment - March 31, 1993

TOTAL	MALE	FEMALE	BLACK	HISPANIC	ASIAN PACIFIC IS.	NATIVE AMERICAN
4,237	3,079	1,158	334	677	224	40

The accompanying text stated, "The Company's Affirmative Action program involves special efforts to employ and advance minorities and females. And it's been successful.

"These figures show that 30 percent of SDG&E employees are minorities and 27 percent are female.

"SDG&E's Affirmative Action Program is not administered as a quota system.

"The Company's objective is to correct imbalances that exist in the utilization of minorities and females in the work force," said Lorraine Goffe-Rush, EEO administrator. She explained that "underutilization" means having fewer minorities or females in a job category than would be expected by their availability in the labor market.

The Denny's restaurant chain, with more than 1500 restaurants, suffered badly in 1993 when charges of racial bias were made against it by African American customers. In a widely publicized incident, six black Secret Service agents—men assigned to guard the President of the United States—said they were refused breakfast service at a Denny's in Annapolis, Maryland, although 15 white Secret Service agents were served. Subsequent news stories reported complaints from black customers at other Denny's outlets that they had been required to pay cover charges or to pay in advance, while other diners were not, and of receiving conspicuously slow, rude service.

Denny's admitted that "some isolated customer concerns" had taken place. It tried to wipe out the stigma with a series of steps to demonstrate its good intentions. It signed an agreement with the National Association for the Advancement of Colored People (NAACP) promising increased employment of African Americans and minorities in management positions and other economic opportunities, arranged for the NAACP to help conduct random checks of Denny's restaurants nationwide for equal rights compliance, hired a black executive as human resources vice president, conducted cultural diversity training sessions for its management, and signed an agreement with the U.S. Department of Justice to settle government claims that it had discriminated against black customers. The chain also ran TV commercials featuring its CEO and restaurant employees, apologetic in tone, promising openness to all. And Denny's announced plans for African American ownership of at least 47 new outlets.

America's Restaurant Is Everybody's Restaurant.

An Open Letter to Denny's Customers and Communities:

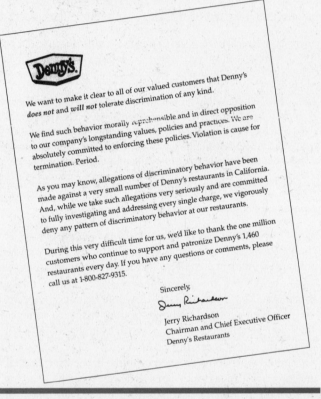

FIGURE 14.4
As part of its campaign to overcome charges of racial discrimination against customers in its restaurants, the Denny's chain ran this full-page newspaper advertisement. Its television commercials emphasized the same message. (Reproduced with permission from Denny's Inc., a division of Flagler Companies, Inc.)

EMPLOYEE COMMUNICATIONS

The employees of a company form a crucial audience for its public relations department. The department, often working with or within the human resources department, must concentrate on communicating with employees just as vigorously as it does on delivering the corporate story to the outside world. A work force that respects its management, has pride in its products, and believes that it is being treated fairly is a key factor in corporate success.

In these days of corporate turmoil, with companies being bought and sold almost casually and mass layoffs resulting from cost-cutting moves, unrest and uncertainty among employees create a greater need than ever for effective employee communications. Surveys indicate a dropoff in employees' loyalty to their companies, based in part on their belief that remote corporate managements feel no loyalty to them.

Job security and financial protection against illness are two principal concerns among employees. As much as the facts justify, they need to be reassured on these points. Stimulation of company loyalty helps to stabilize the work force, an important need of management.

Company magazines, brochures, newsletters, and policy manuals written for employees, such as the one shown in Figure 14.4, are a fundamental form of internal communication. These are discussed in detail in Chapter 22.

Much employee communication work is relatively standard—distribution of information about working conditions, retirement benefits, new company products, changes in management and supervisory personnel, and corporate plans for expansion or alterations in operating procedures. *The better informed employees are, the less likely they are to spread erroneous and possibly damaging misinformation.* Gossip flourishes in an information vacuum. The company grapevine always exists, because humans like to talk and speculate, but a flow of accurate information from management can make the company grapevine a positive rather than a negative force.

HEALTH AND SOCIAL ISSUES

Communication with employees involves much more than the nuts and bolts items just described. Critical health and social issues are involved, in which the company must steer a cautious course.

The skyrocketing cost of health insurance for employees has become a heavy and still growing burden on employers. Yet with personal medical and hospital bills so high, employees regard medical insurance for themselves and their families as extremely important. Company attempts to trim health benefits have encountered fervent resistance.

Circle K, which operates convenience stores nationwide, found that out when, with little preparation, it denied new employees coverage for illnesses and accidents related to "personal life-style decisions."

This meant no coverage for new employees if they became ill with acquired immune deficiency syndrome (AIDS) or had drug or alcohol problems. Circle K was accused, among other things, of making a thinly veiled attack on homosexuality. The dispute was covered on national television and the front pages. Reaction was so severe that Circle K suspended implementation of the plan.

President Clinton's plan to revise American health policy sought to provide medical insurance for all Americans. Much of the huge cost involved would be borne by employers. The intense political battle that followed his announcement included strident opposition by many small companies, which contended that the extra financial burden would bankrupt them.

"STONEWALLING" CAN BE COSTLY

As the Christmas shopping season approached, the management of the large University Park mall at the northeast edge of South Bend, Indiana, refused to let the municipal bus line run a holiday shopping service to the mall. The bus company manager informed his board that the mall managers had told him the shuttle would bring mostly "downtowners" and "West Siders," whom they called "undesirable."

A local TV news show broke the story on a Wednesday evening, and the next day the South Bend *Tribune* covered it extensively.

A surge of anger hit the city. Everyone knew that the downtown has a heavy black population and the West Side is predominantly Polish. The refusal had strong racial and ethnic connotations.

Mall managers refused to talk to the media, referring them to the mall's owners, the Edward J. DeBartolo Corporation in Youngstown, Ohio. For three days DeBartolo headquarters ignored calls from the media. This brush-off increased public displeasure.

The postal clerks union proposed boycotting the mall. So did letter-writers in the newspaper. Shopkeepers in the mall, facing a loss of business, protested. A Polish city councilman held a news conference demanding an apology.

After three days the corporation issued a vague statement about a possible misunderstanding. Then on Monday, the fifth day, it published a full-page ad in the newspaper, in which it apologized for "any misunderstanding" and claimed that the refusal was based solely on limited bus parking space.

This ad didn't even mention any offensive statements. The evasion increased community irritation. Eight of the nine city council members and the acting mayor called for dismissal of the mall managers.

Finally, on the seventh day of the furor, the corporation held a news conference in South Bend at which it distributed a release announcing that the two mall managers involved had been relieved of their duties.

Officially, the episode was closed, but the bad taste lingered in the community. A serious initial mistake that could have been mitigated by a quick public apology was made much worse by the corporation's foolish decision to stonewall.

Management efforts to identify and halt use of drugs on the job is a tricky social issue. How much on-the-job drug testing, if any, should a company do? When does a company's right to maintain strong, safe production levels intrude upon the individual rights of employees? Decisions on such questions must be made by top management, but the manner in which they are communicated to employees heavily influences how the work force accepts them.

Still another aspect of behavior by employees involves smoking. Evidence that exposure to smoke from others may injure nonsmokers has increased pressure for no-smoking rules in company work and recreation areas. Yet some smokers vehemently insist that they have rights, too. Once management has decided the extent of a no-smoking policy on company property, public relations has the task of "selling" it to employees.

Sexual harassment in the workplace worries both employees and management, the latter for legal as well as ethical reasons. The U.S. Supreme Court ruled in *Monitor Savings Bank* v. *Vinson* (1986) that a company may be held liable in sexual harassment suits even if management is unaware of the problem and has a general policy against discrimination.

One major corporation, the DuPont Company, meets the problem of sexual harassment thus, as reported in *Public Relations Journal:* a travel safety seminar for female employees, a personal safety program that includes a rape-prevention workshop, a managers' workshop to define their role in helping employees who have been assaulted, legal assistance, liability coverage, and public relations assistance in handling publicity that might result from a rape trial. The company promotes the program in internal publications, on the company news hotline, and in monthly safety meetings.

With so many mothers working and the cost of private day care so high, should companies provide day-care facilities? Some companies do. To what extent should a company offer general education programs beyond direct job-training education? Is there a danger that companies, in trying to keep employees happy, will do too much and assume a big brother role that causes resentment?

Employee attitudes toward these and similar issues should be closely considered by managements as they make decisions. The public relations department's role in gathering employee opinion, and in providing employees with management's thinking, thus becomes vital.

CASE PROBLEM

Drug abuse increasingly is a problem in the workplace. Although no one knows exact figures about the percentage of employees who might be popping pills, using cocaine, or even abusing alcohol, evidence exists that drugs in the workplace are causing problems in employee morale, absenteeism, and loss of productivity.

The president of Zebra Company, a manufacturer of computer software, decides to create an employee awareness program that will (1) inform employees about the health dangers of drug abuse and (2) encourage them to seek company-funded counseling. The issue, however, is sensitive and has the potential of alienating employees if the wrong approach is taken.

As director of public relations for the company, you are asked to present a public relations plan at the next meeting of the company's officers. What message themes and communications strategies would you recommend?

QUESTIONS FOR REVIEW AND DISCUSSION

1. Why is the public perception of a corporation so important to its success?

2. What caused the growth of the consumer movement between 1960 and 1980 in the United States? Who was its best-known leader?

3. Have you ever participated in a boycott? If so, do you believe the boycott achieved its goal? If it failed, why did it?

4. As a corporate public relations director, what actions might you recommend to top management in order to establish your company's public image as an environmentally responsible organization?

5. How did the 3M Company attack its pollution problem?

6. How do corporate public relations and marketing public relations differ? How does marketing public relations function?

7. Do you approve or disapprove of tobacco and beer companies' sponsorships of sporting events in the social environment of the 1990s? Why?

8. What complaints do corporate executives and business reporters have against each other?

9. Explain the double role of public relations practitioners in the relationship between companies and the news media.

10. How did the Denny's restaurant chain respond to charges of bias against African American customers?

SUGGESTED READINGS

"Are Communicators the Cause or the Solution to the Environmental Dilemma?" *Communication World,* February 1991, pp. 13–25. Various perspectives on the role of public relations spokespersons in the debate about the environment.

Barr, John M. "Maximizing the Value of Sponsorships." *Public Relations Journal,* April 1993, pp. 30–31.

Bird, Laura. "Denny's TV Ad Seeks to Mend Bias Image." *Wall Street Journal,* June 21, 1993, p. B6. Restaurant chain's response to discrimination charges.

Bird, Laura. "Olympic Sponsorship Too Pricey for Some." *Wall Street Journal,* June 28, 1993, p. B6.

Davids, Meryl. "How Now, IR?" *Public Relations Journal,* April 1989, pp. 15–19. Investor relations.

"Employee Communication in the 1990s: Challenges in an Era of Corporate Change." *Communication World,* September 1993, p. 33. Roundtable discussion of experts.

Foehrenbach, Julie, and Goldfarb, Steve. "Employee Communication in the '90s." *Communication World,* May–June 1990, pp. 101–106.

Grunig, James E., editor. *Excellence in Public Relations and Communication Management.* Hillsdale, NJ: Lawrence Erlbaum, 1992. A series of essays and research studies dealing with how organizations approach communications and public relations.

Hauss, Deborah. "Giving Employees Bad News: How to Minimize the Damage." *Public Relations Journal,* December 1993, pp. 18–23.

Hayes, Arthur, and Pereira, Joseph. "Facing a Boycott, Many Companies Bend." *Wall Street Journal,* November 8, 1990, p. B1.

Heger, Kyle. "Exploring the Inner Space of Employee Communication." *Communication World,* May 1993, pp. 28–31.

Howard, Carole M. "Five Principles of Integrated Marketing." *Public Relations Quarterly,* Fall 1993, pp. 35–36.

"Implants and the Press." *Wall Street Journal,* January 27, 1992, p. A14. Editorial about Dow Corning's media relationships in the controversy about the safety of breast implants.

"It's a Whole New World of Internal Communication." *Communication World,* December 1990, pp. 13–55. Special issue devoted to employee communications.

Kleiner, Art. "Beyond Advertising: Marketers Find New Credibility Promoting Their Products as News." *Utne Reader,* January/February 1992, pp. 61–63.

Marston, Robert. "CEOs Are a Breed Apart." *Public Relations Quarterly,* Fall 1993, pp. 29–33. Working with top executives.

McCathrin, Zoe. "Beyond Employee Publications: Making the Personal Connection." *Public Relations Journal,* July 1989, pp. 14–20.

McCauley, Kevin. "Dow Corning Fumbles PR in Breast Implant Crisis." *O'Dwyer's PR Services Report,* March 1992, pp. 1, 8, 10–11.

McGoon, Cliff. "Still Searching for Excellence." *Communication World,* October 1989, pp. 20–22. Results of research showing what types of organizations have excellent public relations.

Murray, Kathleen. "The Unfortunate Side Effects of Diversity Training." New York *Times,* August 1, 1993, p. F5.

Norton, Erle. "Pro Volleyball Sponsors Enjoy the Beach Life." *Wall Street Journal,* September 1, 1993, pp. B1, B7.

Ramirez, Anthony. "From Coffee to Tobacco, Boycotts Are a Growth Industry." New York *Times,* June 3, 1990, p. E1.

Ruffenach, Glenn. "Visa to Sponsor Atlanta as Well as the Olympics." *Wall Street Journal,* January 11, 1993, p. B1.

Shellenbarger, Sue. "Work-Force Study Finds Loyalty Is Weak, Divisions of Race and Gender Are Deep." *Wall Street Journal,* September 3, 1993, pp. B1, B5.

Sims, Calvin. "The Politics of Dealing With the Threat of Boycott." New York *Times,* March 14, 1993, p. E2.

Skolnik, Rayna. "A Full Plate: Consumer Concerns Challenge Food and Beverage Practitioners." *Public Relations Journal,* October 1993, pp. 24–27, 34–35.

Smith, Randolph B. "Environmentalists, State Officers See Red as Firms Rush to Market 'Green' Products." *Wall Street Journal,* March 13, 1990, p. B1.

Stern, Gary M. "Candor: The New Byword in Internal Communication." *Communication World,* September 1993, pp. 37–40.

Theus, Kathryn T. "Organizational Response to Media Reporting." *Public Relations Review,* Winter 1988, pp. 45–57. Media relations.

"Top Executives Weigh Media's Fairness." *Wall Street Journal,* February 11, 1993, p. B1. A roundup of quotes from CEOs about media performance.

Webster, Philip J. "Strategic Corporate Public Relations: What's the Bottom Line?" *Public Relations Journal,* February 1990, pp. 18–21.

15

Public Affairs and Government

P R E V I E W In this chapter, the objective is to provide an understanding of the activities performed by public affairs specialists in business and government, and to show the role of public relations in political campaigning.

Topics covered in the chapter include:

- Corporate citizenship

- Government relations

- Lobbying

- Political action committees

- Public affairs in government

- White House public relations

- State and municipal information services

- Public relations and political campaigns

"Corporate citizenship" is a basic tenet of business and industry for several reasons.

First, many business executives have realized that the only way to stem the tide of government regulation is to take the initiative and voluntarily exercise a sense of social responsibility. Indeed, history shows that business has been regulated in direct proportion to its social abuses.

The so-called robber barons of the late nineteenth century exploited labor and resources, generating considerable regulation of railway, utility, oil, and other companies (see Chapter 3). In more recent times industry's failure to solve many of the environmental problems caused by manufacturing generated more public demands for government regulation. One result was the creation of the Environmental Protection Agency (EPA).

The second reason for the rise of corporate citizenship is the realization by business and industry that they can survive and prosper only in a stable society that provides safety, security, and economic well-being for its citizens. Thus it is to the advantage of business to help find solutions to a number of societal problems. Such assistance not only improves the quality of life but creates a reservoir of public support for business and industry.

Third, corporate citizenship makes good sense from the standpoint of enhancing a company's reputation and its ability to market goods and services. A survey conducted by Opinion Research Corporation for *Fortune* magazine, for example, showed that 89 percent of adults said a company's reputation often determined what products they bought. *California Business,* commenting on the survey, added, "Companies involved in social issues are considered more sensitive to their customers."

With this thought in mind, companies in recent years have undertaken a variety of projects under the rubric of public affairs and community relations. Some examples:

■ Coors Brewing Company committed $40 million over a five-year period with a goal of reaching 500,000 adults with literacy services. It is estimated that 27 million U.S. adults are functionally illiterate.

■ Dayton-Hudson Corporation, a Minneapolis-based retailer, conducted a "Child Care Aware" program to help educate parents about quality child care and how to find it. The program included in-store information booths, distribution of 1.7 million brochures, and a toll-free national hotline.

■ Liz Claiborne, the apparel manufacturer, commissioned leading American women artists to create works of public art to address issues of concern to women. In San Francisco, for example, six artists created a public service campaign on the issue of domestic violence. The company also funded a domestic violence hotline.

■ Arby's restaurant chain set up a "Neighbors in Need" program with local social service groups to give families down on their luck two meals a day for one month. Through its various franchises, the chain provided more than 670,000 meals to families in need.

■ Lenscrafters, in association with Lions Clubs International, sponsored a program in England to recycle eye glasses for distribution to underprivileged families in developing nations. More than 50,000 pairs of glasses were collected.

Corporate public affairs specialists engage in a wide range of activities that foster cooperation and interaction at the community and government levels.

A survey by the Public Affairs Research Group at the Boston University School of Management, for example, indicates that the top four activities are (1) community relations, (2) government relations, (3) corporate contributions, and (4) media relations.

The following sections describe in detail the role corporations play in the areas of (1) community relations, (2) philanthropy, (3) government relations, (4) lobbying, and (5) political contributions.

COMMUNITY RELATIONS

A business slogan says, "Think globally, act locally." An important part of public affairs consists of community relations, particularly in those towns and cities where the company maintains an office, retail outlets, or a manufacturing facility.

Because a corporation relies heavily on local governments for construction permits, changes in zoning laws, and even tax concessions, a good working relationship with city hall and various community groups is important. A community relations program also helps in the recruitment of employees and gives the company an influential voice in community affairs.

Public affairs specialists often serve as representatives of their companies on various community boards, task forces, and commissions. They may be on the mayor's economic advisory council, a task force studying the redevelopment of the downtown area, or a county commission wrestling with the problem of an inadequate mass transit system. In addition, public affairs specialists are members of key civic clubs, serve on boards of nonprofit agencies, and are usually found at any fund-raising dinner of a local politician.

The purpose of this activity is to develop a dialogue between the company and the community. Although the public affairs personnel are responsible for presenting the company's viewpoint, they also fulfill a valuable function by listening and monitoring emerging issues. In this way, they can inform management about any public or governmental concerns that directly or indirectly affect the company.

Environmental concerns, for example, tend to require a great deal of community relations work in the 1990s. Bayer Australia, for example, acquired a chemical plant near Wyong, New South Wales, which had $2.5 million of environmental protection and safety systems. However, a local residents' action group was concerned about the effect of the plant's operation on sensitive local wetlands and filed a lawsuit aginst the company.

Bayer believed the problem was one of misinformation, so it began a community relations campaign to explain how its operations were environmentally sound. Communication tools included formation of an employee advisory committee, a com-

PRESERVATION
PLAN ON IT

Planning on restoring a house, saving a landmark, reviving your neighborhood?

No matter what your plans, gain a wealth of experience and help preserve our historic and architectural heritage. Join the National Trust for Historic Preservation and support preservation efforts in your community.

Make preservation a blueprint for the future.

Write:

**National Trust for Historic Preservation
Department PA
1785 Massachusetts Ave., N.W.
Washington, D.C. 20036**

FIGURE 15.1
Preserving landmarks and restoring buildings is a growing concern in the United States, for which the National Trust for Historic Preservation is a focal point. This advertisement arouses public interest and solicits memberships.

munity newsletter, a video explaining how the plant operated, and plant tours for local media, community leaders, and government officials. The result was improved community relations and a better understanding of the plant's operation.

BP Lima Chemicals faced a similar environmental problem at its plant in Lima, Ohio. The company needed to earn public confidence and U.S. Environmental Protection Agency (EPA) approval to continue disposing of waste in underground wells. Failure to gain approval would cause the closing of the plant and the loss of 600 jobs.

Since the EPA had expressed concern about the geology of the Lima area and whether deep wells would prevent the wastes from spreading, BP volunteered to drill a $4 million test well to obtain geologic data. On another level, however, it was necessary to generate public support and understanding of the project.

BP's education program included video and print descriptions of the deep well construction and technology. Specific communication tools included (1) a slide presentation for the BP Lima Speakers' Bureau, (2) plant tours, (3) meetings with concerned groups and elected officials, and (4) a public exhibit showing the geology of the Lima area. A popular part of the exhibit was a tour down the test well.

A public hearing on the deep well disposal program was attended by 350 people, including representatives of the community and business leaders. EPA, considering the scientific data and public support, approved the company's petition.

Responding quickly to environmental concerns is only one dimension of community relations. Another is good citizenship and making the community a better place to live. Syntex Corporation in Palo Alto, California, maintains an art gallery for the community. Allis-Chalmers provides construction equipment to help build youth and community centers. Merrill Lynch supports productions of operas and other fine arts events.

In recent years, a large number of corporations have also become more involved in education by "adopting" a local school and providing resources no longer provided by tax funds. Other corporations traditionally sponsor community festivals and celebrations.

Japanese-owned firms in American communities also are becoming increasingly involved in community relations as part of good citizenship. They are reacting to polls that show 25 percent of the U.S. population have a "generally negative" feeling toward Japan and its economic clout.

In many ways, the problem is cross-cultural. In Japan, companies think they are contributing to the community by creating jobs and paying taxes. Tsutomu Karino, executive director of the Japanese Chamber of Commerce and Industry, told *O'Dwyer's PR Services Report,* "It is a different way in the U.S.; a corporation plays two roles. It produces a product or service with the goal of making money and is also supposed to support community activities. . . . Americans expect more from their employers."

The Japanese Chamber of Commerce and Industry of New York, representing 320 top Japanese firms operating in the United States, has sought to counter some of these cross-cultural problems by producing a community relations handbook for local managers. The handbook encourages Japanese firms to:

■ Include mention of your community involvement program in company publications distributed externally.

■ Link philanthropy to involvement; create a fund to contribute to the organizations your employees work for.

■ Create corporate volunteer pins, caps, T-shirts, and emblems to be used in all volunteer activities.

The ideas seem to be catching on. Hitachi America Ltd. in Tarrytown, New York, funds a $20,000 college scholarship, finances a teacher-exchange program with Japan, and operates a local homework hotline to help high school students. Fujitsu-America,

---

COMMUNITY RELATIONS LEADS THE BIG MAC ATTACK

McDonald's Corporation used a program of community relations to convince a Boston zoning board that it should approve a new restaurant across the street from historic Faneuil Hall.

To counter the opposition of competing restaurants and preservation groups, McDonald's made a concentrated effort to contact area residents and tell them how the fast-food chain would be a "good neighbor."

This included (1) sponsorship of a youth athletic team, (2) free beverages for senior citizens, (3) a daily sweep-up of the neighborhood, (4) sponsorship of school programs on issues such as ecology and drug awareness, and (5) the possibility of grants from Ronald McDonald Children's Charities.

When the zoning board met, McDonald's presented a petition for the restaurant signed by 500 area residents. In addition, more than 50 supporters attended the meeting.

The zoning board gave the building permit.

Inc., in Santa Clara, California, is the primary sponsor of the Cable Car Classic Basketball Tournament, a national invitational hosted by the University of Santa Clara.

CORPORATE PHILANTHROPY

Another area of public affairs, which often overlaps community relations, is corporate donations.

In 1992, American companies and their foundations contributed $6 billion to charitable organizations, according to statistics compiled by the American Association of Fund-Raising Counsel (AAFRC). This amount represented 4.8 percent of the $124.3 billion given to charitable organizations during the year (see Chapter 18).

Although no breakdown of categories is provided by the AAFRC, a Conference Board report based on a survey of more than 400 major firms shows that education gets the lion's share of corporate donations. In 1992, for example, about a third of the corporate giving ($2.2 billion) was to colleges and universities. Other areas of giving, in descending order, are health and human services, civic and community activities, and culture and art.

The rationale for giving has been summarized by Frank Saunders, vice president for corporate relations of Philip Morris, Inc. He stated:

Corporate executives speak of putting something back into the community, improving the quality of life for employees, attracting prospective employees, practicing corporate citizenship—what boils down to enlightened self-interest. Business doesn't get anything tangible or real that you can put in your pocket and walk away with. This is a way that corporations make friends.

The idea of "enlightened self-interest" means that corporations formulate specific policies regarding the kinds of charitable organizations they will support. In other words, they select forms of philanthropic giving that assist company goals and objectives.

Hewlett-Packard, for example, is a manufacturer of computers, medical equipment, and test equipment. Product gifts account for most of its philanthropy. The company's philosophy is simply stated: "HP giving to college and universities meets university needs for products while attracting highly skilled workers to the industries we support."

On the other hand, Philip Morris uses philanthropy for constituency building and generating favorable perceptions among opinion leaders. The giant beer, tobacco, and food conglomerate donated more than $17 million in one recent year to schools, hospitals, cultural organizations, and charity groups. Many of these funds, activist critics say, were targeted to minority organizations that might help defeat tax and antismoking bills. In other words, corporate giving is based on where there might be political benefit.

Although cash grants and equipment are the most popular methods of corporate philanthropy, many companies have additional programs that get employees involved. A widely used technique is matching funds; for every dollar an employee gives to an organization, the corporation matches it. The matching gift program of Mobil Corporation constituted more than 30 percent of the $13.7 million that was given away.

Corporations also encourage employees to work with charitable groups, either on company time or after work hours. American Express estimates that 25 to 50 percent of its 83,000 U.S. workers do some kind of volunteer work. If such work is done on the employee's time, American Express and other firms say this is considered when the employee is up for a promotion. Other companies, such as Ryder System, "loan out" executives for up to a year to groups like the National Urban League.

Corporate philanthropy does have its limitations. Contributions can generate a reservoir of public support, but they are not a substitute for corporate performance in other areas.

David Finn, a founder of the Ruder Finn public relations firm, said in a speech at Columbia University:

The practical risk of being dishonest or deceptive in [public affairs] programs can be considerable. A consumer advocate who believes that nonreturnable containers should be banned for environmental reasons is not likely to change his mind because a major company in one of these industries subsidizes a series of marvelous films on the history of civilization or a related subject. If the advocate believes that such an expenditure is made in the hope of changing his mind, he is likely to be more vigorous than ever in his attack on the company.

Corporate philanthropy, despite a company's performance, also may come under attack from special-interest groups. This is particularly true regarding extremely emotional issues. Pro-life groups, for example, often target companies that give grants to Planned Parenthood and ask supporters to boycott the company's products.

Pioneer Hi-Bred International, a seed corn company headquartered in Iowa, cancelled its $25,000 annual gift to Planned Parenthood of Greater Iowa after a pro-life group called Rescue the Perishing started distributing leaflets to farmers asking them to boycott the company's products. The company president flatly told the *Wall Street Journal,* "We were blackmailed" but added, "You can't put the corn business at risk."

Pro-life groups had originally forced Dayton-Hudson Corporation, a department store chain, to cancel its contribution to Planned Parenthood, but the company reversed its decision after hundreds of irate customers sent in cut-up credit cards.

The Bank of America, headquartered in San Francisco, was also caught in a no-win situation when it decided to stop funding the Boy Scouts of America because of the group's refusal to admit gays. Although gay activists were pleased by the action, a storm of protest arose from other bank customers who supported the Boy Scouts. Many cancelled their accounts and encouraged others to do the same.

The bank, caught in the crossfire, first tried to explain that its corporate philanthropy policy was not to give funds to any group that discriminated. However, because of the protest, the bank then reversed itself and decided to support the Boy Scouts.

Patrick Jackson, editor of *PR Reporter,* wonders if this was a wise strategy. He wrote, "The question is first one of ethics—not easily answered on such an issue. Also, one of numbers: are there more Scout supporters . . . and homophobes than there are gays and people who oppose discrimination? More important: who is likely to take action?"

In the case of Dayton-Hudson, the numbers question was a consideration. Jackson points out studies showing that the choice movement has higher income and education levels, which ought to translate into more desirable retail customers.

If a corporation's contributions do come under fire, there are several steps to take:

■ Have the company's chief executive write opinion articles for the local newspaper.

■ Return all calls and answer letters from concerned citizens.

■ Publicly correct opponents when they misstate the company's policies.

■ Hold meetings with leaders of adversary groups.

GOVERNMENT RELATIONS

A major component of public affairs is government relations. This activity is so important that many companies, particularly in highly regulated industries, have separate departments of government relations. The reason is simple. The actions of governmental bodies at the local, state, and federal level have a major impact on how a business operates.

Government relations specialists have a number of functions: they gather information, disseminate management's views, cooperate with government on projects of mutual benefit, and motivate employees to participate in the political process.

As the eyes and ears of a business or industry, practitioners spend much time gathering and processing information. They monitor the activities of many legislative bodies and regulatory agencies to keep track of issues coming up for debate and possible vote. Such intelligence gathering enables a corporation or an industry to plan ahead and, if necessary, adjust policies or provide information that may influence the nature of government decision making.

Monitoring government takes many forms. Probably the most active presence in Washington, D.C., and many state capitals is the trade association that represents a particular industry. The Boston University survey previously mentioned showed that 67 percent of the responding companies monitored government activity in Washington through their trade associations. Second on the list were frequent trips to Washington by senior public affairs officers and corporate executives; 58 percent of the respondents said they engaged in this activity. Almost 45 percent of the responding firms reported that they also had a company office in the nation's capital.

A more recent survey by the Foundation for Public Affairs essentially confirms the Boston findings, but it also found that visits to company locations by government officials are a common activity.

Many of these visits, at the expense of the corporate host, are not without controversy. Critics, including Common Cause, assert that legislators should not be the guests of the industries that they oversee on various congressional committees.

John Dingell (D. Mich), while chair of the House Energy and Commerce Committee, is an example. He and his wife spent six days in Florida paid for by utility and pharmaceutical interests. Other lawmakers and spouses went to England and Scotland at the expense of Pfizer, Inc., and British Petroleum Co. Lawmakers defend these "fact-finding" missions as a necessary part of doing their job.

Government relations specialists, when not hosting visiting lawmakers, spend a great amount of time disseminating information about the company's position to a variety of key publics. Spoken tactics may include an informal office visit to a government official or testimony at a public hearing. In addition, public affairs people often are called upon to give a speech or write one for a senior executive.

Written tactics may include writing letters and op-ed articles, preparing position papers, producing newsletters, and placing advocacy advertising. Although legislators are a primary audience, the Foundation for Public Affairs reports that nine of ten companies also communicate with employees on public policy issues, while another 40 percent communicate with retirees, customers, and other publics such as taxpayers and government employees.

A relatively new communication tool is the advocacy video. According to *O'Dwyer's PR Services,* "Sharp visuals, drama, and compelling dialog spoken by professionals ... is an attention grabber, cutting through the piles of position papers received by Congressmen each day."

Larry Pintak, who heads his own video firm in Washington, D.C., adds, "A five-minute video can spark interest in an issue and hook a Congressional staffer. If you send a three-inch thick document supporting your position over to a Capitol Hill office, it probably won't be read."

McDonnell Douglas used advocacy videos in its extensive campaign to convince the Bush administration that it should be allowed to sell its F-15 jets to other nations. In addition, the company's public affairs staff used union hall meetings, a grass-roots letter campaign to the president, endorsements from Missouri's congressional delegation, and newspaper editorials to hammer home the point that such a sale would avoid layoffs of 30,000 workers. During the election campaign of 1992, President Bush did announce the sale of F-15 jets to Saudi Arabia.

This is just one example of the important role that public affairs personnel play in the economic well-being of a company. A New York *Times* writer emphasized this importance thus:

Public relations executives can rightly point out that, with the cacophony of interests clamoring for attention in Washington, there is a role for professional advice on how to insure that one's message is heard. With the expanding role of Congress and the increasing complexity of government, this probably is true now more than ever. There are undoubtedly times that public relations firms can help journalists, politicians and clients.

ETHICAL GUIDELINES FOR BUSINESS PUBLIC AFFAIRS PROFESSIONALS

A. The Public Affairs Professional maintains professional relationships based on honesty and reliable information, and therefore:

1. Represents accurately his or her organization's policies on economic and political matters to government, employees, shareholders, community interests, and others.

2. Serves always as a source of reliable information, discussing the varied aspects of complex public issues within the context and constraints of the advocacy role.

3. Recognizes diverse viewpoints within the public policy process, knowing that disagreement on issues is both inevitable and healthy.

B. The Public Affairs Professional seeks to protect the integrity of the public policy process and the political system, and therefore:

1. Publicly acknowledges his or her role as a legitimate participant in the public policy process and discloses whatever work-related information the law requires.

2. Knows, respects and abides by federal and state laws that apply to lobbying and related public affairs activities.

3. Knows and respects the laws governing campaign finance and other political activities, and abides by the letter and intent of those laws.

C. The Public Affairs Professional understands the interrelation of business interests with the larger public interests, and therefore:

1. Endeavors to ensure that responsible and diverse external interests and views concerning the needs of society are considered within the corporate decision-making process.

2. Bears the responsibility for management review of public policies which may bring corporate interests into conflict with other interests.

3. Acknowledges dual obligations—to advocate the interests of his or her employer, and to preserve the openness and integrity of the democratic process.

4. Presents to his or her employer an accurate assessment of the political and social realities that may affect corporate operations.

Source: Public Affairs Council, a Washington-based organization of public affairs executives for major corporations.

Lobbying is closely aligned with governmental relations, and the distinction between the two areas often blurs. In general, government relations is a broader term that denotes a number of activities related to the monitoring of government and the dissemination of information to various publics, including elected officials.

Lobbying, on the other hand, is a more specific activity. *Webster's New World Dictionary* defines a *lobbyist* as "a person acting for a special-interest group, who tries to influence the voting on legislation or the decisions of government administrators." In other words, a lobbyist directs his or her energies to the defeat, passage, or amendment of proposed legislation and regulatory agency policies.

Lobbyists can be found at the local, state, and federal levels of government. California, for example, has about 900 registered lobbyists who represent more than 1600 special-interest groups. The interests represented in Sacramento include large corporations, business and trade groups, unions, environmental groups, local governments, nonprofit groups, school districts, and members of various professional groups.

The number and variety of special interests multiply at the federal level. One directory of Washington lobbyists lists 13,500 individuals and organizations. The *Public Relations Journal* reports that more than 10,000 corporations, trade groups, labor unions, and special-interest groups have representatives in Washington. The interests represented include virtually the entire spectrum of U.S. business, educational, religious, local, national, and international pursuits.

The diversity of groups lobbying in Washington to influence legislation can be illustrated with President Clinton's proposal for an energy tax. It was a tax on all forms of energy consumption, but was considerably watered down by concessions to various business and trade groups that lobbied hard for exemptions from the tax.

Michael Wines, a reporter for the New York *Times,* wrote that the Clinton administration gave up on enacting a tax on the heat content of fuels

. . . after the proposed tax on coal was lowered; after aluminum smelters and barge operators got a break; after farmers and city dwellers won exemption for the diesel that heats homes and runs combines; after oil refiners and gas and electric companies moved the tax off their backs and onto consumers; after grain merchants won and then lost a battle to exempt ethanol; after chemical and glass makers secured protection against untaxed foreign competitors. . . .

And how was all this accomplished? According to the New York *Times,* lobbyists launched a "juggernaut" against the tax. It continued, "Powered by satellite feeds and talk radio and opinion polls and a blizzard of newspaper advertisements, they had whipped up a froth of outrage over the tax. Mass mailings urged citizens to complain to Congress, and lobbyists offered a toll-free number to make it painless."

Not everyone working on this campaign, however, was an officially recognized lobbyist. Federal law requires registration only by paid lobbyists whose "principal purpose" is to influence the course of legislation in Congress. It doesn't cover executive branch "lobbying," and the courts have ruled that registration only applies to lobbying of lawmakers themselves, not congressional staffers.

In other words, the law is somewhat toothless in its application. The General Accounting Office, for example, found that nearly three-fourths of the individuals listed in one Washington directory of lobbyists were not registered. Consequently Congress, in 1993, considered new legislation about lobbyists—which, of course, became the target of another lobbying campaign by various interests.

The reality is that registered lobbyists represent only a small percentage of those who work in the field. A large number of public relations and public affairs specialists who support lobbying activity by handling grass-roots campaigns, building coalitions, and disseminating information to the media are not formally registered as lobbyists.

Burson-Marsteller and Hill and Knowlton, the largest public relations firms in Washington, are examples. Each firm has more than 125 employees, but only a few are registered lobbyists. The majority of the personnel conduct a broad range of public relations efforts to disseminate background information on issues and generate public support for a particular client's viewpoint.

Peter Carlson, in an extensive Washington *Post* article, "The Image Maker," described the activities of public relations people and lobbyists as follows:

They send out press releases and audio releases and video press releases. They teach their clients how to appear on television without looking foolish and how to appear before congressional committee without looking foolish. They write speeches and brochures and congressional testimony. They ghostwrite editorials and op-ed pieces and then try to persuade newspaper editors to run them. They lobby Congress and they run grass-roots campaigns to persuade constituents to bombard Congress with letters. They stage press conferences and other media events. And they serve as the Washington equivalent of matchmakers, introducing their clients to the movers and shakers of government and the media.

THE NATURE OF LOBBYING

Although the public stereotypes a lobbyist as a fast-talking person twisting an elected official's arm to get special concessions, the reality is quite different.

Today's lobbyist, who may be fully employed by one industry or represent a variety of clients, is often a quiet-spoken, well-educated man or woman armed with statistics and research reports.

Robert Gray, former head of Hill and Knowlton's Washington office and a public affairs expert for 30 years, adds, "Lobbying is no longer a booze and buddies business. It's presenting honest facts and convincing Congress that your side has more merit than the other." He rejects lobbying as being simply "influence peddling and button-holing" top administration officials.

Although the public has the perception that lobbying is done only by big business, Gray correctly points out that a variety of special interests also do it. These may include such groups as the Sierra Club, Mothers Against Drunk Driving, National Association of Social Workers, American Civil Liberties Union, and the American Federation of Labor. Even the American Society of Plastic and Reconstructive Surgeons hired a Washington public relations firm in their battle against restrictions on breast implants.

Lobbying, quite literally, is an activity in which widely diverse groups and organizations engage as an exercise of free speech and representation in the marketplace of ideas. Lobbyists often balance each other and work toward legislative compromises that not only benefit their self-interests but society as a whole.

The clash between competing interests, all claiming the "public interest," must be weighed by legislators and regulatory personnel before a vote is taken or a decision made. Lobbyists, as *Time* magazine puts it, "do serve a useful purpose by showing busy legislators the virtues and pitfalls of complex legislation."

FIGURE 15.2
Stimulating public opinion for or against a pending piece of legislation is a specialized form of public relations work. This advertisement by a Washington, D.C., consulting firm lists ways in which the company generates grassroots response to impress lawmakers.

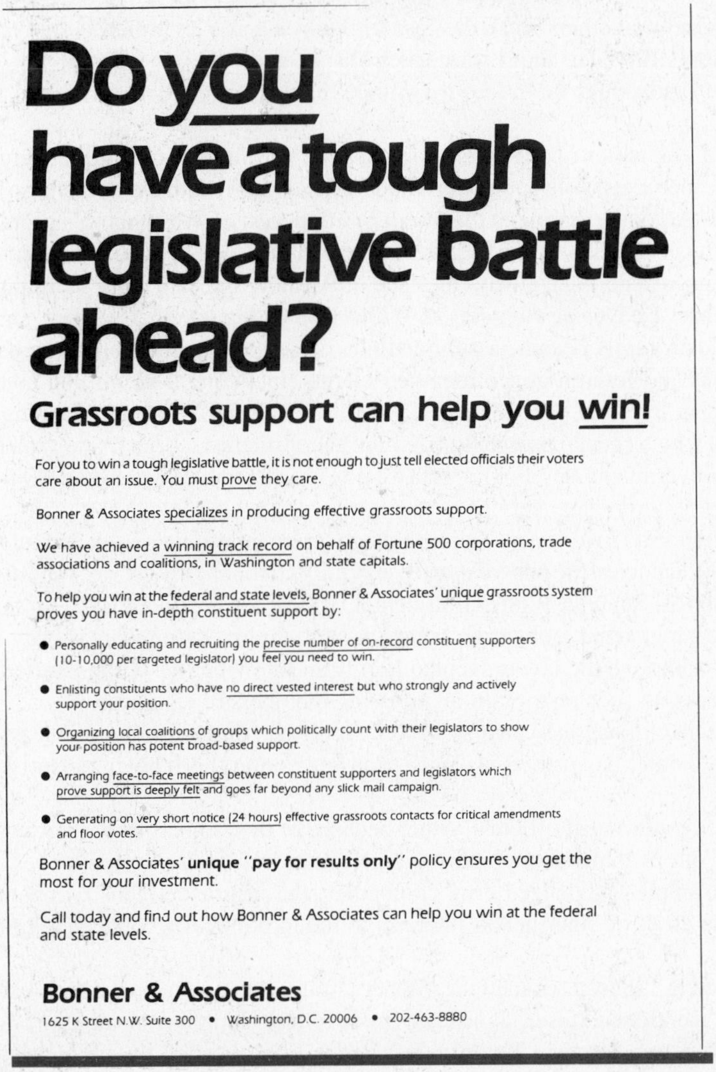

A classic conflict is the debate between saving jobs and improving the environment. A coalition of environmental groups constantly lobbies Congress for tougher legislation to clean up industrial pollution or protect endangered species. Simultaneously, local communities and unions often argue that the proposed legislation would mean the loss of jobs and economic chaos.

Environmental groups argue the "public interest"; so do opposing groups. Is it in the "public interest," they ask, to throw thousands of people out of work or to legislate so many restrictions on the manufacture of a product that it becomes more expensive to the average consumer? The answer, quite often, depends on whether the person is a steel worker, a logger, a consumer, or a member of the World Wildlife Federation.

THE PROBLEM OF "INFLUENCE PEDDLING"

Although Gray and others make the case for lobbying as a legitimate activity, deep public suspicion still exists about former legislators and officials who capitalize on their connections and charge large fees for doing what is commonly described as "influence peddling."

Indeed, the roster of registered lobbyists in Washington includes a virtual "who's who" of former legislators and government officials from both Democratic and Republican parties. A good example is the Wexler Group, one of Washington's premier lobbying firms. It is headed by Anne Wexler, a White House aide in the Carter administration.

"Influence peddling," always an issue in Washington, came into sharp public focus when Michael Deaver quit his job as White House deputy chief of staff for President Reagan and promptly became a public affairs consultant. In short order, he had a list of corporations and foreign governments as clients, including a $1 million contract with South Korean interests. Although he claimed to be doing "strategic planning," Deaver was indicted by a special prosecutor for conflict of interest, perjury, and violation of the Ethics in Government Act. Found guilty, he was ordered to pay a $100,000 fine and do 1500 hours of community service.

The Ethics in Government Act forbids government officials from actively lobbying their former agencies for one year after leaving office, but critics say it has little or no impact. John H. Sununu, White House chief of staff for President Bush, is an example. He became a registered lobbyist on behalf of W.R. Grace & Company shortly after leaving office. Although the law prevented him from lobbying the White House for a year, the law places no such restriction on lobbying members of Congress.

Members of Congress can also become lobbyists immediately upon leaving office. Congress, to date, has passed no legislation restricting the lobbying efforts of former legislators.

Former government officials, either because of their expertise or their connections, are sought out as lobbyists by many groups. President Clinton's goal to reform health care, for example, galvanized drug companies, the insurance industry, hospitals, doctors, and an array of other health interests to retain politically connected lobbyists and lawyers.

Johnson & Johnson retained the Wexler Group. It just so happens that Anne Wexler, previously mentioned, raised significant funds for the Clinton campaign. In addition, the firm employs two former Clinton aides. Bruce Fried headed the Clinton campaign's health advisory group and was a member of the health transition team. Betsey Wright was Clinton's chief of staff when he was governor of Arkansas.

Another drug company, SmithKline Beecham, hired Patson, Boggs, & Blow to represent it on childhood-vaccine issues. The firm also happens to be the former home of Ron Brown, who became Secretary of Commerce in the Clinton administration.

Such connections give the press and the public an uneasy feeling that "influence peddling" is alive and well in the nation's capital. It also gives credence to the cliché, "It's not what you know, but who you know." In a 1993 *Wall Street Journal*/NBC News poll, 26 percent of those surveyed said reducing the influence of lobbyists and campaign contributions should be one of the federal government's top priorities. (Lobbying in the United States for foreign governments is discussed in Chapter 16, "International Public Relations.")

POLITICAL ACTION COMMITTEES

A specialized area of public affairs and lobbying is the organization and administration of political action committees, commonly known as PACs. They were created as a labor union mechanism during the 1930s, but campaign finance reforms in the 1970s, which prohibited corporate contributions to candidates for federal elections, made PACs an effective alternative.

Today, there are more than 4000 PACs organized by labor, business, trade groups, professional societies, and single-issue groups. Under the law, a PAC can give a maximum of $5000 to a federal candidate in a primary election and another $5000 for the general election, a maximum of $10,000 total.

This doesn't sound like much, but a corporation with multiple plant sites and operations may have a score of individual PACs. In addition, each local of a national labor union may have its own PAC. During the 1991–92 election cycle, PACs of all kinds contributed $180.5 million to support congressional candidates, or about 27 percent of the $658.5 million raised by all the candidates.

Labor PACs gave $43 million, about 23 percent of all PAC donations. Finance, insurance, and real estate interests gave $29 million, about 15 percent of all PAC giving. The health industry, which has received a lot of attention because of President Clinton's health reform agenda, contributed $14.8 million through PACs.

This money comes from employees or members of organizations. Corporations encourage employees (particularly managers) to contribute through payroll deduction or by writing an annual check. The National Association of Business Political Action Committees estimates that the average employee donation is less than $100 a year. Union members usually contribute through their local union. Professionals such as architects, doctors, and lawyers use PACs organized by their membership societies.

PACs are a major way of funding politics, particularly at the federal level. A major part of their importance is the high cost of campaigning. During the 1992 elections, for example, 23 Democrats and 7 Republicans spent more than $1 million each to win seats in the U.S. Congress. The top spender was Majority Leader Richard Gephardt (D) of Missouri who spent $3.1 million, according to Federal Election Commission records.

Incumbents, in particular, are recipients of PAC funds. Rep. John Oliver (D-Mass) received $343,000 from labor PACs, or 49 percent of his total receipts. Majority Whip David Bonior (D-Mich) received $283,000, or 22 percent of all the funds he raised.

Such dependence on PAC money has stirred controversy and calls for campaign finance reform. Many citizens' groups believe that vested interests exercise undue influence on legislation and elected representatives by making substantial political contributions. The Association of Trial Lawyers of America PAC, for example, gave $2.3 million in 1992 in an effort to fend off tort reform legislation. And the United Parcel Service PAC gave $1.4 million to key legislators as a way of defending its domination of the lucrative consumer shipping business.

Defenders of PACs say, however, that the threat of undue influence is overrated. They contend that there are so many PACs, each with its own special interests, that they cancel each other out. They also say that no PAC sector, except perhaps labor, is big enough to have a major impact on Congress. Health industry PACs, for example, give only 7.8 percent of all PAC funding. And finally, defenders say PAC contributions simply ensure that a group will be able to express its free speech rights and present its case to legislators.

Nevertheless, campaign finance reform remains a topic of debate in Washington. The objectives are to (1) reduce the role of special interests in the political process, (2) reduce the amount of money candidates spend, and (3) make elections more competitive. Such legislation, no doubt, would also reduce the amount of contributions by PACs. One proposed bill would reduce the maximum contribution from $5,000 to $1,000.

Campaign finance reform is also subject to lobbying. Many members of Congress, who are dependent on PAC funds, find it difficult to give up this source of money. In addition, organizations like the National Association of Broadcasters are lobbying hard to make sure no new legislation gives political candidates free time on the airwaves instead of paying for advertising.

PUBLIC AFFAIRS IN GOVERNMENT

Since the time of the ancient Egyptians 5000 years ago, governments have always engaged in what is known in the twentieth century as public information, public relations, and public affairs.

The Rosetta Stone, discovered by Napoleon's troops and used by scholars as the key to understanding Egyptian hieroglyphics, turned out to be a publicity release for the reign of Ptolemy V. Julius Caesar was known in his day as a master of staged events in which his army's entrances into Rome after successful battles were highly orchestrated.

There has always been a need for government communications, if for no other reason than to inform citizens of the services available and the manner in which they may be used. In a democracy, public information is crucial if citizens are to make intelligent judgments about the policies and activities of their elected representatives. Through information it is hoped that citizens will have the necessary background to participate fully in the formation of government policies.

The objectives of government information efforts have been summarized by William Ragan, former director of public affairs for the United States Civil Service Commission:

1. Inform the public about the public's business. In other words, communicate the work of government agencies.

2. Improve the effectiveness of agency operations through appropriate public information techniques. In other words, explain agency programs so that citizens understand and can take actions necessary to benefit from them.

3. Provide feedback to government administrators so that programs and policies can be modified, amended, or continued.

4. Advise management on how best to communicate a decision or a program to the widest number of citizens.

5. Serve as an ombudsman. Represent the public and listen to its representatives. Make sure that individual problems of the taxpayer are satisfactorily solved.

6. Educate administrators and bureaucrats about the role of the mass media and how to work with media representatives.

"PUBLIC INFORMATION" VERSUS "PUBLIC RELATIONS"

Although many of the objectives described by Ragan would be considered appropriate goals in almost any field of public relations, in government such activities are never referred to as "public relations." Instead, various euphemisms are used. The most common titles are (1) public information officer, (2) director of public affairs, (3) press secretary, (4) administrative aide, and (5) government program analyst.

In addition, government agencies do not have departments of public relations. Instead, the FBI has an External Affairs Division; the Interstate Commerce Commission has an Office of Communications and Consumer Affairs; and the Environmental Protection Agency has an Office of Public Awareness. The military services usually have Offices of Public Affairs.

Such euphemisms serve to reconcile two essentially contradictory facts: (1) the government needs to inform its citizens and (2) it is against the law to use appropriated money for the employment of "publicity experts."

Congress, as early as 1913, saw a potential danger in executive branch agencies' spending taxpayer dollars to sway the American public to support programs of various administrations. Consequently, the Gillett Amendment (Section 3107 of Title V of the United States Code) was passed; it stated, "Appropriated funds may not be used to pay a publicity expert unless specifically appropriated for that purpose." The law was reinforced in 1919 with prohibition of the use of any appropriations for services, messages, or publications designed to influence a member of Congress. Another law that year required executive agencies to utilize the U.S. Government Printing Office so that publications could be more closely monitored than in the past. Restrictions also prohibit executive departments from mailing any material to the public without a specific request.

Congress clearly was attempting to limit the authority of the executive branch to spend taxpayer money on public relations efforts to gain support for pet projects of the president. Some presidents chafed at this, but others thought it was entirely proper that the government should not be in the business of propagandizing the taxpayers. President Eisenhower, for example, ordered all executive branch agencies to dispense with field office information activity. The only problem was the great number of public and press requests for information. Consequently, information offices lost their titles but continued their dissemination functions under such titles as "technical liaison officers" for the Corps of Engineers and "assistant to the director" in the Bureau of Reclamation.

In 1972, alarmed by Richard Nixon's expansion of the White House communications staff, Congress reaffirmed prior legislation by stating that no part of any appropriation bill could be used for publicity or propaganda purposes designed to support or defeat legislation before Congress.

Although most citizens would agree that government should not use tax money to persuade the public of the merits or demerits of a particular bill or program, there is a thin line between merely providing information and using information as a lobbying tool.

If a public affairs officer for the Pentagon testifies about the number of surface-to-air missiles deployed by Iraq or Libya, does this constitute information or an attempt to influence congressional appropriations? Or, to use another example, is a speech by the Surgeon General about the dangers of passive smoking only information or support of legislation that would ban cigarette smoking from all federal buildings?

While ascertaining the difference between "public relations" and "public information" may be an interesting semantic game, the fact remains that the terms *public relations* and *publicity* are seldom used by a government agency.

SCOPE OF FEDERAL GOVERNMENT INFORMATION

The U.S. government is often said to be the world's premier collector of information. It is also maintained, without much disagreement, that the federal government is one of the world's great disseminators of information.

Ascertaining the exact size of the government's "public relations" efforts is like trying to guess the number of jelly beans in a large jar. One of the major difficulties is coming up with a standard definition of what constitutes "public affairs" activity.

The General Accounting Office (GAO) once estimated that $2.3 billion is probably spent each year by federal agencies and the White House. According to the GAO, $337 million was spent on "public affairs" and another $100 million on "congressional affairs." An estimated $1.9 billion went into a catch-all category, "public affairs-related activities."

Other studies have estimated that between 10,000 and 12,000 federal employees are engaged in what can be called "public relations" work. The Department of Defense and the Department of Agriculture each have about 1000 people working in public affairs/information jobs.

The size and scope of governmental information efforts are given in other ways. At last count, there were about 12,000 government publications ranging from a monthly law enforcement magazine published by the FBI to a Department of Agriculture pam-

FIGURE 15.3
The U.S. government publishes huge amounts of consumer information, much of it free, and promotes its distribution with advertisements. This example appeared in the Washington *Post* weekly edition.

phlet titled, "Making Pickles and Relishes at Home." The armed services have so many magazines, newsletters, and pamphlets that, says one media reporter, it would take a truck to deliver everything on the list. Another writer, probably on a slow news day, estimated that the federal government's production of everything from news releases to magazines would fill four Washington Monuments every year.

This mass of paper, of course, does not include the films and videos the government produces every year. The government's output makes the efforts of Hollywood studios puny by comparison, but few government films are blockbusters. Most are produced by the Department of Defense and used in training. Other films and videos are shown primarily to school and civic groups.

Advertising is another governmental activity. Federal agencies spend several hundred million dollars a year on public service advertising, primarily to promote military recruitment, government health services, and the U.S. Postal Service. In a new approach to recruiting, the U.S. Navy purchased advertising spots on the MTV cable TV music channel.

Government Agencies Public information specialists and public affairs officers engage in tasks common to the public relations department of a nongovernmental organization. They typically answer press and public inquiries, write news releases, work on newsletters, prepare speeches for top officials, and oversee the production of brochures. Senior-level public affairs specialists also counsel top management about communication strategies.

One of the longest running public relations efforts has been the preparation and distribution of "hometown" releases by the military. The Fleet Home Town News Center, established during World War II, sends news releases about the promotions and transfers of U.S. Navy personnel (including the Marine Corps and the Coast Guard) to their hometown media. In 1992, more than 1 million releases were written and distributed.

Another long-term effort has been the FBI's legendary list of the ten most-wanted fugitives. Initiated in 1950, the list immediately captured the attention of the public and the media. Over the years, the list has led to the apprehension of more than 400 fugitives.

Other federal agencies also conduct public relations programs to inform citizens. Some examples include (1) the U.S. Census Bureau promoting participation in the 1990 census, (2) the Immigration and Naturalization Service explaining a new law to employers and a multilingual pool of illegal immigrants, (3) the Food and Drug Administration (FDA) using video news releases to inform the public about health issues, and (4) the Environmental Protection Agency (EPA) communicating new regulatory information to companies responsible for underground storage of chemicals. And every year, at income tax time, the Internal Revenue Service distributes news releases loaded with graphics to help people fill out their tax forms.

Government agencies in other nations conduct similar types of information programs. The British government, for example, spends about $20 million annually on a public information campaign about AIDS awareness and prevention.

Congressional Efforts   Although the expenses of Congress are not included in the GAO study, one report in the mid-1980s estimated that the House spent $68 million and the Senate $43 million on a barrage of news releases, newsletters, recordings, brochures, taped radio interviews, and videotapes—all designed to inform voters back home about the operations of Congress.

Critics complain that most of the materials are designed for self-promotion and have little value, but the legislators say that voters have a right to know what is being done on their behalf. The franking privilege (free postage) is singled out for the most criticism.

James Bennett and Thomas DiLorenzo, authors of *Official Lies: How Washington Misleads Us,* say members of Congress spent about $1 billion between 1972 and 1988 on mailing 8.74 billion pieces of mail. The late Senator John Heinz (R) of Pennsylvania sent out 15 million pieces of mail financed by taxpayers in one election year.

White House Efforts   At the apex of government public relations efforts is the White House. The president receives more media attention than all the federal agencies and Congress combined. It is duly reported when the president goes jogging, tours a housing development, or gives a speech. All presidents have taken advantage of the intense media interest to implement public relations strategies that would improve their popularity, generate support for programs, and explain embarrassing policy decisions.

Ronald Reagan, by most accounts, is still considered the master communicator. He was extremely effective on television and was able to read a teleprompter with perfect

FIGURE 15.4
Seeking to project an image of
helpfulness to customers, the
U.S. Postal Service distributes
pamphlets describing its automated telephone information
service and urges patrons to
use it.

POSTAL ANSWER LINE

**The new U.S. Postal
Service automated
telephone information
service.**

PENALTY FOR PRIVATE
USE TO AVOID PAYMENT
OF POSTAGE, $300

Postal Customer

UNITED STATES POSTAL SERVICE
15421 GALE AVENUE
CITY OF INDUSTRY CA 91715-9996

Directory of postal consumer information.
Please keep for future reference.

September 1988

inflection. Reagan also understood the importance of symbolism and giving simple,
down-to-earth speeches that often ended with "God bless you."

Reagan's approach was the carefully packaged sound-bite and staged event. One
time, during a presidential address, Nancy Reagan "surprised" her husband with a birthday cake.

George Bush was no Ronald Reagan as a public relations figure, but he did project
enthusiasm for his job and had a friendly, but formal, working relationship with the
White House press corps. Although he took advantage of photo opportunities and gave
frequent news interviews, one media analyst said Bush's ultimate form of communication was the thank-you note. Bush also had a sense of humor, saying that he was so busy
"planting trees all over the country that I might have to open a branch office."

While Bush came across as somewhat formal and reserved, Bill Clinton's communications style is more populist. He is at home with today's information technology,
analysts say, and he makes effective use of television. Unlike Reagan, however, he often
departs from the prepared text on the teleprompter and improvises as he goes along. He
puts a high premium on the personal encounter, and he is most effective when he is talking on a one-to-one basis with an interviewer or a member of an audience.

All presidents, however, have assistance in their constant quest to be popular, sell
their policies, and be perceived as an effective leader. On every White House staff are
experts in communications strategy, media relations, and speech writing.

POST OFFICE GOES FOR OLYMPIC GOLD

The U.S. Post Office became a sponsor of the 1992 Olympics in Barcelona and also raised more than $500,000 for the U.S. Olympic Team in the process.

Public and congressional support for the sponsorship, as well as the Olympic team, was generated by a "Sign, Seal, & Deliver" program executed by Burson-Marsteller public relations.

The centerpiece of the program was the creation of a giant postcard (larger than three football fields) symbolizing America's support for its Olympic team. Individual pieces of the card were mailed to post offices nationwide to collect signatures and $1 donations. Donators were given two standard-sized postcards; one to send a personal message to Olympians during the Games and one to save as a souvenir.

The giant postcard, requiring 62,000 square yards of material, was "delivered" to Washington, D.C., and installed on the Ellipse behind the White House. It became the centerpiece for a ceremony that attracted 25,000 people, including many members of the U.S. Olympic team.

The "Sign, Seal & Deliver" program, in addition to raising funds for the Olympic team, improved the public perception of the post office and increased employee morale.

Also, a number of "advance" people plan every presidential appearance and trip in meticulous detail. They confirm that the person who heads the receiving line is politically correct and that the sound system works. They make arrangements for the press, organize the cheering crowds, select the best symbolic photo and television possibilities, and plan everything down to the minute. A good example of a timeline for a presidential visit was illustrated in Chapter 8, "Planning the Action" (p. 198).

The top public relations person in the White House is the director of communications. Several months into his presidency, and after a series of public relations blunders, Bill Clinton appointed David R. Gergen to this job, saying, "We want to improve our ability to communicate what we believe and what we're doing. Yes, we do."

Gergen, described by the New York *Times* as "the consummate Washington insider," was also a senior White House communications consultant to Nixon, Ford, and Reagan, having served the latter as director of communications in his first term. In the Clinton White House, Gergen described his job as someone who will be at "the intersection of policy, politics, and communication."

One of Gergen's first jobs was to repair relations with the White House press corps. Taking a cue from his campaign for the presidency, Clinton and his aides had originally decided that they could ignore the various constituencies in Washington and just make contact with people through access media such as radio and television talk shows.

Clinton, responding to media demands to hold a press conference, bluntly told the White House Correspondents Association, "You know why I can stiff you on the press conferences? Because Larry King liberated me by giving me to the American people directly."

What Clinton and his aides didn't realize, however, is that the Washington press corps (large metropolitan dailies and national networks) are still influential in agenda-setting and forming images on a daily basis of how people perceive the effectiveness of

Dear Fellow American,

We have put before the American people a dramatic blueprint for reforming our nation's health care system.

Now, it is up to every American to assure that this essential reform occurs. We cannot let this historic opportunity fall victim to the partisan fighting and special-interest group lobbying seen so often in our nation's capital.

The health care crisis is the greatest continuing threat to the personal security of many American families, and the economic strength of our country.

As it is, every month in this country 2 million people will lose their health care coverage. And those who currently have health insurance run the risk of losing it if they change jobs, or even if they become sick.

This summer we began to bring to an end the gridlock that has paralyzed our government in Washington, by passage of such key legislation as the Family Leave Act, National Service, Campaign Finance Reform, and our economic growth plan.

Despite the importance of these hard fought victories, health care reform is essential to continuing our efforts to bringing about meaningful change in this country.

By the end of the decade, American workers will lose $655 in income each year if health care costs continue to eat up wage increases. And, health care costs per family will double by the year 2000.

Today, we have a once-in-a-lifetime opportunity to make health care protection affordable and more secure for all Americans.

For the first time in our nation's history, we can guarantee that virtually no American family will fall through the cracks in America's health care system.

In the weeks ahead, people all across America will form their first impressions of this landmark health care proposal. And, in that time, we know that many groups will be trying hard to define the debate through "scare tactics" and misleading information.

(over, please)

If you'd like to volunteer, simply check the box on the enclosed support form. An Action Network health care organizer will get in touch with you to discuss how you'd like to help.

That brings me to my final but most important request.

I am hoping that I can count on you to send as generous a contribution as possible to support the Democratic Action Network's National Health Care Campaign.

You and I have a chance not many people get -- the chance to make history.

Democrats in other generations led America forward with Social Security, Medicare, and other far-reaching initiatives.

Now it is our responsibility to bring quality, affordable health care within the reach of each and every citizen of our great nation.

I am counting on you to personally commit yourself to achieving this goal. The National Health Care Campaign can only succeed with a genuine, personal commitment from people like you.

This endeavor deserves that kind of support -- because, measured by the dramatic changes it can create in peoples' lives and the economic health of our country, health care reform is one of the most vital efforts to shape the direction of our nation that you and I will ever undertake.

I have dedicated myself to doing everything I possibly can to see the National Health Care Campaign through to victory.

I urge you to do the same.

Sincerely,

Bill Clinton

P.S. In the upcoming months, you will hear a lot of opposing views taking issue with how we propose to solve our nation's health care problems. But, what we must remember is that the cost of doing nothing is a cost this nation cannot afford. Please act now, support the National Health Care Campaign with your contribution and, if possible, with your time.

FIGURE 15.5
President Clinton used a nationwide mass mailing of a letter to "Dear Fellow American" in the campaign for his health care reform program. The letter urged its recipients to approve the plan and to contribute volunteer time and money.

a president. Not everyone, it appeared, listened only to Larry King on CNN or tuned into C-SPAN.

Indeed, the media portrayal of Clinton as a bumbling president, who sometimes appeared to back off when opposition rose to some of his appointments and policies, seemed to dissipate after the appointment of Gergen, whom the New York *Times* called a "master of image." Dan Rather, anchor of CBS News, commented on the change when Clinton attended a summit meeting in Tokyo. Rather reported, "Every morning they had

David Gergen, left, chats with President Clinton in the Rose Garden after Clinton announced Gergen's appointment as White House communications director.

the headline they wanted, and every evening they had it on everyone's evening news. You could only marvel at it. Are they expert at manipulating coverage? Damn right."

Clinton, although now paying more attention to the national press, is also tapping grass-roots media and using the communications of the computer age. Jeff Eller, the White House director of media affairs, works constantly to get coverage in local media outside Washington.

One day, for example, Eller arranged to have the White House budget director on the Dakota radio network, Tipper Gore interviewed by eight small Florida papers, and Clinton give an informal press conference to reporters and editors of California dailies where base closings were scheduled. Clinton aides estimate that they help stage at least one major media event a day, sometimes more. In addition, press briefings and documents are constantly and instantly transmitted on computer networks like CompuServe and America Online. Despite these efforts and Clinton's energetic coast-to-coast campaigning, the Democratic party suffered a disastrous defeat in the 1994 election and gave up control of Congress to the Republicans.

Media Concern All this public relations activity on the part of the White House and other federal government agencies often is disdained by the media and other political commentators. The media constantly referred to David Gergen and others as "spin doctors," "handlers," and masters of manipulation.

The Washington *Post,* in an editorial about the Clinton administration in its early months, warned the president that his problems were "not about public relations, but about governing."

Although the editors of the Washington *Post* have a point, a *New Yorker* editorial defended the president's use of public relations. Responding to the *Post* editorial, it said, "That is certainly true if public relations means the usual round of sound-bites and photo-ops geared toward the evening news and if the tone is the usual one or relentless rah-rah."

However, the *New Yorker* editorial noted that public relations should also mean a serious, sustained airing of such issues as health-care reform and campaign-finance so the public can understand what compromises and costs are involved. The magazine continued,

... who is to say that government is not "about" (among other things, of course) public relations? Why would President Clinton work any less hard to win the consent of the governed for a set of specific proposals . . . whose purpose is to mend an ailing economy?

As for other federal agencies, Stephen Hess thinks the media concern about managing, manipulating, or controlling the news is overblown. In his book, *The Government Press Connection,* he wrote:

The hypothetical time sheet of the press officers I observed might have the following allocation: responding to reporters' inquiries, 50%; keeping informed and working on agency business, 25%; and initiating materials and events, 25%. . . . I observed no press officer, outside of the White House, who spent most of his time staging events or initiating material as innocuous as handouts. . . . The typical government agency initiates very few events, especially when compared with the daily menu of congressional hearings. . . . There is one significant exception to the modest behavior, however; the White House is expected to put on a daily show.

Every state provides public information services. In California, for example, there are about 175 information officers in about 70 state agencies. Some examples of their activities include:

- The Department of Health and Human Services uses extensive public relations and paid advertising to inform citizens about the issues of smoking and teenage pregnancy. In one commercial, a girl tells her boyfriend, "Just what part of 'no' don't you understand?"

- The AIDS Education Campaign operates a hotline giving information about the disease and conducts an advertising campaign.

- The Commerce and Trade Agency promotes tourism to the state with a variety of news releases, pamphlets, brochures, and advertisements. Its latest campaign, costing $23 million, was aimed at the Japanese tourist market.

The Illinois Department of Transportation provides an example of an information campaign. This covered the rebuilding of the John F. Kennedy Expressway in Chicago, the region's busiest highway. The construction, obviously, would disrupt commuting (270,000 vehicles a day) and a number of businesses served by the Expressway, including O'Hare International Airport.

The agency's program objectives were to (1) reduce travel demand on the Kennedy, (2) increase public and media awareness of the need to rebuild the expressway, (3) inform the public about the project's status during construction, and (4) update the media and the public on a day-to-day basis about construction that may affect the flow of traffic.

A number of communication tools were used, including (1) news releases, (2) daily briefings of traffic reporters, (3) brochures, (4) speaker's bureau, (5) presentations to civic clubs, (6) posters and counter cards at airports and hotels, and (7) on-site radio and television coverage of major reconstruction events.

The result was greater public understanding and support of the reconstruction. Traffic on the Kennedy expressway dropped 25 percent; there was a significant increase in the use of mass transit. Media coverage, instead of being hostile, was thorough and positive throughout the project.

On occasion, state and municipal agencies combine their efforts on a public information campaign. The Maryland Stadium Authority, which includes the city of Baltimore and the Maryland Department of Transportation, teamed up to inform citizens on the best transportation routes to reach the new stadium for the Baltimore Orioles.

MUNICIPAL INFORMATION SERVICES

Cities employ information specialists to disseminate news and information from numerous municipal departments. Such agencies may include the airport, transit district, redevelopment office, park and recreation, convention and visitor's bureau, police and fire, city council, and the mayor's office.

Tell Your Kids About AIDS Now. Or Someone Else May Have To Later.

How can we protect our young people from AIDS? With information. Tell them frankly that the safest protection is to avoid sex altogether. If they do have sex, they can reduce their risk by using a latex condom with every partner, every time. And they must never share needles—for drugs, tattoos, or even pierced ears. For more information, call the AIDS hotline in Northern California at 1-800-367-2437, or in Southern California at 1-800-922-2437.

AIDS.
It's Up To You.
State of California AIDS Education Campaign

FIGURE 15.6
State governments frequently conduct public relations programs to promote health, safe driving, and similar public
issues. This advertisement is one of a series sponsored by the
State of California AIDS education campaign.

The information flow is manifested in a number of ways, but all have the objective of informing citizens and helping them take advantage of opportunities. The city council holds neighborhood meetings; an airport commission sets up an exhibit showing the growth needs of the airport; the recreation department promotes summer swimming lessons; and the city's human rights commission sponsors a festival promoting multiculturalism.

Cities also spend considerable money promoting themselves in an effort to increase business investment and tourism. This is further explored in Chapter 20, but Columbia, South Carolina, provides a good example of a successful city event.

Columbia was able to draw thousands of visitors by restoring a B-25 bomber from World War II and staging the 50th anniversary reunion of Doolittle's Raiders, a group of veterans who used the plane in the war. The three-day civic celebration included (1) a reception for civic and business leaders to meet the Raiders, (2) an original play about the Raiders, (3) a '40s style dinner dance, (4) the B-25 dedication ceremony at the state museum, (5) a statewide school essay contest, and (6) a documentary on educational television.

The Doolittle reunion shows that anniversaries are a good "hook" for creating national visibility and tourism for a city, but extensive information efforts are also needed when a natural disaster hits.

Des Moines, Iowa, found this out when a major flood in the spring of 1993 put many parts of the city under water and contaminated the city's drinking water. The city conducted an aggressive information campaign to keep the public informed of flood developments and hold anxiety to a minimum.

City information officers gave regular press briefings and provided experts from the U.S. Army Corps of Engineers to answer questions. Media from around the nation were told about the cooperative spirit of local citizens and how life still went on in the city. After the flood waters receded and the drinking water supply was restored, the Des Moines Convention and Visitors Bureau used a video news release to announce the city was still a good place to have a convention.

The importance of public information and public relations at the municipal level is best described by the International City Management Association:

Public relations is one of many important variables which affect the ability of an administrator to accomplish program objectives. It involves cooperation between the agency (its personnel, decisions and programs) and the attitudes and desires of persons and groups in the agency's external environment. It imposes on administrators the necessity for dealing with public relations as an inherent and continuing element in the managerial process. The administrator must be mindful of public relations considerations at every stage of the administrative process, from making the decision to the final point of its execution.

CRITICISMS OF GOVERNMENT INFORMATION SERVICES

Although the need for government to inform citizens and publicize programs is generally accepted in principle, many critics still express skepticism about the activity, as mentioned earlier.

To some, like book authors James Bennett and Thomas DiLorenzo (*Official Lies: How Washington Misleads Us*), the federal government operates a huge self-serving propaganda machine with tens of thousands of employees paid for by taxpayers.

Indeed, taxpayer groups often oppose the employment of information officers as costly and unnecessary. In California, for example, a bill was introduced into the legislature that would eliminate all public information jobs in the state. Such an action would have saved $5.5 million of California's 1993 budget of $52 billion.

Although the bill was defeated by the California Senate, it did cause enough anxiety that a number of agencies switched their Public Information Officers (PIOs) to such titles as "analyst," "special assistant," and "deputy director." One PIO was quoted by the Los Angeles *Daily News:* "It (the bill) doesn't prohibit the function, it prohibits the title."

Others, including journalists, criticize legislators for sending reams of useless news releases that often do nothing but promote themselves. Such abuse, coupled with snide news stories about the cost of maintaining government "public relations" experts, rankles dedicated PIOs who work very hard to keep the public informed and the press supplied with a daily diet of news stories.

One PIO for a California agency says, "I'd like to see the press find out what's going on in state government without us. The press would be frustrated. People are not going to be informed unless you have people like us bending over backward for them." Her comments are echoed by another PIO in the Department of Water Resources. He is now called a "government analyst" but says that his department, the news media, and the public still want and demand information about the state's water supply.

A major source of press hostility toward government information effort seems to stem from the fact that the press is heavily dependent on handouts. One text, *Media: An Introductory Analysis of American Mass Communications* by Peter M. Sandman, David M. Rubin, and David B. Sachsman, puts it bluntly: "If a newspaper were to quit relying on press releases, but continued covering the news it now covers, it would need at least two or three times as many reporters."

These handouts and news releases supplied to the media have been called "information subsidies" by O. H. Gandy, author of *Beyond Agenda Setting: Information Subsidies and Public Policy.* He explains that such materials are considered a subsidy because the source "causes it to be made available at something less than the cost a user would face in the absence of a subsidy." In other words, public relations materials save media outlets the cost of time, money, and effort to gather their own news.

Various studies show that government news releases are extensively used by media. Professor Judy Van Slyke Turk, now at the University of South Carolina, found that 51 percent of the releases sent by Louisiana state agencies in one eight-week period were used by the media.

Professors Lynne Masel Walters (Texas A&M) and Timothy Walters (Stephen F. Austin State University) looked at press acceptance of news releases from a state government agency in 1992 and found that 86 percent of the releases were placed in daily newspapers with a combined circulation of nearly 135 million readers.

News releases, however, are only one aspect of helping the media do their job. The city of Homestead, Florida, spent $70,000 on facilities and staff just to handle the deluge of reporters who descended on the city in the aftermath of Hurricane Andrew. Congress also subsidizes the media by spending millions of dollars annually on press facilities and services for working reporters.

And although there is much congressional and media criticism of the government's extensive publications, these are defended on the basis of cost efficiency. A deputy director of the Department of Agriculture publications branch, for example, reported that his office alone receives about 350,000 inquiries a year. Two-thirds of the requests, he says, can be answered with pamphlets that cost between half a cent and 12 cents each, whereas individual responses could cost up to $20 each when personnel costs are included. In other words, the sheer volume of public requests requires a large array of printed materials.

An Associated Press reporter acknowledged in a story that government information does have value. He wrote:

While some of the money and manpower goes for self-promotion, by far the greater amount is committed to an indispensable function of a democratic government—informing the people.

What good would it serve for the Consumer Product Safety Commission to recall a faulty kerosene heater and not go to the expense of alerting the public to its action? An informed citizenry needs the government to distribute its economic statistics, announce its antitrust suits, tell about the health of the president, give crop forecasts.

PUBLIC RELATIONS AND POLITICAL CAMPAIGNS

This chapter so far has dealt with business public affairs and government information efforts. Another important area of widespread public relations activity is in behalf of political candidates.

American political campaigns, according to one estimate, are a $100 million industry. Thousands of political consultants and their firms, often called by critics the "mercenaries of American politics," help candidates at every level of government get elected.

One example is Bob Squier, called the "doyen of the big media consultants" by the *Wall Street Journal,* who helped 20 Democratic candidates run for office in 1992. His firm, consisting of about 25 employees, is a full-service operation that handles a number of activities for a candidate. This may include such traditional techniques as advertising, direct mail, mass telephone calls to specific audiences, speechwriting, staged events, and press kits.

The apex of political campaigning, as it is in government information work, is the presidency. Several hundred million dollars were spent by each of the major parties in 1992 to get their candidate elected. The election also marked the advent of what was dubbed "access media," "new media," "interactive media," and even "teledemocracy."

According to James Perry, writing in the *Wall Street Journal:*

The new media label covers a broad band of new technologies. With satellites, candidates can, and do, hold rallies in several places at once; strategists in different parts of the country meet in teleconferences; direct mail gives way to videocassettes delivered door to door; voters with personal computers log on to candidate bulletin boards and call up vast amounts of information. It's an explosion of technology.

An example of the "new media" is a satellite service operated by the Democratic National Committee at its convention in New York City. It allowed local news anchors to interview Bill Clinton's childhood friends, who testified that he had strong character. Meanwhile, the Clinton campaign was feeding radio actualities, or recorded sound bites, into an 800 number that radio stations around the country could call. In another location, computers were automatically dialing media facsimile machines (fax) and sending reams of news releases and position papers.

Particularly noteworthy was the idea that political candidates discovered cable television and the talk show circuit as a way of talking to the voters without being filtered (mediated) through the critical judgment of traditional journalists.

Ross Perot, for example, used an interview on CNN's Larry King show to announce that he was running for the presidency. And Clinton found that he could project a "real" image by playing the saxophone on the Arsenio Hall show. George Bush was slower to pick up on the talk show circuit, but he eventually appeared on a number of shows and answered questions from audiences.

The three major candidates appeared on so many major talk shows during the election campaign that Jay Leno, host of the *Tonight Show,* announced his lineup of guests one night by saying "And no presidential candidates."

Although the candidates made unprecedented use of modern technology to reach the audience directly in 1992, the concept has been around since the turn of the century. Dirk Smillie, writing in a monograph published by The Freedom Forum at Columbia University, says Theodore Roosevelt—like Perot—harnessed unconventional media back in 1900 by using the mass circulation tabloid papers instead of the mainstream press. About the same time and through the 1920s, the *Saturday Evening Post* allowed presidential hopefuls to write articles outlining their views. Candidate Woodrow Wilson, for example, wrote an article on civil service reform.

Although the new media make it easier to reach millions of people directly, it still goes back to how a candidate is perceived by the audience. Clinton, for example, had to overcome a number of unfavorable images on his way to becoming president.

Advisers, midway through the campaign, decided that he had to project the image of an honest, plain folks idealist with a warm and loving wife. Several strategies were used:

- Appearances on popular talk shows to show Clinton's human side and "plain folks" background

- A series of speeches criticizing special-interest groups to show that Clinton had the courage of his convictions

- More photo opportunities showing Bill and Hillary Clinton together to make them seem warm and affectionate to voters. *People* magazine, for example, was persuaded to write a cover article "At Home with the Clintons."

Symbolism and image are important in any election; they are particularly crucial in a presidential election. There are several ethical guidelines, however, for people working in political public relations. Here are some of them, as formulated by the Public Relations Society of America:

1. It is the responsibility of professionals practicing political public relations to be conversant with the various local, state, and federal statutes governing such activities and to adhere to them strictly. This includes laws and regulations governing lobbying, political contributions, disclosure, elections, libel, slander, and the like.

2. Members shall represent clients or employers in good faith, and while partisan advocacy on behalf of a candidate or public issue is expected, members shall act in accord with the public interest and adhere to truth and accuracy and to generally accepted standards of good taste.

3. Members shall not issue descriptive material or any advertising or publicity information or participate in the preparation or use thereof which is not signed by responsible persons or is false, misleading, or unlabeled as to its source, and are obligated to use care to avoid dissemination of any such material.

4. In avoiding practices which might tend to corrupt the processes of government, members shall not make undisclosed gifts of cash or other valuables which are designed to influence specific decisions of voters, legislators, or public officials.

5. Members shall not, through the use of information known to be false or misleading, conveyed directly or through a third party, intentionally injure the public reputation of an opposing candidate.

During the 1994 campaign, however, many candidates and their advisers ignored these principles. The public was deluged by mean-spirited "attack" TV commercials in which candidates denounced their opponents, frequently using misleading, unsubstantiated allegations. Many voters, disgusted, grew even more cynical about the men and women who run their government.

CASE PROBLEM

The city council of Lakewood (population 150,000), in cooperation with a citizens' commission, has decided that there is a need to improve citizen participation in the city's curbside recycling program. Such a program is environmentally sound, and there are other reasons. The city's only landfill is rapidly filling up and there are new state mandates for recycling.

Recycling is still a relatively new concept for the majority of Lakewood households—only 45 percent of them are separating their trash for recycling. The percentage is even lower among residents in the mid- to lower-income brackets. The objective is to get 80 percent of the households to use the curbside recycling program.

What kind of public information program would you recommend to accomplish this objective? Develop a list of program strategies and communication tac-

QUESTIONS FOR REVIEW AND DISCUSSION

1. Name three reasons why companies should engage in corporate citizenship.

2. List some activities that are typically done by a specialist in community relations.

3. In what ways can corporate philanthropy be beneficial to a company? Can philanthropy cause public relations problems for the company?

4. What are some things a company can do if its philanthropic contributions come under attack?

5. What is the difference between someone working in government relations and someone who is a lobbyist?

6. Name at least five ethical guidelines for business public affairs professionals.

7. Name and explain a federal law that regulates lobbying.

8. What kinds of communications technology are now being used by lobbyists and organizers of grass-roots campaigns?

9. Explain how a political action committee (PAC) works. What are the pros and cons?

10. What societal and environmental factors have led to the growth of government information programs?

11. In what ways are reporters dependent on government information programs? What is the concept of "information subsidies"?

12. What are the concerns and criticisms of government information activities?

13. What role does public relations play in political campaigns? What is the role of campaign consultants?

14. Name some of the new media technologies that political candidates use to disseminate their messages.

15. Some critics say that the appearance of presidential candidates on entertainment talk shows trivializes the political process. Do you agree or disagree?

SUGGESTED READINGS

Abramson, Jill, and Stout, Hillary. "Health Industry Enlists Prominent Lobbyists for Fight After Being Spurned by Policymakers." *Wall Street Journal,* March 18, 1993, p. A16.

Alexander, Suzanne. "McDonald's Moves into Historic Boston District Using Grass-Roots Lobby to Reverse Zoning Vote." *Wall Street Journal,* October 28, 1991.

Blumenthal, Sidney. "The Syndicated Presidency." *New Yorker,* April 5, 1993, pp. 42–47. White House public relations and working with the press.

Carlson, Peter. "The Image Makers." Washington *Post* magazine, February 11, 1990, pp. 12–17, 30–35. Lobbying and public relations in Washington, D.C.

Childers, Linda. "Credibility of Public Relations at the NRC (Nuclear Regulatory Commission)." *Public Relations Research Annual,* ed. James and Larissa Grunig, Vol. 1, Hillsdale NJ: Lawrence Erlbaum Associates, 1989, pp. 97–114.

Dyer, Sam. "The Story of a Community Relations Fiasco." *Public Relations Quarterly,* Summer 1993, pp. 33–35. New Zealand utility case study.

Engelberg, Stephen. "A New Breed of Hired Hands Cultivates Grass-Roots Anger." New York *Times,* March 17, 1993, p. A10–11. Using computers and the telephone to generate citizen feedback to legislators.

Epstein, Marc J. "The Fall of Corporate Charitable Donations." *Public Relations Quarterly,* Summer 1993, pp. 37–39.

Freedman, Alix, and Cohen, Laurie. "Smoke and Mirrors: How Cigarette Makers Keep Health Question Open Year After Year." *Wall Street Journal,* February 11, 1993, pp. A1,6. Lobbying efforts of the tobacco industry.

Gibson, Richard. "Boycott Drive Against Pioneer Hi-Bred Shows Perils of Corporate Philanthropy." *Wall Street Journal,* June 10, 1992, p. B1.

Goldman, Kevin. "Military Struggles with Image Problem." *Wall Street Journal,* February 1, 1993, p. B4.

Kelly, Michael. "A Pragmatist and a Master of Image." New York *Times,* May 30, 1993, p. Y13. Profile of David Gergen, White House director of communications.

Kelly, Michael. "David Gergen: Master of the Game." New York *Times Magazine,* October 31, 1993, pp. 62–71, 80, 92–93, 97, 103. Profile of David Gergen and overview of White House public relations through the years.

Lewis, Charles, and Ebrahim, Margaret. "Can Mexico and Big Business USA Buy NAFTA?" *The Nation,* June 14, 1993, pp. 826–839.

Mack, Charles S. *Lobbying and Government Relations.* Westport, CT: Quorum Books, 1990.

McAvoy, James. "Tactics for the Military in the Media War." *Wall Street Journal,* February 7, 1991, p. A14. Media relations in the Gulf War.

McEwen, Laura. "Communicating Under Fire: Using the Media to Promote Peace." *Communication World,* August 1993, pp. 9–12. Public affairs for UN peacekeeping force in Bosnia-Hercegovina.

Mundy, Alicia. "Is the Press Any Match for Powerhouse PR?" *Columbia Journalism Review,* September–October 1992, pp. 27–34. The influence of Washington lobbyists and public relations executives on media agenda-setting.

Micklin, Julie L. "Many Fortune 500 Companies Curtail Donations to Higher Education." *Chronicle of Higher Education,* May 26, 1993, pp. A25–26.

Noah, Timothy. "Clinton's Campaign Uses Technology to Bypass Traditional News Outlets." *Wall Street Journal,* July 17, 1992, p. A14.

Perry, James M. "Call It New Media, Teledemocracy or Whatever, It's Changing the Way the Political System Works." *Wall Street Journal,* June 24, 1992, p. A22.

Phair, Judith. "The Battle for Support: Pro and Anti NEA Forces Wage Grass-Roots Campaigns." *Public Relations Journal,* August 1990, pp. 18–23, 34–36. National Endowment for the Arts controversy about censorship.

Ponder, Stephen. "Progressive Drive to Shape Public Opinion, 1913–1983." *Public Relations Review,* Fall 1990, pp. 94–104. History of public relations in government agencies.

Rothstein, Edward. "You Can't Please All the People. . . " New York *Times,* July 26, 1992, Section 2, p. R1. Public relations problems of the National Endowment for the Arts.

Sebastian, Pamela. "Attaching Strings: With Coffers Less Full, Big Companies Alter Their Gifts to Charities." *Wall Street Journal,* November 26, 1993, pp. 1A, 5A.

Trahan, Joseph V., III. "Media Relations in the Eye of the Storm." *Public Relations Quarterly,* Summer 1993, pp. 31–32. The U.S. Army's public affairs unit in action after Hurricane Andrew.

Trento, Susan. *Power House: Robert Keith Gray and the Selling of Access and Influence in Washington.* New York: St. Martin Press, 1992.

Walters, Lynne Masel, and Walters, Timothy. "Environment of Confidence: Newspaper Daily Use of Press Releases." *Public Relations Review,* Spring 1992, pp. 31–46. Use of government news releases by the press.

Wartzman, Rick. "In Washington, Groups with Conflicting Views Hire Same Lobbyists Without Creating Problems." *Wall Street Journal,* October 4, 1993, p. A14. Health reform legislation.

16

International Public Relations

P R E V I E W   The objective of this chapter is to provide students with an understanding of international public relations and the complications of cross-cultural and multilingual problems.

Topics covered in the chapter include:

- Global marketing

- Language, culture, and other problems

- Representing foreign corporations in the United States

- Representing U.S. corporations in other countries

- International government public relations

- International group public relations

- Foreign public relations organizations

- Opportunities in international work

A DEFINITION

International public relations may be defined as the planned and organized effort of a company, institution, or government to establish mutually beneficial relations with the publics of other nations. These publics, in turn, may be defined as the various groups of people who are affected by, or who can affect, the operations of a particular firm, institution, or government. Each public is united by a common interest vis-à-vis the entity seeking acceptance of its products or programs.

International public relations also may be viewed from the standpoint of its practice in individual countries. Although public relations is commonly regarded as a concept developed in the United States at the beginning of the twentieth century, some of its elements, such as countering unfavorable public attitudes by means of disclosure of operations through publicity and annual reports, were practiced by railroad companies and at least one share-holding corporation in Germany as far back as the mid-nineteenth century, to mention only one such country. (See Chapter 3.)

Even so, it is largely American techniques that have been adapted to national and regional public relations practices throughout the world, including many totalitarian nations. Today, although in some languages there is no term comparable to *public relations,* the practice has spread to more than 100 countries. This is primarily the result of worldwide technological, social, economic, and political changes and the growing understanding that public relations is an essential component of advertising, marketing, and diplomacy.

INTERNATIONAL CORPORATE PUBLIC RELATIONS

THE NEW AGE OF GLOBAL MARKETING

For decades, hundreds of corporations based in the United States have been engaged in international business operations including marketing, advertising, and public relations. These activities swelled to unprecedented proportions during the 1980s and early 1990s, largely because of new communications technologies, development of 24-hour financial markets almost worldwide, the lowering of trade barriers, growth of sophisticated foreign competition in traditionally "American" markets, and shrinking cultural differences bringing the "global village" ever closer to reality.

Today almost one-third of all U.S. corporate profits are generated through international business. In case of Coca-Cola, probably the best-known brand name in the world, international sales account for 80 percent of the company's operating profit.

At the same time, overseas investors are moving into American industry. It is not uncommon for 15 to 20 percent of a U.S. company's stock to be held abroad. The United Kingdom, for example, has a direct foreign investment in the United States exceeding $122 billion, followed by Japan and the Netherlands with nearly half that sum each, according to the U.S. Department of Commerce.

The worldwide explosion in advertising that began more than two decades ago has been marked by the formation of huge multinational advertising conglomerates and, during the 1980s, by the rise of mega-agencies such as Britain's Saatchi & Saatchi Company and the WPP Group. Saatchi & Saatchi's acquisitions included Ted Bates Worldwide, then America's third largest agency. The WPP Group's U.S. acquisitions included the J. Walter Thompson Company, Hill and Knowlton, and the Ogilvy PR group. In 1989 WPP, a holding company that owns a number of mostly independently operating marketing, advertising, and public relations firms, became the world's largest marketing operation, with 21,000 employees serving more than 5,000 clients in 50 countries.

Public relations is an essential ingredient in the global megamarketing mix being created. (Chapter 5 examines the outreach of U.S. public relations firms abroad through their own offices, full or partial ownership of foreign companies, and affiliations with foreign public relations companies.)

"Everyone realizes now that they have to be part of an international structure, because the big agencies are getting bigger and the small ones are disappearing," said Edward M. Stanton, chief executive of MSL Worldwide, public relations arm of the D'Arcy Benton & Bowles advertising agency.

The fact that advertising agencies own six of the top ten U.S. public relations firms points up the overall objective of the marketing conglomerates: to develop on a global scale seamlessly blended operations involving public relations, creative advertising campaigns, direct mail, special events (often in sports), special promotions or sweepstakes, in-store merchandising, sponsored publications, and other such efforts.

Fueling the new age of global marketing are satellite television, computer networks, electronic mail, fax, fiber optics, cellular telephone systems, and emerging technologies such as integrated services digital networks (ISDN) allowing users to send voice, data, graphics, and video over existing copper cables. For example, Hill and Knowlton has its own satellite transmission facilities, and the General Electric Company has formed an international telecommunications network enabling employees to communicate worldwide, using voice, video, and computer data, by simply dialing seven digits on a telephone. Using three satellite systems, Cable News Network (CNN) is viewed by more than 200 million people in more than 100 countries. A number of newspapers and magazines are reaching millions with international editions. *Reader's Digest,* to cite one instance, distributes about 11.5 million copies abroad—almost 40 national editions in more than a dozen languages, and the *Wall Street Journal* has both Asian and European editions.

David Miln, business development director of Saatchi & Saatchi, declared that it is now possible "to produce the same product, in the same packaging, with the same name, at the same price, wherever you want within the world markets, in the cheapest place probably, and, if there are enough people out there who want it—terrific. But first come finding the need and branding the product."

Differences in language, laws, and cultural mores among the countries (to be discussed shortly) pose serious problems for such a marketing program. Another problem lies in the need for both managers and employees to learn to think and act in global terms as quickly as possible. Already, Burson-Marsteller, with offices in many countries, has been spending more than $1 million a year on training tapes and traveling teams of trainers and seminars, to foster a uniform approach to client projects.

Much of the new business jousting took place on West European terrain, where expectations of a commercially unified European Community (EC) after 1992 attracted

When McDonald's brought American fast food to Moscow, throngs of Russian customers stood in line to buy hamburgers and to enjoy the restaurant's bright lights and friendly service.

enormous attention. Although hampered by recession, public relations expenditures increased significantly. The growth was precipitated in part by expansion of commercial television resulting from widespread privatization, the desire of viewers for more varied programming, satellite technology, and slowly developing EC business patterns. Satellite TV reached 30 million people, mostly through cable systems; one of the most striking changes, however, involved the direct transmission of programming to homes by high-powered satellites, bypassing conventional networks, local stations, and cable systems. On the print side, the business press was growing about 20 percent every year, and there were about 15,000 trade publications in Western Europe.

Although the EC promoted the phrase "a single Europe," corporations and public relations firms still faced the complex task of communicating effectively to 320 million people in 12 countries speaking nine languages.

As the forces of democratization and free market economy strengthened across Eastern Europe and the former Soviet Union, corporations established financial, manufacturing, and distribution bases. Public relations efforts began to grow. In Hungary, for example, the Hungarian Public Relations Association was formed with about 100 practitioners, 10 corporate members, and 10 public relations firms, including Burson-Marsteller, Hill and Knowlton, and the GCI Group.

Burson-Marsteller and its parent, Young & Rubicam, started the first American-style public relations/advertising agency in Russia in the late 1980s. "There was much more PR work to do in the early days because the shops had little (merchandise) to sell," Gary Burandt, who handled advertising for the firm, told *PR News.* "We set up trade shows and media interviews. We'd also arrange meetings with key officials . . . " Public relations clients in 1994 included AT&T, Intel, and an office operated jointly by the United States and the Commonwealth of Independent States to promote privatization of industry.

LANGUAGE, CULTURAL, AND OTHER PROBLEMS

Fundamentally, companies operating in foreign countries are confronted with essentially the same public relations challenges as those in the United States, as Figure 16.1 shows. These include (1) the formation and maintenance of favorable climates for their operations, involving relationships with local and national government officials, consumer groups, the financial community, and employees; (2) the monitoring and assessment of potentially adverse situations and the establishment of ways to counteract them; and (3) the containment of crises before serious damage is done.

These problems, however, may be aggravated by conditions such as the following:

■ Differences in languages and the multiplicity of languages in some countries

■ Longer chains of command, stretching back to the home country

■ Evident and subtle differences in customs

■ The varying levels of development of the media and public relations

■ Antipathy expressed toward "multinationals," a pejorative word in many countries

■ A dislike grounded in such factors as national pride, past relationships, envy, and apprehension, especially in regard to the United States, concerning foreign cultural, economic, political, and military influence

FIGURE 16.1
This advertisement for a position in England shows the similarity between qualifications and objectives for public relations work in the United States and other countries.

PUBLIC AFFAIRS CONTROLLER

To develop high profile Public Relations for leading music industry organisation

c.£38,000, mortgage assistance + car   Central London

Held in high regard in the British music industry, this organisation plays a major role in supporting creative talent. To increase public awareness of this and its many other roles, we have been asked to fill a new position, which will report directly to the Chief Executive. Its essence is the development of innovative, co-ordinated strategies for all aspects of internal and external PR – and the direction of their implementation. Administrative and organisational support is already in place, producing highly professional corporate information and arranging sponsorship, exhibitions, and award ceremonies. We are looking for a cerebral, even inspirational, input, to add immediate spark and long-term fire. Ideal candidates, probably mid thirties/early forties, will almost inevitably be graduates (they'll certainly have graduate intellect) and will have outstanding inter-personal skills and communication flair. They will have already established high personal credibility with the media, including broadcasting, and will have first hand experience of a wide range of PR activities; their track record will demonstrate all this quite clearly. We would like to see some experience in broadcasting or publishing, while a real, if amateur, interest in music would be a distinct advantage.
It's a growth organisation and this is a growth job: above all, it's an exciting one (a cliché we promised ourselves we'd never use, but this time it's really justified!). Please send full career details, quoting reference WE 0143, to Judy Brasier, Ward Executive Limited, Academy House, 26-28 Sackville Street, London W1X 2QL. Tel: 071-439 4581.

WARD EXECUTIVE
LIMITED
Executive Search & Selection

The following are some examples of the types of language problems encountered:

■ Chevrolet executives could not figure out why the Chevy Nova was not selling well in Latin America. Then they learned that although *Nova* means "new" in Spanish, *No va* means "It doesn't go."

■ A Deere & Company marketing manager, addressing a group of German dealers, chose the German word for *mouth* to describe the feeder opening of a forage harvester, inadvertently declaring that "John Deere is the biggest braggart."

■ An interpreter assigned during President Jimmy Carter's visit to Poland was fired for saying in Polish that the President "has a lust for Polish women" rather than "admires Polish women."

■ American practitioners in some foreign countries have discovered that much local conversation and writing is in Pidgin English, of which Figure 16.2 is an example.

FIGURE 16.2
The campaign against AIDS has many international ramifications. The Vanuatu government distributed this poster in Pidgin English urging precautions against the disease. Read it carefully and you probably can decipher the message.

Cultural differences provide additional pitfalls, as shown by the following examples:

- In China, tables at a banquet are never numbered. The Chinese think such tables appear to rank guests, so it is better to direct a guest to the "primrose" or "hollyhock" table.

- German and Swiss executives think a person is uncouth if he or she uses first names, particularly at public events.

- The English start and end their work later in the day, so breakfast meetings are unpopular.

- The proper etiquette for drinking in Korea is to fill your neighbor's glass as well as your own.

- News releases in Malaysia should be distributed in four languages to avoid alienating any segment of the press.

- Americans, perhaps because of their strong freedom-of-expression tradition, tend to be perceived throughout the world as extremely vocal and opinionated—traits not particularly admired or emulated in many cultures.

- In the Middle East, the color white signifies mourning, so no executive should be pictured in white. In that same region care also must be taken in portraying or photographing women.

- If an American executive lacks time to have a negotiating proposal typed and submits a handwritten version, Arabs may consider the gesture so bizarre that they will analyze the proposal intensely, seeking significant messages, or conclude that the American considers the contract unimportant.

- When Japanese executives suck in air through their teeth and exclaim, "*Sa!* That will be *very* difficult," they really mean just plain "no." The Japanese consider an absolute "no" offensive and try to respond euphemistically.

- When an Asian business executive changes the date of a projected meeting, the American executive should not be offended; the Asian may simply have consulted with a religious adviser who urged a more auspicious date for the visit.

- Americans, generally punctual, must learn not to be offended when people in many other countries arrive a half-hour or more late for an appointment. Time traditionally has a different meaning in those nations.

All of these illustrations indicate that Americans not only must learn the customs of the country to which they are assigned but should rely on native professionals to guide their paths. And, although they should study the language both before and after their arrival, they must realize that only by residing in the country for many years will they be free—if ever—of language problems.

Courses of study to prepare Americans to conduct business in other countries have been developed at a number of universities. Since 1970 the business school at New York University has nearly tripled its international business faculty. The University of South

Carolina and the University of Denver, among others, have greatly expanded their international business programs, as has also the Georgetown Center for Strategic and International Studies. The American Graduate School of International Management in Glendale, Arizona, is devoted entirely to preparing students for world business careers. The nonprofit Business Council for International Understanding produces films that help Americans learn about practices in other countries. The Language and Intercultural Research Center at Brigham Young University publishes a variety of booklets which, though intended primarily for missionaries of the Church of Latter Day Saints, are useful for international business purposes.

REPRESENTING FOREIGN CORPORATIONS IN THE UNITED STATES
Industries in other countries frequently employ American public relations firms to advance their needs in this country. Carl Levin, vice president and senior consultant, Burson-Marsteller, Washington, D.C., tells why:

- To hold off protectionist moves threatening their company or industry.

- To defeat legislation affecting the sale of a client's product.

- To support expansion of the client's markets in the United States.

- To provide ongoing information on political, sociological, and commercial developments in the United States that could bear on the client's business interests, not only here but worldwide. In the well-organized foreign company, this information is factored into day-to-day policy decisions as well as periodic strategic plans.

More than 25 counseling firms are registered by the U.S. Department of Justice as doing work for Japanese companies, more than for any other nation. When the sales of imported automobiles soared and those of U.S. manufacturers declined during the 1980s, the Japan Automobile Manufacturers Association mounted a public relations campaign to counteract rising public sentiment in America for curbs on the sale of imported cars.

As Japanese companies began to build their cars in the United States with American labor, additional public relations efforts were required. With Chrysler Corporation sales suffering, Lee A. Iacocca, Chrysler president, personally headed a two-month advertising and public relations media blitz in 1990. The "Advantage Chrysler" campaign was based on a surprising research finding that new car buyers preferred Chrysler cars over those of the highly rated Honda Motor Company. This claim ran counter to vast industry research and public perception that had given Honda vehicles the highest rating for quality. Honda's reply was voiced by a Detroit spokesman: "The sales speak for themselves."

In 1989 Japan's Sony Corporation purchased Columbia Pictures Entertainment Company for $3.4 billion after earlier acquiring CBS Records. Japanese government officials and business executives were taken aback by the negative publicity that followed. Some of them contended that the American reaction amounted to racism toward the Japanese.

Meanwhile, Japanese business interests increased their real estate investments in the United States to a total exceeding $10 billion. Japan's wealthy Mitsubishi Estate

Company reportedly was so sensitive to American reaction that it obtained only a 51 percent interest instead of a planned 80 percent interest in its 1990 acquisition of New York's Rockefeller Center. Even so, American reaction was intense.

Less pronounced was U.S. public reaction to the purchase later in 1990 of MCA, Inc., one of the nation's largest entertainment companies, by Matsushita Electric Industrial Company of Japan for $6.13 billion and stock in a television station. It was by far the largest U.S. acquisition by the Japanese. Although most financial experts approved the purchase as in the United States' interest, a number of persons said they were disturbed by the thought of Japanese owning two American movie companies.

Among the public relations tactics employed by the Japanese to allay American fears of their business moves was to place special advertising supplements in U.S. magazines and newspapers emphasizing the contribution that Japanese companies were making to the U.S. economy.

Noting that about 6000 Japanese companies, employing more than a half-million Americans, were doing business in the United States in 1993, Takashi Kiuchi, chairman and CEO of Mitsubishi Electronics America, urged Japanese employees to build cultural bridges with their American co-workers. Communication he said, has become the "most fundamental issue" facing Japanese businesses in the United States.

REPRESENTING U.S. CORPORATIONS IN OTHER COUNTRIES

On a global basis, public relations as an occupation has achieved highest development in the industrialized nations of the world—United States, Canada, Western Europe, and parts of Asia. It emerges more readily in nations that have multiple-party systems, considerable private ownership of business and industry, large-scale urbanization, and relatively high per capita income levels—which also relate to literacy and educational opportunities. By the same token, public relations as a specialized activity is less developed in Third World nations in which the vast majority of the citizens are still rural villagers.

U.S. and other Western public relations firms began exporting their expertise to the People's Republic of China during the mid-1980s. Hill and Knowlton, active in Asia for almost 30 years, began its Beijing operation with three U.S. expatriates and a locally hired employee dispatching news releases and organizing receptions and conferences from headquarters in a hotel. (A case study later in this chapter tells how the firm helped an international soft-drinks manufacturer achieve its goals in China.) Today more than 30 other PR firms have been established across the country, and the concept of public relations has spread widely. After the first Chinese nongovernmental public relations organization, the Guangdong Public Relations Club, was formed in 1986, more than 400 others have been established, including the Public Relations Society of China. More than 20 universities and 300 institutes and colleges offer public relations courses.

In the Republic of China on Taiwan public relations experienced rapid growth in recent years, paralleling the economic growth of the country.

Australia and New Zealand have public relations industries that are among the most active and developed in the Western world, according to David Potts, a senior public relations counselor in Sydney, Australia. Global public relations firms, as well as many small and medium-sized companies, operate in the two countries. "Some overseas corporations, however, make the mistake of assuming that public relations styles and cam-

Aramco World, a free magazine published by the Aramco Services Company, provides an international audience with information and illustrations about the history, culture, geography, and economy of the Middle East, presented from the oil company's point of view.

paigns which have worked overseas, especially in the U.S.A., will work in [these countries]," said Potts. "They don't always."

Potts has additional observations about public relations in other Pacific Rim countries:

■ Hong Kong, because of its international financial, trading, and tourist links and the fact that Western management techniques are widely used, exhibits a widespread understanding of public relations. There are more advertising and public relations practitioners in Hong Kong than in any other Asian country. Their expertise, however, will stand its greatest test when Britain relinquishes the country to China late in the decade.

■ Singapore and Malaysia enjoy well-developed public relations practices, both local and global. Singapore operations are heavily oriented to visual public relations, and many firms have strong graphics capabilities. The press is freer in Malaysia, and the intricacies of federal, state, and local politics offer wide scope for public relations activity.

■ In Indonesia public relations consultancies and advertising agencies must be domestically owned.

■ Thailand has a great deal of foreign investment and international tourism. The public relations industry is handicapped by a lack of skilled practitioners.

■ Unlike most major Asian countries, no global public relations firm operates in the Philippines; instead outside companies work through local firms on a referral basis. P. A. Chanco III, of the Orientations firm in Manila, advises public relations representatives of foreign corporations to "know the Filipino culture and how it works before anything else."

■ In Japan public relations practice is centered on reaching the media through one or more of the 400-plus reporters' "clubs," with about 12,000 members representing 160 news-gathering organizations. Japan has no public relations tradition.

Japan's Dentsu, one of the world's largest advertising agencies, has joined Burson-Marsteller to form two joint ventures that provide public relations services to Western clients in the country and to Japanese clients in the United States. James H. Dowling, president and chief executive of Burson-Marsteller, said the arrangement "makes Burson-Marsteller Japanese in Japan" and helps Western corporations solve regulatory problems, market Western goods and services, and recruit employees.

On the continent of Africa, South Africa is the only nation that has a sufficient industrial base to support an extensive number of public relations professionals. South African practitioners are increasingly getting involved in employee communications, issues management, community relations, and investor relations.

The new orientation of South African practitioners, of course, is related to factors in the environment of that nation. More than 1 million South African workers, predominantly black, have joined trade unions since the right to organize was granted in 1979. Now, for the first time, South African industry must deal with large organized groups that want more pay and better employment opportunities. At the same time, the nation is running out of skilled workers to fuel its robust economy. This means increased competition among companies for the available pool of skilled workers.

Productivity is another aspect. South Africa, like many other nations, must raise productivity to compete with foreign markets. One way to do this is to motivate workers through effective communications. Consequently, there is considerable interest in newsletters for the rank-and-file, increased training programs, and pressure to increase recruitment of black workers now that apartheid practices have officially ended. (South Africa also will be discussed later in this chapter.)

INTERNATIONAL GOVERNMENT PUBLIC RELATIONS

INFLUENCING OTHER COUNTRIES

The governments of virtually every country have one or more departments involved in communicating with other nations. Much effort and millions of dollars are spent on the tourism industry—attracting visitors whose expenditures aid their hosts' economies. Even larger sums are devoted to lobbying efforts to obtain favorable legislation for a country's products; for example, Costa Rica urged the U.S. Congress to let its sugar into the nation at favorable rates, and the Department of State threatened to enact trade sanctions against countries such as Korea and Taiwan that persisted in "pirating" U.S. products such as computers and books without payment.

Many countries send shortwave broadcasts throughout the world to achieve several objectives, including fostering their national interests and prestige, keeping in touch with nationals abroad, disseminating news, and influencing the internal affairs of other nations.

For decades people throughout the People's Republic of China have listened to Western radio broadcasts, particularly those of the U.S.-based Voice of America (VOA) and the British Broadcasting Corporation (BBC). During and after the pro-democracy uprisings in China in 1989, the VOA's 24-hour service in English and particularly its nearly 13 hours of Mandarin and Cantonese broadcasts each day helped get the facts out to the Chinese population even as the state- and Communist Party–controlled media tried to hide them. The BBC supplemented its regular English-language broadcasts with two and one-half hours of programming in Chinese each day.

For more than 40 years the broadcasts of the VOA, BBC, other European stations, and America's Radio Liberty, which transmitted programs in 14 languages from Munich, Germany, conveyed Western-style news and values to the former Soviet Union and Eastern bloc nations. Despite the jamming that persisted into the late 1980s, millions of Soviet citizens listened. The effect of these broadcasts and of TV programming from (then) West Germany in helping to provide the climate for acceptance of Mikhail Gorbachev's perestroika and glasnost campaigns in the midst of economic deprivations may never be known, but many consider it substantial.

For four decades Radio Free Europe in Munich transmitted programs in native languages to Eastern-bloc nations. In Romania, where demonstrations in December, 1989, ended with the capture and execution of President Nicolae Ceauşescu and his co-dictator wife Elena, student leaders told reporters they would not have taken to the streets had they not been listening for months to British and American shortwave reports about changes taking place elsewhere in Eastern Europe. Said a national student magazine editor: "There was something like a wind of liberty coming from the radio stations from other countries."

The U.S. Information Agency (USIA) operates the Voice of America, and Radio Liberty and Radio Free Europe also are financed by Congress. With the communist threat to world peace virtually eliminated, Congress and an interagency group working under the National Security Council debated the future of the stations. The USIA budget was cut severely. The agency's director, Bruce S. Gelb, was offered the option of eliminating VOA programs for one day a week in all of the 43 languages in which it broadcasts. He chose to keep the VOA on the air seven days a week and to make up the more than $1 million shortage by trimming other USIA projects such as cultural exchange programs with other nations.

In 1990 the United States also reaffirmed its 1985 decision to withdraw from membership in the United Nations Educational, Scientific, and Cultural Organization (UNESCO) on grounds of mismanagement, politicization, and "endemic hostility" toward a free press, free markets, and individual human rights. A State Department announcement stated that the United States would continue to support educational, scientific, cultural, and communications activities through other global agencies.

Since the mid-1970s, Department of State officials have been aided materially by American news media organizations, operating mainly through the World Press Freedom Committee, to respond to complaints of Third World countries. These nations have sought, among other goals, independence and equity in access to global communication resources in order that their own views, values, and developmental efforts might be reported more fully.

Soviet Union In the former USSR, after decades during which the "vulgarity" of Western capitalism and advertising was condemned, Soviet television in 1988 carried commercials by Visa, Pepsi, and Sony during a five-part series examining life in the United States. In 1989 the Soviet government newspaper *Izvestia* began running advertisements weekly in its foreign and Moscow editions. The Soviet Union even offered advertising space on the side of a space shuttle.

Public relations practice began gradually under government monitoring as USSR firms entered into partnership arrangements with foreign companies. "The Soviets are waking up to the fact that they can adopt Western-style public relations and dress up their world," said Stuart Loory of Cable News Network. One of the opening shots in the Soviet public relations offensive was cosponsorship with CNN owner Ted Turner of a major sports event in Moscow, aired in the United States and elsewhere, and repeated in the United States in 1990 and 1994. Soviet spokespersons appeared on U.S. network television programs. Numerous other U.S.–Soviet exchanges followed.

The epitome of glasnost occurred when the USSR opened the doors of its infamous Lubyanka prison to journalists in 1990. KGB General Alexander Karbayinov, the first chief of the KGB's newly created public relations department, welcomed the visitors to the security agency's facility. Other elements in the public relations drive included newspaper interviews with KGB officials, magazine articles about outstanding Soviet spies, and even a television phone-in. "The point of the public relations department is to show that society is no longer subordinate to the KGB or to the state," Karbayinov said.

South Africa The Republic of South Africa, in response to rising worldwide criticism of its apartheid policies, for many years engaged in an extensive information and lobbying campaign in the United States and Western Europe. Its aim was to forestall severe trade sanctions while the government sought a solution to its multiracial problem. In the United States, TransAfrica, a Washington-based lobbying organization, devised strategies to increase pressure on the South African government to hasten the end of apartheid. As the movement gained momentum, Congress passed a law in 1986 that banned new U.S. investments in South Africa, prohibited imports of ore and farm products, and revoked the landing privileges of South African Airways. And by 1990 more than 150 colleges and universities, 26 states, 17 counties, and 80 cities had divested their stock in companies doing business with South Africa.

President F. W. deKlerk, elected in 1989, became the chief architect of improving South Africa's image abroad by cancelling many of the petty apartheid laws and releasing Nelson Mandela, president of the African National Congress (ANC), from a 27-year imprisonment.

The 71-year-old Mandela made a highly successful tour of the United States and Great Britain, during which he urged continuation of economic sanctions against South Africa until further progress was made. Late in 1993 the South African parliament took an historic step by giving blacks their first official role in the government, in preparation for the country's first election open to all races. Appearing before the United Nations in New York the next day, Mandela called for removal of all economic sanctions against South Africa. The U.S. Congress immediately did so, as did other countries. The way was cleared for South Africa's reentry into world trade. Mandela and deKlerk were jointly awarded the Nobel Peace Prize in 1993.

PUBLIC RELATIONS IN BEHALF OF FOREIGN GOVERNMENTS

For fees ranging upward of $1 million or more per year, more than 150 American public relations firms work in this country for other nations. In recent years, for example, Hill and Knowlton has represented Indonesia and Morocco; Burson-Marsteller, Argentina, Costa Rica, Hungary, and the USSR (the latter mainly in trade fairs); and Ruder, Finn & Rotman, El Salvador, Israel, and Japan. Especially active in representing foreign countries is Doremus & Company, whose clients have included Egypt, Iran, Jordan, the Philippines, Saudi Arabia, and Tunisia.

The Countries' Goals What do these countries seek to accomplish? Burson-Marsteller's Carl Levin says that, among other things, the countries pursue several goals:

- ■ To advance political objectives

- ■ To be counseled on the United States' probable reaction to the client government's projected action

- ■ To advance the country's commercial interests—for example, sales in the United States, increased U.S. private investment, and tourism

- ■ To assist in communications in English

- ■ To counsel and help win understanding and support on a specific issue undermining the client's standing in the United States and the world community

- ■ To help modify laws and regulations inhibiting the client's activities in the United States

Under the Foreign Agents Registration Act of 1938, all legal, political, fund-raising, public relations, and lobbying consultants hired by foreign governments to work in the United States must register with the Department of Justice. They are required to file reports with the attorney general listing all activities on behalf of a foreign principal, compensation received, and expenses incurred.

Action Programs Normally hired by an embassy after open bidding for the account, the firm first gathers detailed information about the client country, including past media coverage. Attitudes toward the country are ascertained both informally and through

PLENTY OF FOREIGN BUSINESS FOR U.S. PUBLIC RELATIONS FIRMS

American public relations firms handle a variety of international accounts. The following is a sampling of clients reported in *Jack O'Dwyer's Newsletter* and *O'Dwyer's Washington Report* in 1993:

Client	Public Relations Firm	Contract
Hong Kong	GCI Group, New York	$500,000
Mexican tourism	Edelman PR Worldwide	$10 million +
Ukraine	P/C Advisors	$500,000
Central American and Caribbean Textile and Apparel Council	Greenberg, Trautig, Hoffman, Lipoff, Rosen & Quentel	$200,000
Ruder Finn	Umberto Severi Foundation	$7,000/month

surveys conducted by a specialist such as George Gallup, Lou Harris, or Daniel Yankelovich.

The action program decided on likely will include the establishment of a national information bureau to provide facts and published statements of favorable opinion about the country. Appointments are made with key media people and other influential citizens, including educators, business leaders, and government officials. These people often are invited to visit the client country on expense-paid trips, although some news media people decline on ethical grounds. (Ethical questions are discussed in more detail shortly.)

Gradually, through expert and persistent methods of persuasion and the expenditure of what may run into millions of dollars, critical public attitudes may be changed or reinforced. Success is difficult to judge. So high are the stakes that although the nations may change agencies from time to time, the image-polishing and fact-dissemination operation generally is made permanent.

Problems and Rewards The toughest problems confronting the firm often are as follows:

- Deciding to represent a country, such as Argentina, whose human rights violations may reflect adversely on the agency itself.

- Persuading the heads of such a nation to alter some of its practices so that the favorable public image sought may reflect reality.

- Convincing officials of a client country, which may totally control the flow of news internally, that the American press is independent from government control and that they should never expect coverage that is 100 percent favorable.

- Deciding to represent an autocratic head of state, such as Mobutu Sese Seko of Zaire, whose lavish living and large Swiss bank accounts stand in stark contrast to an average family income among the lowest in the world.

Amnesty International, the Nobel Prize–winning human rights monitor, picketed Burson-Marsteller's offices because of the Argentine account. The Council on Hemispheric Affairs criticized Ruder, Finn & Rotman for working for the government of El Salvador. Norman Wolfson, chairman of Norman, Lawrence, Patterson & Farrell, fled Nicaragua with would-be assassins close on his heels after serving during most of 1978 as the public relations counselor for the late dictator General Anastasio Somoza. A Doremus & Company executive working for the economic development of the Philippines, whose government, headed by Ferdinand Marcos, had placed the country under military law, also was threatened with death.

Why then do these firms work for unpopular governments? Wolfson put it this way: "I felt that I was performing a better service for my country by trying to help Americans understand Somoza than I did even by serving my country in the Navy during the Second World War." Said Burson-Marsteller's Carl Levin: "I do not think it is over-reaching to state that in helping friendly foreign clients we also advance our national interests. And we help in ways that our government cannot." Black, Manafort, Stone & Kelly felt the same way, but dropped its $950,000 contract with an agency close to former Philippines President Ferdinand Marcos when President Reagan called on Marcos

HIGH-COST LOBBYING FOR NAFTA

The fight for ratification of the North American Free Trade Agreement (NAFTA) by the U.S. Congress was one of the most expensive lobbying campaigns ever seen in Washington.

Mexico assembled a high-powered team of public relations specialists, lobbyists, lawyers, and consultants to promote passage of the agreement at an annual cost of about $15 million, according to Justice Department records. Those employed included former U.S. Trade Representative William Brock; Toney Anaya and Jerry Apodaca, past governors of New Mexico; Robert Herzstein, former Commerce Department trade chief; and retired Navy Secretary Edward Hidalgo.

The effort may have been the single most expensive foreign lobbying ever, Charles Lewis, executive director of the Center for Public Integrity, said. U.S. public relations firms helped line up speaking engagements for Mexican officials; the former government officials mapped strategy; and congressional lobbyists worked Capitol Hill. Many members of Congress and their staffs took trips to Mexico provided by the campaign. Lobbying expenditures by Mexico and U.S. corporations in 1993 alone were estimated at $100 million by political writer Pat Choate (whose book *Agents of Influence* criticized Japan's Washington lobbying machine).

Burson-Marsteller public relations was paid $4.5 million to develop brochures about the advantages of NAFTA, organize a speakers bureau, monitor media coverage, produce speeches, and supervise the work of several lobbying firms. In a separate contract, the Office of the President of Mexico paid the firm $1.5 million in fees and expenses to develop a series of television and newspaper ads that promoted Mexico's efforts to combat drug trafficking.

Joining Mexico's lobbying effort were a number of large U.S. companies, which organized under the umbrella of USA*NAFTA. This group, including such organizations as the U.S. Chamber of Commerce and the National Association of Manufacturers, spent at least $2 million to get the trade agreement passed.

FIGURE 16.3
Logo of the North American Free Trade Agreement.

to resign. And, of course, retainers are large: Wolfson earned $20,000 to $30,000 per month, including expenses; Sydney S. Baron & Company was paid $650,000 annually, plus expenses, to promote investment opportunities in South Africa; and Burson-Marsteller received more than $800,000 a year to improve Argentina's reputation.

Publicity for Antigovernment Groups   Although public relations counsel is usually retained by foreign governments, groups opposed to a foreign government also use public relations. *The Wall Street Journal,* in an editorial titled "Guerrilla P.R.," thought it interesting that the guerrillas battling the government in El Salvador had their own press kit. The editorial said, in part: "A few days ago, U.S. editors received a slick-looking press packet bearing the imprint of 'Fenton Communications' on behalf of something called the 'El Salvador Education Project.' It was a job any Madison Avenue house would have been proud of. What it said was that the Salvadoran guerrillas aren't participating in the elections because they are afraid of the 'death squads.'"

The Ethical Questions   Gift giving, entertainment, hospitality, and junkets are long-established practices of foreign governments, or the public relations and lobbying firms that represent them. Those who attend these parties—whether members of Congress and their staffs, regulatory agency personnel, members of the president's cabinet, business leaders, or even members of the press—do so advisedly, for there is a thin line between hospitality and bribery or illegal "influence peddling."

It is generally conceded that the wheels of government are lubricated by countless receptions and cocktail parties in capitals around the world, and there is generally no ethical problem for those attending. Adlai E. Stevenson, when he was chief American delegate to the United Nations, said that "protocol, Geritol, and alcohol" were endemic to a diplomat's life.

"Gift giving" by American corporations also reached an all-time high in the 1970s, and Congress passed the 1977 Foreign Corrupt Practices Act that forbids corporations from giving major gifts or bribes to foreign business contacts or government officials. (Acceptance of such payments is a widely condoned practice in some countries.) In 1982, for example, Boeing pleaded guilty to federal charges of failing to disclose more than $7 million in payments by top-level executives to overseas agents. Today, corporations are extremely careful about giving expensive gifts to potential foreign clients. (See Chapter 6.)

Intervention Tactics   Placing full-page advertisements in major papers such as the Washington *Post* and New York *Times* is almost invariably the first action taken by agents of foreign governments in seeking to influence American public opinion during a crisis (see Figure 16.4). Surveys have shown that a high percentage of the nation's lawmakers and administrators read the *Post* before or soon after arriving in their offices. The *Times,* in particular, is read by opinion leaders throughout the country, and the advertisements gain important visibility, influencing editorial writers and others. Members of Congress often use these political statements in addresses to their colleagues and obtain permission to insert their remarks in the *Congressional Record.* The advertisements generally are followed by personal visits and telephone calls by foreign government agency people and their key supporters. Arrangements are made to place representatives on broadcast network programs. Press conferences are arranged, and newsletters are hastily dispatched to media, government, and other leaders.

Some examples of such campaigns include:

■ An appeal with the headline, "Don't Let Sarajevo Die," called on the international community to "issue an ultimatum to the Serbian leadership in both Serbia and in Bosnia that prevention of delivery of humanitarian assistance to beleaguered civilians will not be tolerated." The appeal was signed by five persons asked by philanthropist George Soros to handle disbursement of $50 million donated for humanitarian assistance.

■ An appeal for support of Koreans fighting eviction from the town of Utoro in Japan, began:

> Fifty years ago, on the eve of World War II, in Korea, Japanese soldiers raped our mothers and took our fathers to Japan to labor in mines and factories. Thousands of other young Korean women were kidnapped or enticed into "comfort battalions" and used by Imperial Army units. . . . Four years ago, in the middle of winter, a developer came with eviction notices and demolition crews to destroy our homes. Nissan [Nissan Motor Company]— which profited from our labor during the war—had sold our village without telling us. Now Nissan refuses to talk to us.

■ A plea to the American people to "help stop the desecration of Japan's ancient capital, Kyoto!" began: "Kyoto, a sacred Buddhist site and center of Japanese culture, has recently become in danger of losing its unique character and appearance. The construction of high-rise buildings by large Japanese enterprises who are only interested in realizing higher profits on their land investments is rapidly spoiling Kyoto." The Kyoto Buddhist Association asked that protest messages be sent to three backers of the enterprise.

INTERNATIONAL GROUP PUBLIC RELATIONS

Hundreds of noncorporate groups depend upon international support for their undertakings. Such organizations as the International Red Cross, World Council of Churches, International Council of B'nai B'rith, and International Chamber of Commerce, along

DON'T LET SARAJEVO DIE

A grave crisis endangers the lives of as many as a million men, women and children as a consequence of the failure of the international community to stop the crime of "ethnic cleansing" in Bosnia-Hercegovina.

Those at risk are Bosnians of all ethnic and religious groups who have not yet been driven out of their homeland by Serbian forces.

Over the last nine months, they have endured the deliberate use of terror as a military tactic: mass murder, rape, torture, detention in subhuman conditions, indiscriminate shelling and pillage.

Peace talks for Bosnia-Hercegovina are still underway. However, the situation in Sarajevo and the other besieged cities of Bosnia is so critical that it cannot wait for implementation of peace agreements. This may be a lengthy and incomplete process anyway. In the meantime, hundreds of innocent people are dying everyday. We must act now.

Bosnian lives are threatened by hunger, cold and disease caused by extended sieges that have blocked deliveries of food, fuel and medical supplies and cut off electricity and water.

In an attempt to alleviate their suffering and save their lives, the philanthropist George Soros has donated $50 million for humanitarian assistance for the victims of violence in Bosnia and Hercegovina. The five signers of this appeal were asked by Mr. Soros to guide the disbursement of those funds.

We issue this statement to draw attention to the impossibility of saving large numbers of lives solely by humanitarian means. We call on the international community to do what is required to ensure that humanitarian aid reaches those in dire need. Prompt action is imperative.

We base this call on our own monitoring of the crisis; on our consultations with the United Nations High Commissioner for Refugees, the International Committee of the Red Cross and those few non-governmental relief organizations that are active in Bosnia; on interviews with refugees from Bosnia, including civilian inmates of detention camps; and on our visit to the besieged Bosnian capital of Sarajevo.

For a brief period in Sarajevo, we experienced the icy conditions, indoors as well as outside; and saw how the frequent shelling, the lack of heat, food, running water or electricity and the destruction of buildings combine to create great hardships and life-endangering hazards in a modern city.

In Sarajevo, we met with Hakija Turajlic, Deputy Prime Minister of Bosnia-Hercegovina, who spoke to us of the 35-40,000 Serbs who have remained in the besieged city to share its hardships with Muslims and others, and of his commitment to the maintenance of a multi-ethnic society. We are deeply shocked at the cold-blooded murder by Serbian troops just four days later of this decent and humane man.

We call on the international community to issue an ultimatum to the Serbian leadership in both Serbia and in Bosnia that prevention of the delivery of humanitarian assistance to beleaguered civilians will not be tolerated. This ultimatum must be backed by the use of United Nations troops to protect the delivery of humanitarian assistance.

In making this call, we note the highly unusual public statements issued by the International Committee of the Red Cross. As never before in its long history, this distinguished and admirable organization has repeatedly spoken out publicly to denounce abuses of human rights and war crimes in Bosnia. In an unprecedented statement on December 4, 1992, the ICRC said that "the UN forces' mandate must be expanded" to provide for "the protection of ethnic minorities in their places of residence."

Ethnic cleansing must not be allowed to succeed. The people of Bosnia need to be saved now. It requires urgent humanitarian efforts, political pressure and, if necessary, force.

TO: LIONEL ROSENBLATT, REFUGEES INTERNATIONAL, 21 DUPONT CIRCLE N.W., WASHINGTON DC 20036
I want to help stop ethnic cleansing in Bosnia: I am sending a contribution to support running this ad elsewhere.
Name: _____
Address: _____
Enclosed please find $ _____

MORTON ABRAMOWITZ	PRINCE SADRUDDIN AGA KHAN	KURT BOLLIGER	MARK MALLOCH BROWN	ARYEH NEIER
President of Carnegie Endowment for International Peace	Former United Nations High Commissioner for Refugees	Former President of the Swiss Red Cross	Vice Chairman of Refugees International	Executive Director, Human Rights Watch

FIGURE 16.4

This plea, published by Refugees International in the New York *Times,* is part of the relief organization's campaign to enlist financial and political help for victims of war in former Yugoslavia. Similar campaigns seek help for refugees in other areas of conflict and hunger.

with numerous foundations, educational enterprises, labor unions, and government-support agencies, maintain vigorous public relations programs. For effective operation, their image must be kept as spotless as possible; like corporations, they must constantly monitor their environments, maintain proper relationships with the governments and publics of the countries in which they operate, and be prepared to handle crises.

The International Red Cross often is plagued with reports that relief goods and services are diverted into private hands or that aid has not been forthcoming as quickly as it might have been in major disasters around the world. Rumors that Red Cross representatives sold rather than gave cigarettes to troops in past wars still provide people who heard those reports years ago with an excuse for not giving.

UNICEF, a United Nations agency that provides food, medical supplies, and other aid for millions of children on three continents, constantly must respond to charges, leveled mainly by those who dislike the United Nations, that too many of the dollars raised through card and gift sales and Halloween door-to-door solicitations are used improperly, in part to pay heavy administrative expenses.

In 1993 the World Council of Churches again defended itself from charges published in a *Reader's Digest* article alleging that much of the council's Special Fund to Combat Racism, allocated only for humanitarian purposes, has gone "to revolutionary Marxist governments in Africa." In 1982 the same staff editor had accused the council of funding armed rebels against white minority groups. The Rev. William Rusch of Chicago, ecumenical officer of the Evangelical Lutheran Church in America, said most of the allegations "have been raised years ago" and were fully investigated by Lutherans and found invalid.

FOREIGN PUBLIC RELATIONS ORGANIZATIONS

In virtually every country where public relations has become an economic and social force, practitioners have organized to exchange information, maintain and improve standards of professional performance, and aid in the development of international public relations. Codes of conduct are commonplace, and many organizations seek to enhance the standing of their members through certification and accreditation programs. Journals or newsletters are published, awards recognize outstanding performance, and scholarships and other assistance are provided to educational centers.

Public relations associations have been formed in about 70 countries. In Great Britain more than 2500 practitioners belong to the British Institute of Public Relations, founded in London in 1948. Other European groups include the Association Française des Relations Publiques (France), Deutsche Public Relations Gesellschaft (West Germany), Federazione Italiana Relazioni Publiche (Italy), and Sociedada Portugesa de Relacoes Publicas (Portugal). The Public Relations Society of Japan includes well over 1000 members. Other examples are the Public Relations Institute of South Africa, Zimbabwe Institute of Public Relations, Public Relations Society of India, and the Public Relations Association of Trinidad and Tobago.

In addition to these national public relations groups, many nations also have organizations comparable to the International Association of Business Communicators (IABC) in the United States before it enlarged the scope of its operations. They include the Society of Business Communicators in Australia, Danish Association of Industrial Editors, Finnish Association of Organizational Communicators, and Asociacion Mexicana de Comunicaciones Internas (Mexico).

There also are regional groups of public relations practitioners. Some examples are the Federation of African Public Relations Associations, Federation of Asian Public Relations Organizations, Federation Inter-American of Public Relations Associations, and the Pan Pacific Public Relations Federation.

On a global basis, there is the International Public Relations Association (IPRA), founded in 1955, an individual membership society for professionals with overseas interests. IPRA has almost 1000 members in more than 60 countries and is seeking further expansion, primarily in Latin America, the Middle East, and Asia. Every third year IPRA sponsors a World Congress of Public Relations, which often attracts 600 or more practitioners. IABC (discussed in Chapter 4) is primarily a North American organization, but it has chapters in Great Britain, Belgium, Hong Kong, the Philippines, and southern Africa.

IPRA has its own code of ethics, known as the Code of Athens. This document speaks in general terms about the responsibility of members to observe "the moral principles and rules of the Universal Declaration of Human Rights." Then it declares that members:

Shall Refrain From:

- Subordinating the truth to other requirements
- Circulating information which is not based on established and ascertainable facts
- Taking part in any venture or undertaking which is unethical or dishonest or capable of impairing human dignity and integrity
- Using any "manipulative" methods or techniques designed to create subconscious motivations which the individual cannot control of his/her own free will and so cannot be held accountable for the action taken on them.

In addition to the various associations that have been noted, numerous networks of public relations agencies provide clients with services almost anywhere in the world. One of the largest is IPR, which links agencies in almost 50 countries.

OPPORTUNITIES IN INTERNATIONAL WORK

The 1990s, according to many experts, represent a new golden age of global marketing and public relations. The opening of the European Market, coupled with economic and social reforms in East European countries and the former Soviet Union, will hasten the reality of a global economy.

All of these developments led Jerry Dalton, immediate past president of the Public Relations Society of America, to say, "I think more and more American firms are going to become part of those overseas markets, and I expect a lot of Americans in public relations will be living overseas." Indeed, Dalton believes that the fastest-growing career field for practitioners is international public relations. He adds: "Students who can communicate well and are fluent in a foreign language may be able to write their own ticket." But the coming of the "global village," as Marshall McLuhan once described it, still means that there will be a multiplicity of languages, customs, and values that public relations professionals will have to understand.

Many transnational corporations, putting an increased emphasis on international customer relations, are hiring "corporate protocol" officers to be responsible for doing everything from booking hotels, planning banquets, and hiring limousines to scheduling plant tours, arranging security, and selecting gifts for foreign officials and major customers. They even brief company executives on current events, advise on the correct protocol for greeting royalty, and "hand out sheet music for sing-alongs at Korean banquets," according to a New York *Times* article.

Its author, Paul Finney, says, "Corporations tend to fill their protocol jobs with people who have backgrounds in public relations, marketing, [and] meeting planning and who have a knowledge of the industry." Although knowledge of foreign languages is a plus, it is not a prerequisite. One protocol officer is quoted as saying, "At AT&T, we're dealing with over 100 countries. You can rent language skills—interpreters, translators—if you need them."

Gavin Anderson, chairman of Gavin Anderson & Company, which has several offices abroad, is an expert in international public relations. He writes:

Practitioners of either global or international public relations are cultural interpreters. They must understand the business and general culture of both their clients (or employers) and the country or countries in which they hope to do business. Whether as an outside or in-house consultant, the first task is to tell a U.S. company going abroad (or a foreign party coming to the United States) how to get things done. How does the market work? What are the business habits? What is the infrastructure? The consultant also needs to understand how things work in the host country, to recognize what will need translation and adaptation. . . .

The field needs practitioners with an interest in and knowledge of foreign cultures on top of top-notch public relations skills. They need a good sense of working environments, and while they may not have answers for every country, they should know what questions to ask and where to get the information needed. They need to know where the potential dangers are, so as to not replenish the business bloopers book.

COMPUTER ERROR COSTS PEPSI MILLIONS

A sales promotion for Pepsi-Cola International became a nightmare when a half million Filipinos claimed the million-peso ($37,000) prize after the number 349 was drawn on May 25, 1992.

Pepsi refused to pay, saying the wrong number had been announced because of computer error. The refusal spawned fury. Rioting took place outside Pepsi plants. More than 30 delivery trucks were set on fire or bombed. Company officials received death threats and a grenade tossed at a truck killed a woman and child.

As a public relations gesture, Pepsi paid $18 each to anyone holding one of the caps. About $11 million was distributed. Said Kenneth Ross, a company spokesman: "It's a horribly unfortunate situation. But there was no attempt on Pepsi's part to deceive anybody . . . and we acted very quickly and very aggressively to correct the mistake."

EXTRACTING OIL FROM THE RAIN FORESTS

Chevron went to unusual lengths to protect the environment when it developed a $1 billion oil field in Papua New Guinea. But villagers in the jungles and mangrove swamps there have been hard to please.

Determined to make the Kutubu operation a practical model of sustainable development, Chevron, among other actions:

■ Laid a 159-mile pipeline underground to minimize damage to the rain forest.

■ Spent about $45 million in building a highway, schools, and clinics.

■ Tried to ensure that money and other benefits actually get to the local people—members of the Fasu, Foi, and other tribes who, according to the *Wall Street Journal,* speak about 800 dialects and "lived in Stone Age isolation until the 1930s."

"We've tried to make this a model effort for development that is environmentally sound and socially responsible," said William Fraizer, the project's director of development.

But, demanding even more development such as a highway all their own (shut off to outsiders), the clans have complained of hunting and fishing disruption and fewer benefits than expected. Villagers carrying spears, axes, and bows and arrows have attacked Chevron officials and set up roadblocks.

". . . If the clans shut down production—or if oil prices fall—Chevron could have a very expensive engineering showcase on its hands," said the *Journal.*

The decision to seek an international career should be made during the early academic years, so a student can take multiple courses in international relations, global marketing techniques, the basics of strategic public relations planning, foreign languages, social and economic geography, and crosscultural communication. Graduate study is an asset. Many students serve internships with international corporations as a desirable starting point.

Taking the U.S. Foreign Service Officers' examination is the first requirement for international government careers. Foreign service work with the innumerable federal agencies often requires a substantial period of government, mass media, or public relations service in this country before foreign assignments are made.

CASE STUDY: TURKEY AS SAFE HAVEN

A multinational program marked 500 years of peaceful living in Turkish lands by Jews expelled from Spain in 1492. Managed by the GCI Group, New York, it sought to create goodwill for Turkey and encourage tourism.

In focus-group research in the United States, more than 90 percent of those interviewed had a negative opinion of Turkey. Interviews with U.S. Jewish leaders disclosed that they had almost no knowledge of Turkey's role in Jewish history.

The campaign included an information kit, news releases, by-lined articles, a calendar of events in the United States and Turkey, a trilingual quarterly newsletter reaching 25,000, a community resource guide for North America, a teacher's guide, a student's handbook, and teaching collaterals. Two video news releases were distributed to 150 television stations, and a series of five "mat" releases went to smaller newspapers nationwide.

Briefings were held for Turkish press and for foreign correspondents based in Turkey. Groups of journalists were taken to Turkey from the United States, the United Kingdom, Italy, and France.

Spokespersons toured the United States to address local foreign affairs committees and Jewish and Turkish groups, and meet with the press. An exhibition of 50 photographs depicting modern Jewish life in Turkey toured 20 cities across North America. The public relations group set up cooperative efforts with important U.S. Jewish groups. Journalists and Jewish leaders traveled to Turkey to promote Jewish-heritage tours.

Print publicity included 95 articles reaching more than 28 million people, appearing in such media as *Newsweek,* the New York *Times,* and the European, as well as Jewish press in 20 metropolitan areas. Radio spots totaled 96 minutes of air time. The video news release was aired on 115 stations with a viewership of nearly 14 million. An information center fulfilled more than 11,000 requests for materials.

The program also raised funds for restoration of an ancient synagogue and construction of historical monuments in Turkey. More than 600 attended a $1,000-a-plate dinner in New York at which humanitarian awards were presented to the president of Turkey and others. Publicity about it appeared in the New York *Times,* London *Times,* Reuters, Associated Press, and Agence France-Presse.

The campaign won not only the 1992 Golden World Award (international category) but also the 1992 Overall Golden World Award of the International Public Relations Association.

INTERNATIONAL CRISIS COMMUNICATIONS

Union Carbide faced an international public relations nightmare in December of 1984, when a tragic gas leak at its plant in Bhopal, India, resulted in the almost immediate deaths of more than 2,500 of an estimated half-million people in the affected area, caused another 50,000 or more to be treated, and brought lingering illness for lung damage and other complications from chemical poisoning to tens of thousand others. By 1992 the death toll exceeded 3,800.

This was the worst industrial disaster in history. *Time* magazine reported, "There is no way to put a price tag on the damage done to Union Carbide's image in 38 countries, from Nigeria to New Zealand, where it has factories, and the 130 nations in which it sells products."

But Union Carbide was able to generate a level of public respect in the days immediately following the disaster by implementing a crisis communication plan that portrayed genuine company concern for the victims.

The corporation chairman, Warren M. Anderson, flew to India within hours of the accident. Serving as the company's chief spokesperson on the disaster, he made himself available to hundreds of reporters clamoring for information. Reporters were impressed with his open manner and found him believable when he said the disaster was Union Carbide's "highest priority."

To back up his statements, Anderson pledged $1 million in immediate relief funds for victims and their families. In addition, he offered a team of technical experts to the Indian government probing the disaster and volunteered to close the company's methyl isocyanate plants around the world. Operations at a similar plant in West Virginia were immediately suspended until the cause of the gas leak was determined.

All this activity—quick action, genuine concern, openness with the press, Anderson as a central spokesperson, and the company's record of corporate responsibility—illustrated the basic concepts of effective crisis communications on an international level.

Union Carbide's legal and public relations problems in India, however, were just beginning. The Indian government filed suit for victims' compensation in the United States, but a federal judge refused to accept the case, saying that India was the proper site for the trial. In 1989 the Indian Supreme Court ordered Union Carbide to pay $470 million to the government for relief for the victims.

The settlement was negotiated by Union Carbide and the government of Prime Minister Rajiv Gandhi. Contentions that the sum was inadequate helped Gandhi's opponent, V.P. Singh, defeat the prime minister in his re-election bid.

The new government began distributing $210 million of the award in the form of individual payments of $12 per month for three years. The remaining $260 million was to be distributed after India's Supreme Court ruled on motions by the government and victims' advocates to overturn the settlement in the hope of winning a larger one.

The court, however, overturned only the part of the settlement that gave the company and its executives immunity from criminal prosecution and threatened to take over the firm's property unless officials appeared to face the criminal charges.

AUSTRALIA INVITES THE WORLD TO EXPO

Australia may be "down under" for most of the world, but thousands of visitors, including more than 5000 media representatives from 20 nations, found their way to Brisbane for World Expo 88, thanks to a full-blown public relations and marketing campaign. The favorable impression of Australia created by Expo helped Sydney win the right to host the 2000 Summer Olympic Games.

Planning   Several years in advance, the organizing committee established a communications division to create national and international awareness and anticipation of the exposition. Its departments—community relations, information services, media relations, media operations, entertainment publicity, and promotions—worked up a comprehensive program.

Execution   *Media Alert,* a press kit and media guide, was prepared, and the Australian media were invited to a series of briefings before Expo opened.

A full-staffed media center was created. It included a briefing auditorium, photo darkroom, broadcast facilities, telex machines, phone banks, and computers.

Publications. Specialized magazines, brochures, and newsletters included:

- *Expo Down Under*—sent monthly to the media, travel industry, and national and international corporations

- *Travel Industry Update*—distributed to national and international travel people. Targeted were travel agents, recipients also of a six-page brochure printed in six languages and a brochure called a "travel shell," on two blank pages of which the agents could work up their own tour packages.

- A newsletter for Australian school children, encouraging group travel

- *Neighborhood Update*—a community newsletter advising area residents about logistics and how Expo organizers were working to assure that local neighborhoods would suffer a minimum of disruption.

In addition, feature stories and photos were distributed to in-flight magazines and Australian civic club publications.

Video. A ten-minute promotional video briefed media representatives and accompanied talks about Expo were provided to service clubs throughout the country. For the foreign market: four-minute videos in Japanese, French, and German.

Direct Marketing. Australians were invited to nominate friends and relatives abroad to compete for free trips to Expo. The approximately 125,000 names and addresses submitted produced a mailing list for Expo promotional materials.

Results Media representatives included a contingent of 293 reporters and photographers from Japan, accompanying Japan's Prime Minister Noboru Takeshita. Other large media delegations accompanied King Juan Carlos of Spain and Prime Minister Margaret Thatcher of England. Interpreters were provided.

The Expo staff compiled approximately 22,000 newspaper and magazine clippings from around the world and received reports of about 2,000 television and 3,000 radio stories.

CASE STUDY:
A 90-COUNTRY CAMPAIGN—THE DALKON SHIELD STORY

By court order the A.H. Robins Company had *only six weeks* in which to notify users of its Dalkon Shield contraceptive device *in 90 countries,* by public relations means alone, that claims of infection-related deaths and other health problems allegedly associated with the device had to be filed by a certain date.

After four years of worldwide distribution, the company had withdrawn the device in 1974. Numerous lawsuits followed. A decade later there was concern that some women were still using it, so Robins conducted a national campaign to urge women with the device to have it removed.

The financial strain of continuing litigation, however, forced Robins to file for reorganization under Chapter 11 of the U.S. Bankruptcy Code. In November 1985, the federal judge in the case set April 3, 1986, as the date after which no further claims could be filed. Declaring that advertising would be too expensive, the judge ordered that a public relations program be designed and executed in all countries where the 4.5 million devices had been distributed. The notification program, he said, had to be completed by January 31, 1986.

Robins conducted an informational campaign in the United States during January 1986. The company then asked Burson-Marsteller to design and execute a public relations program in the 90 other countries—the largest such targeted problem in history.

Strategy/Research   Working with the Robins staff, Burson-Marsteller decided to reach as many people as possible through a simultaneous, multiple-tiered notification program directed at the media, medical associations, and health officials. Each of the audiences would receive special packets of explanatory materials written in local official languages. Press conferences were planned in 16 cities regarded as international media centers, from which the message could be spread.

Planning   The 90 countries were divided among 29 Burson-Marsteller offices and affiliates. The Washington, D.C., office coordinated and monitored the planning, which included preparation of a news release, background document, letter to U.S. ambassadors, letter to medical organizations, and print and broadcast public service announcements (PSAs). The Berlitz Translation Services translated materials into 29 languages, and the New Zealand affiliate later translated them into four languages used in the southern Pacific islands. Nine Robins officials were trained to serve as spokespersons.

Execution   Each Burson-Marsteller field office compiled targeted media, medical, and other lists, made dialectal adjustments to the translated materials, distributed the information, arranged press conferences, and prepared to document contacts.

Obstacles that had to be overcome included (1) accomplishing everything within six weeks, including religious holidays; (2) censorship and intervention by some countries; (3) documentation in countries where no such services existed; and (4) international politics.

Evaluation   The program generated worldwide coverage: 352 reporters attended the 16 press conferences; more than 4800 news media outlets received the information directly; 570 medical organizations, 447 Planned Parenthood organizations, and more than 7000 other groups received the materials; more than 2000 news clippings were obtained; and 300 instances of broadcast coverage were documented.

In all, more than 25,000 potential claims were filed from foreign countries, far more than the court had anticipated. The judge proclaimed the effort an overwhelming success. And Burson-Marsteller completed the assignment $200,000 below its allocated $1 million budget.

By 1993 well over 100,000 women had been notified of their options for collecting from a $2.4 billion trust fund set aside as compensation. The two-decade dispute neared an end.

CASE STUDY: CHINA—A PUBLIC RELATIONS SUCCESS STORY

An international soft-drinks manufacturer turned to Hill and Knowlton Asia Ltd. to handle and publicize events marking the opening of its second bottling plant in China and a six-day tour of that country by the company's international board of directors.

Hill and Knowlton staff members in Hong Kong and Beijing researched and prepared an extensive briefing booklet for the directors, senior executives, and their spouses. The booklet included daily agendas, biographies of key guests, current events, history, cultural pointers, and economic briefs on the five cities to be visited. The more than 30 production items included glossy bilingual brochures, banquet invitations, bus banners, and gift items such as calligraphy books, lapel pins, and bottle-opener pens.

A satellite feed was arranged from Guangzhou, site of the plant opening, for broadcast to key media in Asia, Europe, South America, and the United States. Invitations to local media were dispatched, and 19 journalists from Hong Kong's leading English and Chinese media, including an Associated Press photojournalist with portable transmission equipment, were flown to Guangzhou.

Hill and Knowlton drafted, edited, and translated more than 17 speeches and releases, issued simultaneously during the six-day period throughout Hong Kong, China, and the United States. A comprehensive bilingual press kit was prepared for each of the five cities visited.

Advance teams of bilingual executives ensured that all arrangements were set before arrival of the board, which included directors who also represented five of the world's top corporations.

More than 100 stories were published by newspapers and magazines in Hong Kong and Beijing alone, including dailies with circulations exceeding 2.5 million. CCTV, the leading television station in China, broadcast a two-minute clip reaching an estimated 200 million viewers. Radio Beijing, on both its Chinese and English channel aired a two-minute report heard by an estimated 80 percent of its 800 million listeners.

Hill and Knowlton's expertise and experience in government affairs resulted in confirmed attendance at the client-hosted banquets by top government officials, a feat reportedly unheard of in China. Even Premier Zhao Ziyang participated, delivering a major policy statement during a meeting with the board members. He reaffirmed the commitment of the People's Republic of China to its "open door" policy to foreign investment and continued commitment to expanding the soft-drink industry.

With the help of the New York office of Hill and Knowlton, the satellite feed was transmitted to major stations on four other continents. From Hong Kong, news clips were sent to major broadcast stations throughout Asia.

Major U.S. newspapers covered the events, and *Fortune* magazine ran a four-page exclusive story in its national and international editions about the bus tour. The client rated the project a resounding success.

441

INTERNATIONAL
PUBLIC
RELATIONS

CASE STUDY: THE NESTLÉ INFANT FORMULA CONTROVERSY

Successive public relations campaigns have become a way of life for Nestlé, S.A. Until the late 1970s the Swiss conglomerate "had virtually no public relations programs and felt no need for anything resembling issues management," a company official said.

Since then activists have conducted a seven-year boycott of the company's products sparked by its infant-formula-marketing practices in Third World countries. The boycott ended in 1984 but was renewed in 1989. In that same year attorneys general in three states began investigating whether the marketing and advertising of Good Start H.A., a new infant formula made by Nestlé's Carnation unit, were deceptive.

Nestlé learned its damage control lessons the hard way. Fighting accusations in the early 1970s that "thousands of babies in Third World countries have died or suffered malnutrition" because of its marketing and publicity practices, Nestlé at first treated the matter as a nutrition issue. That defense was dismissed as self-serving and simply not to be believed. Then Nestlé made the mistake of suing a Swiss activist group for libel. The prolonged trial was a public relations disaster that led directly to the first boycott.

Church and charitable groups, concerned scientists, consumer advocates, labor organizations, leftist activists, and other groups were drawn into the boycott, initiated by the Minnesota-based Infant Formula Action Coalition (INFACT).

The scientific case against Nestlé and other infant formula companies (although Nestlé was the sole target of the boycott) was based on five major assumptions, according to Carol Adelman, writing in the *Policy Review* publication of the Heritage Foundation:

(1) There had been a dramatic decline in breastfeeding in developing countries: (2) bottlefed infants came largely from the poorest families in developing countries; (3) bottlefed babies in both developing and developed countries had higher disease and death rates than those breastfed; (4) mother's milk was the "perfect" food; and finally (5) corporate promotional practices contributed significantly to a mother's decision to bottlefeed.

None of these assumptions had been proved, but emotions ran high as INFACT supporters angrily charged that Nestlé's publicity and advertising tactics were causing infant malnutrition and disease from nonsterile bottle-feeding.

Stunned by the highly organized protests, Nestlé in 1980 hired Rafael D. Pagan, Jr., to formulate a public relations campaign to resolve the dispute. Pagan embarked upon what he termed a *social action management* program designed, as he put it, "to listen with political antennae to the concerns of others . . . to bridge the gap between opposing perceptions involving the corporation and the public." The following steps were taken:

1.   The issues were defined and a diagnosis made of the nature of the criticizing groups—"ideologues . . . trendy clergy and lay persons . . . and [those] who were sincerely and morally concerned regarding the problems of poverty and hunger," according to Pagan.

2.   A strategy was developed to deal with perceptions, not with facts alone, in the highly emotional environment. "Bold new approaches and flexibility were required to seize the initiative," Pagan told the Public Relations Society of America at a national conference. "High levels of risk in terms of market share losses and a high corporate visibility had to be accepted by management."

3.   A decision was made to "stick to the issue" at all costs and "not be distracted by the obviously preposterous claims of some critics"—essential to avoid counterproductive confrontation.

4.   The social base of the controversy was expanded. "A good number of highly credible church leaders, scientists and opinion makers, who were not in agreement with the critics' questionable tactics and arguments, had remained silent for too long. They now had to be encouraged to speak out."

Two key decisions helped shift the initiative to Nestlé:

1.   The company organized the Nestlé Coordination Center for Nutrition, Inc., with Pagan as president. The aim was to focus Nestlé's activities "on the positive task of performing its nutrition work so as to benefit the mothers and babies of the world—especially the Third World. . . ."

2.   In addition to steps previously taken to change its marketing policy, Nestlé in 1981 accepted the aims of the World Health Organization's recommended Code of Marketing Breastmilk Substitutes. Detailed instructions enforcing the code were sent to all field managers.

In order to gain complete credibility, the company created an independent audit commission, with former U.S. Secretary of State Edmund Muskie as chairman. The commission met with successive groups of critics and dispatched members to countries throughout the world to monitor Nestlé's implementation of the code.

"We discovered that because business is viewed as aloof, smug, and happiest when left alone to make money," Pagan said, "people are willing to believe the most ridiculous charges against us.

"But once we became aware of the world around us and opened up to human political give-and-take, we were listened to. More important, we were ourselves changed by the process, and we feel better off for it."

The first boycott ended when the International Nestlé Boycott Commission cited Nestlé's progress in adopting standards of the World Health Organization Code of Marketing Breastmilk Substitutes and called on member organizations to cease activities.

But the issue of marketing infant formula in the Third World did not go away. Five years later, opponents began a second boycott, claiming that Nestlé had not done enough and that problems still existed. Nestlé responded by conducting an information campaign to explain how it was conforming to standards set by the World Health Organization.

By 1991, however, protracted criticism by various public interest groups and pressure from Nestlé's independent infant-formula audit commission caused the company to announce a new policy. It committed Nestlé to stop providing free or low-cost formula in developing nations "except for the limited number of infants who need it."

Nestlé had been providing formula to Third World hospitals on a request basis. Over the next several years, according to the *Wall Street Journal,* "the company intends to halt virtually all such supplies and to help government officials define the infants who are truly at risk if the free formula is discontinued."

Nestlé had learned an important public relations lesson: company performance speaks louder than words.

CASE PROBLEM

As part of the liberalization of Eastern Europe, the former Czechoslovakia is now two republics with freely elected governments. In the Czech Republic, to improve the country's economy, the national tourist agency wants to promote Prague as the premier tourist destination in Eastern Europe for foreign tourists.

The Czech Republic has many features to recommend it. Much of the country was spared extensive bombing during World War II, and it has ancient castles, buildings, and medieval churches that are among the finest in Europe. Prague, the capital, is a particularly beautiful city with Old World charm. Food and lodging are relatively inexpensive, in comparison to costs in other European capitals.

Your public relations firm is retained by the Czech Tourist Agency to attract American tourists. What are your recommendations regarding (1) specific audiences to be reached, (2) key themes that should be emphasized, and (3) the publicity and promotional techniques that would be used?

QUESTIONS FOR REVIEW AND DISCUSSION

1. What is meant by international public relations? What are some of the reasons for its growth in recent decades?

2. Organizationally, in what several ways do public relations firms operate internationally?

3. What are some of the difficulties that a corporation is likely to encounter when it conducts business in another country? Enumerate some of the pitfalls that may await its public relations, advertising, and marketing personnel in such enterprises. How may these be partially or fully overcome?

4. What public information activities on an international scale does the U.S. government conduct?

5. Name three reasons why the United States and many other countries engage in shortwave broadcasting.

6. List some examples of how the Soviet government has used public relations and advertising under its new policy of openness.

7. List several objectives that foreign governments may have in conducting public relations programs in the United States. How do they seek to achieve their goals? What legal steps are required?

8. What problems did Burson-Marsteller encounter in informing Dalkon Shield users and former users in 90 countries about the deadline for filing claims?

9. Enumerate the steps taken by Hill and Knowlton to publicize the opening of a soft-drink bottling plant in China.

10. How did Australia attract thousands of visitors and obtain international publicity for its World Expo 88?

SUGGESTED READINGS

Armbrecht, Wolfgang, and Zabel, Ulf J., editors. "Image as an International Public Relations Concept." *Journal of Public Relations Research,* Vol. 5, no. 2, 1993, pp. 63–151. Series of articles about the perception of image in other cultures.

Arfield, George. "As the World Changes, So Must Communicators." *Communication World,* June/July 1993, pp. 33–54. Special issue featuring articles on public relations practice in Hong Kong, Argentina, Slovenia, Taiwan, India, Finland, Malaysia, and Spain.

Black, Sam. "Chinese Update." *Public Relations Quarterly,* Fall 1992, pp. 41–42. Development of public relations in China.

Bovet, Susan Fry. "Trends in the 'New' Europe: Four Practice Areas Will Dominate Business." *Public Relations Journal,* September 1993, pp. 18–24. Includes profiles of U.S. public relations firms active in Europe.

Chen, Ni, and Culbertson, Hugh M. "Two Contrasting Approaches of Government Public Relations in Mainland China." *Public Relations Quarterly,* Fall 1992, pp. 36–41.

Crockett, Eddie. "A Single Europe: So Far and Yet So Near." *Communication World,* May–June 1990, pp. 123–128. Profile of the European Economic Community.

Dempsey, Gerry. "Global Communication Comes into Its Own." *Communication World,* December 1992, pp. 21–23. Impact of the global economy on public relations.

Fawcett, Karen. "An Embassy Can Be a Communicator's Ally." *Communication World,* May 1993, pp. 24–27. Embassies as a source of information and assistance to public relations practitioners.

Fawcett, Karen. "The (PR) Mouse That Roared in Six Languages." *Public Relations Journal,* December 1992, pp. 13–16. The opening of Euro-Disney in France.

Freivalds, John. "Creating a Verbal Identity." *Communication World,* December 1993, pp. 32–33. Consistency in cross-cultural communications.

Freivalds, John. "Six Strategies for Doing Business in Former Soviet Republics." *Communication World,* July 1992, pp. 20–24.

Fry, Susan L. "How to Succeed in the New Europe." *Public Relations Journal,* January 1991, pp. 17–21.

Gargan, Edward A. "Chinese Propaganda Turns Black into White: Seeing Is Not Believing." *Far Eastern Economic Review,* July 13, 1989, pp. 57–58. Propaganda efforts of the Chinese government after the Tiananmen Square massacre.

Hagerty, Bob. "Trainers Help Expatriate Employees Build Bridges to Different Cultures." *Wall Street Journal,* June 14, 1993, pp. B1, B3. Cross-cultural training.

Howard, Carole M. "Perestroika from Pleasantville: Lessons Learned from Launching *Reader's Digest* in the Soviet Union and Hungary." *Vital Speeches,* April 15, 1992, pp. 405–409.

Josephs, Ray, and Josephs, Juanita W. "Public Relations in France." *Public Relations Journal,* July 1993, pp. 20–26. Includes list of leading French public relations firms.

Josephs, Ray. "Japan Booms with Public Relations Ventures." *Public Relations Journal,* December 1990, pp. 18–21.

Lublin, Joann S. "Companies Use Cross-Cultural Training to Help Their Employees Adjust Abroad." *Wall Street Journal,* August 4, 1992, pp. B1, B6.

McCarthy, Michael J. "PepsiCo Is Facing Mounting Lawsuits from Botched Promotion in Philippines." *Wall Street Journal,* July 28, 1993, p. B6.

McCoy, Charles. "Good Intentions: Chevron Tries to Show It Can Protect Jungle While Pumping Oil." *Wall Street Journal,* June 9, 1992, pp. 1, 12A.

Morrow, David J. "Need Ink Abroad?" *International Business,* February 1992, pp. 25–26. Product publicity in Europe.

Pintak, Larry. "Counselors Eye Business in Asia." *Public Relations Journal,* July 1992, pp. pp. 8–9.

Reitman, Valerie. "Enticed by Visions of Enormous Numbers, More Western Marketers Move into China." *Wall Street Journal,* July 12, 1993, pp. B1, B12.

Sharlach, Jeffrey R. "A New Era in Latin America: Free Markets Force Changes in Five Key Nations." *Public Relations Journal,* September 1993, pp. 26–28. The growth of public relations activity in Latin America.

Sharpe, Melvin L., editor. "International Public Relations." *Public Relations Review,* Summer 1992, pp. 103–221. Theme issue featuring 11 articles and research reports on various aspects of international public relations.

Shell, Adam. "American-style Public Relations Greeted Warmly in Red Square." *Public Relations Journal,* November 1992, p. 6. American practitioners visit Moscow.

Shell, Adam. "Communications Revolution Reaches China," *Public Relations Journal,* July 1993, p. 4.

Wells, Ken. "Selling to the World: Global Ad Campaigns, After Many Missteps, Finally Pay Dividends." *Wall Street Journal,* August 27, 1992, pp. A1, A8.

"When It's Not the Media Doing the Sniping." *Inside PR,* December 1992, pp. 43–44. An American public relations firm takes on Croatia as a client.

Wouters, Joyce. *International Public Relations.* New York: Amacom Books, 1991.

Membership Organizations

P R E V I E W   Membership organizations such as trade groups and professional societies, unions, chambers of commerce, and environmental groups are an important element of society. The objective of this chapter is to explain their role and describe their public relations activities.

Topics covered in the chapter include:

- Trade associations
- Labor unions
- Professional associations
- Chambers of commerce
- Environmental and social issue groups

TRADE ASSOCIATIONS

At last count, there were about 6000 trade and professional associations in the United States. Because federal laws and regulations often can affect the fortunes of an entire industry, about one-third of these groups are based in the Washington, D.C., area. There, association staffs can monitor congressional activity, lobby for or against legislation, communicate late-breaking developments to the membership, and see government officials on a regular basis.

The membership of a trade association usually consists of manufacturers, wholesalers, retailers, or distributors in the same field. Memberships are held by corporate entities, not individuals. The following are a few examples:

- American Plastics Council
- Electronic Industries Association
- American Hospital Association
- International Taxicab & Livery Association
- Pharmaceutical Manufacturers Association
- National Cable Television Association
- American Quarter Horse Association
- National Shoe Retailers Association
- National Association of Home Builders

Although individual members may be direct rivals in the marketplace, they work together to promote the entire industry, generate public support and share information of general interest to the entire membership.

By representing its entire industry, an association often is more effective as a news source than is an individual company. When a news situation develops involving a particular field, reporters often turn to the spokesperson of its association for comment.

A TYPICAL PROGRAM

To understand how a trade association uses public relations, let us examine the program of a group representing the plastics industry. Formerly the Council for Solid Waste Solutions, it is now named the American Plastics Council.

Like similar bodies, the council is financed by assessments and dues from companies in the plastics industry. It has a board of directors and a paid staff, and uses the services of a public relations firm. The council's primary objective is to create a political climate conducive to the marketing of plastic products.

The plastics industry has been under attack by consumer and environmental groups because plastic containers and products contribute to solid waste and are not easily biodegradable. In order to head off possible legislation, the council was formed to find effective, long-term solutions to the solid waste management headache. The plastics industry sought to position itself as committed to producing recyclable products.

The council's objective was to become an information/educational resource available to waste management policymakers and influential people. Its 36-page booklet *The Solid Waste Problem: No Single Cause, No Single Solution* traces the history of American waste management practices. Factsheets were developed on topics relating to plastics, and an advertorial (combined advertising and editorial) insert, *The Urgent Need to Recycle,* appeared in such magazines as *Time*. Direct mailings to elected officials introduced the council and its programs. A conference of policymakers discussed the problems of solid waste management.

Survey data later showed that more than a third of the opinion leaders perceived the plastics industry to be committed to producing recyclable products, up from about 20 percent before the program. Recycling of plastics is gaining momentum as the public reacts favorably to the publicity campaign and the industry finds new markets for recycled products. As just one example, the United States recycled 640 million pounds of plastic packaging in 1991, an increase of 9.3 percent from the previous year.

A VARIETY OF APPROACHES

Trade associations communicate to the public in a number of ways. One is the preparation of news stories and features for newspapers. Thus, the Air Conditioning and Refrigeration Institute prepares consumer tips on how to use an air conditioner economically in the home, while the Distilled Spirits Council of the U.S. distributes a recipe for cheese fondue that calls for two ounces of Scotch or bourbon. Cotton Inc., representing U.S. cotton growers, runs TV commercials promoting uses of cotton; also it places advertising and news in garment industry trade papers.

Sometimes a tongue-in-cheek approach achieves distinctive results, as in the case of the lowly catfish. The producers of Mississippi farm-raised catfish, anxious to improve the culinary image and consumption of their product, created the Catfish Institute with the help of Golin/Harris Communications. The campaign began with an elegant dinner in New York at which food editors ate catfish mousse and catfish with artichokes, served by waiters in tuxedos.

The Institute held a World Catfish Festival in Mississippi and, still in whimsical mood, created the "Loyal Order of Catfish Lovers." Well-known personalities are made honorary members, and others such as Burt Reynolds and Barbara Mandrell have been named "Catfish Lovers of the Month"—all with suitable publicity releases. The Loyal Order even has a secret catfish handshake.

Heavy distribution of media kits in which the fun is blended with recipes and nutritional information has kept the campaign going for years. Media tours by prominent food specialists reinforced the outpouring of publicity. The result: members of the Catfish Institute more than doubled their annual sales volume to 400 million pounds.

Trade groups of food growers are particularly adept at getting information in the food sections of newspapers and magazines. They send to editors a steady stream of recipes, features, and photographs of products arranged in mouth-watering servings. Typical is the following, published in a newspaper food section:

Men and women in their sixties and seventies need about one-third less calories than they did in their twenties. However, the need for nutrients apparently does not decline but may actually increase. The National Broiler Council notes that chicken is an ideal protein source for the elderly because it contains fewer calories and has a lower fat content than most red meat. . . .

Another kind of public information campaign was launched by the National Institute of Infant Services, a rather grandiose name for a trade association of diaper-supply companies. After its business had been devastated by the highly advertised use of disposable plastic and paper diapers, the institute began a public relations campaign to bring young parents back to using professionally laundered cotton diapers.

The institute's approach was to employ a child-care writer to prepare recorded radio spots and newspaper columns in which the virtues of the reusable diaper are emphasized. The writer talked about such problems as comforting a teething child and hiring babysitters, while working in her suggestions about diapers. Newspapers and radio stations used these advice items without charge. The writer also prepared a booklet, "The ABCs of Diaper Rash," distributed by members of the trade association. As a result of this campaign, the companies stopped the trend toward exclusive use of disposable diapers and increased their own business.

Makers of cloth diapers have also gained ground competitively by depicting disposable plastic diapers as an environmental hazard that clutters trash landfills. Disposable diaper companies retorted that their rivals exaggerated, because used throwaway diapers constitute only about 1 percent of trash in landfills. What's more, they told the press, washing diapers uses scarce water. Numerous states are considering bans or taxes on disposable diapers, urged on by cloth diaper manufacturers.

Other trade groups may spend the bulk of their money on advertising campaigns. To combat the perception that the chemical industry is an air polluter, the Chemical Manufacturers Association prepared a full-page magazine advertisement dominated by the photograph of a young man holding his small daughter in a swing. The headline stated, "I'm a chemical industry engineer in charge of my plant's air quality. We breathe that air. You can be sure I keep it clean." Figure 17.1 shows an organization's poster aimed at college audiences.

A LOCAL CAMPAIGN

The city of Blooming Prairie, Minnesota—population 2500—was the site of a week-long demonstration of energy-saving, conducted by the Natural Gas Council of Minnesota in conjunction with the local Lions Club, supported by numerous other civic organizations.

By making a single community the focus of its conservation program, the Natural Gas Council dramatized the fact that a concerted campaign can reduce individual energy bills. The council is a nonprofit group composed of representatives from various investor-owned utility companies. Its sole purpose is energy conservation education. This effort was intended to show that the utility companies care for the public welfare and don't coax customers into using unnecessary gas.

FIGURE 17.1
A college fraternity, Pi Kappa Phi, created this poster featuring
the classic *Rape of the Sabine Women* as a contribution to the
campaign against a campus social problem.

By working with them on this money-saving community project, the Natural Gas Council sought to establish good long-range relationships with civic leaders as well as regional and state government officials.

Called "Less-Energy Days," the Blooming Prairie project was publicized by multiple stories in the local newspaper and by news releases to regional newspapers and television and radio stations, all prepared by the council. Articles described the various events and listed tips for saving energy.

Other methods used included the following:

■ Formation of a local energy committee, through which a special publication on money-saving methods was issued and participation encouraged.

■ Publication of endorsements from state and federal energy authorities, making local residents feel "special."

■ Provision of free home energy audit services to residents and distribution of a home energy audit questionnaire.

■ Construction of a large thermometer in the center of the city that indicated daily energy usage. This injected a competitive spirit into the week.

■ Distribution of packets on energy-saving to the local schools for students to read.

Aided by local enthusiasm, the campaign achieved an 11.5 percent reduction in natural gas consumption and a 7.1 percent reduction in use of electricity. Blooming Prairie received the President's Award for Energy Efficiency, a national distinction that created pride in the community.

On another level, membership groups often cooperate with a manufacturer to educate and inform the public. The American Veterinary Medical Association (AVMA) cooperated with Merck & Co., makers of a pill to prevent heartworm disease in dogs. The company offered each chapter of AVMA a $5000 grant to generate heartworm awareness among pet owners, and gave veterinarians kits of publicity materials for distribution to local media.

As a result of a nationally coordinated campaign, conducted primarily at the local level, an additional 3 million dogs were tested and placed on preventive medication. The program increased the business of veterinarians and helped to cause a 27 percent increase in prescriptions for Merck & Co.'s product. This campaign, conducted by Ketchum Public Relations, generated 22 million print and broadcast impressions—that is, the total circulation and listening audience of the print and broadcast media that used the firm's material.

LABOR UNIONS

Since the mid-1970s, labor unions in the United States have suffered serious losses in membership and consequently in political clout. A perception of unions as money-hungry, inflexible, lacking in concern for the public interest, and at times arrogant created a severe image problem. Media coverage often showed union members in negative, adversarial positions that sometimes inconvenienced the public.

Today total union membership amounts to 16.1 percent of all American workers; the figure among private sector workers is 11.5 percent, slightly less than half what it was in 1973.

Nevertheless, labor unions still are very much a part of the American scene, and they are using public relations tools in an attempt to regain strength and influence.

Shifts in American industry contributed to the unions' decline. So did several particularly unpopular strikes. Traditional heavy industry strongholds of unionism have suffered severe reductions in employment, while nonunionized fields have enlarged their work forces. In addition, the unions' problems were increased by the strong anti-union attitude of the Reagan administration during the 1980s and by cutbacks in union work forces by some corporations during the flurry of acquisitions and mergers in the

1980s. Thus the unions must try to increase their appeal among white-collar workers and those in light industry.

Recognizing this challenge, the AFL-CIO in 1988 began a two-year, $13 million advertising and public relations campaign built around television commercials starring Jack Lemmon. The theme was "UNION, YES!" Union leaders, whose relations with the media often have been chilly, have sought to improve them. Several unions began formal training programs on media practices. Two large unions in particular—the Communications Workers of America and the United Steelworkers of America—showed a creative flair with videos, television spots, and other techniques used by corporations.

Despite these efforts, the recession of the early 1990s weakened the unions' position. A sharp reduction in defense plant work, job cutbacks by companies in trouble, and pressure on unions to give up certain benefits at contract-renewal time contributed to organized labor's problems and the challenges facing its public relations departments.

Like corporations, union managements need to employ public relations extensively with their internal audiences. They must keep their memberships informed about what they receive in return for their dues, including social and recreational programs and the representation to company management the union leadership supplies. As a whole, the unions' internal public relations have been more effective than their external relations.

PROFESSIONAL ASSOCIATIONS

Members of a profession or skilled craft organize for mutual benefit. In many ways, their goals resemble those of labor unions in that they seek improved earning power, better working conditions, and public acceptance of their role in society. Unlike their labor union counterparts, however, members of professional organizations place emphasis on setting standards for professional performance, establishing codes of ethics, determining requirements for admission to the field, and encouraging members to upgrade skills through continuing education.

In some cases, professional organizations have quasi-legal power to license and censure members. This is true of organizations such as the American Medical Association and the American Bar Association. In most cases, however, professional groups use the techniques of peer pressure and persuasion to police the particular profession or skilled craft.

In general, professional associations are national in scope with district, state, or local chapters. Many scientific and scholarly associations, however, are international, with chapters in many nations. A good example is the International Communication Association (ICA), a group of academics and communication experts. Another is the International Communications Executives Association. There is even an international association of executives who specialize in managing trade groups and professional societies.

Organizations such as the Public Relations Society of America and the International Association of Business Communicators are classified as professional associations. Here is a sampling of other organizations:

- American Association of Cereal Chemists

- International Society of Appraisers

- American Academy of Dermatology

- International Chiropractors Association

- National Association of Life Underwriters

- American Association of CPAs (accountants)

FIGURE 17.2

This sampling of logos indicates the wide range of national trade, professional, and membership organizations that cultivate public support for their products and causes. (The Seal of Cotton is a registered trademark/service mark of Cotton Incorporated.)

Public relations specialists for these organizations use the same techniques as their colleagues in other branches of practice. They address both internal and external audiences through a variety of communication tools, including newsletters, brochures, videotapes, slide presentations, radio and television spots, news releases, and direct mail packets.

Like their counterparts in trade groups and labor unions, professional associations are responsible for monitoring legislation that may affect the status or earning power of members. Many professional associations maintain a Washington office or one in the state capital and employ lobbyists to advocate positions. One of the most politically active groups is the American Medical Association (AMA).

The lobbying power exercised in Washington by major professional associations was especially evident during the Clinton administration's preparation and promotion of its health-care reform plan in 1993 and 1994. The American Medical Association, with 220,000 physician members, applied both public and backstage pressures in an effort to shape the plan to its advantage. So did other health organizations. Hillary Rodham Clinton, who headed the task force that prepared the program, addressed the AMA convention shortly before the plan was announced, seeking to win support of AMA members, who feared that their income might be restricted.

A barrage of full-page advocacy advertisements by health organizations appeared in Washington newspapers and magazines, and in national magazines with strong congressional readership. They contained such lines as "Price controls on health care would be a costly mistake" (AMA) and "What we're doing to hold down the high cost of cancer" (pharmaceutical companies).

This partial list of advertisers indicates the broad variety of professional associations trying to influence legislation: American Medical Association, Pharmaceutical Manufacturers Association, Committee for National Health Insurance, United States Surgical Corporation, HealthRight, the American Occupational Therapy Association,

---

LAWYERS PLEAD, "PLEASE LIKE US"

Movie audiences watching *Jurassic Park* laughed loudly when a dinosaur ate a lawyer. Comedians tell such jokes as:

Q. Why does California have the most lawyers and New Jersey the most toxic dumps?
A. Because New Jersey had first choice.

Such lawyer-bashing upset the American Bar Association (ABA) so much that it hired a media expert at $170,000 a year to give the legal profession a better image. President Harvey Saferstein of the California Bar Association called criticism of lawyers a form of "hate speech" and urged the public to stop saying nasty things.

The ABA campaign had to combat public conceptions that lawyers are too powerful, overpaid, often tricky, and sometimes more concerned with haggling over points of law than with determining true justice.

How much will the ABA campaign accomplish? It won't be easy. A frequent reaction to the ABA's complaints was that the lawyers were being too thin-skinned. *Time* magazine's headline on its report set the tone: "First, Kiss All the Lawyers."

and the American Speech-Language-Hearing Association. In another approach to the same end, the American Dental Society gives more than $1 million a year to political action committees.

A number of associations offer helpful services to the public. Both the Public Relations Society of America and the International Association of Business Communicators maintain a reference library available to the public or to answer queries by telephone. Another method of public service is a speakers' bureau directory, listing members willing to talk at meetings of civic and business groups. Such a directory was published, for instance, by the Society of Die Casting Engineers. The Scientists' Institute for Public Information has a toll-free referral service; journalists who dial it are given names of scientists from among the 20,000 experts on call who will answer the journalists' particular questions.

Public relations activity on behalf of individual professionals is a relatively new development. Traditionally, lawyers and medical doctors did not advertise or seek to publicize themselves in any way. The taboo arose in part from the rules and regulations of the professional societies. Until recently, many medical societies prohibited their members from hiring public relations firms. The Supreme Court, in several cases, however, said that such regulations infringed on free speech. And the Federal Trade Commission ruled in 1980 that the American Medical Association couldn't tell its members not to advertise.

Many attorneys and physicians still feel uncomfortable about advertising their services, but competition for clients and patients is breaking down the traditional taboos. A survey by *Attorneys Marketing Report,* for example, shows the majority of lawyers using Yellow Pages advertising. In descending order of frequency, they also use (1) entertainment of clients, (2) brochures, (3) seminars, and (4) newsletters.

Public relations specialists work to get lawyers on radio and television talk shows and on the programs of groups that include potential clients. Having a law firm as a public relations client, however, can create problems. One public relations counselor told the *Wall Street Journal:* "They wanted press and a lot of it. But working with them was a nightmare. Some partners refused to talk to me because they were so opposed to PR. But then, if partner X got in the paper, partner Y got jealous and mad. I tried to tell them to get the firm's name in the paper, but the partners were more interested in getting their own names in." Admits the law firm, "We had no idea what we were doing. We're just not used to hawking our services."

The *Wall Street Journal* observed another trend: "Medical associations are also hiring public relations firms to publicize new or controversial techniques. 'Fat suctioning' was the focus of a press briefing publicized by Doremus & Co. for the American Society of Plastic and Reconstructive Surgeons." As the *Journal* article suggests, such factors as the increased competition among medical doctors in urban areas and the national craze for physical fitness have stimulated physicians' reliance on public relations specialists. Both as individual professionals and as members of professional societies, doctors, like their counterparts at the bar or in the dentist's office, find it useful to let the public know what they have to offer.

A *chamber* is an association of businesspersons, often joined by professionals, who work to improve their city's commercial climate and to publicize its attractions. State chambers of commerce and, nationally, the Chamber of Commerce of the United States provide guidance to local chambers and speak for business interests before state legislatures and the federal government. The primary interest of most members, however, is focused on local affairs.

The local interest is manifested in many ways. Often, the chamber of commerce is the public relations arm of city government. The chamber staff often produces the brochures and maps sent to individuals who seek information about visiting the city or are considering moving to the area. Chambers also conduct polls and compile statistics about the economic health of the city, including data on major industries, employment rates, availability of schools and hospitals, housing costs, and so on. Attracting conventions and new businesses to the city is also an important part of chamber work.

Chambers of commerce play the role of community booster: they spotlight the unique characteristics of a city and sing its praises to anyone who will listen. Chambers often coin a slogan for a city, such as "Furniture Capital of Indiana" or "Artichoke Capital of the World." Ironically, the small city of Coalinga, California, whose downtown was devastated by a severe earthquake, has as its slogan, "Coalinga—A City Going Places!" To which columnist Herb Caen in the San Francisco *Chronicle* added, "Right. In all directions."

Because of the nature of their membership, chambers of commerce tend to be conservative politically and to support business growth actively. Generally, they campaign for expansion of their cities in the belief that "bigger is better." This attitude at times places chambers in opposition to other community groups, who want slower, more controlled growth that will reduce the impact of massive urbanization.

ENVIRONMENTAL AND SOCIAL ISSUE ACTIVIST GROUPS

Environmental cleanup holds a high place on the public agenda, primarily because of vigorous campaigns by environmental organizations. By promoting recycling, elimination of toxic waste sites, purification of air and water, and preservation of natural resources, they strongly influence our collective conscience. Organizations that fight for their favorite social causes also have achieved significant impact, both positive and negative.

Some of these organizations work relatively quietly through lobbying, litigation, and public education. Others are stridently confrontational. They draw attention to their causes with shouting demonstrations and picketing in which they challenge the police and often provoke mass arrests.

No matter what approach they take, all environmental and social issue organizations depend heavily upon public relations methods. Indeed, they could accomplish virtually nothing without doing so.

MAJOR ENVIRONMENTAL ORGANIZATIONS

Greenpeace USA, whose membership soared to 1.9 million at the start of the 1990s, is perhaps the best known of the confrontational groups. Television viewers are familiar with the daredevil efforts of some members in small boats to stop nuclear warships and other vessels they regard as perilous to the public welfare.

Greenpeace operates in 30 countries with 1000 employees and has 5 million contributors. Recently its contributions have declined; so has its political influence. Within Greenpeace a dispute exists over whether the organization should abandon its confrontational approach and concentrate on research and lobbying.

In total membership, Greenpeace is outnumbered by the much less flamboyant National Wildlife Foundation, which has 6.5 million members. Ranking next behind Greenpeace are the World Wildlife Fund, the Sierra Club, and Nature Conservancy.

All these organizations have broad agendas concerned with several forms of environmental dangers. Many other groups devote their efforts primarily to single causes. The radical Earth First! group, for example, fights to stop logging in the Pacific Northwest forests, while Clean Water Action works to keep water safe, concentrating on control of toxic chemicals.

METHODS OF OPERATION

The principal ways in which environmental organizations work to achieve their goals include the following:

- *Lobbying.* Much of this is done at state and local government levels, because environmental problems often can be resolved there. For example, approximately 150 organizations campaigned for laws to forbid smoking in public places and restrict the sale of tobacco. This campaign achieved a major success in 1993 when the Los Angeles city council made smoking illegal in the city's 7000 restaurants as well as in theaters, grocery stores, public buildings, and elevators.

- *Litigation.* Through litigation, organizations file suits seeking court rulings favorable to their projects, or attempting to block unfavorable projects. The Sierra Club did so in a years-long action that resulted in a decision by the U.S. Fish and Wildlife Service declaring the northern spotted owl a threatened species. While the Sierra Club rejoiced at the ruling, the lumber industry asserted that it would cost thousands of lumber industry employees their jobs.

- *Mass demonstrations.* Designed to demonstrate public support for a cause and in some cases to harass the operators of projects to which the groups object, mass demonstrations require intricate public relations organizational work. Organizers must obtain permits, inform the media, arrange transportation and housing, plan programs, and provide crowd control. Earth First! organizers have gained much news attention from their confrontational tactics used to counter clear-cutting of California forests.

FIGURE 17.3
An intriguing photograph and challenging headline promote
the Chesapeake Bay Foundation's drive to enlist volunteers in
its fight against bay pollution, with a minimum of text.

■ *Boycotts.* "Hit them in the pocketbook" is the principle underlying use of the boycott to achieve a goal. Group members in particular, and the public in general, are
urged not to purchase or use the products or services of companies accused of environmental offenses. Some boycotts achieve easily identifiable results. Others stay
in effect for years with little evident success because too few people participate.
One environmental success story occurred when the Rainforest Action Network

boycotted Burger King for buying Central American beef raised in cleared rain forests. The fast-food chain agreed to stop such purchases.

■ *Reconciliation.* Some environmental organizations find good results by cooperating with corporations to solve pollution problems. The Environmental Defense Fund joined a task force with McDonald's to deal with the fast-food chain's solid waste problem, leading to a company decision to phase out its polystyrene packaging. Another group, the Coalition for Environmentally Responsible Economies (CERES) created the Valdez Principles, a code of conduct for business, and sucessfully urged a number of companies to sign them.

FUND-RAISING

Direct mail fund-raising and publicity campaigns are a basic tool of environmental groups. Raising money to conduct their programs is an unending and costly problem for them. Early in the 1990s Greenpeace sent out 4.5 million pieces of mail a month for this purpose. With so many groups in the field, competition for donations is intense. Some professional fund-raisers believe that as a whole the groups depend too much on direct mail and should place more emphasis on face-to-face solicitation from wealthy individuals, foundations, and environmentally concerned corporations. Ironically, while some environmental groups denounce direct mail for creating mountains of waste paper and destroying trees, they use "junk mail" themselves to raise funds.

SOCIAL ISSUE ORGANIZATIONS

Similar to the environmental groups in structure, but with social and behavior-modification goals, are several widely known organizations. They use public relations methods such as those just described.

Mothers Against Drunk Driving (MADD) is one such group. The National Rifle Association, extremely powerful politically, is another. The antiabortion Right to Life movement and the prochoice National Organization for Women (NOW), bitter enemies, frequently clash in rival public demonstrations. The Animal Rights movement resorts at times to extreme confrontational tactics such as raiding animal research laboratories and seeking to shame the wearers of fur.

Other groups, such as the American Family Association, pressure advertisers to drop sponsorship of television shows that they consider contrary to family values. As a result of massive letter campaigns by this group, Coca-Cola and Procter & Gamble decided to cancel commercials on *Married . . . with Children.* Members of the AFA also pressured Pepsi to cancel its Madonna ads after seeing the star's video clip for her song "Like a Prayer." Cancellation of the contract with Madonna cost Pepsi $5 million, according to the *Wall Street Journal,* but probably preserved sales among members of fundamentalist groups.

THE BURNING MUST STOP.
NOW!

The world's rain forests are burning. And a wealth of wildlife is trapped in the fire's path.

Rain forests occupy just 2% of the earth's surface. Yet, these rain forests are home to half of the planet's tree, plant and wildlife species. Tragically, 96,000 acres of rain forest are burned every day.

You can help stop this senseless destruction. Right now you can join with The National Arbor Day Foundation, the world's largest tree-planting environmental organization, and support

Rain Forest Rescue. When you join, you will help establish natural rain forest barriers to stop further burning and support on-site conservation management plans to protect threatened forests.

Each and every second, a rain forest area the size of a football field goes up in smoke. You'd better call now.

Rain Forest Rescue.

The National
Arbor Day Foundation

Call Rain Forest Rescue.
1-800-255-5500

FIGURE 17.4
Rain Forest Rescue, an environmental project supported by the National Arbor Day Foundation, dramatizes its call for public support with alarming statistics and the warning, "You'd better call now."

CASE STUDY: THE EARTH TRAIN ROLLS

The goals: Inspire high school students nationwide to participate in environmental issues and give 150 youth leaders an opportunity to express their views to mass audiences.

The program: Select outstanding high school leaders, take them across the United States from Los Angeles to Washington, D.C., by rail aboard a special Earth Train, and have them talk with youth groups and the media at stops in five cities.

The organization: Working with youth groups, the Gateway Pacific Foundation sponsored the train. Ketchum Public Relations of San Francisco handled operations and helped to obtain corporate sponsors.

Applications for the 150 places on the train were solicited by letters to youth groups across the country. Train arrangements were made with the Southern Pacific Railroad and AMTRAK. At stops en route, the passengers participated in Youth Forums and Environment Expos. They met foreign ambassadors at the United Nations and U.S. senators in Washington.

CASE PROBLEM

The Vision Council of America is a trade group representing the optical industry. Its three core membership groups are ophthalmologists, opticians, and optometrists.

The group decides to launch a consumer education program after research reveals a reluctance to take children for eye exams because parents rely on free in-school screenings. Additional research shows that 80 percent of learning before age 12 is accomplished through vision, yet traditional in-school vision screenings miss between 70 and 80 percent of children's vision problems.

Your public relations firm is retained to conduct a national consumer education program emphasizing the importance of annual eye exams for children. What would you suggest? Program elements that you should consider include key publics, message themes, time of year, strategies, and types of communication tools.

The program generated more than 155 million impressions, including features on CNN, NBC radio, Entertainment Network, Voice of America, *Seventeen,* and *Teen Beat.* Associated Press distributed two wirephotos. Ten thousand Earth Train educational curriculum books were distributed.

QUESTIONS FOR REVIEW AND DISCUSSION

1. Trade associations, like other membership organizations, often have headquarters in Washington, D.C., or a state capital. Why?

2. Describe how the Council for Solid Waste Solutions seeks to influence public opinion about the role of plastic.

3. How did the growers of catfish more than double their annual sales?

4. What challenges do labor unions face today?

5. What are the differences and similarities among trade groups, labor unions, and professional associations?

6. Professional associations recently applied heavy public relations and advertising pressure on the government concerning a major political issue. What was it?

7. What decisions stimulated the trend for members of the professions to use public relations counsel?

8. Chambers of commerce often are described as the public relations arm of city government. Why?

9. Give an example of how social-cause lobbying at the local level achieved a result affecting many people.

10. Name four methods environmental organizations use to further their cases.

SUGGESTED READINGS

Abrahmson, Jill. "Lobbyists Threaten to Use Leverage to Protect a Very Special Interest: Their Prized Tax Break." *Wall Street Journal,* July 19, 1993, p. A16. The lobbying of national membership organizations.

Anders, George. "Doctors Lobby Patients in a Campaign to Shape Clinton Health-Care Package." *Wall Street Journal,* July 26, 1993, pp. B3, B5. American Medical Association seeks grass-roots support.

Andrews, Michael C. "Today the Goodyear Blimp, Tomorrow the Moon." *Public Relations Quarterly,* Spring 1993, pp. 39–40. Shriners organization.

Badaracco, Claire, editor. "Public Relations and Religion." *Public Relations Review,* Fall 1992, pp. 231–314. Series of articles on religion in this special issue.

Burton, Thomas M., and Schwadel, Franchine. "Greenpeace Is Battling Slide in Contributions and in Political Clout." *Wall Street Journal,* March 3, 1993, pp. 1A, 6A.

Goldman, Kevin. "NRA Calls Ads for Women Educational." *Wall Street Journal,* September 28, 1993, p. B6. National Rifle Association launches campaign to increase female membership.

Graham, Ellen. "Sprawling Bureaucracy Eats up Most Profits of Girl Scout Cookies." *Wall Street Journal,* May 13, 1993, pp. 1A, A9.

Grunig, James. "Sierra Club Study Shows Who Become Activists." *Public Relations Review,* Fall 1989, pp. 3–24.

Holmes, Paul. "Have Plastics Gotten a Bad Rap?" *Inside PR,* February 1993, pp. 32–34. Industry fights stereotype of being a major polluter.

Milbank, Dana. "Union's Woes Suggest How the Labor Force in U.S. Is Shifting." *Wall Street Journal,* May 5, 1992, pp. 1A, 6A.

Ostrowski, Helen I. "Drug Makers Prescribe Cure for Ailing Reputation." *Public Relations Journal,* October 1993, pp. 18–23. Pharmaceutical industry defends itself against Clinton criticisms.

Schmitt, Richard B. "Lawyers Plan to Accentuate the Positive." *Wall Street Journal,* June 23, 1993, pp. B1–B2. American Bar Association campaign to polish the image of lawyers.

Ybarra, Michael J. "Public Media Go for Jugular to Push Causes." *Wall Street Journal,* September 7, 1993, pp. B1, B5. Use of advertising by activist groups.

18

Social, Cultural, and Health Agencies

P R E V I E W   The objective of this chapter is to show students the wide range of nonprofit agencies that exist, the role public relations plays in them, and the way in which fund-raising is organized and conducted to support them.

The chapter includes these topics:

- Public scrutiny of nonprofit organizations
- The seven categories of social agencies
- Public relations goals
- Importance of volunteer workers
- Organization, motivation, and types of fund-raising
- Use of direct mail solicitation
- Health-care public relations
- Hospitals' use of public relations

THE CHALLENGES OF PUBLIC RELATIONS
FOR PHILANTHROPIC ORGANIZATIONS

Social service, cultural, medical, educational, and religious organizations exist to improve the human condition. Communication is essential to the success of these organizations. Since these groups are not profit-oriented, the practice of public relations in their behalf differs somewhat from that in the business world.

As discussed in Chapter 14, public relations in corporate life includes a defensive factor, to protect the company from attack and defend it if an attack or crisis comes. Traditionally, nonprofit social agencies have been seen as the "good guys" of society—high-minded, compassionate organizations whose members work to help people achieve a better life. Recently, that perception has changed in some cases.

Numerous agencies have been caught by the recent American urge to scrutinize all aspects of the governmental and social establishment. Famous organizations usually regarded as sacrosanct have found themselves in trouble. The Girl Scouts of America were accused of having such heavy overhead expense for their annual national cookie sale that the girls themselves received little direct benefit. The Boy Scouts of America ran into difficulty for barring homosexuals from membership. The United Way of America, which collects charitable contributions to aid many agencies, suffered scandal and public indignation when news stories revealed that its president received an annual salary of $463,000 and used United Way funds to support a lavish lifestyle. Other investigative reporting disclosed that most top executives of major nonprofit institutions receive salaries above $100,00 and some above $300,000.

These controversies and disclosures, coupled with the economic recession of the early 1990s and the imposition of higher federal taxes on the wealthy in 1993, have created difficult fund-raising and image problems for nonprofit organizations. This in turn puts additional pressure on public relations representatives to tell their stories more effectively and, like their colleagues in the corporate world, to prepare crisis management plans.

For many nonprofit groups, obtaining operating funds is a necessity that dominates much of their effort. Without generous contributions from companies and individuals whose money is earned in the marketplace, nonprofit organizations could not exist. As an indication of the scope of philanthropy in the United States, and of the money needed to keep voluntary service agencies operating, American contributions to charity were $124.3 billion in 1992, according to the American Association of Fund-Raising Counsel (see Figure 18.1). Additional funds are donated to specialized nonprofit organizations that do not fall under the "charity" mantle, and still more are contributed by federal, state, and local governments. Competition among nonprofit agencies for their share of donations is intense.

In general terms, nonprofit organizations are of two types—*service,* typified nationally by the Visiting Nurse Association and the Boys Clubs of America, and *cause,* whose advocacy role is exemplified by the National Safety Council and the National Association for the Advancement of Colored People (NAACP). Frequently organizations have dual roles, both service and advocacy.

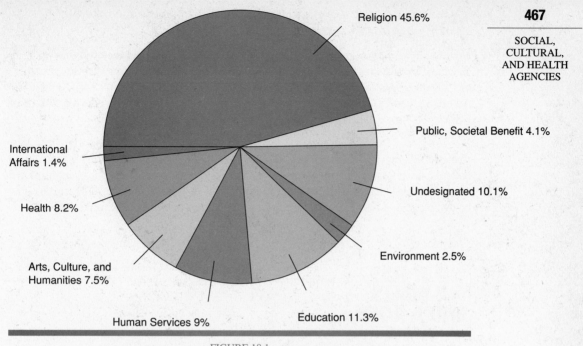

FIGURE 18.1
This pie chart shows how the $124.3 billion given to charity in
1992 was allocated. Individual gifts accounted for $101.8 bil-
lion of the total, foundations gave $8.3 billion, corporations $6
billion. Bequests accounted for $8.2 billion.

Independent Sector, a nonprofit coalition of more than 850 foundation, corporate,
and voluntary organizations, in 1990 estimated the existence of 983,000 tax-exempt
voluntary and philanthropic organizations in the United States.

Demands on volunteer service agencies to enlarge their programs of aid to the needy
are growing, in part because of efforts in recent years to reduce federal welfare services
and shift increased responsibility for humanitarian work to service organizations.

THE SEVEN CATEGORIES OF SOCIAL AGENCIES

For purposes of identification, nonprofit organizations and their functions may be
grouped into seven categories:

1. *Social service agencies.* Serving the social needs of individuals and families in
many forms are social service agencies. Among prominent national organizations of
this type are Goodwill Industries, the American Red Cross, Boy Scouts and Girl Scouts

of America, and the YMCA. Local and regional chapters of these organizations carry out national programs at the community level.

2. *Health agencies.* Many health agencies combat a specific illness through education, research, and treatment, while others deliver generalized health services in communities. Typical national organizations include the American Heart Association, the American Cancer Society, the National Multiple Sclerosis Society, and the March of Dimes.

3. *Hospitals.* Public relations work for hospitals is a large and expanding field. The role of a hospital has taken on new dimensions. In addition to caring for ill and injured patients, hospitals conduct preventive health programs and provide other health-related social services that go well beyond the traditional institutional concept. Hospitals may be tax-supported institutions, nonprofit organizations, or profit-making corporations.

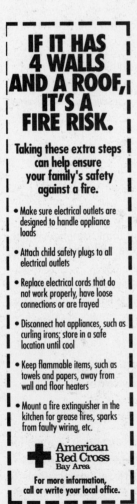

FIGURE 18.2
The American Red Cross emphasizes preventive action to save lives in its public relations campaigns, as well as providing assistance in times of disaster and tragedy.

4. *Religious organizations.* The mission of organized religion, as perceived by many faiths today, includes much more than holding weekly worship services. Churches distribute charity, conduct personal guidance programs, provide leadership on moral and ethical issues in their communities, and operate social centers where diverse groups gather. Some denominations operate retirement homes and nursing facilities for the elderly. At times, religious organizations assume political roles to further their goals. The nondenominational Salvation Army provides the needy with shelter, food, and clothing. It has a vigorous public relations program to generate support and raise funds.

Churches in particular feel the pressure for increased private agency participation in welfare work. Some churches operate food lines, and as the number of homeless Americans multiplied in the late 1980s and early 1990s, churches have taken a prominent role in providing shelters for them.

A recent study by the Brookings Institution, *Fiscal Capacity of the Voluntary Sector,* stated in this regard: "Because religion occupies a stable, central role in American life, religious institutions will be looked to as a backup finance and delivery mechanism by other subsectors . . . particularly . . . in the human service field."

Commenting on these developments in a speech to the Baptist Public Relations Association, Don Bates, a prominent New York public relations counselor, pointed out: "Certainly the shift from government to private initiative provides more opportunities to serve people in need and to prove a case in the process for what your organization does and how it benefits the community."

5. *Welfare agencies.* Most continuing welfare payments to persons in need are made by government agencies, using tax-generated funds. Public information officers of these agencies have an important function, to make certain that those entitled to the services know about them and to improve public understanding of how the services function.

6. *Cultural organizations.* Development of interest and participation in the cultural aspects of life falls heavily into the hands of nonprofit organizations. So, in many instances, does operation of libraries, musical organizations such as symphony orchestras, and museums of art, history, and natural science. Such institutions frequently receive at least part of their income from government sources; many are operated by city, state, and federal governments. Even government-operated cultural institutions depend upon private-support organizations such as Friends of the Museum to raise supplementary funds and help operate their facilities.

Regardless of their ownership and management, government or private, cultural institutions require vigorous public relations activity. Creation and publicizing of programs, formation of support groups, development of a volunteer staff, and fund raising involve the public relations staff either directly or on a consulting basis.

7. *Foundations.* The hundreds of tax-free foundations in the United States constitute about 6 percent of total charitable giving. Money to establish a foundation is provided by a wealthy individual or family, a group of contributors, an organization, or a corporation. The foundation's capital is invested, and earnings from the investments are distributed as grants to qualified applicants in the field for which the foundation was established. Often foundations offer matching grants, in which recipient organizations

FIGURE 18.3
Social, cultural, and health agencies such as those whose logos
are shown here depend on extensive fund-raising programs to
finance their work.

are given money equal to the amount they raise from other sources. A variation is the challenge grant, in which the foundation offers a gift of a specified amount if the recipient organization can raise an identical sum.

The public knows about such mammoth national organizations as the Ford Foundation, the Rockefeller Foundation, and the National Science Foundation. It is probably not aware, however, of many smaller foundations, some of them extremely important in their specialized fields, that distribute funds for research, education, public performances, displays, and similar purposes.

Giving away money constructively is more difficult than most people realize. Again, public relations representation has a significant role. The requirements of a foundation must be made known to potential applicants for grants. Inquiries must be handled and announcements of grants made. In the case of the very large national foundations, at least, general information explaining the organization's work and its social value needs to be circulated. This is necessary, among other reasons, to allay uneasiness among some persons who suspect that the tax-exempt status of foundations is a device to avoid paying a fair share of the tax burden. In small foundations, public relations work is handled by the executive secretary, but most larger foundations have a public relations staff of one or more persons.

From this summary, the student can see what diverse, personally satisfying opportunities are available to public relations practitioners in the social agency fields.

PUBLIC RELATIONS GOALS

Every voluntary agency should establish a set of public relations goals. In doing so, its management should heed the advice of its public relations staff members, for they are trained to sense public moods and are responsible for achieving the goals. Emphasis on goals will vary, depending on the purpose of each organization. In general, however, nonprofit organizations should design their public relations to achieve these objectives:

1. Develop public awareness of the organization's purpose and activities

2. Induce individuals to use the services the organization provides

3. Create educational materials—especially important for health-oriented agencies

4. Recruit and train volunteer workers

5. Obtain funds to operate the organization

The sections that follow discuss ways in which each of these goals can be pursued.

PUBLIC AWARENESS

The news media provide well-organized channels for stimulating public interest in nonprofit organizations and are receptive to newsworthy material from them. Newspapers usually publish advance stories about meetings, training sessions, and similar routine activities. Beyond that, much depends upon the ingenuity of the public relations practitioner in proposing feature articles and photographs. Television and radio stations will broadcast important news items about organizations and are receptive to feature stories and guest appearances by organization representatives who have something interesting to tell. *Stories about activities are best told in terms of individuals, rather than in high-flown abstractions.* Practitioners should look for unusual or appealing personal stories—a retired teacher helping Asian refugee children to learn English, a group of Girl Scouts assisting crippled elderly women with their shopping, a volunteer sorting donated books for a Friends of the Library booksale who discovers a rare volume. A physician who speaks to the American Heart Association and explains warning signs for a certain heart ailment in an unusually compelling manner perhaps would be willing to give the same lecture on a local magazine-type television show.

Creation of events that make news and attract crowds is another way to increase public awareness. Such activities might include an open house in a new hospital wing, a concert by members of the local symphony orchestra for an audience of blind children, or a Run-for-Your-Life race to publicize jogging as a protection against heart trouble. A museum of history may sponsor a history fair for high school students with cash prizes for the best papers and projects.

Novelty stunts sometimes draw attention to a cause greater than their intrinsic value seems to justify. For example, a bed race around the parking lot of a shopping center by teams of students at the local university who are conducting a campus fund drive for the March of Dimes could be fun. It would draw almost certain local television coverage and raise money, too. Each team would have a banner over the bed it pushed, and a streamer across the finish line would proclaim the cause. The possibilities of event publicity are countless.

Publication and distribution of brochures explaining an organization's objectives, operation of a speaker's bureau, showings of films provided by general headquarters of national nonprofit organizations, and periodic news bulletins distributed to opinion leaders are quiet but effective ways of telling an organization's story. Fund raising, which will be discussed later, always stimulates public awareness.

USE OF SERVICES

Closely tied to creation of public awareness is the problem of inducing individuals and families to use an organization's services. Free medical examinations, free clothing and food to the urgently needy, family counseling, nursing service for shut-ins, cultural programs at museums and libraries, offers of scholarships—all these and many other services provided by nonprofit organizations cannot achieve their full value unless potential users know about them.

The news media are valuable in this work. So is word of mouth. Boys and girls become interested in joining the Scouting organizations when they hear about the good times their friends are having in them. Awareness of Planned Parenthood's counseling services and Meals on Wheels food delivery to shut-ins is spread in neighborhood conversations.

Because of shyness or embarrassment, persons who would benefit from available services sometimes hesitate to use them. Written and spoken material designed to attract these persons should emphasize the ease of participation and, in matters of health, family, and financial aid, the privacy of the consultations. A health organization attracts clients with material describing the symptoms of a disease and urging those who suspect such symptoms in themselves to see a physician or to inquire at the organization's office. The American Cancer Society's widely publicized warning list of cancer danger signals is an example of this approach.

CREATION OF EDUCATIONAL MATERIALS

Public relations representatives of nonprofit organizations spend a substantial portion of their time preparing written and audiovisual materials. These are basic to almost any organization's program.

The quickest way to inform a person about an organization is to hand out a brochure. Brochures provide a first impression. They should be visually appealing and contain basic information, simply written. The writer should answer a reader's obvious questions: What does the organization do? What are its facilities? What services does it offer me? How do I go about participating in its activities and services? The brochure should contain a concise history of the organization and attractive illustrations. When appropriate, it may include a membership application form or a coupon to accompany a donation. Videotapes also are very effective as introductory tools.

Organizations may design logos, or symbols, that help them keep their activities in the public eye. Another basic piece of printed material is a news bulletin, usually monthly or quarterly, mailed to members, the news media, and perhaps to a carefully composed list of other interested parties. This bulletin may range from a single duplicated sheet to an elaborately printed magazine. Tax-exempt organizations that meet Postal Service standards as religious, educational, scientific, philanthropic, agricultural, labor, veterans', or fraternal groups may be able to obtain special bulk third-class nonprofit rates that let them mail their bulletins at approximately one-third the first-class rate.

A source of public relations support for national philanthropic organizations is the Advertising Council. This is a not-for-profit association of advertising professionals who volunteer their creative and technical skills for organizations such as the American Red Cross, the National Alliance of Business, and the National Committee for the Prevention of Child Abuse. The council creates public service advertising campaigns in the public interest. Figure 18.4 shows an American Red Cross educational poster.

The council handles more than 30 public service campaigns a year for nonsectarian, nonpartisan organizations, chosen from 300 to 500 annual requests. Newspapers and radio and television stations publish or broadcast free of charge the advertisements the council sends them. The sponsoring agency reimburses the council for the cost of campaign materials.

One of the best ways to tell an organization's story succinctly and impressively is with an audiovisual package. This may be a slide show or a video, usually lasting about 20 minutes, to be shown to community audiences and/or on a continuing basis in the organization's building. As described earlier, an organization can create its own slide show and perhaps make its own videotape program, or specialists may be hired to do the work. Local chapters of national organizations usually are able to obtain audiovisual materials from their national headquarters.

VOLUNTEER WORKERS

A corps of volunteer workers is essential to the success of almost every philanthropic enterprise. Far more work needs to be done than a necessarily small professional staff can accomplish. Recruiting and training volunteers, and maintaining their enthusiasm so they will be dependable long-term workers, is an important public relations function. Organizations usually have a chairperson of volunteers, who either answers to the public relations (often called community relations) director or depends upon the director for assistance.

The statistics are impressive. One in five American adults volunteers time for charitable causes, according to a Bureau of Labor Statistics survey. The median weekly time volunteers contribute is slightly more than four hours. Yet the demand for more volunteers is intense. A major problem is that since so many women now hold jobs and have less free time, they can do less volunteering than earlier generations did.

FIGURE 18.4
This striking poster featuring singer Patti LaBelle was issued
by the American Red Cross and the U.S. Public Health Service
as part of the campaign to educate Americans about the causes
of AIDS, the deadly acquired immune deficiency syndrome.

The concept of voluntary, private charity activity, so strongly developed in the
United States, is spreading to other parts of the world. It has taken root recently in
Eastern Europe and in those Asian countries that are prospering with new wealth.
Volunteerism long has been a factor in Western Europe.

More than 400 U.S. voluntary agencies also do work overseas. The fundamental changes in the global political and social picture, led by the collapse of communism in Eastern Europe, have created new opportunities and challenges for them. Experts foresee the development of worldwide voluntary organizations that may substantially replace government-operated foreign programs. Rotary International, for example, has raised millions of dollars in a drive to eliminate polio from the world by the year 2000.

FIGURE 18.5
A promotional campaign built around a popular cartoon figure is an excellent way for a social agency to attract volunteer workers, because the familiar character gives the agency an aura of significance. Legal permission from the cartoonist before such use is essential.

What motivates men and women to volunteer? The sense of making a personal contribution to society is a primary factor. Volunteer work can fill a void in the life of an individual who no longer has business or family responsibilities. It also provides social contacts. Why does a former business leader living in a retirement community join a squad of ex-corporate executives who patrol its streets and public places each Monday, picking up wastepaper? The answer is twofold: pride in making a contribution to local well-being and satisfaction in having a structured activity that partially replaces a former business routine. For the same reasons, the retired executive spends another day each week as a hospital volunteer, working in the supply room. Those motives are basic to much volunteerism.

Social prestige plays a role, too. Appearing as a model in a fashion show that raises funds for scholarships carries a social cachet. So does selling tickets for a debutante ball, the profits from which go to the American Cancer Society. Serving as a docent, or guide, at a historical museum also attracts individuals who enjoy being seen in a prestigious setting. Yet persons who do well at these valuable jobs might be unwilling to stuff envelopes for a charity solicitation or spend hours in a back room sorting and mending used clothing for resale in a community thrift shop—jobs that are equally important. Such tasks can be assigned to those volunteers who enjoy working inconspicuously and dread meeting the public.

Religious commitment is another powerful motivating force. Churches provide the base for many social service organizations that depend on workers who donate their time.

Retirees Make Excellent Volunteers   Retired men and women, who are increasing in number, form an excellent source of volunteers. The Retired Senior Volunteers Program (RSVP) operates 750 projects nationwide, staffing them from its membership of 365,000. The largest organization of seniors, American Association of Retired Persons (AARP), directs its members into volunteer work through its AARP Volunteer Talent Bank. With well over 34 million members, AARP also operates an insurance program for older citizens, publishes the magazine *Modern Maturity,* and provides discounts on drugs and travel.

How to Recruit Volunteers   Recruiters of volunteers should make clear to potential workers what the proposed jobs entail and, if possible, offer a selection of tasks suitable to differing tastes. A volunteer who has been fast-talked into undertaking an assignment he or she dislikes will probably quit after a short time.

The public relations practitioner can help in recruiting by supplying pamphlets, videotapes, slide shows, speakers, and other information resources to explain the organization's purpose, to show the essential role its volunteers play, and to stress the sense of achievement and social satisfaction that volunteers find in their work. Testimony from successful, satisfied volunteers is an excellent recruiting tool. Instruction materials and speakers should be provided to train new volunteers. Those who meet the public may receive small badges with their names and the word *Volunteer* printed on them.

Like all persons, volunteers enjoy recognition, and they should receive it. Certificates of commendation and luncheons at which their work is praised are just two ways of expressing appreciation. Hospital auxiliaries in particular keep charts showing how many hours of service each volunteer has contributed. Service pins or similar tokens are awarded for certain high totals of hours worked. Whatever form of recognition it chooses, every organization using volunteers should make certain that it says "Thank you!"

Active, satisfied volunteers do more than provide a work force for an organization. They also form a channel of communication into the community.

FUND-RAISING

Because fund-raising is one of the key goals of all voluntary agencies, it warrants more developed discussion here.

At board meetings of voluntary agencies, large and small, from coast to coast, the most frequently asked question is, "Where will we get the money?" Discussion of ways to maintain present programs and to add new ones revolves around that inevitable query. Obtaining operating funds is a never-ending problem for organizations, except for a few blessed with endowments sufficient for their needs.

Although some voluntary organizations receive funds from government sources, many depend entirely upon money they raise in contributions. Because agencies receiving government funds frequently find the subsidies inadequate, they must join in the scramble for donations.

Fund-raising has been elevated to a highly developed art involving sales psychology, financial skill, ingenuity, and persistence. It may be as simple as the sale of raffle tickets to neighbors, or as complex as intricate forms of accounting that provide donors with cherished tax shelters. Although the largest, most publicized donations are made by corporations and foundations, the total of individual contributions far exceeds combined corporate and foundation giving, amounting to about 84 percent of the more than $100-billion annual U.S. philanthropic donations. Depending on their needs, voluntary organizations may try to catch minnows—hundreds of small contributions—or angle for the huge marlin—large gifts from big-money sources. Some national organizations raise massive sums. The Salvation Army, the biggest fund-raiser in 1992, received $726 million in contributions that year; Catholic Charities USA was second with $410 million, and the United Jewish Appeal third with $407 million.

Public relations representatives participate directly in fund-raising by organizing and conducting solicitation programs, or they may serve as consultants to specialized development departments of their organizations. If their needs are substantial, organizations often employ professional firms to conduct their campaigns on a fee basis. In that case, the organization's public relations representatives usually have a liaison function.

Fund-raising on a major scale requires high-level planning and organization. Various departments and divisions, each with a particular area of responsibility, may be set up. An organizational chart for a typical fund-raising campaign is shown in Figure 18.6.

THE RISKS OF FUND-RAISING

Fund-raising involves risks as well as benefits. Adherence to high ethical standards of solicitation and close control of money-raising costs, so that expenses constitute only a reasonable percentage of the funds collected, are essential if an organization is to maintain public credibility. Numerous groups have suffered severe damage to their reputations from disclosures that only a small portion of the money they raised was applied to the cause they advocated. The rest was consumed in solicitation expenses and administrative overhead.

These fund-raising and administrative costs fluctuate widely among organizations, depending on circumstances, and it is difficult to establish absolute percentage standards for acceptable costs. New organizations, for example, have special start-up expenses. In general, an organization is in trouble if its fund-raising costs are more than 25 percent of what it takes in, or if fund-raising and "administrative overhead" exceed 40 to 50 percent.

Some examples among respected national organizations include the following: the American Cancer Society applies 78.2 cents of every dollar it raises to its anticancer work; solicitation costs are 12.1 cents and administrative overhead 9.7 cents. The American Heart Association applies 75 cents to its work, with 14 cents for solicitation and 11 cents for administration. The Girl Scouts of America applies 71 cents to its work;

FIGURE 18.6
This chart shows the basic structure of a fund drive.
Specialized groups should be added in each division as necessary to meet local organizational and geographical needs.

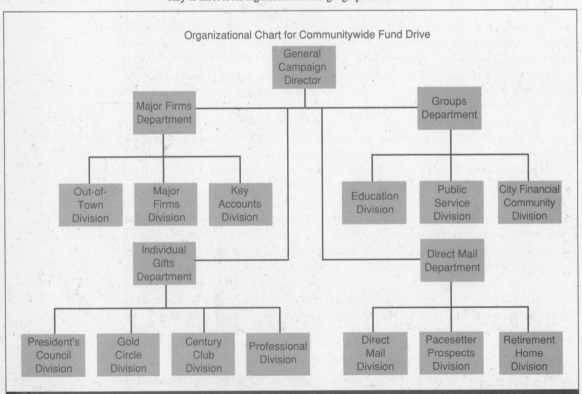

1.9 cents go to solicitation and 27.1 cents to administration. The United Way of America averages about 13 percent for fund-raising and overhead costs.

The National Charities Information Bureau, which reported the cancer organization's performance, sets a standard that 70 percent of funds raised by a charity should go into programs.

The United Way of America scandal, in which the offending president was forced to resign, is the most dramatic of recent disclosures, but recurring reports of nonprofit organizations devouring most of their contributed funds in overhead costs and extravagances have added to public concern about contributing. Some causes have involved outright fraud. The State of California, for example, filed fraud charges against three charities that claimed to fight drug abuse, help homeless veterans, and aid abused children. The suit alleged that 95 percent of the agencies' $8.6 million in contributions had been funneled into the hands of the man who had created all three organization and his associates.

To protect its reputation, a social agency should publish an annual report that specifies expenses as well as income. It should encourage its solicitors to know the financial facts so they can answer questions. Reputable agencies do this (see Figure 18.7).

Charitable groups should be extremely cautious about lending their names to promoters and telemarketing firms that sell merchandise or conduct events on their behalf, using their names. Often the marketing firm takes 80 to 90 percent of the funds raised, and the charitable organization receives only 10 to 20 percent. The charity's credibility often is damaged by deceptive, high-pressure methods the promoter employs. In one California city, a telemarketing firm used a collection agency in an attempt to collect pledges for a staged softball tournament to benefit abused children. The resulting public anger and unfavorable media coverage dealt a crippling blow to the sponsoring charitable agency.

FIGURE 18.7
The scandal caused by extravagant spending of the United Way national administration caused a severe drop in contributions from the public. This headline from *Today*, published by Weyerhauser Corporate Communications, is an example of the campaign to regain support.

Hill urges employees to support United Way

Weyerhaeuser campaign chair Steve Hill says United Way has shaped up, and remains a great way to donate to charity

MOTIVATIONS FOR GIVING

An understanding of what motivates individuals and companies to give money is important to anyone involved in fund-raising. An *intrinsic desire to share* a portion of one's resources, however small, with the needy and others served by philanthropic agencies is a primary factor—the inherent generosity possessed in some degree by almost everyone. Another urge, also very human if less laudable, is *ego satisfaction.* Those who are motivated by it range from donors to large institutions who insist that the buildings they give be named for them, down to the individuals who are influenced to help a cause by the knowledge that their names will be published in a list of contributors. *Peer pressure* is a third factor; saying "no" to a request from a friend is difficult. The cliché about "keeping up with the Joneses" applies here, openly or subtly. Some organizations exploit this pressure almost ruthlessly by holding dinner meetings at which those present are urged to announce their pledges publicly before their fellow guests.

FIGURE 18.8
The March of Dimes builds public confidence in its integrity
and efficiency by inviting possible donors to request audited
financial statements showing how it spends the contributions
it receives.

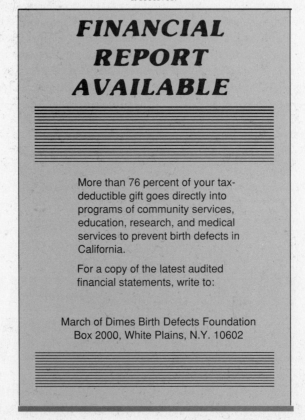

FINANCIAL REPORT AVAILABLE

More than 76 percent of your tax-deductible gift goes directly into programs of community services, education, research, and medical services to prevent birth defects in California.

For a copy of the latest audited financial statements, write to:

March of Dimes Birth Defects Foundation
Box 2000, White Plains, N.Y. 10602

While many companies are truly desirous of contributing a share of their profits to the community well-being, they also are aware that news of their generosity improves their images as good corporate citizens. Individuals and corporations alike may receive income tax deductions from their donations, a fact that is less of a motivating factor in many instances than the cynical believe.

Fund-raisers know that while many contributors desire nothing more than the personal satisfaction of giving, others like to receive something tangible—a plastic poppy from a veterans' organization, for example. This fact influences the sale of items for philanthropic purposes. When a neighbor high school girl rings the doorbell, selling candy to raise a fund for a stricken classmate, multiple forces are at work—instinctive generosity, peer pressure (not to be known in the neighborhood as a tightwad), and the desire to receive something for the money given. Even when householders are on a strict diet, they almost always will accept the candy in return for their contribution rather than merely give the money.

The poorest U.S. households, with incomes of less than $10,000, gave a greater percentage to charity in 1990, than did households with incomes above $100,000.

Independent Sector commissioned the Gallup Poll in 1990 to do a survey on volunteerism and giving. The survey found that 53 percent of those responding cited "assisting those who are less fortunate" as their personal motive for volunteering and giving. The second most frequently cited reason was gaining a feeling of personal satisfaction; religion was third. Only 6 percent cited tax considerations as a major reason for giving.

THE COMPETITIVE FACTOR

The soliciting organization also should analyze the competition it faces from other fund-raising efforts. The competitive factor is important. The public becomes resentful and uncooperative if approached too frequently for contributions. Deserving causes may fail in their campaigns if other organizations have been vigorously in the field ahead of them. That is why the United Way of America exists, to consolidate solicitations of numerous important local service agencies into a single unified annual campaign.

The voluntary United Way management in a community, with professional guidance, announces a campaign goal. Pledges are collected from corporation managements, from their employees through voluntary payroll deduction, from other individuals, and from any additional available sources during a specified campaign period. The money is distributed among participating agencies according to a percentage formula determined by the United Way budget committee.

LOOK-ALIKE ORGANIZATIONS

A vexing problem for major, nationally known organizations is the growing number of look-alike groups. Using names almost like the well-known ones, they solicit funds by direct mail, siphoning off donations the givers thought they were sending to the long-established groups.

The Cancer Fund of America, with a name that imitates the renowned American Cancer Society, even used a return mail address on Peachtree Street in Atlanta, the street on which the American Cancer Society headquarters is located. The big organizations try to combat such diversionary tactics through public education and legal actions.

TYPES OF FUND-RAISING

Philanthropic organizations raise funds in several ways:

- Corporate and foundation donations
- Structured capital campaigns
- Direct mail
- Sponsorship of events
- Telephone solicitations
- Use of telephone numbers with "800" and "900" area codes for contributors
- Entrepreneurship

Corporate and Foundation Donations Organizations seeking donations from major corporations normally should do so through the local corporate offices or sales outlets. Some corporations give local offices a free hand to make donations up to a certain amount. Even when the decisions are made at corporate headquarters, local recommendation is important. Requests to foundations generally should be made to the main office, which will send application forms if the organization's request falls within the scope of the foundation's purpose.

Corporations make donations estimated at more than $5 billion a year to all causes, of which roughly 40 percent goes to education. Much of this is distributed in large sums for major projects, but an increasing amount is going to smaller local programs. A directory, *Guide to Corporate Giving,* published by the American Council for the Arts in New York, describes the contribution programs of 711 leading corporations, which provide $1 billion of the more than $5 billion total. As an example, in a typical recent year the largest contributor was PPG Corporation, with $120 million over five years to the Scripps Research Clinic. Corporations often fix the amount they will contribute each year as a certain percentage of pretax profits. This ranges from less than 1 percent to more than 2.5 percent. The timing of applications is important, because many corporations set aside money for donations in their annual budgets. Corporate years often begin on July 1, so requests should be made well in advance of that date.

Increasingly, corporations make donations on a matching basis with gifts by their employees. The matching most commonly is done on a dollar-for-dollar basis; if an employee gives $1 to a philanthropic cause, the employer does the same. Some corporations match at a 2-to-1 rate or higher. This system tends to spread corporate gifts on a wider basis in a community to smaller, less prominent, voluntary agencies in which individual employees take an interest. By the early 1990s, nearly 900 companies had matching-gift programs, although some were limited to higher education.

Corporations make contributions to charities in less direct ways, too, some of them quite self-serving. (The practice of cause-related marketing is explained in Chapter 14.) Well over 13 million consumers received a mailing from the Arthritis Foundation containing cents-off coupons for pain-relief consumer products from two pharmaceutical companies. One company offered to donate 25 cents to the Arthritis Foundation for each coupon it received, up to $50,000, and the other offered 50 cents each, up to $100,000.

The Arthritis Foundation's local chapters strongly supported the program, and the foundation permitted use of its logo in grocery ads.

Structured Capital Campaigns   The effort to raise major amounts of money for a new wing of a hospital, for an engineering building on a campus, or even for the reconstruction and renovation of San Francisco's famed cable car system is often called a capital campaign.

Because of the significant amounts involved, campaign organization and fund-raising techniques become much more sophisticated than soliciting funds through bulk direct mail or selling candy and cookies from door to door. In a capital campaign, emphasis is placed on substantial gifts from corporations and individuals. One key concept of a capital campaign, in fact, is that 90 percent of the total amount raised will come from only 10 percent of the contributors. In a $10 million campaign to add a wing to an art museum, for example, it is not unusual that the lead gift will be $1 or $2 million.

Capital campaigns require considerable expertise and, for this reason, many organizations retain professional fund-raising counsel. There are a number of firms in the country that offer these services, but the most reputable are those belonging to the American Association of Fund-Raising Counsel.

Traditionally, professional fund-raisers were paid by organizations for their work either in salary or by a negotiated fee. In a controversial decision, however, the National Society of Fund-Raising Executives changed its code of ethics in 1989 to permit its members to accept commissions based on the amount of money their drives raise. It did so because its attorney said the old arrangement violated federal antitrust law as a restraint of trade.

The preparation for a capital campaign, whether managed by a professional counseling firm or by the institution's own development staff, is almost as important as the campaign itself.

The first step is a survey among community leaders and influential people to determine support for the proposed campaign. Do community leaders, particularly those who will be asked to make major donations, think the cause is just and needed by the community? Is this the right time for a capital campaign? Do the proposed plans make sense? In many cases, this kind of feedback causes revision in plans and cost of the project. A finding that community leaders are not sold on the idea signals the need for an intensive cultivation program to brief potential backers thoroughly on the project and to get their support. Cultivation programs also (1) encourage community leaders to participate in the project at an early stage and (2) identify major donor prospects.

The next step is to compile a list of companies and wealthy individuals who will personally be approached for a major contribution. It is common practice for campaign organizers to establish a specific amount of money they will request from each leading potential donor. It is also an axiom of capital fund-raising that prospective donors are asked to contribute by someone who is their peer. Thus the president of one major company will solicit the president of another leading firm. It is also a principle of effective fund-raising that those who ask for gifts have already made their own pledge.

The fund campaign usually is organized on quasi-military lines, with division leaders and team captains. An advance gifts division concentrates on anticipated large donors, so that when the campaign is formally kicked off the leadership can announce that a substantial amount already has been pledged toward the goal. This provides impetus and inspiration to the bulk of the volunteer solicitors, and it creates a bandwagon effect for community support.

Donors often are recognized by the size of their gifts—and terms such as *patron, contributor,* or *founder* are used. In addition, major donors may be given the opportunity to have rooms or public places in the building named after them. Hospitals, for example, prepare "memorial" brochures that show floor plans and the cost of endowing certain facilities.

Direct Mail Direct mail is an expensive form of solicitation because of the costs of developing or renting mailing lists, preparation of the printed matter, and postage. An organization can conduct an effective local, limited direct mail campaign on its own if it develops an up-to-date mailing list of "good" names known to be potential donors and can provide enough volunteers to stuff and address the solicitation envelopes. Regional and national organizations, and some large local ones, either employ direct mail specialists or rent carefully chosen mailing lists from list brokers.

The old days when direct mailing pieces came addressed to "Occupant" are largely gone, thanks to the wonders of computerized mailing lists. Now the letters arrive individually addressed. Inside, the appeal letter may bear a personalized salutation and include personal allusions within the text, such as: "So you see, Ms. Smith, that this opportunity. . . ."

The abundance and diversity of mailing lists for rent is astounding. One company offers more than 8000 different mailing lists. A common rental price is $30 per thousand

---

WRITING DIRECT MAIL LETTERS

A large percentage of fund-raising for charitable institutions is conducted through the direct mail letter. The purpose of the letter, of course, is to produce a response—that is, a donation. Writers of fund-raising letters have learned the best approaches:

1. Make use of an attention-getting headline.

2. Follow with an inspirational lead-in on why and how a donation will benefit clients of the charitable agency.

3. Give a clear definition of the charitable agency's purpose and objectives.

4. Humanize the cause by giving an example of a child or family that benefited.

5. Include testimonials and endorsements from credible individuals.

6. Ask for specific action, and provide an easy method for the recipient to respond. Self-addressed stamped envelopes and pledge cards often are included.

7. Close with a postscript that gives the strongest reason for reader response.

names. Other lists cost more, depending on their special value. The best lists contain donors to similar causes. Direct Media List Management Group, for example, offers a list of almost 1.5 million "aware" women who have contributed to at least one of 27 causes. Or a person can order the Doris Day Animal League list of 400,725 donors. These people are described as "compassionate animal lovers who have responded to a direct mail appeal requesting donation and petition signatures to protect animals from unnecessary laboratory experimentation."

In direct mail campaigns, economic success depends on getting the mailing pieces into the hands of potential donors while not wasting postage in mailing to those who probably are not. Marketing research firms feed demographic, geographic, and psychographic information into computers; the computers then produce mailing lists focused on the desired audience. Such targeting greatly increases the predictable percentage of successful contacts from the mailing. A response of 1 percent on a mailing usually is regarded as satisfactory; 2 percent is excellent.

One marketing research firm, for example, identified 34 human factors such as age, gender, education, and levels of economic well-being. It fed these factors into computers along with a list of 36,000 ZIP code markets and produced 40 neighborhood types. An organization interested in reaching one of these types—the supereducated top income level, for example—could use suitable mailing lists broken down to postal area routes.

Attractive, informative mailing pieces that stimulate recipients to donate are keys to successful solicitation. The classic direct mail format consists of a mailing envelope, letter, brochure, and response device for making a contribution, often with a postage-paid return envelope.

Another essential factor in direct mail solicitation is getting recipients to open the mailing piece. This need has resulted in development of many attention-getting graphic and psychological devices. Publishers Clearing House, a major, aggressive user of direct mail, put the large words "NOTICE OF FORFEITURE" on the envelope of a mailing piece that urged recipients to send in the enclosed entry form for a sweepstakes drawing. The words looked threateningly official but merely meant that by failing to return the form the recipient would forfeit the chance to win. Another attention-getting device that generates curiosity is to omit the name of the organization on the envelope. An address is given, but the receiver must open the envelope to determine who sent the letter. Once a well-chosen recipient has been induced to open the envelope and begin reading the message, much of the selling work has been done. After that, the appeal of the message and the degree of ease with which the recipient can respond will determine the result.

Direct Mail List Rates and Data, updated bimonthly by Standard Rate & Data Service, Inc., is a basic reference book for direct mail lists.

Sponsorship of Events   The range of events a philanthropic organization can sponsor to raise funds is limited only by the imagination of its members.

Participation contests are a popular method. Walkathons and jogathons appeal to the current American emphasis on using the legs for exercise. Nationally, the March of Dimes holds an annual 32-kilometer WalkAmerica in 1100 cities on the same day. Local organizations do the same in their own communities. Bikeathons are popular, too. The money-raising device is the same in all such events: each entrant signs up sponsors who promise to pay a specified amount to the fund for each mile or kilometer the entrant walks, jogs, runs, or cycles. If an entrant obtains several sponsors, at rates from a few cents up to $1 a mile, the contributions mount up.

Staging of parties, charity balls, concerts, and similar events in which tickets are sold is another widely used approach. Often, however, big parties create more publicity than profit, with 25 to 50 percent of the money raised going to expenses. Other methods include sponsorship of a motion picture opening, a theater night, or a sporting event. Barbecues flourish as money-raisers in western cities. Used-book sales can be excellent profit-makers. Raffles, either on their own or in connection with a staged event, are profitable. So are home tours. This is only a sampling of methods popular with smaller organizations, which normally do the work themselves without professional assistance.

Sale of a product, in which the organization keeps a portion of the selling price, ranges from the church baked-goods stand, which yields almost 100 percent profit because members contribute homemade products, to the massive national Girl Scout cookie sale, which grosses about $375 million annually. Light bulbs, candy, grapefruit, Christmas fruitcake, and magazine subscriptions are other commodities sold in this manner.

A key to success in all charity-fund sales is abundant publicity in the local news media. Posters, movable-letter signs, and announcements at organization meetings also help. Use of paid advertising rarely is worthwhile because its cost eats seriously into the profit margin.

Direct solicitation of funds over television by *telethons* is used primarily in large cities. A television station sets aside a block of air time for the telethon, sponsored by a philanthropic organization. During the telethon, the host and a parade of well-known guests take turns making on-the-air appeals for contributions. Donors telephone an announced number, where a battery of volunteers record the pledges. Mixed in with the appeals are bits of entertainment by the guests and prearranged on-camera presentations of large checks by corporations and other givers. Best known of the national telethons is the one conducted annually by comedian Jerry Lewis for muscular dystrophy. Telethons have become increasingly expensive to stage and usually are suitable only for organizations that can command entertainment talent. Collection of the telephoned pledges also may be a problem.

Telephone Solicitations   Solicitation of donations by telephone is a relatively inexpensive way to seek funds but of uncertain effectiveness. Many groups hold down their cost of solicitation by using a WATS (Wide Area Telephone Service) line that provides unlimited calls for a flat fee, without individual toll charges. Some people resent receiving telephone solicitations. If the recipient of the call is unfamiliar with the cause, it must be explained clearly and concisely—not always easy for a volunteer solicitor to do. The problem of converting verbal promises by telephone into confirmed written pledges also arises. The normal method is for the sponsoring organization to send a filled-in pledge form to the donor for signature as soon as possible after the call, reminding him or her of the promise to contribute and enclosing a reply envelope.

Use of "800" or "900" Telephone Numbers   Toll-free telephone numbers with area codes of 800, permitting callers to phone an organization long distance without cost to themselves, have been in use for years. A 900 code has been added by the telephone companies that requires users to pay a fee for each call placed. The phone company takes a service charge from this fee, and the remainder goes to the party being called.

Charitable organizations increasingly are using "900" numbers in fund-raising. Although the callers must pay for their calls, they have the convenience of making a pledge without having to read solicitation material and write a response. Public television station WNET in New York used a 900 number in its annual pledge drive and received $235,000 in contributions through it.

Entrepreneurship Operation of gift shops, bookstores, coffee shops, and similar businesses is another source of revenue for nonprofit organizations. Museums, hospitals, and institutions of learning often use this method. Some large nonprofit organizations carry this approach much further by participating in real estate syndicates, publishing magazines that carry paid advertising, and entering the cable television business. Volunteer help often staffs the service businesses, enabling them to be profitable. However, many voluntary organizations lack the experience required to enter more complicated ventures than the gift shop level and may lose money if they do so. Another problem is opposition from commercial firms if the nonprofit organization's project impinges substantially on their fields of livelihood.

Any nonprofit organization contemplating operation of a business should check the tax laws, which require that the enterprise be "substantially related" to the purpose of the nonprofit group.

CASE STUDY: A LESSON IN FUND-RAISING

The Old Globe Theater in San Diego's Balboa Park is an integral part of the city's cultural life. It attracts about 300,000 playgoers a year to its 325 evening performances and has a splendid professional reputation.

The theater's board of directors knew that it needed rehearsal space, refurbishing, and a concession area. They also wanted to pay off debt incurred from rebuilding part of the theater damaged by fire in 1984 and to acquire a $2 million endowment and reserve fund.

The board decided to conduct a $10 million capital fund campaign. An article in *The Chronicle of Philanthropy* tells how they did so successfully despite severe obstacles.

First, the directors conducted a feasibility study. This showed that San Diego's community leaders did not regard the theater's financial needs as compelling; it also showed that the theater's volunteer leadership lacked members who could make large personal contributions and solicit major campaign gifts.

After a delay caused in part by the death of the theater's campaign consultant, Robert B. Sharp took the job and the campaign was revitalized. New volunteer leaders were recruited. Several events then occurred:

■ A four-color brochure was published to be given to donor prospects.

■ A few donors made large gifts as a nucleus of the drive.

■ At cocktail parties, board members and major donors heard a presentation about the campaign. They were asked to pick names of people they knew from a list of 20,000 season ticket holders. This provided a list for solicitation.

■ A precise goal was set for each prospect—2 to 5 percent of the donor's estimated "adjusted gross worth." The campaign hired a researcher to examine various credit and public records to determine what these goals should be.

With this list, the campaign reached full speed. The co-chair made a challenge gift of $500,000 that required the theater to raise $1.5 million within seven months.

Prospective donors were invited to dinner and a play, taken backstage, and given a slide presentation before seeing the play. The campaign used slides rather than a videotape because they enabled the speaker to pause during the presentation for questions.

Solicitors went after the largest gifts first, then moved step by step to the smaller prospects. They had a gift model showing the various sizes of gifts sought, from a high of $1 million down to $1000, and the number of prospects for each size (three for $1 million, 1500 for $1000). Actual donors in each category proved to be about one-third of the category's prospects.

So far, everything had been done on a personal basis without major publicity. A total of $8.5 million was raised from individuals, corporations, and foundations.

Then the campaign went public with a media blitz to solicit gifts under $10,000 from the general public. The final phase involved sending direct mail pieces to theater constituents who had not contributed.

Large donors were recognized by having their family coats of arms incorporated in the design of the new facilities and they received framed versions of the coats of arms. An importing company donated research to find coats of arms for families lacking them.

A crucial part of this successful campaign was the identification of potential large donors and the analysis of how much each might donate, so that solicitors could make their calls with specific money targets in mind.

HEALTH-CARE PUBLIC RELATIONS

The $400-billion-a-year health-care industry has an impact on all Americans who are concerned about their personal health and the often-burdensome cost of medical service. Since most medical services—primarily treatments by physicians, hospital stays, sale of medicines, and health insurance—function in a competitive environment, public relations and marketing programs are essential in their operations.

Historically, medical services in the United States have been an uncontrolled part of the free enterprise system. Patients paid the suppliers directly for services or did so through health insurance they purchased. Government-financed Medicaid paid the bills for qualified low-income patients, and Medicare insurance, paid for by recipients, helped older citizens receiving Social Security. But some 37 million Americans, financially unable to afford insurance, took their chances on staying well without financial protection, sometimes with disastrous results.

The American system differed from those in many countries, especially the industrially developed ones, where medical service is under government subsidy and control. Patients receive free medical service but pay high taxes for this benefit.

President Clinton's plan for health-care reform, to assure that every American has medical insurance, cut across the traditional American system. The ensuing debate was stimulated by elements of the health-care industry lobbying to protect their "turf."

Although based on a concept of managed medical care and federal restrictions, the plan retained a strong element of free choice by the patient. That meant a continuation of competition, although in altered form, and consequently a continuing role for public relations and marketing. The vehemence of the arguments about the plan, and the lavish expenditures for lobbying and advertising by medical companies and associations, showed what high stakes were involved.

Some American hospitals are nonprofit institutions, run either by local governments or private organizations. Many, however, are profit-making corporations. Hospitals have aggressively sought to sell services and to present a "caring" image in their communities.

PUBLIC RELATIONS FOR HOSPITALS

The public relations staff of a hospital has two specific roles: (1) to strengthen and maintain the public's perception of the institution as a place where medical skill, compassion, and efficiency are paramount, and (2) to help market the hospital's proliferating array of services. Many hospitals have sought to redefine themselves as community health centers. Basically, hospitals, like hotels, must have high room-occupancy rates to succeed financially. They supplement this fundamental source of income by creating and marketing supplementary services, an area that offers a challenge to public relations people.

These supplementary services include alcoholism rehabilitation, babysitter training, childbirth and parenting education, home care, hospices for the terminally ill, pastoral care, sexual dysfunction treatment, a smokers' hotline giving advice on how to quit, speech pathology, a physician referral service, rental of infant car seats for safety, and Tel-Ed. (Tel-Ed informs telephone callers on scores of health topics such as "Understanding Headaches" and "Are Old-Age Freckles Dangerous?")

HOSPITAL AUDIENCES

Because hospitals sell a product (improved health), parallels exist between their public relations objectives and those of other corporations. Both focus on diverse audiences, external and internal; involve themselves in public affairs and legislation because they operate under a mass of government regulations; and stress consumer relations. In the case of hospitals, this involves keeping patients and their families satisfied, as well as seeking new clients. Hospitals produce publications for external and internal audiences. They have an additional function that other corporate public relations practitioners don't need to handle—the development and nurturing of volunteer organizations whose help keeps hospitals functioning smoothly.

Hospital public relations programs have four basic *audiences:* patients, medical and administrative staffs, news media, and the community as a whole. The four audiences overlap, but each needs a special focus. Careful scrutiny can identify significant subaudiences within these four—for example, the elderly; women who have babies or soon will give birth; victims of heart disease, cancer, and stroke who need support groups after hospitalization; potential donors of money to the hospital; and community opinion leaders whose good will helps to build the institution's reputation. Each group can be cultivated by public relations techniques discussed in this textbook.

A SAMPLE OF PUBLIC RELATIONS EFFORTS

The reputations of some hospitals have been damaged by a public perception of them as cold institutions that don't care enough about individual patients. Complaints by patients about poor food and brusque nurses add to the problem.

Here are a few examples of methods hospitals use to project a positive image:

- Sponsorship of community health fairs, offering free screenings to detect symptoms of certain diseases and low-cost comprehensive blood tests. The largest health fair in the United States, in the Central Valley of California, examines nearly 20,000 poor farm laborers and unemployed workers, entirely free.

- A "direct line" telephone system within the hospital on which patients and visitors can register complaints and suggestions 24 hours a day.

- Bingo games on a closed-circuit television system, for which patients pay a small fee and win cash prizes. This brightens the patients' day.

- Creation of an information team of staff professionals to provide local TV stations and newspapers with immediate comment on health-oriented news stories and offer feature stories on medical procedures and hospital activities.

WRITING A "CASE FOR SUPPORT"

Charitable organizations requesting major funds from wealthy individuals, foundations, and corporations usually prepare a "case for support." The following is an outline of what should be contained in such a document.

Background of the Organization

- Founding date
- Purpose and objectives
- What distinguishes the organization from similar organizations
- Evolution (development) of objectives, services

Current Status of Organization's Services

- Number of paid, volunteer staff
- Facilities
- Number of clients served annually

- Current budget
- Breakdown of how budget is allocated
- Geographical areas served

Need for Organization's Services
- Factual and statistical evidence
- Availability of similar services
- Evidence showing seriousness of the problem
- Uniqueness of the program

Sources of Current Funding
- Public donations
- Foundations and corporations
- Government funding

Administration of the Organization
- Background of executive director
- Qualifications of key staff
- Board of directors (names and titles)

Tax Status of Organization

Community Support
- Letters from satisfied clients
- Letters from community leaders
- Favorable media coverage of programs

Current Needs of the Organization
- Specific programs
- Specific staffing
- Financial costs
- Amount of financial support needed
- Sources of possible funding

Benefits to Community with New or Expanded Program

Request for Specific Amount of Funds
- Need for donor's participation
- Benefits to the donor

STEPS IN RUNNING A CAPITAL CAMPAIGN

Robert B. Sharp, California professional consultant, recommends these steps in running a capital campaign:

Conduct a Feasibility Study   Commission an objective review of the cause behind the proposed campaign. The study should . . . provide a monetary goal for the campaign, as well as a "gift model"—a chart breaking down the goal into individual gift amounts and indicating how many of each are needed.

The study may also suggest breaking the campaign into phases for "sequential solicitation," starting with the largest donations and working down to smaller and smaller gifts.

The review should also lead to the development of a clear "case statement," setting out the goals for the campaign.

Get the Board's Approval for and Support of the Feasibility Study   The board should review the feasibility study, give final approval to the case statement and the goal, and take steps to carry out the recommendations. (This often results in delay.) . . .

Enlist Volunteer Leadership   Recruit volunteer leaders who are capable of making significant gifts to the campaign. Choose a campaign chairman and a committee made up of such volunteers. These volunteers will carry the campaign through a private phase, during which a major portion of the goal is achieved before seeking support from the general public.

Begin Soliciting Gifts   Using the feasibility study's gift model and suggested campaign phases, begin the solicitation of prospects, moving from attempts to get larger gifts to efforts to obtain lesser ones. In some cases, larger-gift solicitation will continue throughout the campaign, with smaller-gift phases being added.

Stop for a Midpoint Evaluation   This evaluation, taking place well into the campaign, should make needed adjustments in the drive's time line, financial goal, or strategy. It is here that the campaign is usually announced to the public through the media. Announcement of the campaign should be made only when the goal is assured. Solicitation of the general public, however, will not come until later. Many groups do not go through a formal evaluation or erroneously think that adjustments mean they have failed. . . .

Determine Closing Strategies   This phase usually means more adjustments as volunteers and staff members determine what changes need to be made to meet or exceed the original goal. They should also determine when and how they will begin to solicit the general public.

Honor Volunteer Leadership   Draw up plans for how the volunteers who led the campaign will be acknowledged with special events and permanent recognition. . . .

Perform "Administrative Wrap-up"   Because many large gifts may be divided into pledge payments that will continue to come in for some time after the campaign closes, the staff should set up procedures to process them and encourage timely payment. And staff members, volunteers, and board members should review what the campaign has achieved and then consider the campaign's implications for future fund-raising efforts.

Source: Condensed from *Chronicle of Philanthropy,* February 2, 1990.

NONPROFITS IN THE LATE 1990S

Challenges and issues facing charitable organizations in the late 1990s require leaders and public relations experts to be more creative in problem solving. Nonprofit leaders surveyed made the following predictions:

■ Competition to raise money will be fierce as more nonprofits form and use sophisticated fund-raising techniques.

■ Environmental issues will get the most increased donor support. Efforts to alleviate poverty and improve education will continue to get attention.

■ Traditional charities, such as those that raise money for major diseases, may face increased resistance from donors.

■ Donors will take a harder look at charity appeals and ask more questions before making a donation.

■ There will be increased efforts to recruit outstanding administrators, and salaries for personnel will go up.

■ More people will be interested in volunteering, but they will expect more responsibility and autonomy from the organizations they help.

■ Rising costs and new federal regulations will make raising money through the mail more difficult.

■ Fund-raising by telephone will become more sophisticated.

■ Charities will do more extensive research on the backgrounds of prospective donors and emphasize planned-giving techniques to take advantage of tax benefits.

■ There will be more battles about on-the-job solicitation, and other groups will challenge United Way's traditional dominance in community fund-raising.

■ The federal government will increase its scrutiny of charities involved in commercial ventures.

■ Foundations will give cluster grants to address a variety of social needs, instead of making grants that deal with a single issue.

■ American charities will increasingly become involved in international philanthropic efforts.

Source: The Chronicle of Philanthropy. January 9, 1990

CASE PROBLEM

The facts: For 20 years a western city of 150,000 population has operated a volunteer Meals on Wheels program, taking food to shut-ins. However, financial contributions to help support the project have dwindled, as has the force of volunteers to deliver the meals, endangering continuation of this humanitarian service. Your public relations firm has been hired by a local church to revitalize the program.

Following the four-step process explained in Part Two of this book, develop a program to achieve this objective. Define the audiences you should address. Explain specifically what you would seek to learn during your research, describe the plan of action you would use, tell how you would communicate your message, and draw up a plan of evaluation.

QUESTIONS FOR REVIEW AND DISCUSSION

1. What has caused the recent intensified scrutiny of nonprofit organizations?

2. Name the seven categories of social agencies.

3. Describe three methods a public relations practitioner might use to raise public awareness of a nonprofit agency.

4. What motivates men and women to serve as volunteer workers?

5. What is a challenge grant?

6. Why is it important for a nonprofit organization that solicits funds from the public to put out a detailed annual financial report?

7. Describe four commonly used types of fund-raising.

8. What two principal roles does a hospital public relations staff fulfill?

SUGGESTED READINGS

Chapel, Gage W. "Ethiopian Relief: A Case Study in Failed Public Relations." *Public Relations Review,* Summer 1988, pp. 22–31.

"Charitable Giving Rises 6.4%; Education Gets $14 Billion." *Chronicle of Higher Education,* May 26, 1993, pp. A25–26.

Dyck, Evelyne J., and Coldevin, Gary. "Using Positive vs. Negative Photographs for Third-World Fund Raising." *Journalism Quarterly,* Fall 1992, pp. 572–579. Photographs as emotional appeals.

Fuchsberg, Gilbert. "Charities Are Stepping Up Recruiting as Good Help Grows Harder to Find." *Wall Street Journal,* March 6, 1990, p. B1.

Gaiter, Dorothy J. "Watchdog Group Calls Effectiveness of United Way Fundraising a 'Myth.'" *Wall Street Journal,* November 20, 1992, p. B8.

Jacobson, Michael. "Museums That Put Corporations on Display." *Business and Society Review,* Summer 1993, pp. 24–27. Problems of excessive commercialism.

"Jerry's Got to Be Kidding: Why Disabled People Aren't Laughing." *Utne Reader,* March/April 1993, pp. 103–104. Criticism of Muscular Dystrophy Association (MDA) telethon.

McPherson, Doug. "Twelve Tips to Stretch Your Nonprofit Media Relations Dollar." *Public Relations Quarterly,* Fall 1993, pp. 41–42.

Montague, William. "Proliferating 'Look-Alikes' Cause Headaches for Many Charities." *Chronicle of Philanthropy,* January 9, 1990, pp. 25–26. Charities with similar names.

Olsen, Bruce L. "Developing a Non-Profit Public Relations Network." *Public Relations Quarterly,* Spring 1992, pp. 27–30. Church public relations.

Overkamp, Sunshine. "Not-for-Profits: A New Ball Game." *Public Relations Journal,* January 1990, pp. 22–23. Trends in the 1990s.

Sebastian, Pamela. "For Charity Groups, 'Tis a Prime Season for Sending Lots of Direct-Mail Appeals." *Wall Street Journal,* December 23, 1993, pp. B1, B8.

Sebastian, Pamela. "Survey Shows Gifts to Major Charities Climbed 4% in 1992." *Wall Street Journal,* November 1, 1993, p. A6.

Sebastian, Pamela. "Fund-Raisers' Own Funds Are Rising." *Wall Street Journal,* March 2, 1993, pp. B1, B9. Salaries of development directors.

Sebastian, Pamela. "AIDS Groups Refine Strategies as Many Court Same Donors." *Wall Street Journal,* December 30, 1992, pp. A1, A8.

Sebastian, Pamela. "Unemployment and Unforgotten Scandal Work Against United Way Campaigns." *Wall Street Journal,* October 21, 1992, pp. B1, B5.

Sebastian, Pamela. "Arts Groups Go After Corporate Sponsors With All the Brashness of the Big Top." *Wall Street Journal,* February 19, 1992, pp. B1, B5.

Skolnik, Rayna. "Rebuilding Trust: Nonprofits Act to Boost Reputations." *Public Relations Journal,* September 1993, pp. 29–32.

Skolnik, Rayna. "Arts and Cultural Organizations Seek Increased Private Support as Public Funding Dwindles." *Public Relations Journal,* February 1992, pp. 18–19.

"State Laws Governing Charitable Solicitations." *Chronicle of Philanthropy,* June 12, 1990, p. 33.

Vogel, Carol. "Dear Museumgoer: What Do You Think?" New York *Times,* December 20, 1992, Section 2, pp. 1H, 32H. Museums turn to marketing research for increased revenues and attendance.

Zagorin, Adam. "Remember the Greedy." *Time* magazine, August 16, 1993, pp. 36–38. Excessive administrative costs of nonprofit organizations.

Education

P R E V I E W   In this chapter the objective is to explain the role and activities of public relations in educational institutions at the university and secondary school levels and to identify the publics they need to reach.

Topics covered in the chapter include:

■ College and university development and public relations offices

■ Audiences to be addressed

■ Fund-raising from alumni and others

■ Student recruitment

■ Contemporary issues in secondary schools

■ Public school financial problems

DEVELOPMENT AND PUBLIC RELATIONS OFFICES

The president (or chancellor) is the chief public relations officer of a college or university; he or she sets policy and is responsible for all operations, under the guidance of the institution's governing board.

In large universities the vice president for development and university relations (that person may have some other title) supervises the office of development, which includes a division for alumni relations, and also the office of public relations; these functions are combined in smaller institutions. Development and alumni personnel seek to enhance the prestige and financial support of the institution. Among other activities, they conduct meetings and seminars, publish newsletters and magazines, and arrange tours. Their primary responsibilities are to build alumni loyalty and generate funding from private sources.

The public relations director, generally aided by one or more chief assistants, supervises the information news service, publications, and special events. Depending on the size of the institution, perhaps a dozen or more employees will carry out these functions, including writing, photography, graphic design, and broadcasting.

Figure 19.1 shows the organization of a public relations staff at a typical sized university.

In addition, scores of specialists at a large university perform diverse information activities in agricultural, medical, engineering, extension, continuing education, and other such units, including sports.

PUBLIC INFORMATION BUREAU

The most visible aspect of a university public relations program is its public information bureau. Among other activities, an active bureau produces hundreds of news releases, photographs, and special columns and articles for the print media. It prepares programs of news and features about faculty activities and personalities for stations. It provides assistance and information for reporters, editors, and broadcasters affiliated with the state, regional, and national media (see Figure 19.2). The staff responds to hundreds of telephone calls from members of the news media and the public seeking information.

SERVING THE PUBLICS

In order to carry out their complex functions, top development and public relations specialists must be a part of the management team of the college or university. At some institutions this is not so, and the public relations program suffers. Ideally, these leaders should attend all top-level meetings involving the president and other administrators, learning the whys and wherefores of decisions made and lending counsel. Only then can they satisfactorily develop action programs and respond to questions from the publics those programs concern. They are indeed the arms and voice of the administration.

Faculty and Staff   As noted in previous chapters, every sound public relations program begins with the internal constituency. Able college presidents involve their faculty in decision making to the fullest extent possible, given the complexities of running a major institution. It is a maxim that the employees of a company or institution serve as its major public relations representatives because they come into contact with so many people. Good morale, a necessity, is achieved in large measure through communication.

Colleges communicate with their faculty and staff members through in-house newsletters and newspapers; journals describing research, service, and other accomplishments (which also are sent to outside constituencies); periodic meetings at which policies are explained and questions answered; and in numerous other ways.

Faculty and staff members who fully understand the college's philosophy, operations, and needs generally will respond with heightened performance. For example, when the University of Georgia sought to obtain $2.5 million in contributions from its faculty members as part of an $80 million bicentennial enrichment campaign, they

FIGURE 19.1

Organizational chart of the University of Miami's public affairs office, showing the division of responsibility for the various areas of operation.

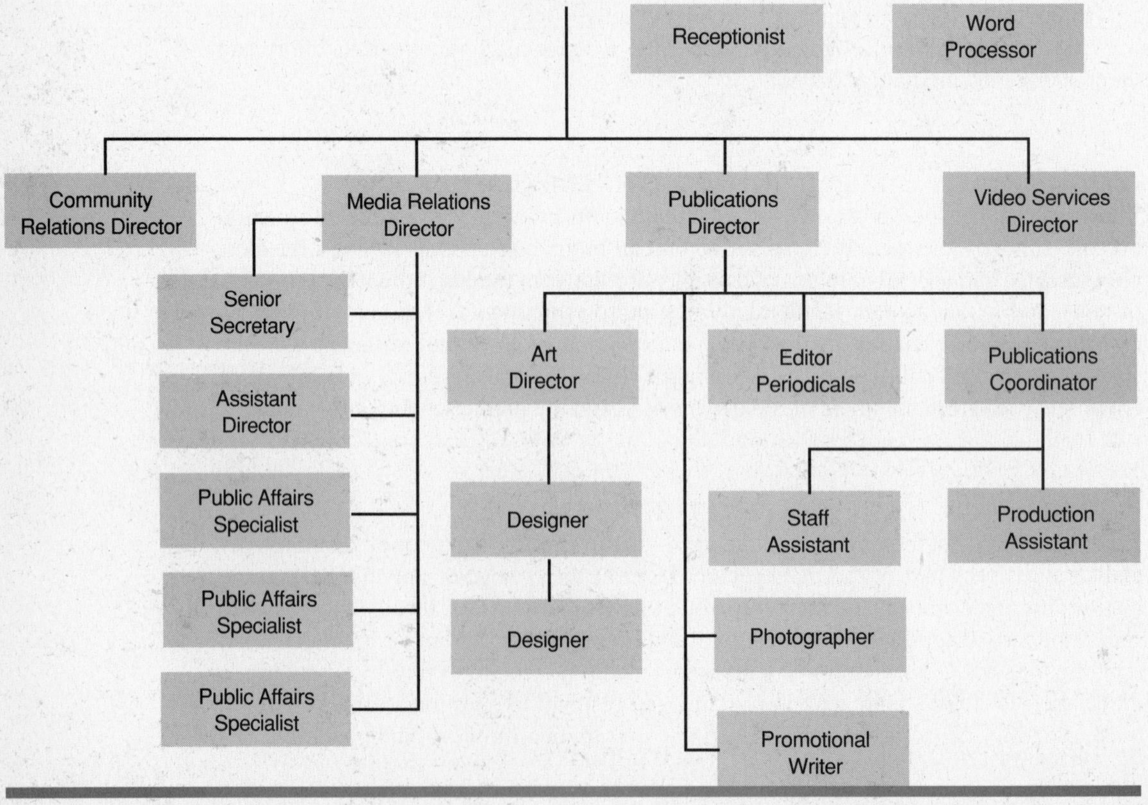

FIGURE 19.2

Some universities try to increase public awareness of themselves by having faculty members quoted in the media as experts when news develops in their special fields. In this advertisement published in *Directory of Experts, Authorities & Spokespersons,* the University of Buffalo invites the media to use its services.

responded with a generous outpouring of nearly $6 million—a signal to outside contributors that helped ensure the success of the program.

Students Because of their large numbers and the many families that they represent, students make up the largest public relations arm—for good or bad—that a university has. The quality of the teaching they receive is the greatest determinant of their allegiance to the institution. However, a sound administrative attitude toward students, involving them as much as possible in decisions that affect their campus lives, is extremely important. So are other forms of communication, achieved through support of student publications and broadcast stations and numerous other ways. When, upon graduation, they are inducted en masse into the university's alumni society, chances are good that, if they are pleased with their collegiate experience, many will support the university in its future undertakings. Public relations effort directed at students is thus essential.

Alumni and Other Donors Fund-raising activities have increased dramatically at most colleges and universities in recent years. As a result, despite the recession, private financial support for these institutions rose 4.9 percent over the preceding academic year to an estimated $10.7 billion during 1991–1992, according to the Council for Aid to Education. Individuals contributed about half of this sum. Alumni giving totaled about $2.84 billion.

With the stakes so high, the demand for experienced fund-raisers has created a shortage among those qualified, and salaries in some instances have skyrocketed well beyond $100,000 or more annually, accompanied by elaborate fringe-benefit packages. Women increasingly are holding top positions in the field.

Colleges and universities use the money mainly to attract and pay new faculty, to buy equipment and provide support for faculty research, and to attract and offer financial aid for students. A common complaint is that few grants are provided to repair or replace aged structures, re-equip obsolete science laboratories, and provide additional classroom and library space. These pressures are accompanied by a number of complications: societal demands that costs be trimmed and management streamlined; rising costs for salaries and benefits for faculty and staff (particularly in health fields); growing public concern over tuition increases; the cost of serving increasingly diverse student bodies including remedial programs and provisions for disabled students; and new developments in scholarship such as the increasing faculty collaboration in combined, expensive research projects across disciplines.

The placement of universities' endowment funds, investments totaling more than $1.7 billion, often poses a public relations problem. During the last decade or so, groups opposed to South Africa's apartheid system persuaded many universities and other entities to sever financial ties with the nation. By 1994, however, with apartheid at an end in South Africa, most institutions had revoked their bans on investment. In 1990, organizations such as the Tobacco Investment Project persuaded Harvard University and the City University of New York to sell their highly profitable stock holdings in the tobacco companies.

The movement's spread brought a similar dilemma to other universities: how and if they could withdraw their holdings in tobacco companies without sacrificing the firms' large annual grants. Particularly at risk was the United Negro College Fund, which has been receiving a total of nearly $500,000 annually from the Philip Morris Companies and RJR Nabisco.

In addition to annual operating expense drives, universities increasingly conduct long-range capital fund campaigns for very large sums, such as the $1.5 billion goal at Yale University and the $1.15 billion goal at Cornell University.

Many institutions employ students to participate in fund-raising phonothons. At the University of Michigan students called 970,000 alumni and raised $8.3 million during a nine-month period. Computerized dialing systems often are used.

At most institutions, letters are mailed to specific graduating classes over the names of members who have agreed to be class agents for that purpose A novel approach was taken by the Texas Christian University alumni office when it mailed a letter composed by Dan Jenkins, a 1953 journalism graduate and longtime *Sports Illustrated* writer and editor. "Billy Clyde Puckett," a character in Jenkins's novel *Semi-Tough,* describing himself as a "semi-tough ex-horny toad," asked fellow alumni to "haul off and give something, no matter how small, and make all those tests you cheated on and all that beer you drank stand for something." Many recipients laughed at the offbeat letter and forwarded contributions; others protested the letter's nature.

Sought are not only year-by-year contributions but bequests and annuities as well. In return, the colleges publish honor rolls listing donors, invite contributors to join hon-

YOUR GIFT COULD PRODUCE A DOCTOR, A LAWYER, OR A KING.

So many United Negro College Fund graduates go on to make royal contributions to society.

But they can't do it without your contribution.

By keeping tuitions low, the United Negro College Fund helps send thousands of deserving students to 42 private, predominantly black colleges.

Please. Give generously to the United Negro College Fund. This country needs another King.

**GIVE TO THE UNITED NEGRO COLLEGE FUND.
A MIND IS A TERRIBLE THING TO WASTE.**

FIGURE 19.3
This appeal for contributions to the United Negro College Fund, prepared by the Ad Council, emphasizes Martin Luther King, Jr., as a role model and includes the fund's widely quoted slogan, "A mind is a terrible thing to waste."

orary clubs (the President's Club, for example), and name rooms and buildings for the largest givers. Educational events and tours to foreign countries often are arranged to build and sustain alumni interest. Class reunions are said to be the most powerful instruments in getting alumni to give.

Universities often use matching grants to make a donor's contribution go further— and thus make giving more attractive. For instance, a donor in Dallas, who wanted to remain anonymous, contributed $8 million toward the establishment of faculty enrichment chairs at the University of Texas at Austin. The sum was matched by foundations,

College fund-raisers have adopted electronic and videotape technology to improve their solicitations. This new Michigan State University telephone system, which cost $350,000. automatically dials donors until a human voice answers the phone.

and the entire $16 million, in turn, was matched by the university, making possible the establishment of 32 new chairs. Such support is essential in order for good universities to become great universities.

Influential alumni and other important friends of colleges and universities also are encouraged, through personal contact and correspondence, to provide political clout with legislative bodies and boards of regents, in support of the institutions' financial and other objectives. Such support also is important in the recruitment of students with outstanding academic or athletic achievement.

Government State and federal governments often hold the vital key to whether universities receive sufficient monies to maintain facilities, faculty, and programs. Most large institutions have someone who regularly monitors the state legislature on appropriations and issues ranging from laboratory experiments on animals to standardized tests and taxes. Their work includes (1) competing with other state institutions for money, (2) defending proposed increases in higher-education budgets and protecting against cuts, (3) establishing an institution's identity in the minds of legislators, and (4) responding to lawmakers' requests for favors. Said Robert Dickens, coordinator of government relations for the University of Nevada at Reno: "When I say I'm a lobbyist, some people look at me as if I need a shower. It's a new business with the universities, and some people think it's a dirty business. But nothing's dirtier than not having resources."

The declining federal support for higher education since the 1960s also has led to an increase in the number of government relations experts representing universities in Washington, D.C. Their work complements that of the American Council on Education, the National Association of Land-Grant Universities, and the Association of American Universities. They not only lobby members of Congress regarding legislation that might have an adverse or favorable effect on their clients but also seek information from federal agencies about new programs and uncommitted funds.

The Community   As in the case of industry, a college or university must maintain a good relationship with the members of the community in which it is situated. The greatest supporters that an institution may have are the people within its immediate sphere of influence, many of whom mingle with its faculty, staff members, and students. Tax dollars are also an immense benefit, although the fact that university property is tax exempt may impose a strain unless the institution voluntarily agrees to some form of compensation for services such as fire and police protection.

The amicable "town-gown" relationship so avidly sought by city leaders and university officials alike generally is tested in other ways as well, including students' loud parties and careless driving. University and local officials cope with these problems as well as they can.

In order to bridge the town-gown gap often evident, faculty and staff members are encouraged to achieve community visibility through work with civic and other organizations. Business groups often take the lead. The Chamber of Commerce in Lawrence, Kansas, for example, for many years sponsored an annual barbecue, including various other activities, to give faculty and townspeople an opportunity to get to know each other better.

Prospective Students   Suffering from declining revenues, increased costs of operation, and a dwindling pool of prospective students occasioned by lower birthrates, many colleges have turned to highly competitive recruiting methods. Some, in the "hard-sell" classification, use extensive advertising in print and broadcast media and on billboards. Other colleges and universities have replaced their catalogues and brochures with four-color, slick materials that use bright graphics and catchy headlines to lure students.

Various other recruiting devices are used. Vanderbilt University sent personalized videotapes to about 40 highly coveted high school seniors. The College of the Atlantic took prospective students on a 90-foot sailing yacht party, Stanford University was host to 750 high school students who stayed overnight in dormitory rooms, visited classes, attended a musical program, and participated in a campus scavenger hunt. Brown University each spring sponsors a party for up to 250 prospects on an Amtrak train traveling between Washington and Providence, Rhode Island. As competition for students has increased, so have the costs of recruiting them. Expenditures on admissions and recruitment have run about $700,000 or more for private universities and in excess of $600,000 for public universities. This high level of activity creates many opportunities for employment in public relations and development.

The purchase of mailing lists is a common tool of student recruitment. Each of approximately 900 colleges annually buys from 10,000 to 15,000 names and addresses of high school students who have taken College Board Examinations. The most sought-after prospects are National Merit Scholarship winners, and it is not uncommon for competing universities to shower a prospect with such lures as free tuition for four years, a private dorm room, guarantees of priority registration, and so on.

Other Publics Examples of other groups requiring special attention are shown in Figure 19.4.

SUPPORT FOR ADVANCEMENT OFFICERS

Most public relations, alumni, and development leaders—known euphemistically as *advancement officers*—enjoy the many services of the Council for Advancement and Support of Education (CASE), with headquarters in Washington, D.C. The aims of CASE are described as building public understanding, stepping up the level of alumni involvement and support, strengthening communication with internal and external audiences, improving government relations, and increasing private financial support. Among CASE current objectives are (1) helping leaders at historically black institutions advance in their careers, (2) publicizing a code of ethics, (3) developing gift and expenditure reporting standards, (4) improving the communication of university research to the public, and (5) studying the impact of new technologies.

FIGURE 19.4
The Burger King restaurant chain, which employs and serves many teenagers, emphasized its concern for education by establishing the Burger King Academy. This consists of alternative schools attended primarily by troubled dropouts from Grades 9–12, who receive classroom instruction and counseling with the ultimate goal of a high school diploma. The schools are operated in conjunction with an educational corporation, Cities in Schools, Inc.

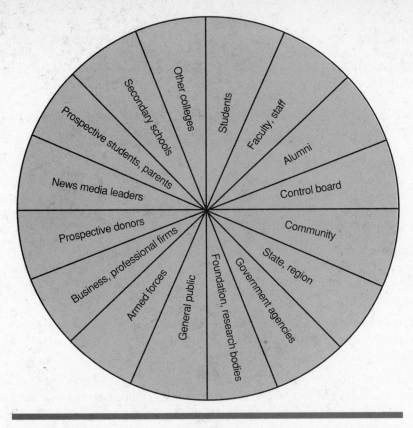

FIGURE 19.5
This wheel shows most of the publics with which college public
relations offices endeavor to maintain two-way communication.

Representing more than 2400 institutional members, CASE serves nationally as a principal public affairs arm for education, monitoring federal rights legislation and regulations and working with the American Council on Education and other associations on education-related issues. The organization provides district conferences and institutes, evaluation and critique services, a certification program, awards, reference materials, and placement opportunities. Thousands each summer attend its four-day assembly, replete with workshops.

ELEMENTARY AND SECONDARY SCHOOLS

RESPONSE TO CONTEMPORARY ISSUES

In 1983 the National Commission on Excellence in Education, citing "a nation at risk," called for massive educational reform. The resulting nationwide debate represented the most searching public examination that education in America has undergone during the last several decades. Integration, busing, accountability, book censorship, sex education, discipline, drugs, and vandalism—all these issues have commanded continuing public attention.

The 18-member commission made recommendations in five major areas, based on the belief that everyone can learn, that everyone is born with an urge to learn that can be nurtured, that a solid high school education is within the reach of virtually all, and that lifelong learning will equip people with the skills required for new careers and for citizenship. Among the recommendations were the following:

1. *Content.* State and local high school graduation requirements should be strengthened, and all students seeking a diploma should be required to take four years of English, three years of mathematics, three years of science, three years of social studies, and one-half year of computer science. Two years of foreign language are strongly recommended for the college-bound.

2. *Standards and expectations.* Schools, colleges, and universities should adopt more rigorous and measurable standards, and higher expectations, for academic performance and student conduct, and four-year colleges and universities should raise their admission requirements.

3. *Time.* Significantly more time should be devoted to learning the New Basics. This would require more effective use of the existing school day, a longer school day, or a lengthened school year.

4. *Teaching.* Teacher candidates should be required to meet high educational standards, and demonstrate an aptitude for teaching and competence in an academic discipline. Salaries should be made more competitive and market-sensitive, with promotion, tenure, and retention tied to teacher evaluation. Teachers should be under 11-month contract. Career ladders should be developed. Substantial nonschool personnel resources should be used to help overcome the shortage of math and science teachers. Incentives should be developed to attract outstanding students to teaching. Master teachers should help design teacher preparation programs and supervise beginning teachers.

5. *Leadership and fiscal support.* Citizens should hold educators and elected officials responsible for providing the leadership necessary to achieve these reforms, and citizens should provide the fiscal support and stability required to bring about the reforms.

Although stung by the commission's indictments, school officials welcomed the nationwide interest aroused. They were hopeful that the spotlight thrown on educational needs would result in another post-Sputnik-type wave of support, which indeed followed.

News of the commission's recommendations reached the offices of thousands of school superintendents almost immediately over the Education U.S.A. Newsline and Information Network, an electronic news and advisory service of the National School Public Relations Association (NSPRA). When local media people called shortly thereafter, many of the more alert superintendents and their communication coordinators were prepared to offer reactions.

NSPRA followed its newsline alert with a special bulletin to members describing the recommendations more fully. The bulletin contained a statement by its president, William J. Banach, urging educators to "initiate the movement toward better educational programming by matching the commission's recommendations against what exists in local districts. Then they should take their findings to the people, explain the value of a well-educated society, and work with citizens, business people, governmental leaders, and others to generate support for the kinds of schools America needs and deserves."

Also enclosed was a telephone survey questionnaire prepared by Banach for use by school public relations people to ascertain community attitudes toward the recommendations—a necessary first step in the coordination of local school response with anticipated state and federal legislation and recommendations.

These actions, and others taken throughout the nation, provided a striking example of the vastly increased appreciation of the role of public relations that has swept many school districts and state and federal school offices in recent years.

And it has come none too soon. Questions had steadily mounted over the teaching of basic reading, writing, and computation skills; the requirements for graduation; the toughness of courses; and more. California's Proposition 13 had been preceded and followed by taxpayer revolts elsewhere in the nation that brought tightened purse strings for school maintenance and the defeat of one capital improvement bond issue after another. Busing and integration—the major problems of the 1960s and 1970s—remained key issues. The campaign seeking tax credits for parents of children enrolled in private schools was troublesome. There were fewer students, more citizens without school-age children, more one-parent families. School-building closings and boundary shifts brought protests.

The issues facing school administrators, teachers, and public relations coordinators became even more complex as the nationwide movement to increase the accountability and efficiency of teachers grew, with quality-based education (QBE) programs sweeping through most state legislatures. Even more pressure resulted from the 1986 report of a 14-member task force appointed by the Carnegie Forum on Education and the Economy. The report called for a wholesale restructuring of the teaching corps designed to provide a profession of "well-educated teachers prepared to assume new powers and responsibilities to redesign schools for the future." Its two major proposals were to (1) set up a national board to certify teachers who meet standards and (2) confine training to graduate school, eliminating the bachelor of education degree.

The pressure for school reform increased in 1989 when the Carnegie Foundation, in a report titled "Turning Points: Preparing American Youth for the 21st Century," declared that schools, community groups, and businesses should work together to educate adolescents between the ages of 10 and 15 to become productive workers, healthy citizens, and responsible members of society.

"Young adolescents are far more at risk for self-destructive behaviors—educational failure, drug and alcohol abuse, school-age pregnancy, contraction of sexually transmitted disease, violence—than their age group ever was before," the report stated.

Schools were urged to create challenging, interdisciplinary curricula that stress health and citizenship, as well as basic education in science, math, history, and English. The report, among other things, recommended that schools be restructured to allow students and staff to meet in small groups, and that every student have an adult adviser.

Meanwhile, increasing amounts of financial aid were being funneled to K–12 (kindergarten through twelfth grade) schools, with corporate contributions rising from $33.9 million in 1987 to $51.9 million in 1988, according to the Council for Aid to Education. Hundreds of corporations, however, were demanding a greater voice in deciding what reforms were needed and how they would be implemented.

In 1990 the monthly *Partnerships in Education Journal* reported the formation of about 140,000 ties between business firms and schools. Many were year-by-year "Adopt-a-School" arrangements, but some extended for ten years or longer. This longer commitment signals strong business concerns, among others, that future employees would be ill prepared for demanding industry and service jobs. *Public Relations Journal* reported that programs financed included combating illiteracy, bolstering the recruitment of minority students, providing leadership and technical training for teachers, reducing the dropout rate, using computers as learning tools, and creating innovative plans for urban schools.

As the movement entered its second decade, leaders noted that 42 states since 1983 had toughened teacher certification requirements, a third had strengthened high school graduation requirements, and teacher salaries had jumped 22 percent over the rate of inflation, rising from $22,000 to a national average of $36,000.

However, national student assessment scores, while no longer falling as they had in the 1980s, had not shown a significant turnaround in the 1990s. And the movement had almost totally bypassed the cities. But as part of a coordinated effort, increasingly orchestrated by the federal government, Head Start and Chapter 1 (a program intended to help poor students reach grade level in reading and math) were financially strengthened. Legislation enacting national standards and assessment guidelines was proposed.

Said Ernest L. Boyer, president of the Carnegie Foundation for the Advancement of Teaching: "Time is running out, and in the coming decade our reform efforts simply must become more focused and more effective."

The larger, more progressive public school systems and independent, private schools, as well as thousands of smaller ones, had long maintained public relations programs in an effort to increase public awareness of their critical needs. Budgetary squeezes, however, had constricted many of those programs. But the necessity for sound community relations—at the heart of both management and public relations—was more evident in the 1990s than ever before. If funds were not available or the system too small to warrant a full-fledged public relations program, then a sole information specialist was employed, full- or part-time. School public relations had come into its own.

REACHING THE PUBLICS

The primary publics of a school system are teachers, children, parents, staff, and the community. As in all public relations, research, planning, action, and evaluation comprise the essential steps with which to reach these publics. On the desks of information directors, communication coordinators, and school-community relations specialists (or whatever the title may be, and it varies widely) are booklets prepared by national and state offices detailing hundreds of ways in which they may carry out their mission. Perhaps the best way to describe school public relations in its major aspects is to examine some of the outstanding programs accorded the Gold Medallion award of the National School Public Relations Association.

Cultural Diversity   The Pittsburgh School District adopted a comprehensive multicultural education policy to eliminate racially biased practices, to improve intergroup relationships, and to broaden understanding and awareness of ethnic groups and cultures.

Original research and a review of literature preceded a decision to establish the Prospect Center for Multicultural Education for middle school children. The policy then was extended district-wide and a public campaign begun encompassing lobbying, information dissemination, and parent and community involvement.

Used were news releases, broadcast and print media coverage, professional journal articles, publications, speakers bureau and public forums.

Four years after its adoption, the new policy, "fully inclusive of all cultures and emphasizing the positive aspects of diversity," had yet to come under fire, its leaders reported.

Analysis of Public Opinion   Formal opinion surveys for schools often cost from $7,500 to $15,000, but the Utica (Michigan) Community Schools system conducts Project HEAR (Householder Educational Attitude Reactions) at a cost of only about $250 per year. The system uses volunteers to telephone a random sample of approximately 300 persons and ask questions for about 15 minutes.

Many of the questions are borrowed from the annual Gallup poll of the Public's Attitudes Toward the Public Schools and from a countrywide survey conducted by the Macomb (Michigan) Intermediate School District; other questions reflect local school district issues. A computer generates the phone numbers from names on a voter registration list, and the questions are pretested for proper phrasing. The persistent but courteous callers have achieved a remarkable 100 percent response rate, thus ensuring the reliability of the random-selection method, even though it is restricted to registered voters and does not include the community at large. The responses are used to readjust school programs each year.

Face-to-Face Communication   Supplementing the newsletters and brochures distributed by all systems, the Fairfax County (Virginia) Public Schools, a large district in suburban Washington, emphasizes face-to-face communication. The superintendent meets monthly with advisory councils representing all categories of employees, bimonthly with a planning council representing citizen organizations, and regularly with a county-wide student advisory council.

Members of the office of community relations (1) help the PTA county council conduct semiannual school-community nights, (2) maintain regular contact with other local groups, (3) operate a speakers' bureau equipped with a slide-tape presentation, (4) conduct administration building tours for school staffs, and (5) arrange student award ceremonies at school board meetings with accompanying publicity.

Confronted with the potential defection of parents of preschool children to private schools, the system conducted "kindergarten roundup" programs and tours in all elementary schools. The invitations to parents were accompanied by a brochure describing five preschool classes as well as free vision and hearing tests. Slide-tape shows were screened at the open houses and questions answered. The result: a record kindergarten enrollment the following fall.

The Fairfax County system won a Gold Medallion for its total public relations program because of, among other achievements, its good relationship with the news media, including service to 100 media outlets—suburban weeklies as well as metropolitan dailies and dozens of radio and television stations.

The system's winning techniques included (1) close personal daily contact with news people; (2) special orientations for new press representatives; (3) distribution of systemwide news stories, feature story tips, and memoranda concerning future events: (4) public service announcements for radio and television; (5) weekly taped radio programs about the school system; (6) press packets for board meetings; (7) distribution of photographs; and (8) interviews with board and key staff people.

Public Forums   For only $35 each, the New Jersey School Board Association prepared a kit containing a 33-minute filmstrip, introductory comments, instructions on how to guide a discussion period, and an in-depth questionnaire with which to obtain valuable feedback at public and in-school meetings, as well as a take-home brochure. It was designed so that any volunteer could conduct such a forum. The filmstrip stars students, teachers, and others and relates how public education seeks to respond to social change.

Marketing of Public School Education   A pioneer in public opinion surveying in education, William J. Banach, administrative director at the Macomb Intermediate School District in Mount Clemens, Michigan, developed a two-year plan designed to discover what the public wants in its schools. The plan also sought ways to respond to those desires and to educate citizens about actions the school could and could not take. Banach based the campaign on what he termed "the 90-7-3 concept of school communication":

Ninety percent of the school's image is who we are and what we do 24 hours a day. How school people think, act, and appear and what they say are key factors in marketing. This is why staff training is an integral part of a marketing program—to help people understand their communication roles and how important they are.

Seven percent of the marketing effort is listening—tuning in to find out what people like, don't like, want, don't want. Anything we do to know more about our "customers" is worth doing.

Three percent of marketing is outbound communication—publications, posters, news releases, and other visible and tangible items.

In successive phases, the marketing plan was targeted at (1) elementary parents, with a focus on reading, writing, and arithmetic; (2) secondary students and their parents, emphasizing "the basics and beyond" and beginning with specific objectives based on survey results and meetings with student leaders; and (3) citizens without children in school.

Arrangements were made for teachers to apply "No. 1 apple" stickers to outstanding student papers, and all classroom papers were sent home each Friday. Posters welcoming visitors were placed at each school. The slogan "Your public schools . . . There's no better place to learn" was displayed on billboards, calendars, bookmarks, bumper stickers, T-shirt transfers, and thank-you cards.

A survey made a year after the campaign began revealed enhanced public confidence in the schools. The Macomb Plan, as it is called, has attracted national attention.

Crisis Communication   For emergencies such as earthquakes, sudden loss of utilities, severe storms, hazardous material spills, explosions, fires, tornadoes, nuclear warnings, plane crashes, bomb threats—for all such crises a communication plan should be in readiness. For the Great Falls (Montana) Public Schools, situated in a city near an Air Force base and missile sites, Audrey Olson, the school district's information consultant, embarked on a project of integrating all emergency procedures into one comprehensive crisis procedure manual.

Communication procedures were provided in checklist form. In an attached envelope were important documents addressing unique situations facing individual schools. Copies of the manual were placed near every telephone in the district, and checklist instructions were made available in every classroom without a phone. A special alert radio was installed in the schools and the administration building.

Procedures were included for pupil dismissal, transportation, and media relations. The manual also contains policy statements by top officials and a letter with which explanations may be provided for parents.

CASE STUDY: BIOMEDICAL RESEARCH AND ANIMAL RIGHTS

Animal rights supporters broke into and vandalized the Texas Tech University Health Sciences Center on July 4, 1989. As the movement focused its funds and propaganda on Texas Tech, break-ins decreased in other parts of the country.

Margaret Simon, Ph.D., director of the Office of News and Publications, and Lorenz Lutherer, M.D., Ph.D., professor of physiology and internal medicine and member of Tech's Institutional Animal Care and Use Committee, headed the initial response to the break-in. At their instigation the Texas Tech administration approved a campaign to alert other universities and to explain biomedical research to the public.

The 1990 Campaign   The first phase was aimed at research scientists and university administrators, including presidents, legal counsel, security personnel, and public relations officers. An international conference at Texas Tech, with the theme, "Crisis for the 90s: The Siege by Animal Rights Activists," attracted more than 200 administrators and scientists.

Dr. Simon wrote an issues paper for the Council for the Advancement and Support of Education (CASE). Dr. Lutherer prepared a similar story for the Texas Medical Association, reprinted by the Texas Veterinary Medical Association. They addressed such groups as the Federation of American Societies for Experimental Biology and the New Mexico Conference on Higher Education.

Broadening the Effort   In 1991 a decision was made to conduct a prolonged, proactive public relations campaign. Its aim: to educate students, parents, patients, faculty outside science disciplines, and school children.

To determine what Texans believed about animal research, leaders contacted the Texas Poll, a joint effort of Harte-Hanks Communications and the Institute for Public Policy at Texas A&M University. A survey funded by the Texas Society for Biomedical Research indicated that, although the vast majority of Texans favored humane animal-based research, many misconceptions existed about laws and regulations governing laboratory research and young people sympathized more with the animal rights movement than did their parents.

Organizing a Student Group   Recognizing the importance of students' talking with their peers and with younger students about the issue, campaign leaders helped Texas Tech students found the Student Organization for Animals and Animal Research (SOFAAR). Local physicians donated $5000, and the students produced a training manual, which Dr. Lutherer rewrote and expanded for national distribution to other student groups.

Leaders helped the students develop and print a brochure titled, "A Healthy Respect for Life," distributed in patient waiting rooms. Medical associations endorsed the brochure, which was featured in *Texas Medicine* and *American Medical News.* SOFAAR members addressed public school and civic club meetings.

Other activities included testimony before the Texas Legislature, which enacted an animal research facility protection law in 1991; national speaking engagements; responses to more than 75 letters requesting information; and publication of a book, *Targeted: The Anatomy of an Animal Rights Attack.*

Budget   In addition to the local physicians' support, an anonymous donor provided $15,000 for travel to speaking engagements and other uses. Underwriting for the international conference exceeded costs, so $10,000 paid other bills. No state-appropriated funds were used.

Results   Their handling of the crisis established the Texas Tech campaign leaders nationally as authorities on the issue. Requests for assistance came from numerous groups, including major industrial companies such as General Motors. Groups similar to SOFAAR were started in Texas and elsewhere, using the organization's publications. At the time of this writing, no other national public relations effort had been directed against biomedical research by the animal rights movement.

In 1992 the Texas Tech University Office of News and Publications and Health Sciences Center won a gold medal in the annual competition sponsored by the Council for the Advancement and Support of Education.

The following advertisement appeared in the May 1993 issue of *O'Dwyer's PR Services Report:*

Director of University Communications

The chief communications officer of the university, this individual provides leadership for all major communications functions, interacts closely with senior administration to coordinate major public events, on and off campus, and has administrative responsibility for the publications, media relations, radio and TV broadcast operations of the university. Reporting directly to the president, the director of university communications works with various constituencies within the university (schools and colleges, office of admissions, direct support organizations, etc.) to provide strategic communication planning, foster strong coordination of communications, and assist in making the university's research, teaching and service activities visible and compelling to its various publics. Although a doctor's degree is desirable, the minimum qualifications include a master's degree and three years of directly related professional work experience, or a bachelor's degree and five years of experience. . . . Salary range $41,810 to $75,300.

CASE PROBLEM

The office of Paul W. Hartman, former vice chancellor for university relations and development at Texas Christian University, mailed the fund-raising letter to alumni from "Billy Clyde Puckett, semi-tough ex-horny toad," discussed in this chapter (p. 500).

At the bottom of the letter, Puckett was identified as Dan Jenkins, a 1953 TCU journalism graduate. Jenkins is author of the novel *Semi-Tough* and other best-sellers and longtime associate editor of *Sports Illustrated*—so famous that in 1987 he was inducted into the Texas Walk of the Stars in Austin's Sixth Street entertainment district along with a football coach, state official, country singer, and other widely known sportswriters.

Many alumni laughed at the offbeat solicitation letter and forwarded contributions. Some others, however, sent Hartman what he termed "hate" mail, protesting the letter's nature.

Was the use of the letter justified? In your opinion, what are the special problems of raising university development funds from alumni and friends year after year?

QUESTIONS FOR REVIEW AND DISCUSSION

1. Who is the chief public relations officer on a college or university campus? Why?

2. A college news bureau is involved in a vast array of day-to-day public relations operations. Name five or six of these functions.

3. With what primary public does a sound university public relations program begin? Why? List eight other constituencies that must be addressed in such a program.

4. In what ways may powerful alumni and other friends provide support for an institution of higher learning? What is the role of the development office in gaining this support? What is CASE and what support does it provide for public relations and alumni officers?

5. The National Commission on Excellence in Education called for massive educational reform. What were its main concerns and how did school officials respond?

6. If you were to conduct a formal opinion survey, could you improve on the procedures followed by the Utica (Michigan) Community Schools system? Explain your answer.

7. Tell how the Fairfax County (Virginia) Public Schools system maintains effective community relations.

8. Do you agree with the marketing concept used by public relations people in the Macomb Intermediate School District in Mount Clemens, Michigan? Describe the key points of this plan in explaining your answer.

9. What public relations problems may be evident when a community turns down a bond issue to improve school financing? What public relations actions do you consider important in building and maintaining strong support of schools?

SUGGESTED READINGS

"Anti-Smoking Groups Push Universities and Other Investors to Sell Holdings in Tobacco Companies and Refuse Gifts." *Chronicle of Higher Education,* June 20, 1990, pp. A1, 31–32.

Blumenstyk, Goldie. "Colleges Report 4.9% Gain in Voluntary Gifts in a Year, but Inflation Adjusted Rate Trails Increase in Costs." *Chronicle of Higher Education,* June 16, 1993, pp. A31–A32. Charts show sources of contributions and how the monies are spent.

"Charitable Giving Rises 6.4%; Education Gets $14 Billion." *Chronicle of Higher Education,* May 26, 1993, pp. A25, A27.

Greenberg, Lenore. "The New Education Agenda for the '90s." *Public Relations Journal,* November 1993, pp. 30–33. Business/education partnerships.

McMillen, Liz. "As Women Increasingly Dominate Advancement Posts on Campuses, a Mentor to Many of Them Retires." *Chronicle of Higher Education,* July 17, 1991, pp. A23–24. Profile of Virginia Carter Smith, a pioneer in college development work.

Nicklin, Julie L. "Many Fortune 500 Companies Curtail Donations to Higher Education." *Chronicle of Higher Education,* May 26, 1993, pp. A25–A26.

Nicklin, Julie L. "New Technologies Extend the Reach of Many College Fund Raisers." *Chronicle of Higher Education,* November 25, 1992, pp. A13–A14.

Nicklin, Julie L. "Fund Drives Flourish, but How Much Do They Really Raise?" *Chronicle of Higher Education,* October 21, 1992, pp. A33–A35.

Spigel, Trudi. "Publicize or Perish." *Gannett Center Journal,* Spring–Summer 1991, pp. 71–77. The use of op-ed articles by faculty to publicize Washington University.

Stout, Hilary. "Firms Learn That Subtle Aid to Schools Can Polish Their Images, Sell Products." *Wall Street Journal,* March 25, 1991, pp. B1, B4.

Theus, Kathryn T. "Academic Reputations: The Process of Formation and Decay." *Public Relations Review,* Fall 1993, pp. 277–291. How college reputations are built.

Wilson, Robin. "College Recruiting Gimmicks Get More Lavish as Competition for New Freshmen Heats Up." *Chronicle of Higher Education,* March 7, 1990, pp. 1, A34.

Entertainment, Sports, and Travel

P R E V I E W   In this chapter, the objective is to show students how public relations promotes these three vigorous, growing forms of recreation and helps develop the careers of entertainers, public figures, and athletes.

Topics covered in the chapter include:

- The cult of personality and mystique of celebrity

- The practitioner's responsibility and ethical problems in handling individual clients

- Operation of a personality campaign

- Promotion of an entertainment

- Sports publicity

- Goals of travel promotion

- Reaching target travel audiences

THE USE AND ABUSE OF PUBLICITY

How did a movie with a catchy title, *Sleepless in Seattle,* manage to earn the highest opening weekend box office income ever for a romantic comedy? Not just by luck. Not by the saturation promotion methods used for its action blockbuster competitors such as *Jurassic Park* and *The Firm.* Clever publicity aimed at target audiences is the answer.

The maker of *Sleepless,* Tristar Pictures, timed its release as a change of pace amid the 1993 summer glut of action thrillers, a move known as counterprogramming. Then it arranged for cover stories in four national magazines shortly before the release date. Seeing the picture as a "woman's film," the producers concentrated their commercials during daytime TV programs for women, a shrewd judgment because research shows that the film's opening weekend audiences were 60 percent female.

Publicists and marketing experts also tapped a potent force, word-of-mouth. They held numerous advance invitational screenings, including one for a convention of romance book and magazine editors. To stimulate additional comment, a week before opening night they conducted sneak previews in 720 theaters, open to the public.

That same summer a massive "hype" campaign promoted the violent Arnold Schwarzenegger film *Last Action Hero,* which cost nearly three times as much as *Sleepless* to make and market. It was a dismal flop, losing a huge sum. These are examples of promotion and public taste for practitioners to ponder.

The publicity buildup of individuals and events is an integral part of the American fabric. This area is outside the mainstream of public relations, however, and professional public relations practitioners often are embarrassed by the tactics of press agents and publicity experts. Although only a relatively small number of men and women are engaged in the promotion of entertainers, politicians, and "beautiful people," the exaggerations and "little white lies"—not so little, at times—that some of them use are wrongly viewed by uninformed people as representative of the public relations industry as a whole.

Nevertheless, all students of public relations should learn how the publicity trade functions. At some point in their careers, they may find a knowledge of its techniques useful—for example, if they are engaged to guide the career of a political aspirant or advise an ambitious professional person or business executive. When applied discreetly and honestly, the techniques of publicity can be useful in many situations. They fall into disrepute when employed to create false images and to substitute deceit for truth.

THE CULT OF PERSONALITY

In contemporary society, the cult of personality has attained enormous stature. Newspapers run daily columns of short items about people with whom readers supposedly are fascinated. The magazine *People Weekly* achieved very large circulation quickly after its appearance. The same personalities turn up on television and radio talk shows all over the United States. Weekly gossip tabloids such as *National Enquirer* and *Star* peddle sensational revelations about the private lives of individuals.

Celebrity worship isn't new. A hundred years ago, press agents touring the small cities of the country ahead of traveling theatrical parties showered local editors with publicity stories—and often with gossipy, unprintable asides—about the stars of their shows. The flamboyant P. T. Barnum was the first highly acclaimed press agent in the United States. His success in stirring public excitement about his performers was immense because he knew how to tap the public's desire for entertainment (see Chapter 3).

The objective is the same today, but the methods for achieving it have expanded greatly. Television and radio talk shows have become vital in politics as well as in entertainment. Increasingly, Americans are learning about their candidates through exposure on nightly newscasts and paid TV and radio advertisements. Much campaign coverage consists of ten-second "sound bites" in which a candidate makes an attention-getting statement without supporting facts or arguments. Use of "access media" techniques such as satellite news conferences and one-on-one satellite interviews, plus messages by fax and electronic mail, have added new dimensions.

THE MYSTIQUE OF "CELEBRITY"

WHAT MAKES A STAR?

What constitutes a celebrity? In some instances fame is based on solid achievement that has won recognition on its own merits, perhaps with an assist from professional publicists. In his time, Henry Ford was a celebrity, as were Charles Lindbergh and Admiral Richard Byrd, the polar explorer. Today, people such as Barbra Streisand, Henry Kissinger, Bill Cosby, and Dan Rather are considered celebrities because of their talents and staying power in the public eye.

Michael Jackson was perhaps the most talked-about celebrity of the early 1990s, combining talent, quirky personality, and unending promotion. Suddenly during his world tour of 1993 his career took a catastrophic dive. Charging sexual abuse, a 13-year-old boy filed a civil suit against the star. California authorities opened a criminal investigation of Jackson. Several of his former employees told lurid stories about him. He cancelled his world tour and went into hiding to undergo treatment for addiction to painkiller drugs. His sponsor, PepsiCola, cancelled its deal with him.

Shortly before the trial of the civil case, Jackson paid the boy an undisclosed sum, reportedly between $15 and $25 million, to withdraw his suit. Through his attorney, Jackson proclaimed his innocence. Whether his severely blemished career could ever regain its luster was doubtful. After Jackson's surprise marriage to Elvis Presley's daughter Lisa Marie in 1994, however, he made an apparently well planned series of husband-and-wife public appearances to improve his image. The California prosecutor shelved the child-molestation case against him because the boy refused to testify.

The risk of such a disastrous turn in a celebrity's career makes many corporations fearful of hiring stars to endorse their products.

Donald Trump, a New York real estate high-roller with an insatiable desire for publicity, is another example of a public figure whose highly hyped career took a sour turn.

He put his name on the buildings and casinos he bought and had a personal press agent in addition to the Trump Organization's aggressive public relations department. He telephoned reporters with stories about himself.

Trump's announcement that he planned to divorce his wife, Ivana, leaving her with a mere $25 million of his reputed $1 billion wealth, received major nationwide coverage. The New York tabloids published intimate details of his romance with a young actress, Marla Maples.

But fame is a slippery thing. At the height of his national attention, including sale of his book on "the art of the deal," stories revealed that he was in financial trouble, overextended with massive debt and inadequate cash. People began to tell jokes, not about his reported sexual prowess, but about his money troubles. His second book, *Surviving at the Top,* was panned by critics.

One public relations specialist put it succinctly: "The mystique is off."

Trump regained the public eye, however, first by announcing that he was the father of a boy born to Miss Maples and then marrying her before an audience of 1500 people described by a publicist as "close friends." The cynical tone of media coverage is indicated by the opening sentence of the Philadelphia *Inquirer* story: "Donald Trump finally married Marla Maples on Monday—till death, tabloid scandal or prenuptial agreement do they part."

Michael Jackson delivers a television statement from his California ranch during the controversy about charges of sexual abuse brought against Jackson by a 13-year-old boy.

A REPORTER'S VIEW OF CELEBRITY

Reporters who interview "celebrities" often develop a cynical attitude toward those they talk or write about. They are quick to spot the pompous, the phonies, and those whose egos exceed their talents.

Most interviewers try to keep this attitude from showing in their reports, not always successfully.

Christina Kelly of *Sassy* writes bluntly, "No-talents become celebrities all the time," a fact that she attributes largely to television. "Once TV started, the whole celeb-creation and -worship careened out of control. . . . TV gives the false impression that celebrities are talking right to you, and you feel like they're your friends."

A word of advice to practitioners: When your clients are interviewed, urge them to avoid pretense and exaggerations about themselves. Like reporters, audiences can see through them.

Publicity buildups of this nature led Barbara Goldsmith to write in the *New York Times Magazine:*

The line between fame and notoriety has been erased. Today we are faced with a vast confusing jumble of celebrities: the talented and the untalented, heroes and villains, people of accomplishment and those who have accomplished nothing at all, the criteria of their celebrity being that their images encapsulate some form of the American dream, that they give enough of an appearance of leadership, heroism, wealth, success, danger, glamour and excitement to feed our fantasies. We no longer demand reality, only that which is real-seeming.

Goldsmith adds, "The public appetite for celebrity and pseudo-event has grown to Pantagruelian proportions, and for the first time in history, the machinery of communications is able to keep up with these demands, even to outrun them, creating new needs we never knew existed. To one extent or another, all the branches of the media have become complicitous to this pursuit. . . ."

What she means is that the publicist and the press agent have a ready market for the materials, staged events, and hype that they constantly peddle to mass media outlets.

The staged event is among the publicist's best tools in personality buildup. When Elizabeth Taylor held her carefully staged 60th birthday party at Disneyland, both the actress and the theme park received enormous media coverage. A video news release about the birthday party distributed by Disneyland reached an audience of 47.9 million viewers, according to Nielsen Media Research, the largest audience for any VNR issued in 1992. Similarly, a brief visit by the president of the United States to a flood, hurricane, or earthquake disaster area, also carefully staged, is intended to demonstrate that he cares about the victims.

For years an appearance on *The Tonight Show* with Johnny Carson as host was the most sought-after public relations appearance because of its large late-night audience. Today that show, hosted by Jay Leno, remains a prime outlet, but appearances with Oprah Winfrey, David Letterman, and Phil Donahue have the same impact. These and other hosts in the guerrilla warfare among TV talk shows have greater celebrity status than most of the guests they interview.

If a client is lucky, the publicity from a talk show, in *People Weekly* magazine, or in the Hollywood gossip columns becomes self-multiplying. A press mention confers celebrity status, and this in turn generates even more publicity and invitations to the right events. Through the efforts of a publicist, an aspiring actress may be invited to celebrity parties escorted by a celebrity male. A great deal of media exposure was generated, for example, by having Michael Jackson escort Brooke Shields to a Hollywood gathering. It is not certain which one of them got more publicity mileage from the photographs taken of the two together.

Eventually, the publicist's news releases begin to refer to the person as a celebrity. Presto, the client is a celebrity. Nobody officially proclaims the celebrity status, any more than some mysteriously remote Solomon on a high pinnacle sends down official word that a sports "star" has become a "superstar."

Indicative of the commercialization of personality is the success of Celebrity Service International, which keeps a 400,000-card databank on well-known persons and publishes daily bulletins in five cities on their comings and goings. It also publishes an annual entertainment-industry contact book that gives the names of managers, lawyers, and publicists who represent celebrities. The daily bulletin, priced at $1250 annually, tips off the media as to what prominent people might be available for a television talk show or a feature interview. The contact book helps business, industry, and charities locate celebrities who might serve as a spokesperson or a charity chairperson, or add glamor to a hotel opening.

PSYCHOLOGICAL EXPLANATIONS

Psychologists offer varied explanations of why the public becomes impressed—often *fascinated* is the more accurate word—by highly publicized individuals. In pretelevision days, the publicity departments of the motion picture studios promoted their male and female stars as glamor figures who lived in a special world of privilege and wealth. Dreaming of achieving such glory for themselves, young people with and without talent came to Hollywood to crash the magical gates, almost always in vain. Thousands more back home spun fantasies about being Rita Hayworth or Cary Grant. They cherished machine-autographed pictures of their favorites and read with relish inflated stories about the stars in fan magazines, visualizing themselves in the glamor figures' places.

In the earlier days of personality buildup, *wish-fulfillment* was a compelling force. It still is. Exposure on television in the intimacy of the family living room, however, makes personalities seem much closer to admiring viewers today than the remote gods and goddesses were in the glory days of the major motion picture studios. Such is the power of television, in fact, that reporters and news anchors who talk on camera about the activities of celebrities attain celebrity status themselves.

Many ordinary people leading routine lives yearn for heroes. Professional and big-time college sports provide personalities for *hero worship*. Publicists emphasize the performances of certain players, and television game announcers often build up the stars' roles out of proportion to their achievements; this emphasis creates hero figures for youthful sports enthusiasts to emulate. Similar exaggerated treatment is applied to entertainers and politicians. Syndicated gossip columnist Liz Smith once tried to explain the American cult of personality by saying, "Maybe it's because we all want

ELVIS IMAGE YIELDS BIG PROFIT

When cleverly promoted, public interest in celebrities may continue and create profits for their heirs long after their deaths. Take the case of Elvis Presley.

Since his early death at 42 in 1977, the rock 'n' roll singing star's memory has been marketed into an industry taking in an estimated $100 million a year from music, movies, memorabilia, and tours of his Graceland mansion in Memphis.

Presley has been honored with a postage stamp, introduced by the U.S. Postal Service with fanfare that included Elvis look-alike contests. More than 650,000 visitors a year tour Graceland and visit the singer's grave, paying approximately $16 million in admission and souvenir purchases. Claims that Elvis is still alive and jokes about Elvis "sightings" are commonplace. A group of Elvis impersonators marched in President Clinton's inaugural parade.

A family company, Presley Enterprises, runs the operation, although most of his recording rights are owned by RCA. Presley Enterprises has sold approximately 2000 licenses to market products bearing the Elvis image. On the date of his death each year, the organization conducts a candlelight prayer vigil.

Todd Morgan, director of communications for Presley Enterprises, told a reporter, "Our market is the world. Elvis is everywhere. He died, but the demand for Elvis did not end. It's as if he is still here with us."

What, in addition to publicity and marketing, keeps the Elvis phenomenon booming? Perhaps the best psychological explanation is that his rise from poverty to open-handed wealth through his talent and personality personifies a dream held by millions of people worldwide, and they find vicarious satisfaction in associating themselves with him.

someone to look up to or spit on, and we don't have royalty." Perhaps this explains the American fascination with Princess Diana.

In addition to admiration for individual performers, members of the public develop a *vicarious sense of belonging* that creates support for athletic teams. Sports publicists exploit this feeling in numerous ways. A winning baseball team becomes "our" team in conversations among patrons of a bar. To signify their loyalty, children and adults alike

MAKING THE MOST OF CELEBRITY APPEARANCES

Celebrities attract crowds to special events, fund-raisers, conventions, and even grand openings of stores. Darcy L. Bouzeos in *Public Relations Quarterly* gives the following tips to assure the success of celebrity appearances and speaking engagements:

- Use the services of a consultant who regularly works with celebrities and knows which one might be appropriate for the event.

- Clearly define the event objectives; this helps the celebrity selection process.

- Make a careful study of the audience demographics. A football star may be good for a Lions Club banquet but totally inappropriate for a convention of the American Association of University Women (AAUW).

- For a diverse audience, an entertainer, comedian, motivational speaker, or a well-known journalist may be the best selection.

- Avoid the temptation to seek the most popular celebrity of the day. He or she may not be suited to the needs and objectives of the event.

- Ask the celebrity's agent about prior engagements and how the person relates to various kinds of audiences.

- Have alternatives in mind if the first choice is not available.

- Be realistic about budgets. A top-name speaker such as Mike Ditka or Barbara Walters may cost $15,000 to $25,000 for a one-hour appearance.

- Be realistic about what to expect from a speaker or guest celebrity. Don't expect him or her to sign autographs for three hours, be present for the entire event, or talk for more than 30 minutes.

- Be aware of schedules. Television news anchors are rarely available for dinners. Newspaper writers have afternoon deadlines, and sports reporters attend games in the afternoon or evening. Baseball and football players rarely have free time during the season.

- Review contracts carefully. Information about the celebrity's transportation and hotel needs, the amount of the honorarium, and the length of the appearance should be spelled out.

- Have a back-up plan if the celebrity is delayed or cancels at the last minute.

wear baseball caps bearing the insignia of their favorite major league teams. Enthusiasts decorate their automobiles with bumper stickers and license-plate holders bearing the name of their favorite team. It isn't surprising that alumni of a university gnaw their fingernails while watching their school basketball team in a tight game, but the same intensity of support is found among fans who have no direct tie to the school. For many years, the vehement rooting from afar for Notre Dame's football team by its so-called sidewalk alumni has been notorious. A championship professional sports team stirs widespread community support.

Still another factor is the *desire for entertainment* most people feel. Reading fan magazines, or watching their favorite stars being interviewed, or lining up in front of a box office hours before it opens to be sure of getting a ticket—these are ways to bring variety and a little excitement into the daily routine of life.

A public relations practitioner assigned to build up the public image of an individual, either to increase the client's ego satisfaction or to stimulate sale of tickets to an event involving the individual, should analyze the ways in which these psychological factors can be applied. Since the client's cooperation is vital in promotional work, a wise publicist explains this background and tells the client why various actions are planned.

THE PRACTITIONER'S RESPONSIBILITY

DAMAGE CONTROL

A practitioner handling an individual client is responsible for protecting the client from bad publicity as well as generating positive news. When the client appears in a bad light because of misbehavior or an irresponsible public statement, the publicist must try to minimize the harm done to the client's public image. To use a naval term, the objective is *damage control*.

Often politicians who say something controversial in public, then wish later that they hadn't, try to squirm out of the predicament by claiming they were misquoted. This is a foolish defense unless the politician can prove conclusively that he or she was indeed quoted incorrectly. Reporters resent accusations of inaccuracy and may hold a grudge against the accuser. If the accused reporter has the politician's statement on tape, the politician appears even worse. A better defense is for the politician to explain what he or she intended and to express regret for the slip of the tongue.

ETHICAL PROBLEMS FOR PUBLICISTS

Personal misconduct by a client, or the appearance of misconduct, strains a practitioner's ingenuity and at times his or her ethical principles. Some practitioners will lie outright to protect a client, a dishonest practice that looks even worse if the media show the statement to be a lie. On occasion, a practitioner acting in good faith may be victimized because the client has lied. As a cynical old-time Hollywood publicist put it while describing how he helped cover up for a famous film hero (married) who found his actress girlfriend dead in her bedroom under strange circumstances, "We told him that before we could lie for him, he had to tell us the truth." Generally, experienced publicists advise their clients in trouble to remain out of sight and talk to as few persons as possible during the critical period.

Issuing a prepared statement to explain the client's conduct, while leaving reporters and their editors dissatisfied, is regarded as safer than having the client call a news conference, unless the client is a victim of circumstances and is best served by talking fully and openly. The decision about holding a news conference also is influenced by how articulate and self-controlled the client is. Under questioning, a person on the defensive may say something that compounds the problem. Guiding a personality through a period of trouble is an unpleasant, difficult aspect of a practitioner's job and may test his or her standards of good professional behavior. (Defensive news conferences are discussed further in Chapter 23.)

CONDUCTING A PERSONALITY CAMPAIGN

A campaign to generate public awareness of an individual should be planned just as meticulously as any other public relations project. This is the fundamental process, step by step, for the practitioner to follow.

INTERVIEW THE CLIENT

The client should answer a detailed personal questionnaire. The practitioner should be a dogged, probing interviewer, digging for interesting and possibly newsworthy facts about the person's life, activities, and beliefs. In talking about themselves, individuals frequently fail to realize that certain elements of their experiences have publicity value under the right circumstances.

Perhaps, for example, the client is a little-known actress who has won a role as a midwestern farmer's young wife in a motion picture. During her get-acquainted talks with the publicist, she happens to mention in passing that while growing up in a small town she belonged to the 4-H Club. The feature angle can be the realism she brings to the movie role: when she was a member of the youth organization, she actually did the farm jobs she will perform in the film.

Not only must practitioners draw out such details from their clients, they must also have the ingenuity to develop these facts as story angles. When the actress is placed as a guest on a television talk show, the publicist should prompt her in advance to recall incidents from her 4-H experience. Two or three humorous anecdotes about mishaps with pigs and chickens, tossed into the TV interview, give it verve. The audience will remember her. The television show host should be tipped off to lead the interview in this direction.

PREPARE A BIOGRAPHY OF THE CLIENT

The basic biography should be limited to four typed pages, perhaps less. News and feature angles should be placed high in the "bio," as it is termed, so an editor or producer can find them quickly. The biography, a portrait and other photographs of the client, and, if possible, additional personal background items should be assembled in a press kit for extensive distribution. Usually the kit is a cardboard folder with inside pockets to hold the contents.

PLAN A MARKETING STRATEGY

The practitioner should determine precisely what is to be sold. Is the purpose only to increase public awareness of the individual, or also to publicize the client's product, such as a new television series, motion picture, or book? Next, the practitioner should decide which types of audience are the most important to reach. For instance, an interview with a romantic operatic tenor on a rock-and-roll radio station would be inadvisable. But an appearance by the singer on a public television station's talk show would be right on target. A politician trying to project herself as a representative of minority groups should be

This depiction of frantic activity symbolizes the role of Liz Beth Rosenberg, Madonna's publicist and "spin doctor." As a vice president at Warner Brothers Records, she spends about two-thirds of her time promoting the controversial singer.

scheduled to speak before audiences in minority neighborhoods and placed on radio stations whose demographic reports show that they attract minority listeners.

CONDUCT THE CAMPAIGN

The best course normally is to project the client on multiple media simultaneously. Radio and television appearances create public awareness and often make newspaper feature stories easier to obtain. The process works in reverse as well. Using telephone calls and "pitch" letters to editors and program directors, the publicist should propose print and on-air interviews with the client. Every such approach should include a news or feature angle for the interviewer to develop. Since magazine articles require longer to reach print, the publicist should begin efforts to obtain them as early as feasible, once the exposure process has begun to gain momentum.

An interview in an important magazine—a rising female movie star in *Cosmopolitan* or *Ladies' Home Journal,* for example—has major impact among women readers. Backstage maneuvering often takes place before such an interview appears. Agents for entertainers on their way up eagerly seek to obtain such an interview. When a personality is "hot" or at the top of the ladder, however, magazine editors compete for the privilege of publishing the interview. The star's agent plays them off against each other, perhaps offering exclusivity but demanding such rewards as a cover picture of the star, the right to choose the interviewer (friendly, of course), and even approval of the manuscript.

News Releases   News releases are an important avenue of publicity, but the practitioner should avoid too much puffery. *Bulldog Reporter,* a West Coast public relations newsletter, once gave a "fireplug" award to a press agent who wrote a release about a Frank Sinatra concert in the Dominican Republic. The release said, in part:

The Sinatra concert represented the first time a legendary star has ever performed for a subscription pay television service. The historical event, in a balmy night that could only rival, not surpass, the audience's decibel level for enthusiasm, should overshadow any in-person star appearance ever offered on subscription television. The Sinatra and Santana/Heart doubleheaders may well be recorded as pay TV milestones.

Photographs   Photographs of the client should be submitted to the print media as often as justifiable. Basic in the press kit is the standard head-and-shoulders portrait, often called a "mug shot." Photographs of the client doing something interesting or appearing in a newsworthy group may be published merely with a caption, without accompanying story. If the client seeks national attention, such pictures should be submitted to the news services so that, if deemed newsworthy, they will be distributed to hundreds of newspapers. (Newspaper and magazine requirements for photographs are discussed in Chapter 24.)

The practitioner and the photographer should be inventive, putting the client into unusual situations. The justification for a successful submission may be thin if the picture is colorful and/or timely.

Sharply increased awareness among editors of women's concern about sexual exploitation has largely eliminated from newspaper pages "cheesecake" pictures—photographs of nubile young women in which the news angle often is as skimpy as their attire. At one time such pictures were published frequently as editors tried to spice up their pages. Occasionally such a picture shows up in print today, blatantly contrived and perhaps in bad taste, such as the one of a smiling man pointing to the replica of a check painted on the bare stomach of a belly dancer. The caption read: "Julian Caruso, an entertainment manager, arrived in court in Stafford, England, yesterday to pay a parking fine. He didn't want to pay the fine, the equivalent of $17, because, he said, Stafford lacks adequate parking. To emphasize his displeasure, he presented the court a check written on the stomach of a belly dancer, Sandrina. Court officials took a look at her—real name, Sandra Audley—and decided they couldn't handle the check in that form."

Stunts like this are a throwback to old-time gimmick press agentry, yet sometimes they succeed. The picture was distributed by the Associated Press and published large size in at least one metropolitan newspaper.

Cheesecake photographs still are printed in the trade press, even though they are seldom seen in daily newspapers. Certain British and Australian newspapers, however, continue to publish large photos of skimpily clad young women, often topless. Some practitioners persist in having bikini-clad models appear at trade shows and shopping center openings, but in doing so they risk having the events picketed.

Public Appearances   Another way to intensify awareness of individual clients is to arrange for them to appear frequently in public places. The appearances may be as modest as cutting the ribbon at a new supermarket or attending opening ceremonies at a county fair.

Commercial organizations at times invite celebrities of various types or pay them fees, to dress up dinner meetings, conventions, and even store openings. A major savings and loan association employed a group of early-day television performers to appear at openings of branch offices. Each day for a week, for two hours, an entertainer stood in a guest booth, signing autographs and chatting with visitors, who received a paperback book of pictures recalling television's pioneer period. Refreshments were served. A company photographer took pictures of the celebrity talking to guests. Later, visitors who appeared in the pictures received them as a souvenir. These appearances benefited the commercial sponsor by attracting crowds and helped the entertainers stay in the public eye.

Awards   A much-used device, but still successful, is to have a client receive an award. The practitioner should be alert for news of awards to be given and nominate the client for appropriate ones. Follow-up communications with persuasive material from the practitioner may convince the sponsor to make the award to the client. In some instances, the idea of an award is proposed to an organization by a practitioner, whose client then conveniently is declared the first recipient. The entertainment business generates immense amounts of publicity for individuals and shows with its Oscar and Emmy awards. Winning an Academy Award greatly strengthens a performer's career and means much additional box office revenue for a film. There is a myriad of lesser awards. Psychologists believe that televised awards ceremonies are popular in part because they give viewers a sense of structure in life.

Question-and-Answer Columns   Another source of exposure in print is the question-and-answer column in newspapers and magazines. The format is for well-known persons to answer questions that readers have submitted to the columnist. Some of the questions published do in fact come from readers; the columnist often asks public relations representatives of the personalities involved to supply answers. However, less legitimately, practitioners sometimes submit questions about their clients along with the answers, and the columnist publishes both—an easy way for the writer to fill a column.

Nicknames and Labels   Creating catchy nicknames for clients, especially sports and entertainment figures, helps the practitioner get their names into print. Celebrity-worshipers like to call their heroes and heroines by nicknames, as though the practice denoted a personal relationship. Thus we see and hear such familiarities for professional basketball players as "Air Jordan" and "Sir Charles" Barkley, and "Old Blue Eyes" and "The Boss" for entertainers. Cliché-prone reporters and columnists help to perpetuate these appellations.

A questionable variation of the nickname consists of adding a descriptive word to the name of a person being publicized, to create a desirable image or career association. Sometimes this is done to provide a respectable veneer for a person of dubious background. In the Palm Springs resort area, to cite an instance, a socially active figure named Ray Ryan hired a practitioner whose task was to build up the image of Ryan as a well-to-do oilman. In every news release about Ryan and every telegram inviting social, business, and media individuals to Ryan's elaborate parties, the practitioner referred to his client as "oilman Ray Ryan." Publications in the area consistently printed "oilman Ray Ryan," giving the publicist the effect he desired. Actually, Ryan also was involved in big-time professional gambling—an involvement apparently responsible for the fact that when he turned the ignition key of his automobile one day, a bomb planted in the car killed him.

RECORD THE RESULTS

Those who employ practitioners want tangible results in return for their fees. The practitioner also needs to compile and analyze the results of a personality campaign in order to determine the effectiveness of the various methods used. Tearsheets, photographs, copies of news releases, and, when possible, videotape clips of the client's public appearances should be given to the client. Clipping services help the practitioner assemble this material. At the end of the campaign, or at intervals in a long-term program, summaries of what has been accomplished should be submitted. Estimates of the audiences reached, based on circulation figures of publications, audience estimates of radio and television stations, and similar statistical criteria often impress clients, although their value as indicators of a campaign's true effectiveness is doubtful (see Chapter 10).

PROMOTING AN ENTERTAINMENT

PUBLICITY TO STIMULATE TICKET SALES

The primary goal of any campaign for an entertainment is to sell tickets. An advance publicity buildup informs listeners, readers, and viewers that an event will occur and stimulates their desire to attend it. Rarely, except for community events publicized in smaller cities, do newspaper stories and broadcasts about an entertainment include detailed information on ticket prices and availability. Those facts usually are deemed too commercial by editors and should be announced in paid advertising. However, some newspapers may include prices, times, and so on in tabular listings of scheduled entertainments. Performance dates usually are included in publicity stories.

Stories about a forthcoming theatrical event, motion picture, rock concert, or similar commercial performance should concentrate on the personalities, style, and history of the show. Every time the show is mentioned, public awareness grows. Thus, astute practitioners search for fresh news angles to produce as many stories as possible. Even two-paragraph items are valuable if they mention the names of the show and its stars. Newspaper entertainment pages frequently use such short pieces.

AN EXAMPLE: PUBLICIZING A PLAY

Let us look at the way a new play can be publicized. The methods are the same, whether the work will be performed on Broadway by professionals or in the local municipal auditorium by a little-theater group.

Stories include an announcement that the play will be presented, followed by releases reporting the casting of lead characters, start of rehearsals, and opening date. Feature stories, or "readers," discuss the play's theme and background, with quotations from the playwright and director inserted to emphasize an important point. In print, radio, and television interviews the play's star can tell why he or she finds the role significant or amusing.

Photographs of show scenes, taken in costume during rehearsal, should be distributed to the media, to give potential customers a preview glimpse. As a reminder, a brief "opening tonight" story may be distributed. If a newspaper lists theatrical events in tabular form, the practitioner might submit an entry about the show, to make the editor's work easier and increase the likelihood that the listing will appear correctly.

THE "DRIP-DRIP-DRIP" TECHNIQUE OF PUBLICITY

Motion picture studios, television production firms, and networks apply the principle of "drip-drip-drip" publicity when a show is being shot. In other words, there is a steady output of information about the production. A public relations specialist, called a unit man or woman, assigned to a film during production, turns out a flow of stories for the general and trade press and plays host to media visitors to the set. The television networks mail out daily news bulletins about their shows to media television editors. They assemble the editors annually to preview new programs and interview their stars. The heaviest barrage of publicity is released shortly before the show openings.

A much-publicized device is to have a star unveil his or her star in the cement of the Hollywood Walk of Fame, just before the star's new film appears. Videotaped recordings of the event turn up on TV stations across the country.

One danger of excessive promotion of an event, however, is that audience expectation may become too high, so that the performance proves to be a disappointment. A skilled practitioner will be judicious in his or her use of publicity and stay away from "hype" that can lead to a sense of anticlimax.

A LOOK AT THE MOTION PICTURE INDUSTRY

By market research and interpretation of demographics and psychographics, motion picture public relations departments define target audiences they seek to reach. Most motion picture publicity is aimed at 18- to 24-year olds, where the largest audience lies. Seventy-five percent of the film audience is under age 39, although increased attendance by older moviegoers has become evident recently.

Professional entertainment publicity work is concentrated in New York and Los Angeles, the former as the nation's theatrical center and the latter as the motion picture center. (American television production is divided primarily between the two cities, with the larger portion in Los Angeles.)

A typical Los Angeles–area public relations firm specializing in personalities and entertainment has two staffs: one staff of "planters," who deliver to media offices publicity stories about individual clients and the projects in which they are engaged, and another staff of "bookers," whose job is to place clients on talk shows and in other public appearances. Some publicity stories are for general release; others are prepared especially for a single media outlet such as a syndicated Hollywood columnist or a major newspaper. The latter type is marked "exclusive," permitting the publication or station that uses it to claim credit for "breaking" the story.

A cardinal sin of "exclusive" publicity is to give a story to two media outlets simultaneously, in the hope that one or the other will use it. This practice is called "double-planting."

Another device is to provide supplies of tickets for a new movie or show to radio stations, whose disc jockeys award them to listeners as prizes in on-the-air contests. In the process, these announcers mention the name of the show dozens of times. Glamorous premieres and trips for media guests to distant points so that they can watch the filming or attend an opening are used occasionally, too.

For such services to individual or corporate entertainment clients, major Hollywood publicists charge at least $3000 a month, with a three-month minimum. The major studios and networks have their own public relations staffs.

SPORTS PUBLICITY

The sports mania flourishing in the United States and in various forms around the world is stimulated by intense public relations efforts. Programs at both the big-time college and professional levels seek to arouse public interest in teams and players, sell tickets to games, and publicize the corporate sponsors who subsidize many events. Increasingly, too, sports publicists work with marketing specialists to promote the sale of booster souvenirs and clothing, a lucrative sideline for teams.

Sports publicists use the normal tools of public relations—press kits, statistics, interviews, television appearances, and the like—to distribute information. But dealing with facts is only part of their role. They also try to stir emotions. For college publicists, this means creating enthusiasm among alumni in order to stimulate their loyalty and contributions to the old school, and making the school glamorous and exciting in order to recruit high school students. Publicists for professional teams work to make them appear to be home-town representatives of civic pride, not merely athletes playing for high salaries.

Sometimes this effort succeeds spectacularly, if the team is a winner. When the Phoenix Suns unexpectedly reached the championship finals in the National Basketball Association in 1993, only to lose to the Chicago Bulls in the playoffs, a crowd of 300,000 turned out in 100-degree heat to cheer the Suns in a postseason parade. Enormous numbers of purple-and-orange Sun T-shirts, neckties, banners, posters, and souvenir books appeared. On Mother's Day a local Sunday newspaper headline urged, "Win one for Mom!" and ministers wished the Suns well from their pulpits.

When a team is an inept loser, however, the sports publicist's life turns grim. He or she must find ways to soothe public displeasure and, through methods such as having players conduct clinics at playgrounds and make sympathetic visits to hospitals, create a mood of patient hopefulness: "Wait 'til next year!"

Since the public yearns for heroes, publicists focus on building up the images of star players, sometimes to excess. They know that stars sell tickets.

The ultimate in sports hype is the National Football League's championship playoff game, the Super Bowl. A football game, frequently no more exciting and often less so than many regular season games, has been turned into a weeklong spectacular. To suggest stature and great importance, each year's game is known by a Roman numeral—not just Super Bowl 22 but Super Bowl XXII.

Reporters fall all over each other during the week before the game, hunting story angles. Parties roar as free-spending ticketholders swarm into the host city. Corporations create tie-ins to the event and entertain hundreds of guests, wooing important customers. The telecast of the game is seen worldwide by more than 100 million viewers, according to the ratings. During the 1994 game, NBC charged $900,000 for 30 seconds of commercial time. The network whose turn it is to telecast the game uses more than 20 cameras, a dozen or so videotape machines for replays, and about 100 microphones to inundate viewers with pictures and commentary.

Anyone responsible for staging a sports event, in fact, can benefit from studying the public relations effort at a Super Bowl, then reducing it in scope to fit the particular need.

At Super Bowl games, the National Football League usually issues more than 2200 media credentials. To offer adequate press service, the NFL public relations department supplements its staff by bringing in the publicity directors of several league teams. During the week preceding the game, the league runs buses for the media from hotels to the practice fields, and operates a central media headquarters in a hotel.

To assist sportswriters, publicity departments compile sets of facts about teams. At the stadium on game day, the league provides a main press box, an auxiliary press section, and extra workrooms below the stands. After the Sunday afternoon game, the department opens a large dining room at the headquarters hotel, to which news people are invited as NFL guests.

By paying close attention to detail, providing ample staff personnel, and arranging adequate working space, the NFL keeps the media throng satisfied in a situation that, poorly handled, could become chaos. Discussion of commercial sponsorship of sports appears in Chapter 14.

TRAVEL PROMOTION

With money in their pockets, people want to go places and see new things. Stimulating and harnessing that desire is the goal of the travel industry, and wise, innovative use of public relations techniques is a principal step in reaching that goal. Anyone doubting the size of the travel market need only face the mob in a major airport at Christmas or read the abundance of alluring cruise ads in magazines.

The federal government has estimated that $269 billion is spent annually on travel and tourism in the United States. Competition for these dollars among states, cities, transportation companies, hotels, theme parks, restaurants, and rental car firms is fierce.

Like entertainment and sports, travel draws upon the public's recreational dollars. Often its promoters intertwine their projects with those of entertainment and sports entrepreneurs.

HOW MANY "FREEBIES" TO ACCEPT?

Creation of newspaper and magazine stories about travel destinations, so essential in tourism promotion, poses a problem for writers and public relations people. Who should pay the writer's expenses in researching them?

Some large newspapers forbid their travel writers to accept free or discounted hotel rooms, meals, and travel tickets. They believe that such subsidies may cause writers to slant their articles too favorably, perhaps subconsciously.

Many smaller publications and most freelance writers cannot afford such an expensive rule, however, and by following it would be unable to prepare travel articles. They contend that pride in their professional objectivity keeps them from being influenced by their hosts' "freebies." Some point to critical articles they have written on subsidized trips.

For the public relations director of a resort, cruise, or other travel attraction, the situation presents two problems: (1) How much hospitality can be given to the press before the "freebies" become a form of bribery? and (2) How does the director screen requests from self-described travel writers who request free housing or travel?

The Society of American Travel Writers (SATW) sets this guideline:

Free or reduced-rate transportation and other travel expenses must be offered and accepted only with the mutual understanding that reportorial research is involved and any resultant story will be reported with the same standards of journalistic accuracy as that of comparable coverage and criticism in theater, business and finance, music, sports, and other news sections that provide the public with objective and helpful information.

THREE PHASES OF TRAVEL PROMOTION

The practice of travel public relations can be divided into three steps:

1. Stimulating the public's desire to visit a place

2. Arranging for travelers to reach it

3. Making certain that visitors are comfortable and well entertained when they get there

Stimulation is accomplished by travel articles in magazines and newspapers, alluring brochures distributed by travel agents and by direct mail, and travel films and videos. When a city or country convinces a motion picture producer to shoot a movie in its territory, the film automatically interests viewers in visiting the area. Encouraging companies and associations to hold conventions in a given place stimulates travel by groups.

Some publications have their own travel writers; others purchase freelance articles and pictures. Well-done articles by public relations practitioners about travel destinations often are published too, if written in an informational manner without resort to blatant salesmanship and purple prose.

Arrangements for travel are made through travel agencies or by direct booking at airlines, airports, and rail and bus stations. Complicated tours and cruises are arranged most frequently by travel agencies, which charge customers retail prices for accomodations and receive a 10 percent commission from the travel supplier. Wholesalers create package tours that are sold by travel agencies.

To promote sales, the 38,000 U.S. travel agencies distribute literature, sponsor travel fairs, and encourage group travel by showing destination films at invitational meetings. Cites and states operate convention and travel departments to encourage tourism. Often these invite travel writers and convention planners on familiarization trips (called "fam trips"), on which they are entertained by hotels and restaurants and shown local attractions. Figure 20.2 "sells" warmth to cold newspaper readers.

Good treatment of travelers is a critical phase of travel promotion. If a couple spend a large sum on a trip, then encounter poor accommodations, rude hotel clerks, misplaced luggage, and inferior sightseeing arrangements, they come home angry. And they will tell their friends vehemently how bad the trip was.

Even the best arrangements go awry at times. Planes are late, tour members miss the bus, and bad weather riles tempers. This is where the personal touch means so much. An attentive, cheerful tour director or hotel manager can soothe guests, and a "makegood" gesture such as a free drink or meal does wonders. *Careful training of travel personnel is essential.* Many travelers, especially in foreign countries are uneasy in strange surroundings and depend more on others than they would at home.

This picture of the U.S. rowing team leading the cruise ship Royal Majesty into harbor on its christening cruise creates attention by its novel concept of a fragile hand-powered craft escorting a huge motor vessel. Public Communications, Inc., arranged the stunt.

*An important tool in travel promotion is the familiarization
trip, in which tour operators and travel writers are taken as
guests to inspect a travel destination. Here a group organized
by the Daniel Edelman public relations firm visits Mexico.*

APPEALS TO TARGET AUDIENCES

As in other forms of public relations, travel promotion identifies target audiences and
supplements its general appeals with special messages aimed at them. A few examples:
In addition to its basic message urging visitors to see Britain's historic places and
pageantry, British promotion focuses on such attractions as London theater tours, golf in
Scotland, genealogical research on family roots, and tours of the cathedrals for persons
with architectural or religious interests.

Similarly, Italy urges persons of Italian descent to visit the villages of their ancestors and promotes religious group visits to the Vatican. Ireland stresses family visits to
ancestral homes, its picturesque pubs, and the greenness of its countryside. For
Australia, the kangaroo is a national symbol; in addition, promotion draws water enthusiasts to the Great Barrier Reef and depicts the beauties of the Sydney harbor. Other
countries develop similar appeals.

"Packaging" is a key word in travel promotion. Basically, this means taking tourists
to destinations in groups, usually by air or cruise ship, then leading them on visits to
major local attractions. When California suffered a falloff in its usually heavy flow of
Japanese visitors, the state set up a California Dream sweepstakes in Japan, offering 250
weeklong visits during which the winners would take one of a half-dozen tours in the
state named Gold Rush, Nature, Romance, Sports, Fun and Sun, and Movie Magic.
United Airlines, Coca-Cola, and other companies helped underwrite the cost, an exam-

ple of government and business cooperation in travel promotion. Print, film, and broadcast publicity in Japan was so intense, according to the California Division of Tourism, that more than 60 million people—half the country's population—were exposed to it. One in ten Japanese participated in the sweepstakes.

Appeal to Seniors   The biggest special travel audience of all is older citizens. Retired persons have time to travel, and many have ample money to do so. Hotels, motels, and airlines frequently offer discounts to attract them.

A large percentage of cruise passengers, especially on longer voyages, are retirees. Alert travel promoters design trips with them in mind, including such niceties as pairing compatible widows to share cabins and arranging trips ashore that require little walking. Shipboard entertainment and recreational activities with appeal to older persons—nostalgic music for dancing rather than rock and roll, for example—are important, too. Public relations practitioners charged with creating interest in cruises can find numerous angles of this kind to emphasize.

FIGURE 20.2
The Australian Tourist Commission received publicity in U.S. newspapers with this photo of Santa Claus at Bronte Beach in Sydney. Its message about the warm December weather in Australia is clear. The photo was released to 100 daily and weekly newspapers with circulation from 25,000 to 50,000 in various states except California, Texas, Arizona, and Florida—states with warm weather.

Travel in Eastern Europe   A vast new field for international travel is open in Eastern Europe since the collapse of the Soviet Union and communist regimes in adjacent countries. After being severely restricted for more than 40 years, a half-dozen former Soviet satellites opened their borders and heavy travel began in both directions. American tour organizers conduct parties into remote parts of Russia and the Commonwealth of Independent States once barred to foreigners. In promoting such tours, travel publicists help increase understanding by Westerners of the problems these peoples face and the nature of their cultures.

TIMES OF CRISIS

Public relations in travel has moments that require crisis management, just as corporate work does. When a popular destination suffers a natural disaster, a violent political crisis, or a terrorist incident involving, or possibly threatening, American tourists, timid travelers—of whom there are many—cancel bookings or abandon partially made travel plans.

Egypt faced such a crisis in 1993 when attacks on tourists by Islamic fundamentalists frightened away visitors. Tourism, Egypt's biggest source of foreign currency, took a precipitous 20 percent drop. The Egyptian Ministry of Tourism hired a U.S. public relations firm, Burson-Marsteller, to stem the losses.

Burson-Marsteller attacked the problem by establishing Egyptian information offices in the United States, Great Britain, France, Germany, Spain, and Italy—all important sources of tourists. The company's goal was twofold: stimulate the desire to see Egypt's attractions and minimize the perceived danger to visitors.

Similarly, tourism in Florida, a multibillion dollar source of revenue for the state, suffered a deluge of damaging international publicity in 1993 when nine foreign tourists were killed in separate incidents, mostly by robbers. Some victims were exchange students, while others were gunned down only a few days after their arrival from abroad. Attempting to limit the damage, the Florida Division of Tourism sent faxes to 28,000 travel agents in North America, England, and Europe describing steps being taken to help travelers and giving an 800 number for inquiries. That winter travel to Florida from Europe was down almost 50 percent from normal.

British Airways suffered 27,000 more cancellations than bookings in the week after U.S. bombers raided Libya in retaliation for terrorism. The airline responded with a spectacular promotion to regain the American tourist trade. Its newspaper advertisements offered the possibility of a free flight to Britain (the airline had plenty of empty seats). From 900,000 persons who sent in their names, the airline drew 5,791 winners. They received other discounts and free services in addition to the free flights, and 30 winners were entertained by the British prime minister for tea at 10 Downing Street. Widespread favorable publicity in U.S. newspapers and broadcasts encouraged the perception that Britain was safe and hospitable, and the tourist trade began to recover.

Travel firms need to make certain that they provide equal facilities and service to all races, and that their facilities are free from environmental pollution, as witness a cruise ship that had to pay a heavy fine after an environmentally aware passenger videotaped its crew members tossing debris overboard.

CASE PROBLEM

Kitaro is a Japanese composer and musician in the field now widely known as "New Age" electronic music. One of his most popular compositions is the *Silk Road Suite,* which has been performed by such groups as the London Symphony Orchestra.

His electronic music blends the musical traditions of East and West, and his music is filled with the sounds of wind chimes, ocean surf, and wind rustling through the forest. His haunting melodies of distant places are popular among young professionals burned out on "hard rock."

Kitaro is planning a concert tour of ten major American cities, and you have been hired as his publicist. Your purpose is to make sure that his American tour receives extensive coverage in the mass media. This, ideally, will lead to increased popularity and sales.

What key publics will you try to reach? What communications strategies will you utilize? What media will be most appropriate for your purposes?

QUESTIONS FOR REVIEW AND DISCUSSION

1. Why do public relations students need to understand how the personal publicity trade functions, even if they do not plan to handle theatrical or sports clients?

2. How do you explain the continued popularity of Elvis Presley so long after his death?

3. Name two psychological factors underlying the American obsession with celebrities.

4. When politicians say something they wish they hadn't and it is published, they often claim that they were misquoted. Why is this poor policy?

5. What is the first step in preparing a campaign to increase the public's awareness of an individual client?

6. What is a "bio"? What should it contain?

7. "Cheesecake" photographs once were commonplace in American newspapers, but few are published now. Why is this so?

8. A professional blunder committed by some entertainment practitioners is called "double planting." What does this mean?

9. Why do practitioners put emphasis on certain players on sports teams?

10. What are the three basic phases of travel promotion?

Bouzeos, Darcy L. "How to Make the Most of Celebrity Appearances." *Public Relations Quarterly,* Summer 1989, pp. 25–26.

Carpenter, Teresa. "Madonna's Doctor of Spin." New York *Times,* September 13, 1992, pp. H45, H60. Profile of publicist Liz Rosenberg.

Copper, Helene. "News of Murders May Be Hurting Florida Tourism," *Wall Street Journal,* May 4, 1993, pp. B1, B6.

Forman, Craig, and Thurow, Roger. "The Kings of Rhythm and Schmooze." *Wall Street Journal,* August 6, 1992, p. A11. Corporate parties at the Olympics.

Fuchsberg, Gilbert. "Will U.S. Promoters Give Mandela Time to Fight Apartheid?" *Wall Street Journal,* March 13, 1990, pp. 1, A9. U.S. tour of Nelson Mandela and how it was promoted.

Fuhman, Candice Jacobson. *Publicity Stunt: Great Staged Events That Made the News.* San Francisco: Chronicle Books, 1989.

Gamerman, Amy. "Keeping Authors Happy on Those 20-City Book Tours." *Wall Street Journal,* February 9, 1993, p. A12. The perils and tribulations of a publicist.

Goldman, Kevin. "Candice Bergen Leads the List of Top Celebrity Endorsers." *Wall Street Journal,* September 17, 1993, pp. B1, B10.

Goldman, Kevin. "From Hoops to Nuts: Basketball's Stars Score High on Endorsements." *Wall Street Journal,* June 1, 1993, p. B5.

Harris, Roy J. "The World Will Be Watching—but Will America?" *Wall Street Journal,* October 18, 1993, p. B1. NFL Super Bowl ranks 17th in terms of worldwide audience.

Horovitz, Bruce, and Biederman, Patricia. "Personal PR: Newest Necessity." Los Angeles *Times,* September 23, 1990, pp. A1, 33. Individuals now hiring public relations practitioners for personal publicity.

Jefferson, David J. "Junket Journalism: The Hollywood Foreign Press Association Doesn't Bite the Hand That Feeds It." *Wall Street Journal,* March 26, 1993, p. R12.

Kelley, Christina. "Why Do We Need Celebrities?" *Utne Reader,* May–June 1993, pp. 100–101. Why the public and the media feel the need to create celebrities.

Klein, Frederick C. "The Other Tradition: Hype Week." *Wall Street Journal,* January 29, 1993, p. A6. Pre-Super Bowl festivities.

McCarthy, Michael J. "Sinking Attendance Leads Baseball Clubs to Come Up with a New Play: Marketing." *Wall Street Journal,* July 6, 1993, pp. B1, B3.

Myerson, Allen R. "Are Fallen Barons Victims of Their Own Press Clippings?" New York *Times,* February 7, 1993, p. E7. Business executives as celebrities.

Perilla, Bob. "How to Work with Celebrities." *Public Relations Journal,* April 1988, pp. 33–34.

Ruffenach, Glenn. "Olympic Backers Will Pay Atlanta Plenty for Exclusivity and Ambush Protection." *Wall Street Journal,* June 4, 1992, pp. B1, B6.

"Sydney Wins Olympic Games for Year 2000." *Wall Street Journal,* September 24, 1993, p. B1. City conducts massive public relations campaign to get the games.

Verhover, Sam Howe. "Tourism's Latest Tough Sell: Waco, a Wonderful Place to Visit." New York *Times,* April 4, 1993, p. E6. City's efforts to improve image after shootout between federal agents and a religious cult.

"Violence Against Tourists Forces Miami to Address Safety Issues." *Public Relations Journal,* December 1993, pp. 10–11.

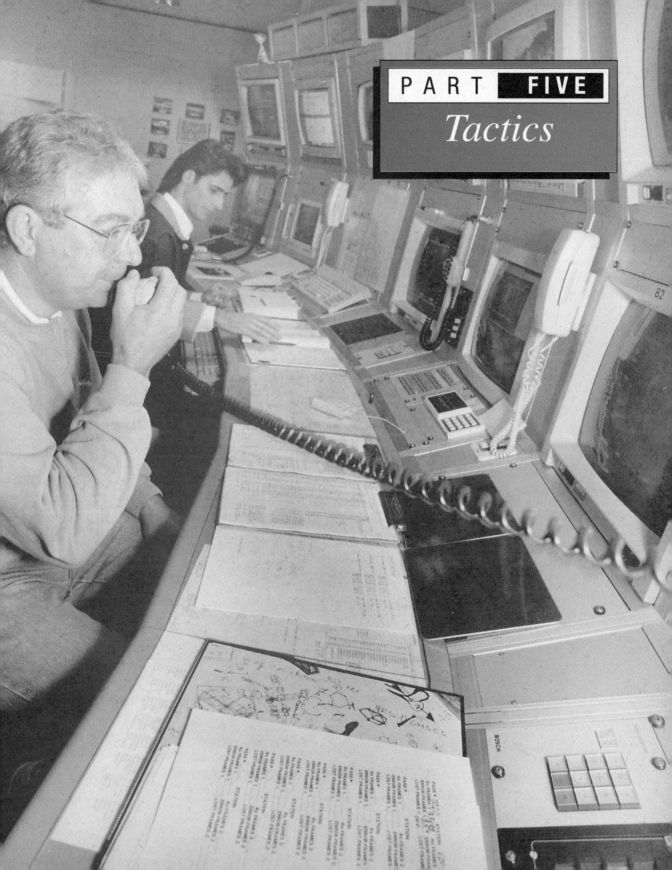

PART FIVE

Tactics

Public Relations and New Technologies

P R E V I E W   The objective of this chapter is to give students an understanding of the global communications explosion caused by development of new technologies and to describe how these can be used in public relations.

Topics covered in the chapter include:

- The interactive "information superhighway"

- Uses of the computer

- Database research

- Facsimile transmission

- Satellite transmission

- Teleconferencing

- Fiber optics

- Other electronic tools

THE COMMUNICATIONS EXPLOSION

Spectacular developments in the speed and scope of electronic communications are taking place around the world. Three familiar forms of communication—telephone, computer, and television—are being blended together in forms of interactive communication such as an "information superhighway."

Massive investments have been made by communications corporations to create worldwide electronic networks, including a main national U.S. system with regional network offshoots. These will transmit masses of information both textually and visually, entertainment on demand, electronic mail, shopping services, and computer conversations, with perhaps hundreds of TV channels. A critical fact is that this abundance of services will be interactive: that is, they will be two-way. Instead of being merely passive receivers of television shows, recipients eventually may be able not only to select pay-per-view movies but to choose the camera angles they wish to see. They also will be able to make video phone calls. Promoters see almost endless uses. Elements of this futuristic dream are already in operation. The Internet computer system, for example, ties together approximately 11,000 smaller networks in about 50 countries. Amnesty International uses Internet for organizing letter-writing campaigns.

Two key factors in this electronic outburst are use of fiber optic cable in place of the traditional copper wire (as described later in this chapter) and digital transmission of sounds and pictures; that is, transmission of messages in coded numbers that are reconstructed at the receiving end as words and pictures.

The enormous cost of laying fiber optic cable, as well as economic questions and legal difficulties, will slow arrival of an ultimate worldwide interlocking system. But as the proposed uses come into place, piece by piece, public relations practitioners will find fascinating new ways with which to present their causes and to receive instant responses.

Until recently, for example, an author on a promotion tour for a new book traveled expensively from city to city in order to visit newspaper critics and appear on local TV and radio interview programs. Today the author can sit in a studio or specialized surroundings and talk by satellite with interviewers from coast to coast, one-by-one. (Satellite tours are discussed later in this chapter.)

In the following pages we describe ways in which the new technology is applied by public relations practitioners today.

THE COMPUTER

By definition, a computer is a machine that accepts and processes information and supplies the results in a desired form. The digital computer processes the information with figures, using binary or decimal notation to solve mathematical problems at high speed. Development of the microcomputer and sophisticated software programs has added flexibility and convenience for users.

Since a computer can store, codify, analyze, and search out information at speeds far beyond human capability, its applications are enormous. When we add its ability to transmit information over long distances at fantastically high speeds, its potential becomes even greater. Still more astounding is the anticipated development of the "thinking" computer. This machine, designed to diagnose and solve problems, in addition to calculating and processing data as present computers do, is in the experimental stages in Japanese and American laboratories.

WORD PROCESSING

With numerous uses, the computer is now standard equipment in public relations offices. A survey sponsored by the Public Relations Society of America and Mead Data Central, Inc., showed that 93 percent of the respondents use computers, and 79 percent agreed very strongly that computers help them do their jobs. Nearly half said they subscribed to at least one electronic information service.

In the computer's function as a word processor, its two principal values are: (1) the capacity to store created material in its memory system for instant recall and (2) the ability to make corrections, insert fresh material, and move material from one portion of a document to another. Ingenious software programs used in the computer greatly enhance the range of services it provides writers. Among these programs are Microsoft Word, WordPerfect, MultiMate, and Apple Write.

Material written on a computer can be transferred electronically to another person's computer for review, correction, and approval. By using a printer attachment, the writer can obtain a "hard copy" version printed on paper.

Business Letters   The word processor can produce professional-quality business letters from material typed into the computer. If a counseling firm wishes to send an identical letter, except for a few personalized touches, to ten prospective clients, some taps on a keyboard will produce a different salutation on each plus individualized copy changes aimed specifically at each recipient. On the typewriter, this special attention would require the time-consuming typing of ten letters. With word processing, the result can be obtained with a small amount of keyboard punching. This instance is merely a sample of how writing business letters can be speeded up with a computer.

Processing of News Releases   Word processing is valuable in preparation of news releases. Like letters, releases can be reworded by computer for different types of publications, such as trade magazines, daily newspapers, and the business press. The draft of a news release can be placed in computer storage while the client makes revisions on a printout copy. These changes can then be made without the time-consuming process of retyping the entire release. Also, the draft of a news release can be entered in storage by its writer and later called up on another screen by the supervisor who must review and approve it.

Correction of Spelling and Grammar   Special software programs—sets of instructions telling the computer what to do—can improve the public relations writer's work by

FIGURE 21.1
Product publicity photographs are important in the computer
industry to help the consumer make the most suitable choice
from the abundance of makes and models on the market. The
caption accompanying this picture of the Macintosh ™ SE
emphasizes that it is a general-purpose business computer
whose functions can expand with communications, video, or
performing acceleration cards inserted in the system's open slot
as the user's needs grow.

correcting spelling and grammatical mistakes. Some programs contain a dictionary of
more than 100,000 words and a thesaurus of more than 10,000 words. Not only will they
detect errors, but they may suggest more appropriate words. Ordinarily, however, they
will not catch a wrong word choice, such as "effect" when the writer should have used
"affect." Writers should give anything on paper a thorough proofreading before submitting it.

Electronic Mail   A piece of writing delivered from the originator's computer into the
recipient's computer, instead of being sent by mail or messenger service, is called *electronic mail,* or simply "E-mail." When a writer creates copy for a brochure, the edited
text can be recorded on a disk for delivery to the printing company. Or, if the printing
company has suitable computer connections, the brochure copy can be transmitted elec-

tronically from the writer's computer into the printing company's computer. No paper is used. That computer in turn can feed the copy into a phototypesetting system, from which it will emerge as type on paper ready to be reproduced, with headlines included. Some companies do electronic publishing by distributing the company newsletter to employees via their computers.

DESKTOP PUBLISHING

Recent advances in computer techniques make possible the creation of professional-looking newsletters and graphically illustrated material on a personal computer right in the office. This is known as desktop publishing.

Desktop publishing allows the public relations writer and editor to design and lay out reports, newsletters, brochures, and presentations by manipulating copy and graphics right on a computer screen instead of on a drawing board. It produces camera-ready pages for offset printing.

The primary advantages of desktop publishing are savings in cost and time. Less than $10,000 will buy all the components necessary for producing high-quality newsletters and graphics: a personal computer, a word-processing program, a graphics program, page-making software, and a laser printer. Producing camera-ready materials in-house reduces the fuss and expense of involving a commercial printer. Apple Computer, a leader in the field, maintains that its desktop publishing systems pay for themselves in six months, from production and cost savings alone. Apple estimates that a 16-page newsletter can be produced by the desktop method in 8 hours, compared with 16 hours by the traditional commercial printing method.

MAILING LISTS

Up-to-date mailing lists are vital in public relations work. Lists of names are typed into a computer and stored in its memory. Changes of address or other alterations can be made by calling up a name and using a few keystrokes. When a mailing is to be made,

FIGURE 21.2
Producing news releases on a computer speeds up production in a public relations office. This graph published in the *Public Relations Journal* shows the steps and elapsed time from origination to finished release.

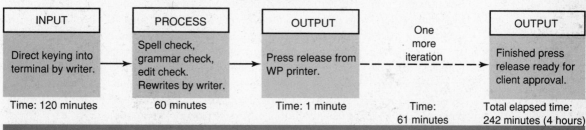

the desired names on the master list can be activated and printed on adhesive labels or on the individual envelopes.

The capability to select groups of names from the master list assists the practitioner in reaching target audiences. For example, when introducing its new models, Ford sought to generate ample publicity for more than 2000 of its dealers located in primarily rural areas. As reported in *Public Relations Journal,* the automaker created a computer file on each dealer including address, phone number, and local spokesperson. By combining this file with its standard news release, Ford created 9600 customized releases. Every release mentioned a local dealer by name. These were sent to carefully culled mailing lists within the dealer's territory.

Public relations departments and firms may compile their own computer lists of media contacts or purchase standard diskettes from press-directory companies. The Gebbie Press media directory is available on PC compatible diskettes. One set contains the addresses of about 1600 daily and 7500 weekly newspapers in the United States; the other gives the addresses of 1100 television stations and 10,000 AM and FM radio stations nationwide.

LISTS OF CONTACTS

In a related application, public relations offices use the storage and call-up facilities of computers to maintain ready-reference lists of individuals with their telephone numbers and addresses, job titles, and other personal data, which can be listed by category.

By keeping names and addresses on a computerized list, the public relations practitioner can easily add new names and make corrections—and the computer keeps everything in alphabetical order. This eliminates the traditional address card file.

With certain software programs, a person can summon a desired telephone number onto the screen and, with a single command, have the computer automatically dial the number.

ON-LINE CONFERENCES

When two or more persons tie their computers together by telephone line, they can hold discussions by exchanging a series of typed messages. In order to do so, their computers must be equipped with a *modem* (short for *modulator/demodulator*), an attachment that converts the computer's electronic signals into signals that can move along the telephone line.

On-line conferences are increasingly valuable in public relations work. Practitioners "converse" with clients and suppliers, or they participate in forums on professional matters with groups of their peers. The text of what has been said can be retained for the record in computer storage or typed out by a hard-copy printer.

As the number of personal computers in use expands, the frequency of on-line conferences will too. Because of their mobility—some are merely lap-size—properly equipped personal computers can be used in out-of-office situations, such as while traveling. The Phoenix (Arizona) *Gazette* created still another use by accepting into its computer system letters to the editor transmitted by personal computer.

GRAPHICS

549

PUBLIC
RELATIONS AND
NEW
TECHNOLOGIES

Use of computers to design for publications eye-catching colored graphics—drawings, graphs and charts, and text—has emerged as a new technology in public relations practice. Recent developments in computer software make such graphics possible, although they remain expensive.

Attractive graphics give visual impact to annual reports and employee publications, as well as to video programs and slide presentations. The techniques of computer graphics are still evolving and somewhat complicated, but the imaginative visual effects that experts can obtain are astonishing.

Slide presentations in particular can be enhanced dramatically with computer-generated graphics. Representations of people, designs, and charts add visual zest that stimulates audiences. Increasingly public relations departments and firms employ such graphics to dress up transparencies used in presentations to gain management approval for their ideas. Still another application of computer graphics is in news releases, especially those reporting on corporate sales and earnings. (Preparation of slide shows is discussed in Chapter 24.)

FACSIMILE TRANSMISSION

An invaluable new tool in public relations practice is facsimile transmission, commonly called *fax.* Such frequently heard remarks as "I'll fax it to you" have added a new verb to the language.

Facsimile transmission moves an exact copy of printed matter and graphics by telephone circuit from a machine in one office to one in another office, across town or to the other side of the world. A news release, a draft of a client's newsletter, instructions from headquarters to a branch office—these are merely three among scores of ways in which practitioners use fax. Office workers even fax their lunch orders to nearby restaurants.

Fax transmission is a tremendous timesaver. Delivery is almost immediate, compared to two days or more by mail. Some machines can deliver copies of an item to multiple addresses.

By using *broadcast fax* a sender can transmit a single document to hundreds of recipients simultaneously. A corporation, for example, can distribute a news release swiftly and equally to competing news media. Candidates used this method extensively in the 1992 presidential campaign. In another application, a customer can call a major vendor such as PR Newswire and Business Wire by toll-free 800 number, request a piece of information, and receive it by fax within minutes.

A word of caution: Discretion should be used in sending news releases to editors by facsimile. Send only those you consider to be truly important and urgent. Editors complain, often quite sharply, about the amount of "junk fax" they receive. They say that the inpouring of materials useless to them, including advertisements and irrelevant announcements, ties up their machines and may delay delivery of important news material. Some states have enacted laws restricting distribution of unsolicited fax items.

Text messages and pictures can be flashed around the world in seconds by using satellite transmission, a fact of enormous significance to public relations communicators.

Satellite transmission on a reliable 24-hour basis became possible when a satellite was shot aloft to the altitude of 22,300 miles above the equator. There a satellite has an orbital period of 24 hours. It thus remains stationary above a fixed point on the earth's surface, available for relaying back to receiving dishes on the earth the transmissions beamed up to it from originating points on the ground. So valuable is satellite transmission that a constantly growing number of satellites are being parked above the equator in what scientists call the *geostationary belt.*

When information is dispatched by computer through a ground "uplink" station to a transponder pad on a satellite, then bounced back to a receiving dish on the ground and into a receiving computer, enormous amounts of material can be transmitted over great distances at breathtaking speeds. One computer can "talk" to another via satellite about 160 times faster than can be done over landlines, and at much lower cost. For instance, transmission of a long novel by this method requires only a few seconds.

The *Wall Street Journal,* New York *Times,* and *USA Today* use satellites to transmit entire page layouts to regional printing plants. The Associated Press, United Press International, and other news services transmit their stories and pictures by satellite. The television and radio networks deliver programs in the same manner.

In public relations practice, satellite transmission has become a tool of impressive dimensions in several ways.

NEWS RELEASE DELIVERY

More than a dozen American companies deliver news releases electronically to large newspapers and other major news media offices. In the receiving newsrooms these releases are fed into computers, to be examined by editors on video display terminals for possible publication or broadcast.

The difference between news release delivery firms and the traditional news services such as the Associated Press is this: newspapers, radio, and television stations pay large fees to receive the reports of the news services, which maintain staffs of editors and reporters to gather, analyze, select, and write the news in a neutral style. On the other hand, the news release delivery companies are paid by creators of news releases to distribute those releases to the media, which pay nothing to receive them. These delivery services are prepaid transmission belts, not selectors of material. They do enforce editing standards and occasionally reject releases as unsuitable.

One of the largest news release companies is Business Wire. Using electronic circuits and satellite communications, the company can simultaneously reach more than 1600 media points in the United States and Canada and more than 500 in Europe, Latin America, East Asia, and Australia. In addition, Business Wire provides rapid dissemination of financial news releases to more than 600 securities and investment community firms worldwide. The company sends an average of 175 news releases daily for a roster of more than 9000 clients.

Electronically delivered news releases have an advantage over the conventional variety. Releases transmitted by satellite tend to receive closer, faster attention from media editors than those arriving by mail.

Another large news release delivery company, PR Newswire, was the first to distribute its releases by satellite. Using time on the SATNET satellite system of the Associated Press, PR Newswire's computers distribute releases and official statements from more than 7500 organizations directly into the newsroom computers of the media. Each day it transmits approximately 150 such releases. The releases by PR Newswire go into several commercial databases. Satellite delivery of public relations news material undoubtedly will increase as other distributors adopt the method.

VIDEO AND AUDIO NEWS RELEASE DISTRIBUTION

Transmission by satellite also makes possible fast distribution of video news releases (VNRs). The picture-and-voice releases are sent primarily to cable television networks, local cable systems, and local television stations. Nearly 30 companies produce and distribute hundreds of video news releases for clients. Only relatively few of the most newsworthy, technically superior VNRs succeed in obtaining airtime. (See Chapter 24 for a discussion of video news releases.) Successful VNRs usually feature people or animals in action, as in these examples:

- Sector Sports Watches featured a user, Gerard d'Abouville, the first man to row alone across both the Atlantic and Pacific Oceans.

- Sea World of California covered the birth of the latest baby killer whale at its San Diego pool.

- A VNR for Aetna Insurance featuring dogs trained to investigate fires received national exposure when broadcast on *CBS This Morning*.

Voice-and-sound news releases for use on radio are also distributed by satellite. Business Wire and Audio Features. Inc., to name two suppliers, send releases over the satellite/audio circuits of the Associated Press and United Press International.

GLOBAL TRANSMISSION OF MESSAGES

Still another use of satellite communication is found in *global electronic mail*. For example, Apple Computer of California regularly communicates with its foreign offices through a Tym-Net system that allows a public relations manager to type a message into an Apple Computer in California and, through a modem, electronically transmit that message via satellite anywhere in the world within seconds.

Some American corporations send facsimile pages of annual reports by satellite to printing firms in Japan and Korea. These corporations find that the cost of overseas transmission, printing, and air shipment back to the United States is lower than if the printing were done by American companies.

TELECONFERENCING

The most spectacular use of satellite transmission for public relations purposes is *teleconferencing,* also called *videoconferencing.* Through it, groups of conferees separated by thousands of miles can interact instantaneously with strong visual impact.

Use of this technique is growing rapidly. Around the United States some 20,000 sites were equipped to handle such events. A traditional conference consists of a group of men and women assembled at a central location for discussion, exchange of information, and inspiration. Participants frequently come from distant points. Their travel costs and hotel bills are often high, they may be plagued by the nuisances of flight reservations and connections, and they may be away from their offices for days.

Satellite-relayed television has changed this concept radically. Now the conferees can remain at their home offices, or gather in groups in nearby cities, and hold their conferences by television. Travel time and cost are reduced or eliminated. In one five-year period, the Boeing Company used teleconferencing for 5699 meetings and eliminated the need for more than 1.5 million miles of travel.

Long-distance discussions among widely separated groups began in the 1930s when the telephone company created conference calls that enabled three or more parties to talk among themselves. The American Telephone & Telegraph Company had videoconferencing in mind when it introduced the ill-fated Picturephone in 1964, but the high cost kept the idea from taking hold.

Now, however, satellites and fiber optics have dropped transmission costs to several hundred dollars per hour, and a company can easily arrange a teleconference by employing a firm that specializes in this form of communication. A company such as Visnews charges less than $2000 for a 30-minute New York-to-Los Angeles videoconference and about $2500 for a New York-to-London connection. Some corporations own their own systems.

The most widely used form of teleconferencing blends one-way video and two-way audio. This one-way video technology, a form of direct broadcast satellite (DBS), broadcasts a live presentation to many locations simultaneously. DBS is the least expensive method because cameras, transmitters, and other expensive equipment are needed only at one end. The video signal can be received by small, relatively inexpensive antennas at locations around the world via satellite. Figure 21.3 shows, in schematic form, how the satellite transmission works.

Guests at receiving locations view the presentation on large screens. Regular telephone circuits back to the point of origin enable the guests to ask follow-up questions. Teleconferencing also has great potential for employee relations. Ford Motor Company, for example, has installed a $10 million system connecting more than 200 Ford locations in North America over which executives in Detroit can speak. Many other large companies have their own internal corporate satellite systems.

Here are examples of teleconferencing in operation:

- ■ The Whirlpool Corporation in the United States and an N. V. Philips division in the Netherlands needed to explain their new $2 billion joint-venture agreement. So they held an international teleconference for their respective stockholders and employees, the media, and financial analysts.

■ Hill and Knowlton, on behalf of several government agencies, arranged a two-hour conference between Cairo, Egypt, and five U.S. cities that permitted several hundred U.S. investors to talk directly with high-ranking Egyptian officials about private investment in that nation.

■ To introduce a newly developed hepatitis B vaccine, Merck Sharp & Dohme used a teleconference beamed to more than 400 locations where doctors, health-care workers, and reporters had gathered. After watching the presentation, the invited guests telephoned questions to a panel of experts.

Technical refinements of teleconferencing are still being developed. Voice-activated cameras can focus on participants in a conference for closeups as each speaks. Hard (printed) copies of documents under discussion can be transmitted from one conference point to another. A more economical system is the "slow scan" conference. This provides for transmission of still pictures or slides over a telephone circuit between conference points, with voice transmission over a separate line.

To decide whether a teleconference will be cost-effective, a potential user should obtain quotations on all expenses involved, and should then compare these figures to the price of travel, lodging, and entertainment if all employees or invited guests were brought to a central conference location. To these travel costs should be added the intan-

FIGURE 21.3
This graph explains how a satellite media tour is conducted, enabling the person being interviewed to remain in one place while appearing on screens in other cities. (Source: Media Link, Inc. ©)

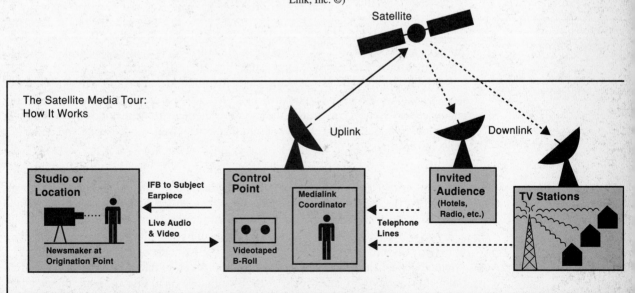

HEWLETT-PACKARD: A LEADER IN VIDEO COMMUNICATION

Hewlett-Packard, with headquarters in Palo Alto, California, spends more than $10 million annually on video communications and produces some of the nation's most sophisticated industrial television.

The company began teleconferencing in 1981 by using a satellite transmitter to reach more than 80 plant and sales sites around the nation, which enabled an executive to address many audiences at the same time. By 1993, HP had 120 sites linked in its video communications network able to receive broadcast signals, including several in Canada and Europe.

Today, HP has 48 teleconference rooms in 44 locations in the United States, Europe, and Asia. These facilities allow participants to hold meetings with people in as many as eight locations. Two-way audio and video allows a truly interactive meeting format, and meeting participants can also share information, including files and graphics on a personal computer.

HP is currently developing desktop interactive multimedia capability so that employees will eventually be able to view videotapes on their personal computers. In addition, they'll be able to receive the chief executive officer's semiannual video message live on their personal computers. This will eliminate the need to schedule a conference room and reserve video equipment.

To communicate with employees, Hewlett-Packard produces a high-quality video magazine. Released six times a year at a cost of $32,000 per show, it is formatted after television's *Evening Magazine*. According to Mary Anne Easley, manager of employee communications, "Television is an effective medium for reaching the baby boomers, the production, and the clerical workers." Surveys of employees, for example, show that HP's print magazine, *Measure,* appeals primarily to the professional and managerial ranks.

gible one of work time lost by employees away from their offices. International teleconferencing is especially attractive for multinational corporations because of the high cost of overseas travel. (For additional information, see Chapter 16.)

Those who use teleconferencing emphasize that it is most effective for reaching large audiences for such purposes as introduction of a product, sales meetings, and announcement of new corporate policies. Like other electronic methods of communication, though, it lacks the personal warmth that comes from a handshake and a face-to-face conversation.

Satellite Media Tours   Instead of having a personality—an actor or author, for example—crisscross the country on an expensive, time-consuming promotional tour, public relations sponsors increasingly use the so-called satellite tour.

The personality is stationed in a television studio, and TV reporters interview him or her by satellite from their home studios. Two-way television is used, permitting a visual dialogue. Each station's reporter is put through to the personality at a specified time; thus a series of interviews, 5 to 10 minutes each, can be done in sequence.

Corporations also employ satellite media tours to promote their products or services, using a well-known performer or other "name" figure as spokesperson.

Actor Christopher Reeve set an endurance record by doing 45 consecutive interviews at one sitting. Tiresome mentally and physically, no doubt, but much faster and cheaper than visiting all those cities!

FIBER OPTICS

As stated earlier, installation of fiber optics cable to replace the traditional copper wire in electrical circuits has begun to have a striking impact on communications, and its significance will grow rapidly. Fiber optics consists of highly transparent strands of glass thinner than human hairs, through which pulses of light in combinations of zeros and ones flash at the rate of 90 million per second. So fine are these strands that 240,000 telephone calls can be transmitted at one time through a single fiber optics cable.

Fiber optics cables laid to date have been primarily for heavy trunk line duty by the telephone companies. As these glass lines are extended into offices and homes, the multimedia uses described at the beginning of the chapter will multiply.

As an indication of the transmission speed and volume possible through fiber optics, a single strand can carry as much information as thousands of regular phone lines. The GTE Corporation reported that the fiber optics lines it installed as part of an electronic information highway could transmit a 500-page novel in slightly more than 2 seconds.

A fiber optics cable the size of a finger (right) can carry 100 times more telephone calls than the standard 3½-inch copper cable.

Electronic methods of communication are expanding rapidly as new techniques become available. Any attempt to name them all is futile, since new developments make the list out-of-date almost instantly. Even so, it is useful to examine a few of the recent additions that are of particular interest to public relations people.

TELETEXT

Teletext is one form of the recently developed concept of *information on demand.* By pushing a few keys, viewers can summon onto the screen indexes of material stored in a computer. From these indexes, the viewers call up what they wish to see. In addition to news, a major component in teletext, the viewer may wish to look for entertainment guides, community service listings, or capsule reviews of restaurants, all of which are targets for public relations practitioners publicizing their clients' services. Teletext is a one-way information service, sender to viewer.

VIDEOTEX

This more complex form of on-demand service is a two-way, or interactive, system. On videotex, viewers call up on a screen what they wish to watch; then by using telephone circuits they can respond to what they have seen.

Videotex usage is still developing as the systems come into commercial service. Among the applications are conducting two-way banking operations, ordering goods displayed on the screen, and having viewers answer poll questions put to them.

These interactive videotex applications, which have not been widely adopted, will of course be absorbed into the "information superhighway" as it develops.

CELLULAR PHONES

While driving, a public relations practitioner can conduct business by using a cellular telephone. A cellular system has interlocking low-power transmitters; as a motorist moves from one zone to another, calls from the car are switched by computer into the next zone, permitting continuous nonfading conversations. Interview calls to radio stations by clients from a practitioner's moving car are one attention-getting use of the system. A cellular phone system with a range enabling communication from one part of the world to another has been announced. The enormous increase in the number of cellular phones during the early 1990s has opened many other possibilities for use in public relations, especially when assignments involve work in the field.

Use of portable telephones is expected to increase tremendously by 2000 as the result of an FCC decision in late 1993 to license as many as seven new wireless systems in every U.S. city. Many innovative uses at attractive prices were predicted.

THE CD-ROM

The CD-ROM (Compact Disc-Read Only Memory) is the multimedia version of the familiar compact disc that plays music, contains video, audio, and text on the same surface. With an enormous capacity, the CD-ROM can display up to 300,000 pages of text, color pictures, and graphics.

As an example of the CD-ROM's potential, Yale University Press issued a disc called Perseus for use in teaching Greek language and history. The disc has 25 volumes of Greek text with English translation, a 35,000-word Greek dictionary, and 6000 photos and drawings of architectural sites and artifacts.

FLOPPY DISKS

The latest form of the informational brochure is the floppy disk, which a person "reads" on a personal computer. Buick, for example, mailed 20,000 floppy disks to users of Apple personal computers to tell them about its new models.

Breakthroughs in software design made it possible for recipients of the Buick floppy disk to "interact" with the information presented. By pushing a few buttons, comput-

A whimsical touch in public relations photographs, as in this picture of a rider using a cellular phone while clearing a jump, catches the eye of editors. The caption under this photo in the GTE Shareholder News said, "You can use a GTE Mobilnet cellular phone on any mode of transportation." The rider is Tom Howland, the horse is Shadow.

er users could load the trunk with luggage and ask questions about mileage, standard equipment, and how the Buick compared with other auto makes.

A "press disk," the floppy disk version of a press kit, has been sent out by at least one company, but reporters made little use of the novelty. A more efficient use of the disk technique is distribution by corporations of their annual reports on diskettes.

ELECTRONIC BLACKBOARDS

Blackboards with chalk now belong to the past as companies begin to use "whiteboards" that serve the same function as facsimile machines. A person can write on a whiteboard with a liquid marker during a presentation, and the image is electronically scanned to allow a printer rapidly to produce multiple copies of the image for future reference by members of the audience.

CASE PROBLEM

Ace Chemical Company publishes and distributes a report to its 10,000 employees on an annual basis. The report reviews the company's progress in the past year, honors employees who made a significant contribution to productivity, and discusses topics of employee interest such as opportunities for advancement, increased benefits, and what the company is doing to make the workplace even safer.

Readership of this annual report has declined in recent years. There is no specific reason, but one comment frequently heard is, "It's a dull report to read." One suggestion is to put the annual report on a videotape; another is to upgrade the current printed report with computer graphics; yet another suggestion is to put the entire report on a floppy disk and mail it to employees who could put the report on a personal home computer.

What are the pros and cons of each of these suggestions? What would you ultimately recommend?

QUESTIONS FOR REVIEW AND DISCUSSION

1. What is the "information superhighway," and what will be some of its uses?

2. Define such terms as *electronic mail, direct broadcast system (DBS), interactive video, desktop publishing, modem, database, teleconference, slow scan, cellular phones,* and *CD-ROM.*

3. Why is facsimile transmission such a popular method of communication?

4. Satellites are placed in geostationary orbit. What does that mean?

5. What is the difference between a news release delivery system such as Business Wire and a news service such as the Associated Press?

6. Teleconferencing is growing in popularity. Explain how it operates.

7. Authors frequently make satellite media tours. How do they work and why do authors prefer them to traditional book promotion tours?

8. What are some of the ways Hewlett-Packard uses its video communication system?

9. As a public relations practitioner, how might you use on-line computer conference calls?

10. Why is transmitting signals by fiber optics superior to sending them over an ordinary telephone line?

SUGGESTED READINGS

Andrews, Edmund L. "Plugging the Gap Between E-Mail and Video Conferencing." New York *Times,* June 23, 1991, p. F9.

"Broadcast Faxing Gaining Popularity." *Public Relations Journal,* April 1990, pp. 10–12.

Bulkeley, William M. "Attention, Clinton: Avoid E-Mail Overload." *Wall Street Journal,* January 8, 1993, p. B6.

Capps, Ian. "What the 'New Technology' Really Means for Communications Professionals." *Public Relations Quarterly,* Summer 1993, pp. 24–25.

Dirks, Douglas. "Setting Up an International Conference ... Online." *Communication World,* March 1991, pp. 28–29.

Elmer-Dewitt, Philip. "The Info Highway: Bringing a Revolution in Entertainment, News, and Communication." *Time,* April 12, 1993, pp. 48–57.

Gayeski, Diane M. "De-mystifying Multimedia." *Communication World,* April 1993, pp. 27–32. An explanation of various terms used in interactive media.

Gleick, James. "The Telephone Transformed—into Almost Everything." New York *Times* magazine, May 16, 1993, pp. 26–27, 50, 53–56. The new information highway.

Grundberg, Andy. "Ask It No Questions: The Camera Can Lie." New York *Times,* August 12, 1990, Section 2, pp. 1, 29. Computer imaging can change photographs.

Heger, Kyle. "Pushing Back the Desktop Frontier." *Communication World,* November 1990, pp. 16–22. Survey of how editors use desktop publishing.

King, Thomas R. "Director Goes On-Line to Push 'Sneakers.'" *Wall Street Journal,* August 28, 1992, p. B1. Computer press kits and on-line services.

"Log On, Download and Start Reading Your Electronic Newsletter." *Public Relations Journal,* September 1991, p. 11.

McGoon, Cliff. "Putting the Employee Newsletter On-Line." *Communication World,* March 1992, pp. 16–18.

Miller, Michael W. "A New Medium: Bulletin Boards Become a Major Means of Communication." *Wall Street Journal,* October 21, 1991, p. R8. Computer bulletin boards.

Mossberg, Walter S. "For Now, the Way to Electronic Papers Goes Through San Jose." *Wall Street Journal,* July 22, 1993, p. B1. Daily newspaper now on-line.

Reilly, Patrick M. "Publishers Design Electronic Newspapers to Keep Control of Information Delivery." *Wall Street Journal,* April 26, 1993, p. B1.

Shewchuk, Ron. "Database Publishing." *Communication World,* November 1991, pp. 34–36. Personalizing direct-mail letters.

"Technology Transforms Media Relations Work." *Public Relations Journal,* November 1993, p. 34. Media directories on-line and on CD-ROM.

Wiesendanger, Betsy. "Electronic Delivery and Feedback Systems Come of Age." *Public Relations Journal,* January 1993, pp. 10–14.

Written Tactics

P R E V I E W   The objective of this chapter is to show students how to write news releases and to understand the preparation and purpose of other written tools of public relations, including the annual report.

Topics covered in the chapter include:

- News releases: Their content and distribution
- Newsletters
- Company periodicals
- Brochures and handbooks
- Annual reports
- Corporate advertising

Basically, a *news release* is a simple document whose purpose is the dissemination of information in ready-to-publish form. Editors of print and broadcast media to whom news releases are sent judge them on the basis of news interest for their audience and timeliness, and in some instances on their adaptability to the medium's form. No payment is made to the publication or station if the material appears in print or on the air. If an organization or individual purchases space in a publication to present its material, this is a paid advertisement and the purchaser controls the content.

Releases should be prepared so that the media can relay their news content to audiences easily, with confidence in their accuracy. Editors want the main facts stated succinctly in the opening paragraph of a release, for quick recognition. A news release is a purveyor of information, not an exercise in writing style, except in those cases of longer releases that are clearly intended to be feature stories. The writer of a basic news release should leave the clever writing to staff members of the media.

A news release faces intense competition when it arrives on an editor's desk, against scores or even hundreds of other releases. As they scan the releases, editors make almost instant decisions, assigning each release to one of three categories:

1. *Obvious news.* Copy that is certain to be used.

2. *Maybe.* Stories possibly worth developing if a reporter has the time. A sharp news angle in a release may put it in the "obvious-news" category instead of the risky "maybe" pile. Potentially good stories placed in the "maybe" pile face the danger of being thrown away after a second reading if the key information is poorly developed.

3. *Discard.* Releases of insufficient interest to the receiving editor's audience and those of marginal value that would require too much effort to develop. These go into the recycling box or the wastebasket.

News releases that are prepared according to the criteria described in the following sections have the best chance of being accepted for publication, assuming that their content is newsworthy.

PHYSICAL APPEARANCE

There is a standard format for news releases:

■ Use plain white 8½-by-11-inch paper.

■ Identify the sender in the upper-left-hand corner of the page, listing name, address, and telephone number. Especially if the sender is a large organization, also give the name of an individual within the organization as a point of contact. It is important that the listed phone be answered by an informed person, usually a public relations specialist, not by a recording.

■ Below the identification state *For Immediate Release* if the material is intended for immediate publication, as most news releases are. If a time restriction is necessary, as with an advance copy of a speech to be delivered at a specified hour, indicate the desired publication time; for example, *For Release at 6 p.m. EST Feb. 12.* This is called an *embargo.* Media recipients of embargoed material have no legal obligation to obey its restrictions, but they normally do so out of courtesy and mutual convenience unless they believe that the embargo is an obvious effort to manipulate the news. Embargoes should be used only when genuinely necessary.

■ Leave 2 inches of space for editing convenience before starting the text.

■ Start the text with a clearly stated summary lead containing timely, relevant, important information.

■ Leave wide margins. Double-space the copy to give editors room in which to edit the material.

■ Never split a paragraph from one page to the next. Put (*more*) at the bottom of each unfinished page.

■ Place an identifying slugline and page number at the top of each page after the first.

Some public relations practitioners place a summary headline above the text, to tell an editor quickly what the release contains.

CONTENT

There are a few essential rules for content:

■ Begin the news release with a tightly written summary lead and state the fundamentals—who, what, when, where, and why—early in the copy. The first sentence should state the most important point in the story. *Do not bury the lead.* The opening paragraph should not exceed five lines, at most.

■ Be concise. Edit the copy to remove excess words and "puff" terminology. A competent editor would cut them out, anyway. Few news releases need to be more than two pages long; most can be written in a single page. A reporter may obtain additional details by telephoning the number listed at the beginning.

■ Caution: Avoid clichés and fancy phrases. When editors receive a news release using such terms as "unique," "revolutionary," and "state-of-the-art," they are likely to throw it away.

■ Never use excessively technical language in a release for a general audience. The objective is communication, not confusion.

■ Be absolutely certain that every fact and title in the release is correct and that every name is spelled properly. Check the copy closely for grammatical errors. Errors can be embarrassing and costly. In a news release announcing a Mexican cruise, distributed nationally, Cunard Lines mistakenly listed the 800 telephone number of a San Francisco optical company instead of its own. The optical company received more than two thousand calls in the first week; its phone lines were tied up and it had to assign personnel to redirect the calls. Cunard compensated for its blunder by giving the optical proprietor and his wife a free cruise to Europe.

For protection against errors and misunderstandings, a public relations counselor is wise to have the client initial a file copy of each news release before its distribution. In company public relations departments, similar initialing by a superior is desirable and in some cases mandatory. Corporate review can become excessive, however. Writing in *Editor & Publisher,* Ron Cantera, a former public relations executive who became a journalism professor, reported: "In one corporate job I held, my news releases were reviewed by at least six different insiders—my boss, his boss, a product manager, the marketing vice president, an agency copyreader and, believe it or not, a word-processing supervisor . . . that led to communication by committee."

Those who issue news releases should welcome follow-up inquiries from reporters and be able to provide additional information. All too often, reporters complain that the public relations personnel aren't available to answer inquiries and don't promptly return phone calls.

To counter this complaint, many public relations people make it a point on news releases to list contact numbers that are direct lines to a real person instead of voicemail or an answering machine. In addition, many practitioners also provide a number where they can be reached after regular business hours. Figure 22.1 shows a typically well-presented news release.

FIGURE 22.1
This news release assists its recipients by including the name and address of the issuing company, plus the name and telephone number of a person at the company who can supply additional information. Date of issuance and the fact that the material is for immediate release also are stated.

NEWS RELEASE

INTERNATIONAL PAPER
6400 Poplar Avenue
Memphis, Tennessee 38197

Contact:
Kaye Dickie
(901) 763-6705

For immediate release
August 20, 1993

POCKET PAL SUPPLIER OFFERS MORE CONVENIENT PAYMENT METHODS

MEMPHIS, Tenn. -- Orders for the 15th edition of *Pocket Pal,* a graphic arts handbook published by International Paper, can now be paid for with all major credit cards, including American Express, Master Card and Visa, as well as by check or money order.

Since its introduction in 1934, *Pocket Pal* has been the authoritative introduction to the graphic arts. It is used worldwide by printers, artists, designers, publishers, advertisers, students and others.

The latest edition features industry changes created by electronics and computers; for example, the conversion of pre-press functions to computer technologies. The new edition consolidates many of the fragmented sections of previous editions into a new pre-press section that includes all the conventional operations and the new electronic functions which help in preparing for printing.

Pocket Pal includes: a guide to selecting printing papers, including the newest recycled and laser grades made by International Paper; information on platemaking, photomechanicals, graphic arts photography, computer art, typesetting, pagination, image assembly, imposition, printing processes, presses, types of printing, inks, process control, binding and distribution. The glossary contains more than 450 terms used throughout the industry.

The book is available at $6.25 a copy, with discounts available for quantities of more than 25. Ordering information is available by calling Print Resource, International Paper's distributor, at (901) 373-4086 or 1-800-854-3212, or by faxing an order to (901) 373-8411.

International Paper is a worldwide producer of a wide variety of paper and forest products. The company is a major producer of printing and writing papers, paperboard and packaging products and wood products. The company also operates specialty products businesses and distributes paper and wood products. International Paper has manufacturing operations in 26 countries and exports its products to more than 130 nations.

###

> ### "WEDDING KISS WORKSHOP" MAKES NEWS
>
> The makers of Moodmatcher lipsticks received prominent media coverage for their products in New York when they invited reporters to a "kissing workshop."
>
> Two stars of an off-Broadway play, *Tony N' Tina's Wedding,* introduced as kissing experts, demonstrated osculatory styles. Then they judged a "Moodmatcher Best Kiss Technique" contest.
>
> Contestants had been attracted by advance publicity inviting brides-to-be to apply. The winner, an editor of *True Story* magazine, won a free dinner, a wedding make-up makeover, and free lipsticks for up to 500 wedding guests.
>
> After the contest, everyone present shared a wedding cake. Both the *Wall Street Journal* and ABC television covered the event, and lipstick sales rose.

When a story is controversial, and the organization or individual issuing the news release is in a defensive position, this openness sometimes diminishes or even vanishes. The attitude of some upper-management executives toward the media in controversial situations is, "Tell them only what we want the public to know. Let them find out the rest for themselves, if they can." This attitude on the part of management may persist even to the point of having the public relations department omit relatively simple information from routine releases, raising questions every good reporter should want answered.

Citing "company policy," Quadrex Corporation refused to answer press inquiries about how many people were being laid off. An editorial in the local newspaper called the company to task. It said, in part: "A public company should be relatively open. There is no reason or excuse—except short-term stonewalling to harbor the company's stock from truth—to withhold such information as the number of persons in a layoff. . . . In the long run, Quadrex would generate a better public image by disclosing rather than withholding information."

This management attitude of playing it close to the vest is a source of mistrust among the media toward companies that follow the practice. A survey by a unit of the J. Walter Thompson advertising agency showed that 55 percent of the business editors who responded criticized corporate press releases for burying important information.

Frequently, as news-oriented persons, public relations practitioners wish they could be more informative in their releases than management policy permits. As the influence of upper-level public relations executives on corporate policy-making increases, which it is doing gradually, many firms are adopting a more forthright approach. A company has no reason to wash its dirty linen in public in a voluntary outburst of confession. Yet greater frankness in news releases and willingness to volunteer answers to reasonable questions that good reporters will ask anyway help to build a company's credibility in the eyes of media and public.

DELIVERY OF NEWS RELEASES

News releases should be conveyed to the media in a timely and effective manner. As pointed out in Chapter 12, releases should be addressed to recipients by name whenever possible. Releases may be sent in a broadside manner to large numbers of recipients, in an approach called *macrodistribution,* or to carefully selected target media sources, in the *microdistribution* technique. The high cost of postage and of specialized delivery services causes most public relations practitioners to select recipients of their news releases with care, not sending to those unlikely to use the material. Therefore, practitioners should familiarize themselves with the appropriate media sources for their firm or their clients.

Locally, releases should be sent first-class if mailed, or delivered by fax or messenger if they contain urgent material. Use of bulk mail to save postage is unwise. Delivery is subject to delay, and recipients of bulk mail tend to dismiss it as of little importance.

Delivery of releases regionally or nationally is more complicated because of timing problems and the need to reach the proper outlets and individuals in areas where the sender lacks knowledge of local situations. Accurate, current mailing lists substantially influence the amount of exposure a news release obtains. For this reason, many organizations employ distribution firms to handle their mailings. One of these firms, Media Distribution Services, states that it maintains current lists of more than 150,000 editors and reporters at more than 40,000 print and broadcast media in the United States and Canada, and lists the media in 2500 categories of editorial interest.

Recent developments in computer techniques give the creator of a release numerous options for its delivery, depending upon the importance of the release and budget allocations. Distribution by mail still is the cheapest, most common, and least attention-getting method. Overnight delivery by Federal Express, Express Mail, or United Parcel Service by messenger is more expensive but gives the news release an aura of importance. Faxed messages are a popular way of delivering invitations to meetings and events.

Electronic Delivery   As pointed out in Chapter 21, distribution of news releases electronically is one result of the satellite and computer revolution. Companies whose services are based on computer programming offer various types of news release delivery, usually aimed at carefully targeted lists of recipients. The public relations practitioner writes a news release and turns over the copy to one of these distribution companies. Depending upon the type of distribution the practitioner chooses, the commercial firm either prints and mails it to a selected mailing list or distributes it by high-speed private wire to outlets chosen by the author. The release arrives in newsrooms on special public relations printers in the same ready-to-publish form as if it had been mailed. Recognizing the growing dependence on computers in newsrooms, distribution companies also will dispatch news releases from their computers directly into the computers of newsrooms, just as news services send copy to most newspapers.

In the growing number of instances in which the public relations practitioner has suitable word-processing equipment, the release can be composed on the writer's video screen, transmitted into the distribution firm's computer, checked there, and dispatched into the computers of designated recipients. Not a word has appeared on paper from the originator to the ultimate recipient. Such electronic distribution is much more expensive than the traditional mailings. However, distribution firms offering the service claim better usage of a release sent electronically. Recipients include commercial databases, whose clients such as stockbrokers and banks may call up the information.

Editorial Promotion Services   Still another way of distributing news about products, services, and events nationally is through an editorial promotion service. A company or firm sends a featurized news release about its project or product to the promotion service. If the service's editors deem the content to be newsworthy and written in competent news story style, they include the release in one of their periodic mailings to newspaper editors. Photographs and appropriate drawings may be included to illustrate the release. Brand names are permitted, although they usually are placed inconspicuously well down in the stories. Smaller newspapers in particular use editorial promotion service copy as textual matter in special advertising sections on such themes as gardening, home repair, Mother's Day, auto repair, and fashions. To win acceptance by an editorial promotion service, copy must be free of hard-sell "puffery," concentrating instead on an informational approach.

LOCALIZING A NEWS RELEASE

National corporations realize that when the releases they send out are localized, media use will be substantially higher. The local angle should be placed in the lead if possible. Inclusion of local names or statistics attracts editors; they know it interests readers. For example, a corporation with offices and plants in 20 cities sends out a release reporting that it currently has 30,000 employees systemwide, who last year received total wages and health benefits of stated amounts. The release may be published rather inconspicuously in the newspapers of some company cities but will receive little or no broadcast attention because it is too general. Even company employees will have difficulty relating to it. However, if the releases sent to the media in each company city tell how many employees the company has in that locality, and how much these workers receive in payroll and health benefits each year, likelihood of widespread use will be high.

In a period of large layoffs such as the 1990s, and the closing and reorganizing of plants, localized information by corporations is especially important because the futures of workers and their families are at stake.

Lack of localization in the news releases they receive is a major cause of complaint by editors. In a comprehensive study of news releases and their usage, Professor Linda P. Morton of the University of Oklahoma found that fewer than 10 percent of the releases reviewed were localized. When they were localized, usage jumped. Of one group she studied, Morton reported, "For instance, of 174 localized releases, 78 were published. Comparably, 1174 general releases resulted in only 87 being used."

Using computer techniques, a corporation can prepare a standard national news release giving general information for use by all recipients. It also can prepare paragraphs containing the local information for each company city. These paragraphs are inserted by computer appropriately into the releases intended for each specific city. The media outlets in that city receive only the releases especially tailored for them.

GETTING EXTRA MILEAGE FROM NEWS RELEASES

Shrewd practitioners find ways to get extra value from published news releases. Clipping services they employ send them stories in newspapers and magazines based on their releases. Some distribution firms also offer clipping services. By sending photocopies of these clippings appropriately to sales representatives and company officials in each territory, practitioners keep the field force informed about what is being published concerning the company and its products. The same system is useful for trade and professional associations. When an individual is mentioned favorably in a news story based on a release, the practitioner can please the individual by sending a copy of the story to him or her with a note of congratulation.

A discussion of video news releases appears in Chapter 24.

THE FACTSHEET

Although factsheets are distributed by public relations personnel to the same media as news releases are, and somewhat resemble releases physically, they are in outline form instead of in news story format.

A *factsheet* is essentially a quick reference tool for reporters: it summarizes the key points about an event, a product, or a company to help reporters get a quick grasp or overview. A file of factsheets proves useful as reference material.

Press kits (discussed in the next section) often contain factsheets, and the sheets may also accompany a single news release or a letter suggesting a story idea to a reporter or editor.

Figure 22.2 shows a factsheet giving basic facts about Napa Valley Wine Train Incorporated.

Susan Antilla, New York bureau chief of *USA Today*'s money section, said in *Jack O'Dwyer's Newsletter,* "PR people can really help a lot by providing background on companies . . . good factsheets are considered gold and are kept on file."

FIGURE 22.2
A factsheet such as this one gives the media the traditional five Ws of news—who, what, when, where, and why—to enable editors to arrange coverage of the event.

THE ROWLAND
COMPANY

MEDIA ALERT *** MEDIA ALERT *** MEDIA ALERT

Contact: Bob Polzoni
Stacy MacLean
(415) 512-3512

(202) 29-NAMES

300,000 EXPECTED IN WASHINGTON, DC OCTOBER 9-11

TO VIEW THE AIDS MEMORIAL QUILT

Tipper Gore, wife of Democratic Vice Presidential Nominee

Al Gore, will be Among Participants in International Display

WASHINGTON, DC -- More than 300,000 celebrities, volunteers, AIDS activists and panelmakers from around the world will assemble in Washington, DC Oct. 9-11 in one of the largest mobilizations ever to draw attention to AIDS. The centerpiece of this mobilization is the NAMES Project AIDS Memorial Quilt, which will be displayed on the grounds of the Washington Monument. The Quilt, comprised of more than 20,000 panels representing persons who have died of AIDS, weighs 30 tons and will cover an area equivalent to 12 football fields.

WHO: The NAMES Project AIDS Memorial Quilt

WHAT: The International Display of the Quilt and a series of events including conferences, concerts, theatre performances and informational talks on AIDS-related issues

WHERE: The grounds of the Washington Monument

WHEN: Friday, October 9 -- 10:00 am - 6:00 pm. Opening Ceremonies
Among those scheduled to participate in the traditional reading of the names are: Tipper Gore; Leanza Cornett, 1992 Miss America; Dr. Antonio Novello, Surgeon General of the U.S.; Liza Minelli, actress; Lily Tomlin, actress; Sharon Pratt Kelly, Mayor of Washington, DC; Representative Pat Schroeder; Dr. Anthony Fauci, Director of the National Institute of Allergy & Infectious Diseases; and Mary Fisher and Bob Hattoy who spoke at the Republican and Democratic Conventions respectively.

Saturday, October 10 -- 10:00 am - 6:00 pm
6:30 - Candlelight March begins at the Ellipse

Sunday, October 11 -- 10:00 am - 4:00 pm. Closing Ceremonies

WHY: Laid on America's front yard three weeks before the presidential election, the Quilt will call the world's attention to the escalating AIDS epidemic. The display in Washington, D.C. will take place in conjunction with an enormous gathering of AIDS-related service organizations. The Quilt's International Display will include panels from 18 countries, providing a unique forum for HIV/AIDS education and prevention and helping to raise public awareness and revitalize volunteerism. Celebrities, AIDS activists and panel makers will be available to speak with the media about their personal experiences with the AIDS pandemic.

THE ROWLAND
COMPANY

September 29, 1992

«data Editorial Dbase»

«sal» «first» «last»
«title»
«company»
«address»
«city», «st» «zip»

Dear «sal» «last»:

Three weeks before the presidential election, a symbol the size of 12 football fields will be laid on America's front yard to call attention to the escalating AIDS epidemic.

Comprised of more than 20,000 panels representing persons who have died of AIDS, the entire NAMES Project AIDS Memorial Quilt will be displayed October 9-11 on the Washington Monument Grounds. Approximately 300,000 people are expected to attend from around the county and the world, including thousands of families, lovers and friends who have made Quilt panels to memorialize loved ones and work through their pain and anger.

We believe that the Quilt display, as symbolic of the AIDS epidemic and its impact on American lives and politics, merits editorial comment by «company». Possible approaches include:

- Having grown ten-fold in five years, the Quilt is a dramatically visual strategy to draw attention to the need for courageous government leadership as the AIDS epidemic streamrolls into its second decade. The events of October 9-11 promise to underscore the continuing political debate over AIDS and other health care issues, less than a month before we choose our next president.

- Behind the Quilt's 20,000 panels are 20,000 personal stories of AIDS and its impact on the families, lovers and friends who must carry on afterwards. Panel makers range from children to grandparents, spouses to significant others, congregations to corporations -- all editorial could pay tribute to this vast tapestry of individual stories, which speaks eloquently of the true state of American "family values."

Enclosed is a press kit with more information on the AIDS Memorial Quilt and the activities planned for October 9-11. I will follow-up with you soon to see if you need more information. If you have questions in the meantime, please call me at 415/512-2512 or Dan Theobald at 415/542-4589.

Sincerely,

Bob Polzoni

A *press kit* is often prepared when a company announces a new product or sponsors a major event; frequently elaborate, it gives media representatives a thorough background and provides information in various formats. Press kits may be sent to the media or distributed at a news conference (discussed in the next chapter).

The basic format consists of a large folder cover with pockets inside that contain news releases, factsheets, backgrounders (background articles), collateral company materials, black-and-white publicity photos, color slides, and even article reprints. The folder usually is visually attractive, incorporating graphic design, color, and the name of the company.

Typical of such press kits is one prepared by LMS International, a new company formed as a joint venture of Control Data and Philips corporations. The public relations objective was to announce the new organization and develop a stronger understanding among the electronic trade media of its products; consequently, the press kit contained the following materials:

- Backgrounders on (1) the company/management team, (2) product areas/markets, and (3) major new products

- Separate news releases on each new product

- A six-page, four-color brochure on glossy paper about the new company and its products

- Black-and-white product publicity photos of major products

- Color slides of major products

The budget for the press kit was $10,000. One thousand press kits were distributed to (1) senior editors and reporters of the computer press around the world, (2) business and financial editors covering computer technology, and (3) market researchers and analysts. As a result, articles and photographs about the company appeared in more than 200 publications worldwide. Secondary articles appeared in more than 400 publications; also, the company received more than 100 requests for special features, industry trend/position articles, and technical articles.

Levi Strauss & Co. also prepared a fairly elaborate kit to publicize the results of a national survey about the fashion and lifestyle tastes of today's college students. The survey, conducted on 25 campuses among 7700 undergraduates, was called the Levi's 501 Report.

This kit contained (1) four news releases, (2) a factsheet on Levi's 501 jeans, (3) a backgrounder on the statistical findings of the survey, and (4) a sampling of fashion publicity photos of college-age models wearing, of course, jeans. A special press kit cover and letterhead were also designed.

The cost to write, produce, and distribute the press kit was $20,000. The cost of the survey was $25,000. The package was distributed to fashion editors at the top 500 newspapers around the United States, the news services, college media news services, and radio syndicates. Within three months, 345 articles appeared.

Designed as an informal publication to deliver information to a target audience at regular intervals, the newsletter is precisely what the two portions of its name indicate: *news* transmitted in the chatty, brisk style of a *letter.* Newsletters are used frequently by corporations to communicate with employees and stockholders, by nonprofit agencies and associations to reach members and friends, and by sales organizations to deliver information and personnel chitchat to representatives in the field. Expert opinion and inside advice in specialized fields also are sold to subscribers in newsletter form by commercial publishing firms. The cover shown in Figure 22.3 is of a well-edited newsletter.

The typical newsletter is a four-page folder of 8½-by-11-inch pages, often set in computer type rather than regular printer's fonts. This style projects an air of informality and urgency. Ample use of white space increases readability.

The newsletter can be double-folded into a No. 10 business envelope, or it can be a self-mailer—that is, when folded, it has space on an outside surface for the address and stamp. A piece of tape sometimes is used to hold the self-mailer shut. While envelope mailing generally is considered to have greater impact, the self-mailer is more economical. The choice is a question of budget. Some newsletters have three holes punched along the fold so that they can be filed in ring binders.

Newsletters for internal audiences typically report to employees on trends in their field of work, forthcoming events, personnel changes and policy announcements within the organization, news from field offices, introduction of new products, unusual achievements by employees, results of surveys, and new publications. The goal is to make employees feel that they are informed about company affairs, right up to the minute.

A newsletter aimed at an outside audience, members of an organization, or both, may contain items about political trends that could affect the organization or field of interest, announcements of new programs and policies, brief human interest stories about personnel or recipients of organization services, promotions and retirements—whatever news the editor believes of interest to readers that can be told succinctly. On complicated stories, the newsletter should give the basic facts and indicate where readers can write or telephone for additional details. A newsletter is a brisk compilation of highlights and tidbits, not a place for contemplative essays or detailed professional discussion.

Punchiness in writing style is essential for a successful newsletter. Sentences are short and direct. The writing is authoritative and no-nonsense in tone, from a busy writer to a busy reader. Another secret of the successful newsletter is to cover several topics that will appeal to a wide variety of readers. The single-topic edition should be avoided as too limited in interest.

For internal use among departments and branches of large corporations with extensive word processing facilities, the electronic newsletter has made its appearance. The editor composes the letter in the usual way. The copy then is coded into the computer system, dispatched, and delivered to everyone on the receiving list on hard copy from the recipients' printout machines.

VISIONS

BISHOP RANCH

BUSINESS PARK

BISHOP RANCH SET FOR BIG EXPANSION

CHOPPER CHOPPER CHOPPER CHOPPER CHOPPER SERVICE LANDS AT BISHOP RANCH

It's a bird, it's a plane, no . . . it's a helicopter. And, because of this new amenity, tenants at Bishop Ranch now can fly in and out of the business park via charter chopper.

The Bishop Ranch Heliport, at 2565 Camino Ramon near the intersection of Executive Parkway, is home to a four-passenger Bell Jet Ranger helicopter operated by Aris Helicopters of San Jose.

According to Jon Miller, the company's primary pilot for Bishop Ranch, the helicopter is available for business and pleasure for employees at Bishop Ranch. "We can fly to any airport in the Bay Area, north to Sacramento and south to the San Joaquin Valley."

Flight time to Oakland's airport is eight minutes and 15 minutes to both San Jose and San Francisco airports, he said. Cost to charter the helicopter is $435 per hour. "It's a bigger toll than taking other forms of transportation, but it's certainly faster, less aggravating, more fun and much more convenient."

Bishop Ranch's helicopter charter service operates from 7 a.m. to 6:30 p.m. Monday to Friday and 9:30 a.m. to 5 p.m. on Saturdays.

For more information contact Jon Miller at Bishop Ranch 2, 2682 Bishop Drive #110, 275-8045.

Bishop Ranch Business Park is booming with business as it readies for the grand opening this fall of Bishop Ranch 7 and the full completion of Bishop Ranch 8.

Opening September 1, the third and final building at Bishop Ranch 8 will welcome 400 employees of Impell Engineers into 60% of the building's 190,000 square feet. The five-story building's impressive interior features a covered atrium surrounded by walkways overlooking a beautiful water sculpture and tranquil sitting area. Its bold, angular exterior faces a carefully landscaped courtyard with fountains, across which sit the structure's two siblings.

According to Gabe Ciccone, Sunset Development Company's vice president of construction, the three buildings

at BR 8 are among the business park's finest structures. "The interior atriums are quite impressive, providing a feeling of openness," Ciccone said. The 27-acre Bishop Ranch 8 complex is located at 5000 Executive Parkway between the Toyota and Pacific Bell facilities.

Opening in November, Bishop Ranch 7, adjacent to the Heliport at 2527 Camino Ramon, offers 220,000 square feet of leasable space in its three stories. Single floor sizes of 75,500 square feet are available.

The building sits on 13.5 acres and features a beautifully landscaped half-acre courtyard accessible through front and rear lobbies. Showers and lockers for employees who jog during their lunch hour, a

restaurant and an abundance of free parking are among the amenities offered. The $34 million project will be the sixth Bishop Ranch complex of 11 planned by Sunset Development Company.

Aerial view of Bishop Ranch 7 (below) highlights the building's half-acre courtyard. Bishop Ranch 8 (right) nears completion.

FIGURE 22.3

The newsletter is more informal in appearance and content than a magazine and usually is produced more quickly. Like magazines, newsletters can be designed for various special audiences. This six-page newsletter from the Bishop Ranch Business Park is exceptionally strong visually.

THE ADVERTORIAL

Illustrated editorial inserts in newspapers and magazines, underwritten by a sponsoring company and known as *advertorials,* have become increasingly common. These usually attempt to emulate the look and tone of the publication, so as to appear an integral part of it. In one instance, a one-page pre-Olympics article in *Time* was underwritten by Visa International.

Some editors oppose having advertorials appear in their publications, contending that the corporate sponsorship blurs the traditional line separating editorial and advertising content.

COMPANY PERIODICALS

Hundreds of well-written, well-edited, and attractive periodicals published in the United States never are seen by the general public. They are produced by public relations departments of companies or their counseling firms and distributed free to carefully selected audiences. Whether designed to be read by employees, stockholders, customers, or combinations of these audiences, periodicals are among the most effective channels of continuing communication that a company can use. Like any publication issued at regular intervals, the company magazine or newspaper creates a sense of anticipation of its arrival. This helps to strengthen the ties between management and the groups it seeks to inform and influence.

Although it is commonly accepted that employees with long-term service in a company are the most avid readers of company newsletters and magazines, research has disputed this. Professor John Pavlik, formerly of Penn State University, studied employees of Honeywell, Inc., in Minneapolis and found that an employee's career aspirations are a much better predictor of readership. Quite simply, Pavlik says, "An employee with higher career aspirations tends to place greater importance on reading to keep track of changes in management and to find out what is going on in the company generally."

The research found that the purpose of reading the company publication varies with gender. Women seem to show strong interest in reading to keep track of their friends, while men primarily want to follow the company's business activities. Of course, this finding may be skewed in the respect that traditionally women have been assigned more to lower-level clerical functions, and many have had no real career path in the company.

Experts emphasize the importance of four elements in maintaining a good relationship between management and employees—employee recognition, communication, a sense of belonging, and emotional security. When all of these elements function well, productivity tends to rise. Workers who believe that their jobs are secure and their personal worth recognized will contribute more than disgruntled ones.

Along with other forms of internal communication—including company brochures, staff-management meetings, audiovisual presentations, and memoranda—company periodicals help substantially in the development of all four elements. The periodicals

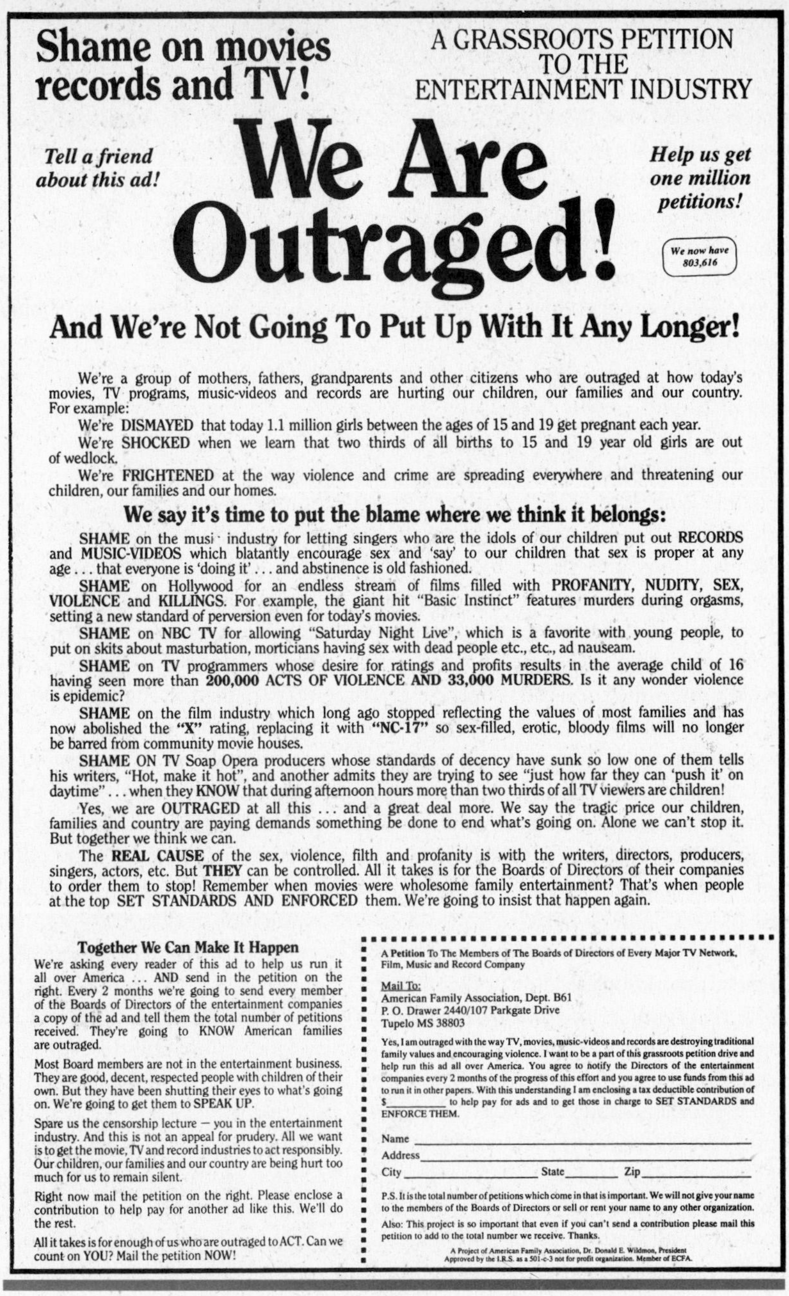

Shame on movies records and TV!

A GRASSROOTS PETITION TO THE ENTERTAINMENT INDUSTRY

Tell a friend about this ad!

We Are Outraged!

Help us get one million petitions!

We now have 803,616

And We're Not Going To Put Up With It Any Longer!

We're a group of mothers, fathers, grandparents and other citizens who are outraged at how today's movies, TV programs, music-videos and records are hurting our children, our families and our country. For example:

We're DISMAYED that today 1.1 million girls between the ages of 15 and 19 get pregnant each year.

We're SHOCKED when we learn that two thirds of all births to 15 and 19 year old girls are out of wedlock.

We're FRIGHTENED at the way violence and crime are spreading everywhere and threatening our children, our families and our homes.

We say it's time to put the blame where we think it belongs:

SHAME on the musi· industry for letting singers who are the idols of our children put out **RECORDS** and **MUSIC-VIDEOS** which blatantly encourage sex and 'say' to our children that sex is proper at any age . . . that everyone is 'doing it' . . . and abstinence is old fashioned.

SHAME on Hollywood for an endless stream of films filled with **PROFANITY, NUDITY, SEX, VIOLENCE** and **KILLINGS**. For example, the giant hit "Basic Instinct" features murders during orgasms, setting a new standard of perversion even for today's movies.

SHAME on NBC TV for allowing "Saturday Night Live", which is a favorite with young people, to put on skits about masturbation, morticians having sex with dead people etc., etc., ad nauseam.

SHAME on TV programmers whose desire for ratings and profits results in the average child of 16 having seen more than **200,000** ACTS OF VIOLENCE **AND 33,000** MURDERS. Is it any wonder violence is epidemic?

SHAME on the film industry which long ago stopped reflecting the values of most families and has now abolished the **"X"** rating, replacing it with **"NC-17"** so sex-filled, erotic, bloody films will no longer be barred from community movie houses.

SHAME ON TV Soap Opera producers whose standards of decency have sunk so low one of them tells his writers, "Hot, make it hot", and another admits they are trying to see "just how far they can 'push it' on daytime" . . . when they KNOW that during afternoon hours more than two thirds of all TV viewers are children!

Yes, we are OUTRAGED at all this . . . and a great deal more. We say the tragic price our children, families and country are paying demands something be done to end what's going on. Alone we can't stop it. But together we think we can.

The **REAL CAUSE** of the sex, violence, filth and profanity is with the writers, directors, producers, singers, actors, etc. But **THEY** can be controlled. All it takes is for the Boards of Directors of their companies to order them to stop! Remember when movies were wholesome family entertainment? That's when people at the top SET STANDARDS AND ENFORCED them. We're going to insist that happen again.

Together We Can Make It Happen

We're asking every reader of this ad to help us run it all over America . . . AND send in the petition on the right. Every 2 months we're going to send every member of the Boards of Directors of the entertainment companies a copy of the ad and tell them the total number of petitions received. They're going to KNOW American families are outraged.

Most Board members are not in the entertainment business. They are good, decent, respected people with children of their own. But they have been shutting their eyes to what's going on. We're going to get them to SPEAK UP.

Spare us the censorship lecture — you in the entertainment industry. And this is not an appeal for prudery. All we want is to get the movie, TV and record industries to act responsibly. Our children, our families and our country are being hurt too much for us to remain silent.

Right now mail the petition on the right. Please enclose a contribution to help pay for another ad like this. We'll do the rest.

All it takes is for enough of us who are outraged to ACT. Can we count on YOU? Mail the petition NOW!

A Petition To The Members of The Boards of Directors of Every Major TV Network, Film, Music and Record Company

Mail To:
American Family Association, Dept. B61
P. O. Drawer 2440/107 Parkgate Drive
Tupelo MS 38803

Yes, I am outraged with the way TV, movies, music-videos and records are destroying traditional family values and encouraging violence. I want to be a part of this grassroots petition drive and help run this ad all over America. You agree to notify the Directors of the entertainment companies every 2 months of the progress of this effort and you agree to use funds from this ad to run it in other papers. With this understanding I am enclosing a tax deductible contribution of $________ to help pay for ads and to get those in charge to SET STANDARDS and ENFORCE THEM.

Name ____________________
Address ____________________
City __________ State _____ Zip ________

P.S. It is the total number of petitions which come in that is important. We will not give your name to the members of the Boards of Directors or sell or rent your name to any other organization.

Also: This project is so important that even if you can't send a contribution please mail this petition to add to the total number we receive. Thanks.

A Project of American Family Association, Dr. Donald E. Wildmon, President
Approved by the I.R.S. as a 501-c-3 not for profit organization. Member of ECFA.

FIGURE 22.4
Advocacy advertising, exemplified in this emotional appeal by an organization that seeks to influence the content of motion pictures, promotes an attitude or an idea, rather than a product. Corporations sometimes use this method to improve their images or advocate legislation helpful to them.

communicate information and decisions from management to employees. They increase the workers' feeling that they know what is going on in the company, and why. Management can use the periodicals to influence the attitudes of employees. However, this purpose must be accomplished with caution and finesse. If employees sense that management is talking down to them and using the periodical merely as a propaganda vehicle, the publication may become an object of derision rather than a tool for achieving the two-way communication management desires. Periodicals also can serve as channels for communication from employees to management through letters to the editor, question-and-answer features, and similar editorial devices.

Major corporations sometimes produce sleek, sophisticated-appearing magazines and colorful newspaper-style publications that are in the forefront of contemporary design. Four-color covers and splashy graphics help attract readers in this age of visual emphasis. Examples of this lavish approach are AT&T's management-oriented *AT&T Magazine* and Transamerica Corporation's *Transamerica.* Some of these, such as the American Express *Dateline International,* circulate worldwide.

From this elaborate and expensive format, company publications range down to four-page folders in black and white that resemble a small tabloid newspaper. The publication interval may be weekly, biweekly, monthly, or quarterly. Decisions on format and frequency depend on the size of the public relations budget and the audience management seeks to reach. Some companies have found that their blue-collar employees get more satisfaction from a periodical which is simple in design and presentation than from an elaborate, multicolored, sophisticated-looking magazine such as those distributed to stockholders and others the company seeks to impress.

Large corporations frequently publish several periodicals, each designed for a different audience. Usually the objective of a publication is stated in small type in its masthead. Typically, *Chevron World,* published quarterly by Standard Oil Company of California, states, "The *Chevron World* is published and distributed by the company's Public Affairs organization for the information of shareholders, employees, and other interested parties." Knowledge of this stated purpose helps a person to scrutinize the content of a periodical and analyze why various elements were included. (*Chevron World* is described in detail later in the chapter.)

Nonprofit organizations publish periodicals for much the same purposes that corporations publish theirs. Instead of trying to please stockholders and customers, nonprofit organizations must seek the support of contributors. Their product is service. Therefore, periodicals aimed at contributors and possible donors emphasize the quality and social value of the service the organization delivers.

Company magazines fall into four major categories, grouped by the audience they serve. To illustrate how the various types function, the following sections analyze the contents of typical magazines in each category: those for employees and retirees, for stockholders and employees, for marketing staff and wholesaler customers, and customers and association members.

MAGAZINES FOR EMPLOYEES AND RETIREES

The employee magazine is a means by which management can inject a personal touch into company affairs. As a humanizing tool, it helps offset the feelings of some employees, especially in large corporations, that they have little significance as individuals to management. Through its pages, the company can recognize the achievements and personal milestones of those who work for it. A well-edited employee periodical helps instill an attitude among employees that they are part of the company. At the same time, the magazine offers management an opportunity to report its policies and explain why they were adopted. When the publication is in newspaper format, the appearance is different but the goals are the same.

Employee publications, like most periodicals, usually have stated objectives. The Clorox Company publishes a quarterly magazine, *The Diamond,* for its 4800 employees. *The Diamond* has the following objectives:

- To assist management in securing employee understanding and support for the company's operations, activities, objectives, and plans

- To recognize employee accomplishments on and off the job to maintain high morale and develop a sense of participation in the company's affairs and its relationship with local communities

- To educate employees about subjects such as the U.S. economic system, safety, and the obligations of responsible citizenship to make employees more valuable members of the Clorox family and their communities.

The editor of *The Diamond* follows a story mix intended to recognize people in different divisions, departments, and various locations while covering issues important to the company such as safety, quality, productivity, cost reduction, and community involvement. One edition of *The Diamond,* for example, contained the following stories:

- *Clorox Community Service.* An article about a company community service project that received a national presidential citation.

- *Pasta Plant in Pennsylvania.* A feature about the operations of a company manufacturing facility. A sidebar article features a salad-dressing plant in West Virginia. Photos show employees at work.

- *Volunteers Helping Kids.* A short employee feature about a Clorox employee who volunteers her time at a shelter for troubled youngsters.

- *A Day in the Life of* . . . A feature about the work of the Cincinnati regional sales manager.

- *Company Profits.* An economic education feature that explains how company profits are reinvested in areas of safety and new plant equipment.

- *A Healthy Heart.* A true-false Q&A article to educate employees about heart disease.

- *Service Anniversaries.* Names of employees who have worked 20, 15, 10, and 5 years for the company.

- *Doer's Profile.* An article highlighting how a manufacturing facility in Chicago slashed workers' compensation costs by more than 99 percent with a well-organized safety campaign.

The Clorox *Diamond* exemplifies effective employee communication with a limited staff and budget. In a primarily one-person operation, the editor plans content, interviews people, writes all copy, handles all approvals, takes most photographs, and supervises design, production, and printing. The editor also handles all phases of a monthly two- to four-page newsletter.

MAGAZINES FOR STOCKHOLDERS AND EMPLOYEES

Because a magazine of this type is aimed at two audiences, its approach must be broader. Although stockholders and employees share concern about the success of their company, their interests are not identical. News about the activities and milestones of individual employees does not interest stockholders. The magazine's focus needs to be more on technical and economic developments in the corporation's field and on the company's strategy to take advantage of them. A magazine distributed to stockholders as well as to employees usually is more visibly management-oriented than one for employees only. It must be kept in mind that many employees also are stockholders, often as participants in company-sponsored stock purchase programs.

An example of the company periodical distributed to both stockholders and employees is *Chevron World,* published quarterly by Standard Oil of California as a colorfully printed, 30-page, slick-paper magazine.

A typical issue of *Chevron World* contains a policy statement by the chairman of the board about oil exploration, articles about natural gas reserves and oil taxation, and a feature about Chevron's TV school in which the company instructs its executives on how to appear on television programs. Other material includes a brilliantly illustrated story about oil exploration in Arctic waters and one about bird life on the company's North Sea oil platforms.

The difference in approach between *Chevron World* and the magazines edited exclusively for employees is obvious. In this publication, employees are given a carefully crafted picture of their company's ambitious search for new energy sources. Their pride in the company's size and ingenuity is stimulated. They receive strong exposure to management's views on taxation and legislation. Corporate image-building is the dominant theme. Another company periodical, *Standard Oiler,* is distributed only to employees and retirees.

MAGAZINES FOR MARKETING STAFF MEMBERS AND WHOLESALERS OF COMPANY PRODUCTS

These periodicals are unabashedly promotional, edited to encourage sales through inspirational essays and how-to-do-it articles.

An excellent example of these direct sales-booster periodicals is *Team Talk,* published by Anheuser-Busch of St. Louis to promote its group of beers. Articles contain cheerleader sentences of a type the reader would be unlikely to find in the magazines previously analyzed. Quotations like this from wholesalers are included in articles about their activities:

Everybody loves a winner and wants to be associated with a class organization . . . our retailers and the general public know we are proud of our products. Anheuser-Busch is a winner, and we want to be one, too.

In general, the content of *Team Talk* urges marketing people to exploit established events by pushing exposure of their products and to create special events for the same purpose. Its goal is stimulation of its readers.

MAGAZINES FOR CUSTOMERS AND ASSOCIATION MEMBERS

As a psychological link to their customers, to remind them of company products and services, some firms publish magazines addressed exclusively to this group. Magazines published by national organizations for their members are similar in purpose and character, although in some instances somewhat wider in editorial range. The cost of a membership magazine normally is included in the annual dues.

The customer magazine is not a catalogue, although it may contain pages offering services or products, often packaged in special offers. Primarily its objective is to present a favorable image of the company, rather than direct selling.

A colorful example of the customer magazine is *Silver Circle,* a 48-page quarterly published by Home Savings of America and distributed free to members of its Silver Circle. The Circle is a device designed to increase deposits in this very large savings and loan association. Home Savings depositors who have at least $10,000 in accounts become Silver Circle members. They receive the magazine and a membership card entitling them to discounts on numerous travel and entertainment items.

The editors of *Silver Circle* can make several important assumptions about their audience: (1) those who receive the magazine have at least a moderate amount of spare money; (2) members may be expected to have substantial interest in travel; (3) all probably have at least a fundamental understanding of financial matters. Relative affluence, money awareness, concern about health, interest in travel—those attributes of the *Silver Circle* audience are the framework on which the magazine is built.

Because of the national worry about failures in the savings and loan industry, a typical issue opens with a reassuring statement by the chairman of Home Savings about the company's financial strength and long-term growth. One article exposes get-rich-quick schemes, another tells how to set up a home fitness center, and a third describes a cruise to South America. Financial tips and medical news items are presented attractively. The magazine also includes a lengthy hotel and resort guide listing places that offer Silver Circle discounts, and discount coupons from amusement centers.

The interlocking tie-ins between the magazines and the hotels, restaurants, and amusement parks offering discounts in it illuminate the techniques of entertainment sales promotion. Those who give discounts know they are reaching an audience with money to spend. Home Savings in turn earns goodwill from magazine recipients by offering such bargains. When presented in the context of a sleek magazine, the discounts avoid the look of being gimmicks that may have a catch in them somewhere.

Another group of magazines in this category are aimed specifically at target audiences of importance to a corporation or association, such as *WEcology* by McDonald's, sent to 4.5 million students and teachers.

BROCHURES AND HANDBOOKS

Writing informational publications to fill innumerable needs is among the most common duties of public relations practitioners. Some printed pieces are issued at stated intervals, such as quarterly reports to stockholders and college catalogues. The majority, however, are designed to last for indefinite periods, subject to updating as required. Most of this material is distributed free, although price tags may be placed on more elaborate and expensive items such as museum catalogs.

Whatever their purpose, these publications share clearly defined writing requirements. Clarity is essential. Frequently the writer must explain technical material or simplify complex issues for a reader who knows little about the topic. This calls for explanations that are straightforward, shorn of jargon, and stated in terms of reference that a casual reader can comprehend quickly. Paired with clarity is conciseness. Informational writing should be tightly done; elaborate literary devices should be left to the fiction writer. The person who delivers information needs to pare excess verbiage from sentences and paragraphs.

Every brochure, handbook, or other form of printed information should be organized on a firm outline that moves the reader forward comfortably through unfamiliar territory. Frequent subheads and typographical breaks are desirable. The writer often operates under budget restrictions that dictate the size of the publication—perhaps a 4-page folder, perhaps a large-format brochure of 30 pages consisting primarily of illustrations with short blocks of type. Space limitations should be regarded as a challenge to the writer's skill at condensation.

The following are the types of publications in this category that a public relations writer is most frequently called upon to create.

INFORMATIONAL BROCHURES

These describe the purposes, policies, and functions of an organization. Tour-guide folders given out at museums are an example of this form.

HANDBOOKS

More elaborate than basic brochures, these usually include policy statements, statistical information, and listings of significant facts about the issuing organization and its field of operation. Handbooks often are designed for distribution primarily to news media sources as handy references for a writer or broadcaster in a hurry. Trade associations and large corporations are among the most frequent users of the handbook as a public relations tool.

GUIDELINES FOR BROCHURES AND HANDBOOKS

Plain English and basic design enhance the communication effectiveness of any document. These attributes not only increase goodwill with key publics but also reduce complaints and confusion among employees and consumers.

The following are research-based criteria for enhancing readability and comprehension:

- Use 8- to 10-point type. Readers often ignore text that is too small.

- Use plenty of white space. Wide margins, indents, and occasional short pages keep the document from looking crowded and too difficult to read.

- Use ragged right, rather than justified, margins. This gives the document a relaxed contemporary look.

- Use short lines. Optimal line length for most text is 50 to 70 characters.

- Use boldface for emphasis. It is easier to read than a word in all capital letters.

Source: Based on material from the Document Design Center of the American Institute for Research, Washington, D.C., as presented in *PR Reporter.*

Typical examples of the handbook are the following:

- *"Sharing the Risk," published by the Insurance Information Institute.* Nearly 200 pages describe property and casualty insurance concepts, regulations, and policies, ranging from homeowners' losses to nuclear risks.

- *"Oil & Gas Pocket Reference," published by Phillips Petroleum Company.* This is a 60-page small-format booklet of statistics about the oil industry. Included are such lists as the top 10 U.S. oil-producing states; the top 15 oil-producing nations, with amounts; oil and gas imports by year; and significant reference dates.

CORPORATE BROCHURES FOR EXTERNAL USE

Frequently aimed at specific audiences rather than at the general public, these may be such items as the inserts utility companies include with their bills, financial documents such as quarterly reports to stockholders and proxy statements for potential stock purchasers, owners' manuals, and teaching materials that help students learn about the issuing industries.

CORPORATE BROCHURES FOR INTERNAL USE

To inform and train their employees, companies issue a broad range of brochures and handbooks. These may be distributed at in-plant meetings or to individuals at work, or mailed to the employees' homes. In simplest form, information sheets may be posted on

FINANCIAL SUMMARY

1993
First
Quarter

1

SDGE

**A Publication of
San Diego Gas & Electric
Investor Relations**

FIGURE 22.4
Quarterly financial reports sent to a company's investors and
the financial community are an essential element in its public
relations program. This report cover is typical.

company bulletin boards. Readership of these boards is high; anything posted there will
be noticed and probably will become a topic of conversation on the job.

Examples of in-company brochures and manuals include the following:

■ *Atlantic Richfield Company's 12-page booklet to assist older employees make the
transition from work to retirement.* It answers questions that concern every employee approaching retirement, such as financial planning, use of leisure time, and
health benefits.

■ *A manual describing proper telephone techniques, given to employees of Washington Federal Savings and Loan Association in Seattle.* Employees discuss the manual in seminars during which they see a 25-minute film depicting "telephone traps"
in which they might find themselves.

GLOSSARIES

Trade associations and corporations in technical fields often issue pamphlets defining
terms, including jargon as well as standard words, commonly used in their work. Like

handbooks, glossaries are distributed extensively to the news media, to help writers understand the special language and use it accurately. Glossaries sometimes are included in other corporate publications.

An oil industry glossary, for example, includes words and terms such as *desiccation, dispersant, huff-and-puff,* and *wrinkle chaser*—hardly the language that a nonspecialist writer runs across in daily life. (*Huff-and-puff* is descriptive of techniques to recover oil by steam injection. A *wrinkle chaser* is a geologist.) These examples were taken from a glossary published by Phillips Petroleum.

THE ANNUAL REPORT

"The principal purpose of the annual report is to tell the company's story to a multiplicity of audiences," says David F. Hawkins, a professor at the Harvard Business School. "It's a public relations document with a regulatory requirement."

Indeed, preparation of a corporation's annual report is a major function of a company's public relations department or counseling firm and is probably the company's most expensive written contact with its stockholders and the financial community. According to a study by the National Investor Relations Institute, investor relations executives devote about 13 percent of their time to preparing annual reports. The estimated 10,000 public companies in the United States spend an average of $3.52 a copy to produce a glossy publication of abundant color, with striking graphics and impressive photography, averaging 44 pages. (See Figure 22.5.)

Technically, the corporate annual report is an informational document required by the Securities and Exchange Commission of all publicly traded companies. But there is no legal requirement that annual reports be extravaganzas. Under Rule 14a–3 of the Securities Exchange Act, publicly traded companies are required to include only basic financial information and other material such as a list of directors and the auditor's opinion letter. Once these requirements are met, the rule states, "the report may be in any form deemed suitable by management."

Companies publish expensive and attractive annual reports for public relations purposes. These include (1) impressing current and potential stockholders that the company is well managed and successful, (2) encouraging potential investors to purchase stock, and (3) using the annual report as a vehicle for recruiting new employees. In other words, annual reports help showcase the company's accomplishments and management philosophy.

Some evidence exists, however, that costly expenditures on such reports don't really influence potential investors. A Hill and Knowlton survey of 501 investors concluded that only 3 percent found annual reports to be the best source of investment information. In that respect, annual reports ranked behind periodicals, stockbrokers, statistical services, friends, and relatives. Some companies recently have reduced the scope of their annual reports, even down to summary size.

A corporate annual report is divided into two general sections:

1. *Detailed financial information about the company's condition and performance during the past year.* A consolidated balance sheet and management's discussion of the

Southern New England Telecommunications Corporation Annual Report 1992

Building On Our Strengths

SNET
We go beyond the call.

FIGURE 22.5
By featuring employees on the cover of its annual report,
Southern New England Telecommunications Corporation
emphasizes the fact that behind its statistics and charts are men
and women who make the company function.

financial condition are essential elements. A letter from the corporation's auditing firm attesting to the validity of the figures is included, along with separate breakdowns of certain financial aspects. The statistical material in this section is prepared by the financial department and approved by top management. The material is coldly objective and must be completely accurate, but some companies also use a profusion of numbers that often confuse everyone except specialists in accounting.

To cite one case, an annual report of Koppers Company had a mass of numbers, charts, and graphs—and even a ten-year financial comparison of 45 items. Yellow lines highlighted the most favorable statistics that the company wanted to emphasize.

Other relevant information about the corporation is published in this section for reference. This may include lists of key executives and their salaries, names of major stockholders, lists of plant sites, and major subsidiaries. Because specific financial data are required by the Securities and Exchange Commission in an annual report, a specialist in financial public relations should be assigned to compile the reports.

2. *Management's presentation of accomplishments during the past year, its goals and outstanding problems.* This material, appearing in the first portion of the report just after a one-page summary of financial highlights, is designed to give a good impression of management's work. While the prose is restrained, use of striking color photographs and other graphics, often in full-page size, helps suggest corporate vigor and achievement.

The centerpiece of this front section is a report to stockholders by the board chairperson or the chief executive officer. This is the "message," and it is sometimes used to rail against government regulation, or to extol the company's contribution to making America a leader of the "free world."

When companies have had a bad year financially, or have been involved in an embarrassing episode, they frequently bury that fact in their annual reports, so that only a close reading—not too common among ordinary stockholders—will disclose it.

Others discuss their troubles with refreshing candor. In the LSI Logic company's 1989 report, Chairman Wilfred Corrigan told stockholders, "this past year was a disappointment, and I'm glad it's behind us." Similarly, Walter Elisha, chairman of Spring Industries, the big textile corporation, commented, "In sum for the '80s, we would, if asked, grade ourselves a 'B' . . . better than most but not yet measuring up to our own standards."

In general, trends in annual reports during the 1990s are toward more informality in writing, more focus on employees, and, when a company's operations justify it, emphasis on its roles in the international market and the environmental movement.

This section of the annual report also contains information about new projects, new acquisitions, new products, and areas of corporate philanthropy. Many companies also comment on social responsibility efforts to hire more minorities, promote more women, and deal with environmental issues.

On occasion, a company breaks out of the usual mold with a creative approach. BellSouth, for example, used an annual report to focus on the year 2000 by including essays from nationally known authors, commentators, and experts about our lives now and in the future. And First Hawaiian, Inc., a bank-holding group, used color photos of its executives in Hawaiian shirts instead of three-piece suits.

As supplements to printed annual reports, but never as replacements for the financial section, some companies issue videotaped annual reports for showing to employees, stockholders, and financial groups. Teleconferencing an annual meeting is an increasingly common practice. But evidence shows that although a video can provide basic information, comprehension is increased if an executive is present to explain and field questions. Research has shown that recipients don't "reread" video reports as they do printed ones.

Traditionally, *advertising* is defined as purchased space or time used to sell goods or services, while public relations space in the media is obtained free. The line of demarcation becomes fuzzy when a company engages in *corporate advertising,* also called *institutional advertising.* Such advertising is processed and purchased in the regular manner. Its purpose, however, is not to sell the company's products or services directly but to enhance public conception of the company or to advocate a company policy.

FIGURE 22.6
This story is an example of free ready-for-publication feature material sent to newspapers by specialized services paid to do so by the companies and organizations featured in the articles.

CAR CARE

R$_x$ for Rock and Roll: New Shocks or Struts

News USA

(NU) - With auto repairs, like dental repairs, the longer you delay the more it will cost you.

A classic example of this theory is the case of the shock absorber or, on most of today's cars, the strut. There's one of these attached to each wheel of your vehicle. They dampen the rebound of the springs and help reduce rock and roll or sway on turns. They keep the tires in contact with the road.

Shocks and struts are the subject of a new pamphlet produced by the Car Care Council in cooperation with the Ride Control Institute. Written in layman's terms, the illustrated folder explains the function of these important components and how they affect a vehicle's safety.

"Vehicle owners traditionally have identified shock absorbers with riding comfort," says Council President Donald B. Midgley. "Our pamphlet shows vehicle owners how this component relates to other aspects of the vehicle's road worthiness as well.

"During that brief period your wheels are skittering and hopping as you make a turn on a rough road, you've lost contact with the road surface. This affects your steering and braking and could take you into a ditch or an oncoming vehicle."

Wear and Tear

In addition to riding comfort and control, there's wear and tear on other parts of the vehicle, often directly attributable to worn shock absorbers or struts. The exaggerated motion can cause fatigue of springs and accelerate wear of steering and suspension parts.

The jar from a chuck hole or road obstruction sometimes will break radiator mounts or exhaust system support brackets, according to Midgley. "This kind of wear or damage, all or partly due to weak shock absorbers, adds to the cost of having procrastinated on maintenance."

For a copy of the free pamphlet, send a stamped, self-addressed envelope to Car Care Council, Department RC, One Grande Lake Drive, Port Clinton, OH 43452.

A corporate advertisement, as defined by Leading National Advertisers, a checking service, must deal with a company's policies, functions, facilities, objectives, ideas, and standards; build favorable opinions of the company's management, skill, technology, or social contributions; enhance the investment qualities or financial structure of the company; or promote it as a good place to work.

Recently some corporate advertising has been used to push products, sometimes rather subtly, to the extent that the distinction between product and corporate advertising becomes blurred.

The largest percentage of corporate advertising is done on television, with consumer magazines a close second. Radio, outdoor advertisements, and newspaper supplements receive much smaller amounts, and daily newspapers receive the least.

Corporate advertising may be divided into three basic types: (1) *general corporate image-building,* (2) *investor and financial relations programs,* and (3) *advocacy.*

IMAGE-BUILDING

Image-building advertising is intended primarily to strengthen a company's identity in the eyes of the public and/or the financial community. Conglomerates whose divisions market unrelated products seek through such advertising to project a unified, readily recognized image. Others use it to correct an unfavorable public impression. Increasingly, corporations use institutional advertising to show their concern for the environment, and by doing so seek to demonstrate what good corporate citizens they are.

Chevron, for example, published a series of advertisements titled "People Do" in which the oil corporation emphasized that its construction crews avoid disturbing nature. One of these image advertisements, built around a drawing of a sage grouse, read:

THE PIPELINE AND THE DANCING BIRD

At sunrise in Western Wyoming, the strange and spiky male Sage Grouse does its mating dance.

It's the beginning of a process of life that could be endangered if anything enters his breeding grounds.

That's why people building a pipeline stopped construction. They worked further down the line and came back to finish the job after the chicks had hatched.

Sometimes doing what's required doesn't make work easier, but it can make it feel more worthwhile.

Do people really put aside human plans so nature can take its course?

People Do.

CHEVRON

A *warning:* Any corporation that strikes a pro-environmental posture, then is caught polluting or otherwise damaging the environment, immediately becomes the object of derision for hypocrisy.

In one instance, Mobil Chemical Company sought to attract environmentalists by advertising that its Hefty brand plastic trash bags are degradable and break down when exposed to the elements. Calling the advertising false, the attorneys general of seven states sued to halt its use and asked civil penalties of at least $500,000 against the company. With its image damaged by the publicity, the company agreed to drop the claim until agreed terminology could be worked out.

FINANCIAL RELATIONS PROGRAMS

The second form of corporate advertising is aimed straight at the financial community. The advertiser tries to depict its financial strength and prospects so favorably that securities analysts will advise their clients to purchase its stock. When a corporation has millions of shares outstanding, even a fractional improvement in their price is beneficial. Such advertising is used extensively during proxy fights for control of companies, or when a company is undertaking a major reorganization and needs to keep the financial community informed.

ADVOCACY

The third, sometimes controversial, form of corporate advertising is advocacy. In such advertisements, a corporation or association tries to influence public opinion on a political or social issue. Only a small portion of corporate advertising expenditure goes into advocacy advertising, but because these advertisements sometimes touch public sensibilities, they receive considerable attention.

Mobil has been among the most vocal corporations in its advocacy advertising, emphasizing its aggressive positions on matters of energy control and chiding the media for what Mobil's advertising has called "irresponsible reporting." The tone of this advertising brought criticism against the giant oil corporation.

Chase Manhattan Bank also encountered criticism for some of its advocacy advertising, as it conceded frankly in a full-page newspaper advertisement. This advertisement was dominated by a drawing of several of the Founding Fathers, above the headline:

In accordance with the wishes of our founding fathers, we'll continue to speak out.

The text stated, in part:

In the past year, Chase has been running a series of advertisements which expressed our views on some of today's important economic issues. These included the need for greater productivity . . . the need to stimulate research and development . . . tax incentives to spur investment, generate capital and modernize our industrial plant . . . government overregulation . . . inflation. And the spurious rhetoric about "excessive" corporate profits.

Since then, these topics have become central issues in this critical election year. For that we're grateful, because the American public surely deserves a full and open debate as to how best these pressing national problems can be solved.

On the other hand, it's caused us to go through some soul-searching in recent weeks. We've frankly asked ourselves whether an institution such as ours should continue to speak out on important and sometimes sensitive issues in the middle of a national election.

So we went back to the First Amendment to our Constitution and took a long and thoughtful look. As a result, we've decided to go right on speaking out, even though we obviously risk causing controversy or alienating a constituency. . . .

How effective is corporate advertising? Because of its abstract nature, measurement of results is difficult. In this sense it resembles public relations programs more than it does traditional advertising, which can be evaluated in terms of units sold.

Ogilvy & Mather, a major advertising agency, studied corporate advertising. It announced these conclusions:

We have learned that good corporate advertising can:

- Build awareness of a company
- Make a favorable impression on investors and securities analysts
- Motivate employees and attract recruits
- Influence public opinion
- Strengthen relations with dealers
- Influence legislation

We have learned that corporate advertising cannot:

- Gloss over a poor record or a weak competitive position
- Boost the price of your stock next month
- Swiftly turn the tide of public opinion

There are no quick fixes. Advertising can spread the truth about your company but cannot *conceal* it.

Thomas F. Garbett, a recognized authority on the subject, offered this justification for corporate advertising, in an article published in the *Harvard Business Review:*

Although many companies assume that the safest course is to keep a low profile, this may in fact be a dangerous tack. If some inadvertent disclosure brings high visibility or even incidental exposure, an unknown company maintains little credibility as it moves to counter public criticism . . . When people first get acquainted with a company through an unfortunate disclosure, they often distort what little they know and make generalizations about missing information. The less filled out a company's image is, the more subject that image is to wild distortions.

CASE PROBLEM

A new 550-room hotel, the Fairmont, will be built in downtown San Jose, California's third-largest city, with a population of 900,000. The hotel, to cost an estimated $30 million, is part of a downtown redevelopment effort that includes a light rail system and a $110 million convention center now under construction.

The hotel, part of the Fairmont chain, will have four restaurants, a health club, lobby bar, and banquet facilities for up to 2000 people. The architect is Skinner and Associates, and the contractor is BK Industries. Estimated completion date and grand opening of the hotel will be in about 18 months. Hotel executives and city officials say that the hotel is the cornerstone of the downtown's revival.

Write a news release on behalf of the hotel chain to announce the decision to build a new facility in San Jose. Use appropriate quotations from hotel and city officials as you deem necessary.

QUESTIONS FOR REVIEW AND DISCUSSION

1. What is an *embargo* on a news release? Does it have any legal standing?

2. What are the physical requirements for an attractive news release?

3. A public relations counselor should have a client initial a file copy of each news release before distribution. Why?

4. Describe the difference between a news release and a factsheet.

5. To what audiences might a corporate public relations department send a newsletter?

6. As editor of a company magazine intended for employees and retirees, what would be your objectives?

7. Handbooks are issued frequently by corporations and trade associations. What types of material do they usually contain?

8. To what federal agency must corporate annual reports be submitted?

9. Corporate or institutional advertising differs in purpose from ordinary advertising. Explain this difference.

10. What risk does a corporation take when it uses aggressive advocacy advertising?

SUGGESTED READINGS

Alvarez, Paul H. "Corporate Advertising Review: Overall Media Buying Stagnates but Targeted TV Booms." *Public Relations Journal,* August 1993, pp. 14–17.

Goldfarb, Roz. "The Outlook for Annual Reports." *Step-by-Step Graphics,* January/February 1993, pp. 18–19.

Kemper, Gary W. "Employee Publications: Achieving Excellence Is a High-Wire Act." *Communication World,* September 1991, pp. 22–26.

Kemper, Gary W. "Employee Publications: Are They a Poor Investment for Many Organizations?" *Communication World,* April 1991, pp. 17–23. Survey of employee publications and their effectiveness.

McCathrin, Zoe. "The 'Should I Print It' Test: Questions to Ask Before Creating Another Brochure or Newsletter." *Communication World,* April 1991, p. 10.

McGoon, Cliff. "Putting Your Employee Newsletter On-Line." *Communication World,* March 1992, pp. 16–18.

Minter, Bobby. "Starting a Newsletter." *Public Relations Journal,* July 1989, pp. 30–32.

Morton, Linda, and Warren, John. "News Elements and Editor's Choices." *Public Relations Review,* Spring 1992, pp. 47–52. Survey of news elements in news releases.

Mullins, Ronald G. "Employee Communications: Fracture for Success and Security." *Communication World,* September 1992, pp. 18–21. How to make periodicals effective.

Palframan, Barbara. "Annual Reports: Examining the Best." *Communication World,* September 1992, pp. 34–37.

Parker, Robert. A. "Employee Publications: Dying? Flourishing?" *Communication World,* February 1993, pp. 31–37. A survey about types of publications and how they are produced.

Rothman, Andrea, and Droscoll, Lisa. "Won't You Please Read Our Annual Report?" *Business Week,* May 13, 1991, p. 50.

Upbin, Bruce. "What Your Annual Report and Cosmo Should Have in Common." *Communication World,* September 1993, pp. 16–18.

Walters, Lynne Masel, and Walters, Timothy N. "Environment of Confidence: Daily Newspapers' Use of Press Releases." *Public Relations Review,* Spring 1992, pp. 31–46.

Watras, Michael. "Going Global With Annual Reports." *Communication World,* September 1991, pp. 16, 18.

Spoken Tactics

P R E V I E W   The objective of this chapter is to explain spoken tactics in public relations and how such assignments as writing speeches and conducting news conferences are handled. The problem of rumors also is examined.

Topics covered in the chapter include:

- Face-to-face discussion

- Speechwriting techniques

- Staging a speech

- Conducting a news conference

- Press parties and tours

- Interviews

- Conducting meetings

- Word-of-mouth

A conversation face-to-face between two persons is widely regarded as the most effective form of interpersonal communication. This is certainly true in the world of work. The chemistry of personality that can develop during a business call is not easily defined but can be tremendously valuable.

Visualize these typical situations: a salesperson soliciting an order from a customer at lunch; a public relations representative at an editor's desk explaining the reasons for her hospital client's fund drive; a corporate vice president for public affairs calling on a city council member to urge the opening of a new street to reduce traffic congestion outside the company's manufacturing plant. In each case, the logic of the persuader's arguments is reinforced (or undermined) by the impact of the individual's personality. Sincerity impresses the listener. An aggressive, demanding approach arouses irritation. A smile, perhaps a casual quip, and a friendly but respectful manner help immeasurably in getting one's message across.

The personal call is among the most potent methods a public relations practitioner can use. It may fail, however, no matter how good the cause, if the caller arrives ill-prepared and handles the presentation clumsily. Here, from a veteran newspaper editor who has listened to hundreds of across-the-desk public relations presentations, is advice on how to present a case effectively:

1. *Telephone in advance for an appointment.* Then be on time. Don't walk in "cold" and expect a hearing.

2. *Identify yourself and your purpose immediately.* Present a business card if possible, so the recipient has your name and affiliation at hand during the discussion and for filing later.

3. *Be concise.* Editors, program directors, and other opinion-makers on whom you call are busy. Even those who appear relaxed and casual have other work waiting to be done. Make your presentation succinctly. Describe what your client plans to do, explain the purpose of the program, tell how it will help the public, and state specifically what support you hope to receive from the person you are addressing. Respond to your host's questions without meandering up side conversational paths, politely seek a commitment if that seems appropriate, then leave. Unless the listener judges your proposal to be excessively commercial or self-serving, you can expect a sympathetic hearing in most instances.

4. *Don't oversell.* Don't plead. Persons who receive presentations dislike being pressured and instinctively build defense mechanisms against excessively emotional "pitches." Never say, "You must help us!" Persons whose aid you seek resent being told that they "must" do anything.

5. *Express appreciation for your host's time and for anything he or she can do to assist your cause.*

6. *Leave behind written material—a brochure, a news release, a factsheet—for your host to study later.* Be certain that the material includes a telephone number at which you can be reached for further information. Asking your host to read the material while you sit there is a poor tactic, unless it is very short; the result may be a hasty, reluctant scanning rather than the thoughtful reading you desire.

If the presentation can be made at lunch, over coffee or perhaps over a drink, outside the office setting, its impact may be stronger—assuming that the person being solicited will spare the necessary time.

7. *Follow up with a note of appreciation for the reception, expressing hope that the recipient can use the information you left.* It subtly reminds the person to read the material, if that hasn't happened, and to do something about it.

If you are working with an editor or program director in a small community, or with a person you know well, the approach can be more informal. However, conciseness, restraint, and the delivery of printed information are important in every situation.

Face-to-face discussion also is an essential tool for open communication within business organizations. Such conversations between management representatives and supervisors, supervisors and foremen, management and union officers, spread understanding of a company policy or a new product among the employees. Slightly less intimate, but almost as effective if well done, is the small-group discussion directed toward the same goal. Internal communication through staff study meetings, employee training sessions, and department meetings creates a more competent, motivated work force and identifies areas of employee dissatisfaction. (A discussion on how to conduct an effective meeting appears later in this chapter.)

A blind spot in company management, in small firms as well as large ones, is the too-frequent assumption that employees down the line know the reasons for company policies. The cynical wisecrack "There's no reason for it, it's just company policy" shows a weakness of management that need not exist if verbal channels of internal communication are used frequently and intelligently. Explaining *why* something is done is just as important as explaining *how* it should be done.

Vital as they are in reaching opinion leaders, person-to-person conversations form only one segment of a campaign to inform the public and mold opinion through the spoken word. A public relations campaign usually must reach many persons at the same time. This can be done orally through speeches, news conferences, and appearances of representatives on radio and television. Although the impact of a speaker's personality on individual listeners may diminish when the message is delivered in a large meeting hall or filtered through a receiving set, the sheer abundance of simultaneous contacts speeds up distribution of the message. Repetition of a message in several forms creates greater awareness, and use of several methods helps to reinforce the message among selected audiences.

Each of these spoken methods will be discussed in detail. The text will first examine the speech: how to plan it, how to write it, and how to assist the speaker who delivers it.

ASSIGNMENT: SPEECHWRITING

Public relations practitioners frequently are called on to write speeches for their employers or clients. As speechwriters, their role is a hidden one. They labor silently to produce the words that may sparkle like champagne when poured forth by their employ-

THE PUBLIC SPEAKS—LOUDLY

A massive upsurge in expression of public opinion about political issues developed through telephone calls and radio talk shows during the 1992 presidential campaign and again during the 1994 congressional elections.

During the first eight days of the 1993 congressional session, the Capitol switchboard handled a record 1,650,143 phone calls, of which 263,947 were logged in a single day. Thousands more were received on direct lines to congressional offices.

Some of these calls were spontaneous. A vast number, however, were generated by special-interest groups using sophisticated electronic "alert" systems that stimulated citizens to support their causes by telephone, fax, or letter.

Bonner & Associates, a firm that specializes in grass-roots lobbying, has a million-dollar phone system with 300 lines. Operators work from computerized lists of names and phone numbers compiled from national organization lists. Membership lists also can be cross-referenced with magazine subscriptions, data on personal purchasing habits, and precincts with particular voting patterns to produce larger lists of sympathetic people.

Among the most powerful public relations systems is the so-called gospel grapevine. Evangelists rally support on issues through their programs on 1200 radio stations, their television and cable TV programs, and a system of telephone calls to churches. In one instance, evangelist Jerry Falwell on his "Old Time Gospel Hour" urged viewers to dial a 900 number and add their names to a petition asking Clinton not to remove the ban on homosexuals in the military services. The calls cost those who responded 90 cents for the first minute. Within hours, 24,000 calls were received.

Other interest groups use similar systems. The U.S. Chamber of Commerce has a phone bank to call its 215,000 members, urging them to speak out on issues it favors or opposes. Those answering with a touchtone telephone are invited to press 1 to have a Mailgram or letter sent in their names to a representative in Congress, press 2 to record a voicemail message, or press 3 to have a computer connect them immediately with the lawmaker's office.

Members of Congress quickly identify the sources of artificially stimulated calls and discount their significance. Nevertheless, the sheer weight of such mass organized call-ins does influence the legislators.

Occasionally, their overburdened staffs find ways to strike back. When Clinton proposed a huge increase in tobacco taxes as part of his attack on the federal budget deficit, the Phillip Morris tobacco company asked smokers to call members of the House Ways and Means Committee in protest. Angry aides to several committee members retaliated by sending masses of "junk" documents to the fax machine in Phillip Morris' Washington office.

Many calls to radio talk programs are similarly stimulated by organized interests. On the better-conducted shows, the production staffs that screen the calls put through to the on-air hosts try to balance the pro and con opinions. Despite this control, the volume of organized call-ins does influence the tone of many shows.

ers from the lecterns of convention halls. In the White House, the wraps of anonymity usually are drawn around the writers who churn out speeches and statements for the president of the United States. A president who utters a memorable phrase gets the credit, but some unknown writer in a back office probably created it. There is nothing discreditable about this. Presidents have more urgent tasks than to think up catchy quotations. Although speechwriters rarely receive ego-building recognition, they find personal satisfaction in creating competent speeches for someone else. Speechwriting is a highly skilled craft.

Most of the largest corporations employ speechwriters, some of whom receive annual salaries from $70,000 to $120,000. Freelance writers often command from $1,000 to $10,000 for a speech. The life of a speechwriter is not easy, however; the writer's copy must be approved by numerous executives, and it sometimes becomes badly mangled in editing battles.

Turning loose a speaker, especially an inexperienced one, before an audience without a text, or at least a careful outline, may be an invitation to boredom. The "and . . . uhs" and "as I was sayings" will proliferate like rabbits. The audience will squirm, inwardly at first and then conspicuously in their chairs, as the speaker stumbles along. The opportunity to deliver a message that informs, persuades, and entertains listeners has been thrown out the window. That is why speakers who lack the time or the skill to do their own preparation need able speechwriters.

Some speakers prefer to work from notes rather than read a text. In that event, the writer should prepare a full speech for the speaker to study, then reduce the main elements of it to note cards arranged in proper sequence. Talking from notes increases the air of spontaneity, if the speaker is experienced and comfortable before an audience. It also magnifies the risk, however, that the speaker will meander and lose control of the time.

A written speech should reflect the personality and voice patterns of the speaker, not those of the writer.

Speeches come in many sizes and serve many purposes. The writer may be called on to prepare a light 20-minute talk for the service club luncheon circuit, a provocative 10-minute statement to open a panel discussion, or a scholarly 45-minute lecture for delivery before a university audience. Possibly the assignment may be for "just a few remarks" to welcome foreign visitors on a plant tour. Or it could be for a hard-sell pitch to raise money for a local charity campaign.

THE BASIC POINTS OF SPEECHWRITING

Whatever the assignment, here are basic points for the speechwriter to keep in mind:

1. *A speech should say something of lasting value.* Even a talk intended to entertain, full of fluffy humor, should be built around a significant point. A speech needs both content and style; without the former, the latter is empty.

One veteran speechwriter for a large corporation and an influential trade organization applies what he calls the "Door Test" to the speeches he writes. After hearing a dinner speaker, the listeners go out the door of the banquet room and on entering the doors of their homes are greeted by their spouses and asked what the dinner speaker said. In reply, the listeners give the essence of the speech as they remember it. Was there a message clear and concise enough to remember? Did the speech pass the Door Test?

2. *A speech should concentrate on one, or at most two, main themes.*

3. *A speech needs facts.* The information must be accurate. The writer's skill as a researcher is put to the test, to dig up information that will illustrate and emphasize the

speaker's theme. Before a speaker makes a statement, the information in it should be verified beyond any doubt.

4. *The type of audience should influence the style and content of the speech.* When a company celebrates its fiftieth anniversary with a reception and dinner dance for its employees, they don't want to hear the president drone on for 30 minutes about the corporate financial structure. The setting calls for some joking, a few nostalgic stories, references to some individuals by name, words of appreciation for what the employees have contributed, and a few upbeat words about the future. On the other hand, the president may ask the writer for a speech about the company for delivery at a meeting of securities analysts. This is not the place for droll stories. The audience wants facts on which to base investment decisions, not entertainment.

5. *Clarity in speechwriting is essential.* If the listeners don't understand what the speaker is saying, everyone's time is wasted. This happens when the speech contains complicated sentences, technical information that the speaker fails to explain in terms the audience can comprehend, and excessive jargon or "inside" talk. The speechwriter's challenge is to simplify and classify the speaker's message without destroying its significance.

AN EXAMPLE OF SPEECHWRITING

To determine how the speechwriting process works, consider how a specific assignment could be handled. The assistant public relations director of a large regional restaurant chain is assigned to prepare a speech for the general manager to deliver at a chamber of commerce banquet in a middle-sized city where the company has recently opened a luxury restaurant. What does the practitioner do?

First, she must know what the speaker desires to emphasize. The management has heard extensive word-of-mouth criticism about the high dinner prices the new restaurant charges. Some business has been lost because of this. The general manager sees the speech invitation as an opportunity to explain why the restaurant must charge these prices and to stress what good values the dinners really are. To do so, he must give the audience a frank behind-the-scenes look at the restaurant business—an opening for the speechwriter to spice up the necessary financial information with whimsical backstage anecdotes.

Twenty minutes of such material, brightly presented, will entertain and inform this business-oriented audience. It will demonstrate that the restaurant organization is efficiently run and does its best to provide residents with a distinctive place to dine at the lowest feasible cost. Indeed, here is an excellent public relations moment.

The speechwriter rarely talks with the general manager. So she must use her speech-planning appointment with him not only to learn what he wants to say but to study his style. Does he speak intensely or in a casual, wry manner? Is his speech staccato or a bit fulsome? The words she writes should be shaped to his natural style. Probably he can provide her with one or two of his favorite restaurant anecdotes. She can talk later with other officials of the company to obtain additional stories.

With this guidance in hand, how does the practitioner organize and write the speech?

A speech is built in blocks, joined by transitions. The following pattern for assembling the blocks provides an all-purpose outline on which most speeches can be built:

1. *Introduction (establishment of contact with audience)*

2. *Statement of main purpose of speech*

3. *Development of theme with examples, facts, and anecdotes.* Enumeration of points in 1, 2, 3 order is valuable here. It gives a sense of structure and controlled use of time.

4. *Statement of secondary theme, if there is one*

5. *Enunciation of principal point to which speaker has been building, the heart of the speech*

6. *A pause at this plateau, with an anecdote or two.* This is a soft place while audience absorbs principal point just made.

7. *Restatement of theme in summary form*

8. *Brief, brisk conclusion*

This plan of speech organization is *deductive;* that is, the central theme is stated almost at the beginning, and the points that follow support and illustrate the theme. A less common type of organization is *inductive.* In it the speaker presents points of information and arguments leading up to a statement of the principal theme near the end of the speech.

Introduction   Following the preceding deductive outline, the speechwriter uses the first 2 minutes of the allotted 20 to build rapport between the general manager and the audience. The manager explains that when his company first considered coming to this city, he doubted that the area would support the luxury type of restaurant it operates. But the chamber of commerce convinced him that it would, and he is delighted that he had the good sense to listen (a light, slightly self-disparaging touch). He congratulates the chamber on the excellent statistical material it provided, thanks the membership for the organization's aid in solving the problems of setting up business, and mentions by name a few individuals who were especially helpful.

Then come the building blocks leading up to the conclusion.

Statement of Main Purpose   The speaker says he wants to tell the audience about how a luxury restaurant operates, what its problems are, and why the customer sees things done a certain way. A summary of purpose in a single theme sentence at this point gives the speech a solid foundation. Almost as an aside he remarks, "Perhaps this will help you understand why our dinners cost as much as they do."

Development   The manager states his company's total investment in opening this restaurant and reveals the number of people needed to run it . . . mentions kitchen jobs the diner never knows about . . . lists how many potatoes, steaks, heads of lettuce, and pounds of coffee are consumed in a week . . . relates a story about the night when the maitre d' had a full book of reservations and the salad chef walked out in a huff after a quarrel with his waitress girlfriend . . . describes how the chain's bill for pork and beef has soared.

Statement of Secondary Theme   The speaker explains how the restaurant chooses its menus. He describes research into which entrees sell well or poorly, nutritional factors, and the difficulties in finding reasonable prices for the high-quality foodstuffs that will maintain the restaurant's standards of excellence.

Enunciation of Principal Point   Operation of a top-flight restaurant in a time of high labor costs and rising food prices is a risky business, subject to the vagaries of weather, the economy, and the largely unpredictable turns of public fancy. By its steady growth, his organization has proved that a significant percentage of the public, "including here in this city," will patronize a restaurant that serves fine food with alert service in a distinctive setting. "Our challenge is to provide these things at the lowest prices we can offer while earning a legitimate profit from our investment."

Pause on Plateau   The manager relates an anecdote about a diner who tried to steal some silverware, only to have it drop out of his pocket near the front door. The story illustrates problems of operating a restaurant.

Restatement of Theme   The speaker's summary emphasizes his pride in the way local diners have patronized the new restaurant, proving his belief that the establishment provides the city with a type of high-quality dining that its citizens want and appreciate.

Brief Conclusion   The audience hears a bit of news: the speaker announces that the restaurant has arranged to receive ample supplies of a popular but relatively rare fish. Next week the restaurant will add the fish, prepared in an unusual manner, to the menu at a special low introductory price. He invites everyone to come and try it.

One more step remains to make this a thoroughly successful public relations appearance. The speaker knows that the audience will be invited to ask questions; he has had the speechwriter give him a list of antagonistic queries he may receive. These include such challenges as, "Why do you hold people with dinner reservations in the bar so long before seating them—to make more money on liquor?" and "Is it true that you require waitresses to surrender a percentage of their tips to management?" His ability in answering the tough ones will improve or detract from the good impression his speech has made.

SPEECHWRITING TECHNIQUES

THE DIFFERENCE BETWEEN THE WRITTEN AND SPOKEN WORD

The first principle in writing words to be spoken is to make them flow in the way a person usually talks. Writing intended for the ear must be simpler in construction and more casual in form than writing meant for the eye. Instead of saying, "the Chicago man," make it "the man from Chicago"; it sounds more natural. Contractions such as *don't* and *won't* increase the sense of informality.

Short, straightforward sentences are best. To provide variety, an occasional long sentence is acceptable if its structure is simple. So is a scattering of sentences beginning with brief dependent clauses. Often the ear fails to comprehend as fully and quickly as the eye does because the listener is easily distracted or may not hear clearly. The audio channel becomes clogged. Complex grammatical constructions should be avoided. A person can read a complicated sentence again and again until its meaning is clear. A listener who hears that same sentence spoken has no opportunity to hear it again because the speaker has moved ahead to new material. Thus a speaker, especially when handling difficult information, should repeat key points of the speech, couching them if possible in slightly different form.

Studies indicate that the average person listens four times as rapidly as the average person speaks. Thus the listener may be thinking about other matters while hearing the speaker. Even for a skillful speaker, holding the listener's undivided attention is extremely difficult; recapitulation of main points helps the listener retain at least the main thrust of the speech.

Here, for example, is a sentence from a published news story that would be unacceptable in a speech text because of its intricate structure:

Wright, who has agreed to pay the fine, said she believes the commission's action, which comes three weeks before the Nov. 2 election, will have no effect on her reelection campaign against Democrat C. D. (Dick) Stine.

If the material were written as follows, listeners could comprehend it far more easily:

Wright has agreed to pay the fine. The commission's action comes only three weeks before the November 2nd election. But Wright believes that it will not affect her campaign for reelection against Democrat Dick Stine.

An excellent way to grasp the concept of writing for speech is to close your eyes and listen to people around you talk. Do the same thing while hearing a radio newscast, which has been written especially for the ear. Visualize how the words you are hearing would appear on paper. Notice how often people use fragments of sentences. The words that would complete the sentences are implied, a kind of verbal shorthand. Such fragments in a speech increase the feeling of naturalness.

The incomplete sentence is used quite effectively in this excerpt from a speech by John C. Bedrosian, president of the American Federation of Hospitals. His topic, the high cost of medical care, was complex, and he dealt with the problem in depth. A brief text, however, kept the speech from bogging down. Brief sentences, sentence fragments, and short words are used to offset such necessary long ones as *catastrophic* and *ambulatory:*

Hospital care is expensive. There is no denying that. It is essentially designed to provide care to the critically ill. Catastrophic illnesses. Major surgeries. Serious injuries. Any institution that is equipped and staffed to provide the highest level of care is by its very nature not economically appropriate for low-level care.

That's why we are witnessing the growth of alternative care and treatment sources. Satellite clinics, for example, surgi-centers, and other ambulatory care facilities. Skilled nursing homes for recuperation from illness or surgery. Home health care, a concept that has really only gotten started.

All of these are approaches that match the level of care to the need, and at a significant reduction in cost.

A speaker normally delivers a text at the rate of about 150 words a minute. A standard page of pica-sized typewriter copy contains about 250 words. So, when preparing a 20-minute speech, the writer must produce about 3000 words, approximately 12 typewritten pages. If the speaker is an especially fast talker, this wordage might be increased a bit. Pauses for emphasis and laughter, however, tend to make a speaker's delivery before an audience slower than during practice run-throughs.

SOME TIPS FROM PROFESSIONALS

Here are tips on writing from professional speechwriters:

- *Read aloud the words you have written, to be certain that they sound natural to the ear.*

- *Avoid clauses that complicate sentences.* Instead of writing, "John Williams, chairman of the State Highway Commission, said, etc.," eliminate the clause by writing, "Chairman John Williams of the State Highway Department said, etc."

- *Use smooth transitions to move from one section of the speech to the next, as in these examples:*

"And while discussing the fine art of communications, Japanese style, I would like to mention the role of the press." (K. M. Chrysler of *U.S. News & World Report*)

"Now I'd like to move to a second major challenge facing us—crime." (James B. Jacobson of Prudential Insurance Company of America in a speech on "Challenges and Choice—Inflation and Crime")

- *Use rhetorical questions.* They provide change of pace and are a good device to introduce new ideas. An example:

"Is it too difficult to develop a curriculum whereby students can be fully educated? I think not. It has been done before and quite well." (Benjamin H. Alexander, president of the University of the District of Columbia)

- *Draw verbal pictures.* Help the audience visualize scenes, color, movement.

- *Be wary of jokes.* Some speakers tell them well, others fumble. Never let your speaker use that bromide, "That reminds me of a story." If used, jokes should be woven into the text, not telegraphed in advance. Those involving racial and religious topics are likely to offend some members of the audience. Don't use them.

The light touch desired in a speech can be obtained by anecdotes or quips that provoke a smile or a chuckle.

■ *Quote statistics sparingly.* Provide them in graphic terms when possible. Dixy Lee Ray, former chairperson of the Atomic Energy Commission, did it this way: the amount of energy now being consumed in the United States by one person in one day is equivalent to what would be produced by the human muscle of approximately 300 slaves working all 24 hours, consuming no energy themselves.

ESTABLISHING A BOND WITH THE AUDIENCE

Use of the second-person form of direct address is a clever tool for speakers trying to establish a personal bond with the audience. A physicist delivering a university lecture would avoid such a device; it might subtly lower the intellectual level of his speech. Politicians use it frequently.

President Clinton used the technique in promoting his economic recovery program in 1993. Breaking down the massive figures into individual terms, he told listeners that "you" would pay relatively little in additional taxes and would help "your" government create better times for "you" and others like "you."

Clinton achieved less impact with this approach, however, than President Reagan did a decade earlier when he proposed a tax increase a year after putting through a major tax reduction. A former actor and TV host, Reagan pushed the "you and I together" theme in his principal speech with repeated use of "you" and "us" and such sentences as, "You helped us to start this economic recovery program last year, when you told your representatives you wanted it. You can help us again . . . "

Of such niceties are speeches of persuasion made.

VISUAL AIDS FOR A SPEECH

A speech often can be strengthened by use of visual devices. Graphs and charts, a common kind of visual aid, are only as good as their visibility to the audience. A chart too complicated for easy comprehension or too small to be read from the rear of the room is almost useless. Slides projected onto a screen are frequently used. They must be simple in content; holding a slide on the screen long enough for the audience to study involved information creates restlessness. (Audiovisual aids are discussed in Chapter 24.)

Use of objects is still another form of visual aid for a speaker. The model of a new company product displayed near the lectern is an example. A blown-up reproduction of a United Way fund drive emblem hung behind the head table is another. President Jimmy Carter tried a similar technique by wearing a cardigan on camera, instead of the usual presidential suitcoat, during a nationally telecast speech urging energy conservation. The device was so obvious, however, that criticism of the presidential image-building effort severely weakened its effect.

Effective speeches don't just happen. They have to be rehearsed and prepared—or, in the language of the theater, "staged." Organizations frequently rely upon a practitioner's understanding of potential audiences to ensure that a speaking engagement helps the organization get a positive message across. And to create a pool of talented speakers, some organizations establish training programs.

THE PRACTITIONER'S ROLE

Public relations practitioners who write speeches are frequently called upon by management to give their opinion about whether the company should accept an invitation to speak and, if so, how the firm should use such a forum to present its views and policies in the most favorable light.

When an invitation arrives, the first decision to be made is whether a speech should be delivered at all. This is where the practitioner's advice may be sought by company management. Thought should be given as to whether the size and significance of the audience justify the time and effort involved. Although this may sound a little arrogant, it is only a matter of practicality.

On the other hand, a public relations representative whose employer desires to make speeches can create ample opportunities. Waiting for invitations is unnecessary. Offers to make a speaker available to organizations without charge may be made discreetly by letter, telephone, or word-of-mouth. The approach is to suggest that the speaker has an unusual message that should be of special interest to the group being solicited. If the speaker is a corporation executive, the hosts should be assured that they will not be subjected to a heavy sales pitch.

Management also is likely to seek out the practitioner's opinion when a speaker must appear before a hostile audience—a real test of public relations skill. While not always pleasant, the experience can pay dividends. A land developer who proposes construction of a shopping center close to a school cannot expect a cordial welcome when addressing an audience of parents. If the speaker can command respect by a pleasant, frank manner, however, some members of the audience may realize that he is not the ogre they had imagined. Having achieved this, the speaker can lay out his arguments and at least make the audience aware of his reasoning. People usually admire frankness in others and, while not always admitting it, may grudgingly admire a person for voluntarily facing up to enemies.

Members of the public are not the only audiences an organization's speaker may address. Management representatives—including public relations staff members—frequently make speeches within the organization, as part of an employee relations program. Although the atmosphere normally is friendly, the speaker still must maintain good rapport with the audience. Practitioners themselves may address a group, or they may offer guidance to other speakers in presenting the message. During times of internal hostility such as labor disputes, public relations expertise may be essential.

Even a brilliantly written speech can fail if it is delivered poorly. Upper-echelon executives for whom speeches are a required part of the job should be offered training by professionals in the techniques of public speaking. Progressive organizations also search among their employees for men and women who can be trained to speak effectively.

Employees selected may be assigned to attend on-the-job training sessions in speechmaking. They are instructed in such basics as diction, stage presence, voice projection, reading audience reaction, and handling questions. Videocassette tapes and other teaching aids enhance the instruction.

When a company needs to explain its policy to employees and seek their cooperation, top-echelon officials aren't always the best ones to do it. A well-trained fellow worker in a department may succeed better in convincing his or her colleagues to authorize automatic payroll deduction for United Way contributions than a speaker sent out from the executive offices. When management trains speakers from various work levels, provides them with well-written speeches appropriate for their needs, and gives them a suitable setting, they can fill a valuable role in the internal communication chain. What's more, they can give management enlightening feedback from their colleagues.

HELPING THE SPEAKER POLISH AND PRESENT THE SPEECH

After writing a draft of a speech, the writer should go over it with the speaker, who may request changes. By listening to the speaker read the material aloud, the writer can detect clumsy portions and smooth them out. The more frequently a speaker reads the text aloud in practice, the better the on-stage performance will be. A videotape made of a practice session will show the speaker where improvement is needed.

The finished version of a speech should be typed on 8½-by-11-inch pages in easily read type, without excessive crowding. Some speakers prefer that the typescript cover only the upper two-thirds of a page, to prevent them from dropping their heads too low as they read. If the bottoms of the typed pages are crimped a bit, the speaker can turn them without having two stick together.

Writing an introduction and sending it to the person who will present the speaker is a good tactic. This assures that the information about the speaker will be correct. Although the introducer may alter the material, the content probably will be approximately what the public relations representative desires.

At the scene of the speech, the public relations representative should take several actions:

■ *The microphone and other apparatus should be tested.* The audiovisual equipment should be set up and checked and the slide projector focused. Charts or flipcards should be arranged in correct order on an easel.

■ *Extra copies of the speech should be brought along.* Additional copies are for distribution to the news media and to listeners who request a copy.

■ *The speech should be recorded on tape.* The tape can be used to settle any disputes over what the speaker said, to provide "actuality" excerpts for local radio stations,

KETCHUM PUBLIC RELATIONS
WORLDWIDE

David R. Drobis
Chairman and CEO
KETCHUM PUBLIC RELATIONS

"Balancing Conflicting
Interests of Multiple
Stakeholders"

A Speech Before
The Conference Board

FIGURE 23.1

A spoken communication can reach an important additional audience when printed and sent to opinion leaders such as newspaper editors, government officials, television commentators, academicians, and people who speak for industry. This is the cover of a speech reprint distributed by Ketchum Public Relations.

and to assemble material for a postmortem session between speaker and writer analyzing the performance. If the speaker is well known, especially if he or she is from out of town, the public relations representative may arrange for radio, television, and newspaper interviews as well as provide taped excerpts to the stations.

Two other steps can be taken to obtain additional exposure for an important speech: (1) copies can be mailed to a selected list of opinion leaders and (2) the speech can be rewritten as an article for a company publication or submitted to a suitable trade magazine (see Figure 23.1).

SPEAKERS' BUREAUS AND HOTLINES

Speakers' bureaus operated by trade associations, social agencies, and corporations constitute an important instrument for bringing speakers and audiences together (see Figure 23.2). They function something like a company's pool of internal speakers, but on a more elaborate scale. Speakers developed within an organization are made available by the bureaus upon request. The bureaus also seek to place speakers before influential audiences. Utility companies, which have a constant need to build friendly community

QÚI VỊ CÓ THỂ LIÊN LẠC VỚI CHÚNG TÔI BẰNG TIẾNG VIỆT

Công ty điện Edison Miền Nam California hiện có nhân viên phục vụ bằng tiếng Việt. Chúng tôi có thể giúp qúi vị nếu qúi vị có những thắc mắc về tiền điện hàng tháng hay muốn mở hoặc đóng đồng hồ điện tại nơi mình cư ngụ.

Qúi vị có thể gọi những nhân viên nói tiếng Việt này ở số điện thoại ghi trên, hoàn toàn miễn phí.

Chúng tôi hy vọng như vậy sẽ giúp qúi vị liên lạc với Công ty thuận tiện hơn.

FIGURE 23.2
Recognizing the immense ethnic diversity in its service area, Southern California Edison Company operates a speakers' bureau, the Multi-Lingual Speakers Task Force, consisting of company employees. Speakers are available in several Asian languages and in Spanish. More than 26 percent of Edison customers speak Spanish with limited English capability, and 16 percent speak an Asian language. The language in the illustration is Vietnamese.

relations, are especially heavy users of the speakers' bureau concept. Typically, a telephone company in Illinois has a bureau with 42 trained speakers who talk before all types of clubs and civic organizations. Before being sent out to represent the company, the speakers receive professional training and must pass auditions.

Talent-booking agencies that place professional speakers for a fee sometimes also call themselves speakers' bureaus. The roles of these two types of speakers' bureaus are quite dissimilar: one provides speakers without charge, to promote the cause of the corporation or organization that operates it, while the other does so on a direct profit-making basis. It is important to distinguish between the two.

Somewhat related to the organizational speakers' bureau is the telephone hotline service operated by some trade associations and companies to provide quick answers, especially to the news media (see Figure 23.3). This facility generally offers toll-free telephone service using the 800 prefix. The following advertisement by the Edison

FIGURE 23.3
Trade associations place advertisements in media journals, such as this one in *Editor & Publisher,* to encourage use of their telephone hotlines.

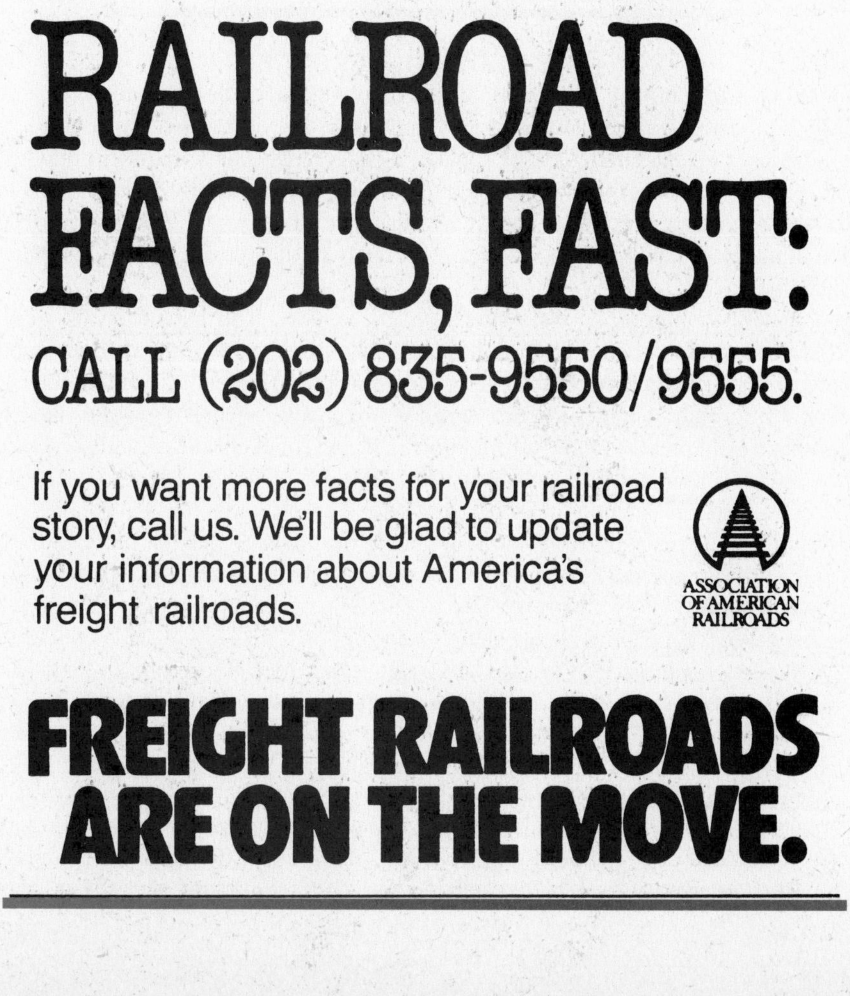

RAILROAD FACTS, FAST:
CALL (202) 835-9550/9555.

If you want more facts for your railroad story, call us. We'll be glad to update your information about America's freight railroads.

ASSOCIATION OF AMERICAN RAILROADS

FREIGHT RAILROADS ARE ON THE MOVE.

Electric Institute Information Service in *Editor & Publisher,* the newspaper trade journal, illustrates how the hotline functions:

YOU DON'T NEED A PRESS CONFERENCE TO GET THE ENERGY STORY

Let's have a conference right now.

And it won't even cost you a dime.

One of our experts is ready to help you with your newsbreak, feature, or editorial.

Ask for facts, background, and the national perspective on electric energy.

Ask about energy sources, economics, and the environment.

Because energy is one of the crucial issues in American life today, there's someone on the hotline, 24 hours a day, 7 days a week.

Just think. By using the phone, you'll be saving energy while writing about it.

Call toll-free 800-424-8897.

SPECIAL TYPES OF SPEAKING OPPORTUNITIES

THE NEWS CONFERENCE

A speaker addressing an audience represents one-way communication. Listeners receive the message, either accepting or rejecting it, but do not engage in a dialogue during which they can challenge the speaker's statements. The speaker commands the situation. The only exception occurs when a speaker agrees to accept questions from the floor—a practice that some speakers relish but others avoid either because they realize that they do not perform well spontaneously or they desire to avoid embarrassing questions.

At a news conference, communication is two-way. The person speaking for a company or a cause submits to questioning by reporters, usually after a brief opening statement. A news conference makes possible quick, widespread dissemination of the sponsor's information and opinions through the news media. It avoids the time-consuming task of presenting the information to the news outlets individually and assures that the intensely competitive newspapers and electronic media hear the news simultaneously. From a public relations point of view, these are the principal advantages of the news conference. Against these important pluses must be weighed the fact that the person holding the conference is open to severe and potentially antagonistic questioning.

In public relations strategy, the news conference can be either an offensive or a defensive device, depending on the client's need.

Most news conferences—or press conferences, as they frequently are called—are *positive* in intent; they are affirmative actions to project the host's plans or point of view. A corporation may hold a news conference to unveil a new product whose manufacture will create many new jobs, or a civic leader may do so to reveal the goals and plans for a countywide charity fund drive she will head. Such news conferences should be carefully planned and scheduled well in advance under the most favorable circumstances.

Public relations specialists also must deal frequently with unanticipated, controversial situations. A business firm, an association, or a politician becomes embroiled in difficulty that is at best embarrassing, possibly incriminating. Press and public demand an explanation. A barebones printed statement is not enough to satisfy the clamor. This is the moment for a news conference that is *defensive* in nature, an effort to put out the fire with the least damage possible. The person who holds the conference will face uncomfortable minutes under sharp questioning. However, the alternative of "stone-walling" silence is worse. It leaves public and press with a feeling of evasion and a suspicion that the truth is even worse than it actually is. A well-prepared spokesperson may be able to achieve a measure of understanding and sympathy by issuing a carefully composed printed statement when the news conference opens.

No matter how trying the circumstances, the person holding the news conference should create an atmosphere of cooperation and project a sincere intent to be helpful. The worst thing he or she can do is to appear resentful of the questioning. The person never should succumb to a display of bad temper. A good posture is to admit that the situation is bad and that the organization is doing everything in its power to correct it. (Further discussion of crisis public relations appears in Chapter 14.)

Rarely, an organization or public person caught in an embarrassing situation foolishly attempts to quiet public concern by holding a news conference that really isn't a news conference. The host reads a brief, inadequate statement, then refuses to answer questions from reporters. This practice alienates the press, which feels cheated. Suspicions of the host's conduct are increased, not minimized. If, for a valid reason, only a brief statement can be issued at the time, this should be done by distribution of a news release rather than by summoning reporters to a nonproductive conference.

Two more types of news conferences are held occasionally. One is the spontaneous conference arising out of a news event: the winner of a Nobel Prize meets the press to explain the award-winning work . . . a runner who has just set a world's record breathlessly describes his feelings . . . a woman appointed to a high-court judgeship tells reporters about her legal philosophy . . . a candidate for mayor makes an election night claim of victory. The other type is the regularly scheduled conference held by a public official at stated times, even when there is nothing special to announce. Usually this is called a briefing—the daily State Department briefing, for example.

Planning and Conducting a News Conference   First comes the question, "Should we hold a news conference or not?" Frequently the answer should be "No!" The essential element of a news conference is *news*. If reporters and camera crews summoned to a conference hear propaganda instead of facts, or information of minor interest to a limited group, they go away disgusted. Their valuable time has been wasted—and it *is* valuable. Editors complain that they never have enough staff hours available to cover everything they would like to cover; if they send reporters to a conference that has been called merely to satisfy the host's sense of self-importance, they resent the fact. The next time, they probably won't send reporters.

If the material involved fails to meet the criteria of significant news, a wise public relations representative will distribute it through a press release. The information has a chance of being published based on its degree of merit without irritating editors and reporters.

Notices usually are sent by fax or mail, but some organizations use special delivery methods for major conferences in the belief that the extra impact justifies the additional cost. Every news outlet that might be interested in the material should be invited. An ignored media outlet may become an enemy, like a person who isn't asked to a party. The invitation should describe the general nature of the material to be discussed so an editor will know what type of reporter to assign.

What hour is best? This depends upon the local media situation. If the city has only an afternoon newspaper, 9:30 or 10 A.M. is good, because this gives a reporter time to write a story before a midday deadline. If the city's newspaper publishes in the morning, 2 P.M. is a suitable hour.

Another prime goal of news conference sponsors is the early evening newscasts on local television stations, or even network TV newscasts if the information is important enough. A conference at 2 P.M. is about the latest that a television crew can cover and still get the material processed at a comfortable pace for inclusion in a dinner-hour show. This time period can be shortened in an emergency, but the chances of getting on a show diminish as the processing time dwindles.

A warning: a public relations representative in a city with only an afternoon newspaper who schedules a news conference after that paper's deadline, yet in time for the news to appear on the early evening television newscasts, makes a grave blunder. Newspaper editors resent such favoritism to television and have long memories. Knowledge of, and sensitivity to, local news media deadlines are necessary elements of a public relations representative's work.

Deadlines for radio news reporters are less confining than those for newspapers and television, because radio newscasts are aired many times a day. The conference hours suggested for newspapers and television are suitable for radio as well, though.

Here are two pieces of advice from longtime public relations specialists to persons who hold news conferences:

1. *The speaker should never attempt to talk off-the-record at a news conference.* If the information is so secret that it should not be published, then the speaker shouldn't tell it to reporters. Many editors forbid their reporters to honor off-the-record statements, because too often the person making them is merely attempting to prevent publication of material that is legitimate news but might be embarrassing. Any statement made before a group will not stay secret long, anyway. If one reporter present ignores the request and publishes the material, those who honored it are placed at an unfair competitive disadvantage.

2. *The speaker should never lie!* If he or she is pushed into a corner and believes that answering a specific question would be unwise, it is far better to say, "No comment" in some form than to answer falsely. A person caught in a lie to the media suffers a critical loss of credibility.

Preparing the Scene   At a news conference, public relations representatives resemble producers of a movie or television show. They are responsible for briefing the spokesperson, making arrangements, and assuring that the conference runs smoothly. They stay in the background, however.

Bulldog Reporter, a West Coast public relations newsletter, suggests the following checklist for a practitioner asked to organize a news conference. The time factors given are normal for such events as new product introductions, but conferences concerning spot news developments for the daily press and electronic media often are called on notice of a few days or even a few hours.

■ Select a convenient location, one that is fairly easy for news representatives to reach with minimal travel time. In some cities, this is the local press club; in others, it is a major hotel. On occasion, the organization's headquarters is appropriate.

■ Set the date and time. Times between midmorning and midafternoon are good. Friday afternoons are deadly, as are days before holidays. Be sure to check media deadlines.

■ When possible, issue an invitation to a news conference about six to eight weeks ahead of time, but one month is acceptable. The invitation should include the purpose of the conference, names of spokespersons, and why the event has significant news value. Of course, the date, time, and location must be provided.

■ Distribute a media release about the upcoming news conference when appropriate. This depends on the importance of the event.

■ Write a statement for the spokesperson to give at the conference and make sure that he or she understands and rehearses it. In addition, rehearse the entire conference, including introductions and presentation of the prepared statement.

■ Try to anticipate questions so the spokesperson can readily answer difficult queries. Problem/solution rehearsals prepare the spokesperson for off-the-wall questions or ones that are designed to put the speaker on the defensive.

■ Prepare printed materials for distribution at the conference. These should include a brief factsheet with names and titles of participants, a basic news release, and basic support materials. This is sometimes called a press kit.

■ Prepare visual materials as necessary. These may include slides, transparencies, posters, or even a short videotape. Television crews particularly need something visual.

■ Make advance arrangements for the room. Be sure that there are enough chairs and leave a center aisle for photographers. If a lectern is used, make certain that it is large enough to accommodate multiple microphones from radio and television crews.

■ Arrive 30 to 60 minutes early to double-check arrangements. Test the microphones, arrange name tags for invited guests, and distribute literature.

Some organizations provide coffee and possibly sweet rolls for their media guests as a courtesy. Others find this gesture unnecessary because most of the newspeople are in a hurry, more concerned with getting the story than with enjoying social amenities. Liquor should not be served at a regular news conference. Such socializing should be reserved for the press party, discussed in the next section.

At some news conferences, still photographers are given two or three minutes to take their pictures before questioning begins. Some photographers complain that, thus restricted, they cannot obtain candid shots. If free shooting is permitted, as usually is the best practice, the physical arrangements should give the photographers operating space without allowing them to obstruct the view of reporters.

Relationships between print and television reporters sometimes become strained at news conferences. A practitioner should take particular care to arrange the room in such a way that the electronic equipment does not impede the print reporters. Some find it good policy for the speaker to remain after the news conference ends and make brief on-camera statements for individual TV stations, if their reporters request this attention. Such statements should not go beyond anything the speaker has said to the entire body of reporters.

A final problem in managing a news conference is knowing when to end it. The public relations representative serving as backstage timekeeper and watchdog should avoid cutting off the questioning prematurely. To do so creates antagonism from the reporters. Letting a conference run down like a tired clock is almost as bad. At every conference there comes a moment when the reporters run out of questions and the danger of dull repetition arises. A speaker may, or may not, recognize this. If not, the practitioner may step forward and say something like, "I'm sorry, but I know some of you have deadlines to make. So we have time for just two more questions."

Presidential press conferences do not have this problem. Long-standing custom limits these conferences to 30 minutes. At that point, the senior news service reporter present calls out, "Thank you, Mr. President!" and the conference ends. Everyone concerned with public relations should study a presidential press conference on television. The kinds of questions asked, the manner in which the president answers them, the nature of any opening announcements, and the physical facilities—all of these provide clues for organizing news conferences of a more mundane nature.

THE PRESS PARTY AND THE PRESS TOUR

In the straightaway news conference, the purpose is to transmit information and opinion from the conference speaker to the news media in a businesslike, time-efficient manner. Neither side wishes to turn the meeting into a social event. It is part of the day's work. Often, however, a corporation, an association, or a political figure wishes to deliver a message or build rapport with the media on a more personal basis; then a social setting is desirable. Thus is born the press party or the press trip.

The Press Party   This gathering may be a luncheon, a dinner, or a reception. Whatever form the party takes, standard practice is for the host to arise at the end of the socializing period and make the "pitch." This may be a hard-news announcement, a brief policy statement followed by a question-and-answer period, or merely a soft-sell thank-you to the guests for coming and giving the host an opportunity to know them better. Guests usually are given press packets of information, either when they arrive or as they leave. Parties giving the press a preview of an art exhibit, a new headquarters building, and so forth are widely used.

The press party is a softening-up process, and both sides know it.

The advantages of a press party to its host can be substantial under the proper circumstances. During chitchat over food or drink, officials of the host organization become acquainted with media people who write, edit, or broadcast material about them. Although the benefit from the host's point of view is difficult to measure immediately, opening the channels of communication with the media at multiple informal levels may prove highly advantageous in the future.

Also, if the host has an important policy position to present, the assumption—not necessarily correct—is that editors and reporters will be more receptive after a social hour. The host who expects that food and drink will buy favorable press coverage may receive an unpleasant surprise. Conscientious reporters and editors will not be swayed by a free drink and a plate of prime rib followed by baked Alaska. In their view, they have already given something to the host by setting aside a part of their day for the party. They accept invitations to press parties because they wish to develop potential news contacts within the host's organization and to learn more about its officials.

Until a few years ago, though, *freeloading* by news people at parties was widespread and accepted as normal practice. Often press guests were given expensive gifts. In large cities, the expectations of certain reporters, especially those covering business and entertainment, became absurdly high. One co-author of this book recalls attending a new-model announcement dinner for the press given some years ago by the Chevrolet division of General Motors. During dinner, the public relations director announced that there would be gifts for the guests when they went home. Each guest was asked to fill out a color preference card—blue, green, or tan.

One guest at the author's table asked another, quite seriously, "Do you think they are going to give us cars?" The other responded, with equal gravity, that perhaps they might. The actual gift proved to be an expensive blanket of the preferred color, packed in an individualized cedar chest. This type of payoff for attending the presentation became known as "loot." None of the media guests refused to accept the gift. (Present practice concerning gifts will be described shortly.)

Here are two actual examples of press parties:

1. Officials of Blue Cross in a midwestern state regularly hold a series of dinners in major cities for invited members of the local media. The guest lists include men and women who cover the health field, have a role in editing stories about it, or comment on it editorially. During a cocktail party before dinner, Blue Cross officials mingle with the guests. The public relations consultant accompanying them helps with introductions. During dinner, the host group spreads itself around to sit with guests.

After dinner, the chief executive speaks briefly, explaining what Blue Cross regards as the significant trends and problems in health care. Then he opens the meeting to questions. Inevitably, queries center on why medical costs are so high and what Blue Cross is doing to control them. Some questions are friendly, some barbed. The public relations consultant distributes packets of news releases, factsheets, and charts. No gifts are offered to the guests.

2. A land developer invited local media guests and civic leaders to a luncheon at which he disclosed plans for a major shopping center at the edge of the city. Printed invitations announced a reception at noon and lunch at 12:30. Acceptances by phone were requested by a certain date. Arriving guests received paste-on tags imprinted with their names, large folders containing news releases, photographs of the developer and of an artist's rendering of the project's exterior and interior, and a factsheet giving the developer's biography and a list of projects he had built. The artist's renderings stood on

> ## "JUNKET JOURNALISM" AT DISNEY WORLD
>
> Disney World in Florida threw a press party to celebrate its fifteenth anniversary, and more than 10,000 people came.
>
> The fact that Disney World paid the entire expense of some guests—and offered to do so for all of them—created a debate on media ethics that almost overshadowed the celebration. The party, incidentally, was a classic example of a created news event.
>
> Disney World was well aware of the trend in the media against allowing reporters to accept free trips because the gift might influence the tone of their stories. Its invitations, sent nationwide, offered guests three alternatives:
>
> **1.** Disney World and its travel-promotion partners would pay a guest's entire travel, lodging, and food costs.
>
> **2.** The hosts would pay $150 a day of a guest's expense, and the guest's company would pay the balance.
>
> **3.** A guest's employer would pay his or her entire expense.
>
> Some guests used each method, but Disney World refused to say how many.
>
> The New York *Times* in an editorial claimed that media guests who accepted the free-trip offer had "debased" journalism and given the impression that the entire press was "on the take." The St. Petersburg *Times* called the party "junket journalism." Rebutting this position, some guests from smaller newspapers and broadcasting stations said that their companies could not afford such expensive travel, so this was the only way they could visit the entertainment center and write about it.
>
> Disney World did not require its expense-paid guests to do anything in return. The park did receive a very large amount of publicity, generally favorable except for the media-ethics dispute. The total cost to Disney World and its cosponsors was estimated at around $7.5 million, according to *Editor & Publisher.*

easels around the room; a scale model of the project was displayed on a table. Drinks were served, followed by a large luncheon. After the meal, the developer spoke about the project and answered questions.

The normal adjournment hour for luncheon sessions is 1:30 P.M. This one ran a few minutes past that hour because of the number of questions. No press luncheon ever should run past 2 P.M.

The Press Tour There are three kinds of press tours. The most common is a trip, often disparagingly called a "junket," during which editors and reporters are invited to inspect a company's manufacturing facilities in several cities, ride an inaugural flight of a new air route, or watch previews of the television network programs for the fall season in Hollywood or New York. The host picks up the tab for transporting, feeding and housing the reporters.

A variation of the press tour is the familiarization trip. "Fam trips," as they are called, are offered to travel writers and editors by the tourism industry (see Chapter 20).

Convention and visitor bureaus, as well as major resorts, pay all expenses in the hope that the writers will report favorably on their experiences. Travel articles in magazines and newspapers usually result from a reporter's "fam trip."

In the third kind of press tour, widely used in high technology industries, the organization's executives travel to key cities to talk with selected editors; for example, top Apple Computer executives toured the East Coast to talk with key magazine editors and demonstrate the capabilities of the new Macintosh computer. Depending on editors' preferences, the executives may visit a publication and give a background briefing to key editors, or a hotel conference room may be set up so that the traveling executives may talk with editors from several publications at the same time.

The Ethics of Who Pays for What   In recent years, severe self-searching by media members, as well as by professional public relations personnel who feel it is unethical to offer lavish travel and gifts, has led to increased self-regulation by both groups as to when a press tour or "junket" is appropriate and how much should be spent.

The policies of major dailies forbid employees to accept any gifts, housing, or transportation; the newspapers pay all costs associated with a press tour on which a staff member is sent. In contrast, some smaller dailies, weeklies, and trade magazines willingly accept any and all offers for an expense-paid trip. The managers of these publications maintain that they don't have the resources of large dailies to reimburse an organization for expenses and such trips are legitimate if the reporter is covering a newsworthy activity.

Some newspapers with policies forbidding acceptance of travel and gifts don't extend the restrictions to all departments. Reporters in the "hard news" area, for example, cannot accept gifts or travel, but such policy may not be enforced for reporters who write "soft news" for sports, travel, and lifestyle sections. Few newspapers, for example, pay for the press box seats provided for reporters covering a professional football game, nor does the travel editor usually pay the full rate for rooms at beach resorts that are the focus of travel articles.

Given the mixed and often confusing policies of various media, the public relations professional must use common sense and discretion. He or she, first of all, should not violate the PRSA code of ethics that specifically forbids lavish gifts and free trips that have nothing to do with covering a legitimate news event. Second, the public relations person should be sensitive to the policies of news outlets and should design events to stay within them. A wise alternative is to offer a reporter the option of reimbursing the company for travel and hotel expenses associated with a press tour. Hewlett-Packard, when it invites an editor to have a hosted lunch with an executive during a press tour, even asks the editor to select the restaurant, so the company cannot be accused of trying to "buy" favorable coverage by taking the editor to the most expensive restaurant in town.

In terms of gift-giving, the sensible approach is a token of remembrance such as a pen, note pad, or a company paperweight. (Ethics are discussed extensively in Chapter 6.)

Organizing a Press Party or Press Tour   The key to a successful event is detailed organization. Every step of the process should be checked out meticulously.

In planning the press event, the practitioner has to consider a variety of details. Menus for a luncheon or dinner should be chosen carefully. Do any of the guests have dietary restrictions? Has the exact hour of serving been arranged with the restaurant or caterer, to allow sufficient time for the program? The usual check on microphone and physical facilities is essential.

Even such a seemingly trivial item as a name tag requires the practitioner's careful attention. Paste-on tags written in advance are lined up on a check-in table at the entrance to the room. A host or hostess hands the tags to the arriving guests. A guest who can be welcomed by name, without having to state it, feels subtly flattered. Almost inevitably, though, some name tags will be unclaimed because individuals who accepted fail to show up. In a perfect world, absentees would telephone to cancel their acceptances, but public relations life doesn't work that way. Occasionally, an invited person who failed to answer the invitation will arrive unexpectedly: blank name tags should be kept available for such a situation. (Arrangements with the restaurant should include agreement on the percentage of meals ordered that can be canceled at the last moment without charge. Press kits should be sent to the absentees.)

Fouled-up transportation is perhaps the worst grief for a person conducting a press tour. Buses that fail to arrive at the departure point on time and incorrect booking on airliners irritate the guests and give tour managers gray hairs. Some guests may be prima donnas with inflated egos who will be dissatisfied with almost any hotel room assigned to them. None of the tour guests should be allowed to feel that others are receiving favored treatment. Booking and maintaining a firm tour schedule is essential. When stops are made, the host should specify their length, then begin to round up the strays a few minutes before departure time. Otherwise, the trip may bog down in confusion.

As much as possible, the tour host should "walk through" the entire route to confirm arrangements and look for possibly embarrassing hidden troubles. When North American Aviation introduced a new jet fighter to the national press at the Palmdale, California, airport in the Mojave desert, it asked the pilot to impress the guests by diving and creating a sonic boom. He did so—and pieces of glass went flying through the reception area from windows broken by the impact of the boom. The pilot climbed to do it again, but the public relations hosts stopped him in time by yelling into the radio, "Call it off!"

THE INTERVIEW

Another widely used spoken method of publicizing an individual or a cause is the interview, which may appear in print form in newspapers and magazines or be transmitted electronically via television and radio. In both versions, the ability of the person being interviewed to communicate easily is essential to success. Although required to stay in the background during a client's interview, with fingers crossed that all goes well, a public relations specialist can do much to prepare the interviewee for the experience.

Andrew D. Gilman, president of CommCore in New York City, emphasizes the need for preparation. Said he: "I would no more think of putting a client on a witness stand or through a deposition without thorough and adequate presentation than I would ask a client to be interviewed by a skillful and well-prepared journalist without a similar thorough and adequate preparation."

Techniques for arranging interview appearances by clients are discussed in Chapter 12. This section will examine the steps the public relations representative can take to increase the odds for an effective performance.

In all interviews, the person being questioned should say something that will inform or entertain the audience. Otherwise, the public exposure is wasted. The practitioner should prepare the interviewee to meet this need. An adroit interviewer attempts to develop a theme in the conversation—to draw out comments that make a discernible point or illuminate the character of the person being interviewed. The latter can help the interviewer—and his or her own cause as well—by being ready to volunteer specific information, personal data, or opinions about the cause under discussion as soon as the conversational opportunity arises.

In setting up an interview, the public relations person should obtain from the interviewer an understanding as to its purpose. Armed with this information, the practitioner can assemble facts and data for the client to use in the discussion. The practitioner also can aid the client by providing tips about the interviewer's style and approach.

Some interviewers on the radio talk shows that have proliferated in recent years ask "cream puff" questions, while others bore in, trying to upset the guest into unplanned admissions or embarrassment. Thus it is especially important to be well acquainted with the interviewer's style, whether it be Larry King before a national audience of millions or a local broadcaster. Short, direct answers delivered without hesitation help a guest project an image of strength and credibility.

A significant difference exists between interviews in print and those on radio and television. In a print interview, the information and character impressions the public receives about the interviewee have been filtered through the mind of the writer. The man or woman interviewed is interpreted by the reporter, not projected directly to the audience. On radio and television, however, listeners hear the interviewee's voice without intervention by a third party. During a television interview, where personality has the strongest impact of all, the speaker is both seen and heard by the audience. Because of the intimacy of television, a person with a weak message who projects charm or authority on the air may influence an audience more than one with a strong message who does not project well. When a charismatic speaker is armed with a strong message, the impact can be enormous.

The following sections describe these two types of interview in detail.

When an organization or individual is advocating a particular cause or policy, opportunities to give newspaper interviews are welcomed, indeed sought after. Situations arise, however, when the better part of public relations wisdom is to reject a request for an interview, either print or electronic. Such rejection need not imply that an organization has a sinister secret or fails to understand the need for public contact.

For example, a corporation may be planning a fundamental operational change involving an increase in production at some plants and the closing of another, outdated facility. Details are incomplete and company employees have not been told. A reporter, either suspecting a change or by sheer chance, requests an interview with the company's chief executive officer.

Normally, the interview request would be welcomed, to give the executive public exposure and an opportunity to enunciate company philosophy. At this moment, however, public relations advisers fear that the reporter's questions might uncover the changes prematurely, or at least force the executive into evasive answers that might hurt the firm's credibility. So the interview request is declined, or delayed until a later date, as politely as possible. The next week, when all is in place, the chief executive announces the changes at a news conference. *Avoiding trouble is a hidden but vital part of a public relations adviser's role.* At a later time, the public relations representative might make a special effort to do the would-be interviewer a favor on a story, to remove any lingering feeling of having been slighted.

An alternative approach would be for the chief executive officer to grant the interview, with the understanding that only topics specified in advance would be discussed. Very rarely is such an approach acceptable, however, because reporters usually resent any restrictions and try to uncover the reasons for them.

The Print Interview   An interview with a newspaper reporter may last about an hour, perhaps at lunch or over coffee in an informal setting. The result of this person-to-person talk may be a published story of perhaps 400 to 600 words. The interviewer chooses bits from the conversation, weaves them together in direct and indirect quotation form, works in background material, and perhaps injects personal observations about the interviewee. The latter has no control over what is published, beyond the self-control he or she exercises in answering the interviewer's questions. Neither the person being interviewed nor a public relations representative should ask to approve an interview story before it is published. Such requests are rebuffed automatically by newspapers as a form of censorship.

A talk with an entertainment personality is among the most common forms of newspaper interview. Many personality interview stories carrying Hollywood or New York datelines are proposed by practitioners endeavoring to build up a performer's image or to publicize a new motion picture or television series.

Excellent promotional results can be achieved in far less popular fields of endeavor than entertainment when the person interviewed has something unusual to offer. The following excerpt from an interview with a grower of kiwis demonstrates the point. Many readers, uncertain what kiwis are, would never guess that a man could become a millionaire by growing them. Notice how well prepared the grower was with quotable comments and pertinent facts about his unusual business. Publication of this San Francisco *Chronicle* interview was timed to the kiwi harvesting season; interest it created could be translated readily into purchases at the food store.

KIWI PIONEERS HAVE LAST LAUGH

When the three Tanimoto brothers planted their first acre of kiwi fruit 17 years ago, "we put it in back of our peach groves so people wouldn't laugh at us." recalled George Tanimoto.

"Everybody laughed anyway, and we laughed too," Tanimoto said last week. "Now they say he's laughing all the way to the bank and it's true."

Year after year, the Tanimoto brothers waited for a crop. Finally, in 1970—after 5 years of fruitless ridicule—the first fuzzy brown egg-shaped pods of kiwi appeared on their vines.

Tanimoto sold his maiden kiwi crop to Frieda Kaplan, a Los Angeles fruit dealer who happened to be allergic to kiwi. At first, he shipped the fruit south in three wooden boxes that looked suspiciously like coffins, then individually wrapped them in packages called "flats," because kiwis are very sensitive and will shrivel and shrink when exposed to gas fumes or other ripening fruit.

Today, the 56-year-old Tanimoto is a millionaire because he didn't quit on what he affectionately calls the "Ugly Fruit.". . .

This interview is not a direct hard-sell job, nor can it be described as outright "puffery." The purpose from the newspaper's point of view was to tell readers something interesting.

From a public relations point of view, the story distributes knowledge of the product involved, with the possibility that this knowledge will stimulate purchases of the product.

Magazine interviews usually explore the subject in greater depth than those in newspapers, because the writer may have more space available. Most magazine interviews have the same format as those in newspapers. Others, such as those published in *Penthouse* and *U.S. News & World Report,* appear in question-and-answer form. These require prolonged questioning of the interviewee, sometimes at several tape-recorded sessions, by one or more writers and editors. During in-depth interviews, the person interviewed must be alert against letting down his or her guard and saying something that has unfortunate repercussions.

A famous instance of this occurred when Jimmy Carter was running for president against President Gerald Ford. Carter was a deeply religious man, a fact his public relations advisers emphasized by publicizing his work as a Sunday School teacher and lay preacher in a Southern Baptist church. When they sensed that these pursuits made Carter appear too sanctimonious to voters less religiously inclined, his advisers sought to have him offset this image by being interviewed in *Playboy.*

In the published interview Carter, although happily married, admitted that he had "looked upon a lot of women with lust" and "committed adultery in my heart many times." Angry reactions from his conservative followers were swift. He had besmirched their perceived image of him. Although this frank admission of a common enough male trait made Carter seem more "human" to some voters, overall the interview statements damaged his campaign. He was, of course, elected anyway.

A third, even more elaborate, form of magazine interview story is the long profile, such as those published in *The New Yorker.* Reporters doing profiles usually travel with the interviewee, observing the subject at close range over extended periods. Before trying to interest a magazine in doing such a profile on a client or employer, the public relations adviser should be satisfied that the intended subject of the profile is willing to accept the interviewer on an intimate basis for long periods and will wear well under close scrutiny. Outbursts of anger, a dictatorial manner toward assistants, excessive drinking, and similar private habits produce a bad effect when revealed in print. The profile when published might have a negative result instead of a positive one.

Radio and Television Interviews   With more than 10,000 AM and FM radio stations operating in the United States, the possibilities for public relations people to have their clients interviewed on the air are immense. The current popularity of talk shows, both on local stations and syndicated satellite networks, provides many opportunities for on-air appearances in which the guest expresses opinions and answers call-in questions from listeners. Chapter 12 discussed the public relations opportunities radio and television provide. This discussion will be concerned with the preparation and techniques of on-the-air appearances.

A successful radio or television broadcast interview appearance has three principal requirements:

1. *Preparation.* Guests should know what they want to say.

2. *Concise speech.* Guests should answer questions and make statements precisely and briefly. They shouldn't hold forth in excessive detail or drag in extraneous materi-

al. Responses should be kept to 30 seconds or less, because seconds count on the air. The interviewer must conduct the program under severe time restrictions.

3. *Relaxation.* "Mike fright" is a common ailment for which no automatic cure exists. It will diminish, however, if the guest concentrates on talking to the interviewer in a casual person-to-person manner, forgetting the audience as much as possible. Guests should speak up firmly; the control room can cut down their volume if necessary. (Personal appearances on television are discussed in more detail in Chapter 24.)

A public relations adviser can help an interview guest on all of these points. Answers to anticipated questions may be worked out and polished during a mock interview in which the practitioner plays the role of broadcaster. If a tape recording or videotape can be made of a practice session, the guest-to-be will have an opportunity to correct weaknesses in manner and content that may be revealed.

All too often, the hosts on talk shows know little about their guests for the day's broadcast. The public relations adviser can overcome this difficulty by sending the host in advance a factsheet summarizing the important information and listing questions the broadcaster might wish to ask. On network shows like David Letterman's, nationally syndicated talk shows like Oprah Winfrey's, and local programs on metropolitan stations, support staffs do the preliminary work with guests. Interviewers on hundreds of smaller local television and radio stations, however, lack such staffs. They may go on the air almost "cold" unless provided with volunteered information.

Training business executives in speaking techniques, described earlier in the section on speechmaking, also helps to prepare them for broadcast appearances.

CONDUCTING A MEETING

Meetings are a major public relations tool in contemporary American life. They can be an extremely effective form of communication, or they can be incredible bores. Speakers who drone on too long and discussions that degenerate into petty quibbling act as soporifics on the audience. The hardness of chairs seems to increase by geometrical progression as the presiding officer introduces speaker after speaker. Collective attempts at mental telepathy by audience members urging the chairperson, "Please, please, let us go home," never seem to work. Far from accomplishing a worthwhile purpose, such meetings alienate their audiences. Everyone's time is wasted.

Meetings held for public relations purposes take many forms and vary greatly in size. Sessions may be informational and friendly, they may be heated and controversial, or they may be largely formalized gatherings such as banquets and dedications. Within a company or an organization, they are held to explain and discuss policy, to plan programs, and to train employees. Half a dozen persons may participate, or more than a hundred. Whatever the size and form of a meeting, good planning and an alert presiding officer can assure that the meeting accomplishes its purpose without leaving participants glassy-eyed with fatigue.

A computer information magazine, *MIS,* estimated after a survey that 12 million meetings are held in North America every business day. The survey also reported that executives spend an average of 16 hours a week in meetings for a total of 21 weeks a year. Many of these meetings, called for informational purposes, could be avoided by distribution of the material in printed form.

Guidelines for Meetings Preparation and firmness discreetly applied can control the dynamics of a meeting. The program should move briskly toward a goal. Few people have ever been heard to complain that a meeting was too short. Participants should have a feeling of movement without the appearance of hurry. By following these 12 guidelines, the organizers and presiding officer can create an effective session:

1. If the meeting is open to the public, an audience should be built through distribution of news releases and through other forms of publicity such as posters and announcements at clubs.

2. An agenda should be made and followed.

3. The meeting should start promptly at the announced hour.

4. Speakers should be allotted specified amounts of time and urged to cooperate.

5. Physical arrangements of the hall should be checked in advance—acoustics, seating of the audience so that it is centered in front of the speakers, adequate lighting and fresh air, advance placement of visual aids, and the like.

6. If possible, the reading of minutes and reports should be avoided. Distribution of these documents in printed form is one way to solve this time-consuming problem.

7. Printed material should be distributed to an audience at the start or the close of a meeting, not while the session is in progress. The latter is distracting.

8. Discussion should be controlled even-handedly so that the audience has adequate opportunity to express itself but isn't allowed to wander from the theme. In a controversial situation, a time limit should be set on each speaker from the floor—5 minutes, perhaps—and enforced. When the discussion lags, it should be cut off. One or two verbose individuals should not be permitted to dominate a discussion.

9. In a panel discussion, the presiding officer should give all panel members equal opportunity to be heard. The moderator should try to distribute questions from the floor equitably among the panelists.

10. In long meetings such as a seminar or a training session, periodic recesses should be called; the meeting should resume promptly after the allotted time. A recess should be at least 10 minutes, 15 or 20 if the crowd is large. Comfortable chairs should be provided.

11. The meeting should be brought to a constructive conclusion. If there are several speakers, the best one should be scheduled last, if possible. At the end of a discussion, the presiding officer should summarize for the audience what was said. If a motion for action will be needed, arrangements may be made in advance for someone to offer it.

12. A closing time should be set and strictly adhered to, especially if it has been announced in advance.

AUDIO NEWS RELEASES

Another form of spoken public relations is the audio news release, sent to radio stations in ready-to-broadcast form. The following release, distributed by the American Red Cross promoting Earthquake Preparedness Month in the San Francisco Bay area, is typical. At the top of the page, the release specifies how much air time the announcement will consume, information essential to a radio station.

IN THE CAR

Imagine for a moment that you're in your car when a major earthquake strikes.

At first, it may feel like you've blown a tire, so you pull over. What do you do next? Is it safe to keep driving, or not?

Now image that you are familiar with emergency procedures. You knew when and where it was safe to stop your car, and what to do next.

Now, stop imagining. The reality is that a major earthquake *will* strike the Bay Area again. Call your local chapter of the American Red Cross Bay Area. They'll tell you exactly what you need to do to lessen the impact.

WORD-OF-MOUTH

Often called "interpersonal communication" by academics, "word-of-mouth" is an ephemeral form of spoken communication difficult to isolate or measure but which has a major impact on the formation of public opinion. (See Chapters 9 and 11.)

Research shows that people seldom accept new ideas or products unless friends and relatives also endorse them. Studies also show that informal conversations among peers and friends influence our thinking and behavior more than television commercials or newspaper editorials do.

What people tell one another about a political candidate, a product, a play, or a movie often circumvents the multimillion-dollar expenditures of advertising and marketing experts. *Sleepless in Seattle,* a summer movie hit in 1993, was released quietly in the midst of high-powered promotion for *Last Action Hero,* yet heavily outdrew the violent action film because of enthusiastic word-of-mouth support.

Word-of-mouth is instrumental in making or breaking many products. The American automobile industry provides an example. The message traveled by word-of-mouth that imported cars were more reliable and better crafted than American cars. Despite massive advertising campaigns to change public perception, American automakers lost millions of buyers. Then, subtly, the mood changed and talk among buyers became more favorable to American cars.

One study shows that a person dissatisfied with a product tells a minimum of 10 to 15 people about the experience; in turn, these people tell others in an ever-widening ripple effect that condemns the product. On the other hand, if word-of-mouth designates a product as "trendy," sales soar.

Every professional communicator should understand how rumors start and, more important, how to combat them.

Simply stated, rumors are pieces of "information" that cannot be confirmed or verified by personal experience or a highly credible secondary source. They thrive when a combination of uncertainty and anxiety exists and authentic, official information is lacking or incomplete.

When a company's future is in doubt because of a takeover or merger, employees invariably start a number of rumors about layoffs. The same thing occurs when information is released that the company had a bad fiscal year. The rumors will persist until official information confirms them ("Yes, there will be layoffs") or denies them ("No layoffs are planned"). The key is whether employees trust management to tell the truth. If trust is low, even company announcements may not curtail or kill the rumor.

James Esposito and Ralph Rosnow, writing in *Management Review,* give four strategies for defusing rumors in a company:

1. *Keep employees informed.* Employees are especially sensitive about situations that may affect them directly, such as management-union relations, job advancement, opportunities for relocation, and potential layoffs. Be fully honest, because half-truths encourage additional rumors and destroy the credibility of official spokespersons.

2. *Pay attention to rumors.* If the source of employee anxiety can be determined, the underlying cause of the rumors is obvious. Then, by giving feedback to employees—letting them know how the situation is being dealt with—their fears should be allayed and the prospect of future rumors reduced.

3. *Act promptly.* Rumors become more difficult to control as they harden with time. Get the facts out rapidly but don't repeat a false rumor, because repetition may foster belief. If the rumor is true, it must be confirmed.

4. *Educate personnel.* Actually, conducting a workshop on rumors and their destructive potential can help to stop rumors before they get started. This is especially true when a situation arousing anxiety arises, such as a new boss.

External rumors are more difficult to control, and they can have a devastating effect on a company or its products. A bank in New York City's Chinatown experienced a large outflow of deposits because of a rumor that the bank was in financial trouble. When Johnny Carson did a joke about a supposed toilet-paper shortage, people rushed to the supermarket to stock up. Long lines at the bank and empty shelves at the supermarket tended to reinforce the rumors.

Plagued by rumors that their company was connected with the Ku Klux Klan, the makers of Snapple ready-made teas decided to attack the problem head-on with an advertising campaign in San Francisco denouncing the tales as "outrageous."

One version of the rumor claimed that the illustration of a sailing ship on a label represented a slave ship. Actually, it depicted the Boston Tea Party. Another rumor charged that the encircled letter K on some labels symbolized the Klan. In fact, it indi-

PROCTER & GAMBLE FIGHTS A RUMOR

Despite elaborate efforts to disprove the lie, Procter & Gamble has been plagued for years by a malicious, damaging rumor that it promotes devil worship.

The falsehood is based in part on the soap and food company's circular trademark, which shows a man-in-the-moon face in profile, looking at a field of stars representing the original American colonies. Rumor-mongers claim that this represents Satan.

FIGURE 23.4
The Procter & Gamble trademark.

Anonymous pamphlets distributed in schools and churches are the chief source of the rumor. They claim that a P & G executive appeared on a nationally televised talk show and pledged the company's profits to the Church of Satan.

The rumor became so intense in 1982 that the company received 15,000 calls in one month about it.

Procter & Gamble struck back with statements from the talk show producers that no P & G executive had ever appeared on their programs, and letters of support from ministers. As a last resort, it filed suits against a dozen persons it identified as rumormongers and won judgments against all of them, ordering them to cease.

Throughout the 1980s the rumor kept breaking out—on the East Coast, in the South, the Pacific Northwest, and Indiana. In the early 1990s it surfaced again, in the Southeast and Chicago.

The company immediately mailed "truth packets" to hundreds of churches, schools, newspapers, and radio stations in those areas. These included testimonials for it from the Revs. Jerry Falwell and Billy Graham.

Yet the rumor rolls on. During 1990, the company received about 350 calls a day about it. Altogether, P & G had handled much more than 100,000 phone calls concerning the rumor.

In 1991 the company won its first damage award—$75,000—from a couple found guilty of spreading the rumor. It also slightly revised the trademark.

---

cated that the product was Kosher. The company was unable to discover the source of the rumors.

Rumors that cannot be tracked to any particular cause are more difficult to deal with. McDonald's had to cope with a rumor that its ground beef contained earthworms as a protein supplement, and General Mills had to contend with the rumor that its Pop Rocks candy was explosive.

Little evidence exists to support the suspicion by many people that rumors are started by commercial competitors. Instead, social psychologist Frederick Koening says, "Rumors validate the world view of those who believe them. If you believe in Satan—and many people do—you're likely to welcome a rumor that he's alive and well in Akron, Ohio."

People spread rumors by word-of-mouth for a number of reasons: (1) they are advocates of conspiracy theories and distrust all institutions of society; (2) they feel victimized by a complex, uncaring society and have high anxiety; (3) they seek recognition from peers by claiming to have "inside" information; and (4) they find the rumor somewhat plausible.

The environmental context is also a major factor. The run on the New York bank began shortly after the bank was closed for Election Day and newspaper articles had appeared about the failures of banks in Hong Kong. Many depositors, ethnic Chinese, put these facts together and reached the wrong conclusion.

Another example of environmental context is the continuing recall of products from the American marketplace. People increasingly express anxiety about the general safety of food products they are consuming, and from there it is only a short step to rumors about a particular product.

MEASURING THE EFFECTS OF WORD-OF-MOUTH COMMUNICATION

Although efforts to measure the specific effects of word-of-mouth communication have been relatively few, and of minor value, the Coca-Cola Company did obtain enlightening information from a study it sponsored concerning public reaction to its handling of consumer complaints.

Questionnaires were sent to hundreds of persons who had filed complaints with Coca-Cola's consumer affairs department. Responses showed that individuals who felt that their complaints had not been resolved satisfactorily told a median of nine to ten persons about their negative experience. Those who were completely satisfied told a median of four to five persons about their good results—a word-of-mouth distribution of bad news over good by a ratio of approximately two to one. Nearly 30 percent of those who felt that their complaints had not been resolved satisfactorily said they no longer bought Coca-Cola products. On the other hand, nearly 10 percent of the satisfied complainers reported that they now bought more Coca-Cola products as a result of the

---

TIPS ON COMBATING RUMORS

Here are general guidelines for combating rumors:

1. Analyze the nature and impact of the rumor before taking corrective action. Many rumors are relatively harmless and dissipate within a short time.

2. Attempt to track the cause of the rumor and the geographical locations where it is prominent. This will help determine whether the rumor should be dealt with on a local, state, or national level.

3. Compile complete, authentic information that will either refute or confirm the rumor.

4. When denying a rumor, avoid repeating it more than necessary.

5. Use outside experts and credible public agencies to refute the rumor. The public views the U.S. Food and Drug Administration as more trustworthy than the president of a company defending the firm's product. If the rumor is only among certain highly identifiable groups, enlist the support of the groups' leaders.

good treatment. Two lessons for companies trying to preserve a favorable image with customers emerge from this survey:

1. The best service possible should be given so that complaints are held to a minimum.

2. Complaints should be handled promptly and thoroughly, so that customers feel the company really cares about them. Not only may unhappy customers become noncustomers, but their word-of-mouth criticism may drive away other potential purchasers—how many, no one ever knows. As an example, an eight-year-old girl sued the makers of Crackerjack because she didn't find a prize in a box she purchased. She had written to the company about the mistake, but it failed to answer the letter. The lawsuit she brought gave the company bad nationwide publicity.

CASE PROBLEM

The national headquarters of Continental Oil Company is in Los Angeles. For the past month, a false rumor has been circulating that the company will move its headquarters to Houston. In fact, plans are on the drawing board for a new, larger headquarters building in Los Angeles.

The rumor probably started because the company had a managers' conference in Houston several months ago. This was rumored to be a high-level meeting to take a look at Houston real estate and decide on a site for the new headquarters. The rumor is beginning to affect employee morale in Los Angeles.

The president of Continental Oil, upon the advice of public relations counsel, decides to put the rumor to rest in a speech at the annual employee recognition banquet next week. You are assigned to write the ten-minute speech for the president.

Would you include in the speech a direct reference to the rumor? Would you take the opportunity to ridicule the rumor? Write a draft of the speech for the president.

QUESTIONS FOR REVIEW AND DISCUSSION

1. List three tasks a public relations representative should perform when preparing for and making a face-to-face presentation to an editor.

2. How many themes should a speech have?

3. What are some key building blocks a writer uses in constructing a speech?

4. Which type of sentence structure should a speechwriter use? Explain your answer.

5. Why do companies sometimes use fellow workers rather than high executives to address audiences of employees?

6. How should a company executive prepare to hold a news conference?

7. Should a spokesperson speak off the record at a news conference? Why or why not?

8. What might a corporate host hope to accomplish by holding a press luncheon instead of a morning news conference?

9. How can a public relations representative help a client prepare for a television interview?

10. A company may be harassed by malicious rumors about its policies. If it decided to strike back, how might it do so?

SUGGESTED READINGS

Burns, Robert Edward. "Combating Speech Anxiety." *Public Relations Journal,* March 1991, pp. 28, 30.

DeVito, Joseph A. *The Elements of Public Speaking,* 5th edition. New York: HarperCollins, 1994.

Engleberg, Isa N. *The Principles of Public Presentation.* New York: HarperCollins, 1994.

Jensen, Elizabeth. "Tales Are Oft Told As TV Talk Shows Fill up Air Time." *Wall Street Journal,* May 25, 1993, pp. A1, A7.

Klepper, Michael. "What Are You Talking About?" *Communication World,* October 1990, pp. 20–22. Organizing a speech.

Koranda, Timothy J. "Writing Speeches with Impact." *Public Relations Journal,* September 1990, pp. 31–34.

Marsh, Barbara. "Small Agencies Pop up to Meet Demand for Talk Show Guests." *Wall Street Journal,* December 31, 1992, p. B1.

Noah, Timothy. "Clinton's Campaign Uses Technology to Bypass Traditional News Outlets." *Wall Street Journal,* July 7, 1992, p. A14. Use of packaged radio actualities.

Sandberg, Jared. "When a Penny Falls from Heaven, Can It Kill a Pedestrian?" *Wall Street Journal,* September 22, 1993, pp. A1, A7. Urban legends and rumor.

Sheldon, Keith A. "Build Bridges with a Multilingual Speakers' Bureau." *Communication World,* August 1990, pp. 21–23.

Shell, Adam. "Radio News Releases Make the Hit Parade." *Public Relations Journal,* July 1992, p. 6.

Sklarewitz, Norman. "Press Junkets: Sound Marketing Method or Boondoggle?" *Communication World,* February 1988, pp. 32–35.

Solomon, Jolie. "Executives Who Dread Public Speaking Learn to Keep Their Cool in the Spotlight." *Wall Street Journal,* May 4, 1990, p. B1.

Spalding, Jeannette. "Speech Writers in the Thick of It." *Communication World,* October 1990, pp. 23–27.

Swasy, Alecia. "P&G Once Again Has Devil of a Time with Firm's Logo." *Wall Street Journal,* March 26, 1990, p. B3. Rumor control.

Thaler-Carter, Ruth E. "And Now a Few Words from MYSELF!" *Communication World,* October 1990, pp. 16–20. How to get on the speaking circuit.

Tarver, Jerry, and Geigel, Sara. "It Is with Great Pleasure That I Introduce. . . . " *Communication World,* June 1988, pp. 30–32. How to introduce a speaker.

Theibert, Phil. "Speechwriters of the World, Get Lost!" *Communication World,* December 1993, pp. 28–31. Advice on speechwriting.

Wester, Natalie Y. "Build Confidence with Media Training." *Public Relations Journal,* February 1992, pp. 26–28. Preparing for press interviews.

Winter, Grant. "Improving Broadcast News Conferences." *Public Relations Journal,* July 1990, pp. 25–26.

Visual Tactics

P R E V I E W   The objective of this chapter is to help students understand the advantages and disadvantages of numerous visual and audiovisual techniques, and to explain the visual needs of the various mass media outlets.

Topics covered in the chapter include:

- News delivery to television
- Video news releases (VNRs)
- Personal appearances on television
- Other uses of videotape
- Motion pictures
- Still images for projection
- Still photography
- Comic books and cartoons
- Outdoor displays
- Corporate design

The human eye is a magnificent channel for communication, carrying messages to the brain at astounding speeds, often so subtly that the recipient is not consciously aware of absorbing them. These images are stored in the brain, combining with the intake of audible and tactile impressions to help form opinions, trigger decisions, and generate actions. Since these are the goals of public relations, the role of visual communication in public relations practice obviously is vital.

Television is the dominant form of visual communication in contemporary life. The Nielsen survey reports that the average American family has its TV set turned on about seven hours a day.

Chapter 12 examined how the television industry is organized and listed ways in which public relations practitioners can use television to advance their causes. This chapter will look more closely at techniques employed for this purpose and will discuss the growing use of television for internal corporate communication.

NEWS RELEASES

Practitioners can provide news releases to television stations in several ways, ranging from a simple sheet of paper to an expensively produced videotaped story ready to go on the air. The type of news material, the time factor, and the originator's budget will determine which method is best for each story.

The Printed News Release   Identical to that sent to newspapers, the so-called handout frequently is sufficient (see Chapter 22). If the news director or assignment editor at a station judges the material to be newsworthy, a staff member is assigned to handle the story, rewriting it briefly in television style or, if the material justifies, going to the scene with a camera crew to obtain visual support for the facts. When a television reporter and crew come on assignment in response to a news release, the public relations practitioner who sent out the release should do everything possible to assist them, such as providing an authoritative spokesperson who will appear on camera to state the facts and answer questions, and helping to arrange other shots the reporter and photographer may request.

A fundamental difference between a news story on television and one in a newspaper is *motion*. Stories that can be illustrated easily and effectively often will receive more air time than ones that cannot. The rule for a practitioner trying to place a news story on television is: *think pictures!* The representative never should tell a reporter and photographer what pictures to shoot or what questions to ask but may discreetly suggest possible picture and story angles.

The other primary factor in television news coverage is *brevity*. A story that runs 400 words in a newspaper may be reported in only two or three sentences in a newscast. If a television crew spends an hour shooting a story with a practitioner's help, and the story then receives 30 seconds or less of air time, the inexperienced public relations representative may feel let down. All that work, with such a brief result! As any veteran will advise, however, there is no reason for disappointment. The impact of even a very brief item on a popular newscast can be heavy.

The Prepared Script This second, more elaborate, form of television news release is accompanied by one to four slides to illustrate the text. In this method, the public relations representative does most of the television news department's work on the story. Smaller stations with limited news staffs may be especially willing to air such ready-to-use material if it is newsworthy, perhaps even if only marginally so. In preparing scripted news releases, the writer should avoid terminology that sounds like advertising or "puff" publicity. Graphics created by computers can be used effectively in news releases (see Figure 24.1).

For a fee, specialist commercial firms will prepare a news release script with slides from a practitioner's material, send the script to television stations, and report on the use they made of it.

Videotaped excerpts from local speeches made by the practitioner's client, delivered to a television station along with a written news release explaining the circumstances in which the speech was made, may be used in the station's newscasts if the content is significant or provocative. Prospects for use of the material are improved if it is delivered quickly after the event for same-day use.

FIGURE 24.1
Use of graphic human-like figures to illustrate the results of an employee opinion survey gives the reader a quick grasp of the statistics. The survey was taken by the American States Insurance Company of Indianapolis.

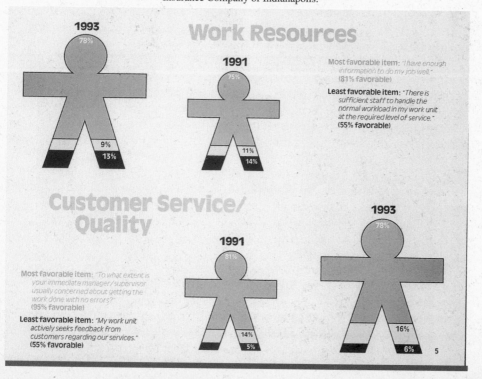

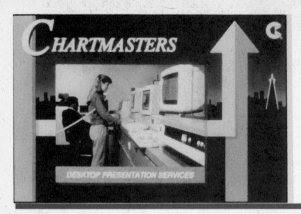
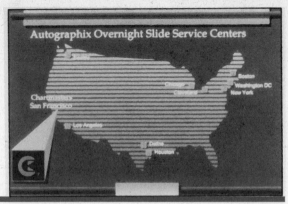

FIGURE 24.2
Colorful computer graphics deliver information effectively and
add visual impact to news releases for television.

The Videotaped News Release   The most elaborate, expensive, and controversial
form of news delivery to television stations is the videotaped news release (VNR). This
report prepared by a public relations organization presents information about a product,
a service, or an idea, usually in featurized style.

Delivered to selected stations by satellite feed or by package, the VNR may be a
ready-to-use tape of visual and voice material that a TV station may put on the air exact-

*A video news release shot in the cockpit of a B-24 Liberator bomber
from World War II, and outside the plane, provided a dramatic setting
for the story of an Army Air Force Medal of Honor winner. Venture
Productions made the VNR, which won air time because of its aura
of nostalgia.*

"ROTTEN SNEAKERS" CONTEST

Makers of Odor-Eaters foot deodorant pads boosted their sales 60 percent with video news releases about an annual contest in which children compete to see who has the smelliest footwear.

In the VNRs the kids tell how their sneakers came to be so filthy. The videos contain footage of the competitors wearing Odor-Eater hats and T-shirts. Each year the VNR contains a different angle, such as having a reindeer sniff the sneakers.

A foot doctor serves as judge and spokesperson. *The Today Show* had the doctor as a guest to answer questions.

ly as received—the use most desired by the supplier. Or, to give the station more editorial control, the release may consist of separate elements an editor can use in preparing the station's own presentation. These may include unedited video pictures, called B-roll footage, any of which the editor may select; brief "sound bites"; a separate voice-over narration by the producer's announcer, which may be aired as-is or instead read by a station announcer; and a script to be used or rewritten.

Obviously preparation and distribution of such VNR packages is expensive, from $5000 to $50,000 for most releases and even higher for elaborate ones. Yet TV stations receive hundreds of VNRs each year, many of inferior technical quality. More than 4000 VNRs are produced each year.

Several factors should be considered before an organization commits that much money to a news release. Is the story sufficiently newsworthy, so that many stations probably will put it on the air? Can the story be told well visually? Does the producer have sufficient time to prepare the release, perhaps as much as six weeks? If the VNR concerns a legitimate health issue or scientific breakthrough, its chances of being widely used are better than those for introductions of commercial products

In producing successful video news releases, sponsoring organizations must create a feeling of news or offer an interesting feature idea. Advertising sales pitch techniques should be avoided; so should glorifying adjectives. The benefit to the sponsoring organization is indirect, by making the viewing public aware of the existence of the service, the idea, or the product. Direct sales efforts must be handled separately. A VNR that is clearly an attempt to obtain free advertising goes automatically into a station's wastebasket.

This restriction creates the need for ingenuity. Writing in the *Wall Street Journal,* Michael Klepper described how a company seeking mass exposure for a new talking doll produced a successful VNR about the history of artificial voice synthesis, using the doll as an example of the technology.

To introduce a new picture book *America Then & Now,* DWJ Television shot part of a video news release from the top of the Brooklyn Bridge, interviewing a still photographer who took a picture from the spot that duplicated one taken from the same place 116 years earlier. The book, published by HarperCollins, compared recent photos of events and locations with pictures taken at the same places many years earlier. Thus the VNR stimulated the viewers' historical interest while simultaneously making them aware of the book.

A tie-in satellite media interview was conducted by the author with TV reporters in more than 30 states in which book pictures had been taken. (See Chapter 21.) A B-roll containing those pictures was sent in advance to each station, so it could select home-state shots for use in its interview.

Ethical Problems in the Use of VNRs   Video news releases are intended to present the sponsoring organization's story in a favorable light, subtly or more obviously. Knowing this, news editors of some television stations refuse to use them, and many stations that use some VNR material refuse to broadcast the ready-to-air versions they receive. That is why the makers of VNRs increasingly supply B-roll footage with their submissions. Small TV stations with limited news staffs are more likely to use the ready-made versions than are their larger colleagues.

Ethical responsibility for the airing of video news releases lies equally with those who produce the VNRs and the television stations that run them. Producers should make clear who is paying for the releases. Stations in turn should tell their viewers the sources of the releases they use (see Chapter 6 for a discussion of this ethical issue).

Infomercials   An expanded form of VNR, called an *infomercial* or *advertorial,* is a lengthy presentation made to look like an editorial examination of a topic when in reality it is a slightly disguised sales pitch for a product or service. Such programs often turn up on the screen in the late-evening hours, especially on cable systems. Some channels and stations announce that the shows are paid programs; others fail to do so or make announcements so inconspicuous that viewers easily miss them.

NEWS ON CABLE TELEVISION

Newscasts on cable television provide fresh opportunities for public relations exposure. Innovative practitioners can find ways to place their news stories before cable-viewing audiences in addition to viewers of the over-the-air television stations and networks.

Numerous newspapers have obtained local cable channels on which they produce newscasts, using their own staff-gathered material as resources. Videotaped news releases, as described above, have a possibility of receiving air time on these newscasts. Using satellite distribution, nationwide superstations such as WTBS-TV in Atlanta and WGN-TV in Chicago, and networks such as Cable News Network, reach large numbers of cable viewers from coast to coast. These outlets are worthwhile targets for the public relations practitioner.

PERSONAL APPEARANCES ON TELEVISION

Anyone invited to appear on television in a talk show or for an interview should prepare for the occasion. The beaming red light of a television camera aimed at a guest, indicating that he or she is on the air, can have a terrifying effect on an inexperienced performer. The throat goes dry. The words won't come out. The guest projects discomfort and uncertainty to thousands of viewers, precisely the opposite of the effect desired. A valuable opportunity is wasted.

Public relations practitioners can help their clients avoid this unpleasantness by coaching them in what to say and how to behave. Playing the role of interviewer in practice sessions, the coach can rehearse the guest by asking anticipated questions. If the subject matter is controversial, the practitioner should fire antagonistic questions to test the guest's mettle. As much as possible, the guest's prepared responses should be honed down to 30 seconds or less. (Preparation for appearances on television is discussed in Chapter 23).

In general, guests on television should dress conservatively. On most shows a business suit is appropriate for men; for women, a suit or dress of simple pattern without conspicuous ornamentation. White clothing, including shirts, should be avoided, as should metallic decorations—all might reflect studio lights. On shows featuring entertainers and sports figures, dress is more informal, to the point of conspicuous casualness. By watching a show in advance or asking production personnel, the public relations person can advise a client how to dress suitably for the appearance.

Professional coaches who prepare guests for television appearances make these suggestions for their personal conduct:

- *Use of gestures.* The guest should create movement for the camera, even though seated, by changing facial expressions and by moving the hands, arms, head, and shoulders to emphasize points. Potential guests can observe these tricks by watching professional actors on talk shows.

- *Use of eye contact.* The guest should look at the interviewer, as in a private conversation. If the camera is focused directly at the guest, he or she should talk to it. The trick is to think of the camera eye not as an electronic device but as another person whom the speaker is trying to inform or convince.

- *Proper placement of the body.* Persons being interviewed should not cross their legs; the position is awkward. It is better to sit with one foot in front of the other. Leaning forward in the chair makes a person appear more aggressive. Keeping the hands apart allows the guest to use them for gesturing. Guests also should be coached to mention key points about the event or product several times.

TELEVISION FOR RESTRICTED AUDIENCES

Television can be used to tell a story to the general public through news releases and personal on-the-air appearances. This is the external face of the medium, aimed at viewers who choose their programs by flicking the dial from channel to channel. Less well known, but growing enormously, is use of television to reach controlled private audiences in selected locations without having the program content seen by the general public.

The uses of *closed-circuit television,* tremendously enlarged by development of satellite transmission, are multiplying. Corporations employ it to deliver information and training material to their employees, to conduct sales meetings, to present financial information to securities analysts and shareholders, to show the proceedings of their annual meetings, and to hold long-distance news conferences. Surgeons, engineers, and other professional groups employ television to discuss technical developments and to solve problems.

OTHER USES OF VIDEOTAPE

Videotape is so flexible and cheap that it is used by public relations people in many ways in addition to video news releases. Commercial firms and nonprofit organizations use it to reach external audiences and to communicate information and instruction to their staffs. Here is a small sample of such uses.

■ American Express sponsored a video, "It Could Never Happen to Me: Preventing Campus Crime," to be loaned free to colleges nationwide, using actual testimony of campus crime victims.

■ The Del Webb Development Company gives videos of its Sun City retirement communities to purchasers of homes and shows them to potential buyers.

■ The Atlanta delegation used videos and computer graphics in the presentation that won the 1996 Summer Olympic Games for that city.

VIDEOTAPED FINANCIAL REPORTS

Corporations increasingly are putting their financial information onto videotape for showing to shareholders and securities analysts. Videotaping of annual meetings is one aspect of this trend. Specially prepared reports with graphs and other visual aids also are taped.

Distribution of videotaped material needs as much attention as preparation of the content. Videocassettes may be mailed to brokers and other financial specialists for their individual viewing. Perhaps more effective is a personal showing of the videotaped material by a company executive to groups of invited guests, who can ask questions after viewing the tape. Another method is to invite interested investors and brokers to request a loan copy of the videotape.

INTERNAL CORPORATE TV NEWS PROGRAMS

Large corporations with thousands of employees scattered in many locations keep hunting for ways to give their employees a sense of company pride and common purpose. Among the print media, company newspapers and magazines have that goal. The audio-visual equivalent is the corporate television news program.

Such programs need a strong professional touch in production: hence, they are expensive to create. They should have a well-defined formula for content. Management-oriented material should be presented discreetly in news style. The techniques of brevity, visual story-telling, human interest, and touches of humor that mark a successful commercial television newscast need to be applied to a corporate news program—not an easy task. Television consultant firms may be employed to produce the program or to provide technical assistance.

Showing of these programs to employees on a voluntary basis is done at lunch hours or other convenient times. Videotape cassettes of the shows can be distributed to sales and other employees working in the field. Playing the programs on cable television in cities where corporate plants are located is another possibility.

TV News, a corporate TV magazine for employees of SmithKline Beecham, is an excellent example. A pioneer in the field, it has appeared weekly since 1972. Although some corporations use a TV newscast format with an anchor person, *TV News* has employees do voice-over narrations of stories involving them, such as veterans of the Persian Gulf War and Hurricane Andrew survivors.

VIDEOTAPED TRAINING AND MARKETING PROGRAMS

An estimated $3 billion is being spent annually on employee video programs, according to the American Society for Training and Development. The flexibility and economy of videotape makes it an ideal vehicle for training employees and updating their work skills.

VIDEOTAPED SALES MESSAGES

A recent development as the electronic revolution changes publicity methods is distribution of sales messages on tape to selected potential customers. *Videocassettes* are mailed upon request to prospective buyers who can play these illustrated sales messages on home recorders. A stamped, self-addressed envelope for return of the cassettes to the firm may be included. Because of the costs involved, this method is used primarily for higher-priced items, by companies selling direct to the consumer rather than through retail outlets.

Looking into the future, some electronics enthusiasts predict that a prospective purchaser, after seeing an item advertised, will be able to dial a toll-free number on a home telecomputer, watch the sales demonstration on the home television screen, and order the item by pushing the proper button on the computer terminal. Payment for the item will be drawn by computer from the customer's bank account. Whether or not future sales methods follow this precise line, the use of electronic demonstration and selling inevitably will grow. Meanwhile, home-shopping channels on cable TV offer a similar service.

HOME VIDEO

Three-fourths of American families now have videocassette recorders (VCRs) with which they record television shows or view rented or purchased movies. A Newspaper Advertising Bureau study showed that VCR owners rented an average of 108 movies a year while the average American visited a movie theater only five times annually.

Taking advantage of this viewing potential, a growing number of organizations and companies now use videotape to reach key audiences.

In politics, candidates and groups use videotapes as today's "high-tech leaflet." A Massachusetts congressional candidate distributed a 15-minute videotape of himself for campaign workers to show in voters' homes. In Orinda, a community across the bay from San Francisco, pro-incorporation forces produced a videotape on the advantages of being a city, for showing at neighborhood meetings and in homes. The incorporation measure passed, and the city's first mayor credited the videotape as a major factor in the victory.

Increasingly, employees can check out videotapes of company-produced materials from the corporate video news magazine to view such material as an explanation of the new health benefits. This gives the company an opportunity to communicate with the employee's family. Stockholders are routinely offered videotape cassettes reporting on company affairs. On another level, a corporation may subsidize production of a videotape to be sold to the public at a nominal charge.

MOTION PICTURES

Hollywood commercial feature films viewed by millions of customers in theaters constitute only a fraction of the films produced in the United States and Canada every year. Hundreds of motion pictures, often equal in quality to theatrical films, are made annually by sponsors for showing to selected audiences. Only a handful of these ever will appear on commercial theater screens, and then only as supporting films on programs of mass market entertainment.

Sponsored films have a major role in public relations work, as noted in Chapter 12. Designed to inform, instruct, and persuade, often subtly, they play to a huge cumulative audience. Unlike commercial films, most of them are shown to viewers without charge. The makers of these films, and in some instances the organizations showing them, bear the cost in order to further their purposes directly or indirectly.

Public relations practitioners can make use of mass market entertainment motion pictures and, more important, of sponsored nontheatrical films.

HOLLYWOOD ENTERTAINMENT FILMS

Moviegoers are frequently exposed to publicity projects in the films they watch, although they rarely are aware of it. Public relations specialists who arrange mentions of their clients' products or causes in movies obtain high visibility because Hollywood motion pictures often are seen by millions of viewers (see Chapter 20).

Such mentions dropped into the middle of the story line are not accidental. They are arranged by negotiations between public relations specialists and the film's producer, in which the filmmaker receives payment in money or services. The show business weekly *Variety* calls the practice "product *pluggola.*"

Two recent examples:

- The producer of *Jurassic Park* selected the Ford Explorer as the sports-utility vehicle in which humans ride while viewing and being chased by dinosaurs. A Ford official said the auto company paid the filmmaker nothing for using the Explorer but supplied vehicles free of charge. Millions of moviegoers around the world watched the Explorer perform.

- A little-known brand of beer, Red Stripe, was featured in *The Firm*, starring Tom Cruise and Gene Hackman. Cost to the brewers was $5000, mostly in the form of free beer supplied to the film crew.

Benefits of such appearances often are difficult to evaluate in terms of sales, but product exposure even at high prices is regarded as a bargain for participants if the film proves to be a hit. When E.T., the lonesome waif from space, ate Reese's Pieces in *E.T., The Extra-Terrestrial,* the makers of that candy, Hershey Food Company, reported a 65 percent increase in sales of the brand. Some companies have paid moviemakers as much as $50,000 for a product placement.

SPONSORED FILMS AND VIDEOS

The range of films and videos made to be shown free of charge, or to be rented or purchased for showing to external audiences, is immense. A well-produced film or video, with minimal commercial emphasis, is an excellent way for companies and organizations to reach members of school, church, social, cultural, professional, and business groups.

Sponsored films and videos, despite their expense, serve several public relations purposes. They can (1) inform audiences about a topic of educational interest, (2) create understanding of a company or organization's activities, and (3) generate goodwill and name recognition among important audiences. Charms Candy, for example, reached an important audience, schoolchildren, by producing a film on school-bus safety that school administrators often show in school assemblies.

Cable television is another important outlet for sponsored films. Consumer education films and videos in which the company's commercial message is reduced to perhaps just the opening and closing credit lines find widespread acceptance by cable operators who need to fill broadcast time at minimal expense.

Production of sponsored films and videos, also called *industrial films,* is a substantial industry involving an estimated 600 firms around the world. Their filming techniques and equipment in many instances are highly advanced and on a par with any Hollywood or television network studio. Indeed, potential viewers are so accustomed to professional television that even a company's training film cannot be amateurish.

Motion pictures are produced in four sizes, from 70 millimeter down to 8 millimeter. The Hollywood-type entertainment picture usually is made on 35-millimeter film for large-screen projection in theaters. Some sponsored films are 35 millimeter, but the majority are produced on 16-millimeter width, the format of the standard movie projector used in classrooms. Increasingly companies are also making films available in video format, and it is often difficult to determine whether a production was originally produced on motion picture film or videotape.

A limiting factor on use of videotape is the projection method. Unless a large group meeting place is equipped with a large television screen or multiple television monitors, viewing is difficult. School-assembly or service-club rooms rarely have large television monitors. And even if the group is small enough for a standard television monitor, there is the problem of standardization in tape size and equipment. Some players take ½-inch tape, others take ¾-inch; the Beta and VHS cassettes are incompatible, with VHS the dominant form. Although the availability of playback equipment is improving, the standard movie projector is still the workhorse in classrooms and small membership organizations. Recently TV monitors have been installed in many classrooms by Whittle Communications and cable TV systems so students can watch their programs.

The length of sponsored films and videos varies greatly. A survey by Modern Talking Picture Service, however, shows a strong audience preference for films 21 to 30 minutes in length. But there are exceptions. "Where's the Cap'n?" is a 4-minute music video sponsored by the Quaker Oats Company to develop awareness among children 6 to 12 years old about a cereal promotion. The video was used on nationally and locally produced video music programs, reaching an estimated audience of 7.9 million viewers.

At the other end of the spectrum, Pepsi-Cola sponsored a 40-minute film titled *Amber Lights* that received widespread acclaim as a high school assembly program. It combined popular film clips and music in an MTV format to address the No. 1 killer of teenagers in the United States—drunk drivers. The company estimates that 3 million teenagers saw the film during one school year.

A Corporate-Image Film   Bechtel Corporation's *Jungle Gold* depicts the company's gold-mining operations in New Guinea. The film discusses a school and a hospital built there by Bechtel and reflects the company's interest in showing that private-sector initiatives can be catalysts in developing countries.

A Government Social-Problem Film   The Utah Department of Health produced a frank film about a serious social problem. *If You Want to Dance . . .* concerns an unwed teenage couple faced with the consequences of an unplanned pregnancy. Candid but constructive, the 14-minute film opens with a locker-room scene in which three high school boys talk about sex, then shifts to a hospital room where two pregnant unwed teenage girls discuss their problems. Much praised, the film has been widely shown to high school classes, church groups, and community organizations. A discussion guide is distributed with the film, which is available for loan or purchase on both 16-millimeter film and ¾-inch videocassette.

STILL IMAGES FOR PROJECTION

Slides, filmstrips, and transparencies—all of them methods for projecting still images onto a screen—often are referred to as *audiovisual aids*. Properly, the word *audiovisual* encompasses all forms of sound-and-picture projection, including motion pictures, but in practice it frequently is applied only to these simpler forms. Inclusion of such visual aids in programs stimulates audiences.

Audiovisual aids are much cheaper than motion pictures and videotapes and have simple projection requirements. All that is needed are a relatively inexpensive slide projector, an electrical outlet, and a small screen. A presentation of still images accompanied by live or recorded narration often is the most efficient method for bringing a message to a small audience. Public relations practitioners find scores of uses for such presentations.

SLIDE SHOWS

Slide presentations range upward from Uncle Chester showing the dinner guests slides he made during his trip to Europe—usually too many and occasionally upside-down—

to the projection of intricate triple-screen, three-dimensional productions issued by some corporations.

For his performance before the captive audience in the living room, Uncle Chester selects the slides he likes best and delivers a rambling ad-lib narration about them as they flash on the screen. This is the exact opposite of the way a professional slide show should be constructed.

A slide show should be built on a well-defined theme, to tell a story and deliver a message. The script should be written and approved first, then the visual elements should be developed to illustrate and emphasize points in the script. Standard technique is for a visually oriented person to study the script, marking places in it that lend themselves to illustration by photograph or drawing. An artist then creates rough storyboards, indicating the illustration perceived for each point. More detailed and refined storyboards may be developed in subsequent story conferences. Photographer and artist go to work, producing 35-millimeter slides that meet the requirements of the storyboards. Slides and motion picture film can be coordinated.

Depending on its purpose, a slide show might consist of photographs, as in a program made by a state tourist board to publicize the scenic attractions of the state. Or, if intended to explain retirement benefits to an internal audience of employees, it might be made entirely with drawings and explanatory text slides. A combination of photographs, drawings, and text also can be effective. Leasing of stock shots of scenery, people, and events from commercial firms such as *Time* specializing in this work is a convenient way to fill out the picture requirements of a show. Some large picture firms have from 2 to 5 million still photos and slides on file to fill requests.

Whatever form the slide show takes, inclusion of humorous bits creates audience interest. These might be cartoons or candid photographs in which individuals are caught in laughable situations.

Text-only slides often help to give a presentation cohesion and to emphasize key points. The content of each text slide should be brief, making a single clear statement in

---

VISUAL AIDS IMPROVE MEETING RESULTS

Speakers who use visual aids such as slides, filmstrips, and overhead transparencies not only keep their audiences more interested but also accomplish greater results. A study sponsored by the Wharton School of Business at the University of Pennsylvania showed the following percentages:

	With Visuals	Without Visuals
Speaker's goal achieved	67%	33%
Group consensus reached	79%	58%
Information retained	50%	10%
Average meeting length	19 minutes	28 minutes

a maximum of 25 words, preferably fewer. A slide containing ten words or fewer can be powerfully effective. Color slides containing text and/or drawings need strong contrast, usually a dark background of blue, black, or brown with letters and pictures in white or yellow. An occasional black-and-white slide mixed into a color sequence can have a strong impact.

A narrator may deliver the script of a slide show live, or it may be accompanied by a taped voice synchronized with the progression of slides. Slides can be shown on an automatic projector controlled by a button the speaker presses to change them.

If a company or organization has competent writing, photographic, or graphic talent on its staff, it may be able to produce an attractive slide show using its own resources. Outside graphic talent may be hired, or the sponsor may employ a firm specializing in audiovisual work to handle the entire production. Specialist organizations are able to produce elaborate slide shows with dramatic graphic effects. Animation and masking that reveals only part of a picture at a time add visual zest, and use of multiple screens and projectors provides dramatic impact.

FILMSTRIPS

A filmstrip consists of a series of 35-millimeter or 16-millimeter slides reproduced in sequence on a short piece of film. The strip can be advanced slowly, one frame at a time, in an inexpensive projector, with each frame held on the screen as long as desired. Filmstrips are economical, small, and easily transported. They are especially useful as instructional tools for single concepts. If a recorded narration accompanies the filmstrip, the frames must be advanced at a coordinated speed.

OVERHEAD TRANSPARENCIES

A simple, economical form of audiovisual aid is a sheet of transparent acetate or similar material on which illustrations and/or lettering have been placed. When this sheet is laid on a flat glass surface in the projector, the images are reproduced on a screen behind the speaker by light transmitted by mirrors and lenses. Overhead transparencies are especially good in classrooms and small discussion groups because of their flexibility. They can be made by running a master on regular paper through a photocopier onto the acetate plastic. Large type should be used on overheads and only a few words of copy.

Masking a transparency permits a speaker to show several steps in a process with only one transparency. If the same series of steps were shown by slides, a separate slide would be necessary for each step.

When a speaker wishes to show the operation of a piece of machinery, for example, masking can be done in the following way: The transparency contains a diagram of the entire machine. A piece of onionskin or white opalescent plastic is laid over each portion of the diagram and taped lightly into place. As the blanked-out transparency appears on the screen, the speaker removes each sectional overlay progressively and explains the revealed portion of the diagram, until the entire diagram is visible. The speaker can draw or write on a transparency while it is being displayed on the screen.

A story in the print media, especially newspapers and magazines, may, and frequently should, be told in pictures as well as words. Still photography is an essential tool for every practitioner who works with publications.

NEWSPAPER REQUIREMENTS

Newspaper editors like to receive black-and-white photographs of persons mentioned in news releases. The presence of a photograph with a release sometimes increases the likelihood that the story will be published. Or, as frequently happens, a photograph of a newsworthy individual or group will be published without an accompanying story, the necessary information having been condensed into the photo caption.

The type of photograph most easily placed in a newspaper by a practitioner is the head-and-shoulders portrait of a client. These portraits, known in the trade as *mug shots,* frequently are published in one-column or half-column size to illustrate textual material. Group shots are published less often than individual pictures because they require multiple-column space. Practitioners submitting group photographs should keep the number of persons in a picture small and have them tightly grouped—a maximum of three or four persons unless the picture is a highly unusual one.

Photographs on the main news pages of a newspaper usually are taken by staff photographers or are provided by the news picture services. They stress spot-news action. The chances for a public relations practitioner to have a submitted photograph published in these up-front pages are relatively small, except for one-column portraits. When spot news is involved, the practitioner is better advised to telephone the photo editor of a newspaper and call attention to a picture possibility that a staff photographer can cover. Staff photographers know their editors' requirements, space limitations, and deadlines. They can respond very quickly to fast-breaking news situations.

Other sections of a newspaper provide abundant opportunities for publication of photographs submitted by practitioners.

The business pages regularly include photographs of meetings, new products, and individuals appointed to new positions. Sports editors welcome photographs of athletes and coaches in various poses. Entertainment editors need pictures of performers, individually and in groups, and publish still photos taken from scenes in locally playing motion pictures and television shows. Travel editors desire photographs of interesting scenes and modes of transportation.

An especially broad target for the practitioner is the section of a newspaper called "Family Living," "Life Styles," "Today's Scene," or something similar. For many years these sections were referred to as "women's," "society," or, in newspaper jargon, "sock." They concentrated on engagements and weddings, parties and club meetings, food, beauty, and fashion. Now their appeal is greatly enlarged, aimed at men as well as women.

While retaining the traditional elements, these sections have added material about family life and problems, personal finances, careers, and contemporary lifestyles. This

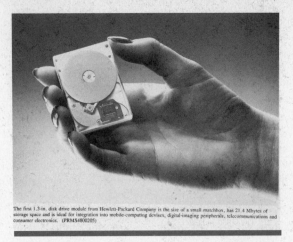

The first 1.3-in. disk drive module from Hewlett-Packard Company is the size of a small matchbox, has 21.4 Mbytes of storage space and is ideal for integration into mobile-computing devises, digital-imaging peripherals, telecommunications and consumer electronics. (PRMS4800205)

Product publicity photographs are frequently printed in trade publications edited for specialized audiences. This shows the first 1.3-inch disk drive module from Hewlett-Packard Company. It is the size of a small matchbox.

broadened appeal has multiplied the photographic possibilities for the public relations practitioner, both to submit photographs and to query editors with ideas for illustrated feature stories by staff members about activities of their clients.

"Family Living" sections often publish pictures of groups planning charity events, civic affairs, and social organization parties. These pictures generate interest in the event, help to sell tickets, and incidentally serve as an ego payoff to workers who appear in them. Unfortunately, far too many such pictures belong to the waxworks school of photography—stilted, self-conscious poses in which the participants appear ramrod-stiff and painfully artificial. A photographer's ingenuity is challenged to invent an interesting piece of business for the participants to do, and to coax them to relax.

When shooting a publicity shot, a clever photographer will include, if possible, a prop that helps to carry the message. A picture promoting a Red Cross blood drive, for example, would be strengthened by inclusion of a Red Cross poster or similar symbol.

Publicity shots may be submitted by the practitioner, or arrangements may be made with an editor for a staff photographer to handle the assignment. If a staff photographer is assigned, the practitioner must make certain that all participants in the picture assemble at the appointed place on time, appropriately dressed. The photographer is busy and, in a sense, the editor is doing the organization a favor.

Creativity also should be applied to news pictures submitted for publication. Groundbreakings, installations of officers, delivery of donation checks—routine events that frequently fall within the domain of the public relations worker—are notorious sources of cliché photos. For that reason, some newspapers refuse to publish photographs of these events. A practitioner taking a picture of such an event, or a commercial photographer hired to do so, should use every ounce of innovative skill to find a new camera angle or piece of action.

Photographs submitted to newspapers normally are 8 by 10 inches in black and white, with caption material attached either to the back or bottom of the picture. *The practitioner should be absolutely certain that the names in the caption are spelled correctly and match up in left-to-right sequence with the photograph itself.* An added precaution is to count the number of persons in the picture and the number of names in the caption, to be sure that they correspond. Smaller prints usually are acceptable for head-and-shoulders portraits.

Use of Color   Many newspapers publish pictures in color daily, and the practice is growing. Although spot pictures, such as those showing fires and wrecks, usually are taken by staff photographers, excellent public relations opportunities exist to place color pictures in feature sections. Living sections often run color photos of prepared foods; travel sections show enticing color shots of destinations.

The practitioner should submit color slides, not color prints. To increase the chances that a picture will be used, it is a wise precaution to determine in advance from the picture editor or chief photographer what special technical requirements for color work the newspaper may have.

Keep File Pictures Current   Since newspapers maintain large files of published and unpublished photographs, it is not unusual for a mug shot of a newsworthy personality to be published more than once—a bonus for the practitioner who submitted it. Individuals change in appearance as they age, and occasionally an editor will reach into the files in a

This photograph of Marilyn Monroe is a classic example of the staged photo arranged for publicity purposes. To promote her film, The Seven Year Itch, she stood over a grating while windblowers hidden beneath it swirled her skirt upward. Publicists claimed that the resulting photo was "accidental."

hurry and publish an obviously outdated picture of a news figure. The public relations person handling a prominent individual can avoid this embarrassment by submitting an up-to-date photograph from time to time, with a request that it replace the old one.

The importance of including a selection of photographs in a press kit introducing such projects as a new shopping center, a sales program, a political campaign, or a fund drive is obvious. The kit should contain pictures of the key persons involved and of physical aspects of the projects.

On a national or regional basis, the alert practitioner may obtain space by appealing to newspaper editors' interest in home-town angles. At trade conventions or sales conferences, the public relations staff can run a "production line" in which individual delegates are photographed in company with a celebrity. A mattress manufacturer, for example, hired Vanna White, the sexy, glamorously gowned costar of the TV game show "Wheel of Fortune," to sit on a new model mattress at a trade show. Company salesmen were invited to come up one by one and pose on the mattress beside her. The opportunity delighted them. One elderly participant exclaimed, "What an experience! Me on a bed with Vanna. I must tell my grandchildren."

At least rudimentary knowledge of photographic techniques is an important asset for all men and women working in public relations. The best way to obtain this is to take a college course in news photography. If this cannot be done, courses in photography are available in many adult education programs. Membership in a camera club is another way.

MAGAZINE REQUIREMENTS

Magazine requirements resemble those of newspapers, although emphasis is primarily on feature photographs. Some magazines use only color photographs, some only black and white, some both. The practitioner should study each magazine before submitting pictures to it. Color slides rather than prints should be sent.

Trade and professional magazines frequently use submitted photographs of individuals, new products, and industrial installations. When sending in a proposal for a feature story about a client, the practitioner should offer to provide photographs to accompany the text, regardless of whether the story is written by the practitioner, by a freelance writer, or by a magazine staff member. Many magazines do not have photographic staffs, or budgets and facilities for acquiring pictures, and so depend upon submitted pictures. Attractive photographs accompanying a manuscript enhance the possibility that it will be accepted for publication.

Public relations departments and counseling firms should include in their annual budgets a substantial amount for photographic service. In addition to submitting pictures to the media, representatives often find it effective to send souvenir prints of these pictures to persons appearing in them and to important persons such as dealers and customers. Such small gestures have a flattering effect.

COMIC BOOKS AND CARTOONS

Another eye-catching way to deliver visual messages in print is to use comic books and cartoons. The artwork must be of professional quality, however, or the effect is dimin-

FIGURE 24.3
A touch of humor brightens certain types of publicity releases
and increases their chances of publication. The California
Strawberry Advisory Board uses this method effectively, showing a strawberry cartoon character in whimsical poses.

ished. Drawings are especially good for illustrating steps in a process, as in an owner's instruction manual. If an artist can create a whimsical cartoon character that symbolizes the service or objective, entire campaigns can be built around it.

A variation is the coloring book, which E. F. Hutton sent to its employees with mixed results. The purpose was to boost employee morale battered by Hutton's guilty plea to a check-overdraft scheme. But one employee told *Time* magazine that he thought the coloring-book idea was disgusting and that management should communicate in an adult fashion.

A note of warning: Published cartoons and comic strips are covered by copyright and may be reproduced only by permission, which the copyright holders often are reluctant to give.

OUTDOOR DISPLAYS

Although billboards, building signs, and other forms of outdoor announcements are erected primarily for advertising and identification, they have potential uses as public relations tools. Billboards may remind motorists and pedestrians of a citywide charity fund drive in progress. A changing electric sign outside a bank showing time and temperature performs a public service and creates goodwill for the bank; so does a signboard on which announcements of forthcoming civic events are placed. An ingenious practitioner working for a nonprofit organization may be able to find numerous outlets of this type to deliver a message, at little or no cost.

A public relations specialist should know the fundamentals of billboard design and economics, in case a situation arises in which outdoor displays will fit into a publicity program. The standard billboard of the type seen along streets and on buildings is 12 by 25 feet. The colorful paper posters pasted onto it are slightly smaller, leaving a white frame around them. The standard poster is called a 24-sheet, because at one time 24 sheets of paper were needed to cover the space on a full-sized billboard. Modern printing processes do it with 10 sheets. Small posters called 3-sheets are designed to attract pedestrian readers at sidewalk level. Recent development of computer-controlled painting on vinyl billboards permits use of larger boards.

Outdoor advertising companies rent display space on their billboards on the basis of what they call a *100-showing*—that is, the number of boards in a market area calculated to expose the advertiser's message to approximately 100 percent of the people at some time during the 30 days it is posted. The number of boards that constitute a 100-showing fluctuates from market to market, based on traffic studies.

When messages are painted onto the billboards instead of being pasted on, their effective life is longer and the space rental price higher.

Successful billboard copy must be short and illustrations simple, because the duration of viewing time as motorists pass is brief. Eye-catching impact is the goal. That requires powerful design and strong colors. Two lively examples: "Heaven Can Wait . . . Wellness Works" and "We Don't Do That in Clarke County," an antilittering billboard in Georgia. One message was five words long, the other seven, quickly absorbed. Perhaps the greatest advantage of billboards is their reinforcement value in support of a program using other methods as well. Design and preparation of billboard posters are handled by advertising agencies, while physical placement is done by the billboard companies.

CORPORATE DESIGN

The need to present a unified visual image to the world is becoming increasingly evident to corporations and nonprofit organizations. Especially among corporations that have grown rapidly by acquiring many subsidiaries, the uncoordinated proliferation of letterheads, signs, publication symbols, news release sheets, packages, and other visual public representations of the organization gives a jumbled, unfocused appearance.

Creation of a simple, powerful logotype for use on all printed matter and signs projects an image of the company as a tightly knit contemporary operation. An impressive logo suggests quality and strength.

In the acquisition-minded climate of corporate life today, companies often add so many subsidiaries that the original names of the parent firms become inadequate to describe their overall function. So these corporations adopt generalized names, usually of one or two words. United States Steel Corporation changed its name to USX Corporation, and American Machinery & Foundry Company became AMF Incorporated.

Because it no longer makes cans but has moved into such varied fields as life insurance, direct mail, recorded music, and stock brokerage, the American Can Company decided to change its name. It paid Lippincott & Margulies consultants $200,000 to help

FIGURE 24.4
Evolution of the City Bank of New York's symbol over 180
years is demonstrated in this series of pictures. The designs
reflect the artistic taste of the periods in which they were used.
In today's version the name has been shortened to Citibank; the
type is simple, strong, and suggestive of movement. (© 1985
Citibank, N.A., Member FDIC)

it choose a new one. The choice was Primerica, a synthetic word intended to reflect the
company's "prime" growth prospects and ability to finance them.

Corporate redesign usually involves coordinated effort by the public relations and
marketing departments. First, management must define the objectives to be sought in
the new design. Should the graphic style be ultramodern, formal and conservative, or
perhaps old-fashioned to suggest historical continuity? A counseling firm and graphics
specialist usually are brought into the discussion. A detailed audit of existing printed
materials and signs is necessary, to establish the areas where the new design will be
used. In a corporation with numerous divisions, the logotype may be color-coded—a
different color for each division, with identification of the division in type below.

As companies enter the international market, they often find that their traditional
identifying logotypes are unsuitable in foreign countries because of language complica-

tions and cultural differences. So they seek logos that are easily identified around the world. The Fuji Bank of Japan, for example, replaced its symbol using Japanese letters with a simple design consisting of a drawing of Mount Fujiyama and the words Fuji Bank.

Corporate designers also must wrestle with the need to create symbols and designs that are effective on computer screens and other electronic outlets, as well as on traditional paper.

Creation of a symbolic person to represent a corporate product is another effective graphic method. Practitioners working with smaller companies and nonprofit organizations can achieve visual unity and focus public attention, just as the huge corporations do.

Goodwill Industries, for example, formerly had as its symbol a cartoon character, a smiling young man, feather in his hat and a lunch box in his hand, pictured rolling along in a wheelchair. The national help-the-handicapped organization found that the symbol, while clever, did not print well and lacked sales appeal on signs outside its retail outlets. The design consultant Goodwill employed replaced the symbol with a rectangular logo in which a large lowercase *g* in the upper-left corner looks like half of a smiling face.

In another piece of clever public relations and marketing, Goodwill put a "Morgie" label on the used jeans it sells, thereby spoofing the current fad for designer jeans that bear high-fashion labels. Sales of the used jeans rose, and Goodwill received excellent national press coverage.

Creation of a graphics standards manual helps a large organization to enforce its unified designs throughout all its operations. Such a manual gives the specification of exact colors, the proper use of stationery, the size of lettering on signs, and similar information.

CASE PROBLEM

The local chapter of the American Lung Association needs to update its ten-minute slide presentation about the activities and services of the organization. Do some research on the American Lung Association and what it does. Then write the script on the right side of the paper. On the left, briefly describe the slides that would be keyed to the basic points of the script.

QUESTIONS FOR REVIEW AND DISCUSSION

1. What is the fundamental difference between a news story in a newspaper and one on television?

2. Under what conditions might a public relations adviser recommend distribution of a videotaped news release?

3. In what ways can a corporation make use of videotaped presentations?

4. If you were handling public relations for an airline, what types of publicity tie-ins might you develop with a Hollywood motion picture producer?

5. A food manufacturer plans to produce a sponsored film about a new oat-bran cereal. What elements might it include in the film? To what target audiences might it show the film?

6. Why is it desirable to write the script of a slide show before the pictures are taken?

7. What is a storyboard?

8. Why is a mug shot a useful photographic tool in public relations practice?

9. Billboard companies rent display space on the basis of a *100-showing*. What does this mean?

10. How can graphics design help to strengthen a corporation's public image?

SUGGESTED READINGS

Ackerman, Laurence D. "Identity in Action." *Communication World,* September 1990, pp. 33–35.

Allen, Gray. "Show." *Communication World,* October 1991, pp. 34–37. Overview of trade show industry.

Allen, Gray. "What's Hot in Corporate TV?" *Communication World,* October 1989, pp. 16–19.

Bauman, Lorraine, and Daniels, Elizabeth. "Making an Open House a Special Event." *Public Relations Journal,* August 1990, pp. 32–33.

Chapnick, Benjamin. "How to Get the Best Photographic Results for Annual Reports, Brochures, and Editorial Placements." *Public Relations Quarterly,* Fall 1990, pp. 27–32.

Dekker, Marla. "Design Management: The Mystery and the Magic." *Public Relations Quarterly,* Fall 1993. Corporate identity through design and graphics.

Gallina, Emil. "VNRs Under Attack." *Communication World,* October 1991, p. 13. FDA rules and guidelines.

Glazer, George. "Let's Settle the Question of VNRs." *Public Relations Quarterly,* Spring 1993, pp. 43–46. Defense of video news releases as a source of news.

Guglielmo, Bob, and McWilliams, Jim. "Planning a Successful Slide Presentation." *Communication World,* March 1989, pp. 18–20.

Holmes, Paul. "Corporate Identity: Beyond Name and Logo." *Inside PR,* November 1992, pp. 43–44.

Johnson, Marti. "Thanks for the Memory." *Communication World,* July–August 1988, pp. 44–45. How to write video scripts.

Kern-Foxworth, Marilyn. "Plantation Kitchen to American Icon: Aunt Jemima." *Public Relations Review,* Fall 1990, pp. 55–67. Historical evolution of a Quaker Oats trademark.

King, Thomas R. "Firms Grow Choosier About Film Tie-Ins." *Wall Street Journal,* June 30, 1992, pp. B1, B8.

"Logos Have Powerful Effect on Company Image." *Communication World,* December 1992, p. 29.

Marken, G. A. "Andy." "Public Relations Photos: Beyond the Written Word." *Public Relations Quarterly,* Summer 1993, pp. 7–12.

O'Hara-Devereaux, Mary, and Pardini, Robert L. "Seeing How We Work Together: Graphic Language Supports Communication Across Cultural Boundaries." *Communication World,* March 1993, pp. 29–32. Using graphics to communicate.

Templin, Neal. "Employers Use TV to Reach Their Workers." *Wall Street Journal,* December 7, 1993, pp. B1, B4.

Shell, Adam. "VNRs: Who's Watching? How Do You Know?" *Public Relations Journal,* December 1993, pp. 14–17, Includes list of VNR suppliers.

Shell, Adam. "VNRs in the News." *Public Relations Journal,* December 1992, pp. 20–23. Critical article in *TV Guide* stirs ethical debate.

Shell, Adam. "Will Europe Be the Next Frontier for VNRs?" *Public Relations Journal,* December 1991, pp. 11–12, 22, 28.

Stecki, Ed, and Corrado, Frank. "How to Make a Video, Part I." *Public Relations Journal,* February 1988, pp. 33–34.

Stecki, Ed, and Corrado, Frank. "How to Make a Video, Part II." *Public Relations Journal,* March 1988, pp. 35–36.

Walter, Kate. "Moving Your Photos on the Wires." *Public Relations Journal,* March 1989, pp. 33–35.

A PUBLIC RELATIONS GLOSSARY

Account executive   A person in a public relations firm or advertising agency who works with a client on a program.

Accreditation   In public relations, the designation *APR* given to members of the Public Relations Society of America with at least five years of experience who have passed written and oral examinations. The International Association of Business Communicators has a designation, *ABC,* standing for Accredited Business Communicator, based on experience and testing.

Actuality   A brief on-the-scene report, live or on tape, inserted into a radio news show.

Agenda-setter   A term often applied to the mass media, whose choice of news stories and headlines suggests to the public what to think about.

Annual report   A corporate information document filed each year with the Securities and Exchange Commission. Many companies expand their reports with illustrations and text for distribution to stockholders, employees, and other interested persons.

Backgrounder   Slang term for an article giving the background of an organization, individual, or situation.

Benchmark study   A measurement of audience attitudes before and after a public relations campaign.

Bill stuffer   Company information or sales material placed in an envelope containing a customer's bill.

Bio   Slang abbreviation for the detailed biography a practitioner prepares for a client.

Booker   Publicist whose assignment is to place clients on talk shows and in other public events.

Bottom line   Popular usage indicating the most important fact; derived from the bottom line of a financial statement, showing net profit or loss.

CEO   Chief executive officer of a corporation.

Channeling   The technique of tapping a group's attitudes with salient messages that propose a course of action.

Cheesecake   Photograph of a scantily clad young woman used as a publicity device. Similar photographs of men are called "beefcake."

Communication audit   A review to determine what public relations material the target audience is receiving and what it desires to receive.

Copyright   The protection of a creative work from unauthorized use.

Copy-testing   The technique of trying out material on a small group before distributing it to an entire audience.

Corporate advertising   Advertising intended to enhance public conception of a company or to advocate a company policy. (See *Institutional advertising.*)

Corporate communications   Term covering all types of communication by a company to both external and internal audiences.

Courtesy bias   Tendency of some survey respondents to give a socially "correct" answer rather than one disclosing their true opinions.

Crisis communications   Methods and policies a corporation uses in distributing information when its operations become involved in an emergency situation affecting the public.

Database   Indexed information held in computer storage, from which a computer user can summon selected material, usually for a fee.

Decoder   In communication theory, one who receives a message. (See *Encoder.*)

Demographics   The characteristics of a human population, including size, density, growth, distribution, and vital statistics.

Editor   Director of a newspaper's news and editorial department; may be subordinate to the publisher or on an equal footing, depending upon the newspaper's organization.
    Associate editor   Director of the editorial and commentary pages.
    Managing editor   Manager of news operations, to whom the city editor and other news editors answer.
    City editor   Director of the local news staff; the person to whom most news releases are addressed.

Electronic mail   Textual messages transmitted from one computer terminal to another, rather than delivered by a mail carrier or messenger.

Embargo   Statement of the day and hour set by the creator of a news release for use by the news media.

Encoder   In communication theory, one who sends a message. (See *Decoder.*)

External publication   One designed to be read by persons not employed by the sponsoring organization. (See *Internal publication.*)

Facsimile   Electronic method of transmitting exact reproductions of printed matter. Often called "fax."

Factsheet   An advisory information sheet about a forthcoming event.

Feedback   Reaction from those affected by an activity or public relations material about the situation.

Fiber optics   Transmission of signals through highly transparent strands of extremely thin glass, instead of by wire.

Filmstrip　Sequence of film frames that, when advanced one by one in a projector, presents a topic on a screen; used as a training tool.

Flack　Derogatory term applied primarily to a person who publicizes entertainment events and personalities. (See *Press agentry*.)

Focus group　Panel of persons, representative of the audience a public relations practitioner desires to reach, who are asked to give their opinions of proposed programs.

Freeloading　The practice of some reporters and editors to accept gifts, entertainment, and travel from organizations seeking to influence them.

Gatekeeper　Editor, reporter, news director, or other person who decides what material is printed, broadcast, or otherwise offered to the public.

Gross impressions　Total circulation and listening audience of the print and broadcast media that use a news release.

Hierarchy of needs　Abraham Maslow's definition of an individual's five levels of needs, a basis for planning appeals to self-interest.

Hotline　In public relations, a toll-free telephone number set up by a trade association or corporation to provide quick answers, especially to the news media.

Hype　The promotion of movie and television stars, books, magazines, and so forth, through shrewd use of the media; used as both noun and verb. (See *Press agentry*.)

Hypodermic needle theory　The belief that people receive information directly without any intervening variable, as in a vacuum.

Image-building　Protection and enhancement of the reputation of an organization or individual.

Impression　Exposure of an individual to a news release through the print or broadcast media. (See *Gross impressions*.)

Information on demand　Computerized information on requested topics called up on a television or computer screen by the user.

Information retrieval　Act of obtaining desired pieces of information from material stored in a computer.

Information superhighway　Popular term to describe the emerging system of transmission that blends television, telephones, and computers to provide vastly expanded two-way communication.

Institutional advertising　Advertising intended to strengthen an organization's image, rather than to stimulate immediate sales of its products or services. (See *Corporate advertising*.)

Internal publication　One designed for distribution primarily to employees. (See *External publication*.)

Internship　Temporary employment by a student to obtain professional work experience.

Interpersonal communication Exchange between two or more persons in close proximity using conversation and gestures.

Issues management Program of identifying and addressing issues of public concern in which a company is, or should be, involved.

Libel Mainly defamation by written or printed words; but also, as interpreted by the courts, by broadcast. (See *Slander.*)

Line function Pursuit of management objectives through supervision, delegation of authority, and work assignments. (See *Staff function.*)

Literary agent Person who represents an author in dealings with publishers.

Lobbyist Person who presents an organization's point of view to members of Congress or other government bodies.

Marketing communications Product publicity, promotion, and advertising.

Marketing public relations Use of public relations techniques to support overall advertising and marketing objectives of a company or client.

Message entropy Tendency for a message to dissipate, or lose information, as it is disseminated.

Muckrakers Writers who seek to expose corrupt and immoral conduct by companies, institutions, and governments; specifically, a group of early 1900s writers and publications in America.

Mug shot Slang term for a head-and-shoulders photograph of an individual for newspaper publication.

News conference Meeting at which the spokesperson for an organization or an individual in the news delivers information to reporters and answers their questions; often called a *press conference*.

News release Timely information about an activity of a public relations practitioner's client or organization, distributed in ready-to-use form.

Off-the-record Practice of giving reporters confidential information with the demand that it not be published.

100-showing Number of billboards needed to expose a message to approximately 100 percent of the population in a designated area within 30 days.

Opinion leader Articulate person knowledgeable about specific issues whose opinions influence others.

Pattern speech Basic speech written so that several speakers can deliver it to different audiences with only minor variations.

People meter A device for measuring how much a person watches television, used in determining the size of TV audiences.

Pilot test Tryout of a public relations message and key copy points on a small audience before general distribution.

Planter   Publicist who delivers news releases to media offices and urges their use.

Positioning   The practice of creating corporate identity programs that establish a place in the market for a company and its products. Also, the effort to get ahead by doing something first.

Press agentry   Term applied primarily to the publicizing of entertainers and shows; often used in a derogatory sense. (See *Hype.*)

Press conference   (See *News conference.*)

Press kit   Folder containing news releases, photographs, and background information, distributed to media representatives.

Preventive public relations   Efforts to maintain goodwill for an organization or individual through reinforcing messages.

Probability sample   Survey in which every member of the targeted audience has a chance of being selected for questioning.

Product recall   Act of calling back from consumers a company's product found to be defective, for repair or replacement.

Public affairs   Term used primarily to describe work in the areas of government and community relations.

Public information   Term used primarily by government agencies, social service organizations, and universities to describe their public relations activities.

Publisher   Chief official of a newspaper who directs financial, mechanical, and administrative operations, and sometimes news and editorial operations as well.

Purposive sampling   Selection of opinion leaders to be interviewed; usually used when approval of the group is necessary for success of a public relations campaign.

Quota sampling   Selection of a group to be polled that matches the characteristics of the entire audience.

Royalty fee   Amount of money received by an author for each copy of a book sold, usually 10 or 15 percent of the retail price; also money received by program distributors for materials used in broadcasting.

Satellite transmission   Method of transmitting text, pictures, and sound by beaming an electronic signal to a transponder on a satellite orbiting 22,300 miles above the earth, from which it bounces back to receiving dishes on the ground.

Semantic noise   Inept language usage that impedes the receiver's ability to comprehend a message; for example, use of trade jargon to a general audience.

Semantics   Study of words and their use and interpretation.

Slander   Oral defamation of character. (See *Libel.*)

Social contract   Popular term for a corporation's set of responsibilities to the public.

Source credibility   Use of representatives who have expertise, sincerity, and charisma to win acceptance from an audience.

Split message   Exposure of two or three different appeals to separate audiences, to determine which is most effective.

Sponsored film   Motion picture paid for by an organization to deliver information or a message, usually shown without charge.

Staff function   Pursuit of management objectives through suggestions, recommendations, and advice. In corporate organization, public relations is a staff function. (See *Line function.*)

Talk show   Television or radio program on which a host or hostess chats with guests or telephone callers.

Teleconference   Presentation or discussion by television, involving groups assembled at scattered receiving points, usually with telephone or television channels that permit distant viewers to ask questions or express reactions.

Teletext   System of delivering news and other information to a television screen, in which the viewer can select certain portions of the material to watch.

Telethon   Fund-raising program on television lasting several hours, in which appeals for donations are mixed with entertainment.

Trade journal   Magazine designed and edited for a special-interest commercial or professional group.

Trademark   Name, symbol, or other device identifying a product, officially registered and legally restricted to the use of the owner or manufacturer.

Transfer   Technique of associating a person, product, or organization with individuals or situations of high or low credibility, depending on the intention of the message.

Transparency   Sheet of transparent acetate or similar material on which text or graphic material is placed, for showing on an overhead projector.

Videocassette   Small container of videotape that can be inserted in a playback machine for projection.

Videoconference   (See *Teleconference.*)

Video news release (VNR)   Pictorial news release distributed on videotape, with or without accompanying spoken commentary.

Videotape   A recording of moving images and sound on magnetic tape.

Videotex   Two-way communication system in which a viewer receives information on a screen and sends messages by keyboard.

BIBLIOGRAPHY

This selected list of recent books is based, in part, on an annual bibliography compiled by the Information Center of the Public Relations Society of America, 33 Irving Place, New York, NY, 10003.

GENERAL BOOKS

Aronoff, Craig, and Baskin, Otis. *Public Relations: The Profession and the Practice,* 3rd edition. Dubuque, IA: Brown, 1991.

Botan, Carl H., and Hazelton, Vincent. *Public Relations Theory.* Hillsdale, NJ: Lawrence Erlbaum, 1989.

Brody, E. W. *The Business of Public Relations.* Westport, CT: Greenwood, 1987.

Brody, E. W. *Public Relations Programming and Production.* New York: Praeger, 1988.

Cantor, Bill. *Experts in Action: Inside Public Relations,* 2nd edition. White Plains, NY: Longman, 1989.

Crable, Richard, and Vibbert, Steven. *Public Relations As Communication Management.* Fort Lee, NJ: Burgess, 1986.

Culbertson, Hugh M., Jeffers, Dennis W., Stone, Donna Besser, and Terrell, Martin. *Social, Political, and Economic Contexts in Public Relations.* Hillsdale, NJ: Lawrence Erlbaum, 1993.

Cutlip, Scott M., Center, Allen H., and Broom, Glen M. *Effective Public Relations,* 7th edition. Englewood Cliffs, NJ: Prentice Hall, 1994.

Grunig, James E., editor. *Excellence in Public Relations and Communication Management.* Hillsdale, NJ: Lawrence Erlbaum, 1991.

Grunig, James E., and Hunt, Todd. *Managing Public Relations.* New York: Holt, Rinehart and Winston, 1984.

Haberman, David, and Dolphin, Harry. *Public Relations: The Necessary Art.* Ames: Iowa State University Press, 1988.

Hausman, Carl, and Benoit, Philip. *Positive Public Relations.* Blue Ridge Summit, PA: Tab Books, 1990.

Hiebert, Ray E. *Precision Public Relations.* White Plains, NY: Longman, 1988.

Jefkins, Frank. *Planned Press and Public Relations.* Philadelphia: Trans-Atlantic, 1992.

Kendall, Robert. *Public Relations Campaign Strategies: Planning for Implementation.* New York: HarperCollins, 1991.

Kruckeberg, Dean, and Starck, Kenneth. *Public Relations and Community: A Reconstructed Theory.* Westport, CT: Greenwood, 1988.

Lesly, Philip, editor. *Lesly's Handbook of Public Relations and Communications,* 4th edition. New York: Amacom Books, 1991.

Nager, Norman, and Allen, T. Harrell. *Public Relations: Management by Objective.* White Plains, NY: Longman, 1984.

Newsom, Doug, Scott, Allen, and VanSlyke, Turk. *This Is PR: Realities of Public Relations,* 5th edition. Belmont, CA: Wadsworth, 1993.

Saffir, Leonard, with Tarrant, John. *Power Public Relations.* Lincolnwood, IL: NTC Publishing, 1993.

Seitel, Fraser P. *The Practice of Public Relations,* 5th edition. New York: Macmillan, 1992.

Simmons, Robert E. *Communication Campaign Management.* White Plains, NY: Longman, 1990.

Toth, Elizabeth L., and Heath, Robert L., editors. *Rhetorical and Critical Approaches to Public Relations.* Hillsdale, NJ: Lawrence Erlbaum, 1991.

Wilcox, Dennis L., Ault, Phillip H., and Agee, Warren K. *Public Relations: Strategies and Tactics,* 4th edition. New York: HarperCollins, 1995.

White, Jon. *How to Understand and Manage Public Relations.* London: Business Books, 1991.

Wragg, David. *Public Relations Handbook.* Cambridge, MA: Blackwell Business, 1992.

SPECIAL INTEREST

BUSINESS/MANAGEMENT

Atkins, Chris, and Sauerhaft, Stan. *The Visible Company: Creating Corporate Goodwill for Market Advantage.* New York: Wiley, 1989.

Buchholz, Rogene. *Business Environment and Public Policy: Implications for Management.* Englewood Cliffs, NJ: Prentice Hall, 1991.

Chajet, Clive, and Shachtman, Tom. *Image by Design: From Corporate Vision to Business Reality.* Reading, MA: Addison-Wesley, 1991.

Ciabattari, Jane. *Winning Moves: How to Survive (and Manage) a Corporate Shakeup.* New York: Penguin, 1989.

Corrado, Frank M. *Getting the Word Out: How Managers Can Create Value with Communications.* Homewood, IL: Business One–Irwin, 1993.

Dilenschneider, Robert. *A Briefing for Leaders.* New York: HarperBusiness, 1992.

Drucker, Peter. *Management: Tasks, Responsibilities, Practices.* New York: Harper & Row, 1985.

Drucker, Peter. *Managing for Results.* New York: Harper & Row, 1986.

Freed, Melvyn N., and Diodata, Virgil I. *Business Information Desk Reference.* New York: Macmillan, 1991.

Garbett, Thomas F. *How to Build a Corporation's Identity and Project Its Image.* Lexington, MA: Lexington Books, 1990.

Gregory, James R., and Wiechmann, Jack G. *Marketing Corporate Image: The Company as Your Number One Product.* Lincolnwood, IL: NTC Business, 1991.

Hart, Norman. *Effective Corporate Relations: Public Relations in Business and Industry.* New York: McGraw-Hill, 1988.

Kotter, John, and Heskett, James. *Corporate Culture and Performance.* New York: Free Press, 1992.

Marsteller, William. *Creative Management.* Lincolnwood, IL: NTC Business, 1992.

Olasky, Marvin N. *Corporate Public Relations and American Public Enterprise.* Hillsdale, NJ: Lawrence Erlbaum, 1987.

Olins, Wally. *Corporate Identity.* Cambridge, MA: Harvard Business School Press, 1992.

Pauchart, Thierry, and Mitroff, Ian. *Transforming the Crisis-Prone Organization.* San Francisco: Jossey-Bass, 1992.

Peters, Thomas, and Waterman, Robert. *In Search of Excellence.* New York: Warner Books, 1988.

Sauerhaft, Stan, and Atkins, Chris. *Image Wars: Protecting Your Company When There Is No Place to Hide.* New York: John Wiley, 1989.

Selame, Elinor, and Selame, Joseph. *The Company Image: Building Your Identity and Influence in the Marketplace.* New York: Wiley, 1988.

Sobel, Marion. *Shaping the Corporate Image: An Analytical Guide for Executive Decision Makers.* Westport, CT: Greenwood Press, 1992.

Tomasko, Robert M. *Downsizing: Reshaping the Corporation for the Future.* New York: AMACOM, 1990.

Walton, Wesley, and Brissman, Charles. *Corporate Communications Handbook.* New York: Clark Boardman, 1989.

Winner, Paul. *Effective PR Management: A Guide to Corporate Success.* Woodstock, NY: Beekman, 1990.

CAREERS

Field, Sally. *Career Opportunities in Advertising and Public Relations.* New York: Facts on File, 1990.

Helitzer, Melvin. *The Dream Job: Sports Publicity, Promotion, and Public Relations.* Athens, OH: University Sports Press, 1992.

Rotman, Morris. *Opportunities in Public Relations Careers.* Lincolnwood, IL: National Textbook, 1988.

Mogel, Leonard. *Making It in Public Relations: An Insider's Guide to Career Opportunities.* New York: Collier Books, 1993.

Public Relations Career Directory, 4th edition. Orange, CA: Career Press, 1993.

CASE STUDIES

Capper, Alan, and Cunard, Peter. *The Public Relations Case Book: Major Campaigns in Action.* Woodstock, NY: Beekman, 1990.

Center, Allen H., and Jackson, Patrick. *Public Relations Practices: Managerial Case Studies and Problems,* 5th edition. Englewood Cliffs, NJ: Prentice Hall, 1994.

Hendrix, Jerry A. *Public Relations Cases,* 2nd edition. Belmont, CA: 1992.

Moss, Danny. *Public Relations in Practice: A Casebook.* New York: Routledge, 1991.

Simon, Raymond, and Wylie, Frank W. *Cases in Public Relations Management.* Homewood, IL: NTC Business Books, 1993.

COMMUNICATION/PERSUASION

Agee, Warren K., Ault, Phillip H., and Emery, Edwin. *Introduction to Mass Communications,* 11th edition. New York: HarperCollins, 1994.

Bovee, Courtland L., and Thill, John v. *Business Communication Today,* 3rd edition. New York: McGraw-Hill, 1992.

Brody, E. W. *Managing Communication Processes: From Planning to Crisis Response.* New York: Praeger, 1991.

Brody, E. W. *Communication Tomorrow: New Audiences, New Technologies, New Media.* New York: Praeger, 1990.

Combs, James E., and Nimmo, Dan. *The New Propaganda: The Dictatorship of Palaver in Contemporary Politics.* White Plains, NY: Longman, 1993.

Corman, Steven R. *Foundations of Organizational Communication.* White Plains, NY: Longman, 1990.

Creedan, Pamela J. *Women in Mass Communications: Challenging Gender Values.* Newbury Park, CA: Sage, 1989.

DeFleur, Melvin L., and Dennis, Everette E. *Understanding Mass Communication.* Boston: Houghton Mifflin, 1994.

DeFleur, Melvin, and Ball-Rokeach, Sandra. *Theories of Mass Communication,* 5th edition. White Plains, NY: Longman, 1989.

Goldhaber, Gerald. *Organizational Communication,* 6th edition. Dubuque, IA: Brown, 1993.

Hamilton, Seymour. *A Communications Audit Handbook: Helping Organizations Communicate.* White Plains, NY: Longman, 1987.

Hunt, Todd, and Rubin, Brent D. *Mass Communication: Producers and Consumers.* New York: HarperCollins, 1993.

Jowett, Garth, and O'Donnell, Victoria. *Propaganda and Persuasion.* Newbury Park, CA: Sage, 1987.

Larson, Charles U. *Persuasion: Reception and Responsibility,* 6th edition. Belmont: CA: Wadsworth, 1992.

Lukaszewski, James. *Influencing Public Attitudes: Strategies to Reduce Media Power.* Leesburg, VA: Issue Action Publications, 1993.

MacArthur, John R. *Second Front: Censorship and Propaganda in the Gulf War.* New York: Hill & Wang, 1992.

McCombs, Maxwell, editor. *Contemporary Public Opinion: Issues and the News.* Hillsdale, NJ: Lawrence Erlbaum, 1991.

Pratkanis, Anthony, and Aronson, Elliott. *Age of Propaganda: The Everyday Use and Abuse of Persuasion.* Salt Lake City, UT: W. H. Freeman, 1992.

Reardon, Kathleen K. *Persuasion in Practice.* Newbury Park, CA: Sage, 1991.

Rice, Ronald, and Atkin, Charles K. *Public Information Campaigns,* 2nd edition. Newbury Park, CA: Sage, 1989.

Ross, Raymond. *Understanding Persuasion,* 3rd edition. Englewood Cliffs, NJ: Prentice Hall, 1990.

Salmon, Charles T. *Information Campaigns.* Newbury Park, CA: Sage, 1989.

Samovar, Larry, and Porter, Richard. *Intercultural Communication: A Reader,* 6th edition. Belmont, CA: Wadsworth, 1991.

Severin, Werner, and Tankard, James. *Communication Theories: Origins, Methods, Uses,* 3rd edition. White Plains, NY: Longman, 1992.

Shockley-Zalabak, Pamela. *Fundamentals of Organizational Communication,* 2nd edition. White Plains, NY: Longman, 1991.

Windahl, Seven, and Signitzer, Benno. *Using Communication Theory: An Introduction to Planned Communications.* Newbury Park, CA: Sage, 1991.

Yankelovich, Daniel. *Coming to Public Judgment: Making Democracy Work in a Complex World.* Syracuse, NY: Syracuse University Press, 1991.

CONSULTING/COUNSELING

Brody, E. W. *Professional Practice Development.* New York: Praeger, 1989.

Budd, John F., Jr. *Street Smart Public Relations.* Lakesville, CT: Turtle Publishing Company, 1992.

Cohen, William A. *How to Make It Big as a Consultant,* 2nd edition. New York: AMACOM, 1990.

Harris, Thomas L. *Choosing and Working with Your Public Relations Firm.* Homewood, IL: NTC Business, 1992.

Holtz, Herman. *The Consultant's Guide to Proposal Writing,* 2nd edition. New York: Wiley, 1990.

Nager, Norman, and Truitt, Richard. *Strategic Public Relations Counseling.* White Plains, NY: Longman, 1987.

Poppe, Fred. *50 Rules to Keep a Client Happy.* New York: HarperCollins, 1988.

Putnam, Anthony O. *Marketing Your Services.* New York: Wiley, 1990.

Shenson, Howard L. *The Contract and Fee Setting Guide for Professionals and Consultants.* New York: Wiley, 1990.

Shenson, Howard L. *Shenson on Consulting: Success Strategies.* New York: Wiley, 1990.

CRISIS/EMERGENCY COMMUNICATIONS

Barton, Lawrence. *Crisis in Organizations: Managing and Communicating in the Heat of Crisis.* Cincinnati, OH: South-Western Publishing Company, 1993.

Bernstein, Alan. *Emergency Public Relations Manual,* 3rd edition. Highland Park, NJ: PASE, 1988.

Charles, Michael, and Kim, John. *Crisis Management: A Casebook for Survival.* Gettysburg, PA: C. C. Thomas, 1988.

Gottschalk, Jack A., editor. *Crisis Response: Inside Stories on Managing Image Under Siege.* Detroit: Visible Ink Press (Gale Research, Inc.), 1993.

Irvine, Robert B. *When You Are the Headline: Managing a News Story.* Homewood, IL: Dow Jones–Irwin, 1987.

Marconi, Joe. *Crisis Marketing: When Bad Things Happen to Good Companies.* Chicago: Probus Publishing Company, 1993.

Pinsdorf, Marion. *Communicating When Your Company Is Under Siege.* Lexington, MA: Lexington Books, 1986.

DEMOGRAPHICS

Ambry, Margaret K. *1990–91 Almanac of Consumer Markets: The Official Guide to the Demographics of American Consumers.* Ithaca, NY: American Demographics Press, 1989.

Asian, Black and Hispanic Research: Pointing the Way to Marketing Effectiveness. New York: Advertising Research Foundation, 1991.

Crispell, Diane. *The Insider's Guide to Demographic Know-How.* Ithaca, NY: American Demographics Press, 1990.

Michman, Ronald D. *Lifestyle Market Segmentation.* New York: Praeger, 1991.

Wolfe, David B. *Serving the Ageless Market.* New York: McGraw-Hill, 1990.

DESIGN/GRAPHICS

Baird, Russell N., McDonald, Duncan, and Pittman, Ronald K. *The Graphics of Communication,* 6th edition. Fort Worth, TX: Harcourt Brace, 1993.

Beach, Mark. *Graphically Speaking—An Illustrated Guide to the Working Language of Design and Printing.* Manzanita, OR: Elk Ridge Publishing, 1993.

Bohle, Robert. *Publication Design for Editors.* Englewood Cliffs, NJ: Prentice Hall, 1990.

Conover, Theodore. *Graphic Communications Today.* St. Paul, MN: West, 1990.

Hoffman, Kenneth E., with Teeple, Jon A. *Computer Graphics Applications: An Introduction to Desktop Publishing and Design, Presentation Graphics, Animation.* Belmont, CA: Wadsworth, 1990.

Lichty, Tom. *Design Principles for Desktop Publishers,* 2nd edition. Belmont, CA: Wadsworth, 1994.

Napoles, Veronica. *Corporate Identity Design.* New York: Van Nostrand Reinhold, 1987.

Shapiro, Ellen. *Clients and Designers.* New York: Watson-Guptill, 1990.

White, Jan. *Mastering Graphics: Design and Production Made Easy.* Ann Arbor, MI: Bowker, 1983.

DIRECT MARKETING

See also "Marketing" section.

Bacon, Mark S. *Do-It-Yourself Direct Marketing.* New York: John Wiley, 1991.

Bird, Drayton. *Commonsense Direct Marketing,* 2nd edition. Lincolnwood, IL: NTC Business, 1990.

Jones, Susan K. *Creative Strategy in Direct Marketing.* Lincolnwood, IL: NTC Business, 1991.

Kramer, John. *The Complete Direct Marketing Sourcebook.* New York: John Wiley, 1992.

Linchitz, Joel. *The Complete Guide to Telemarketing Management.* New York: AMACOM, 1992.

Shepard, Dave. *The New Direct Marketing . . . How to Implement a Profit Driven Database.* Homewood, IL: Dow Jones–Irwin, 1990.

Vogele, Siegfried. *Handbook of Direct Mail: Dialogue Method of Direct Communication.* Englewood Cliffs, NJ: Prentice Hall, 1992.

EDUCATION

Gray, Lynton. *Marketing Education.* Bristol, PA: Taylor & Francis, 1991.

Hayes, Thomas J. *New Strategies in Higher Education Marketing.* Binghamton, NY: Haworth Press, 1991.

Kotler, Philip, and Fox, Karen. *Strategic Marketing for Educational Institutions.* Englewood Cliffs, NJ: Prentice Hall, 1985.

Rowland, A. W. *Handbook of Institutional Advancement,* 2nd edition. San Francisco: Jossey-Bass, 1986.

Topor, Robert. *Institutional Image: How to Define, Improve, Market It.* Washington, DC: CASE, 1986.

West, Philip. *Educational Public Relations.* Newbury Park, CA: Sage, 1985.

EMPLOYEE RELATIONS

Bland, Michael, and Jackson, Peter. *Effective Employee Relations.* London: Kogan Page Ltd., 1990.

Brown, Kathleen, and Turner, Joan. *AIDS: Policies and Programs for the Workplace.* New York: Van Nostrand Reinhold, 1989.

Hartley, Jean F., and Stephenson, Geoffrey M. *Employment Relations: The Psychology of Influence and Control at Work.* Cambridge, MA: Blackwell Business, 1992.

Marchington, Mick. *Managing the Team: A Guide to Successful Employee Involvement.* Cambridge, MA: Blackwell Business, 1992.

Smith, Alvie L. *Innovative Employee Communication.* Englewood Cliffs, NJ: Prentice Hall, 1991.

ENVIRONMENT

Blakey, H. Allen. *Environmental Communications and Public Relations Handbook.* Rockville, MD: Government Institute, 1990.

Carson, Patrick, and Moulden, Julia. *Green Is Gold.* New York: Harper Business, 1991.

Environmental Information Directory. Detroit: Gale Research, 1991.

Harrison, E. Bruce. *Going Green: How to Communicate Your Company's Environmental Commitment.* Homewood, IL: Business One–Irwin, 1993.

Ottman, Jacquelyn A. *Green Marketing: Challenges and Opportunities for a New Marketing Age.* Lincolnwood, IL: NTC Publishing, 1993.

Stilwell, E. Joseph. *Packaging for the Environment.* New York: AMACOM, 1991.

ETHICS

Baker, Lee W. *The Credibility Factor: Putting Ethics to Work in Public Relations.* Burr Ridge, IL: Irwin Professional Publishing, 1993.

Christians, Clifford, Rotzoll, Kim, and Fackler, Mark. *Media Ethics,* 3rd edition. White Plains, NY: Longman, 1991.

Day, Louis A. *Ethics in Mass Communications: Cases and Controversies.* Belmont, CA: Wadsworth, 1991.

Ferre, James. *Public Relations Ethics: A Bibliography.* Boston, MA: G. K. Hall Publisher, 1991.

Henderson, Verne E. *What's Ethical in Business.* New York: McGraw-Hill, 1992.

McElreath, Mark P. *Managing Systematic and Ethical Public Relations.* Dubuque, IA: Brown and Benchmark, 1993.

Walton, Clarence. *The Moral Manager.* New York: Harper Business, 1990.

FINANCIAL/INVESTOR RELATIONS

Dumitrescu, Claudia. *Public Relations for Financial Marketers.* Chicago: Financial Institute Marketing Association, 1990.

Furlong, Carla. *Marketing Money.* Chicago: Probus, 1989.

Nichols, Donald. *The Handbook of Investor Relations.* Homewood, IL: Dow Jones–Irwin, 1989.

Sametz, Arnold. *The Battle for Corporate Control: Shareholder Rights, Stakeholder Interests, and Managerial Responsibilities.* Homewood, IL: Business One–Irwin, 1991.

Samuelson, Paul, and Nordhaus, William. *Economics,* 14th edition. New York: McGraw-Hill, 1992.

Taggert, Philip, and Alexander, Roy. *Taking Your Company Public.* New York: AMACOM, 1991.

FUND-RAISING/DEVELOPMENT

Broce, Thomas. *Fund Raising.* Norman: University of Oklahoma Press, 1986.

Burlingame, Dwight, and Hulse, Lamont. *Taking Fund Raising Seriously.* San Francisco: Jossey-Bass, 1991.

Edles, L. Peter. *Fundraising: Hands-on Tactics for Nonprofit Groups.* New York: McGraw-Hill, 1993.

Kelly, Kathleen S. *Fund Raising and Public Relations: A Critical Analysis.* Hillsdale, NJ: Lawrence Erlbaum, 1991.

Lindahl, Wesley E. *Strategic Planning for Fund Raising.* San Francisco: Jossey-Bass, 1992.

Nichols, Judith E. *Changing Demographics: Fund Raising in the 1990s.* Chicago: Bonus Books, 1990.

Rosso, Henry. *Achieving Excellence in Fund Raising.* San Francisco:

Seymour, Harold J. *Designs for Fund Raising.* Washington, DC: The Taft Group, 1988.

Stolper, Carolyn, and Hopkins, Karen. *Fundraising: A Handbook for Arts and Cultural Organizations.* Phoenix, AZ: Oryx, 1989.

GOVERNMENT/PUBLIC AFFAIRS

Johnson-Carter, Karen S., and Copeland, Gary A. *Negative Political Advertising Coming of Age.* Hillsdale, NJ: Lawrence Erlbaum, 1991.

Kern, Montague. *30-Second Politics: Political Advertising in the Eighties.* Westport, CT: Greenwood, 1989.

Mack, Charles S. *Lobbying and Government Relations: A Guide for Executives.* Westport, CT: Quorum Books, 1989.

Marcus, Alfred. *Business Strategy and Public Policy.* Westport, CT: Greenwood, 1987.

Post, James, and Mahon, John. *Corporate Public Affairs.* New York: Ballinger, 1989.

Remmes, Harold. *Lobbying for Your Cause.* Babylon, NY: Pilot Books, 1986.

Smucker, Bob. *The Nonprofit Lobbying Guide.* San Francisco: Jossey-Bass, 1991.

Wittenberg, Ernest, and Wittenberg, Elisabeth. *How to Win in Washington.* Washington, DC: Basil Blackwell, 1990.

HISTORY/BIOGRAPHY

Barmash, I. *Always Live Better Than Your Clients: The Fabulous Life and Times of Benjamin Sonnenberg.* New York: Dodd, Mead, 1983.

Cutlip, Scott M. *Public Relations: Its Early History.* Hillsdale, NJ: Lawrence Erlbaum, 1994.

Dilenschneider, Robert. *Power and Influence: Mastering the Art of Persuasion.* Englewood Cliffs, NJ: Prentice Hall, 1990.

Fuhrman, Candace J. *Publicity Stunts.* San Francisco: Chronicle Books, 1989.

Hiebert, Ray. *Courtier to the Crowd: Ivy Lee.* Ames: Iowa State University Press, 1966.

Mitchell, Greg. *The Campaign of the Century: Upton Sinclair's Race for Governor of California and the Birth of Media Politics.* New York: Random House, 1993.

Rogers, Henry C. *Walking the Tightrope.* New York: Morrow, 1980.

Saxon, A. H. *P. T. Barnum: The Legend and the Man.* New York: Columbia University Press, 1990.

Wood, Robert, and Gunther, Max. *Confessions of a PR Man.* New York: New American Library, 1989.

Sattler, John E. *Fifty Years Ahead of the News.* Kalamazoo, MI: Sattler International, 1993.

Trento, Susan. *Power House: Robert Keith Gray and the Selling of Access and Influence in Washington.* New York: St. Martin Press, 1992.

INTERNATIONAL

Cateora, Philip. *International Marketing.* Homewood, IL: Business One–Irwin, 1992.

Hornik, Robert C. *Development Communication: Information, Agriculture, and Nutrition in the Third World.* White Plains, NY: Longman, 1988.

Kaynak, Erdener. *Sociopolitical Aspects in International Business.* Binghamton, NY: Haworth Press, 1990.

Lamont, Douglas. *Winning Worldwide: Strategies for Dominating Global Markets.* Homewood, IL: Business One–Irwin, 1990.

Makridakis, Spyros G. *Single Market Europe: Opportunities and Challenges for Business.* San Francisco: Jossey-Bass, 1991.

Nally, Margaret. *International Public Relations in Practice: First Hand Experience of 14 Professionals.* London: Kogan Page Ltd., 1991.

Reed's Worldwide Directory of Public Relations Organizations. Washington, DC: Pigafetta Press, 1990.

Samovar, Larry, and Porter, Richard. *Communication Between Cultures.* Belmont: CA: Wadsworth, 1991.

Weber, Robert E. *The Marketer's Guide to Selling Products Abroad.* Westport, CT: Greenwood Books, 1989.

Williams, Robert. *The World's Largest Market: A Business Guide to Europe 1992.* New York: AMACOM, 1990.

When in Rome . . . A Business Guide to Culture and Customs in 12 European Nations. New York: AMACOM, 1991.

Wouters, Joyce. *International Public Relations: How to Establish Your Company's Product, Service, and Image in Foreign Markets.* New York: AMACOM, 1991.

ISSUES MANAGEMENT

Chase, Howard. *Issues Management: Origins of the Future.* Stamford, CT: Issues Action Publications, 1984.

Ewing, Raymond P. *Managing the New Bottom Line: Issues Management for Senior Executives.* Homewood, IL: Dow Jones–Irwin, 1987.

Heath, Robert. *Strategic Issues Management: How Organizations Influence and Respond to Public Interests and Politics.* San Francisco: Jossey-Bass, 1988.

Heath, Robert, and Nelson, Richard. *Issues Management.* Newbury Park, CA: Sage, 1985.

LAW

Banta, William. *AIDS in the Workplace: Legal and Practical Answers.* Lexington, MA: Lexington Press, 1990.

Lawrence, John, and Timberg, Bernard. *Fair Use and Free Inquiry: Copyright Law and the News Media,* 2nd edition. Norwood, NJ: Ablex Publishing, 1989.

Lively, Donald E. *Modern Communications Law.* Westport, CT: Greenwood, 1991.

Middleton, Kent, and Chamberlin, Bill. *Law of Public Communication,* 2nd edition. White Plains, NY: Longman, 1993.

Posch, Robert J. *The Complete Guide to Marketing and the Law.* Englewood Cliffs, NJ: Prentice Hall, 1988.

Rome, Edwin, and Roberts, William. *Corporate and Commercial Free Speech.* Westport, CT: Quorum Books, 1985.

Watkins, John J. *Mass Media and the Law.* Englewood Cliffs, NJ: Prentice Hall, 1990.

Wilson, Lee. *Make It Legal.* New York: Allworth Press, 1990.

MARKETING

See also "Direct Marketing" section.

Albrecht, Karl. *The Only Thing That Matters: Bring the Power of the Customers into the Center of Your Business.* New York: Harper Business, 1992.

Brooks, William T. *Niche Selling: How to Find Your Customer in a Crowded Market.* Homewood, IL: Business One–Irwin, 1991.

Dirks, Laura M., and Daniel, Sally H. *Marketing Without Mystery: A Practical Guide to Writing a Marketing Plan.* New York: AMACOM, 1991.

Ennew, Christine. *The Marketing Blueprint.* Cambridge, MA: Blackwell Business, 1993.

Harris, Thomas L. *The Marketer's Guide to Public Relations.* New York: Wiley, 1991.

Holtz, Herman. *Databased Marketing.* New York: John Wiley, 1992.

Kassarjian, H., and Robertson, T. *Handbook of Consumer Behavior.* Englewood Cliffs, NJ: Prentice Hall, 1990.

Kotler, Philip. *Marketing Management.* Englewood Cliffs, NJ: Prentice Hall, 1991.

Linneman, R. E. *Making Niche Marketing Work: How to Grow Bigger by Acting Small.* New York: McGraw-Hill, 1991.

Magrath, Allan. *Six Imperatives of Marketing: Lessons from the World's Best Companies.* New York: AMACOM, 1992.

McKenna, Regis. *Relationship Marketing.* Reading, MA: Addison-Wesley, 1991.

Nash, Edward L. *Database Marketing: The Ultimate Tool.* Blue Ridge Summit, PA: TAB Books, 1993.

Nilson, Torsten. *Value Added Marketing.* Blue Ridge Summit, PA: TAB Books, 1992.

Ottman, Jacquelyn. *Green Marketing: Challenges and Opportunities for the New Marketing Age.* Lincolnwood, IL: NTC Business, 1993.

Paley, Norton. *The Strategic Marketing Planner.* New York: AMACOM, 1991.

Schultz, Don E., Tannenbaum, Stanley I., and Lauterborn, Robert F. *Integrated Marketing Communications.* Lincolnwood, IL: National Textbook Company, 1993.

Stevens, Robert E. *Marketing Planning Guide.* Binghamton, NY: Haworth Press, 1992.

Swenson, Chester A. *Selling to a Segmented Market: The Lifestyle Approach.* Westport, CT: Greenwood, 1990.

Vavra, Terry. *Aftermarketing: How to Keep Customers for Life Through Relationship Marketing.* Homewood, IL: Business One–Irwin, 1992.

Zande, Irma, and Leonard, Richard. *Targeting the Trend Setting Customer.* Homewood, IL: Business One–Irwin, 1991.

MEDIA/PRESS RELATIONS

See also "Publicity/Promotion" section.

Blohowiak, Donald W. *No Comment! An Executive's Essential Guide to the News Media.* New York: Praeger, 1987.

Evans, Fred J. *Managing the Media: Proactive Strategy for Better Business and Press Relations.* Westport, CT: Greenwood, 1987.

Hannaford, Peter. *Talking Back to the Media.* New York: Facts on File, 1986.

Howard, Carole, and Matthews, Wilma. *On Deadline: Managing Media Relations.* Prospect Heights, IL: Waveland, 1988.

Irvine, Robert. *When You Are the Headline: Managing a Major News Story.* Homewood, IL: Dow Jones–Irwin, 1987.

Rafe, Stephen C. *Mastering the News Media Interview.* New York: Harper Business, 1991.

Schmertz, Herb. *Good-bye to the Low Profile: The Art of Creative Confrontation.* Boston: Little, Brown, 1986.

Soley, Lawrence C. *The News Shapers: The Sources Who Explain the News.* New York: Praeger, 1992.

Weiner, Richard. *Webster's New World Dictionary of Media and Communications.* Englewood Cliffs, NJ: Prentice Hall, 1990.

MEETINGS

Burleson, Clyde. *Effective Meetings: The Complete Guide.* New York: John Wiley, 1990.

McKenzie, John K. *It's Show Time: How to Plan and Hold Successful Sales Meetings.* Homewood, IL: Business One–Irwin, 1989.

McMahon, Tom. *Big Meetings, Big Results.* Lincolnwood, IL: NTC Business, 1990.

Price, Catherine. *The AMA Guide for Meeting and Event Planners.* New York: AMACOM, 1989.

Shenson, Howard L. *How to Develop and Promote Successful Seminars and Workshops.* New York: John Wiley, 1990.

Simerly, Robert G. *Planning and Marketing Conferences and Workshops: Tips, Tools, and Techniques.* San Francisco: Jossey-Bass, 1990.

NONPROFIT/CHARITABLE GROUPS

See also "Fund-Raising/Development" section.

Connors, Tracy. *Non-Profit Organization Handbook,* 2nd edition. New York: McGraw-Hill, 1988.

Hammack, David C., and Young, Dennis R. *Nonprofit Organizations in a Market Economy.* San Francisco: Jossey-Bass, 1993.

Kennedy, Larry. *Quality Management in a Nonprofit World.* New York: Jossey-Bass Press, 1991.

Kotler, Philip, and Anderson, Alan. *Strategic Marketing For Nonprofit Organizations.* Englewood Cliffs, NJ: Prentice Hall, 1987.

Kotler, Philip, and Clarke, Roberta. *Marketing for Health Care Organizations.* Englewood Cliffs, NJ: Prentice Hall, 1987.

Lewton, Kathleen L. *Public Relations in Health Care: A Guide for Professionals.* Chicago: American Hospital Association, 1991.

Malinowsky, Robert, and Perry, Gerald. *The AIDS Information Sourcebook* 1993–94. Phoenix, AZ: Oryx Press, 1989.

Marlowe, David. *Building a Foundation for Effective Health Care Market Research.* Chicago: American Marketing Association, 1988.

Ruffner, R. *Handbook of Publicity and PR for the Nonprofit Organization.* Englewood Cliffs, NJ: Prentice Hall, 1985.

Stevens, Robert E., and Loudon, David. *Marketing for Churches and Ministries.* Binghamton, NY: Haworth Press, 1992.

Topor, Robert. *Your Personal Guide to Marketing a Nonprofit Organization.* Washington, DC: Council for Advancement and Support of Education (CASE), 1988.

PUBLICITY/PROMOTION

See also "Writing in Public Relations" section.

Baker, Kim, and Baker, Sunny. *How to Promote, Publicize, and Advertise Your Growing Business.* New York: John Wiley, 1992.

Barhydt, James D. *The Complete Book of Product Publicity.* New York: AMACOM, 1987.

Doty, Dorothy I. *Publicity and Public Relations.* Haupauge, NY: Barron, 1990.

Engel, James F. *Promotional Strategy: Managing the Marketing Communication Process.* Homewood, IL: Business One–Irwin, 1990.

Freisleben, Christine G. *The Publicity Process,* 3rd edition. Ames: Iowa State University Press, 1989.

Levine, Michael. *Guerilla PR: How You Can Wage an Effective Publicity Campaign . . . Without Going Broke.* New York: HarperBusiness, 1993.

Quelch, John, and Ferris, Paul W. *Cases in Advertising and Promotion Management.* Homewood, IL: Business One–Irwin, 1990.

Ramacitti, David F. *Do-It-Yourself Publicity.* New York: AMACOM, 1990.

Smith, Jeannette. *The Publicity Kit.* New York: John Wiley, 1991.

Yale, David. *The Publicity Handbook.* Lincolnwood, IL: NTC Business, 1991.

Yearly, Vincent. *Decent Exposure: How to Manage Your Own Publicity.* London: Kogan Page, 1991.

RESEARCH METHODS

Alreck, Pamela L., and Settle, Robert B. *The Survey Research Handbook.* Homewood, IL: Irwin, 1985.

Blakenship, A. B., and Breen, George. *State of the Art Marketing Research.* Lincolnwood, IL: NTC Business, 1992.

Bradburn, Norman, and Sudman, Seymour. *Polls and Surveys.* San Francisco: Jossey-Bass, 1988.

Breen, George, and Blakenship, A. B. *Do-It-Yourself Marketing Research,* 3rd edition. New York: McGraw-Hill, 1991.

Brody, E. W., and Stone, Gerald. *Public Relations Research.* Westport, CT: Greenwood, 1989.

Broom, Glen, and Dozier, David. *Using Research in Public Relations.* Englewood Cliffs, NJ: Prentice Hall, 1990.

Churchill, Gilbert A. *Marketing Research: Methodological Foundations.* Niles, IL: Dryden Press, 1991.

Dickinson, John R. *The Bibliography of Marketing Research Methods.* New York: Free Press, 1990.

Emmert, Philip, and Barker, Larry. *Measurement of Communication Behavior.* White Plains, NY: Longman, 1989.

Lowery, Shearon, and DeFleur, Melvin. *Milestones in Mass Communications Research,* 2nd edition. White Plains, NY: Longman, 1988.

Patton, Michael Quinn. *Qualitative Evaluation and Research Methods.* Newbury Park, CA: Sage, 1990.

Pavlik, John V. *Public Relations: What Research Tells Us.* Newbury Park, CA: Sage, 1987.

Stempel, Guido, and Westley, Bruce. *Research Methods in Mass Communication,* 2nd edition. Englewood Cliffs, NJ: Prentice Hall, 1989.

Templeton, Jane. *Focus Groups: A Guide for Marketing and Advertising Professionals.* Chicago: Probus, 1990.

SPECIAL EVENTS

Burleson, Clyde. *Effective Meetings: The Complete Guide.* New York: Wiley, 1989.

Catherwood, Dwight, and Vankirk, Richard. *The Complete Guide to Special Events.* New York: Wiley & Sons, 1992.

Chase's Annual Events. Chicago: Contemporary Books, 1994.

Harris, April. *Special Events: Planning for Success.* Washington, DC: Council for Advancement and Support of Education (CASE), 1988.

Soares, Eric J. *Promotional Feats: The Role of Planned Events in the Marketing Communications Mix.* Westport, CT: Quorum Books, 1991.

SPEECHES/PRESENTATIONS

DeVito, Joseph A. *The Elements of Public Speaking,* 5th edition. New York: HarperCollins, 1994.

Engleberg, Isa N. *The Principles of Public Presentation.* New York: HarperCollins, 1994.

Fletcher, Leon. *How to Design and Deliver a Speech,* 4th edition. New York: HarperCollins, 1990.

Glenn, Ethel, and Forman, Sandra. *Public Speaking: Today and Tomorrow.* Englewood Cliffs, NJ: Prentice Hall, 1990.

Kaplan, Burton. *The Corporate Manager's Guide to Speechwriting.* New York: Free Press, 1988.

McKenzie, John K. *It's Show Time.* Homewood, IL: Dow Jones–Irwin, 1989.

McMahon, Tom. *Big Meeting, Big Results.* Skokie, IL: NTC Business Books, 1990.

Rafe, Stephen C. *How to Be Prepared to Think on Your Feet.* New York: Harper Business, 1990.

Smith, Terry C. *Making Successful Presentations,* 2nd edition. New York: Wiley, 1990.

Verderber, Rudolph F. *Essentials of Persuasive Speaking: Theory and Concepts.* Belmont: CA: Wadsworth, 1991.

VIDEO/BROADCASTING

See also "Writing in Public Relations" section.

Hausman, Carl. *Institutional Video: Planning, Budgeting, Production, and Evaluation.* Belmont, CA: Wadsworth, 1991.

Hilliard, Robert L. *Writing for Television and Radio,* 5th edition. Belmont: CA: Wadsworth, 1991.

MacDonald, R. H. *Broadcast News Manual of Style.* White Plains, NY: Longman, 1987.

Morley, John. *Scriptwriting for High-Impact Videos: Imaginative Approaches to Delivering Factual Information.* Belmont, CA: Wadsworth, 1992.

Richardson, Alan R., editor. *Corporate and Organizational Video.* New York: McGraw-Hill, 1992.

Willis, Edgar E. *Writing Scripts for Television, Radio, and Film,* 3rd edition. Fort Worth, TX: Harcourt Brace, 1993.

WRITING IN PUBLIC RELATIONS

Aronson, Merry, and Spetner, Don. *The Public Relations Writer's Handbook.* New York: Lexington Books/Macmillan, 1993.

Beach, Mark. *Editing Your Newsletter,* 3rd edition. Portland, OR: Coast to Coast Books, 1988.

Bivins, Thomas H. *Fundamentals of Successful Newsletters.* Lincolnwood, IL: NTC Business Books, 1992.

Bivins, Tom. *Handbook for Public Relations Writing.* Lincolnwood, IL: National Textbook Company, 1991.

Bivins, Thomas, and Ryan, William E. *How to Produce Creative Publications: Traditional Techniques and Computer Applications.* Lincolnwood, IL: NTC Business, 1992.

Brody, E. W., and Lattimore, Dan L.   *Public Relations Writing.* New York: Praeger, 1990.

Hunt, Todd, and Grunig, James E.   *Public Relations Techniques.* Fort Worth, TX: Harcourt Brace, 1994.

Majors, Randall E.   *Business Communication: Writing, Interviewing, and Speaking at Work.* New York: HarperCollins, 1990.

Newsom, Doug, and Carrell, Bob.   *Public Relations Writing: Form and Style,* 4th edition. Belmont: CA: Wadsworth, 1994.

Parsigian, Elisa K.   *Mass Media Writing.* Hillsdale, NJ: Lawrence Erlbaum, 1992.

Rayfield, Robert, Acharya, Lalit, Pincus, David, and Silvis, Donn.   *Public Relations Writing: Strategies and Skills.* Dubuque, IA: Brown, 1991.

Roman, Kenneth, and Raphaelson, Joel.   *Writing That Works.* New York: HarperCollins, 1992.

Tucker, Kerry, Derelian, Doris, and Rouner, Donna.   *Public Relations Writing,* 2nd edition. Englewood Cliffs, NJ: Prentice Hall, 1994.

Wilcox, Dennis L., and Nolte, Lawrence W.   *Public Relations Writing and Media Techniques,* 2nd edition. New York: HarperCollins, 1995.

Williams, Patricia A.   *Creating and Producing the Perfect Newsletter.* Glenview, IL: Scott, Foresman, 1990.

DIRECTORIES

Directories are valuable tools for public relations personnel who need to communicate with a variety of specialized audiences. Media directories, many of which are now available on disk, CD-ROM, or on-line, can provide names of editors and background information for thousands of media. The following is a selected list of the leading national and international directories.

MEDIA DIRECTORIES

Bacon's Media Directories: Newspapers, Magazines, Radio, TV/Cable, Business Media, International Media, and Media Calendar.   Bacon's Information Inc., 332 South Michigan Avenue, Chicago, IL 60604.

Black Media in America.   Hall Company, 70 Lincoln, Boston, MA 02111.

Broadcasting/Cablecasting Yearbook.   Broadcasting Publications, 1705 DeSales NW, Washington, DC 20036.

Bulldog Reporter's Western Media Contacts. Intercom Group, 2115 4th Street, Berkeley, CA 94710.

Burrelle's Media Directories: Newspapers and Related Media, Magazines and Newsletters, Radio, Television and Cable. Burrelle's Media Directory, 75 E. Northfield Road, Livingston, NJ 07039.

Cable & Station Coverage Atlas. Warren Publications, 2115 Ward Court NW, Washington, DC 20037.

Directory of the College Student Press in America. Oxbridge Communications, 150 Fifth Ave., New York, NY 10011.

Editor & Publisher Directory of Syndicated Services. Editor & Publisher, 11 W. 19th St., New York, NY 10011-4234.

Editor & Publisher International Year Book. See above address. Listing of weekly and daily newspapers.

Feature News Publicity Outlets. Morgan Rand, 2200 Sansome Street, Philadelphia, PA 19103.

Gale's Directory of Publications and Broadcast Media. Gale Research Company, Box 441914, Detroit, MI 48244-9980.

Gebbie Press All-in-One Directory. Gebbie Press, Box 1000, New Paltz, NY 12561.

Hispanic Media and Markets Directory. SRDS, 3004 Glenview Road, Wilmette, IL 60091.

Hudson's Newsletter Directory. Hudson Company, 44 W. Market St., Rhinebeck, NY 12572.

Just the Fax: A Media Directory. Public Access, 2000 L St. NW, Washington, DC 20036.

Magazine Handbook. Magazine Publishers Association, 575 Lexington Avenue, New York, NY 10022.

MediaMap. MediaMap, 130 The Great Road, Bedford, MA 01730.

National Directory of Magazines. Oxbridge Communications, 150 Fifth Ave., New York, NY 10011.

National Directory of Weekly Newspapers. American Newspaper Representatives, 1000 Sherland Parkway, Minneapolis, MN 55426.

National Radio Publicity Outlets. Morgan Reed, 2200 Sansome Street, Philadelphia, PA 19103.

Newsletters in Print. Gale Research Company, Box 441914, Detroit, MI 48244-9980.

Oxbridge Directory of Newsletters. Oxbridge Communications, 150 Fifth Ave., New York, NY 10011.

Print Media Editorial Calendars. SRDS, 3004 Glenview Rd., Wilmette, IL 60091.

Radio Talk Shows Need Guests. Pacesetter Publications, Box 101330, Denver, CO 80250.

Senior Media Directory. Gem Publications, 250 E. Riverview Circle, Reno, NV 89509.

Senior Media Guide. CD Publications, 8204 Fenton Street, Silver Spring, MD 20910.

Working Press of the Nation Directories: Newspapers, Magazines, TV and Radio, Feature Writers and Photographers, Internal Publications. National Research Bureau, 225 W. Wacker Drive, Suite 2275, Chicago, IL 60606-1229.

INTERNATIONAL DIRECTORIES

Bacon's International Publicity Checker. Bacon Publishing, 332 S. Michigan, Chicago, IL 60604.

Benn's Media Directory. Benn Business Information Service, Box 20, Sovereign Way, Tonbridge, Kent, England TN9, 1RW. Volume 1 is the United Kingdom, and Volume 2 is international media.

Editor & Publisher International Year Book. Editor & Publisher, 11 W. 19th St., New York, NY 10011.

Gale International Directory of Publications. Gale Research Company, Box 441914, Detroit, MI 48244-9980.

Hollis Press and Public Relations Annual. Contact House, Lower Hampton Rd., Sunbury-on-Thames, Middlesex, England TW16, 5BR.

International Literary Market Place. R. R. Bowker Company, 245 W. 17th St., New York, NY 10011.

International Media Guides: Newspapers Worldwide, Consumer Magazines Worldwide, Business Publications Asia/Pacific, Europe, The Americas, Middle East/Africa. International Media Enterprises, 22 Elizabeth St., South Norwalk, CT 06856.

Ulrich's International Directory. R. R. Bowker Company, 245 W. 17th St., New York, NY 10011.

OTHER DIRECTORIES

Awards, Honors, Prizes. Gale Research Company, Box 441914, Detroit, MI 48244-9980.

Charitable Organizations of the United States. See above address.

Celebrity Directory. Axiom International, Box 8015, Ann Arbor, MI 48017.

Celebrity Service International Contact Book. Celebrity Service, 1780 Broadway, New York, NY 10019.

Chase's Annual Events. Contemporary Books, Two Prudential Plaza, Suite 1200, 180 N. Stetson Ave., Chicago, IL 60601-9847.

Directory of American Firms Operating in Foreign Countries. Uniworld Business Publications, 50 E. 42nd Street, New York, NY 10017.

Encyclopedia of Associations. Gale Research Company, Box 441914, Detroit, MI 48244-9980.

The Foundation Directory. The Foundation Center, 79 Fifth Ave., New York, NY 10003.

Holidays and Anniversaries of the World. Gale Research Company, Box 441914, Detroit, MI 48244-9980.

International Encyclopedia of Communications. Cary, NC: Oxford University Press, 1989. Four volumes.

Literary Marketplace. R. R. Bowker Company, 245 W. 17th St., New York, NY 10011.

National Directory of Corporate Public Affairs. Columbia Books, 1350 New York Ave. NW, Washington, DC 20005.

National Trade/Professional Associations. See above address.

O'Dwyer's Directory of Corporate Communications. O'Dwyer Company, 271 Madison Ave., New York, NY 10016.

O'Dwyer's Directory of Public Relations Firms. See above address.

Professional's Guide to Public Relations Services. AMACOM, 135 W. 50th St., New York, NY 10020.

Reed's Worldwide Directory of Public Relations Organizations. Pigafetta Press, Box 39244, Washington, DC 20016.

Standard Rate and Data Services: Business Publications Rates and Data, Community Publication Rates and Data, Newspaper Rates and Data, and Spot Radio Rates and Data. SRDS, 3004 Glenview Rd., Wilmette, IL 60091.

Trade Shows Worldwide. Gale Research Company, Box 441914, Detroit, MI 48244-9980.

Washington Lobbyists Directory. Columbia Books, 1350 New York Ave. NW, Washington, DC 20005.

Who's Who in America. Marquis Who's Who, 121 Chanlon Road, New Providence, NJ 07974-0043. Regional editions also available.

Worldwide Government Directory. MacFarlane Company, One Park Place, Atlanta, GA 30318.

CASE Currents.   11 Dupont Circle, Washington, DC 20036. Monthly publication of the Council for the Advancement and Support of Education.

Communication Briefings.   700 Black Horse Pike, Suite 110, Blackwood, NJ 08012. Bi-weekly.

Communication World.   IABC, One Hallidie Plaza, Suite 600, San Francisco, CA 94102. Monthly publication of the International Association of Business Communicators.

Community Relations Report.   Box 924, Bartlesville, OK 74005. Monthly.

Inside PR.   235 West 48th Street, Suite 34A, New York, NY 10036. Monthly.

Investor Relations Update.   NIRI, 1730 M St. NW, Suite 806, Washington, DC 20036. Monthly publication of the National Investor Relations Institute.

Jack O'Dwyer's PR Newsletter.   271 Madison Ave., New York, NY 10016. Weekly.

O'Dwyer's PR Services Report.   See above address. Monthly.

Journal of Public Relations Research.   Lawrence Erlbaum Associates, 365 Broadway, Hillsdale, NJ 07642. Quarterly.

PR News.   Phillips Business Information, 1201 Seven Locks Road, Potomac, MD 20854. Weekly.

PR Reporter.   Box 600, Dudley House, Exeter, NH 03833. Weekly.

Public Relations Journal.   PRSA, 33 Irving Place, New York, NY 10003. Monthly publication of the Public Relations Society of America.

Public Relations Quarterly.   Box 311, Rhinebeck, NY 12572. Quarterly.

Public Relations Review.   JAI Press, 55 Old Post Road, Greenwich, CT 06836-1678. Quarterly.

Ragan Report.   407 S. Dearborn, Chicago, IL 60605. Weekly.

Special Events Report.   213 W. Institute Pl., Chicago, IL 60610. Twice a month.

Index

Credits

695